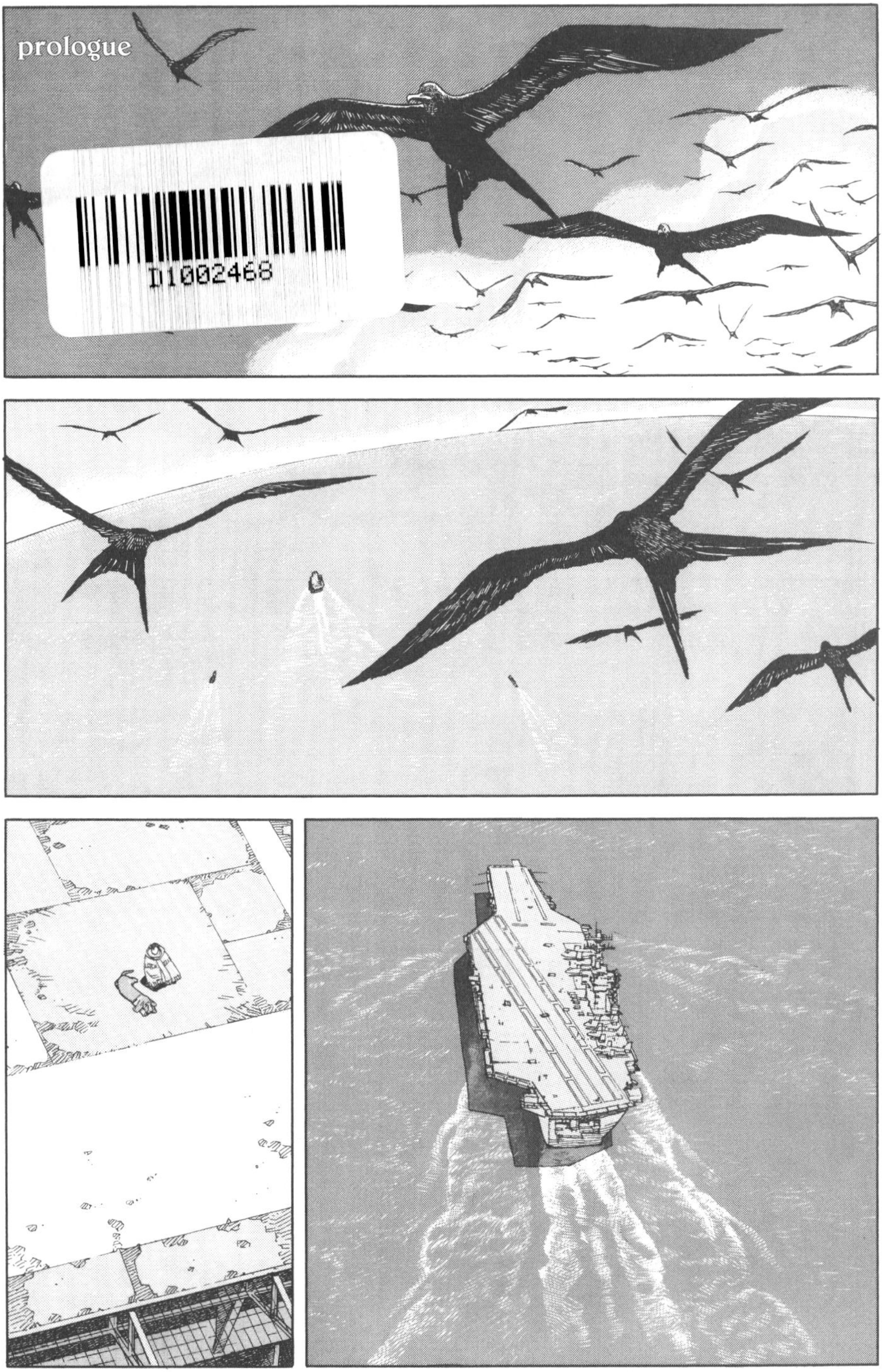
prologue

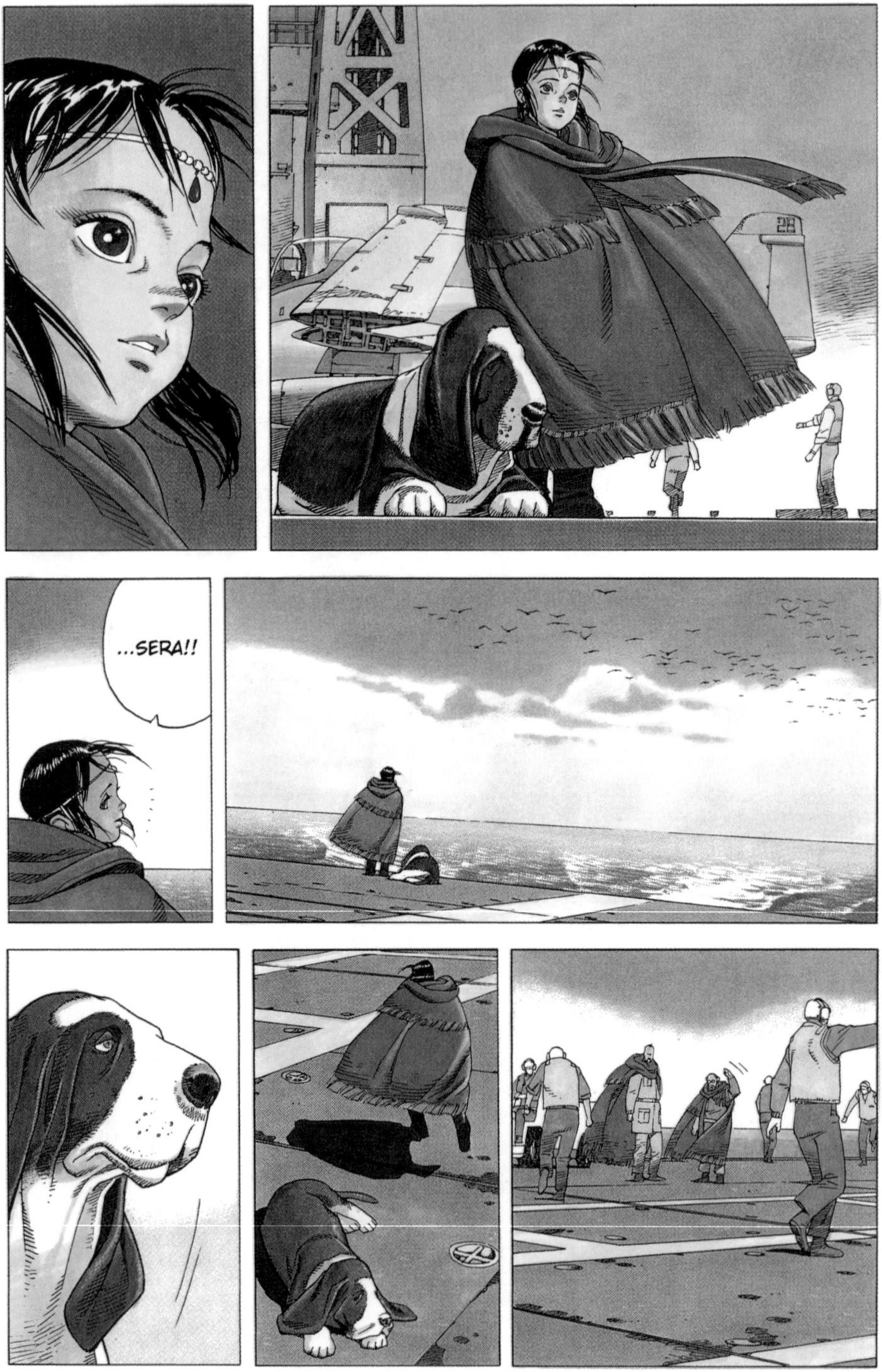
...SERA!!

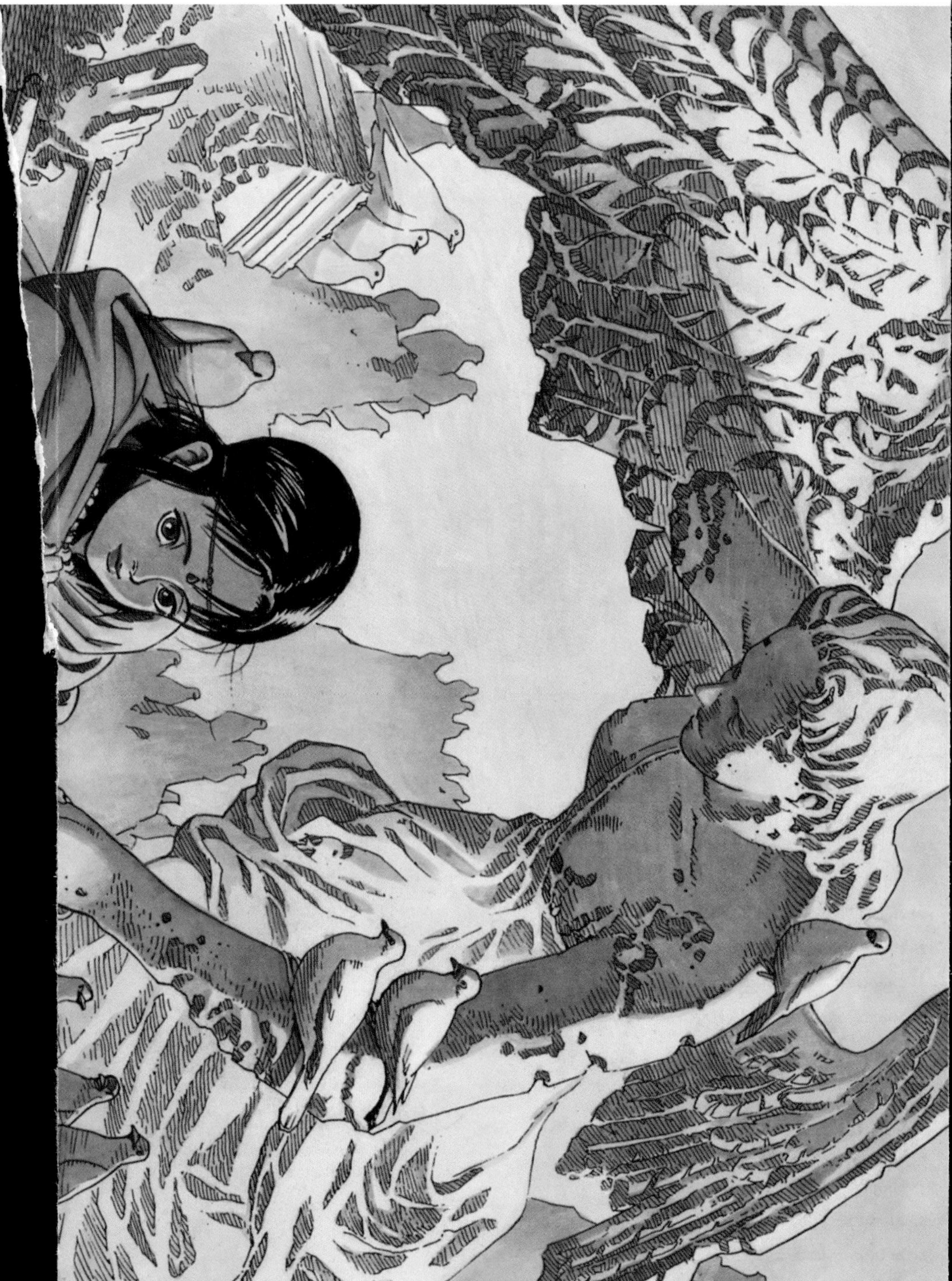

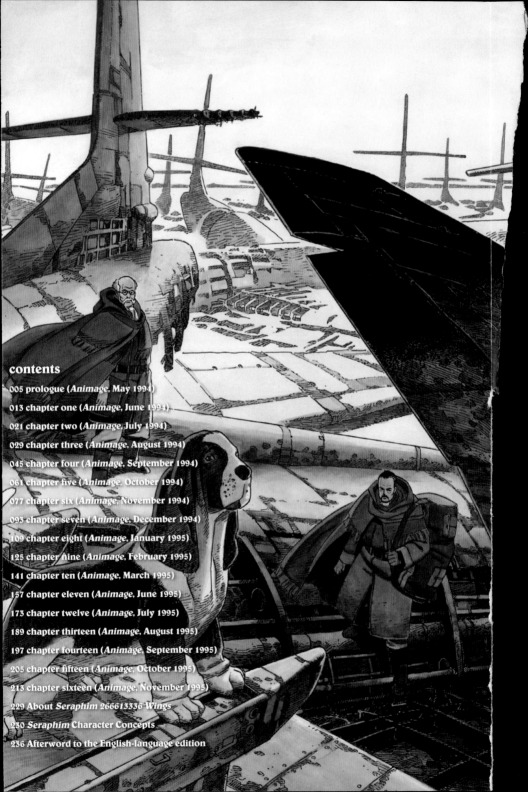

contents

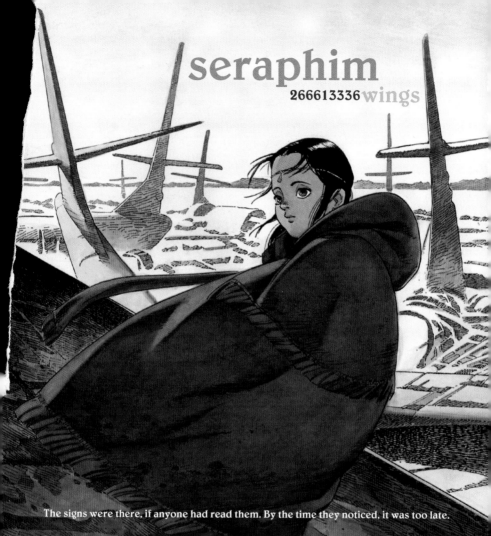

seraphim

266613336 wings

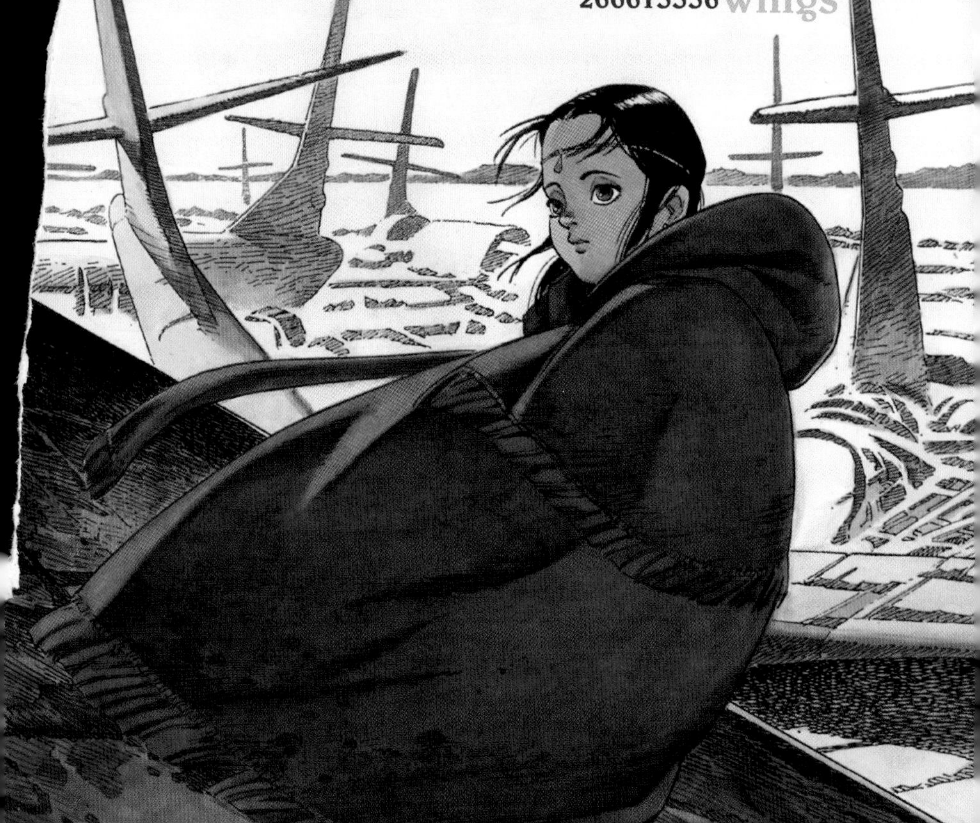

The signs were there, if anyone had read them. By the time they noticed, it was too late.

It began on the cusp of the twenty-first century. An unknown disease appeared from deep inside Eurasia, then spread uncontrollably until it decimated the continent.

Infection caused distortions of the body, accompanied by consuming hallucinations and death. Nothing could halt the plague's advance. Nations collapsed in its wake, leaving swarms of refugees pouring out of contaminated areas. Almost at once, the developed nations sealed their borders. Refugees armed themselves, which triggered battles and mass killings carried out in the name of purification . . .

In a final, desperate bid for survival, a *cordon sanitaire* was imposed around the infected zones, creating what would later be called the Great Quarantine of Eurasia. A new Dark Ages had descended. Inside the quarantine, people succumbed to hopelessness and despair. Outside, civilization began its slow decline.

With no end in sight, the disease was accorded an almost mystical reverence. It was called *Seraphim*—the Angel Plague.

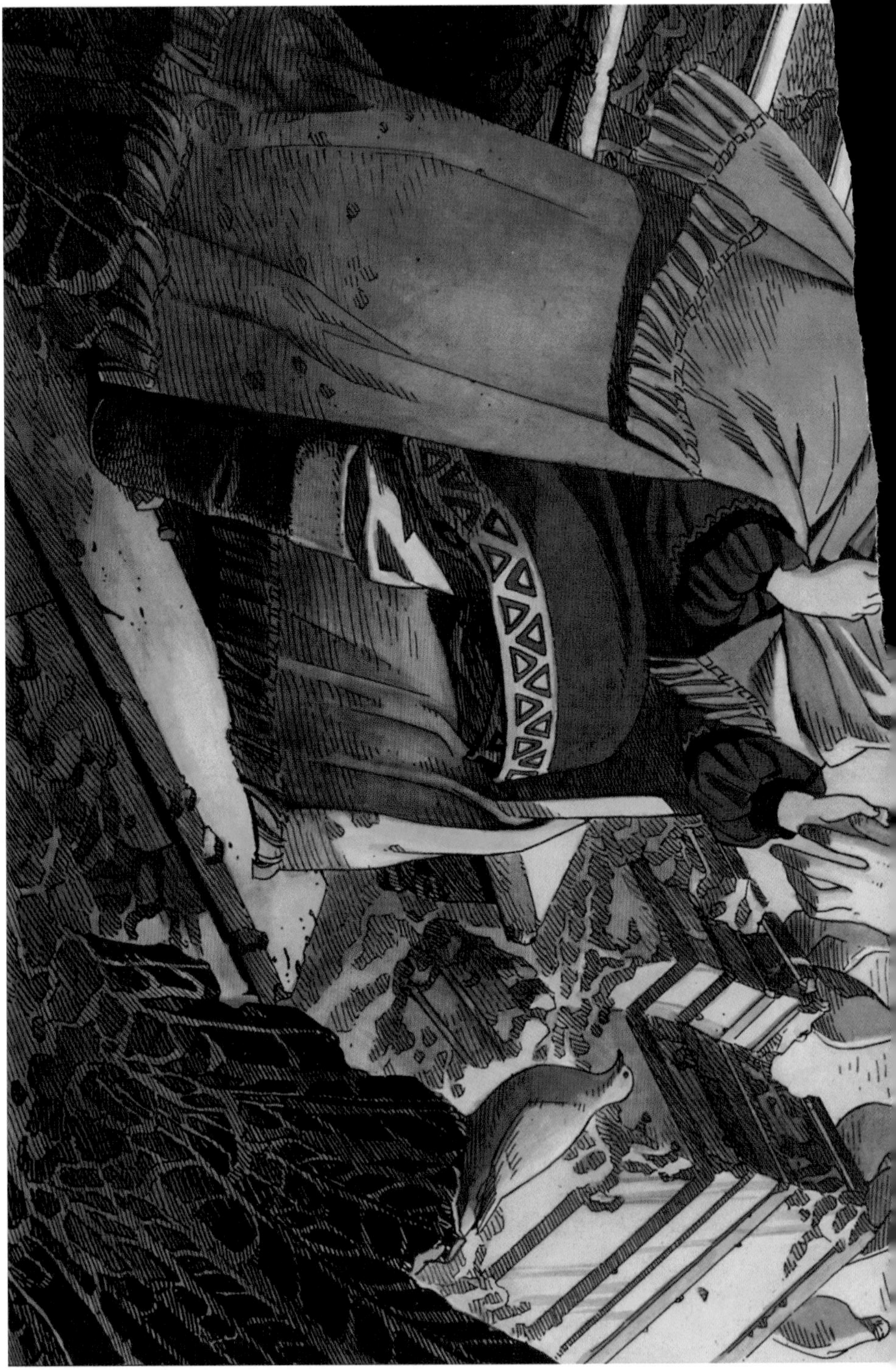

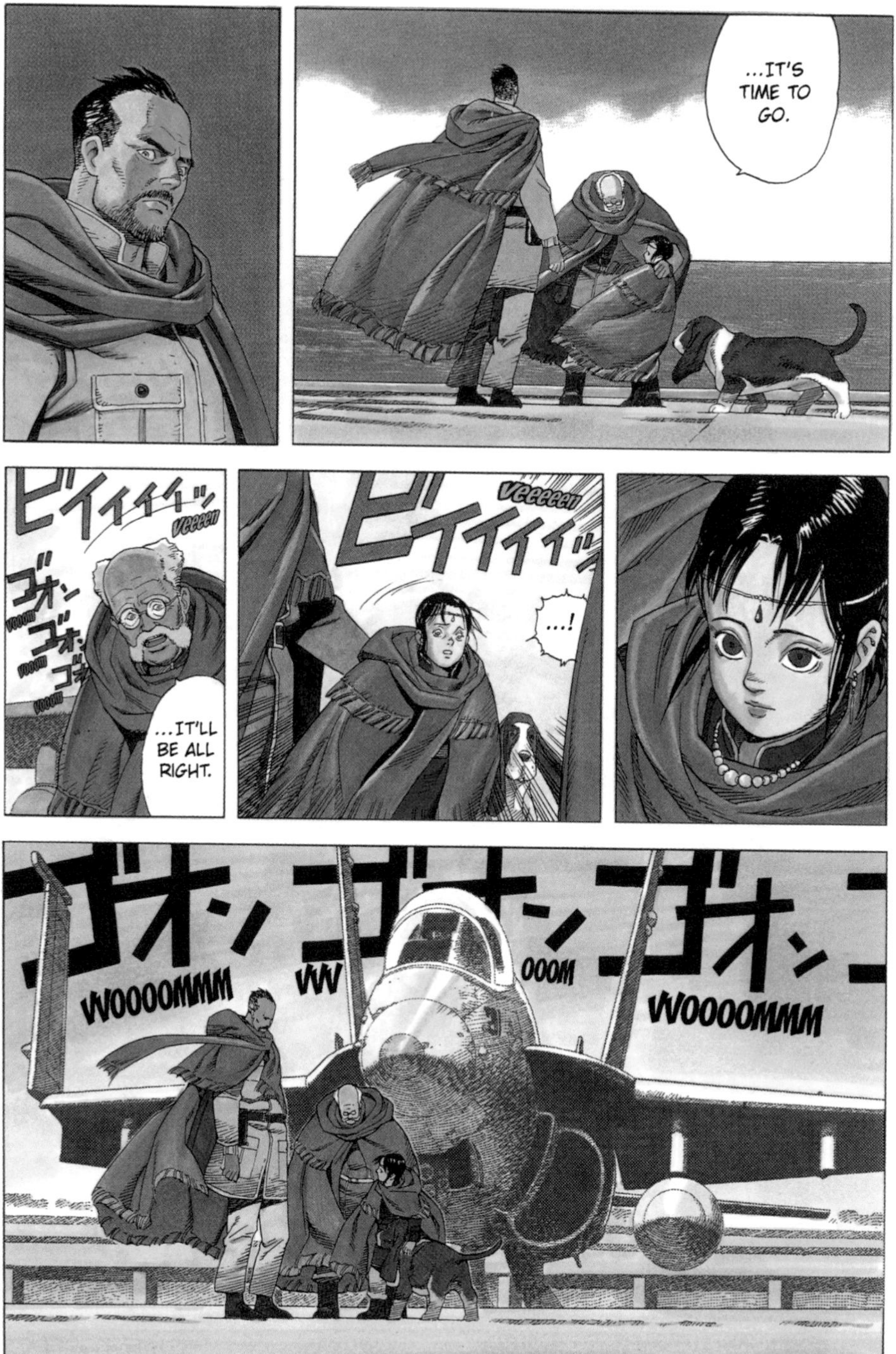
...IT'S TIME TO GO.
ビイイイイッ
veeeeen
...!
ビイイイイッ
veeeen
ゴオン
vooom
ゴオン
vooom
ゴオン
vooom
...IT'LL BE ALL RIGHT.
ゴオン
VVOOOOMMM
ゴオン
OOOM
VVV
ゴオン
VVOOOOMMM

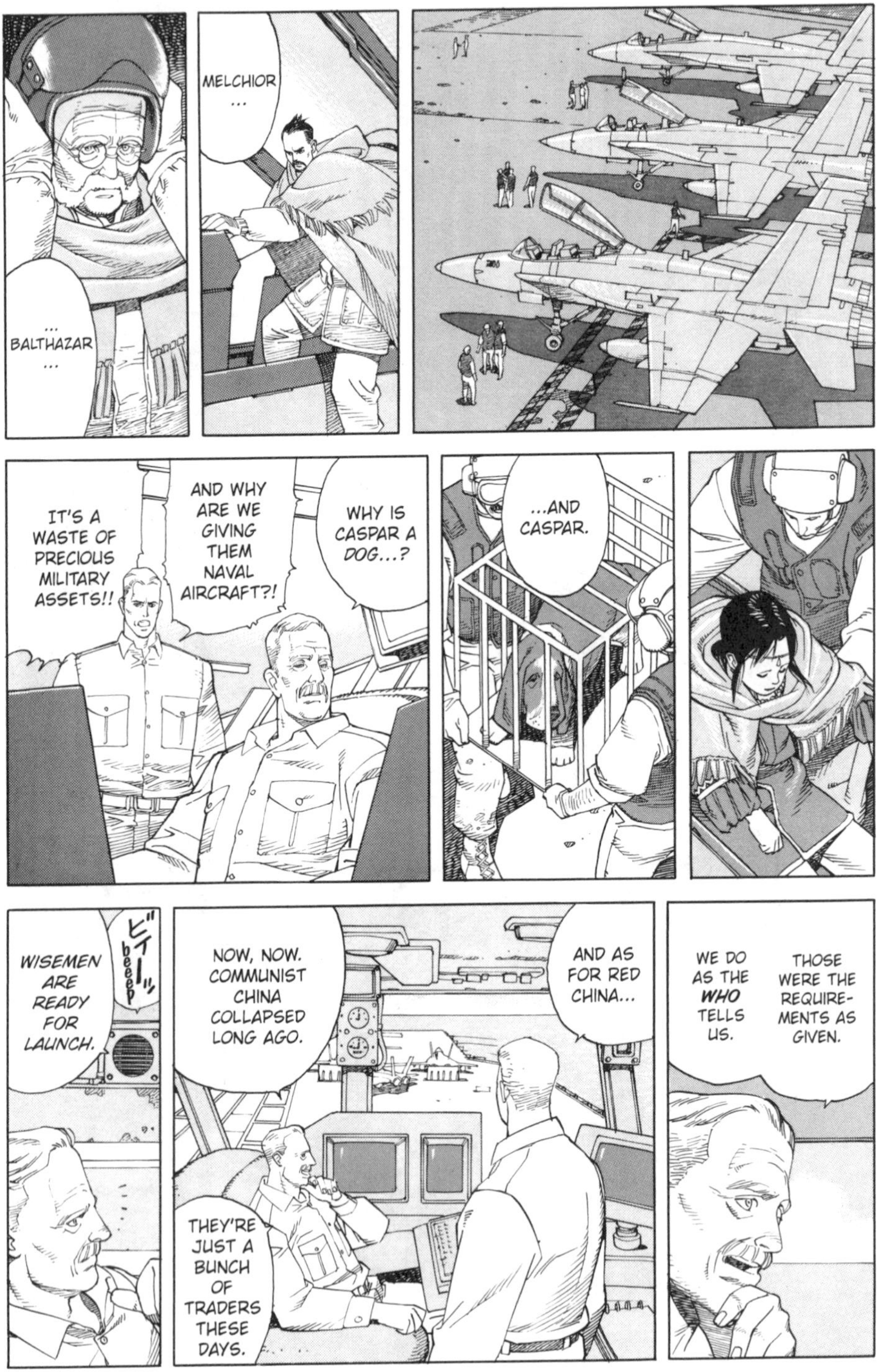
MELCHIOR ...
... BALTHAZAR ...
...AND CASPAR.
WHY IS CASPAR A DOG...?
AND WHY ARE WE GIVING THEM NAVAL AIRCRAFT?!
IT'S A WASTE OF PRECIOUS MILITARY ASSETS!!
THOSE WERE THE REQUIRE-MENTS AS GIVEN.
WE DO AS THE *WHO* TELLS US.
AND AS FOR RED CHINA...
NOW, NOW. COMMUNIST CHINA COLLAPSED LONG AGO.
THEY'RE JUST A BUNCH OF TRADERS THESE DAYS.
ビイーッ beeep
WISEMEN ARE READY FOR LAUNCH.

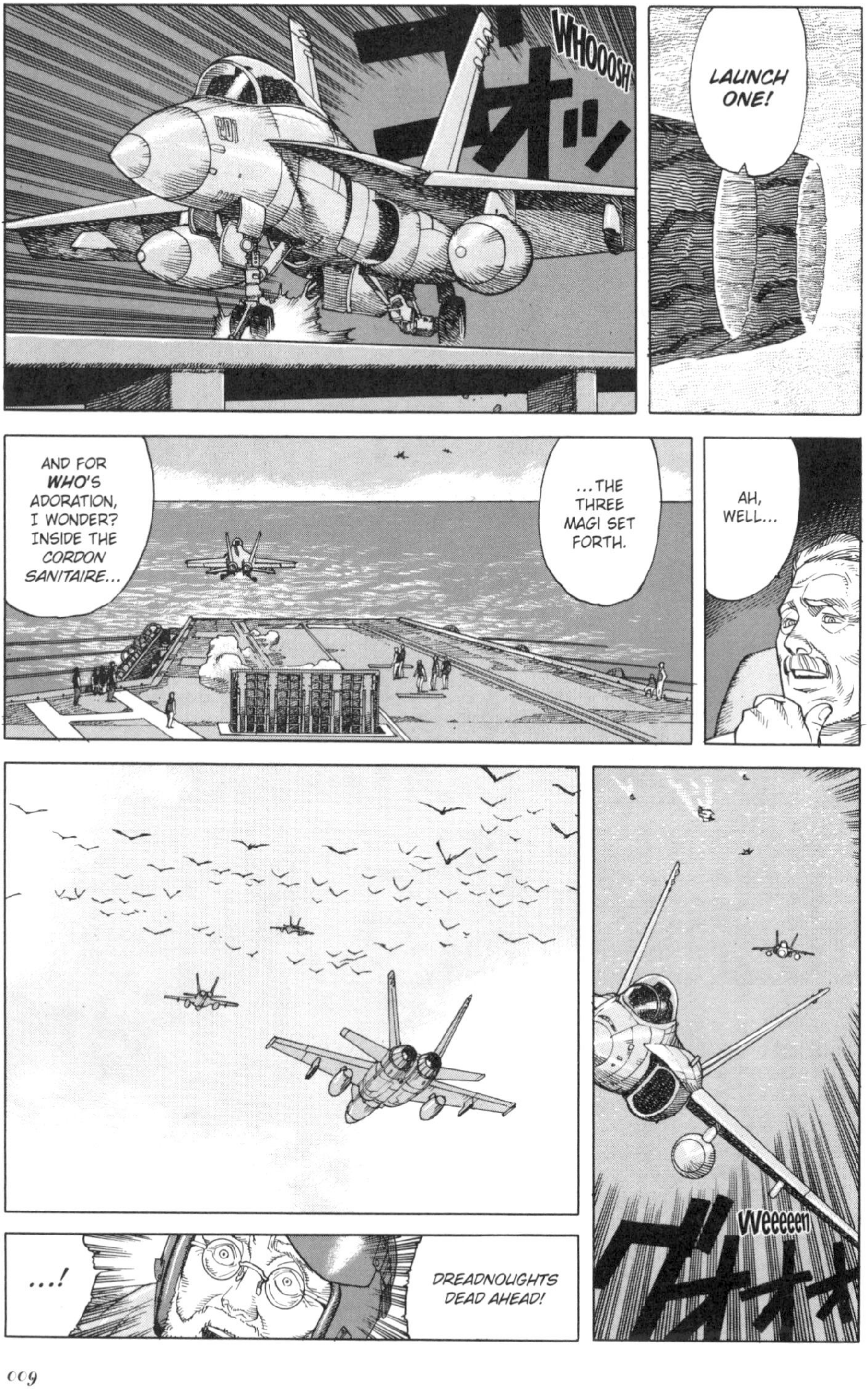
LAUNCH ONE!
WHOOOSH!
AH, WELL...
...THE THREE MAGI SET FORTH.
AND FOR WHO'S ADORATION, I WONDER? INSIDE THE CORDON SANITAIRE...
VVeeeeen
DREADNOUGHTS DEAD AHEAD!
...!

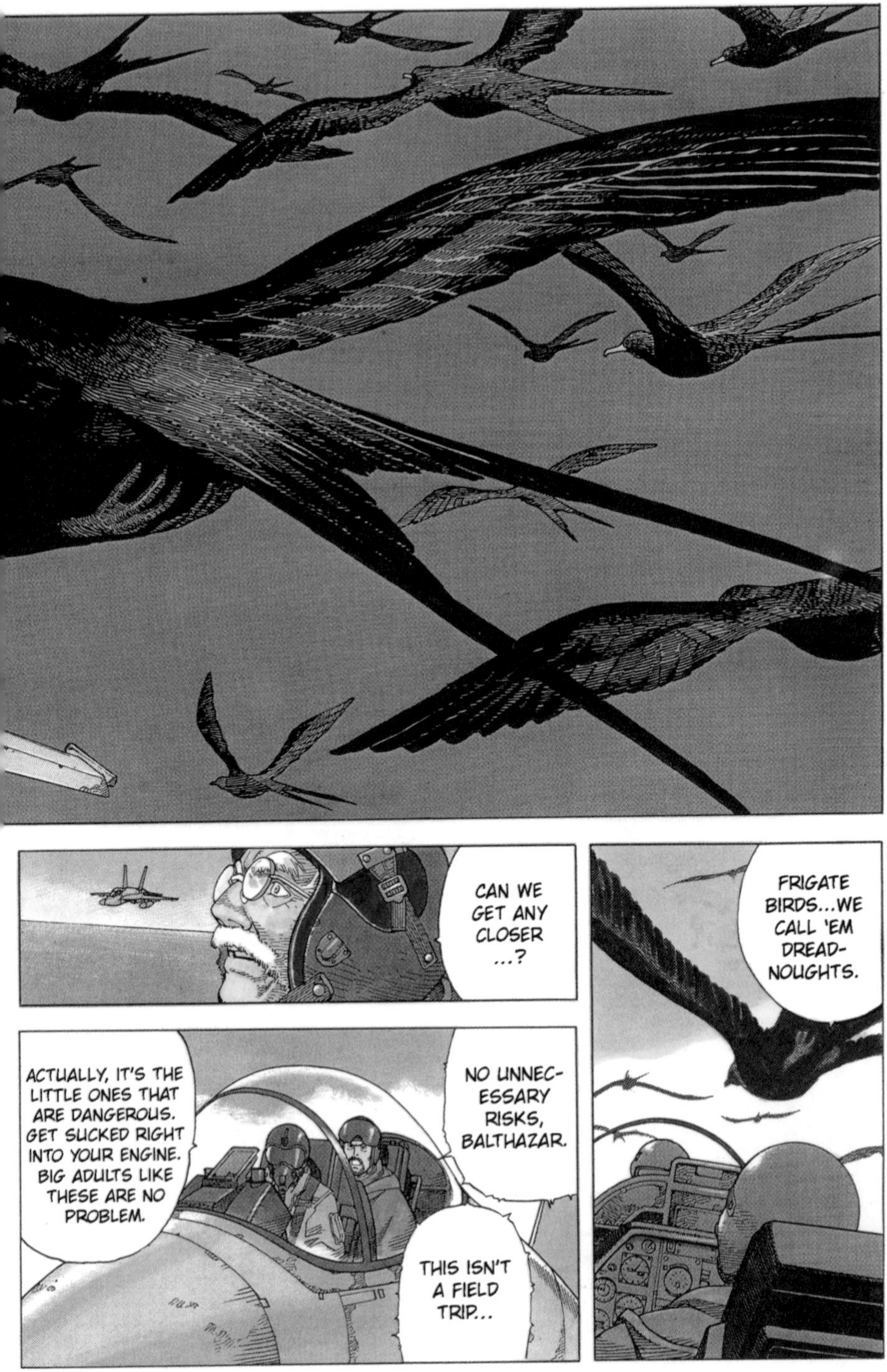
FRIGATE BIRDS...WE CALL 'EM DREAD-NOUGHTS.
CAN WE GET ANY CLOSER ...?
NO UNNEC-ESSARY RISKS, BALTHAZAR.
THIS ISN'T A FIELD TRIP...
ACTUALLY, IT'S THE LITTLE ONES THAT ARE DANGEROUS. GET SUCKED RIGHT INTO YOUR ENGINE. BIG ADULTS LIKE THESE ARE NO PROBLEM.

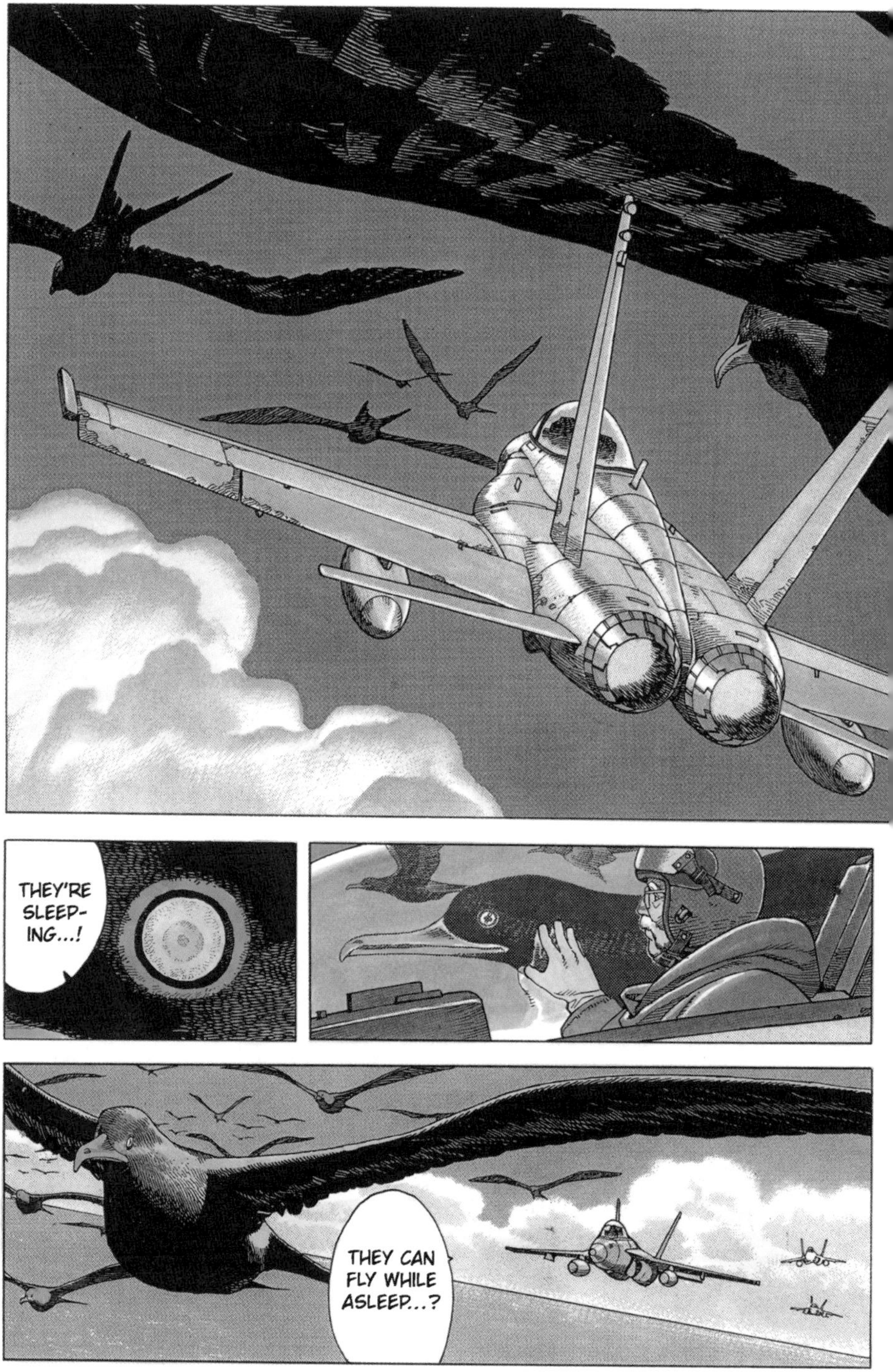
THEY'RE SLEEP-ING...!
THEY CAN FLY WHILE ASLEEP...?

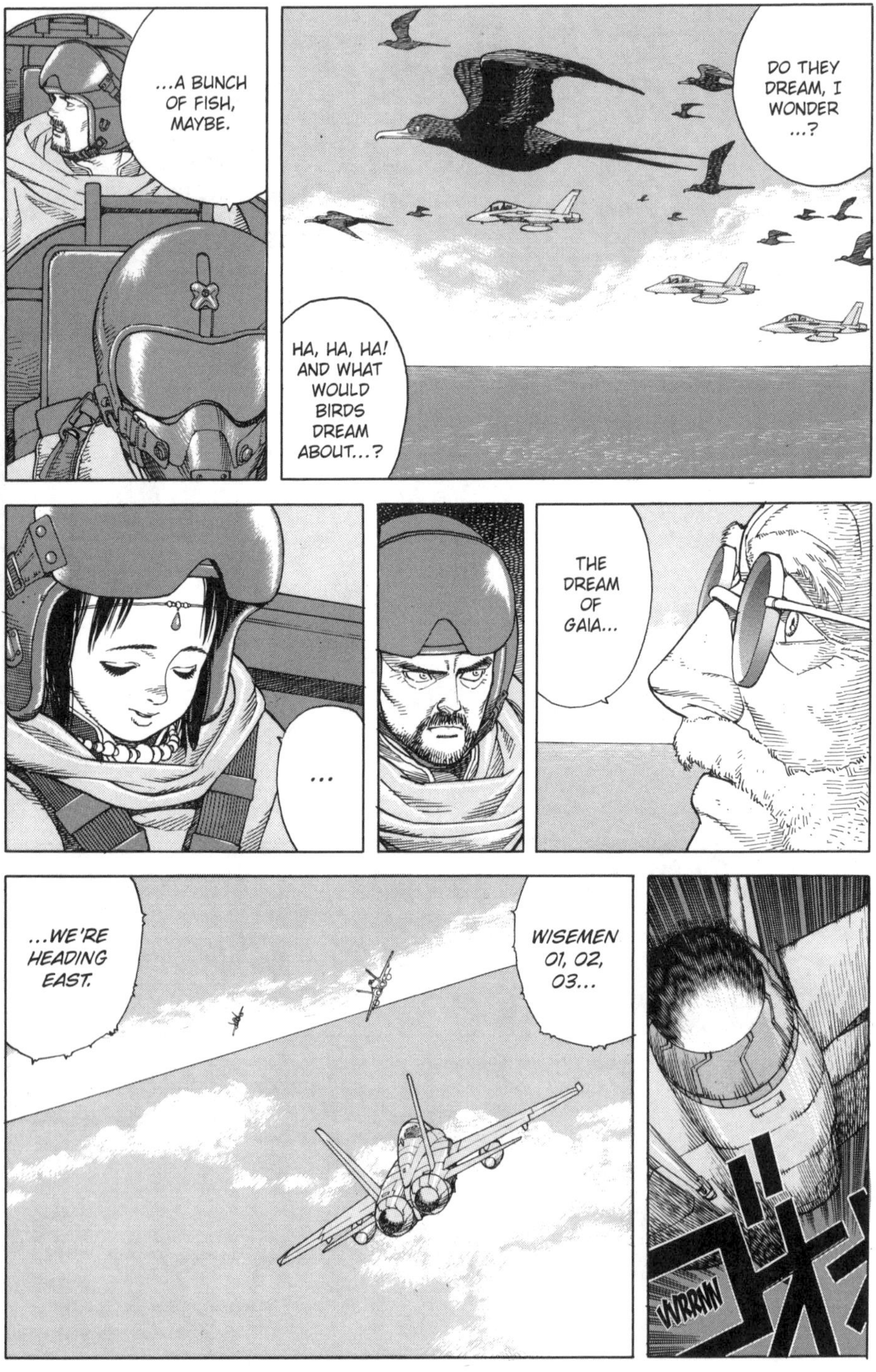
DO THEY DREAM, I WONDER ...?
HA, HA, HA! AND WHAT WOULD BIRDS DREAM ABOUT...?
...A BUNCH OF FISH, MAYBE.
THE DREAM OF GAIA...
...
WRRNN
WISEMEN 01, 02, 03...
...WE'RE HEADING EAST.

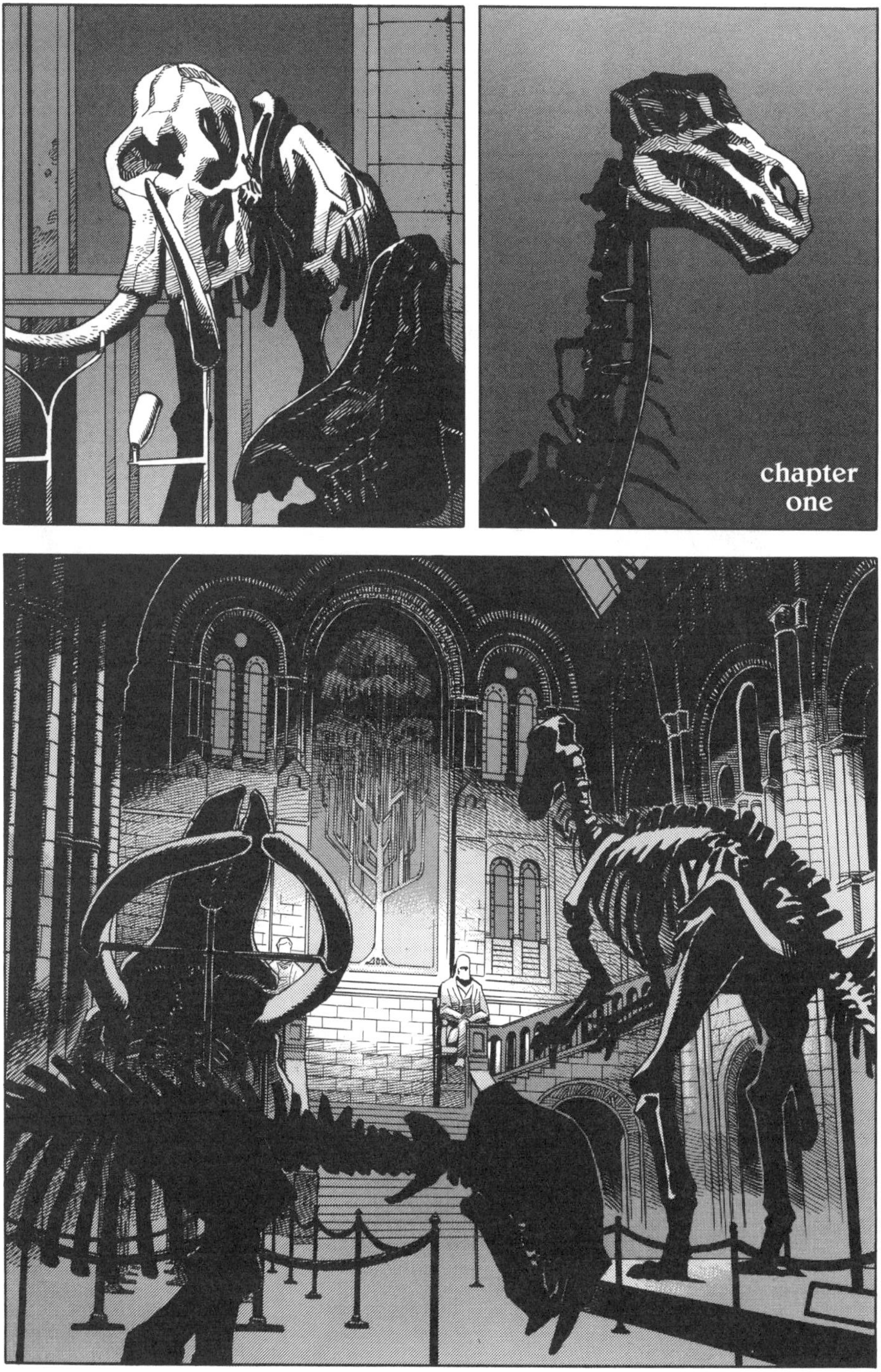
chapter
one

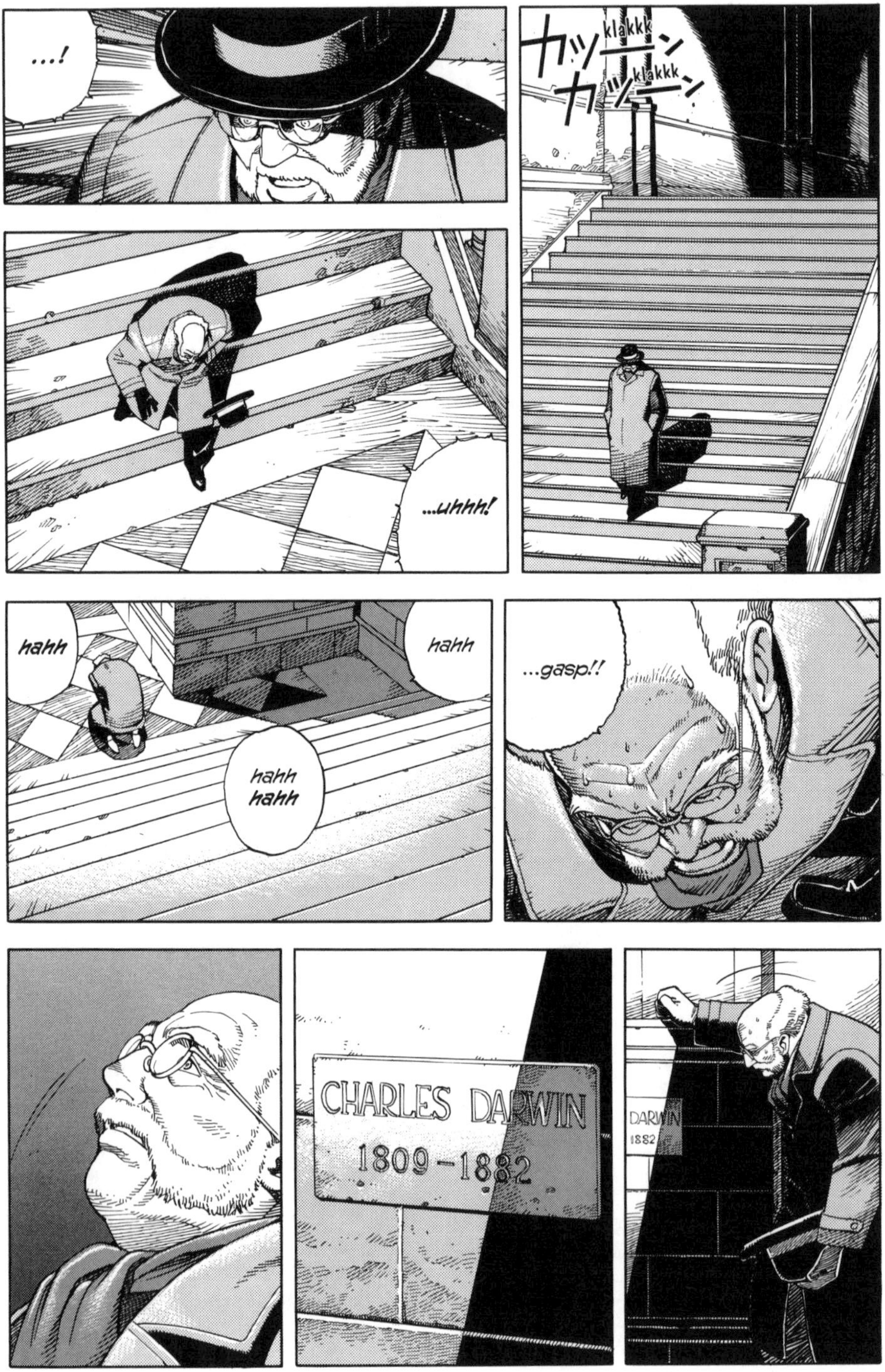
カッーン
klakkk
カッーン
klakkk
...!
...uhhh!
...gasp!!
hahh
hahh
hahh
hahh
DARWIN
1882
CHARLES DARWIN
1809-1882

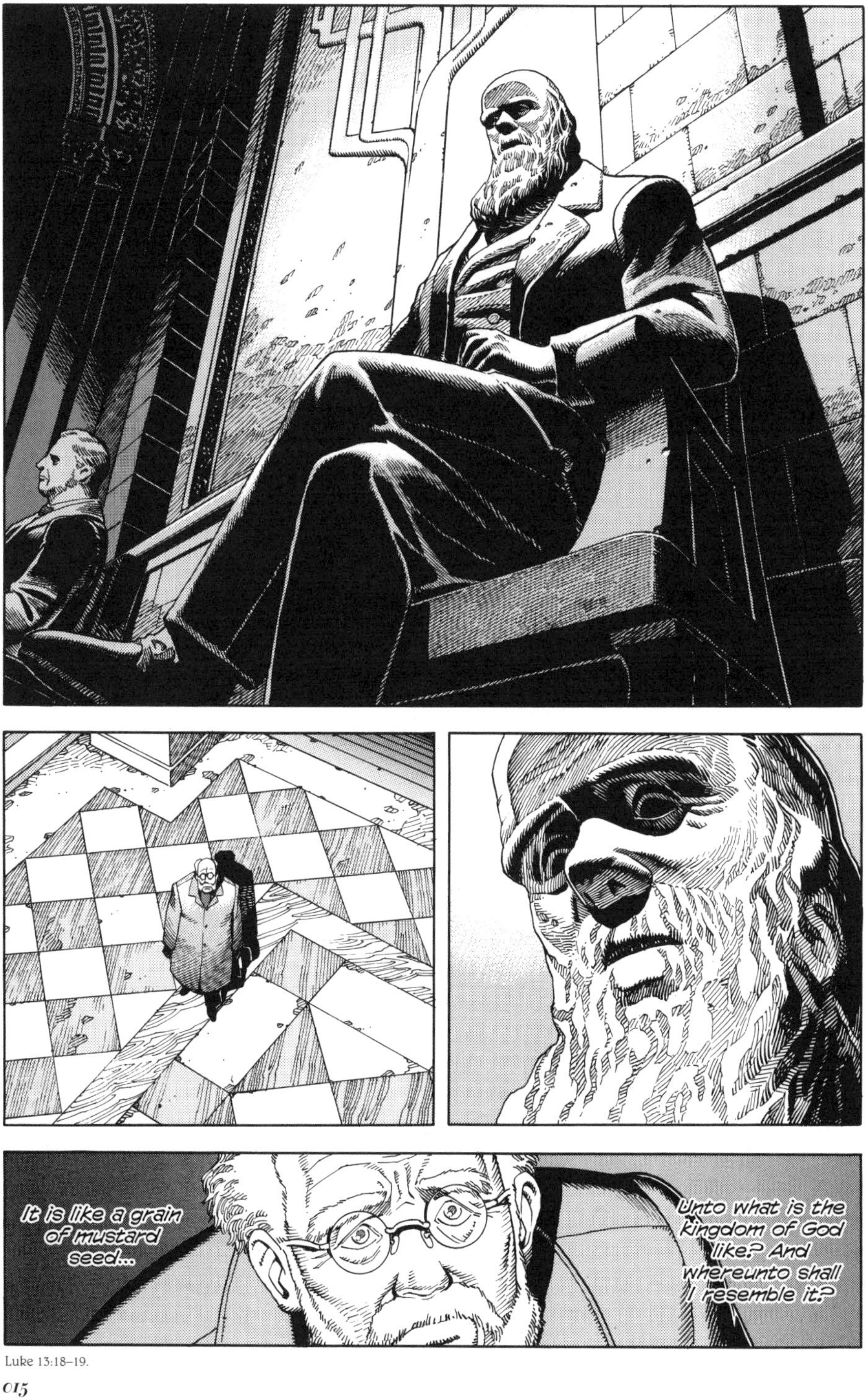
Unto what is the kingdom of God like? And whereunto shall I resemble it?
It is like a grain of mustard seed...

Luke 13:18–19.

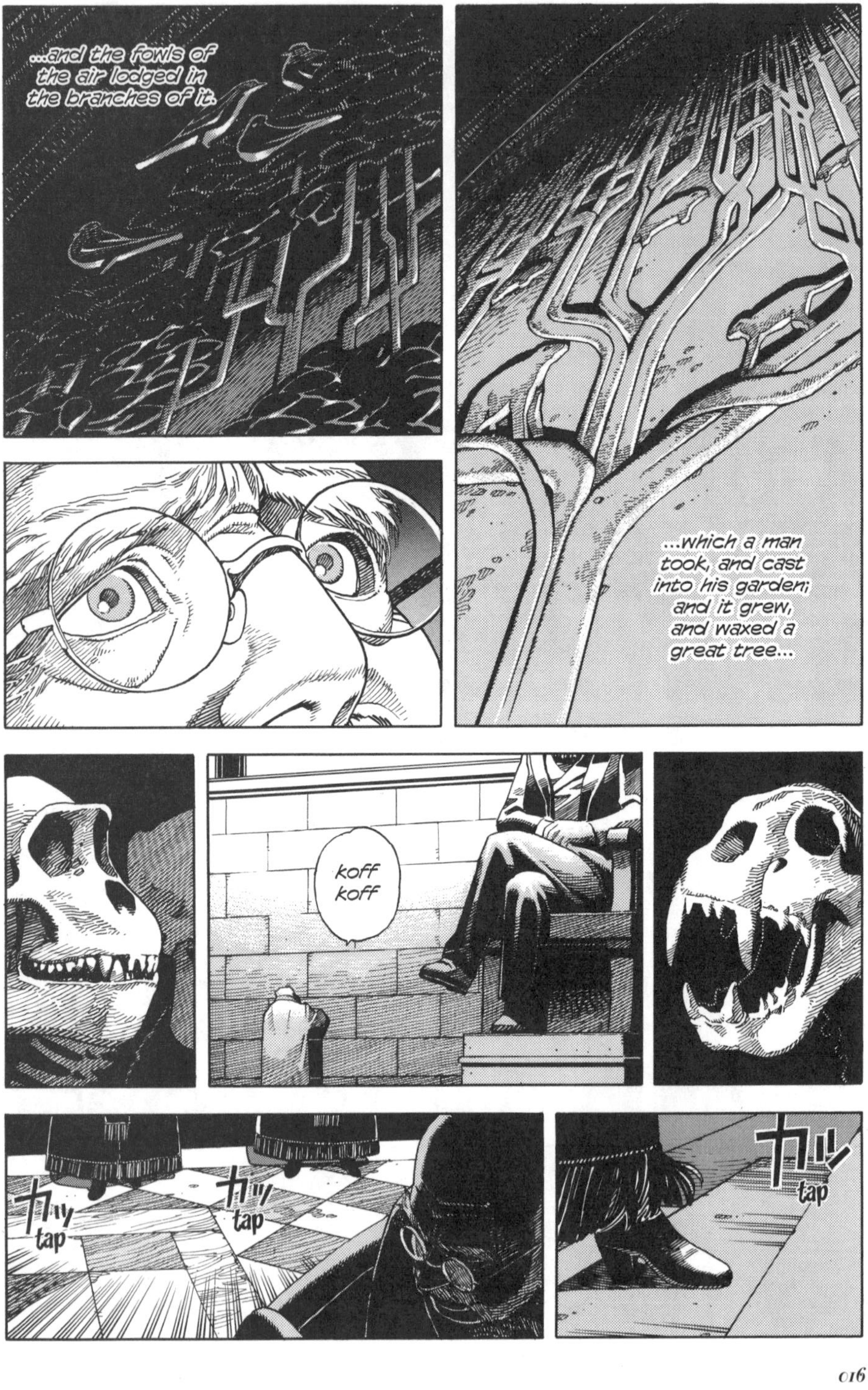
...which a man took, and cast into his garden; and it grew, and waxed a great tree...
...and the fowls of the air lodged in the branches of it.
koff koff
カッ tap
カッ tap
カッ tap

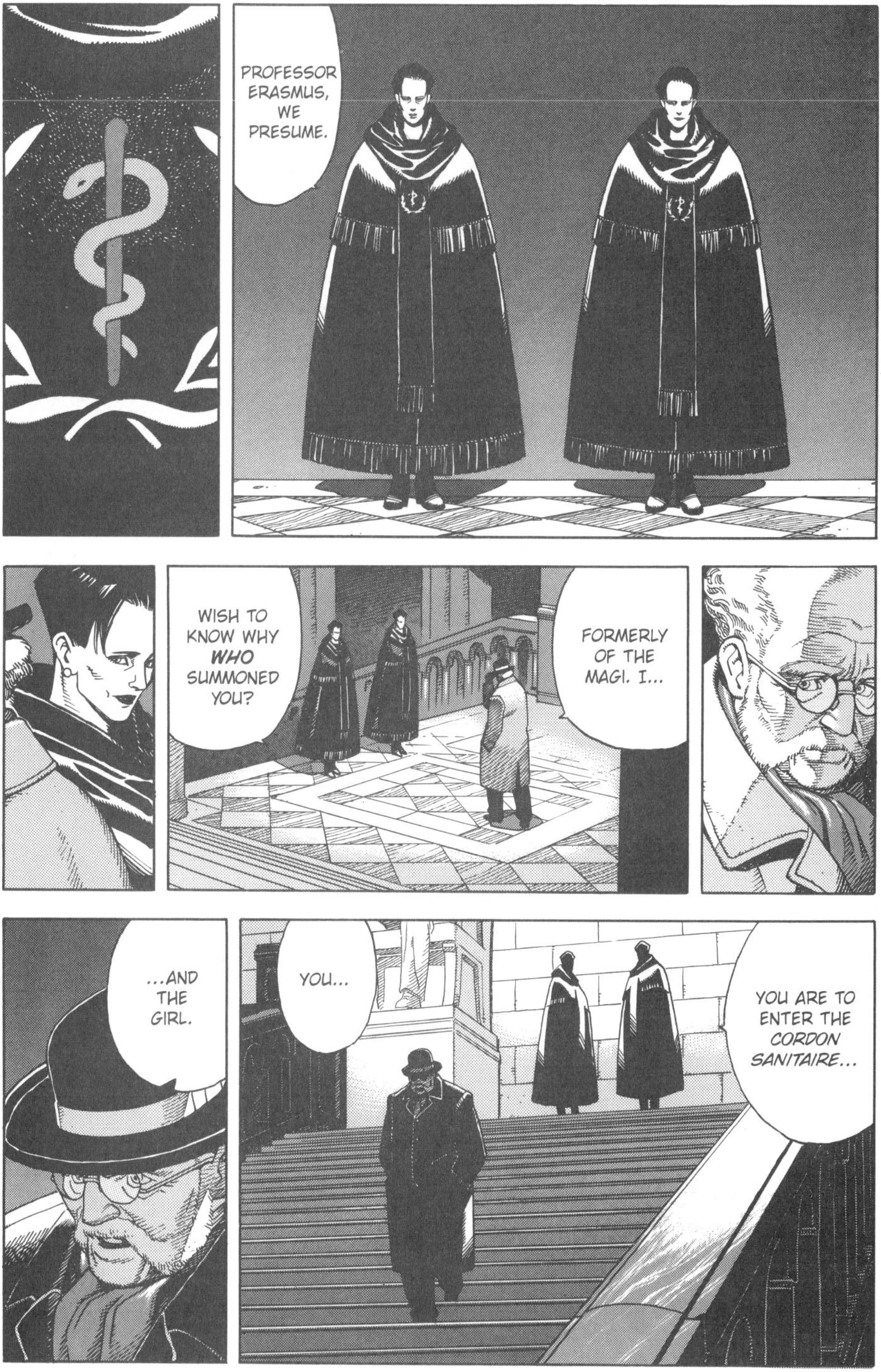
PROFESSOR ERASMUS, WE PRESUME.
FORMERLY OF THE MAGI. I...
WISH TO KNOW WHY *WHO* SUMMONED YOU?
YOU ARE TO ENTER THE *CORDON SANITAIRE*...
YOU...
...AND THE GIRL.

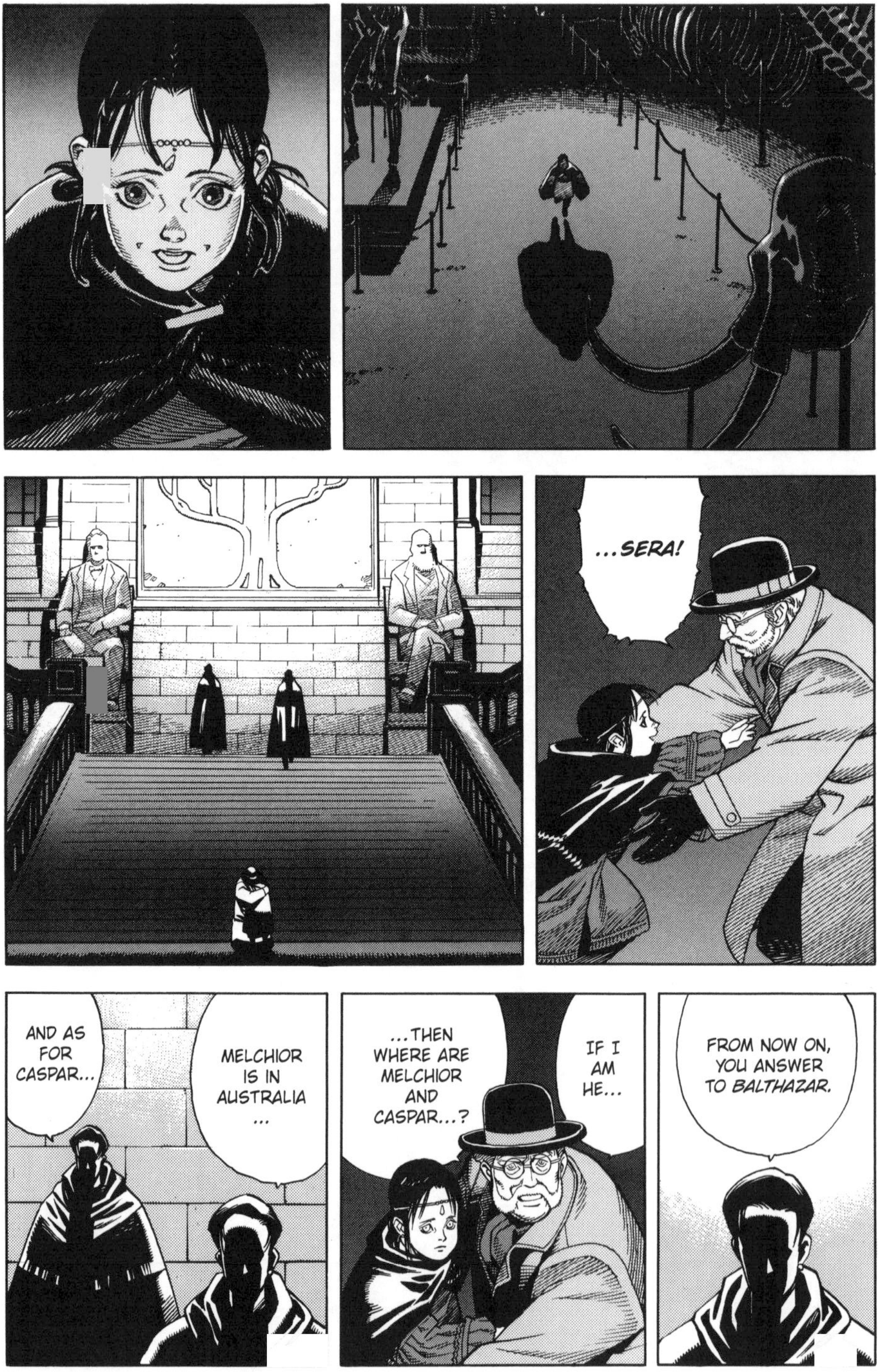
...SERA!
FROM NOW ON, YOU ANSWER TO *BALTHAZAR.*
IF I AM HE...
...THEN WHERE ARE MELCHIOR AND CASPAR...?
MELCHIOR IS IN AUSTRALIA ...
AND AS FOR CASPAR...

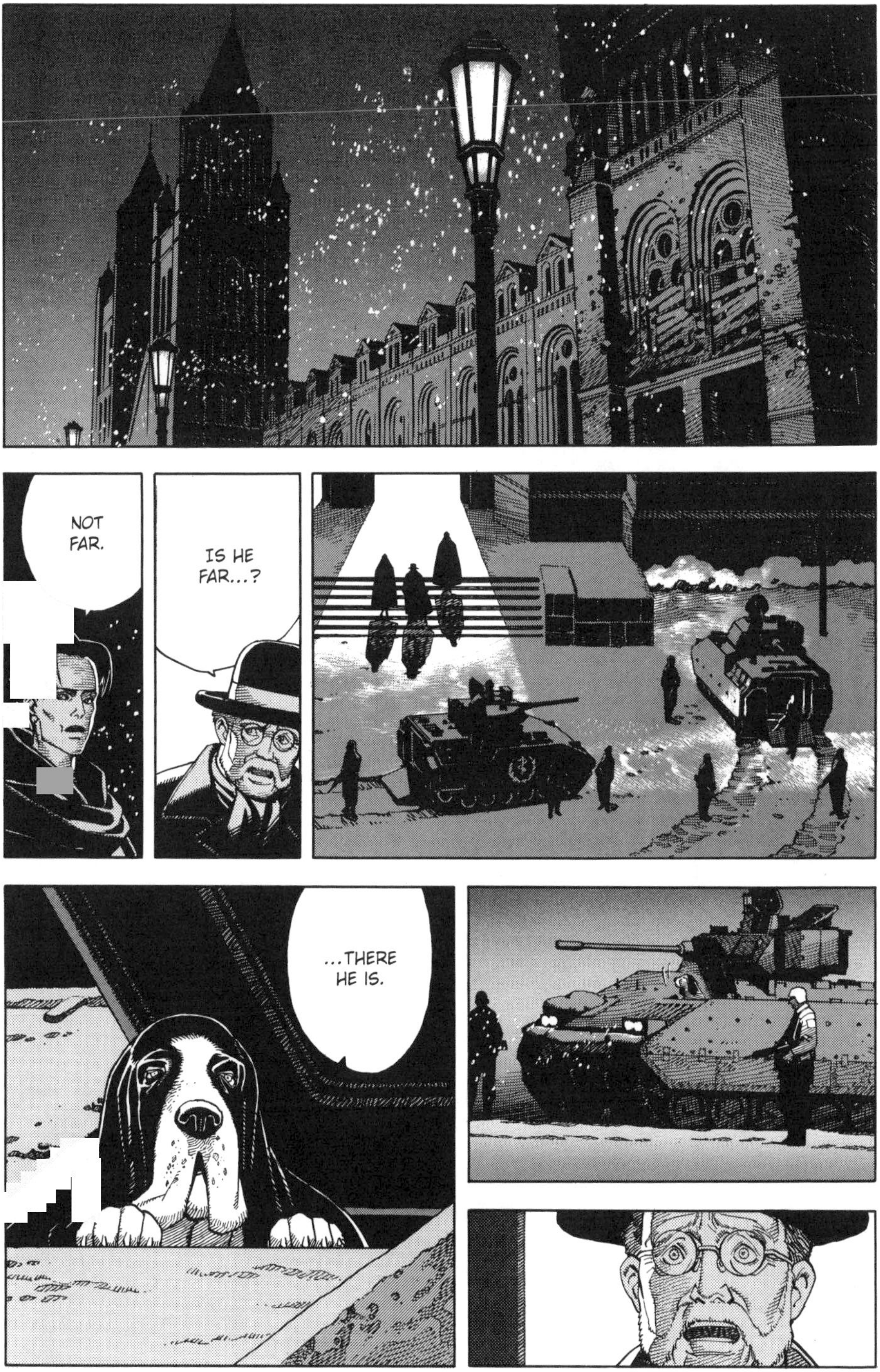
IS HE FAR...?
NOT FAR.
...THERE HE IS.

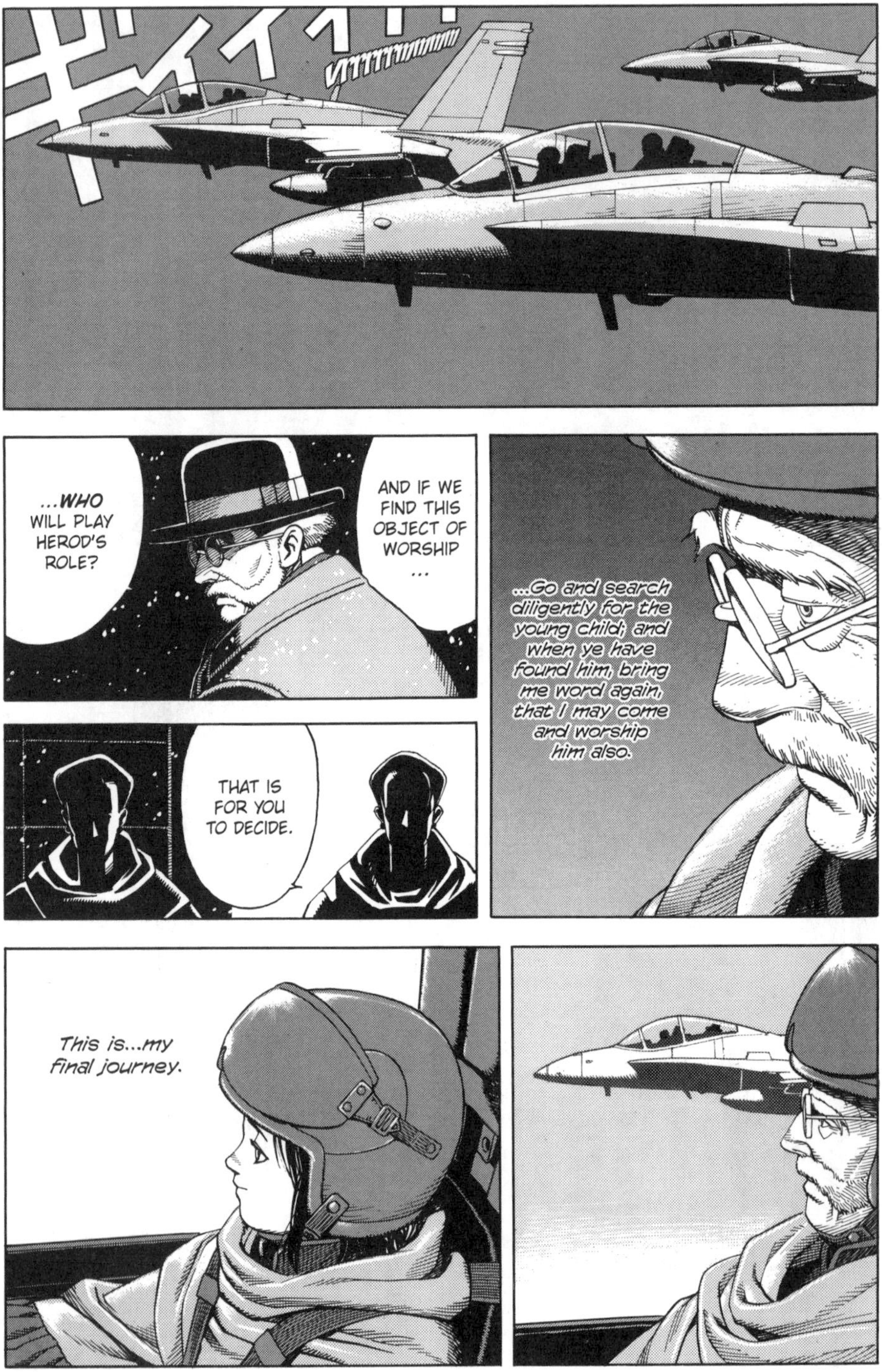
...Go and search diligently for the young child; and when ye have found him, bring me word again, that I may come and worship him also.
AND IF WE FIND THIS OBJECT OF WORSHIP ...
...WHO WILL PLAY HEROD'S ROLE?
THAT IS FOR YOU TO DECIDE.
This is...my final journey.

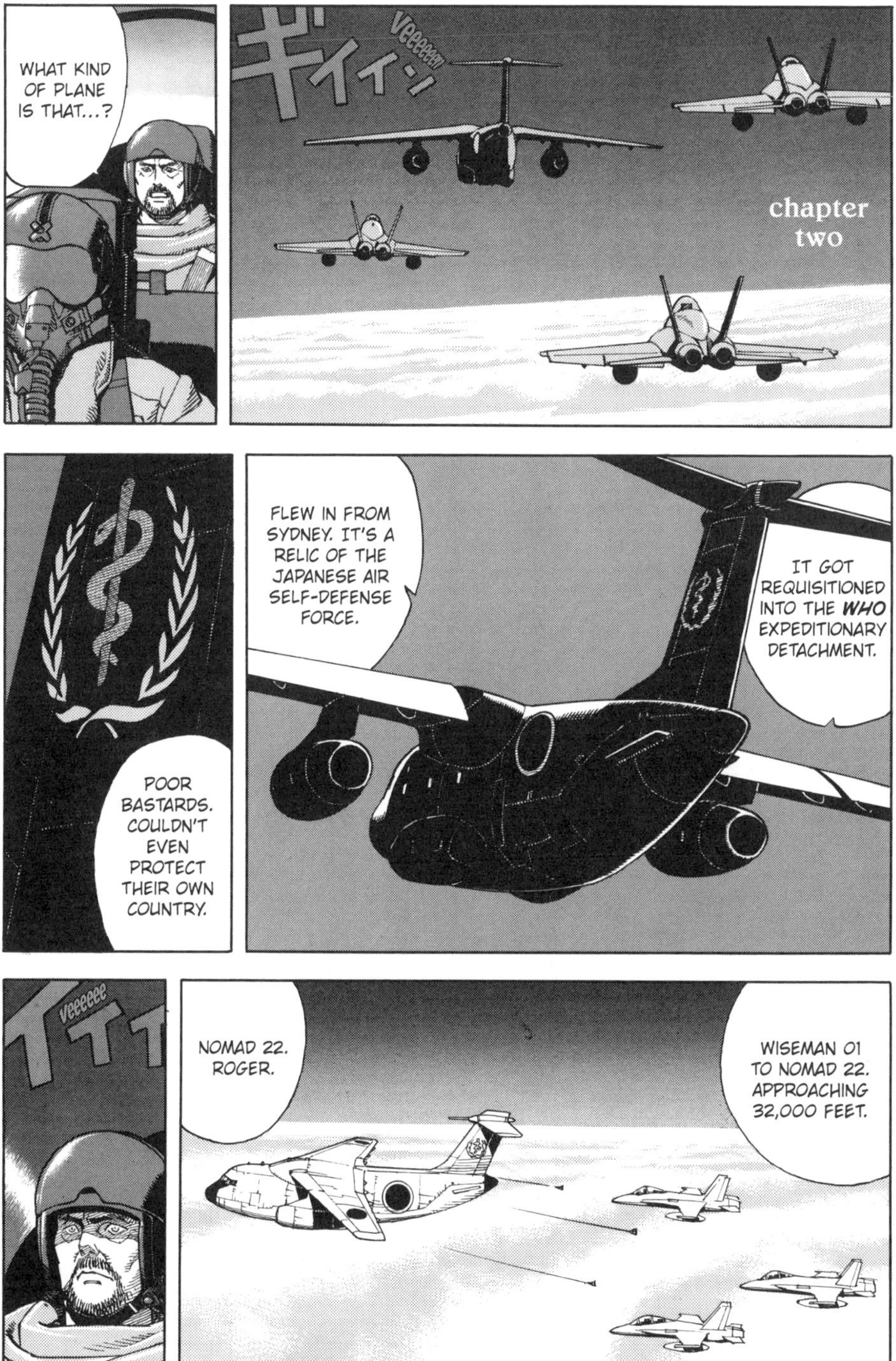
ギイィン
Veeeeeen
chapter two
WHAT KIND OF PLANE IS THAT...?
FLEW IN FROM SYDNEY. IT'S A RELIC OF THE JAPANESE AIR SELF-DEFENSE FORCE.
IT GOT REQUISITIONED INTO THE ***WHO*** EXPEDITIONARY DETACHMENT.
POOR BASTARDS. COULDN'T EVEN PROTECT THEIR OWN COUNTRY.
WISEMAN 01 TO NOMAD 22. APPROACHING 32,000 FEET.
NOMAD 22. ROGER.
Veeeeee

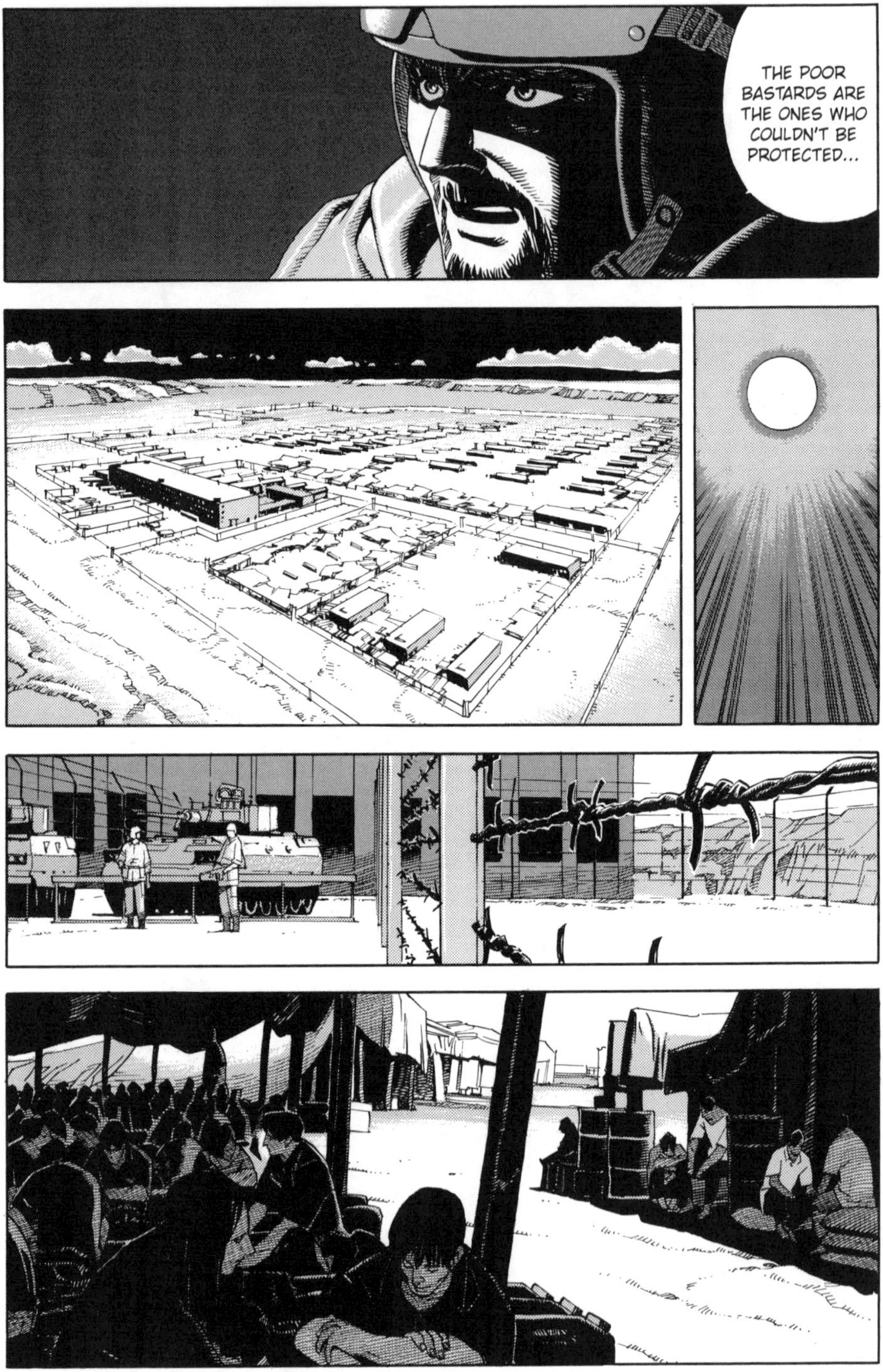
THE POOR BASTARDS ARE THE ONES WHO COULDN'T BE PROTECTED...

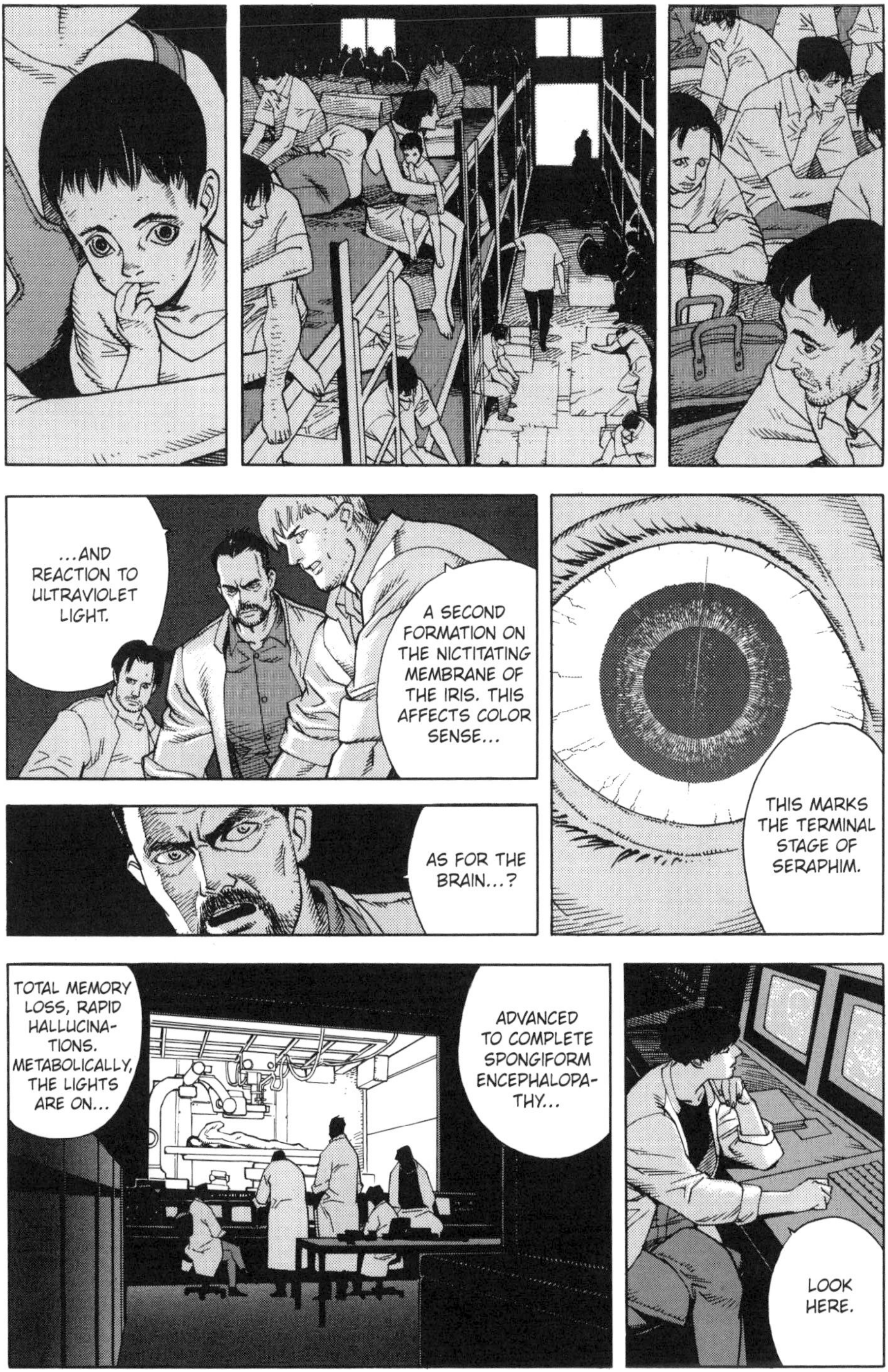

THIS MARKS THE TERMINAL STAGE OF SERAPHIM.
A SECOND FORMATION ON THE NICTITATING MEMBRANE OF THE IRIS. THIS AFFECTS COLOR SENSE...
...AND REACTION TO ULTRAVIOLET LIGHT.
AS FOR THE BRAIN...?
LOOK HERE.
ADVANCED TO COMPLETE SPONGIFORM ENCEPHALOPA-THY...
TOTAL MEMORY LOSS, RAPID HALLUCINA-TIONS. METABOLICALLY, THE LIGHTS ARE ON...

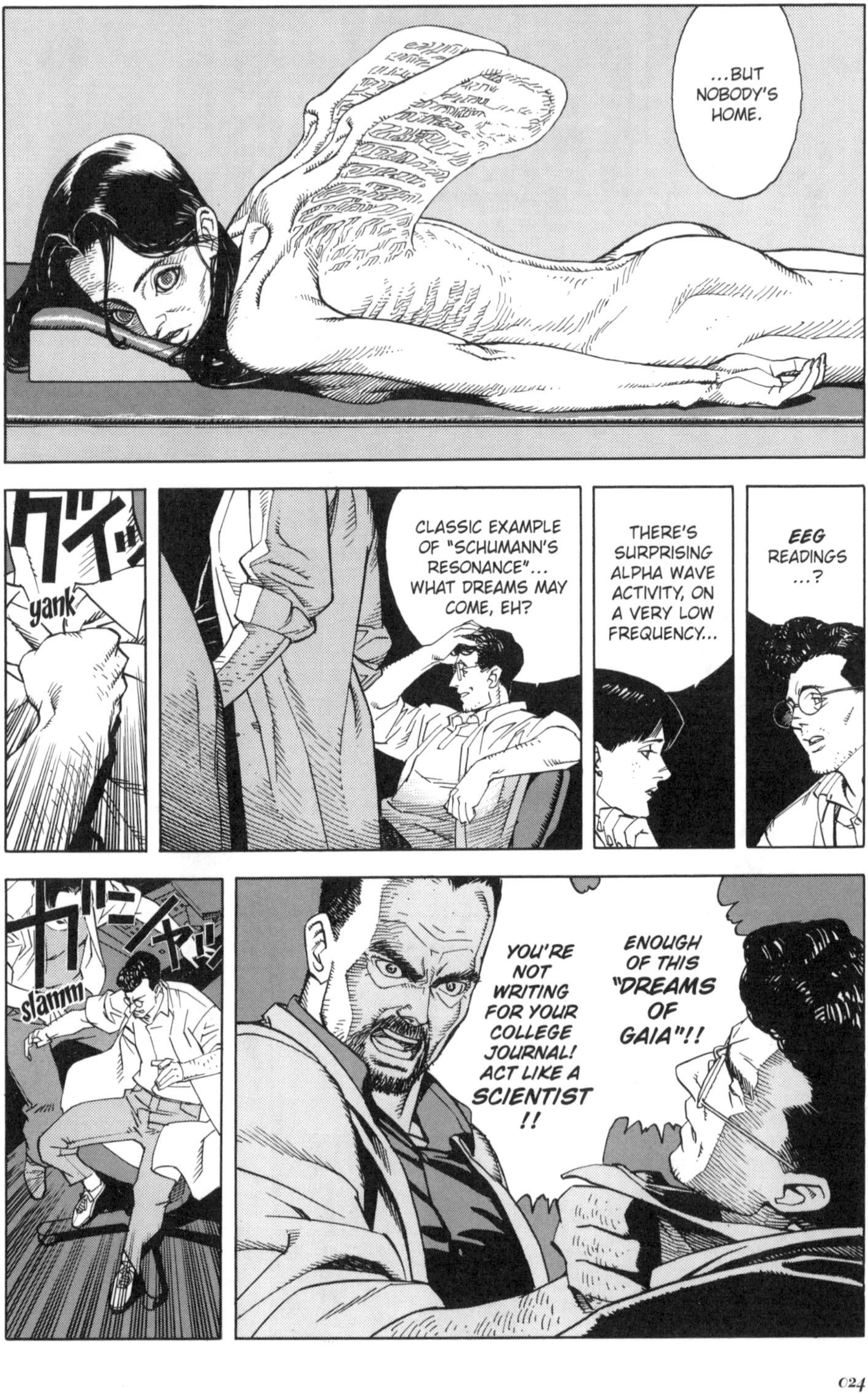
...BUT NOBODY'S HOME.
EEG READINGS ...?
THERE'S SURPRISING ALPHA WAVE ACTIVITY, ON A VERY LOW FREQUENCY...
CLASSIC EXAMPLE OF "SCHUMANN'S RESONANCE"... WHAT DREAMS MAY COME, EH?
yank
ENOUGH OF THIS "DREAMS OF GAIA"!!
YOU'RE NOT WRITING FOR YOUR COLLEGE JOURNAL! ACT LIKE A SCIENTIST!!
slamm

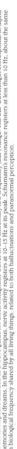

In 1952, physicist W. O. Schumann described a resonant cavity between Earth's surface and the ionosphere that acts as a wave guide for electromagnetic waves in the extremely low frequency (ELF) range. The ELF wavelength corresponds to alpha waves in the main part of the temporal cortex of the human brain, which is said to build memories and dreams. In the hippocampus, nerve activity registers at 10–15 Hz at its peak. Schumann's resonance registers at less than 10 Hz, about the same as the human dream state. The resonance covers the globe, and some speculate that it is a biological frequency shared by all living things, related to both hallucinations and paranormal perception.

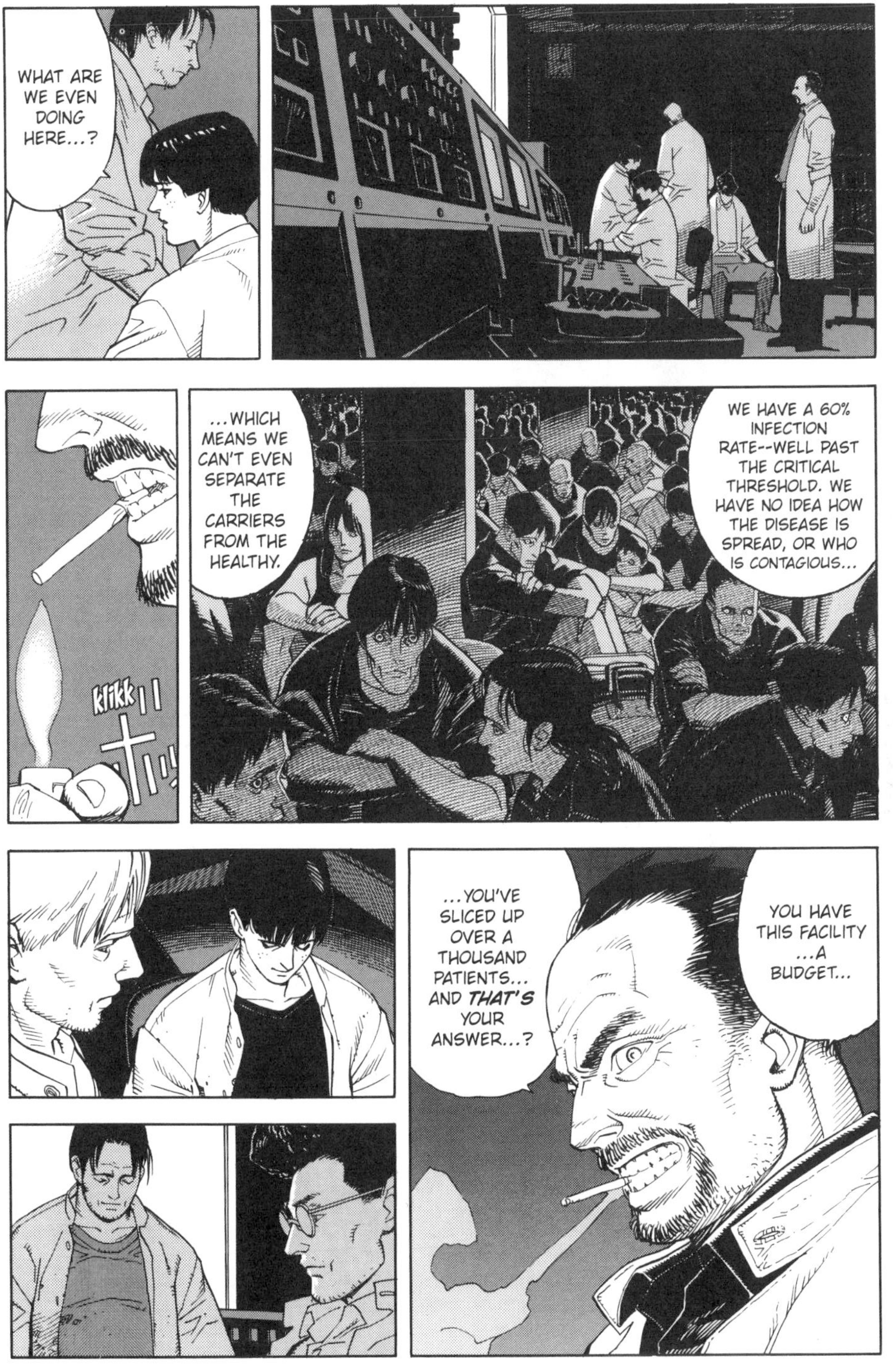
WHAT ARE WE EVEN DOING HERE...?
WE HAVE A 60% INFECTION RATE--WELL PAST THE CRITICAL THRESHOLD. WE HAVE NO IDEA HOW THE DISEASE IS SPREAD, OR WHO IS CONTAGIOUS...
...WHICH MEANS WE CAN'T EVEN SEPARATE THE CARRIERS FROM THE HEALTHY.
klikk
YOU HAVE THIS FACILITY ...A BUDGET...
...YOU'VE SLICED UP OVER A THOUSAND PATIENTS... AND ***THAT'S*** YOUR ANSWER...?

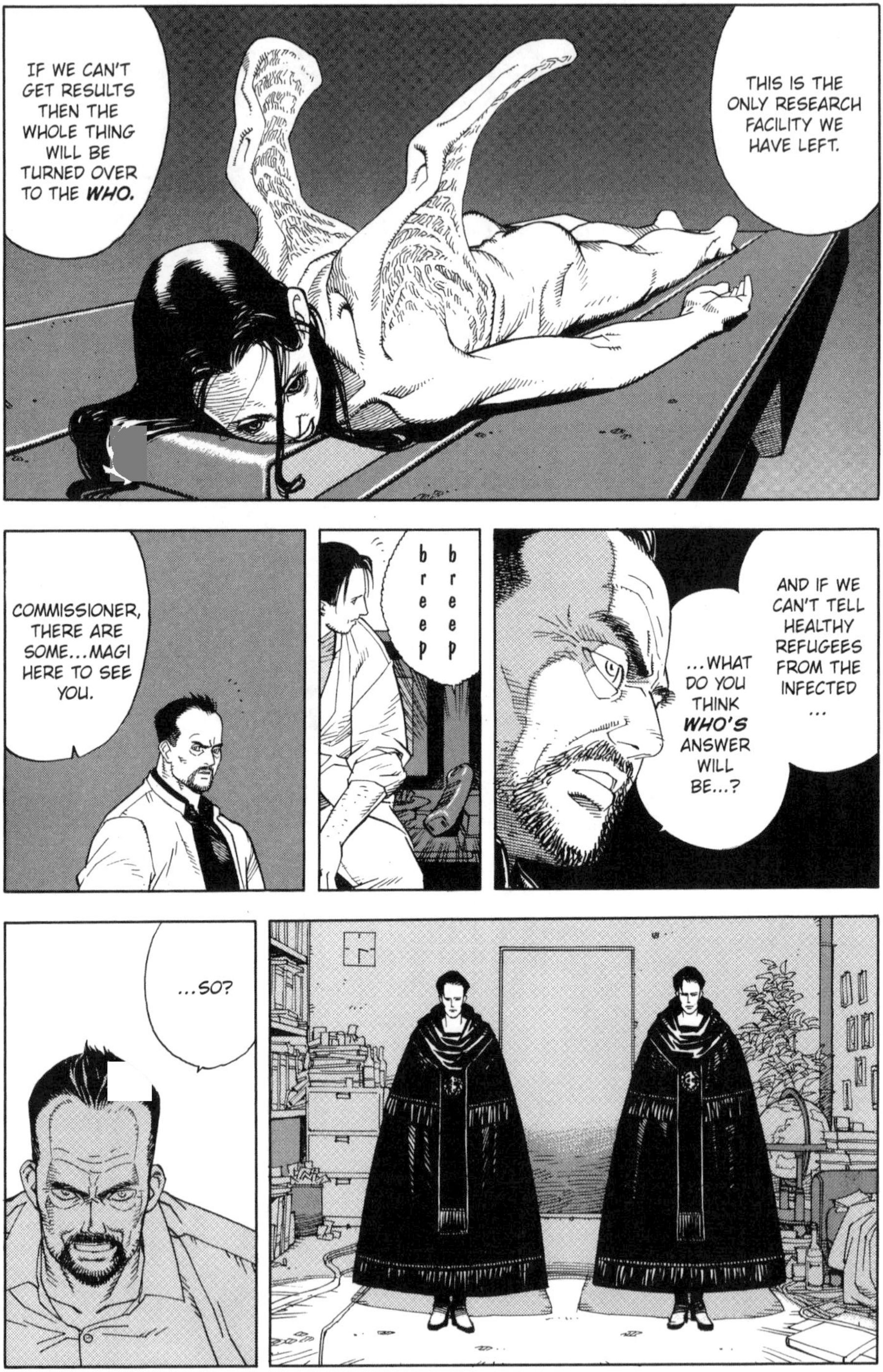
THIS IS THE ONLY RESEARCH FACILITY WE HAVE LEFT.
IF WE CAN'T GET RESULTS THEN THE WHOLE THING WILL BE TURNED OVER TO THE **WHO.**
AND IF WE CAN'T TELL HEALTHY REFUGEES FROM THE INFECTED ...
...WHAT DO YOU THINK **WHO'S** ANSWER WILL BE...?
breep
breep
COMMISSIONER, THERE ARE SOME...MAGI HERE TO SEE YOU.
...SO?

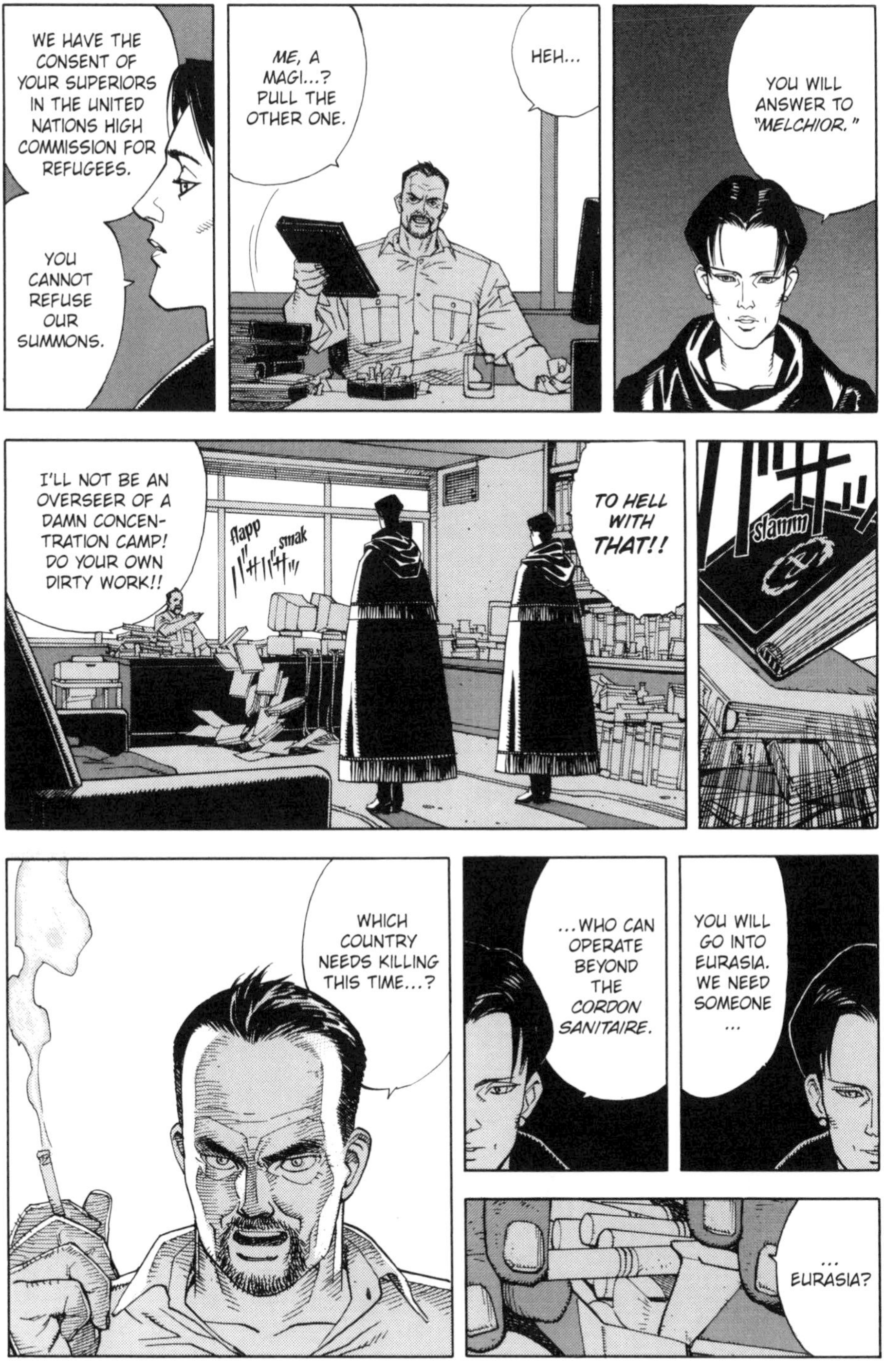
YOU WILL ANSWER TO "MELCHIOR."
HEH...
ME, A MAGI...? PULL THE OTHER ONE.
WE HAVE THE CONSENT OF YOUR SUPERIORS IN THE UNITED NATIONS HIGH COMMISSION FOR REFUGEES.
YOU CANNOT REFUSE OUR SUMMONS.
slamm
TO HELL WITH THAT!!
I'LL NOT BE AN OVERSEER OF A DAMN CONCEN-TRATION CAMP! DO YOUR OWN DIRTY WORK!!
flapp
smak
YOU WILL GO INTO EURASIA. WE NEED SOMEONE ...
...WHO CAN OPERATE BEYOND THE CORDON SANITAIRE.
... EURASIA?
WHICH COUNTRY NEEDS KILLING THIS TIME...?

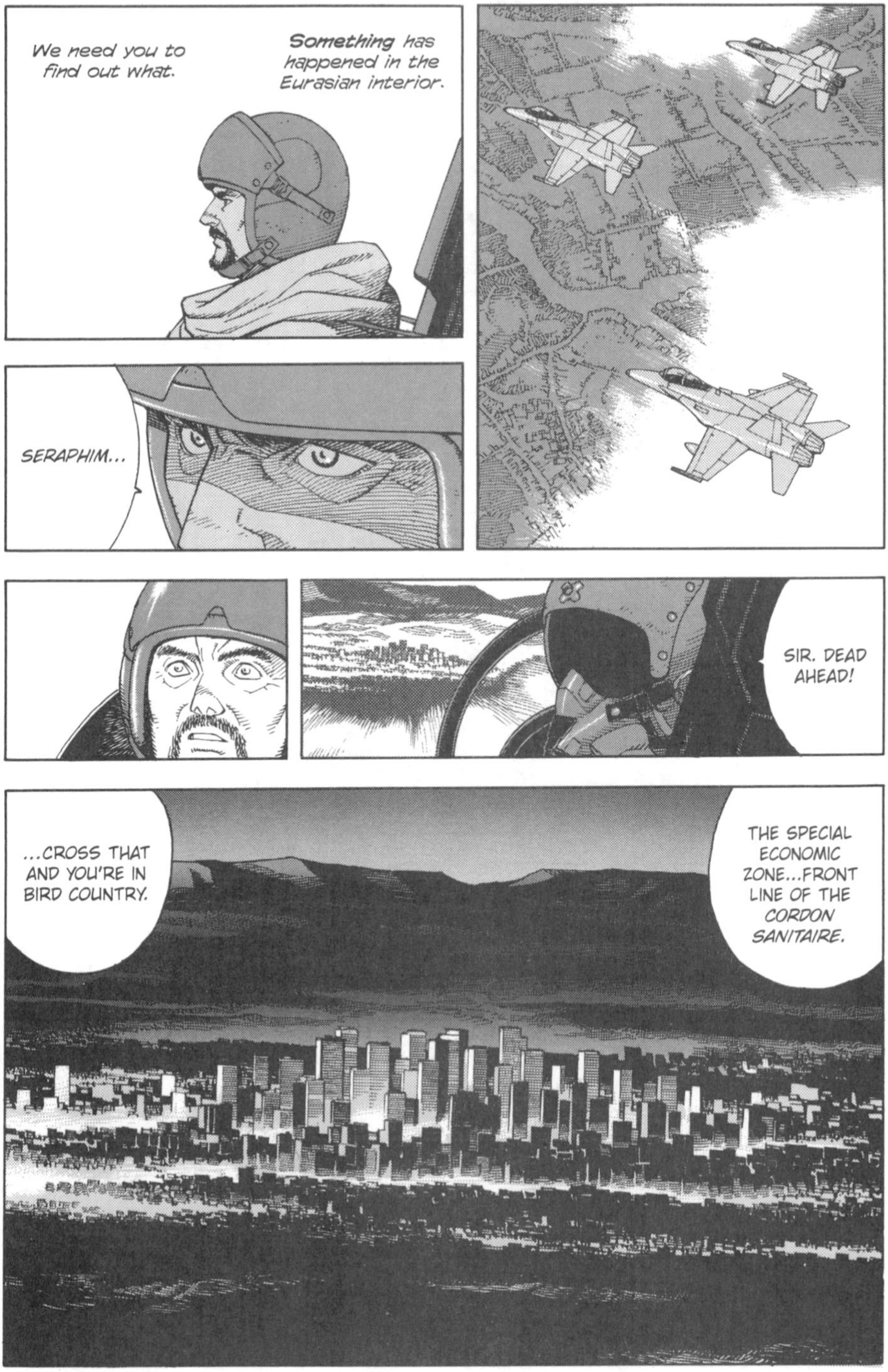
Something has happened in the Eurasian interior.
We need you to find out what.
SERAPHIM...
SIR. DEAD AHEAD!
THE SPECIAL ECONOMIC ZONE...FRONT LINE OF THE CORDON SANITAIRE.
...CROSS THAT AND YOU'RE IN BIRD COUNTRY.

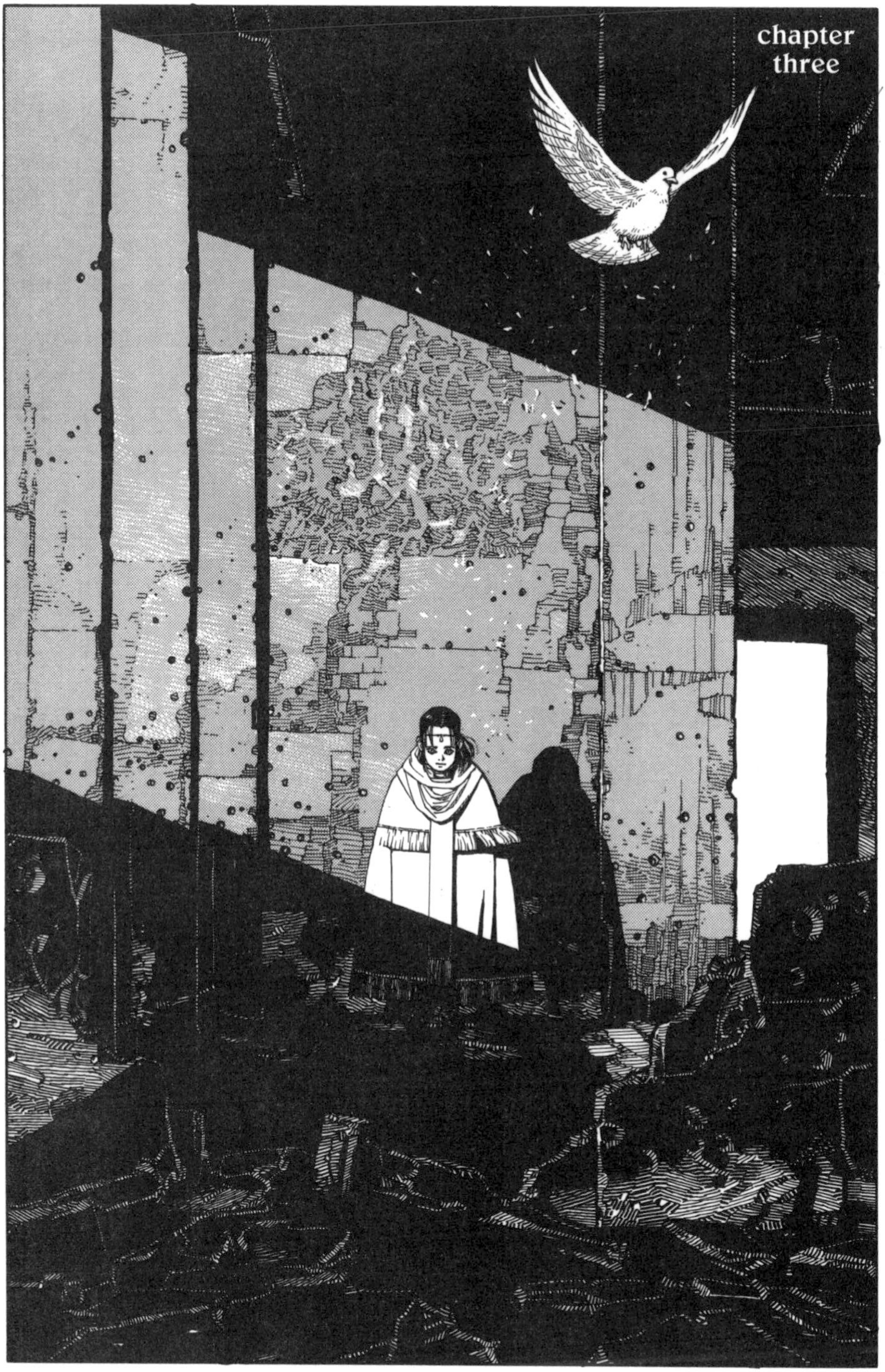
chapter
three

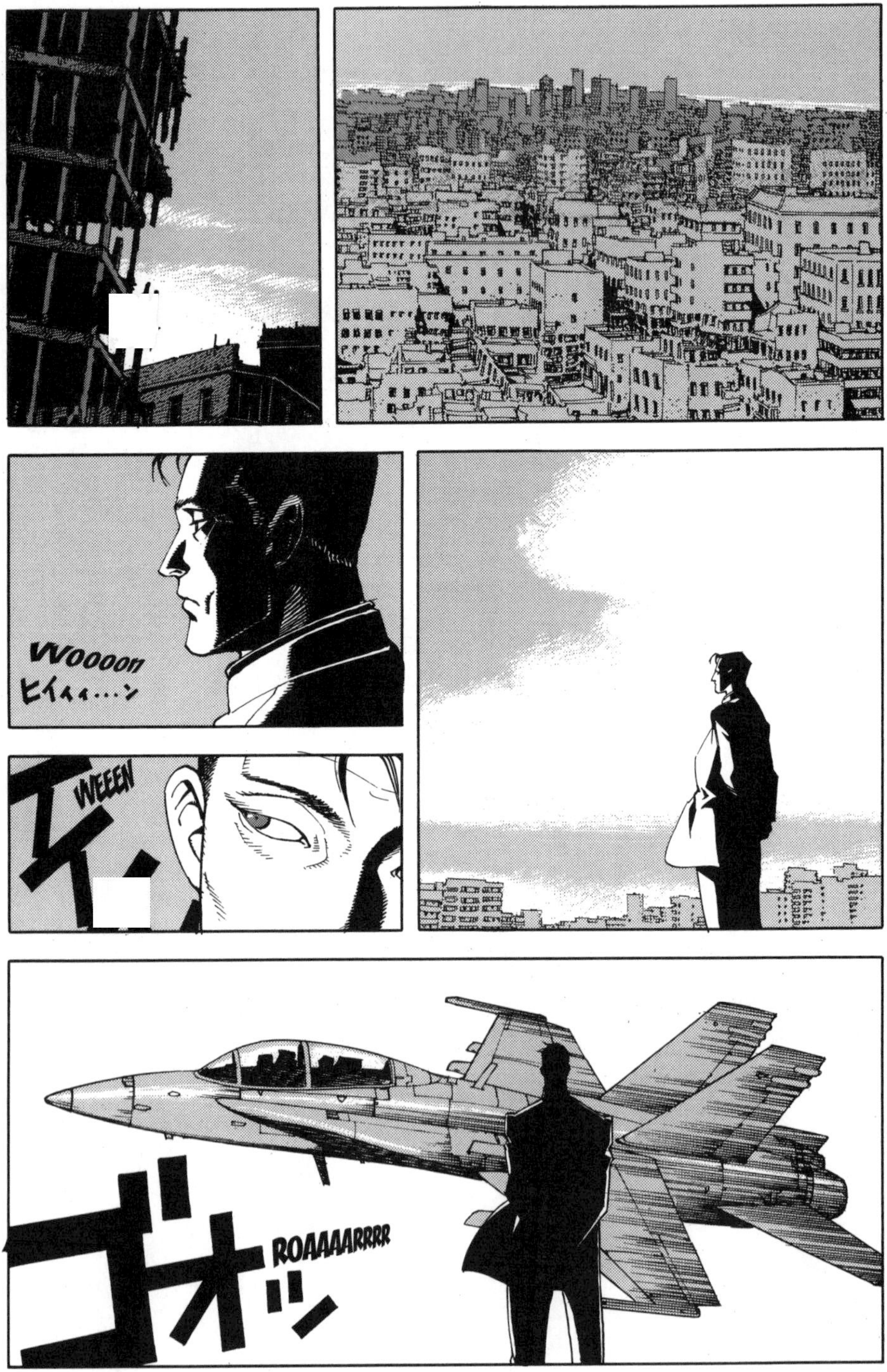
Wooooon
ヒイィィ…ン
WEEEN
ROAAAARRRR
ゴオッ

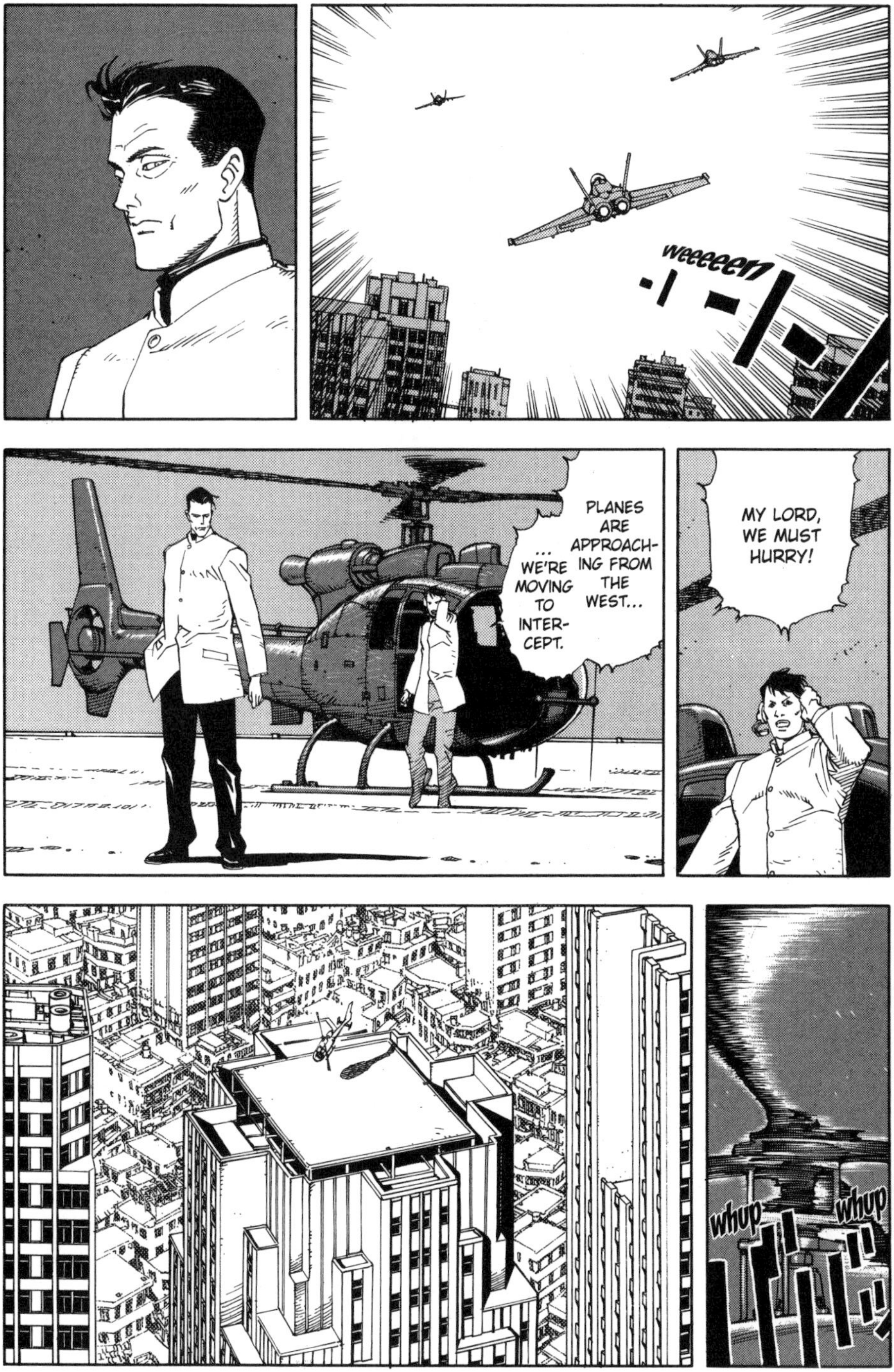
weeeeen
PLANES ARE APPROACHING FROM THE WEST...
... WE'RE MOVING TO INTERCEPT.
MY LORD, WE MUST HURRY!
whup
whup

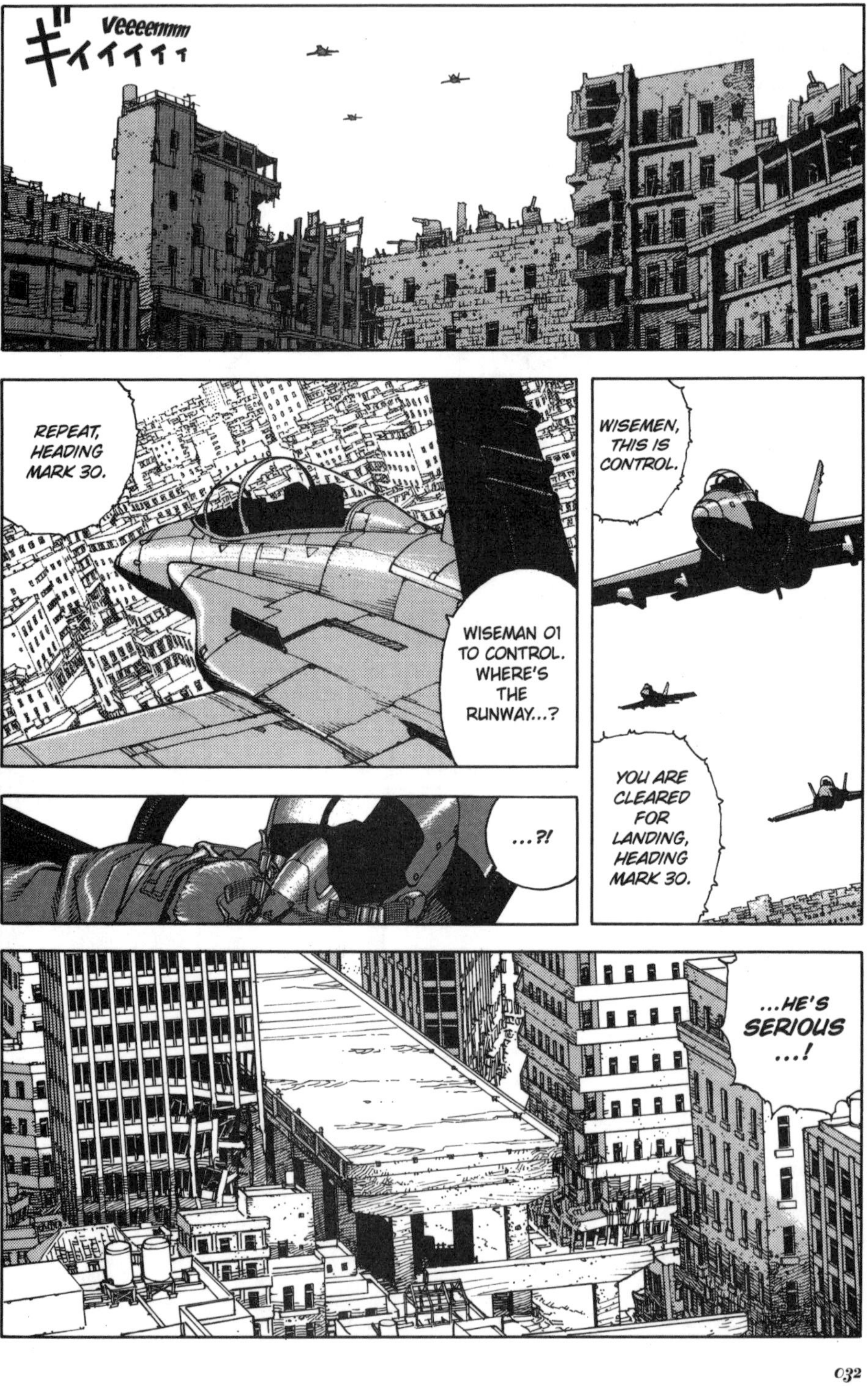

ギイイイイィ
Veeeennnn
WISEMEN, THIS IS CONTROL.
YOU ARE CLEARED FOR LANDING, HEADING MARK 30.
WISEMAN 01 TO CONTROL. WHERE'S THE RUNWAY...?
REPEAT, HEADING MARK 30.
...?!
...HE'S SERIOUS ...!

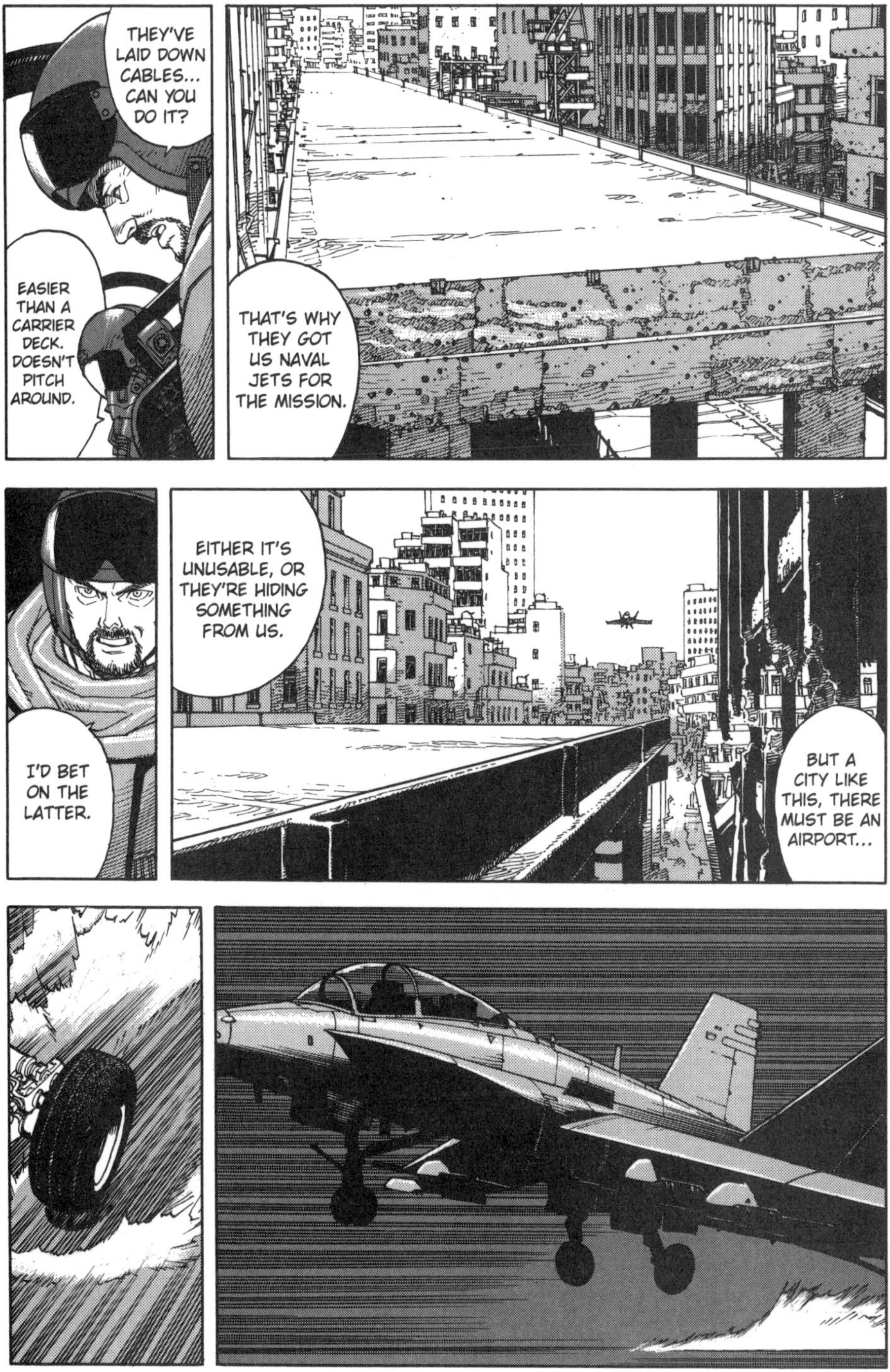
THAT'S WHY THEY GOT US NAVAL JETS FOR THE MISSION.
THEY'VE LAID DOWN CABLES... CAN YOU DO IT?
EASIER THAN A CARRIER DECK. DOESN'T PITCH AROUND.
BUT A CITY LIKE THIS, THERE MUST BE AN AIRPORT...
EITHER IT'S UNUSABLE, OR THEY'RE HIDING SOMETHING FROM US.
I'D BET ON THE LATTER.

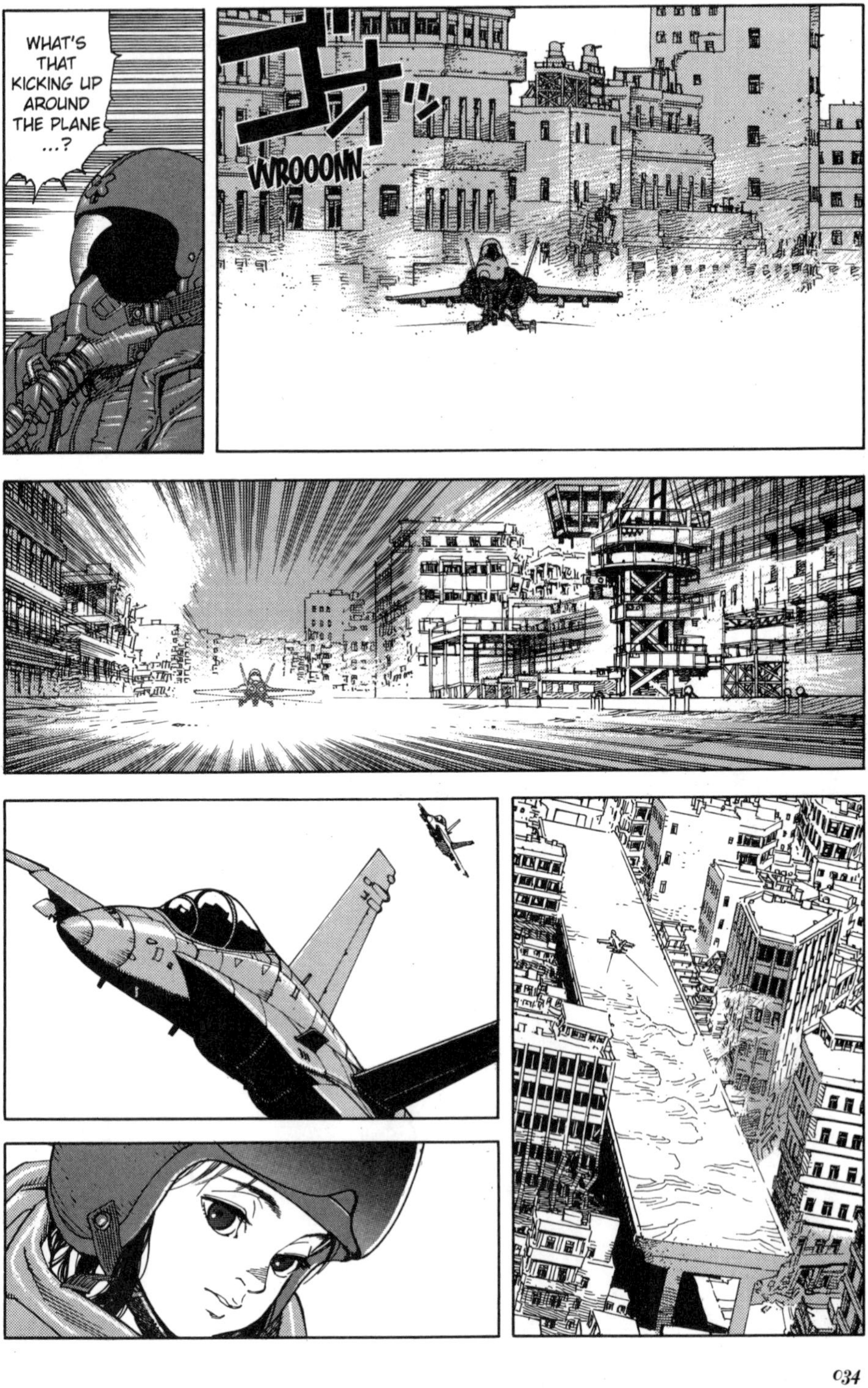
WHAT'S THAT KICKING UP AROUND THE PLANE ...?
ゴォオ
VVROOOMN

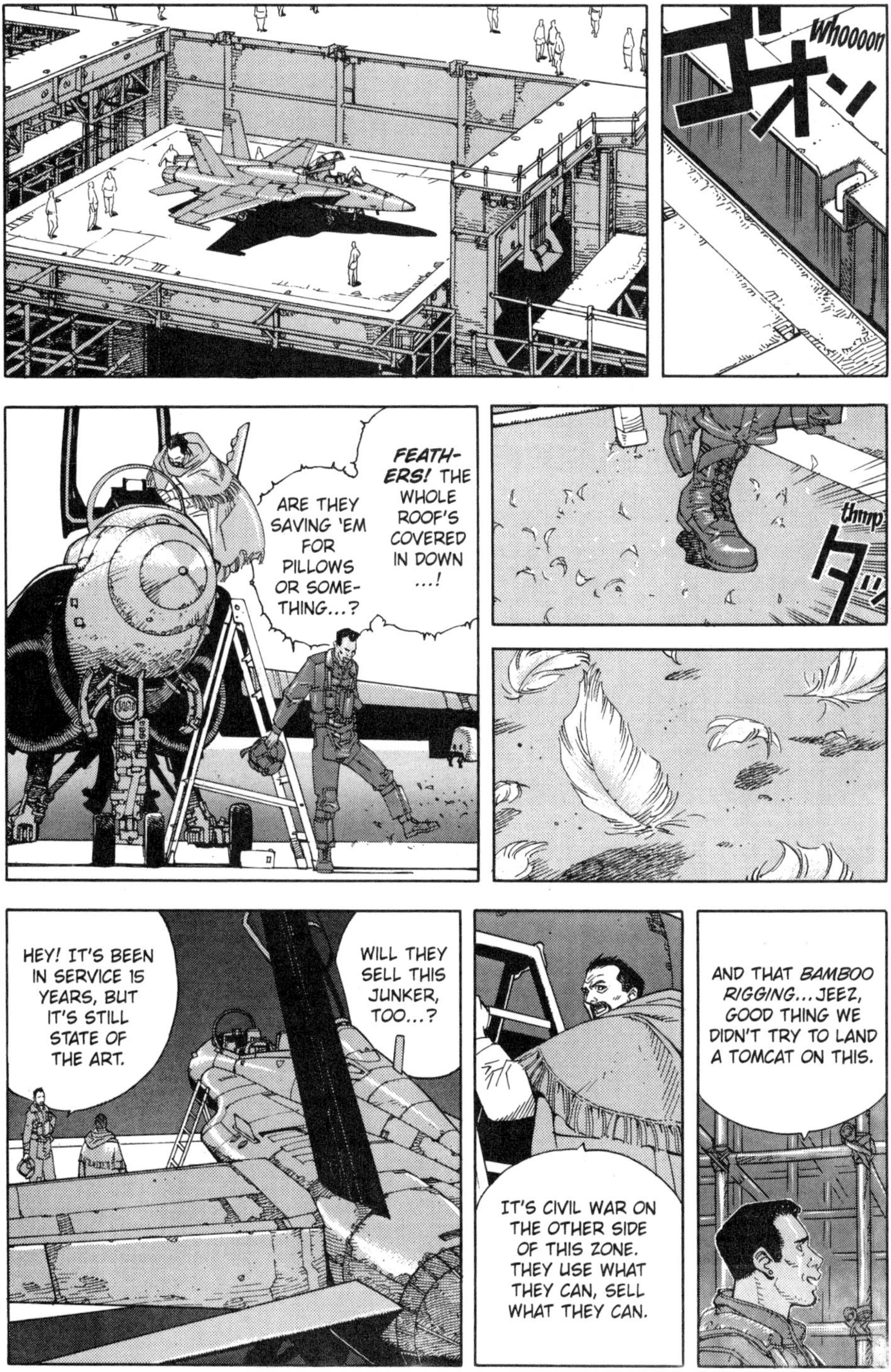

Whoooon
ゴオン
thmp
タッ
FEATHERS! THE WHOLE ROOF'S COVERED IN DOWN...!
ARE THEY SAVING 'EM FOR PILLOWS OR SOMETHING...?
AND THAT BAMBOO RIGGING... JEEZ, GOOD THING WE DIDN'T TRY TO LAND A TOMCAT ON THIS.
IT'S CIVIL WAR ON THE OTHER SIDE OF THIS ZONE. THEY USE WHAT THEY CAN, SELL WHAT THEY CAN.
WILL THEY SELL THIS JUNKER, TOO...?
HEY! IT'S BEEN IN SERVICE 15 YEARS, BUT IT'S STILL STATE OF THE ART.

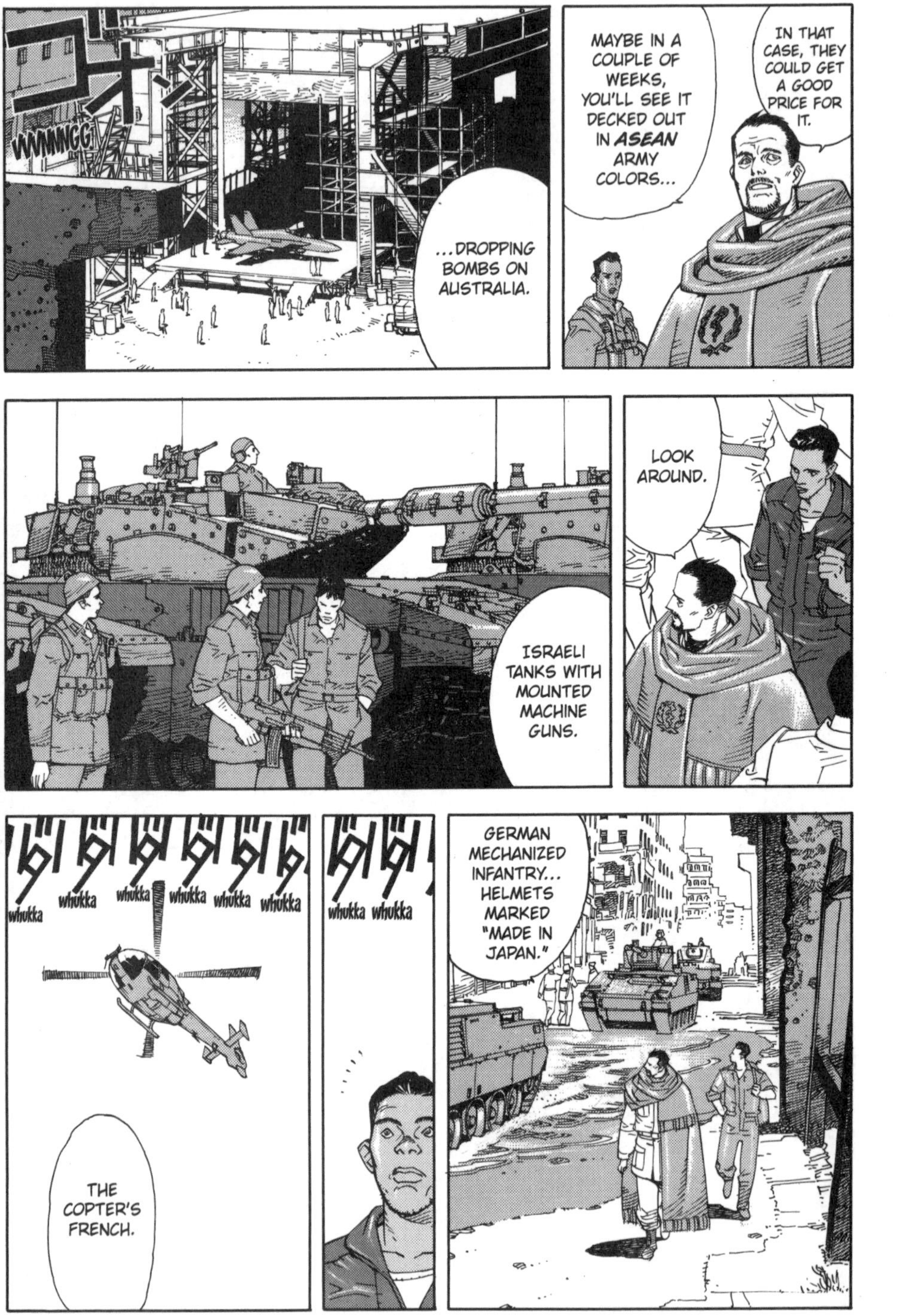
IN THAT CASE, THEY COULD GET A GOOD PRICE FOR IT.
MAYBE IN A COUPLE OF WEEKS, YOU'LL SEE IT DECKED OUT IN ASEAN ARMY COLORS...
WWNNGG
...DROPPING BOMBS ON AUSTRALIA.
LOOK AROUND.
ISRAELI TANKS WITH MOUNTED MACHINE GUNS.
GERMAN MECHANIZED INFANTRY... HELMETS MARKED "MADE IN JAPAN."
whukka whukka
whukka whukka whukka whukka whukka whukka
THE COPTER'S FRENCH.

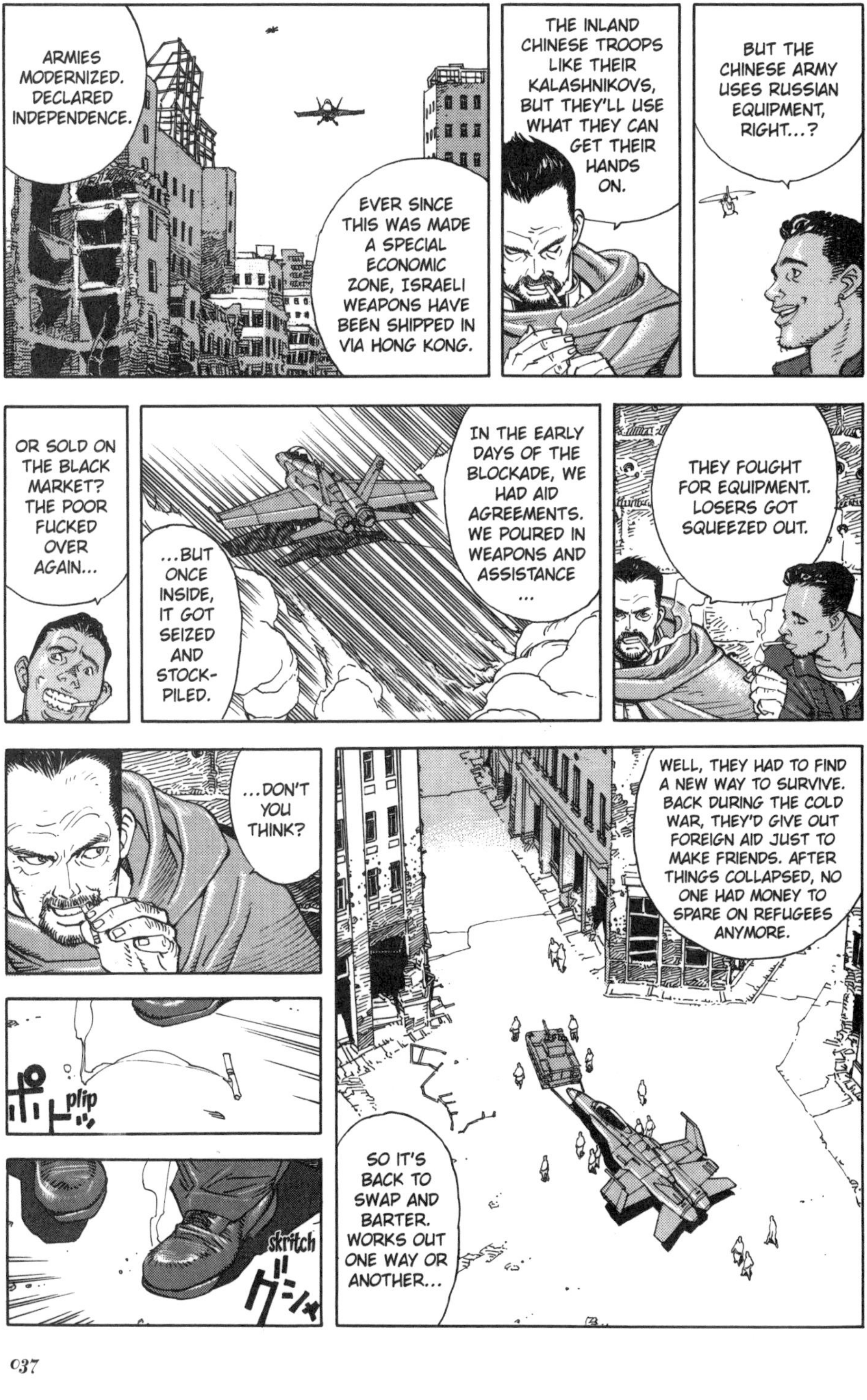
BUT THE CHINESE ARMY USES RUSSIAN EQUIPMENT, RIGHT…?
THE INLAND CHINESE TROOPS LIKE THEIR KALASHNIKOVS, BUT THEY'LL USE WHAT THEY CAN GET THEIR HANDS ON.
EVER SINCE THIS WAS MADE A SPECIAL ECONOMIC ZONE, ISRAELI WEAPONS HAVE BEEN SHIPPED IN VIA HONG KONG.
ARMIES MODERNIZED. DECLARED INDEPENDENCE.
THEY FOUGHT FOR EQUIPMENT. LOSERS GOT SQUEEZED OUT.
IN THE EARLY DAYS OF THE BLOCKADE, WE HAD AID AGREEMENTS. WE POURED IN WEAPONS AND ASSISTANCE …
…BUT ONCE INSIDE, IT GOT SEIZED AND STOCK-PILED.
OR SOLD ON THE BLACK MARKET? THE POOR FUCKED OVER AGAIN…
WELL, THEY HAD TO FIND A NEW WAY TO SURVIVE. BACK DURING THE COLD WAR, THEY'D GIVE OUT FOREIGN AID JUST TO MAKE FRIENDS. AFTER THINGS COLLAPSED, NO ONE HAD MONEY TO SPARE ON REFUGEES ANYMORE.
SO IT'S BACK TO SWAP AND BARTER. WORKS OUT ONE WAY OR ANOTHER…
…DON'T YOU THINK?
ポトッ plip
skritch グシャ

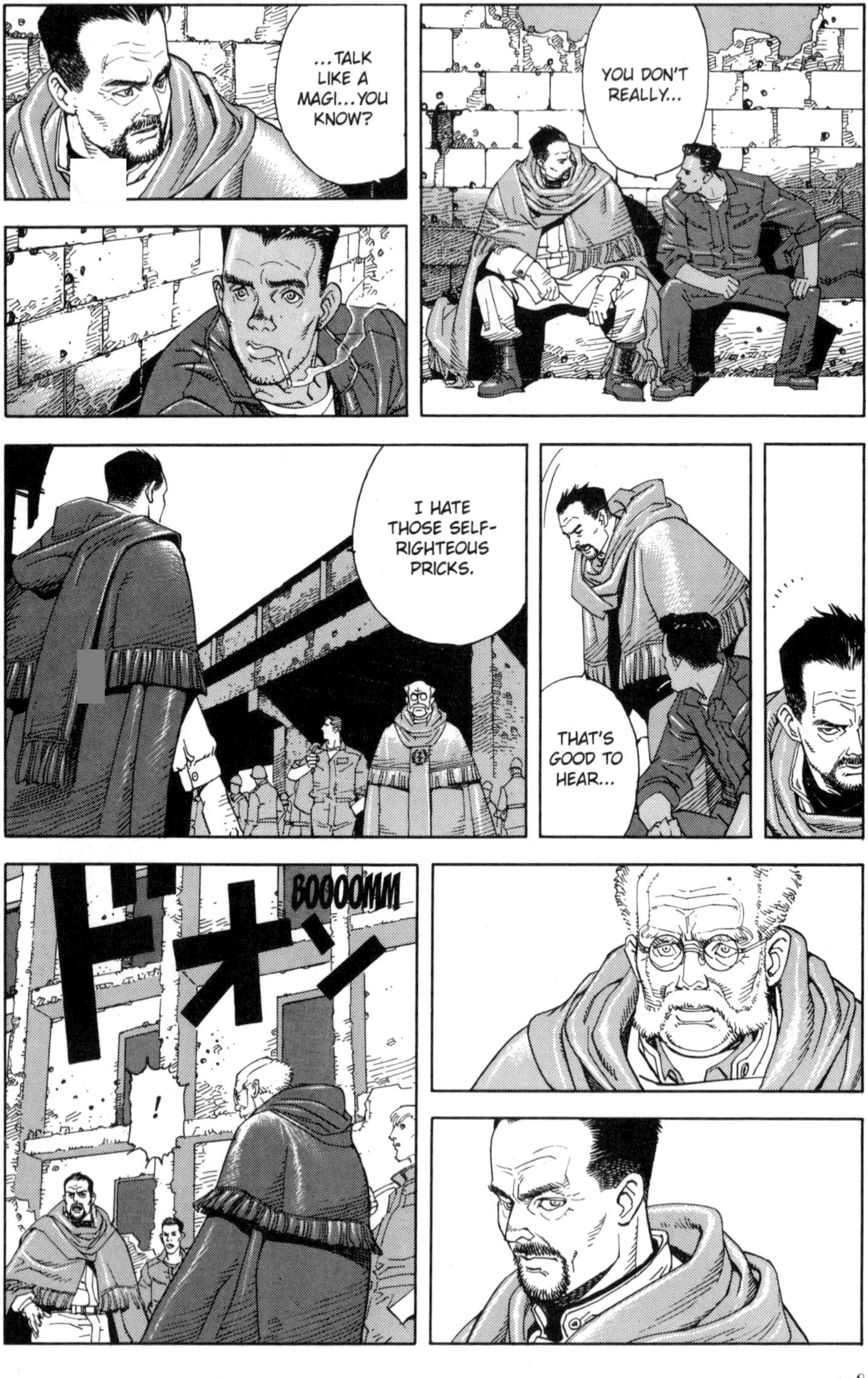
YOU DON'T REALLY...
...TALK LIKE A MAGI...YOU KNOW?
.....
THAT'S GOOD TO HEAR...
I HATE THOSE SELF-RIGHTEOUS PRICKS.
ドオーン
BOOOOMM
!

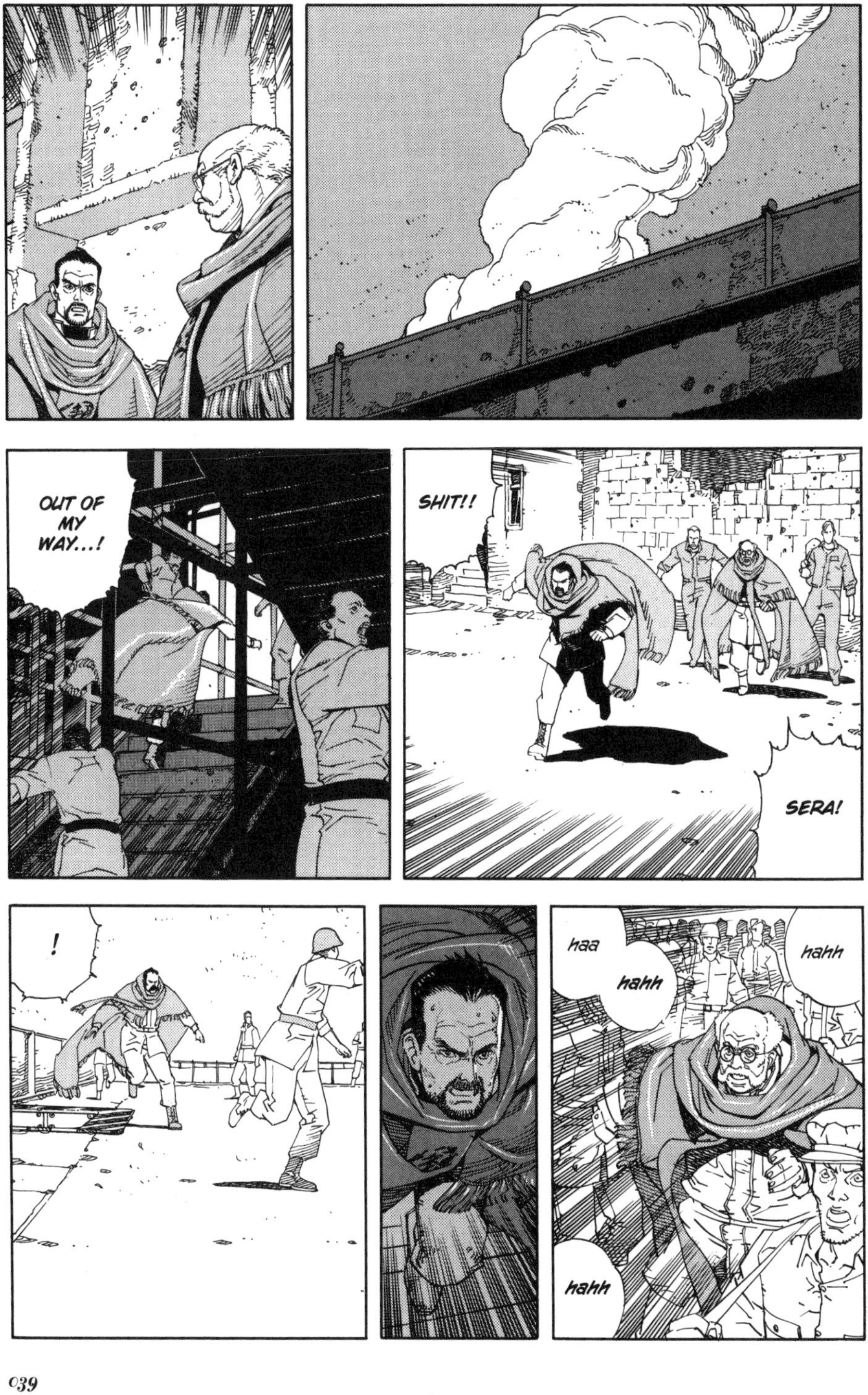
SHIT!!
SERA!
OUT OF MY WAY...!
hahh
haa
hahh
hahh
!

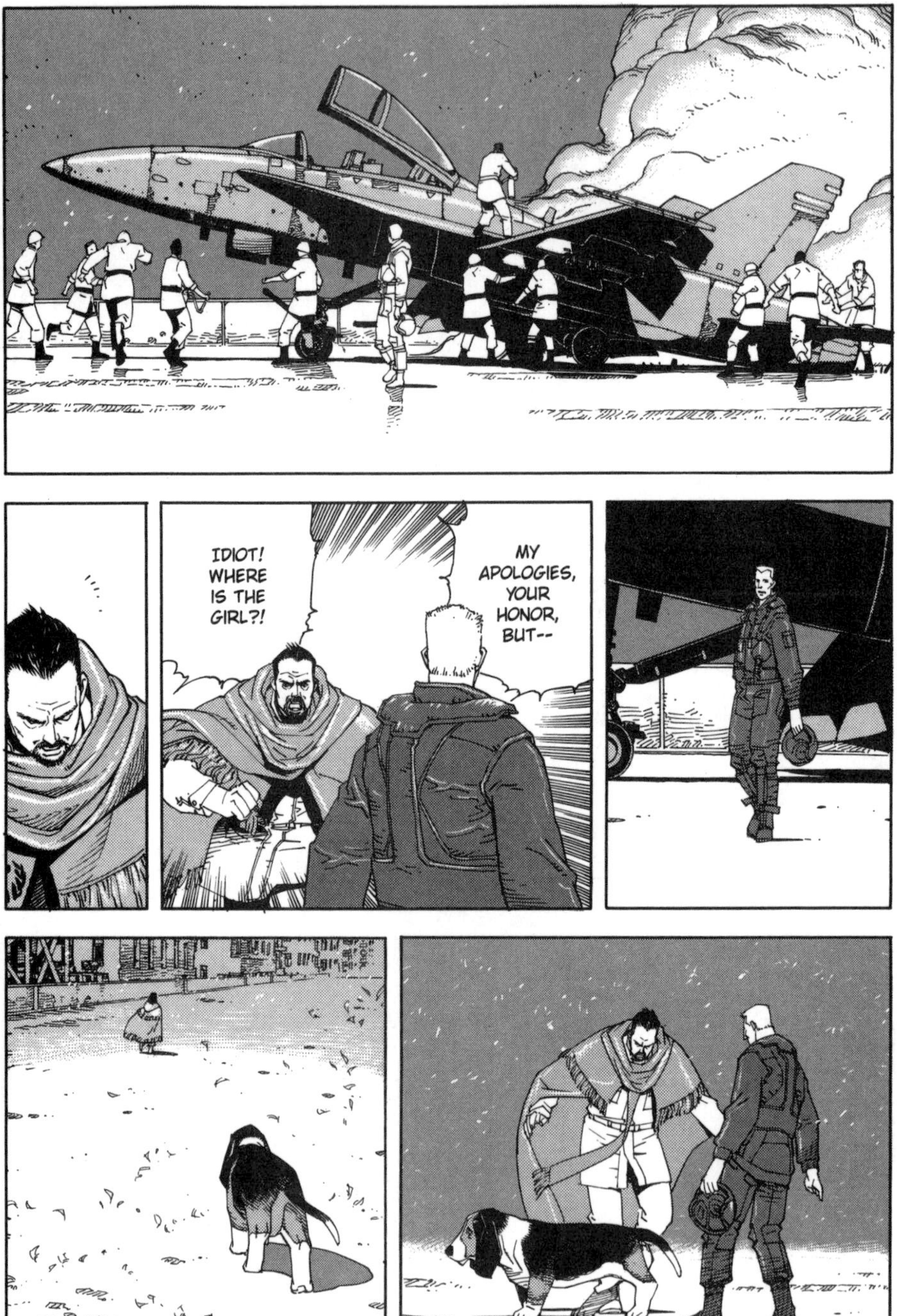
MY APOLOGIES, YOUR HONOR, BUT--
IDIOT! WHERE IS THE GIRL?!

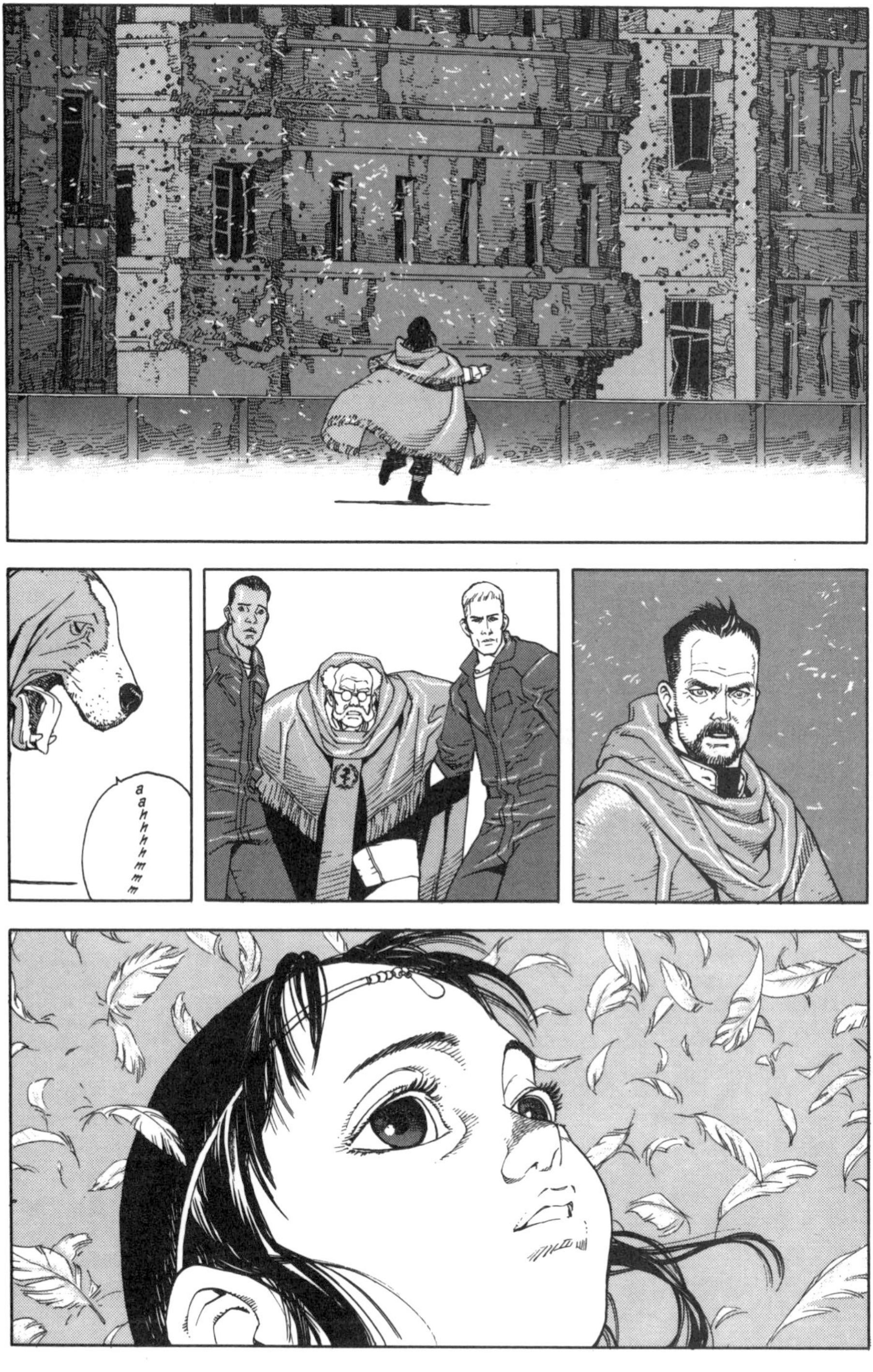
aahhhhmmm

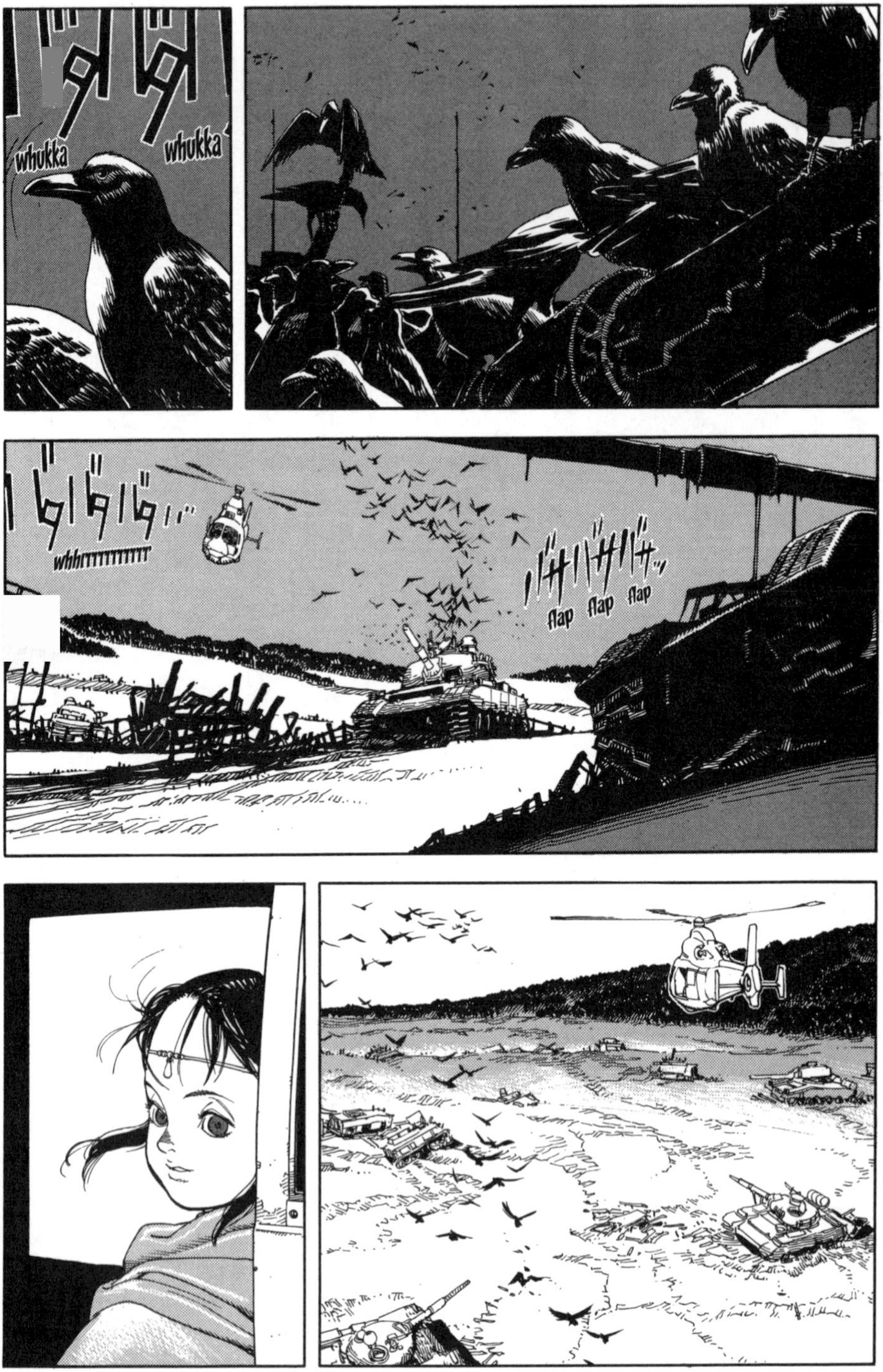
whukka
whukka
flap flap flap
whhrrrrrrrrrrrr

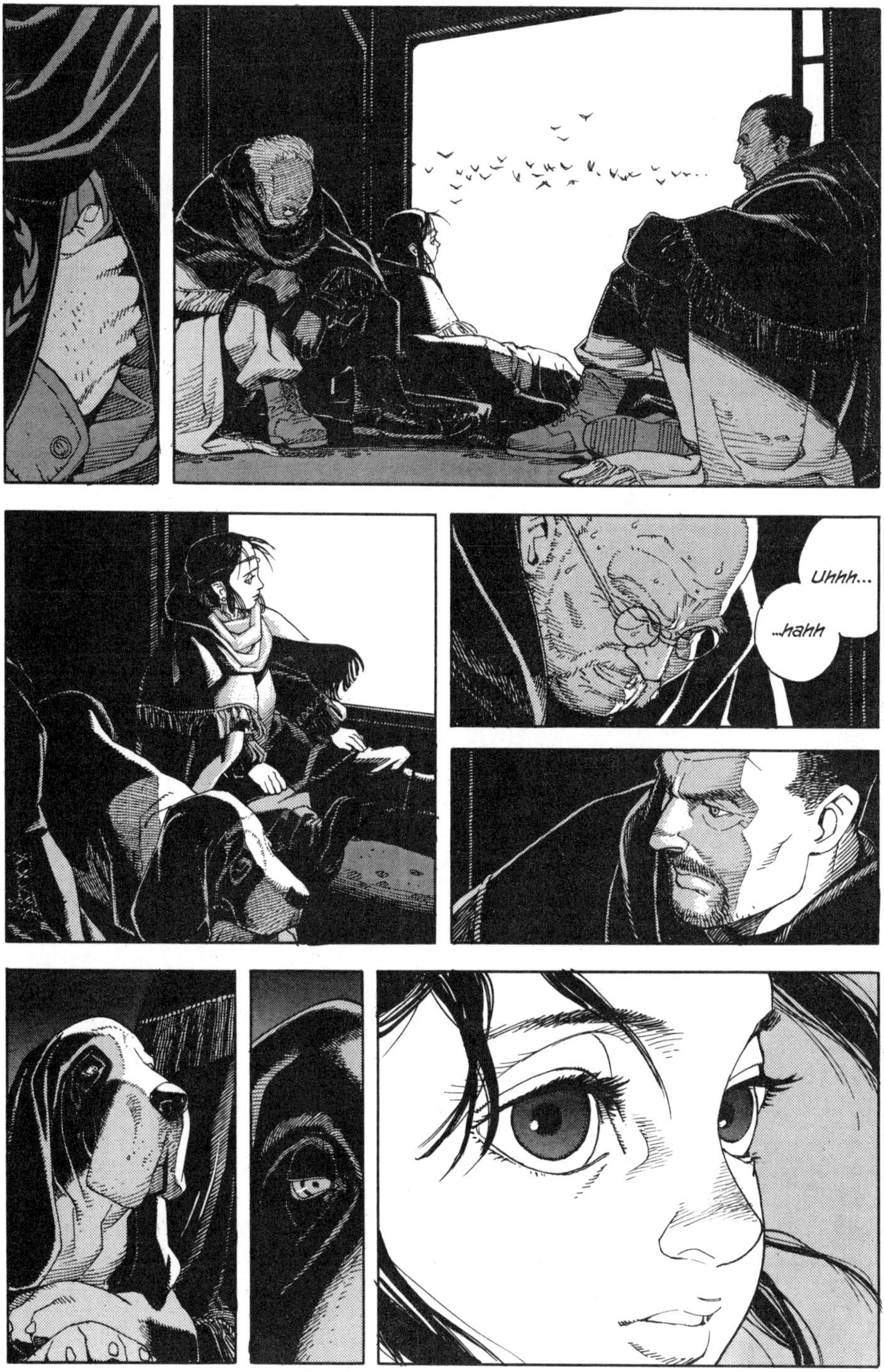
Uhhh...
...hahh

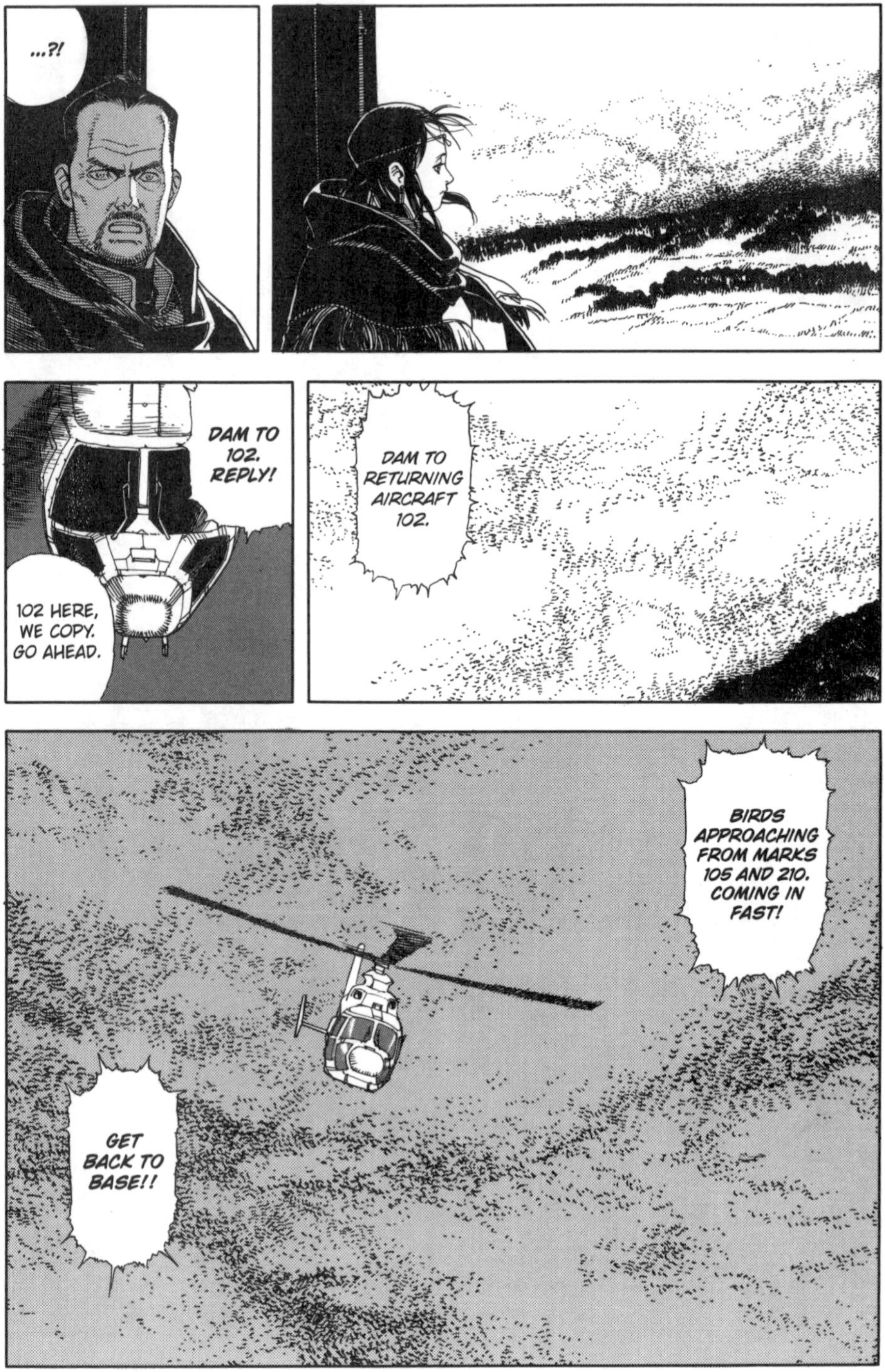
...?!
DAM TO RETURNING AIRCRAFT 102.
DAM TO 102. REPLY!
102 HERE, WE COPY. GO AHEAD.
BIRDS APPROACHING FROM MARKS 105 AND 210. COMING IN FAST!
GET BACK TO BASE!!

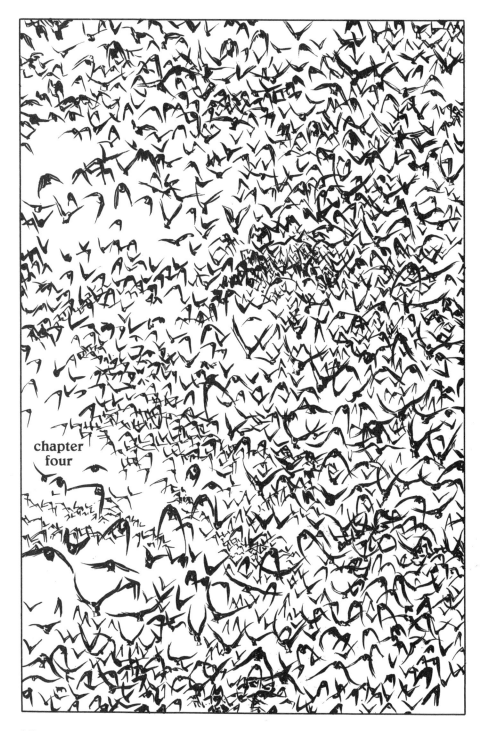

chapter
four

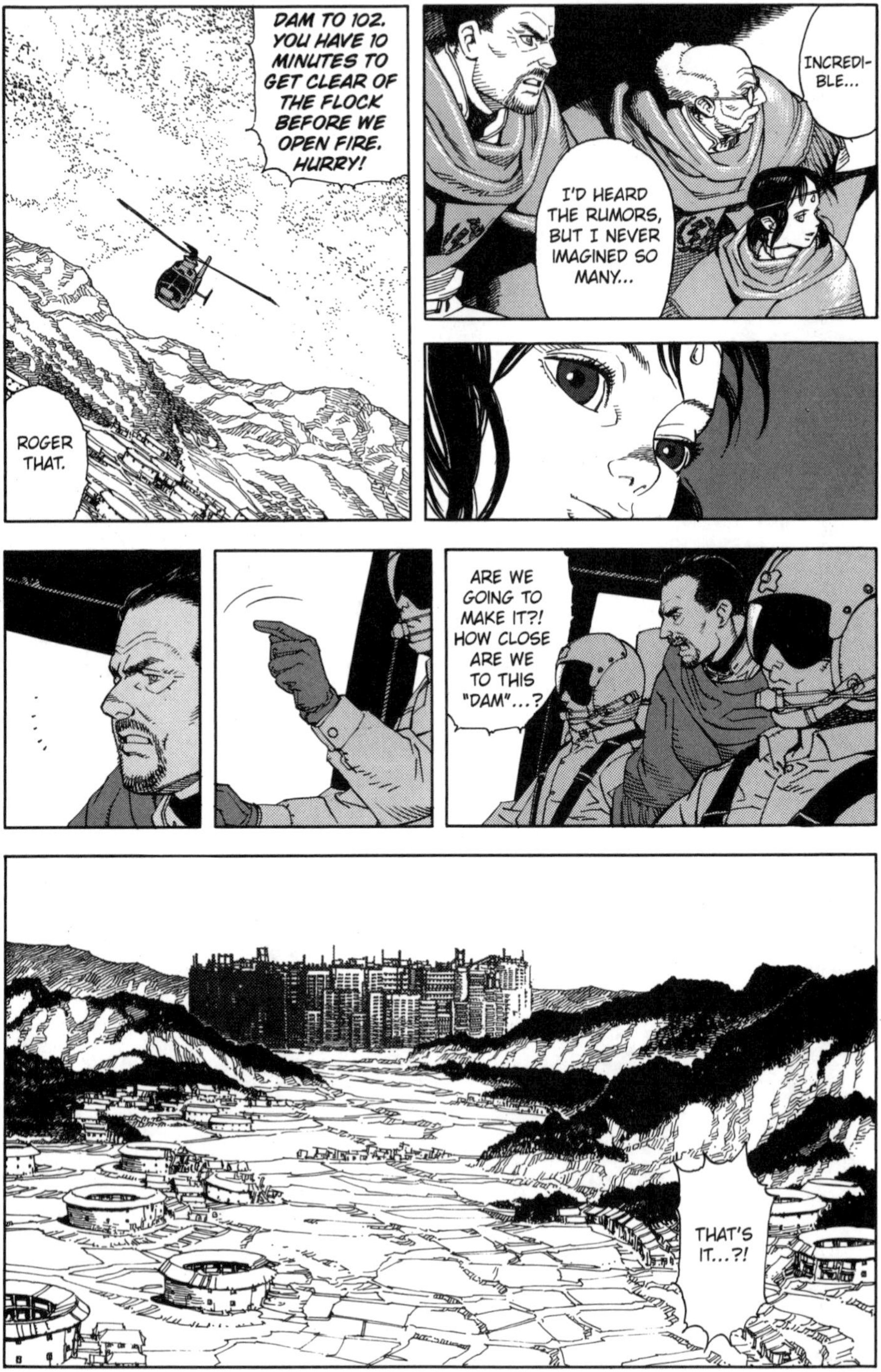
INCREDI-BLE...
I'D HEARD THE RUMORS, BUT I NEVER IMAGINED SO MANY...
DAM TO 102. YOU HAVE 10 MINUTES TO GET CLEAR OF THE FLOCK BEFORE WE OPEN FIRE. HURRY!
ROGER THAT.
ARE WE GOING TO MAKE IT?! HOW CLOSE ARE WE TO THIS "DAM"...?
...
THAT'S IT...?!

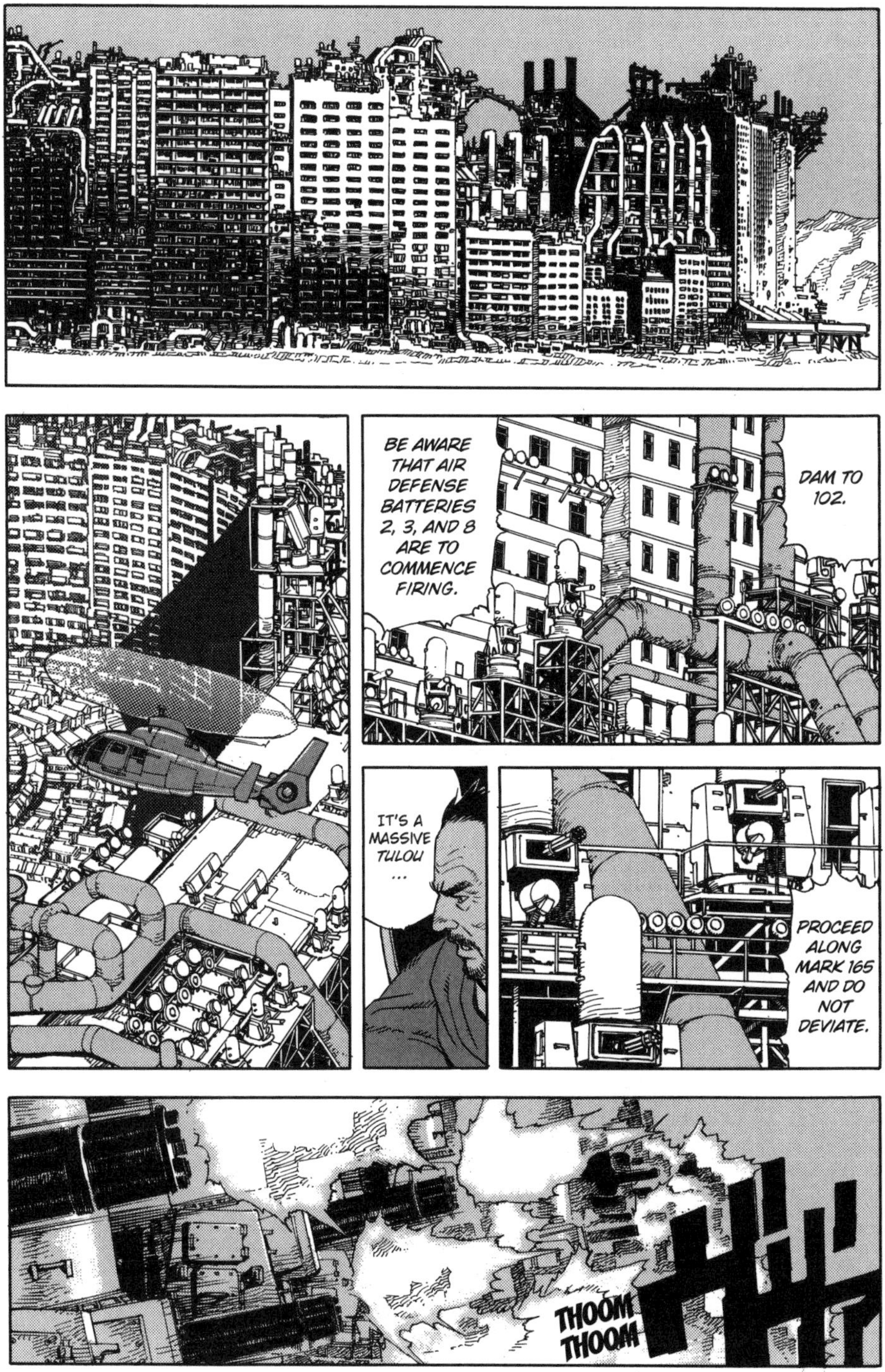
DAM TO 102.
BE AWARE THAT AIR DEFENSE BATTERIES 2, 3, AND 8 ARE TO COMMENCE FIRING.
PROCEED ALONG MARK 165 AND DO NOT DEVIATE.
IT'S A MASSIVE TULOU ...
THOOM THOOM

Tulou are villages built in the shape of a walled compound, an architectural style traditionally associated with the Hakka people.

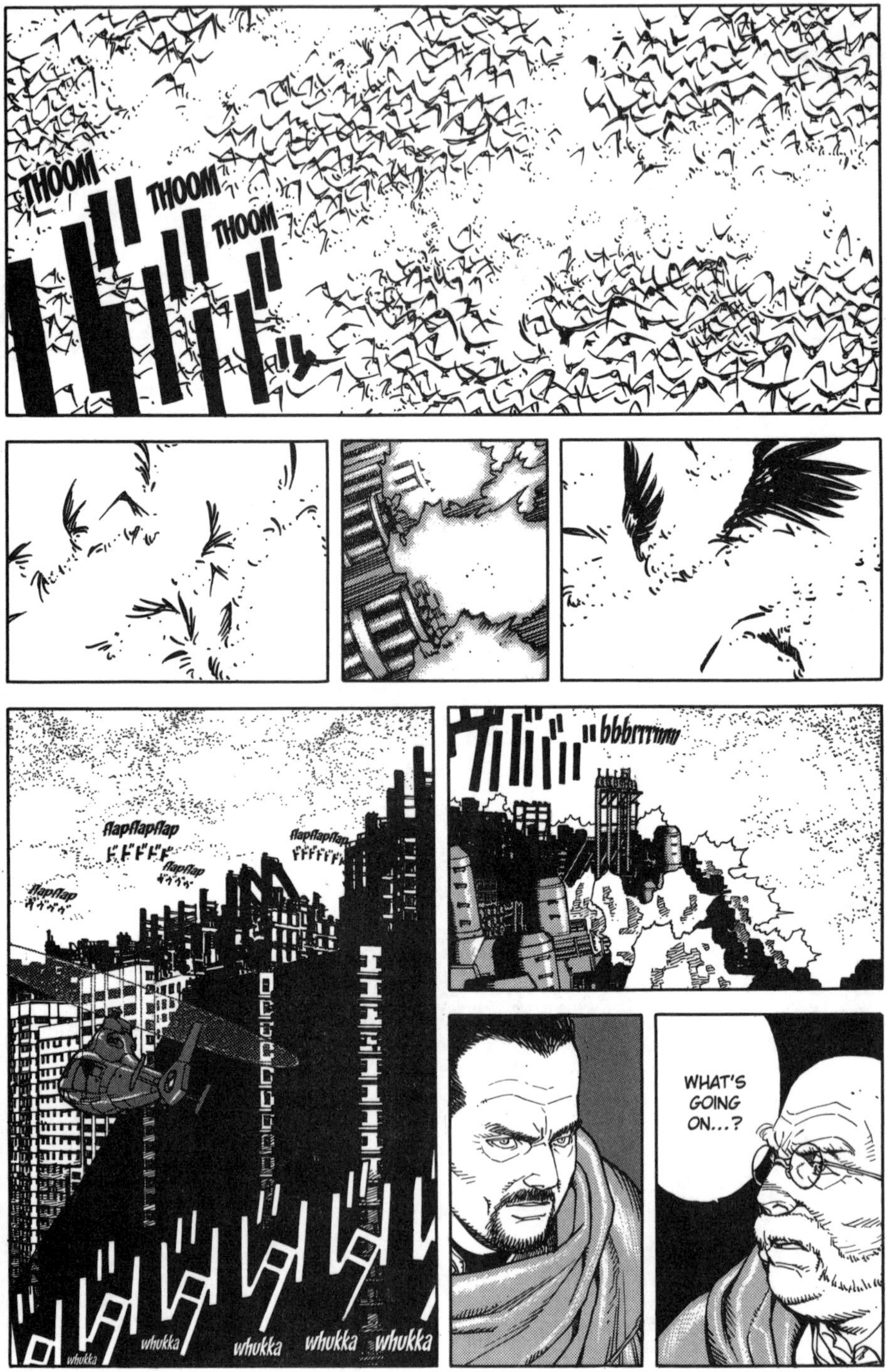
THOOM
THOOM
THOOM
bbbrrrrrrr
WHAT'S GOING ON...?
flapflapflap
flapflapflap
flapflap
flapflap
whukka
whukka
whukka
whukka
whukka

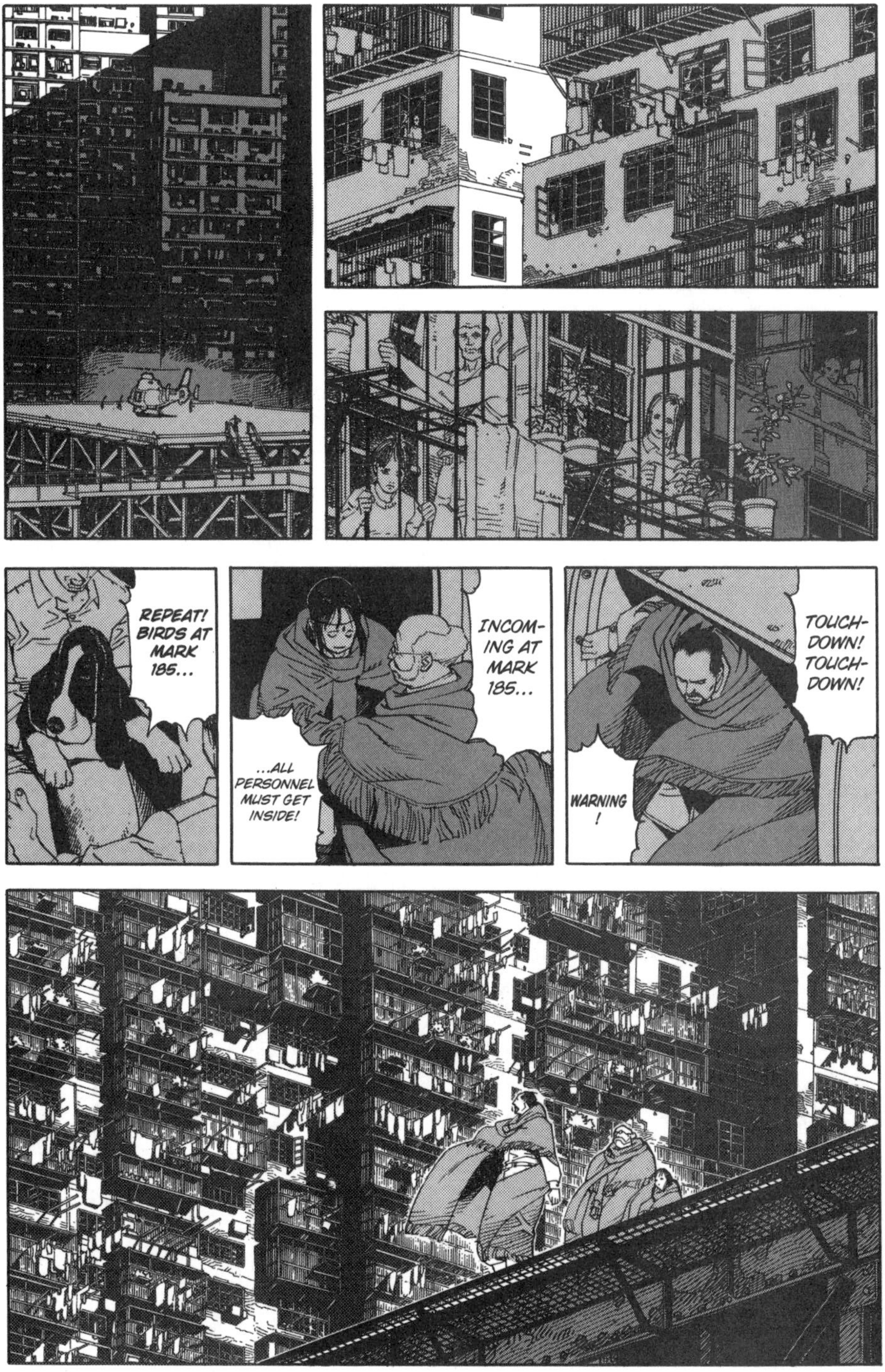
TOUCH-DOWN! TOUCH-DOWN!
WARNING!
INCOMING AT MARK 185...
...ALL PERSONNEL MUST GET INSIDE!
REPEAT! BIRDS AT MARK 185...

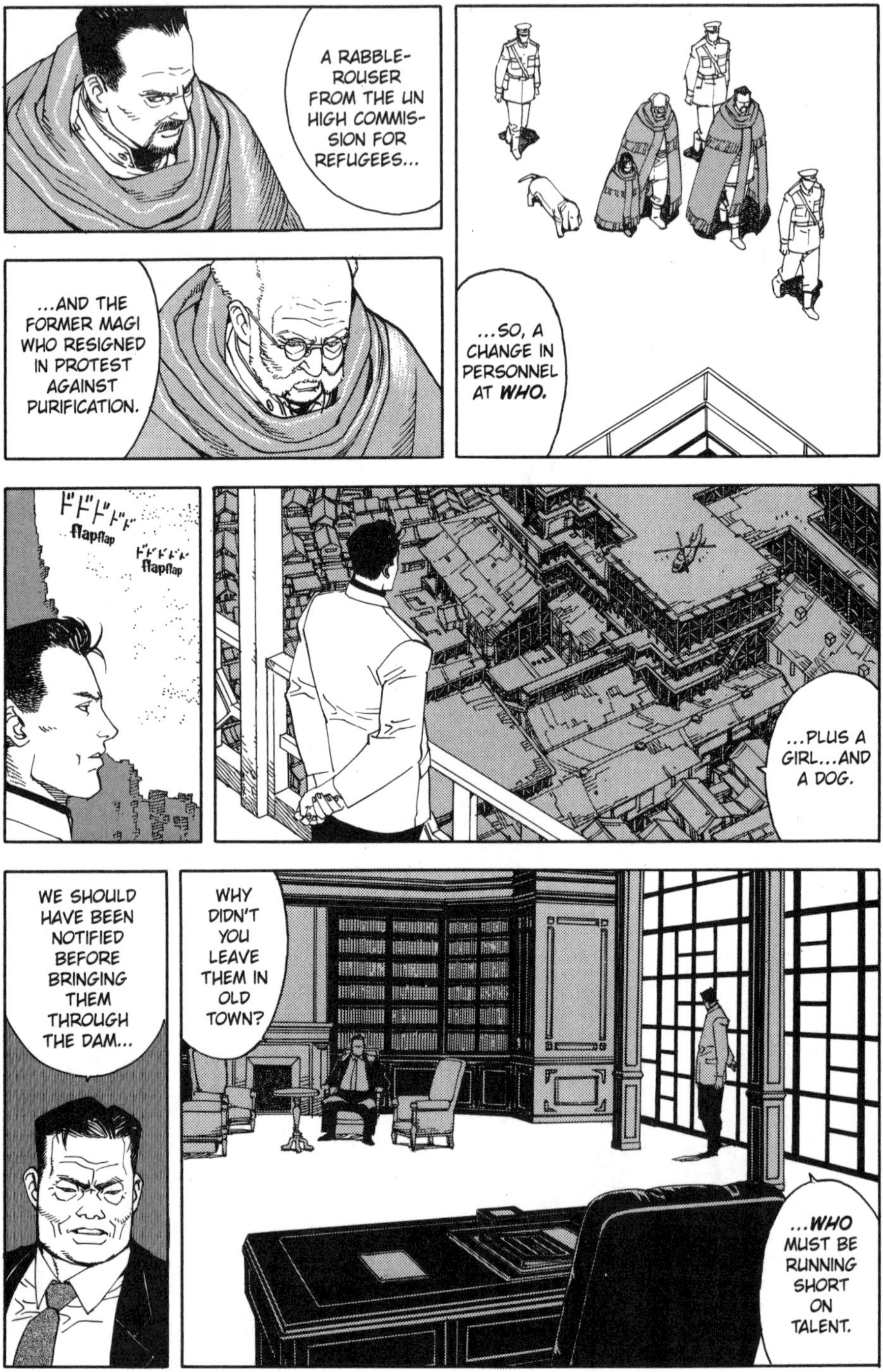
...SO, A CHANGE IN PERSONNEL AT *WHO.*
A RABBLE-ROUSER FROM THE UN HIGH COMMISSION FOR REFUGEES...
...AND THE FORMER MAGI WHO RESIGNED IN PROTEST AGAINST PURIFICATION.
...PLUS A GIRL...AND A DOG.
ドドドドド
flapflap
ドドドドド
flapflap
WHY DIDN'T YOU LEAVE THEM IN OLD TOWN?
...*WHO* MUST BE RUNNING SHORT ON TALENT.
WE SHOULD HAVE BEEN NOTIFIED BEFORE BRINGING THEM THROUGH THE DAM...

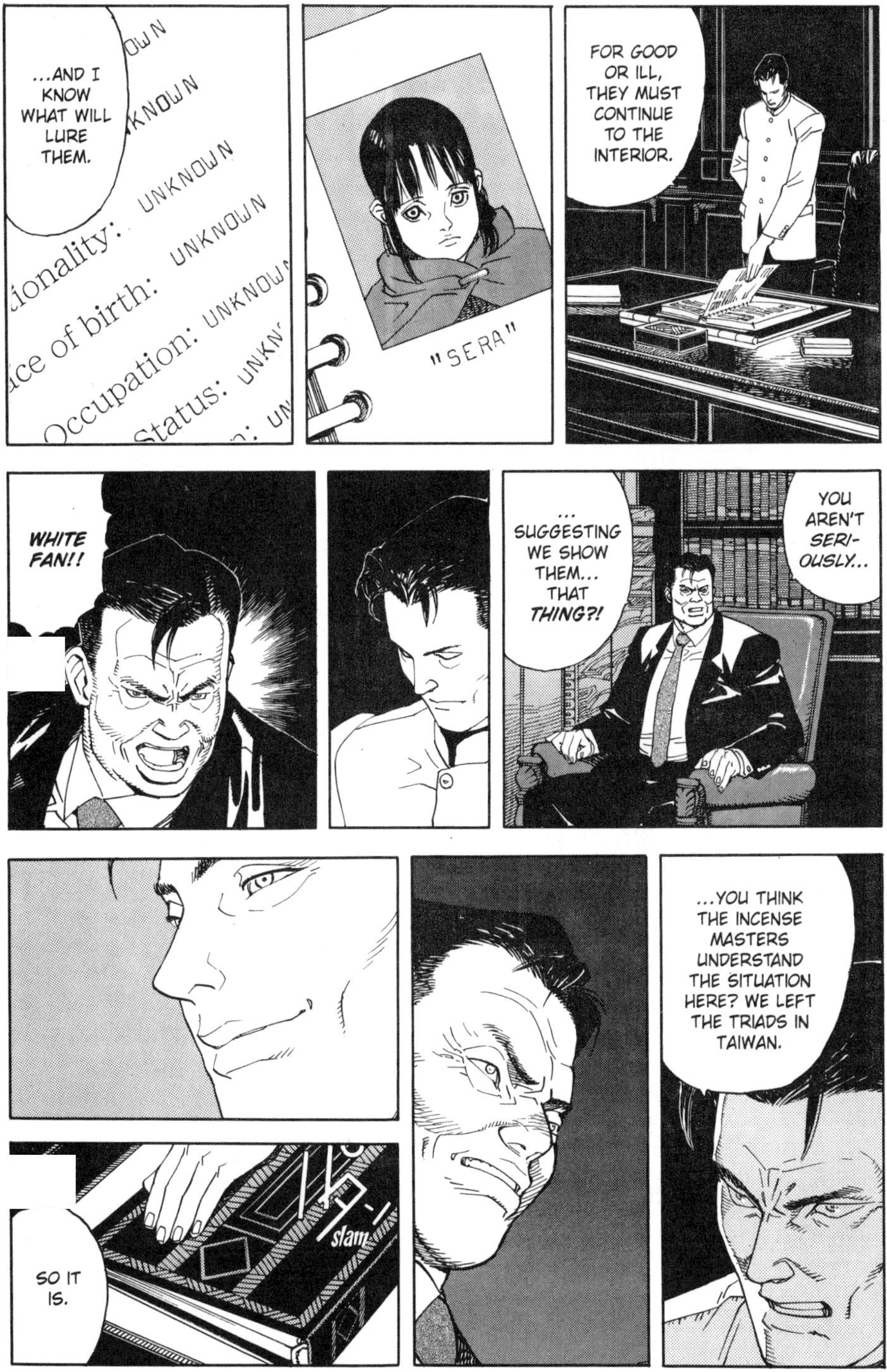
FOR GOOD OR ILL, THEY MUST CONTINUE TO THE INTERIOR.
"SERA"
...AND I KNOW WHAT WILL LURE THEM.
ionality: UNKNOWN
ce of birth: UNKNOWN
YOU AREN'T SERI-OUSLY...
...SUGGESTING WE SHOW THEM... THAT THING?!
WHITE FAN!!
...YOU THINK THE INCENSE MASTERS UNDERSTAND THE SITUATION HERE? WE LEFT THE TRIADS IN TAIWAN.
slam
SO IT IS.

White Fan, in the Chinese Triad system, is a third-tier rank with responsibility for finance and administration. Incense Master is a superior rank in the second tier, with responsibility for Triad initiations.

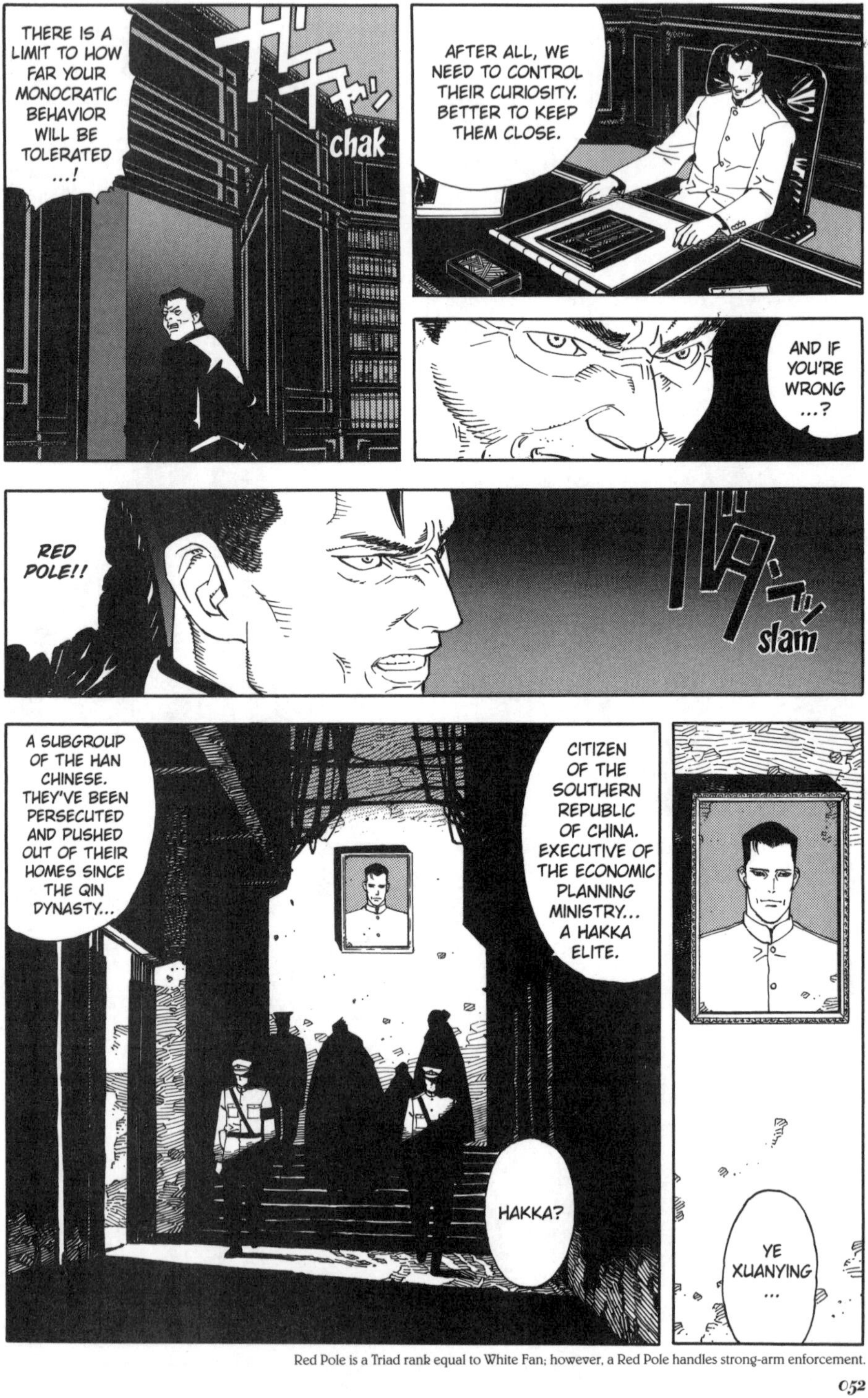
AFTER ALL, WE NEED TO CONTROL THEIR CURIOSITY. BETTER TO KEEP THEM CLOSE.
AND IF YOU'RE WRONG ...?
chak
THERE IS A LIMIT TO HOW FAR YOUR MONOCRATIC BEHAVIOR WILL BE TOLERATED ...!
slam
RED POLE!!
YE XUANYING ...
CITIZEN OF THE SOUTHERN REPUBLIC OF CHINA. EXECUTIVE OF THE ECONOMIC PLANNING MINISTRY... A HAKKA ELITE.
HAKKA?
A SUBGROUP OF THE HAN CHINESE. THEY'VE BEEN PERSECUTED AND PUSHED OUT OF THEIR HOMES SINCE THE QIN DYNASTY...

Red Pole is a Triad rank equal to White Fan; however, a Red Pole handles strong-arm enforcement.

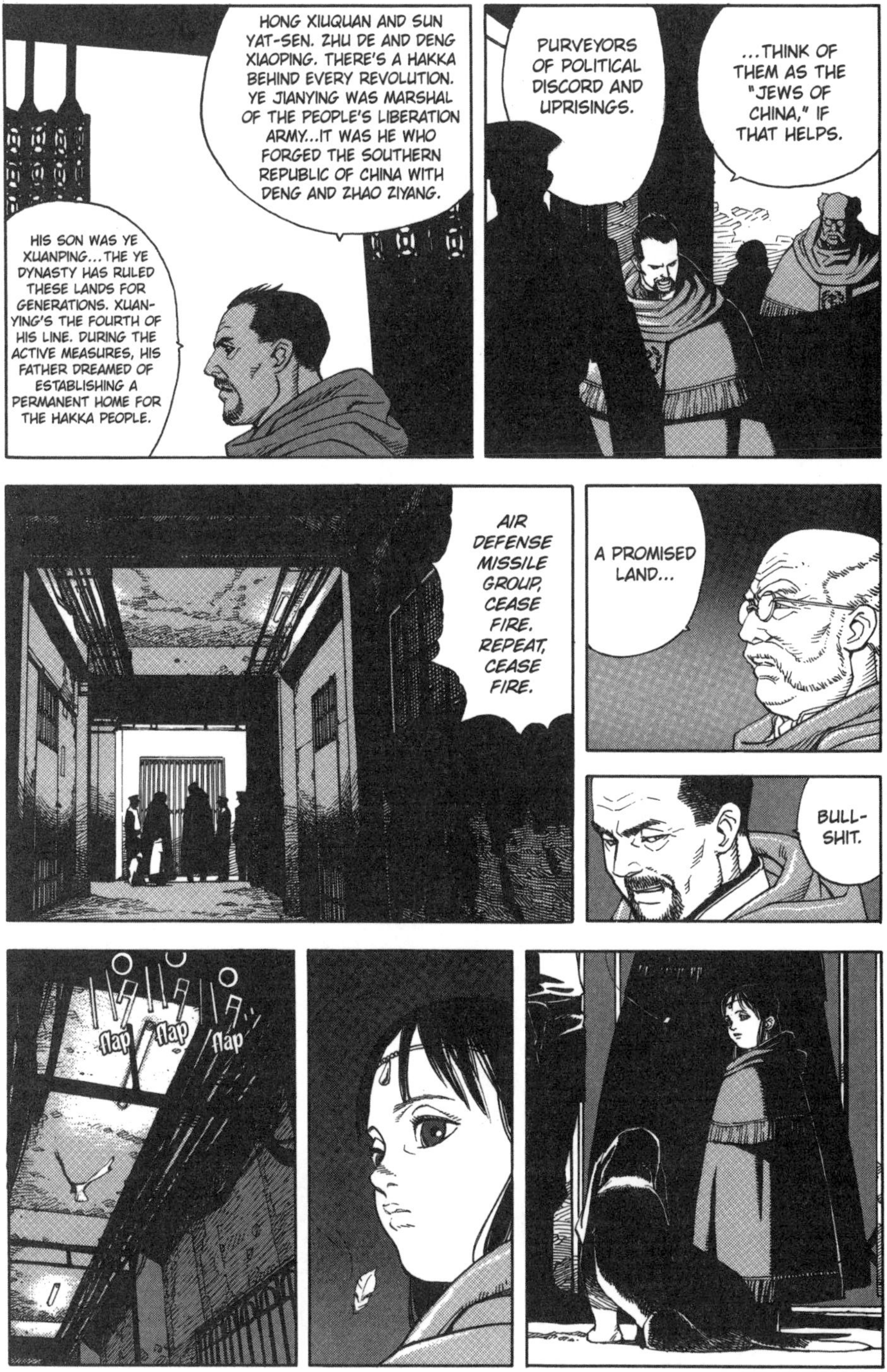
...THINK OF THEM AS THE "JEWS OF CHINA," IF THAT HELPS.
PURVEYORS OF POLITICAL DISCORD AND UPRISINGS.
HONG XIUQUAN AND SUN YAT-SEN. ZHU DE AND DENG XIAOPING. THERE'S A HAKKA BEHIND EVERY REVOLUTION. YE JIANYING WAS MARSHAL OF THE PEOPLE'S LIBERATION ARMY...IT WAS HE WHO FORGED THE SOUTHERN REPUBLIC OF CHINA WITH DENG AND ZHAO ZIYANG.
HIS SON WAS YE XUANPING...THE YE DYNASTY HAS RULED THESE LANDS FOR GENERATIONS. XUAN-YING'S THE FOURTH OF HIS LINE. DURING THE ACTIVE MEASURES, HIS FATHER DREAMED OF ESTABLISHING A PERMANENT HOME FOR THE HAKKA PEOPLE.
A PROMISED LAND...
BULL-SHIT.
AIR DEFENSE MISSILE GROUP, CEASE FIRE. REPEAT, CEASE FIRE.
flap flap flap

Hong Xiuquan was the leader of the 1850–64 Taiping Rebellion, perhaps the deadliest civil war in human history. Sun Yat-sen became the first national leader of postimperial China in 1912. Zhu De (1886–1976) was a crucial military ally of Mao Zedong and one of the founders of the People's Liberation Army.

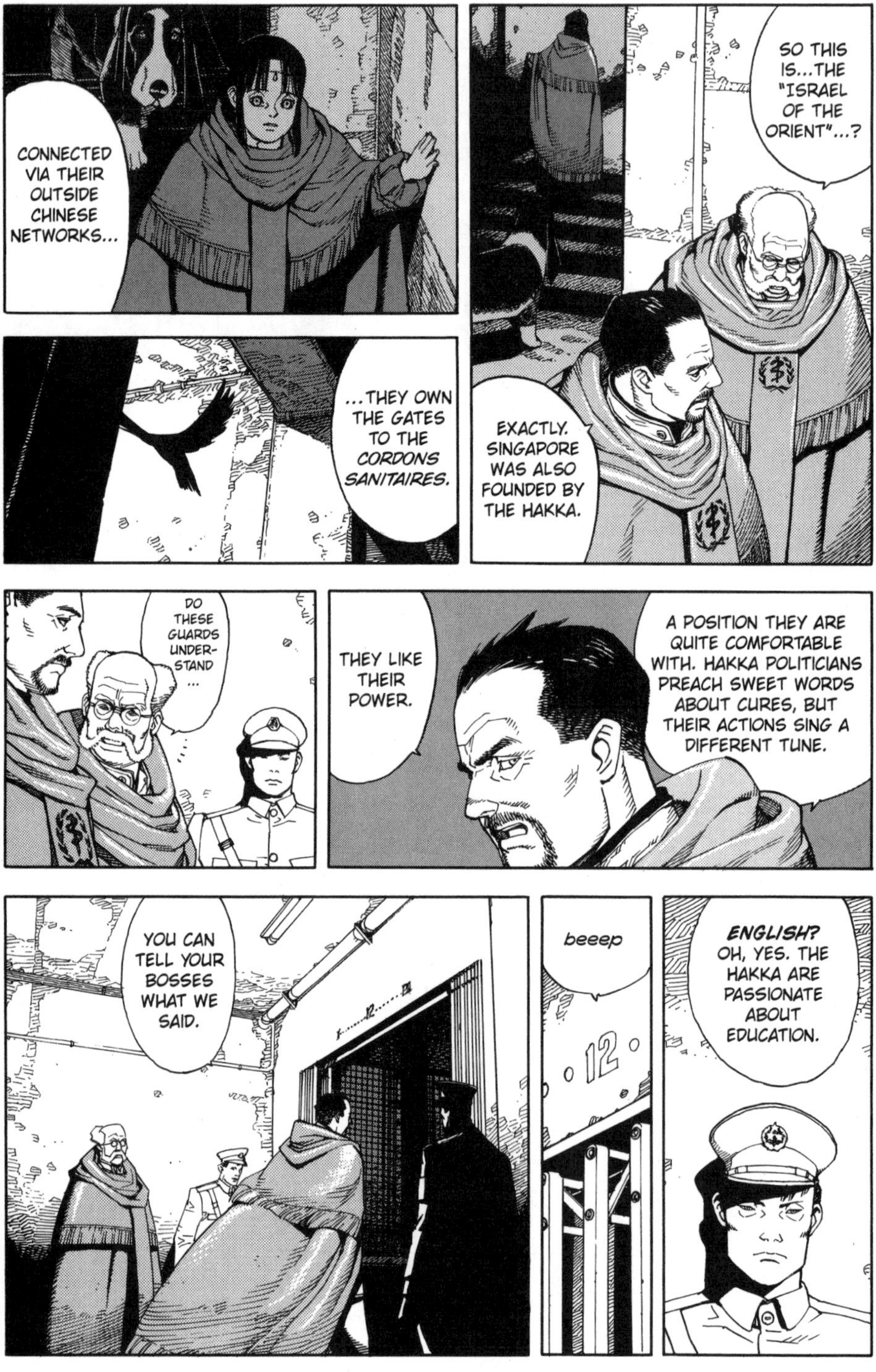
SO THIS IS...THE "ISRAEL OF THE ORIENT"...?
EXACTLY. SINGAPORE WAS ALSO FOUNDED BY THE HAKKA.
CONNECTED VIA THEIR OUTSIDE CHINESE NETWORKS...
...THEY OWN THE GATES TO THE *CORDONS SANITAIRES.*
A POSITION THEY ARE QUITE COMFORTABLE WITH. HAKKA POLITICIANS PREACH SWEET WORDS ABOUT CURES, BUT THEIR ACTIONS SING A DIFFERENT TUNE.
THEY LIKE THEIR POWER.
DO THESE GUARDS UNDER-STAND ...
ENGLISH? OH, YES. THE HAKKA ARE PASSIONATE ABOUT EDUCATION.
beeep
YOU CAN TELL YOUR BOSSES WHAT WE SAID.

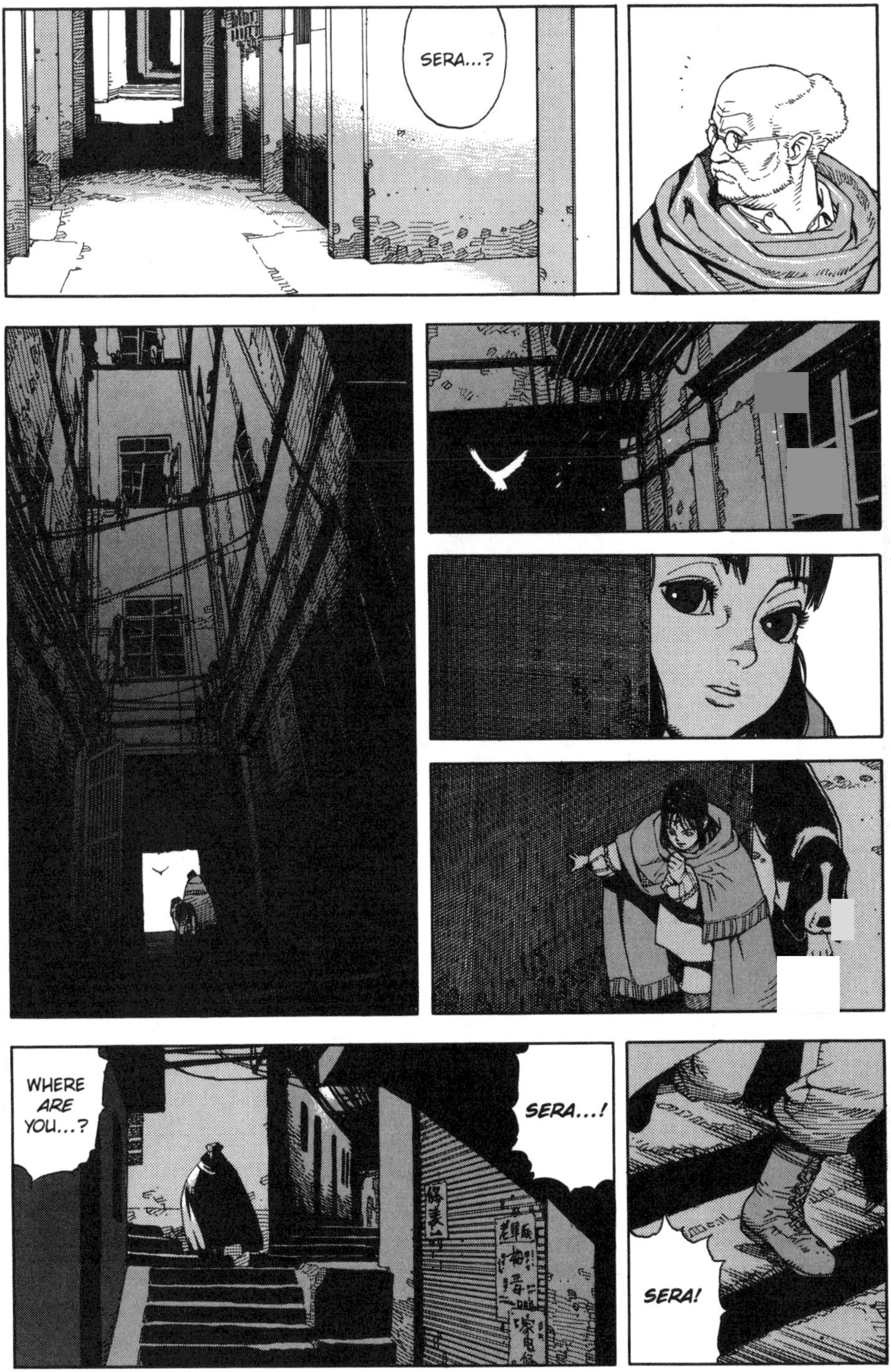
SERA...?
SERA!
SERA...!
WHERE ARE YOU...?

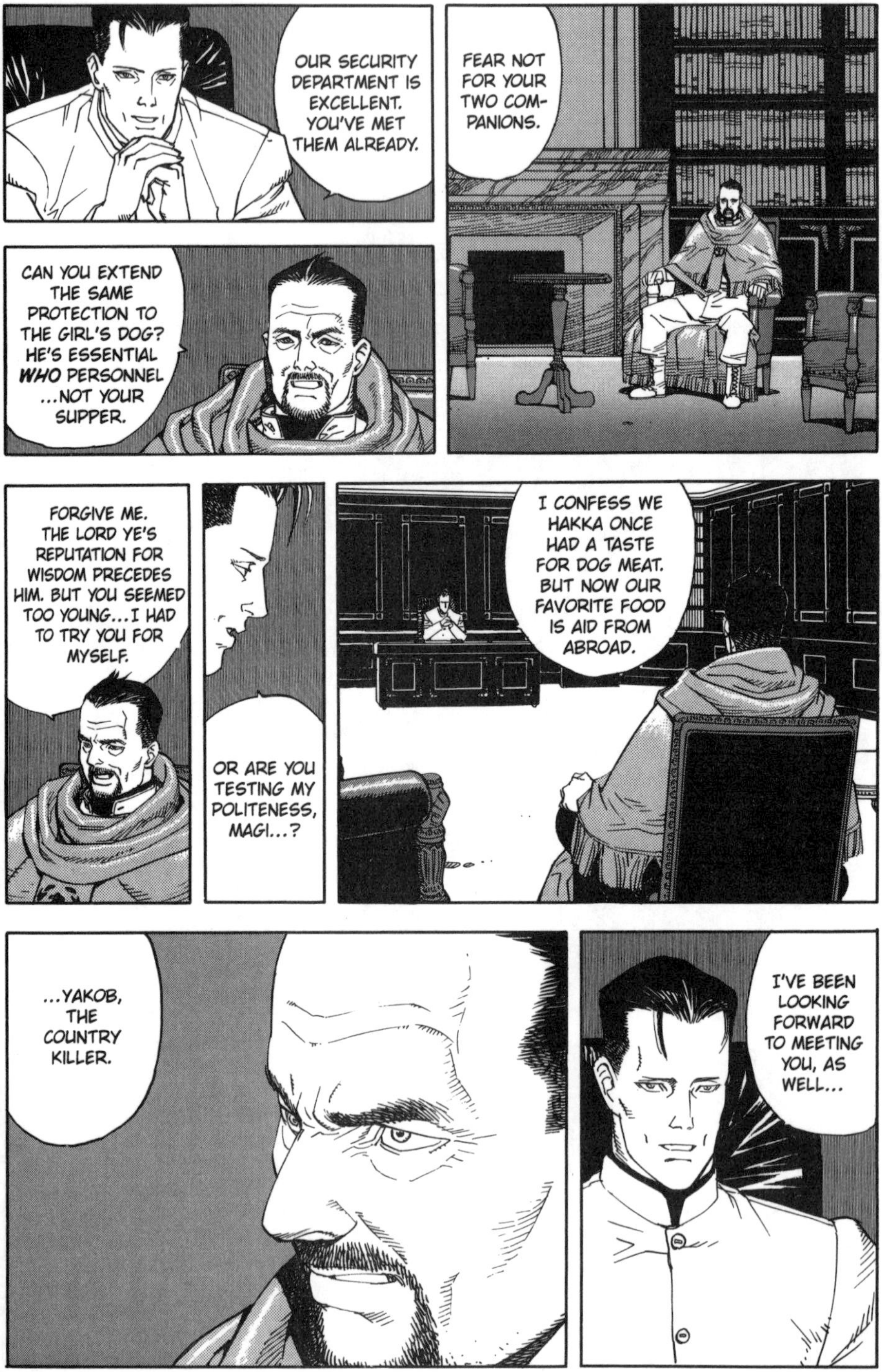
FEAR NOT FOR YOUR TWO COMPANIONS.
OUR SECURITY DEPARTMENT IS EXCELLENT. YOU'VE MET THEM ALREADY.
CAN YOU EXTEND THE SAME PROTECTION TO THE GIRL'S DOG? HE'S ESSENTIAL ***WHO*** PERSONNEL ...NOT YOUR SUPPER.
I CONFESS WE HAKKA ONCE HAD A TASTE FOR DOG MEAT. BUT NOW OUR FAVORITE FOOD IS AID FROM ABROAD.
OR ARE YOU TESTING MY POLITENESS, MAGI...?
FORGIVE ME. THE LORD YE'S REPUTATION FOR WISDOM PRECEDES HIM. BUT YOU SEEMED TOO YOUNG...I HAD TO TRY YOU FOR MYSELF.
I'VE BEEN LOOKING FORWARD TO MEETING YOU, AS WELL...
...YAKOB, THE COUNTRY KILLER.

The Hakka Chinese are often stereotyped as dog eaters.

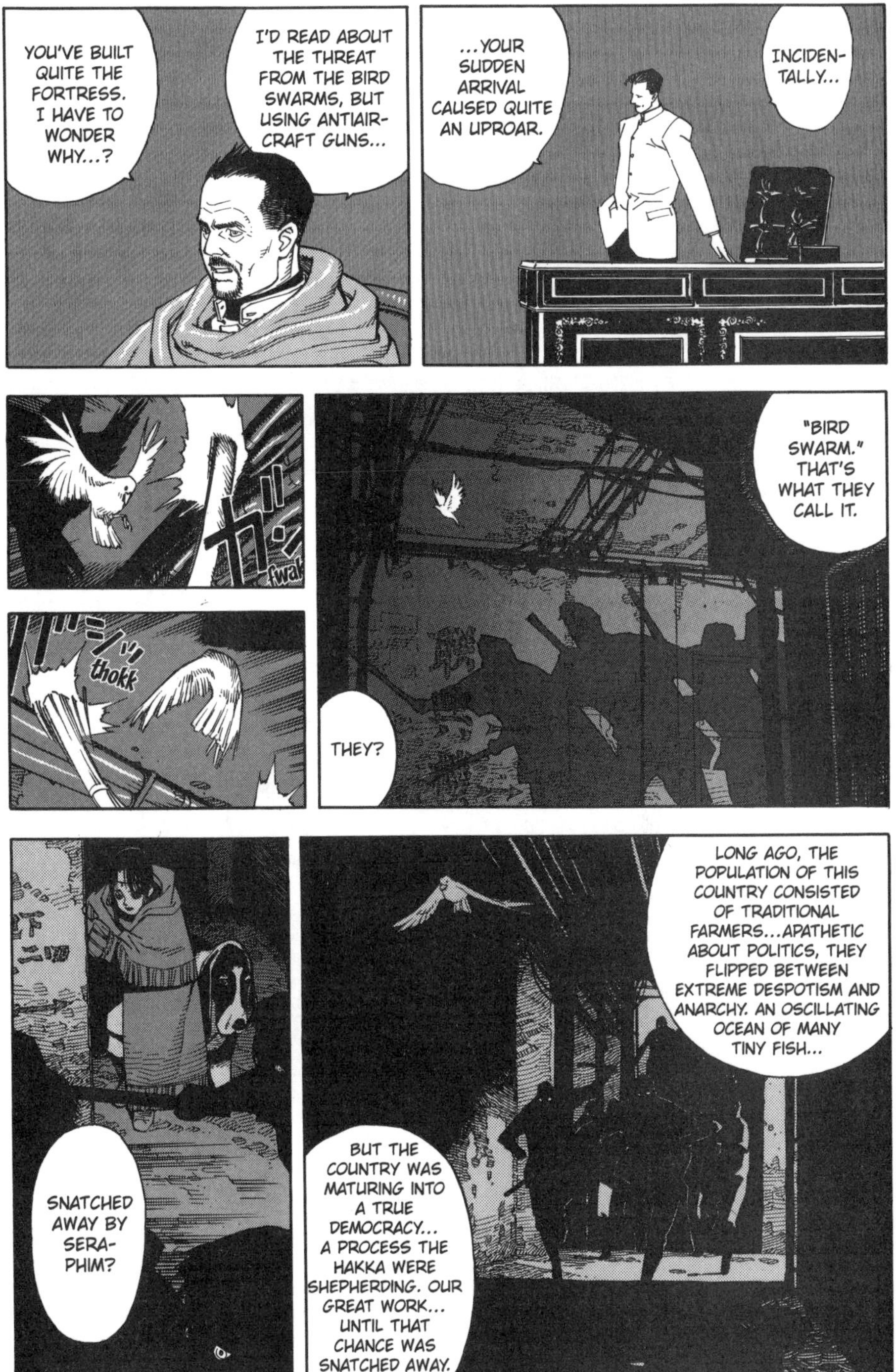
INCIDEN-TALLY...
...YOUR SUDDEN ARRIVAL CAUSED QUITE AN UPROAR.
I'D READ ABOUT THE THREAT FROM THE BIRD SWARMS, BUT USING ANTIAIR-CRAFT GUNS...
YOU'VE BUILT QUITE THE FORTRESS. I HAVE TO WONDER WHY...?
"BIRD SWARM." THAT'S WHAT THEY CALL IT.
THEY?
fwak
thokk
LONG AGO, THE POPULATION OF THIS COUNTRY CONSISTED OF TRADITIONAL FARMERS...APATHETIC ABOUT POLITICS, THEY FLIPPED BETWEEN EXTREME DESPOTISM AND ANARCHY. AN OSCILLATING OCEAN OF MANY TINY FISH...
BUT THE COUNTRY WAS MATURING INTO A TRUE DEMOCRACY... A PROCESS THE HAKKA WERE SHEPHERDING. OUR GREAT WORK... UNTIL THAT CHANCE WAS SNATCHED AWAY.
SNATCHED AWAY BY SERA-PHIM?

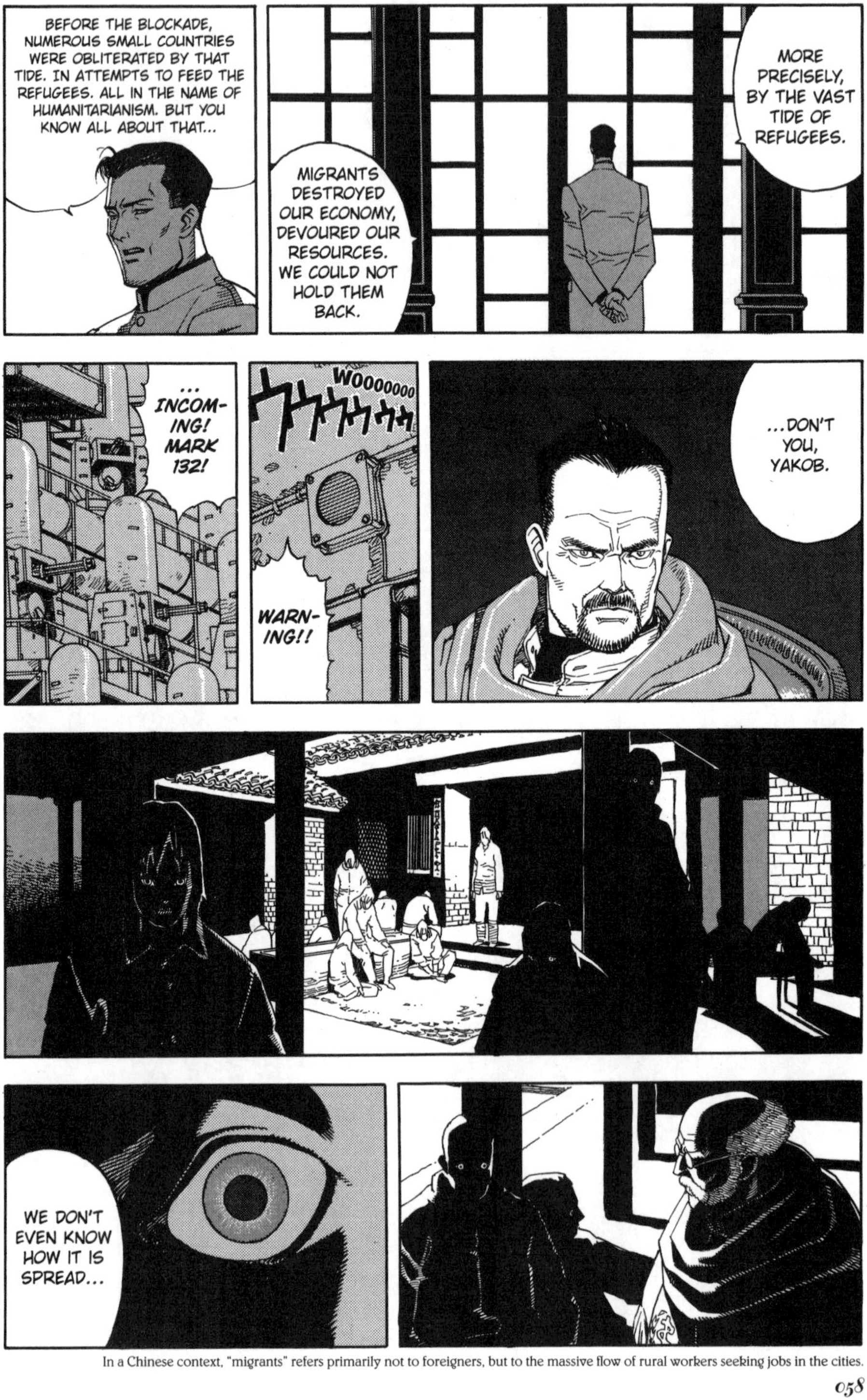
MORE PRECISELY, BY THE VAST TIDE OF REFUGEES.
MIGRANTS DESTROYED OUR ECONOMY, DEVOURED OUR RESOURCES. WE COULD NOT HOLD THEM BACK.
BEFORE THE BLOCKADE, NUMEROUS SMALL COUNTRIES WERE OBLITERATED BY THAT TIDE. IN ATTEMPTS TO FEED THE REFUGEES. ALL IN THE NAME OF HUMANITARIANISM. BUT YOU KNOW ALL ABOUT THAT...
...DON'T YOU, YAKOB.
WOOOOOOO
ウウウウウウ
WARNING!!
... INCOMING! MARK 132!
WE DON'T EVEN KNOW HOW IT IS SPREAD...

In a Chinese context, "migrants" refers primarily not to foreigners, but to the massive flow of rural workers seeking jobs in the cities.

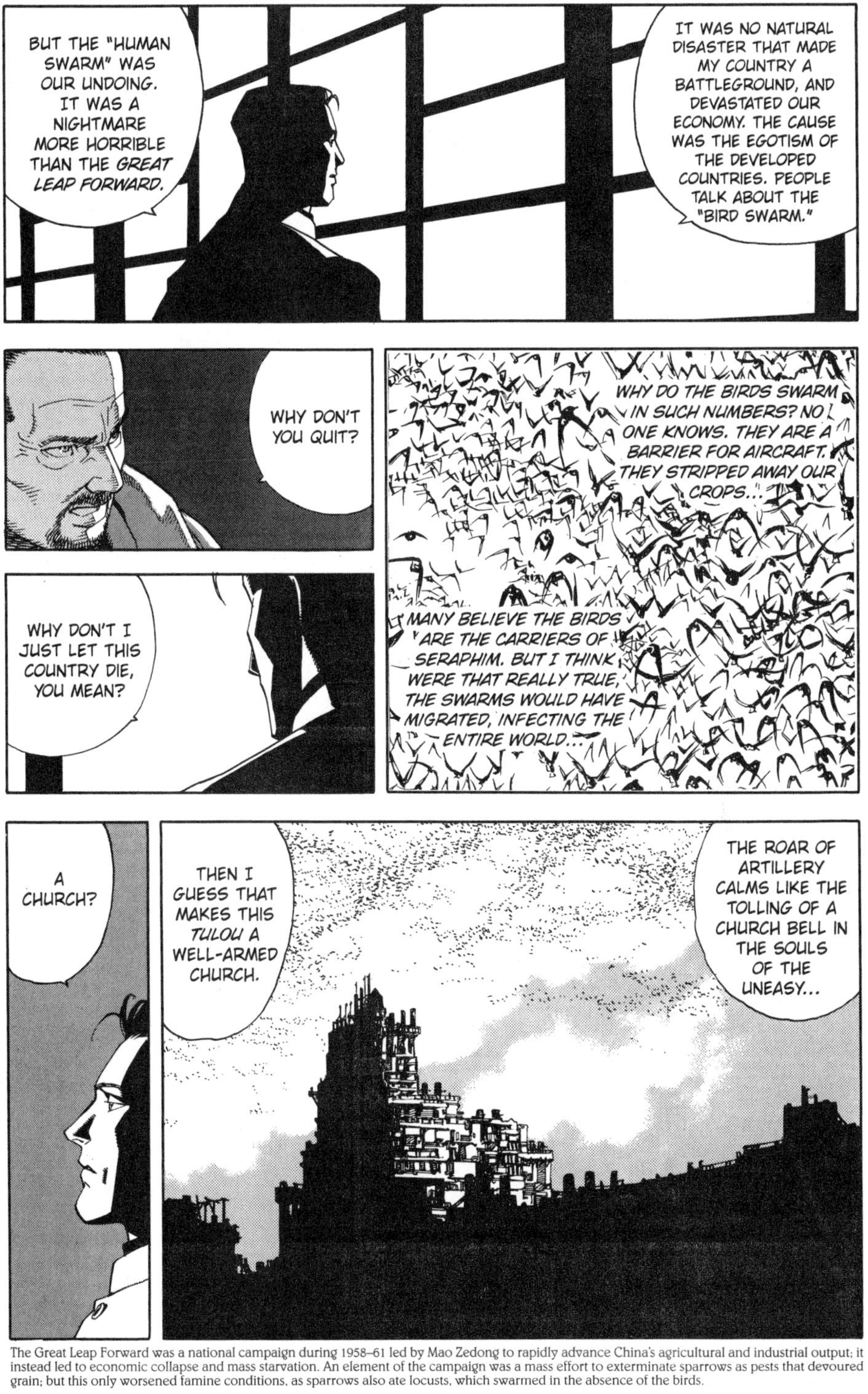
IT WAS NO NATURAL DISASTER THAT MADE MY COUNTRY A BATTLEGROUND, AND DEVASTATED OUR ECONOMY. THE CAUSE WAS THE EGOTISM OF THE DEVELOPED COUNTRIES. PEOPLE TALK ABOUT THE "BIRD SWARM."
BUT THE "HUMAN SWARM" WAS OUR UNDOING. IT WAS A NIGHTMARE MORE HORRIBLE THAN THE *GREAT LEAP FORWARD.*
WHY DO THE BIRDS SWARM IN SUCH NUMBERS? NO ONE KNOWS. THEY ARE A BARRIER FOR AIRCRAFT. THEY STRIPPED AWAY OUR CROPS...
MANY BELIEVE THE BIRDS ARE THE CARRIERS OF SERAPHIM. BUT I THINK WERE THAT REALLY TRUE, THE SWARMS WOULD HAVE MIGRATED, INFECTING THE ENTIRE WORLD...
WHY DON'T YOU QUIT?
WHY DON'T I JUST LET THIS COUNTRY DIE, YOU MEAN?
THE ROAR OF ARTILLERY CALMS LIKE THE TOLLING OF A CHURCH BELL IN THE SOULS OF THE UNEASY...
THEN I GUESS THAT MAKES THIS *TULOU* A WELL-ARMED CHURCH.
A CHURCH?

The Great Leap Forward was a national campaign during 1958–61 led by Mao Zedong to rapidly advance China's agricultural and industrial output; it instead led to economic collapse and mass starvation. An element of the campaign was a mass effort to exterminate sparrows as pests that devoured grain; but this only worsened famine conditions, as sparrows also ate locusts, which swarmed in the absence of the birds.

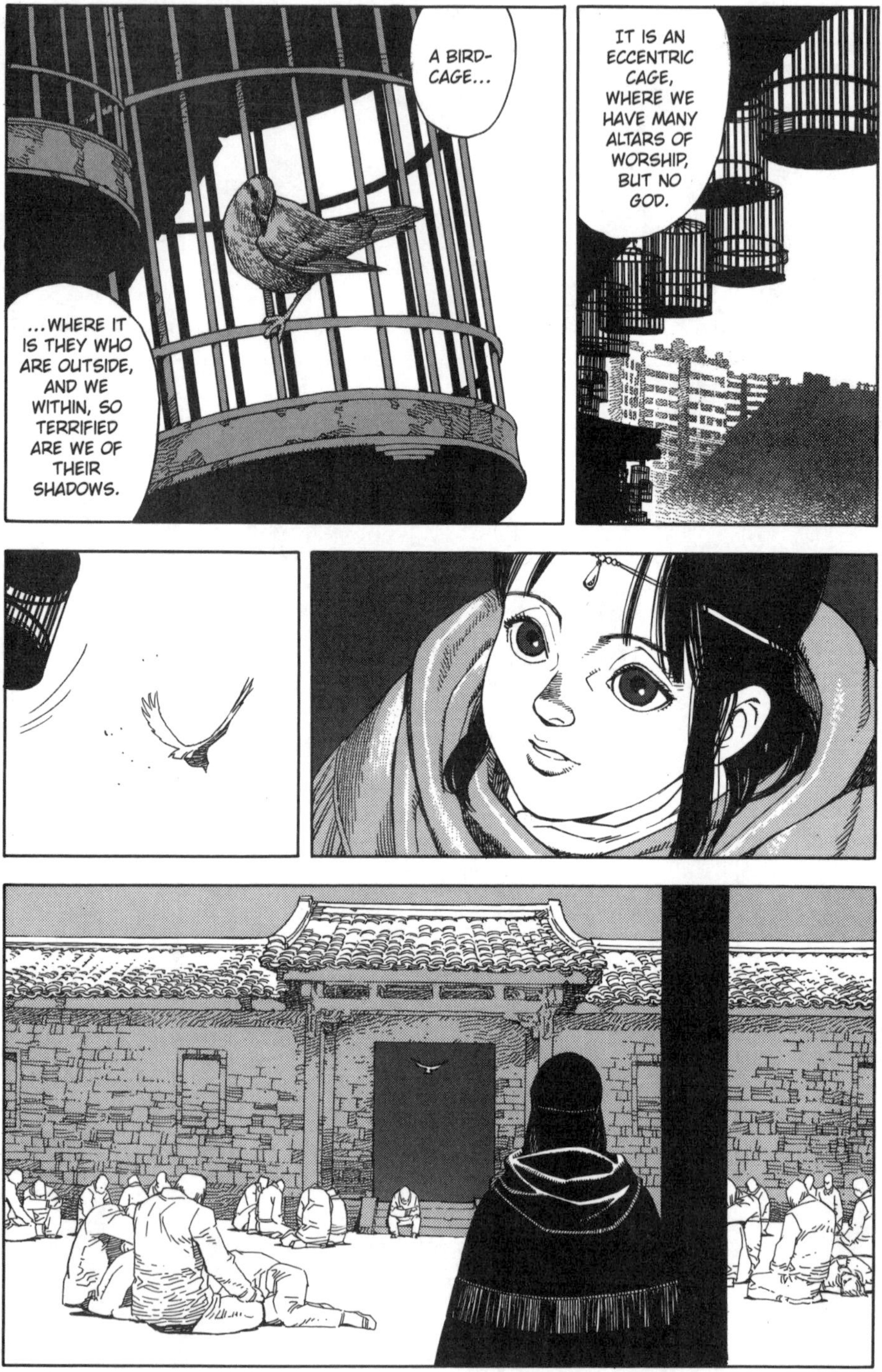
IT IS AN ECCENTRIC CAGE, WHERE WE HAVE MANY ALTARS OF WORSHIP, BUT NO GOD.
A BIRD-CAGE...
...WHERE IT IS THEY WHO ARE OUTSIDE, AND WE WITHIN, SO TERRIFIED ARE WE OF THEIR SHADOWS.

chapter five

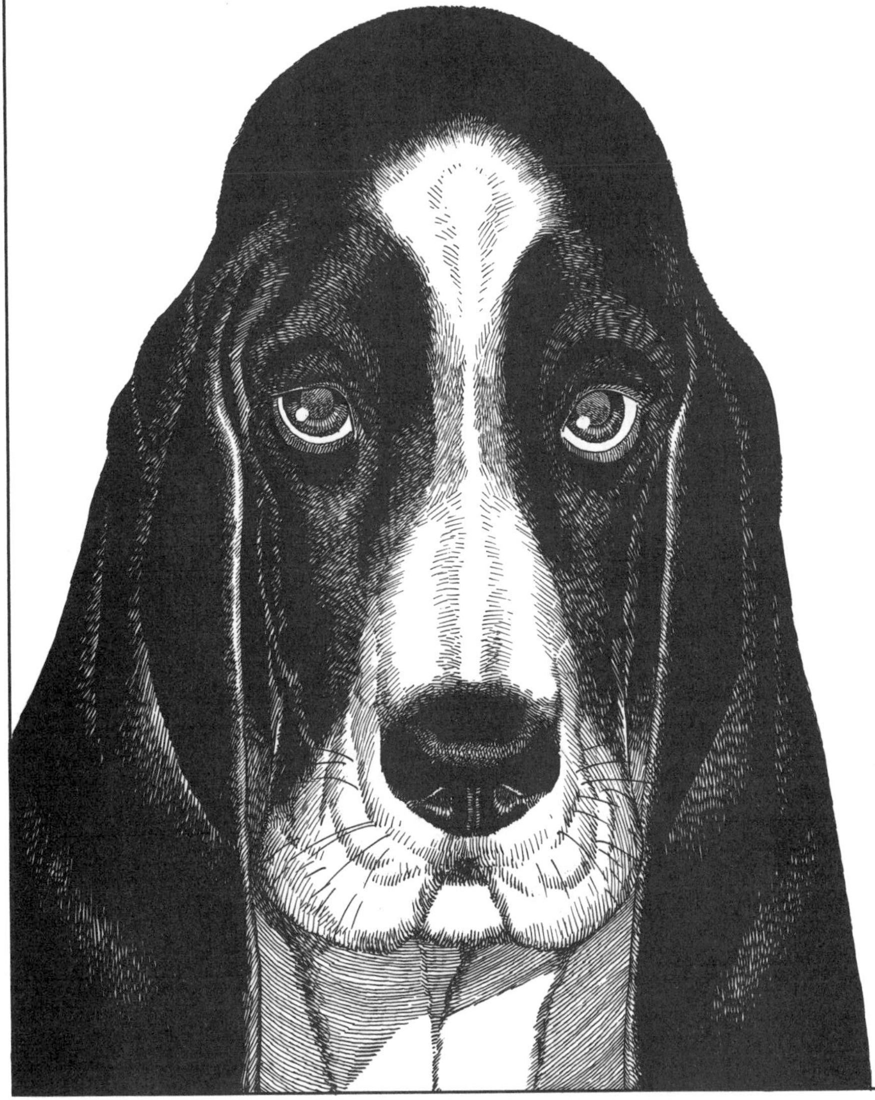

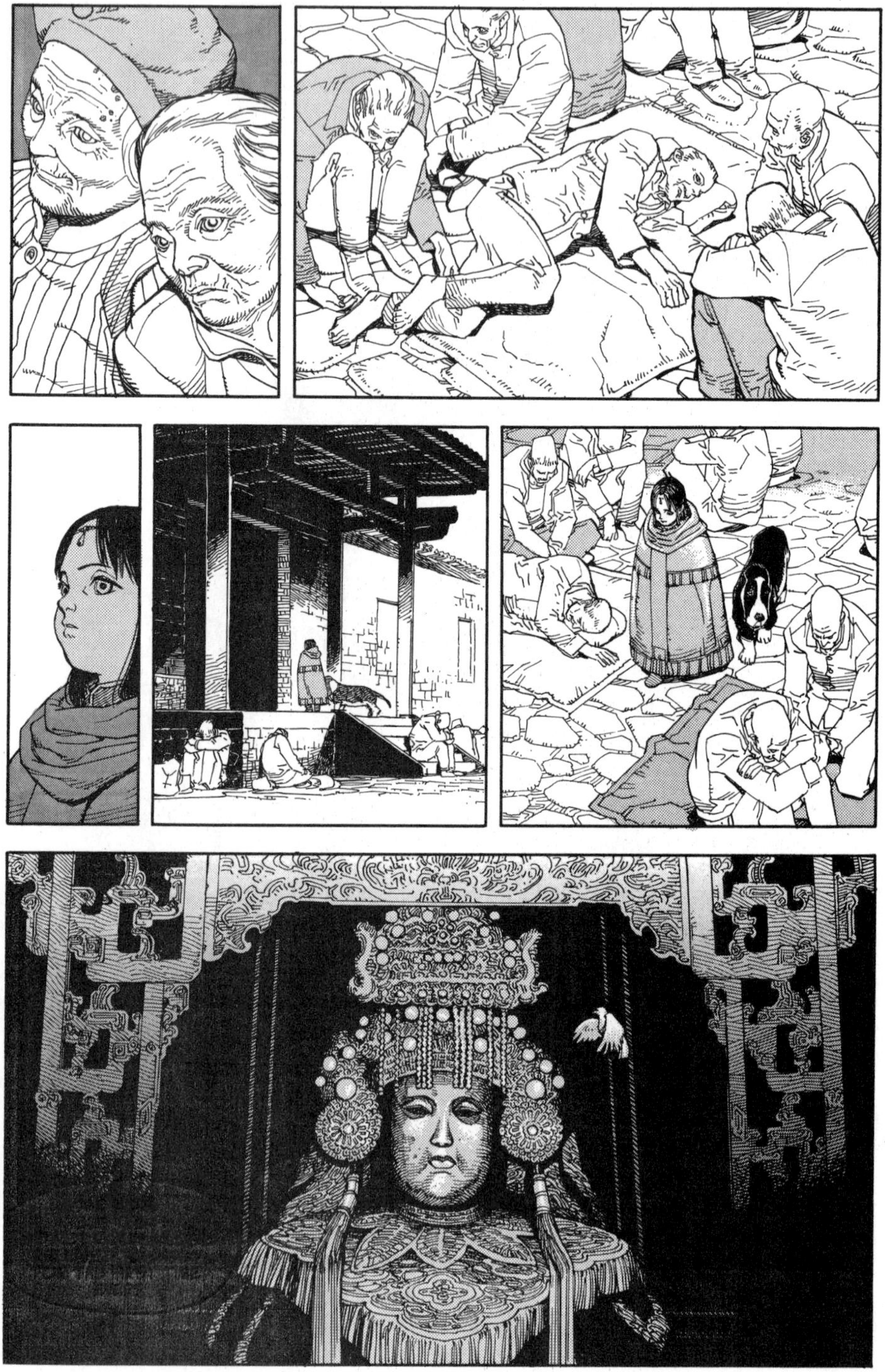

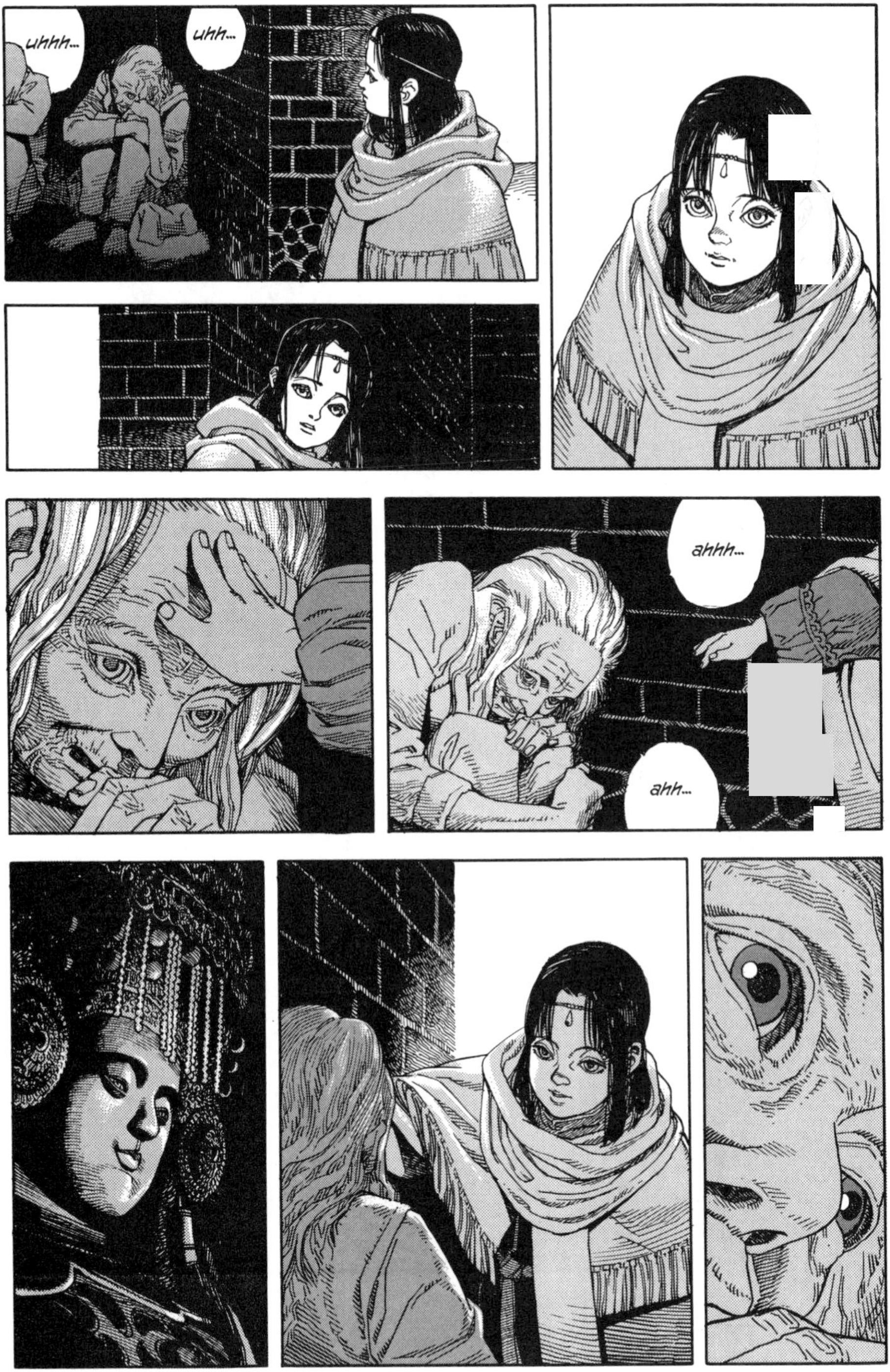
uhh...
uhhh...
ahhh...
ahh...

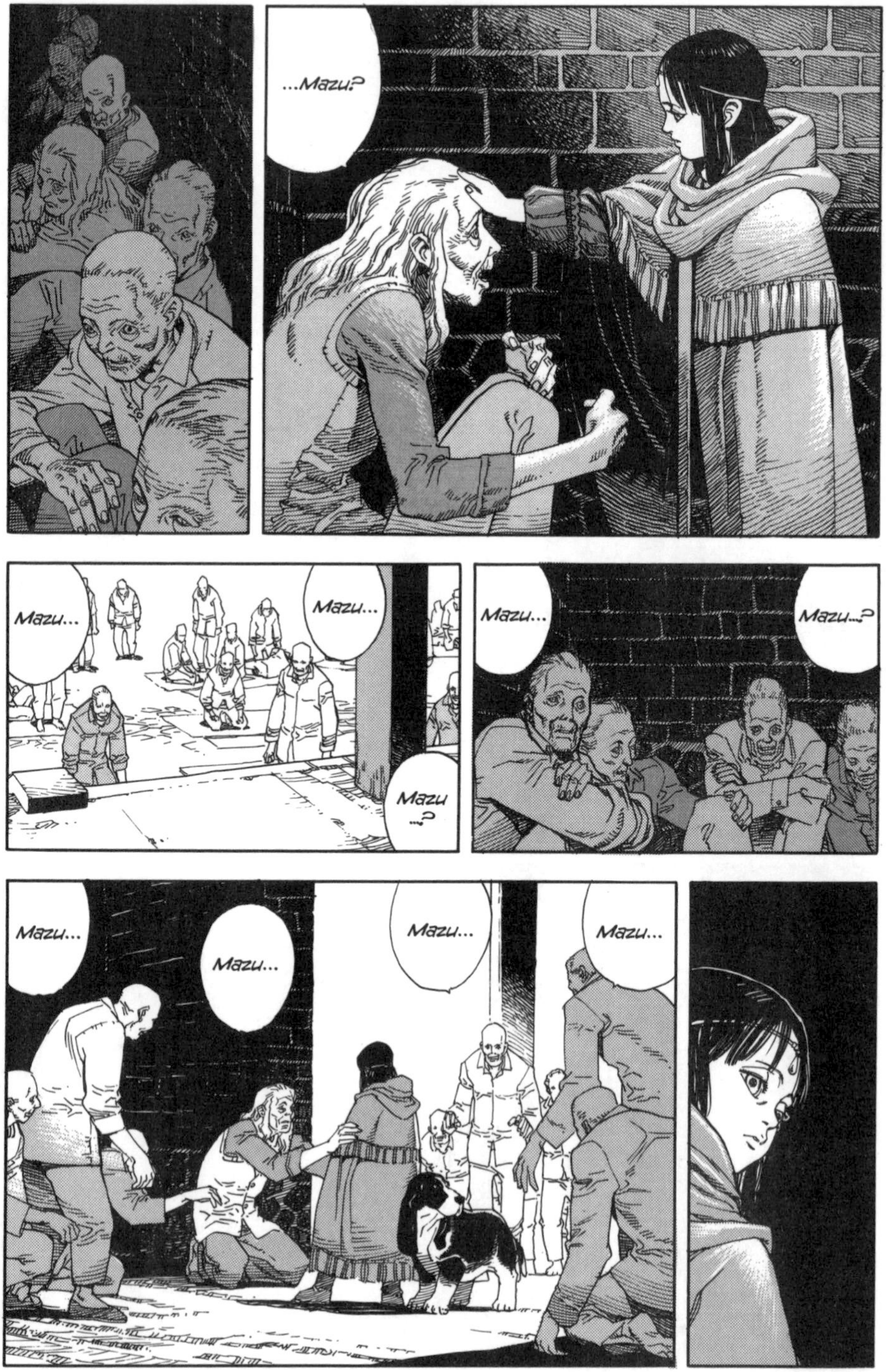
...Mazu?
Mazu...?
Mazu...
Mazu...
Mazu ...?
Mazu...
Mazu...
Mazu...
Mazu...
Mazu...

Mazu!
Mazu!
Mazu!
Mazu!
Mazu!
Mazu!
Mazu!
Mazu!
Mazu!
Mazu!
ギッ
snap
Mazu!
Mazu!

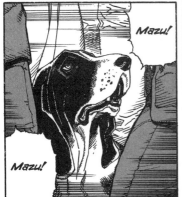

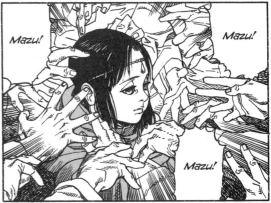

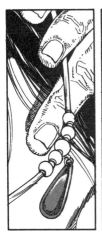

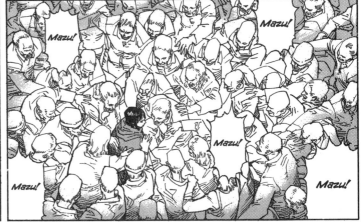

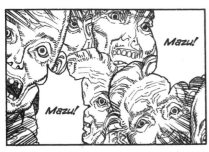

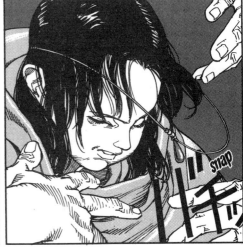

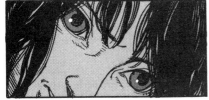

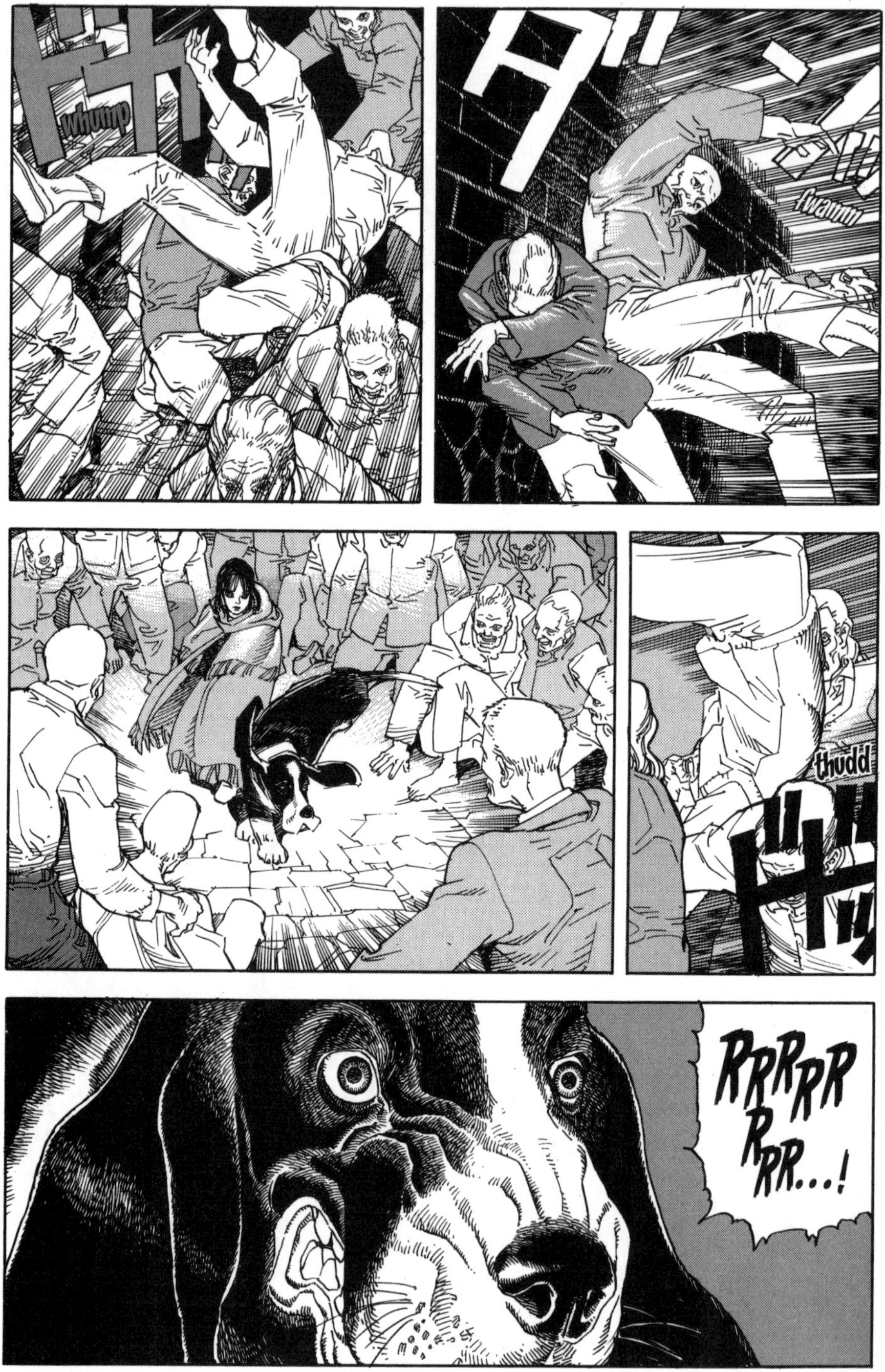
fwamm
whump
thudd
RRRRR
RRR...!

...EH?

GET BACK, YOU...

BACK!

tmp
tmp
tmp
tmp

...SERA!

ド キ
イイイィァン
shiiinnn

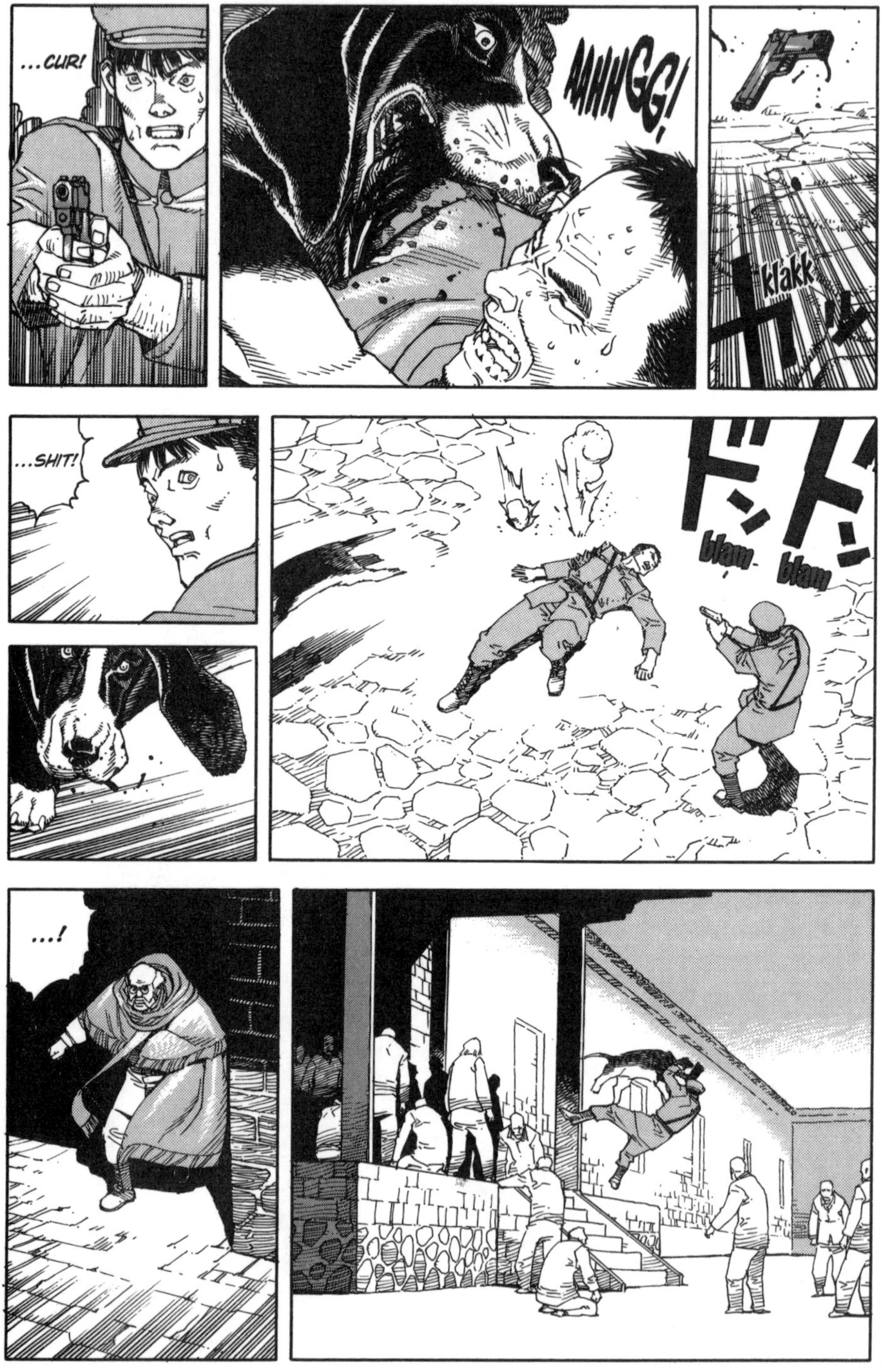
klakk
カッ
AAHHGG!
...CUR!
ドン
ドン
blam-
blam
...SHIT!
...!

...STOP
!!

WAIT...
CASPAR
...!

CASPAR
...

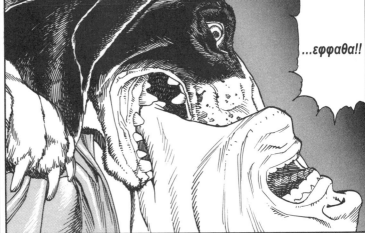

...εφφαθα!!

lick

εφφαθα—Ephphatha; Mark 7:34.

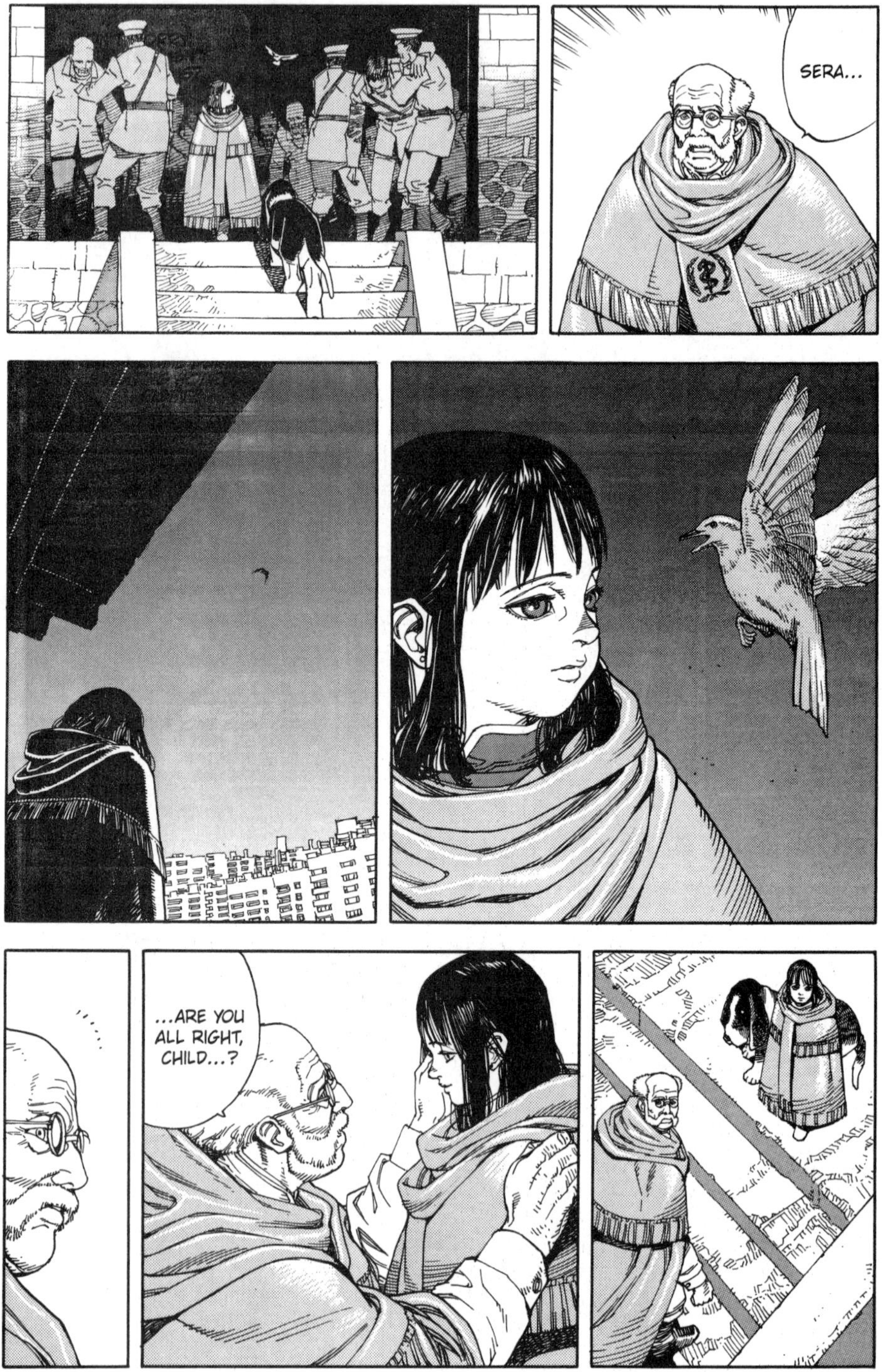
SERA...
...ARE YOU ALL RIGHT, CHILD...?
...

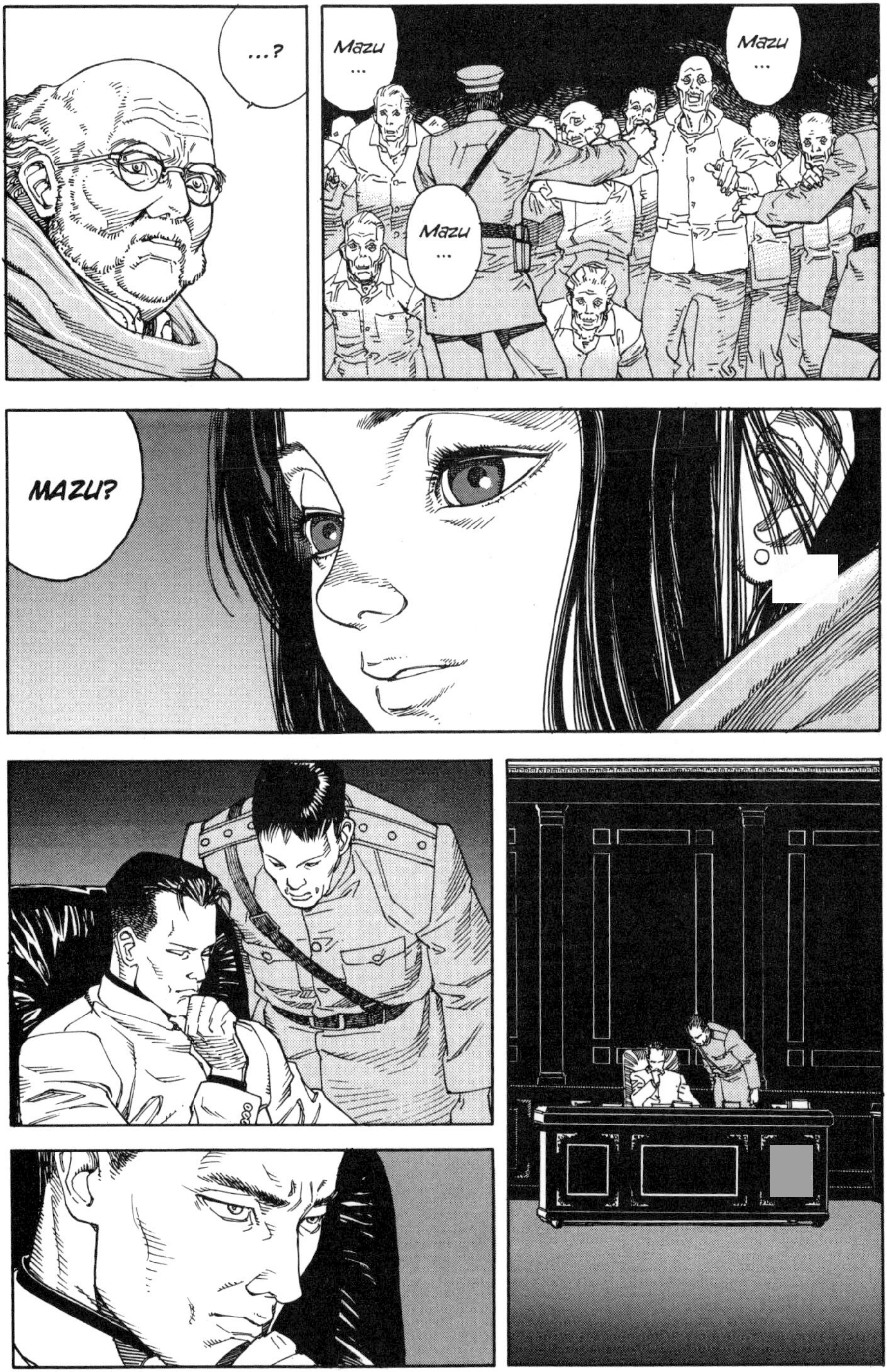

Mazu ...
Mazu ...
Mazu ...
...?
MAZU?

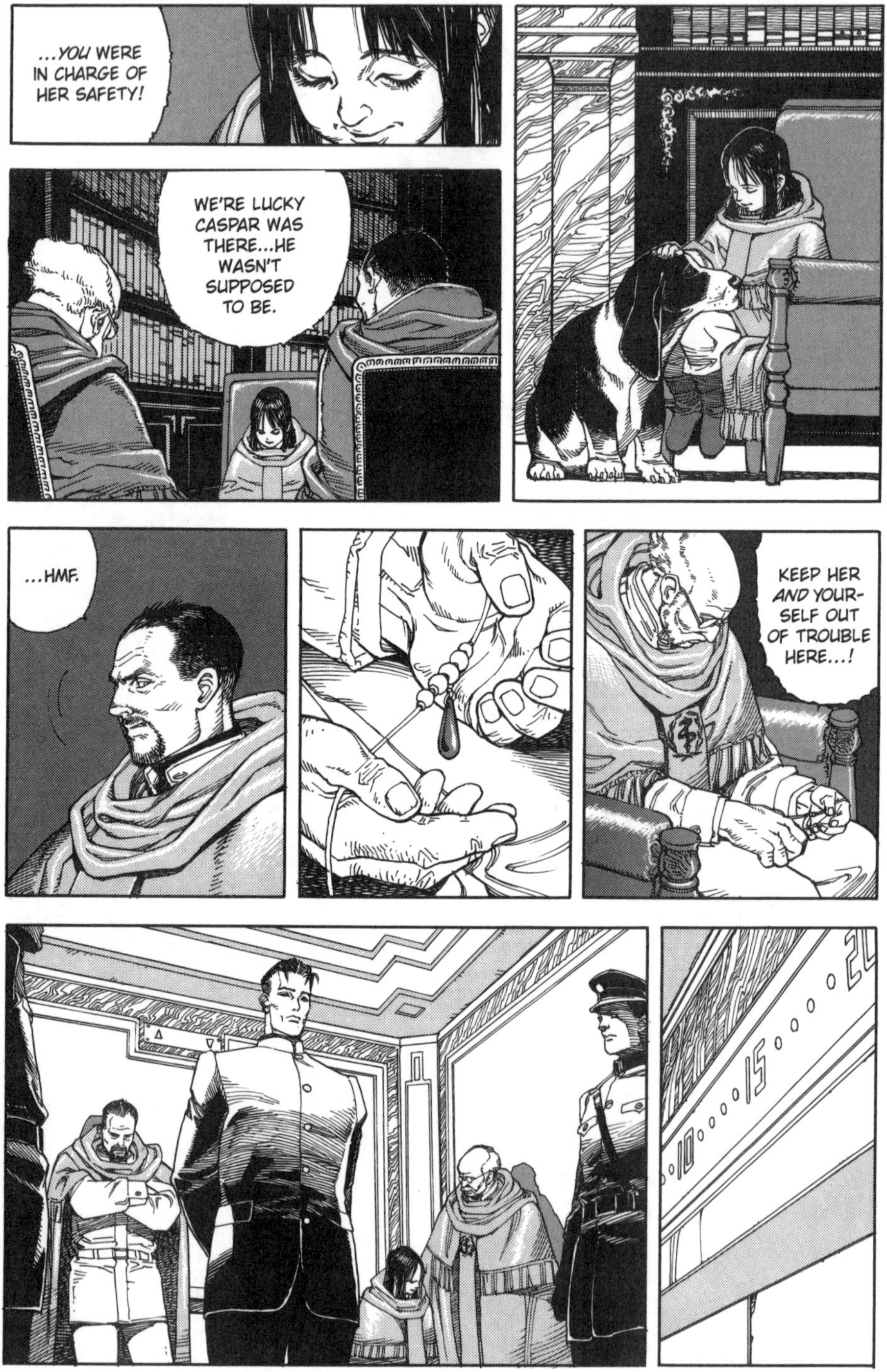
...*YOU* WERE IN CHARGE OF HER SAFETY!
WE'RE LUCKY CASPAR WAS THERE...HE WASN'T SUPPOSED TO BE.
KEEP HER *AND* YOURSELF OUT OF TROUBLE HERE...!
...HMF.

SO WHAT IS
THIS "THING"
YOU WANT TO
SHOW US...?

...

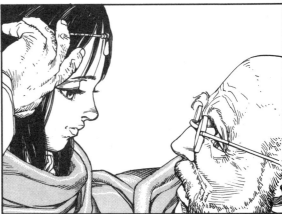

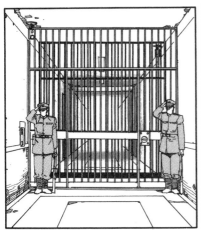

VOOOOM!!

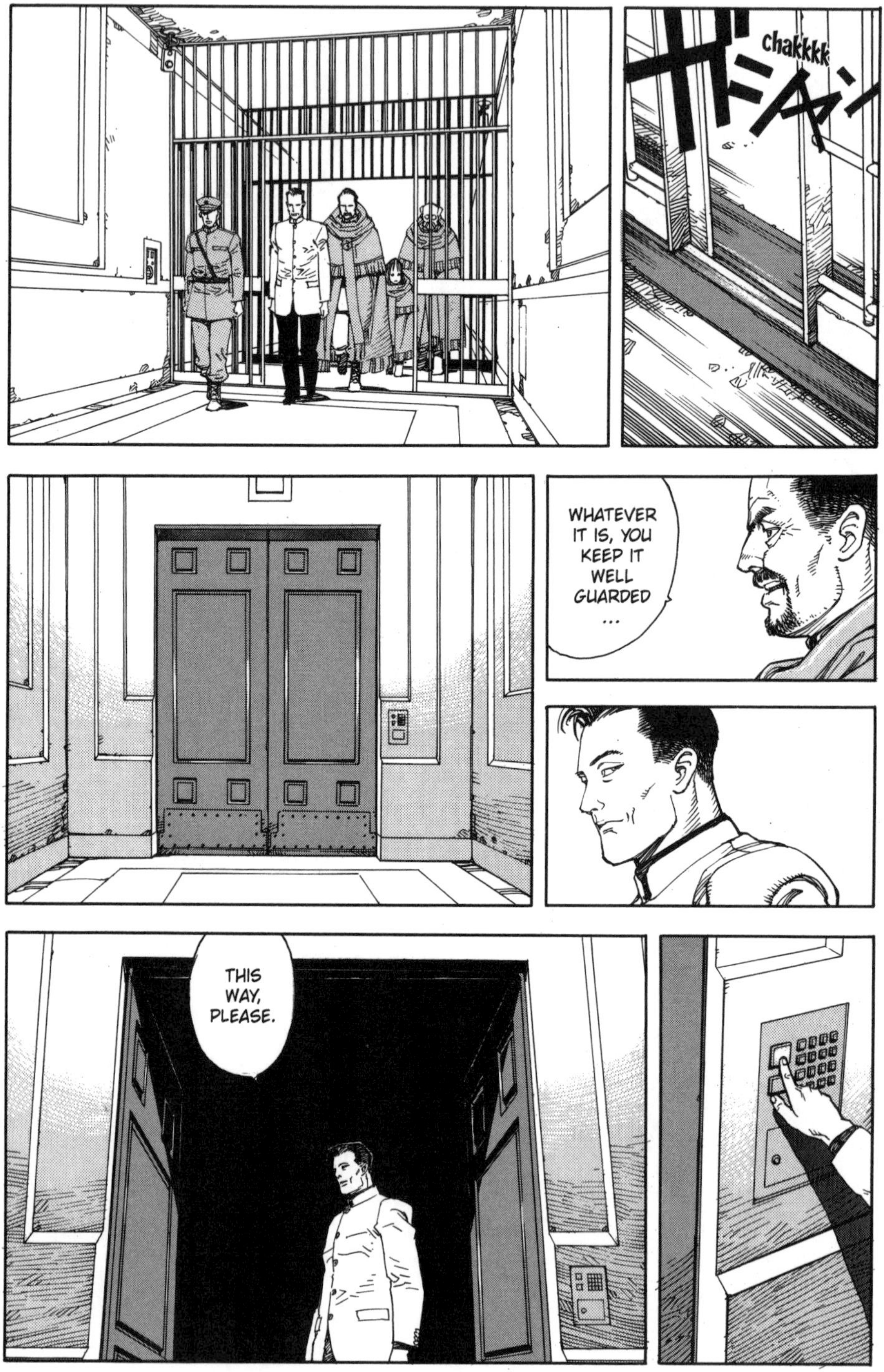
chakkkk
WHATEVER IT IS, YOU KEEP IT WELL GUARDED ...
THIS WAY, PLEASE.

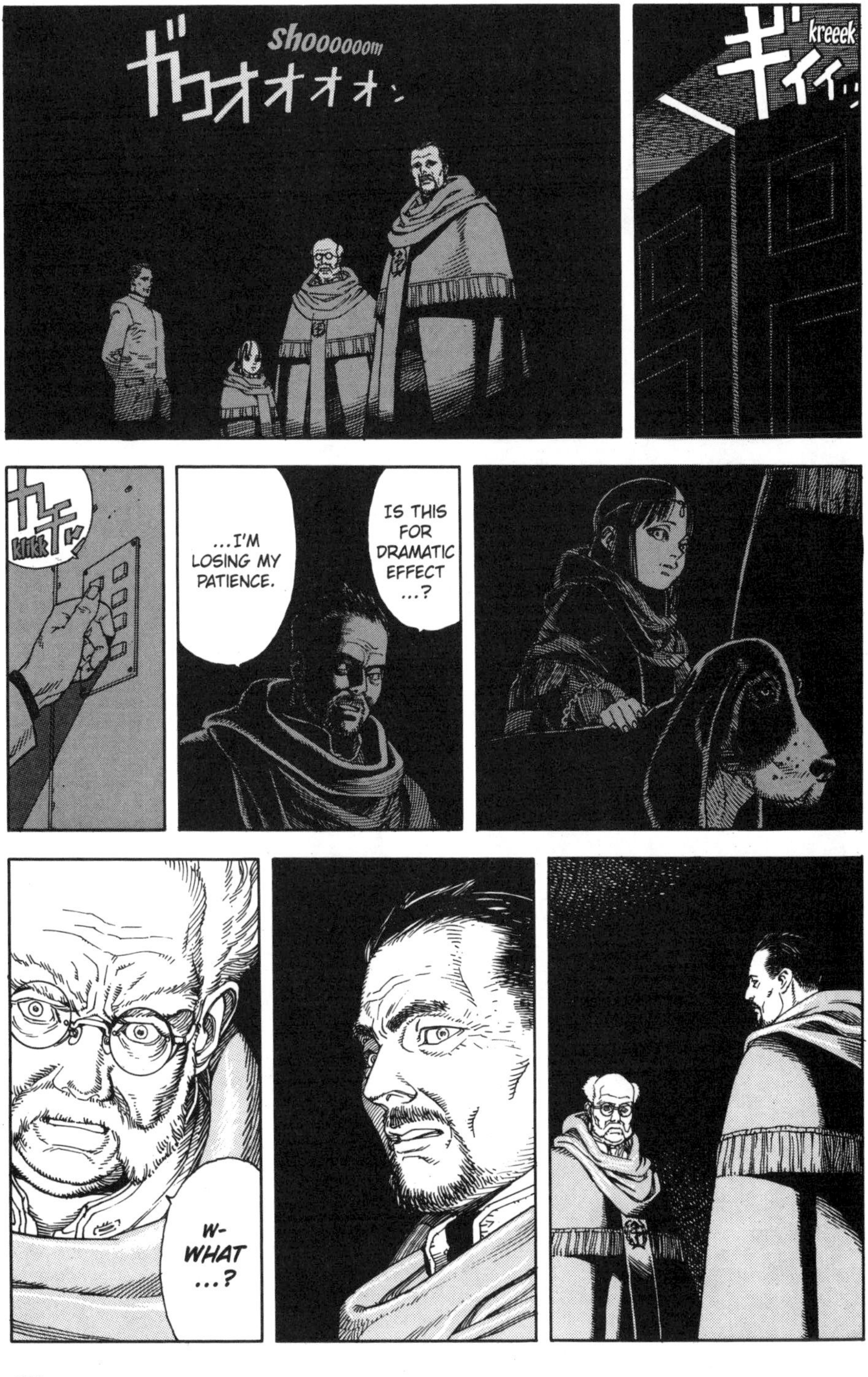
ギイィッ
kreeek
ガコオオオオン
shoooooom
IS THIS FOR DRAMATIC EFFECT ...?
...I'M LOSING MY PATIENCE.
カチッ
klikk
W- WHAT ...?

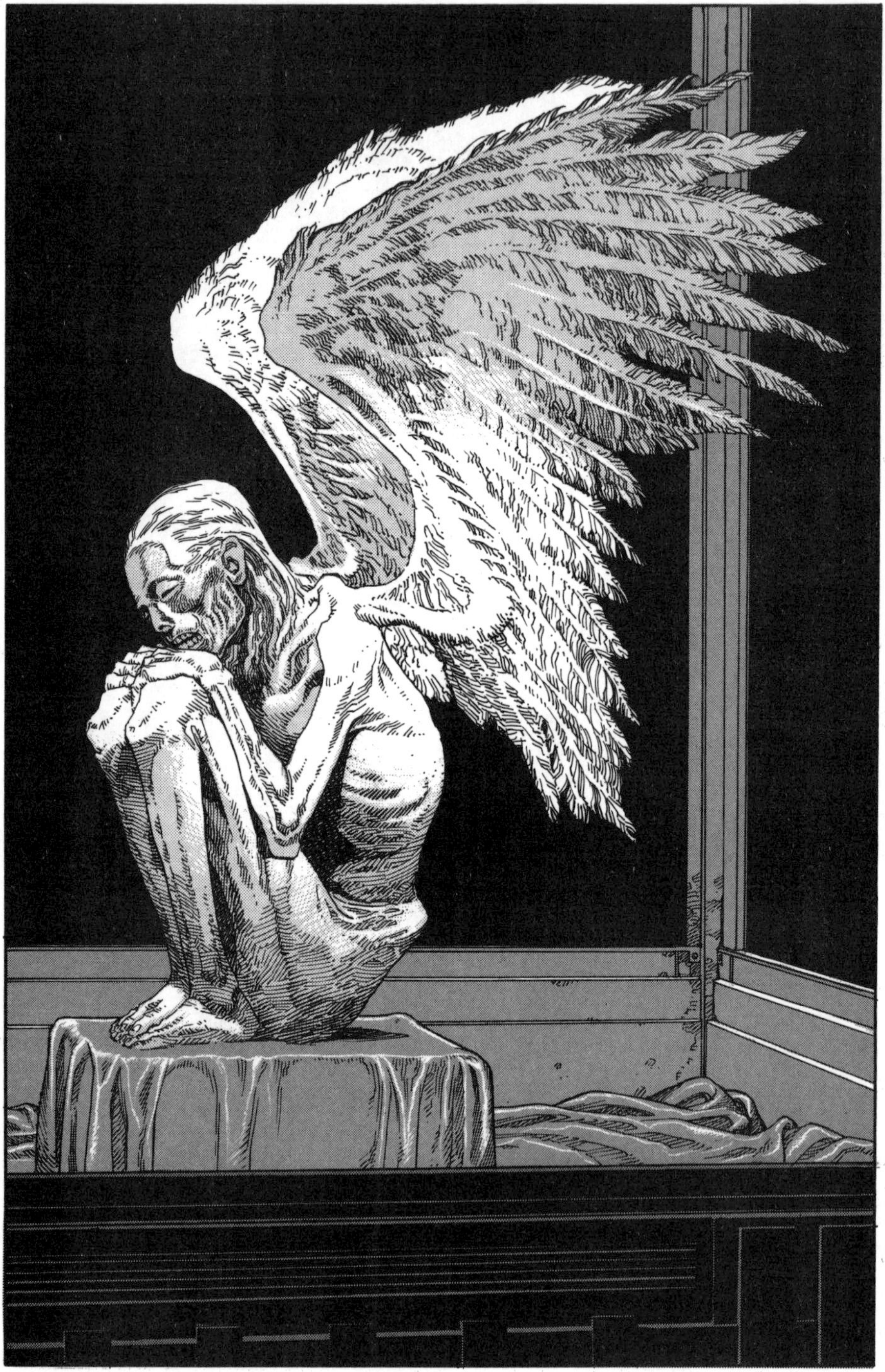

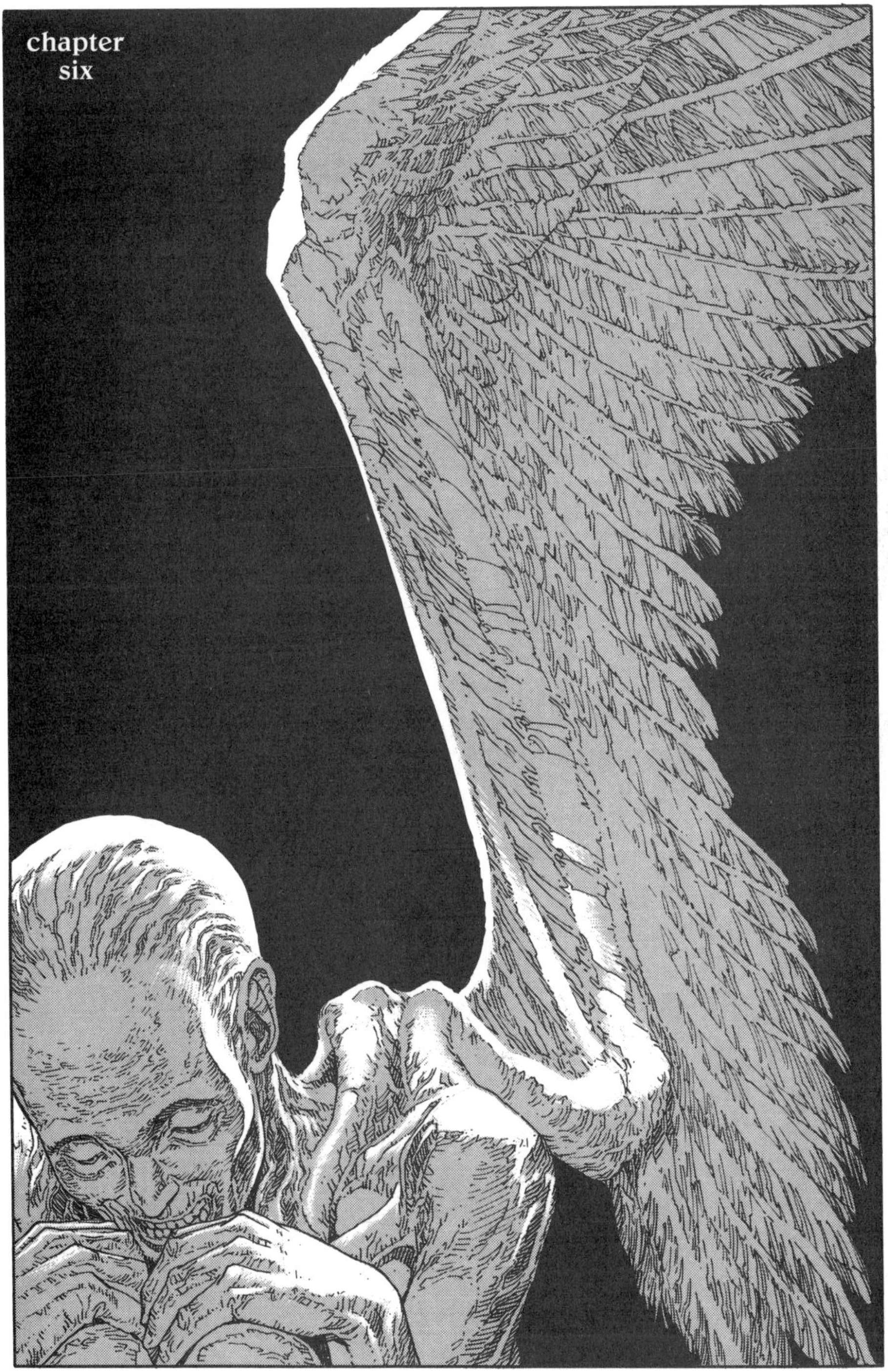
chapter
six

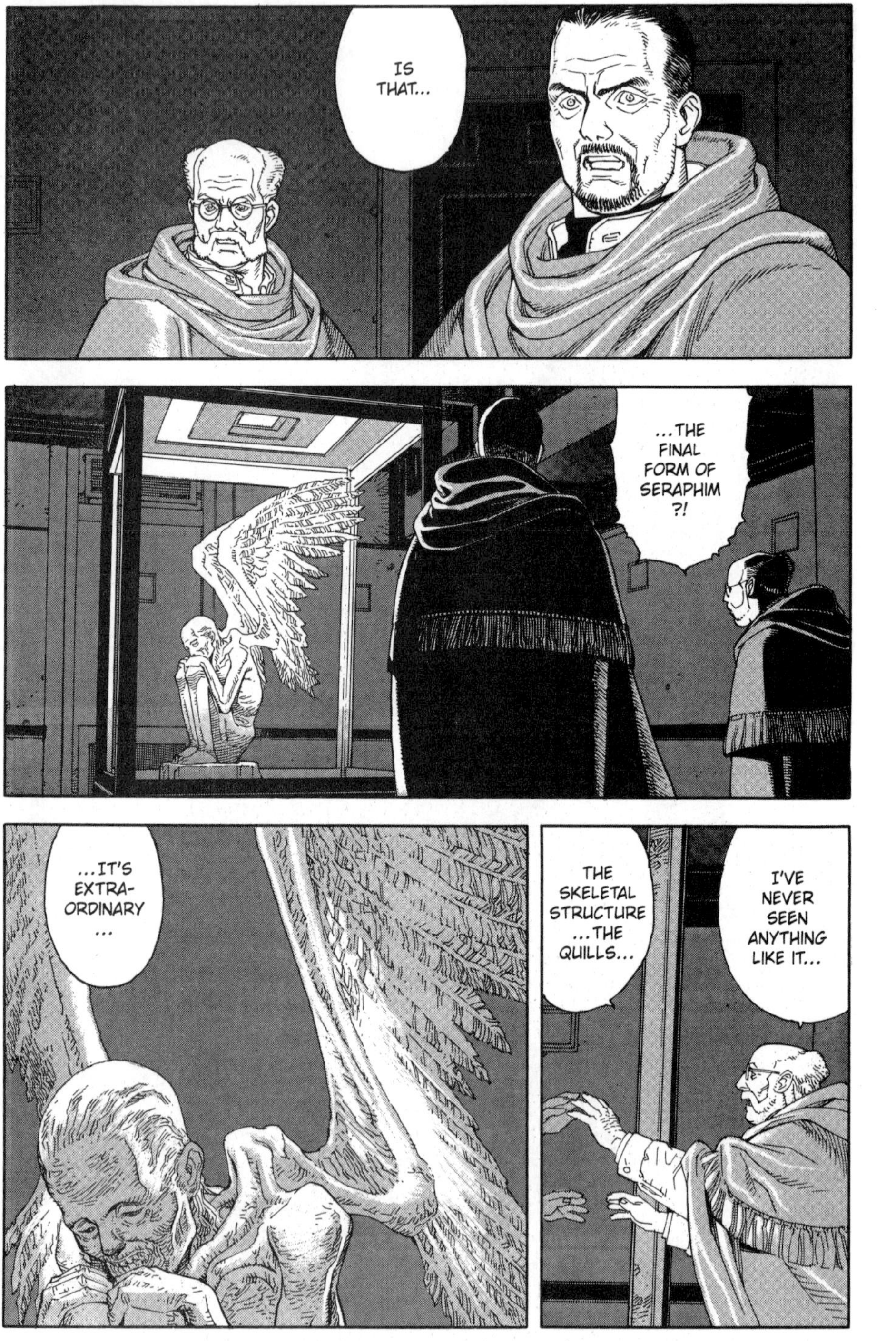
IS THAT...
...THE FINAL FORM OF SERAPHIM ?!
I'VE NEVER SEEN ANYTHING LIKE IT...
THE SKELETAL STRUCTURE ...THE QUILLS...
...IT'S EXTRA-ORDINARY ...

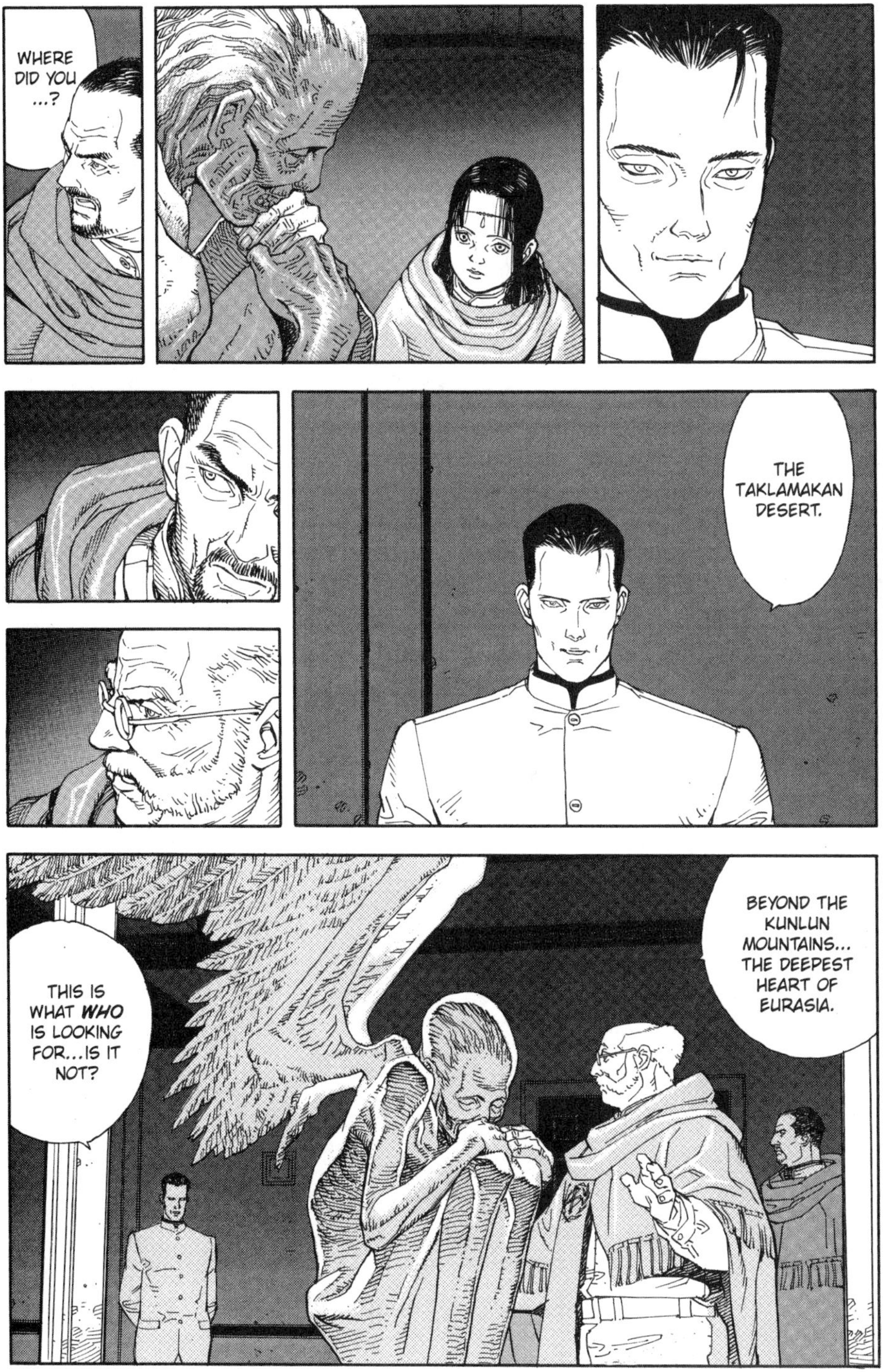
WHERE DID YOU ...?
THE TAKLAMAKAN DESERT.
BEYOND THE KUNLUN MOUNTAINS... THE DEEPEST HEART OF EURASIA.
THIS IS WHAT ***WHO*** IS LOOKING FOR...IS IT NOT?

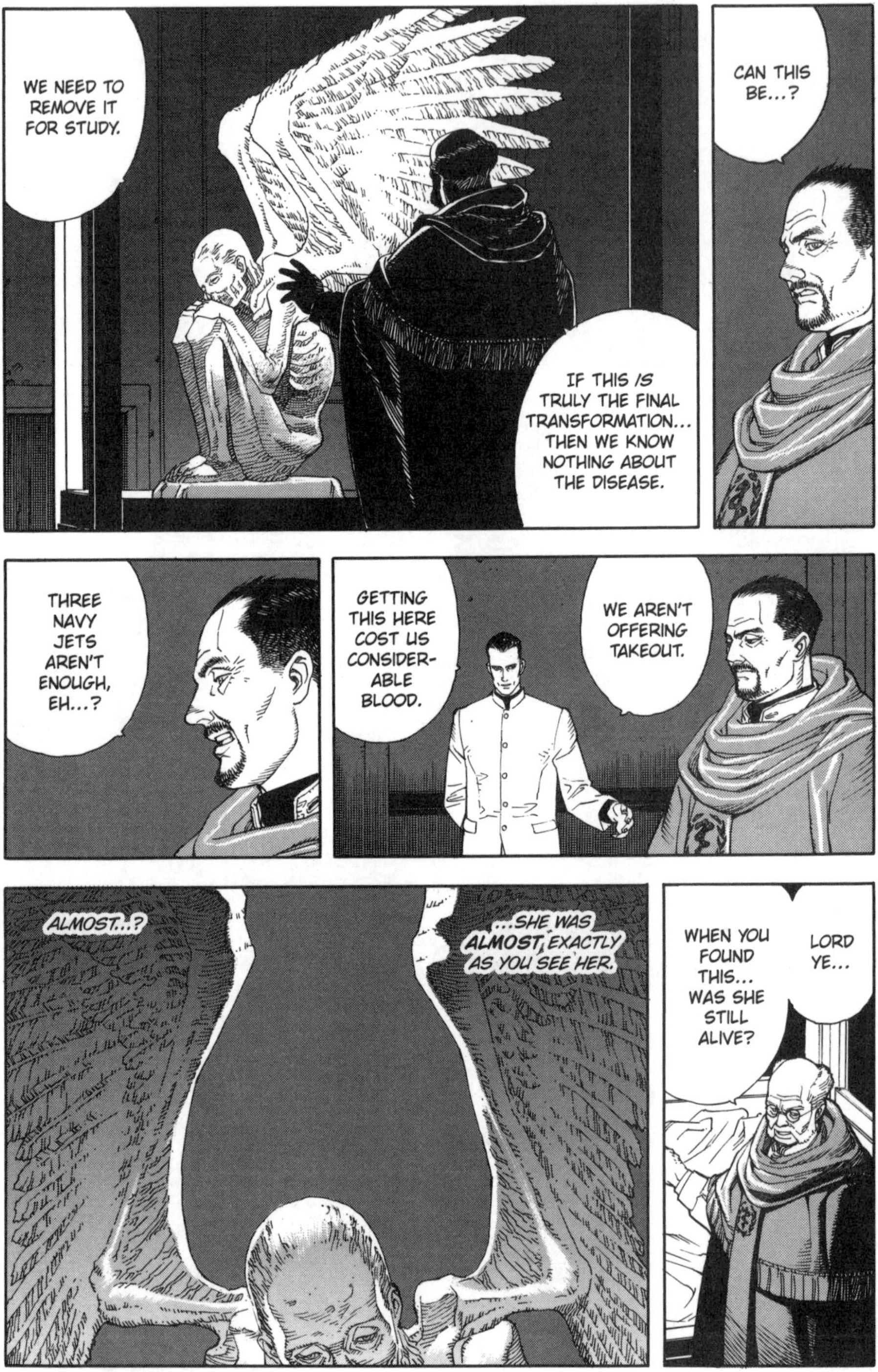
CAN THIS BE...?
IF THIS IS TRULY THE FINAL TRANSFORMATION... THEN WE KNOW NOTHING ABOUT THE DISEASE.
WE NEED TO REMOVE IT FOR STUDY.
WE AREN'T OFFERING TAKEOUT.
GETTING THIS HERE COST US CONSIDERABLE BLOOD.
THREE NAVY JETS AREN'T ENOUGH, EH...?
LORD YE...
WHEN YOU FOUND THIS... WAS SHE STILL ALIVE?
...SHE WAS ALMOST, EXACTLY AS YOU SEE HER.
ALMOST...?

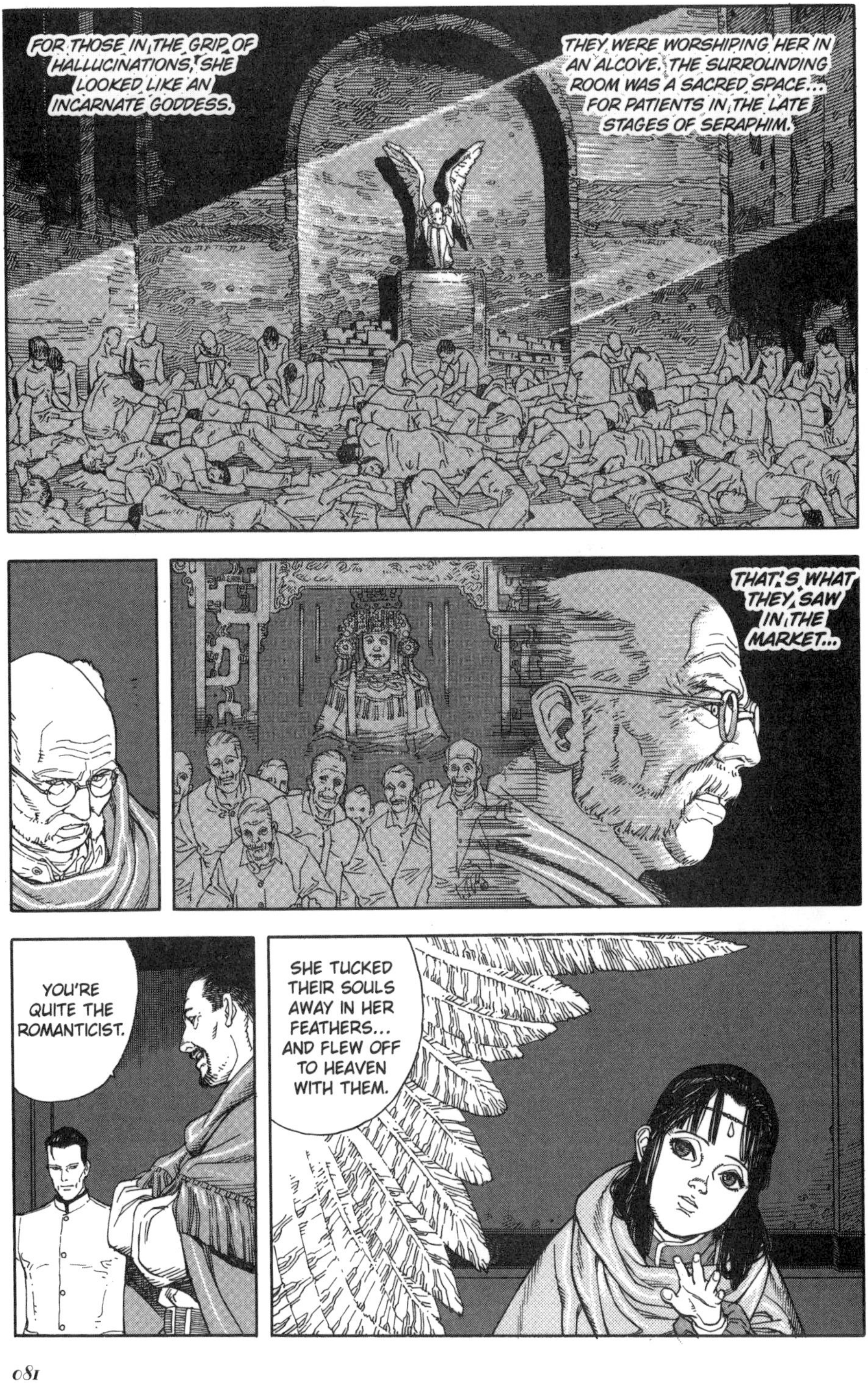
THEY WERE WORSHIPING HER IN AN ALCOVE. THE SURROUNDING ROOM WAS A SACRED SPACE... FOR PATIENTS IN THE LATE STAGES OF SERAPHIM.
FOR THOSE IN THE GRIP OF HALLUCINATIONS, SHE LOOKED LIKE AN INCARNATE GODDESS.
THAT'S WHAT THEY SAW IN THE MARKET...
SHE TUCKED THEIR SOULS AWAY IN HER FEATHERS... AND FLEW OFF TO HEAVEN WITH THEM.
YOU'RE QUITE THE ROMANTICIST.

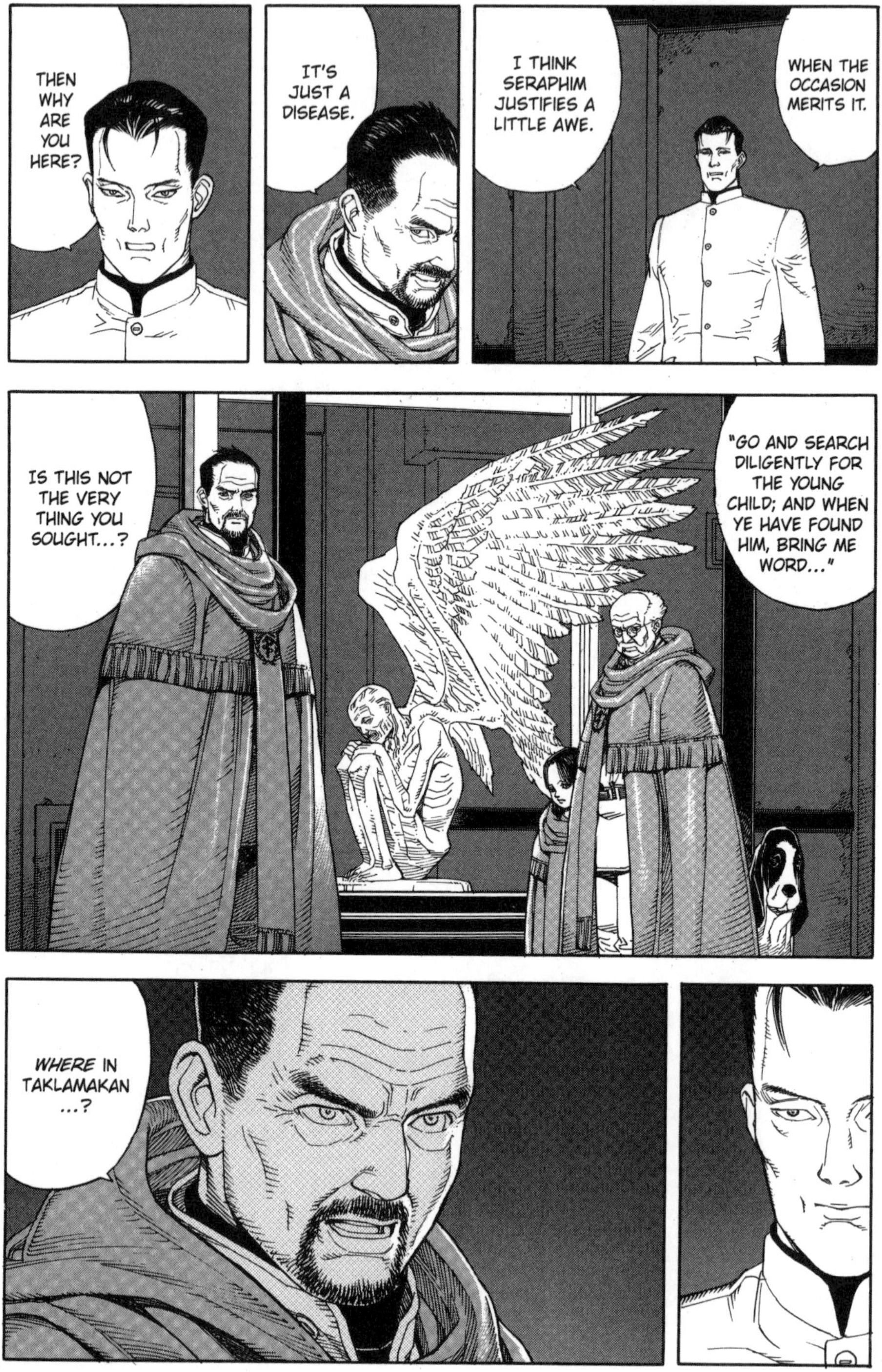
WHEN THE OCCASION MERITS IT.
I THINK SERAPHIM JUSTIFIES A LITTLE AWE.
IT'S JUST A DISEASE.
THEN WHY ARE YOU HERE?
"GO AND SEARCH DILIGENTLY FOR THE YOUNG CHILD; AND WHEN YE HAVE FOUND HIM, BRING ME WORD..."
IS THIS NOT THE VERY THING YOU SOUGHT...?
WHERE IN TAKLAMAKAN ...?

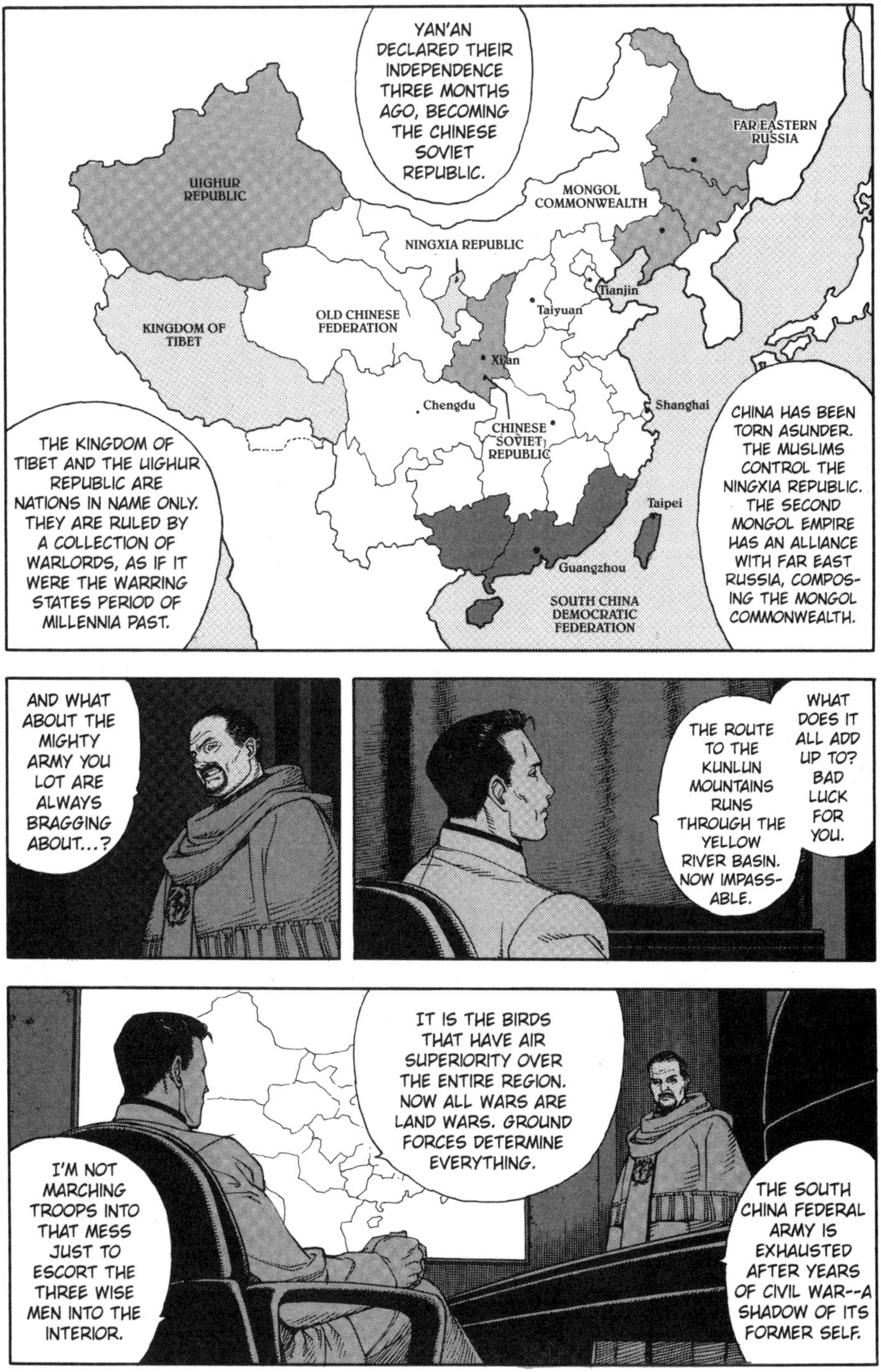
YAN'AN DECLARED THEIR INDEPENDENCE THREE MONTHS AGO, BECOMING THE CHINESE SOVIET REPUBLIC.
CHINA HAS BEEN TORN ASUNDER. THE MUSLIMS CONTROL THE NINGXIA REPUBLIC. THE SECOND MONGOL EMPIRE HAS AN ALLIANCE WITH FAR EAST RUSSIA, COMPOS-ING THE MONGOL COMMONWEALTH.
THE KINGDOM OF TIBET AND THE UIGHUR REPUBLIC ARE NATIONS IN NAME ONLY. THEY ARE RULED BY A COLLECTION OF WARLORDS, AS IF IT WERE THE WARRING STATES PERIOD OF MILLENNIA PAST.
FAR EASTERN RUSSIA
UIGHUR REPUBLIC
MONGOL COMMONWEALTH
NINGXIA REPUBLIC
Tianjin
Taiyuan
OLD CHINESE FEDERATION
KINGDOM OF TIBET
Xi'an
Shanghai
Chengdu
CHINESE SOVIET REPUBLIC
Taipei
Guangzhou
SOUTH CHINA DEMOCRATIC FEDERATION
WHAT DOES IT ALL ADD UP TO? BAD LUCK FOR YOU.
THE ROUTE TO THE KUNLUN MOUNTAINS RUNS THROUGH THE YELLOW RIVER BASIN. NOW IMPASS-ABLE.
AND WHAT ABOUT THE MIGHTY ARMY YOU LOT ARE ALWAYS BRAGGING ABOUT...?
IT IS THE BIRDS THAT HAVE AIR SUPERIORITY OVER THE ENTIRE REGION. NOW ALL WARS ARE LAND WARS. GROUND FORCES DETERMINE EVERYTHING.
THE SOUTH CHINA FEDERAL ARMY IS EXHAUSTED AFTER YEARS OF CIVIL WAR--A SHADOW OF ITS FORMER SELF.
I'M NOT MARCHING TROOPS INTO THAT MESS JUST TO ESCORT THE THREE WISE MEN INTO THE INTERIOR.

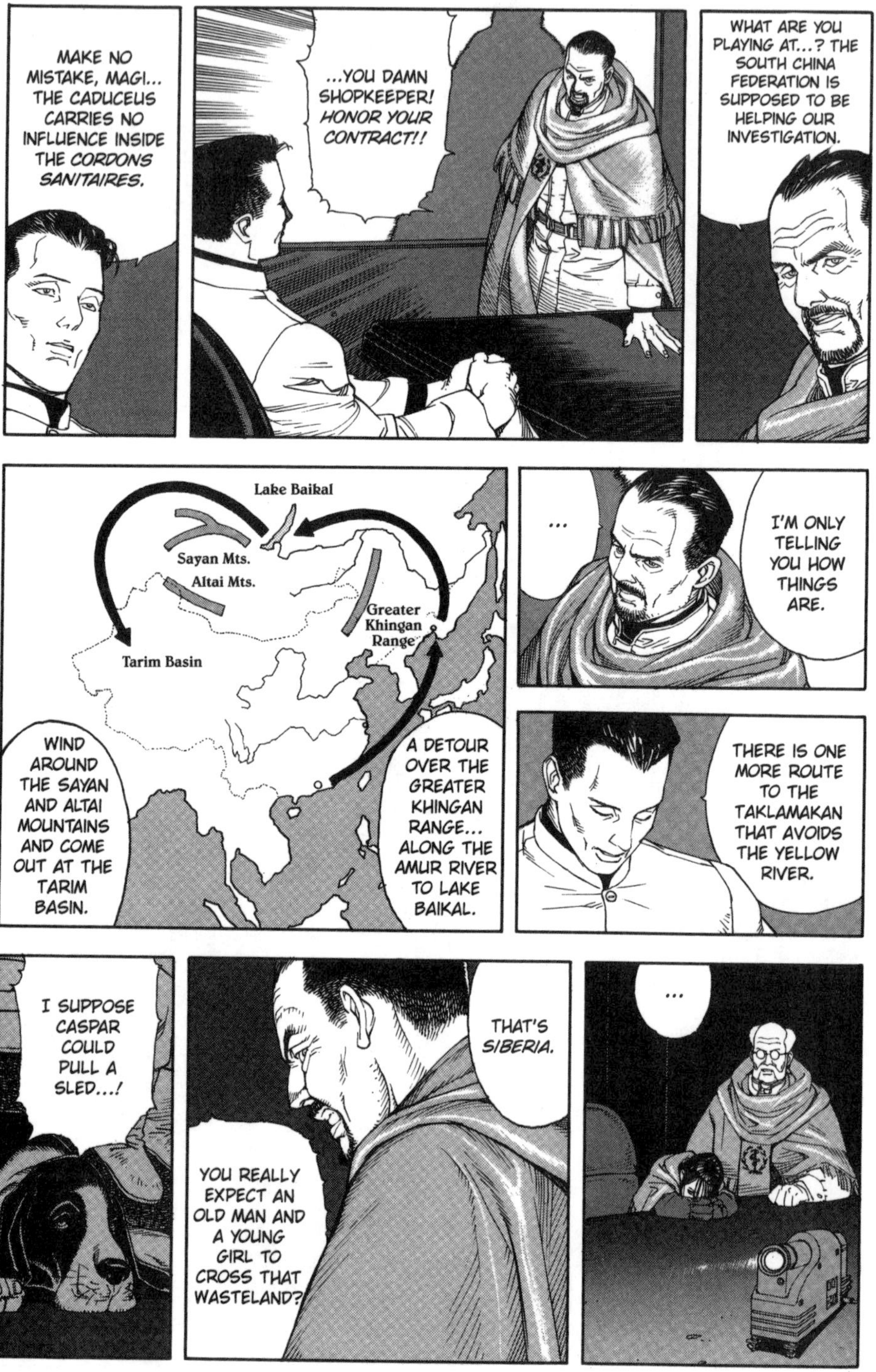
WHAT ARE YOU PLAYING AT...? THE SOUTH CHINA FEDERATION IS SUPPOSED TO BE HELPING OUR INVESTIGATION.
...YOU DAMN SHOPKEEPER! *HONOR YOUR CONTRACT!!*
MAKE NO MISTAKE, MAGI... THE CADUCEUS CARRIES NO INFLUENCE INSIDE THE *CORDONS SANITAIRES.*
I'M ONLY TELLING YOU HOW THINGS ARE.
...
THERE IS ONE MORE ROUTE TO THE TAKLAMAKAN THAT AVOIDS THE YELLOW RIVER.
Lake Baikal
Sayan Mts.
Altai Mts.
Greater Khingan Range
Tarim Basin
A DETOUR OVER THE GREATER KHINGAN RANGE... ALONG THE AMUR RIVER TO LAKE BAIKAL.
WIND AROUND THE SAYAN AND ALTAI MOUNTAINS AND COME OUT AT THE TARIM BASIN.
...
THAT'S *SIBERIA.*
YOU REALLY EXPECT AN OLD MAN AND A YOUNG GIRL TO CROSS THAT WASTELAND?
I SUPPOSE CASPAR COULD PULL A SLED...!

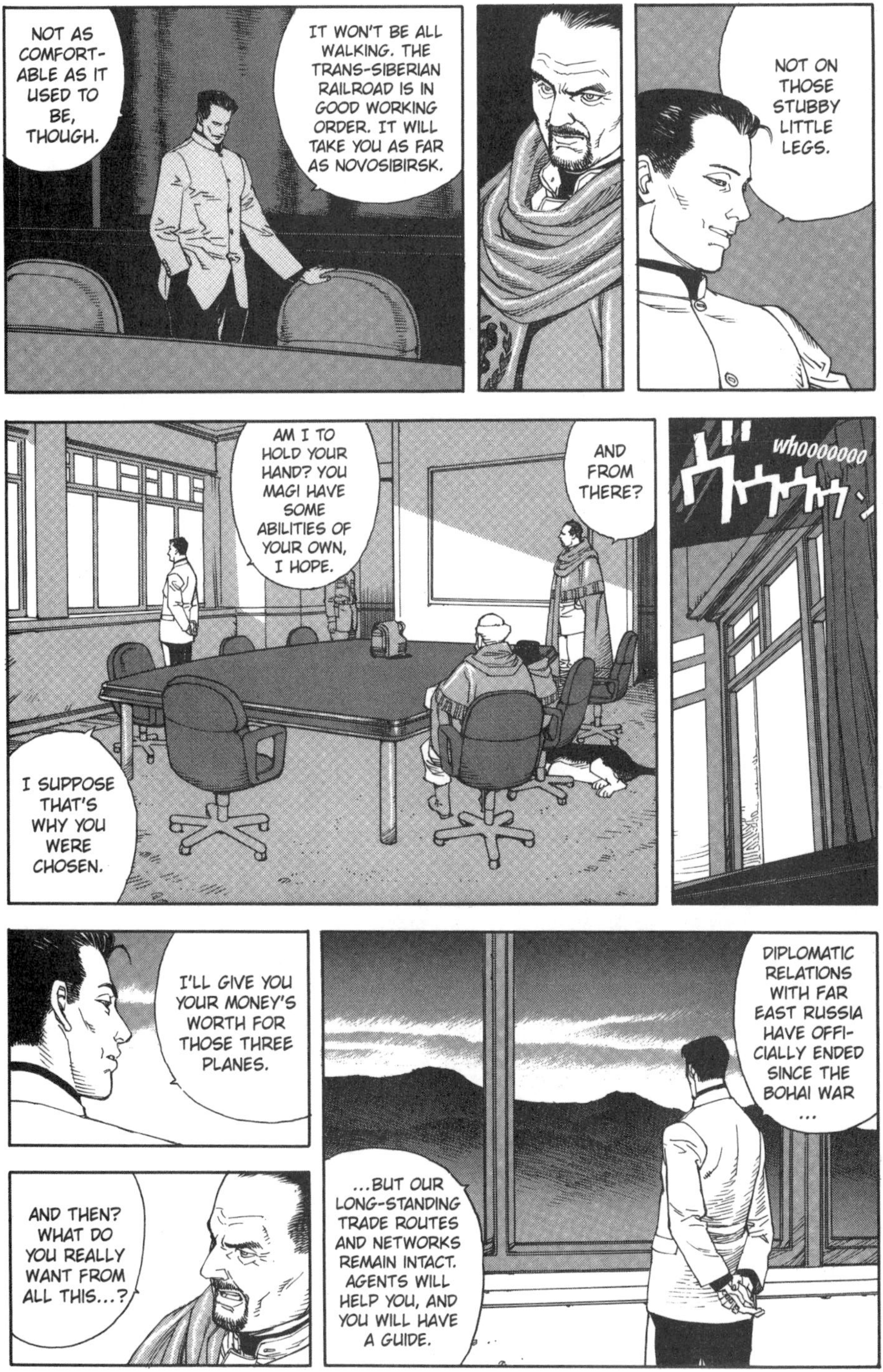
NOT ON THOSE STUBBY LITTLE LEGS.
IT WON'T BE ALL WALKING. THE TRANS-SIBERIAN RAILROAD IS IN GOOD WORKING ORDER. IT WILL TAKE YOU AS FAR AS NOVOSIBIRSK.
NOT AS COMFORT-ABLE AS IT USED TO BE, THOUGH.
whoooooo
AND FROM THERE?
AM I TO HOLD YOUR HAND? YOU MAGI HAVE SOME ABILITIES OF YOUR OWN, I HOPE.
I SUPPOSE THAT'S WHY YOU WERE CHOSEN.
DIPLOMATIC RELATIONS WITH FAR EAST RUSSIA HAVE OFFI-CIALLY ENDED SINCE THE BOHAI WAR ...
...BUT OUR LONG-STANDING TRADE ROUTES AND NETWORKS REMAIN INTACT. AGENTS WILL HELP YOU, AND YOU WILL HAVE A GUIDE.
I'LL GIVE YOU YOUR MONEY'S WORTH FOR THOSE THREE PLANES.
AND THEN? WHAT DO YOU REALLY WANT FROM ALL THIS...?

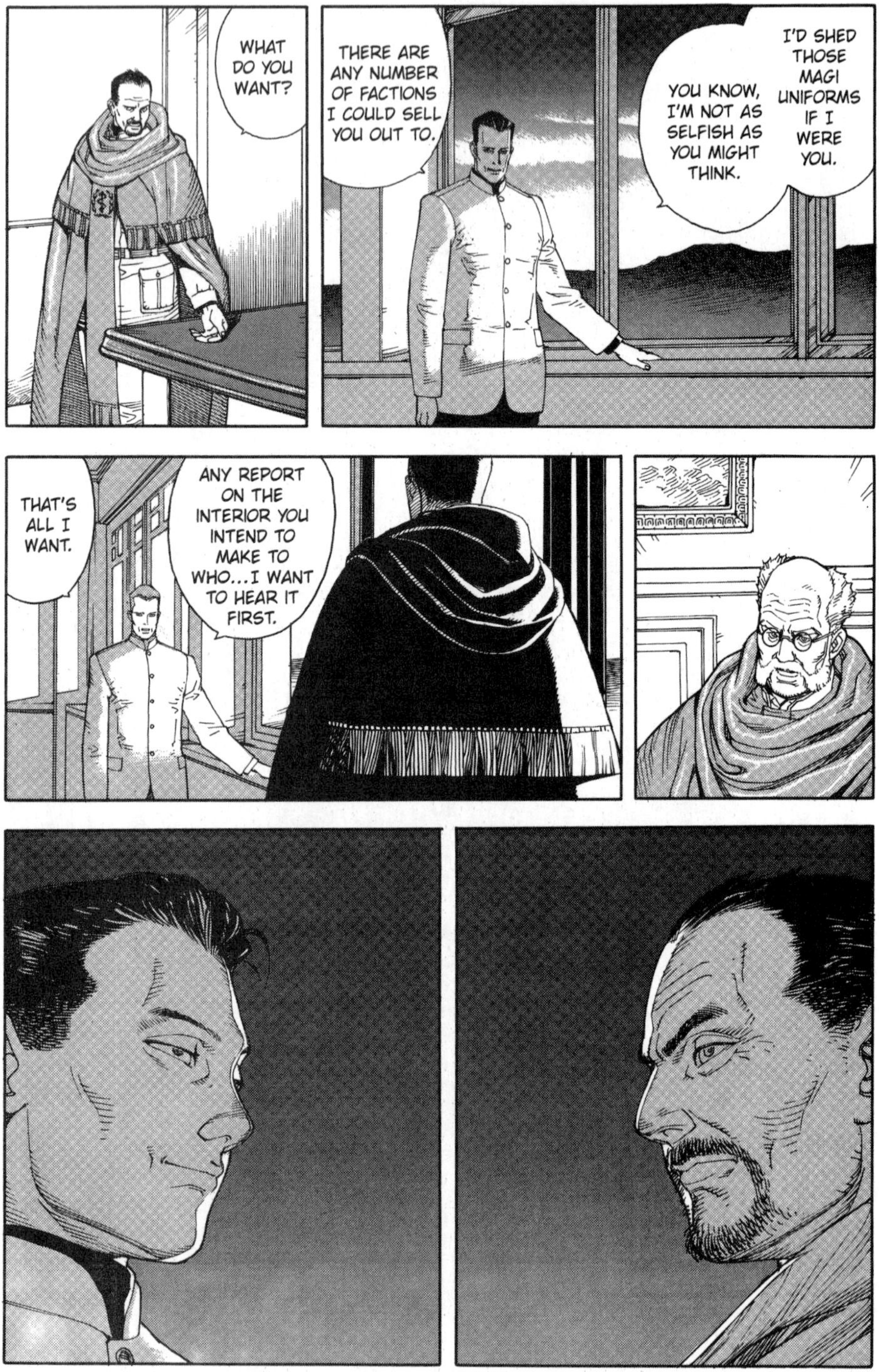
I'D SHED THOSE MAGI UNIFORMS IF I WERE YOU.
YOU KNOW, I'M NOT AS SELFISH AS YOU MIGHT THINK.
THERE ARE ANY NUMBER OF FACTIONS I COULD SELL YOU OUT TO.
WHAT DO YOU WANT?
ANY REPORT ON THE INTERIOR YOU INTEND TO MAKE TO WHO...I WANT TO HEAR IT FIRST.
THAT'S ALL I WANT.

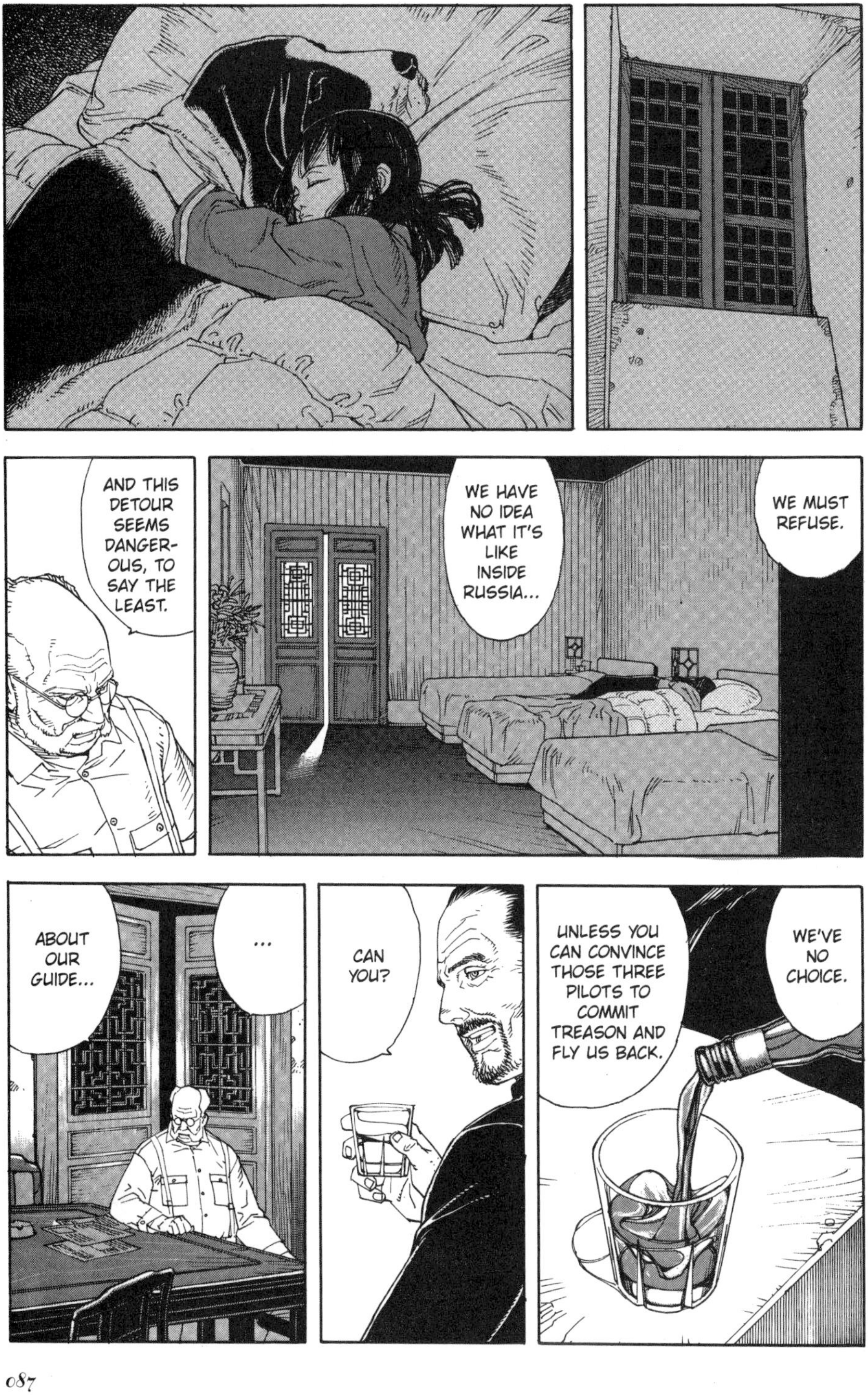
WE MUST REFUSE.
WE HAVE NO IDEA WHAT IT'S LIKE INSIDE RUSSIA...
AND THIS DETOUR SEEMS DANGER-OUS, TO SAY THE LEAST.
WE'VE NO CHOICE.
UNLESS YOU CAN CONVINCE THOSE THREE PILOTS TO COMMIT TREASON AND FLY US BACK.
CAN YOU?
...
ABOUT OUR GUIDE...

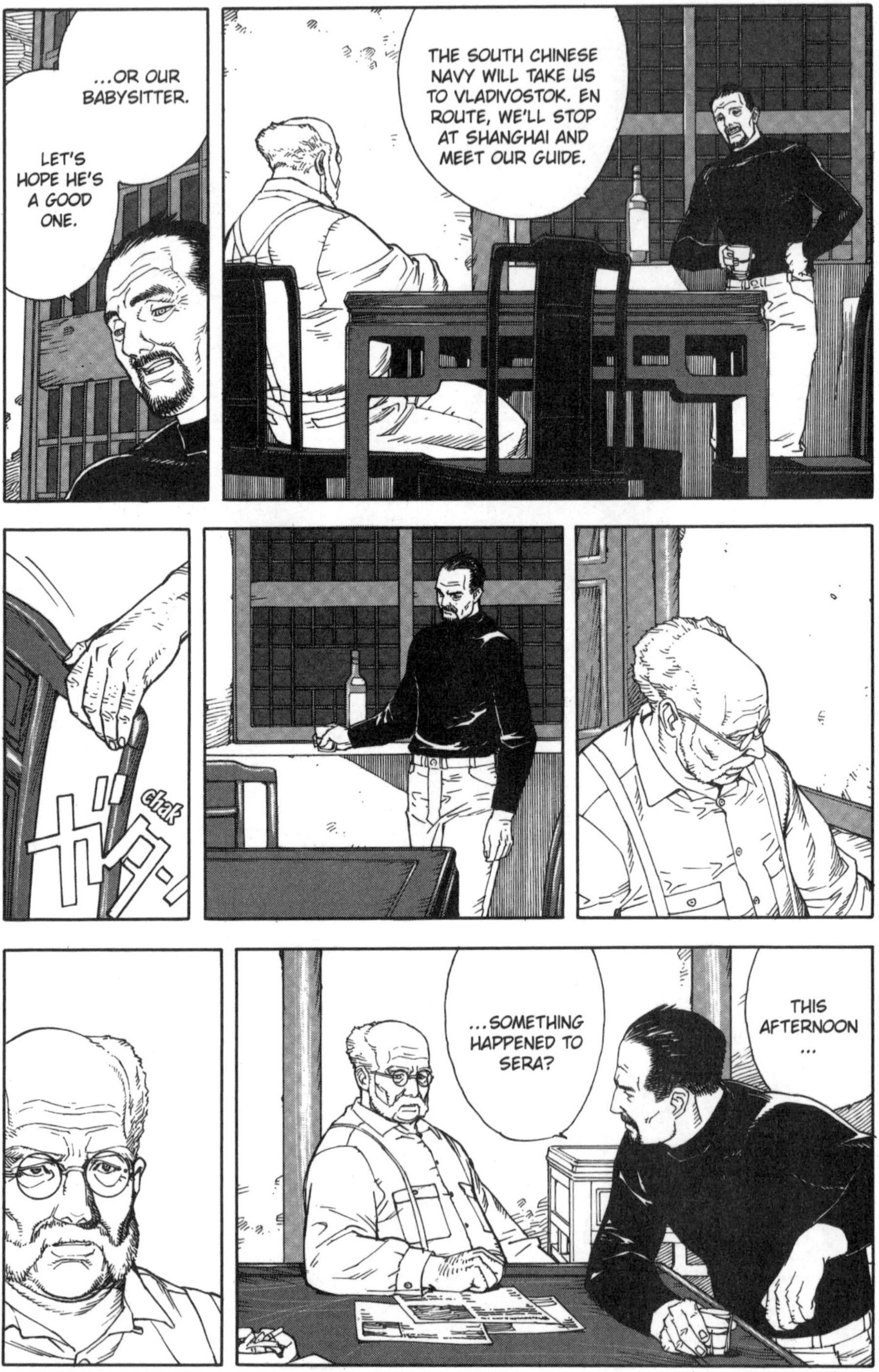
THE SOUTH CHINESE NAVY WILL TAKE US TO VLADIVOSTOK. EN ROUTE, WE'LL STOP AT SHANGHAI AND MEET OUR GUIDE.
...OR OUR BABYSITTER.
LET'S HOPE HE'S A GOOD ONE.
chak
THIS AFTERNOON ...
...SOMETHING HAPPENED TO SERA?

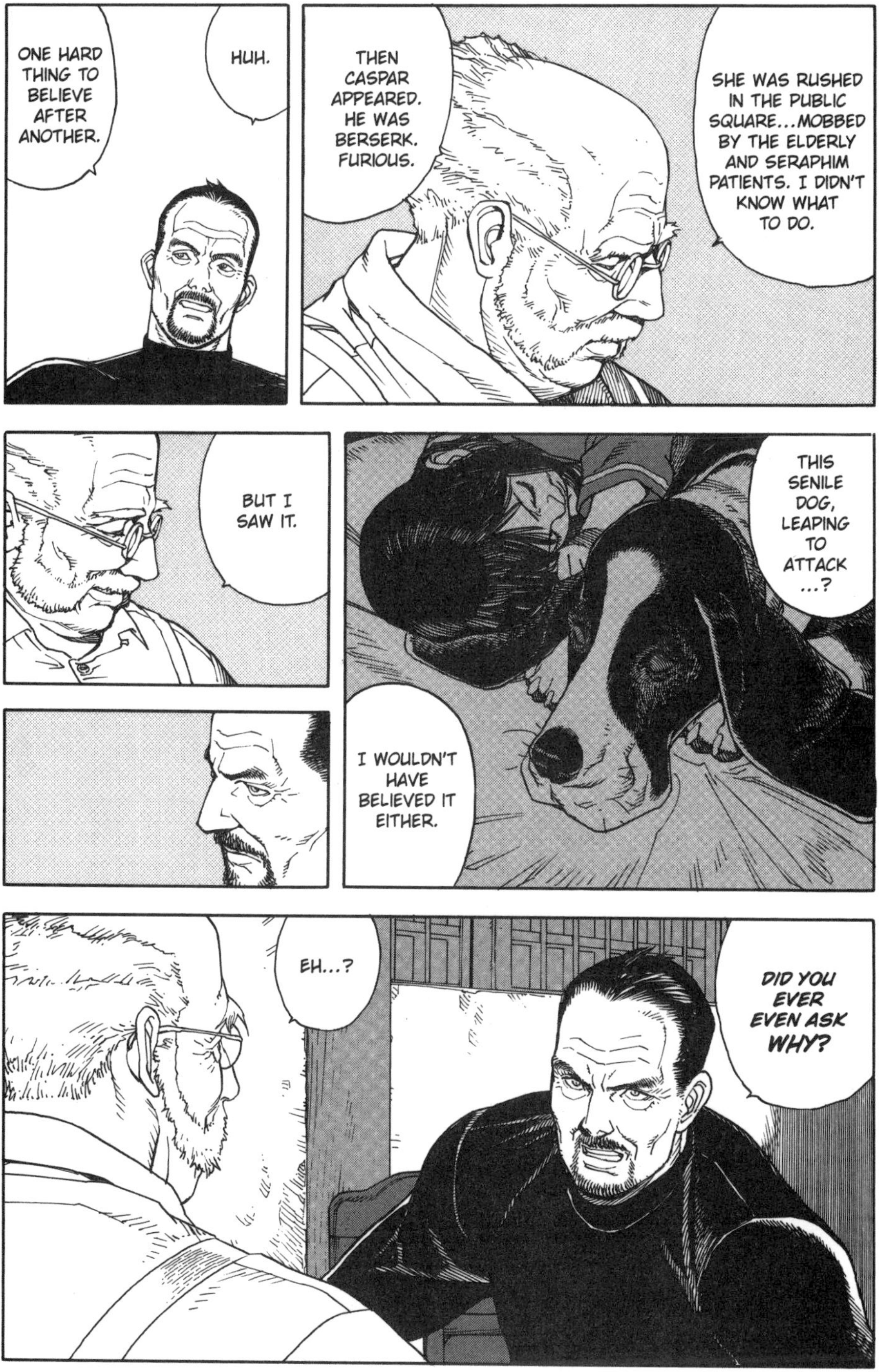
SHE WAS RUSHED IN THE PUBLIC SQUARE...MOBBED BY THE ELDERLY AND SERAPHIM PATIENTS. I DIDN'T KNOW WHAT TO DO.
THEN CASPAR APPEARED. HE WAS BERSERK. FURIOUS.
HUH.
ONE HARD THING TO BELIEVE AFTER ANOTHER.
THIS SENILE DOG, LEAPING TO ATTACK ...?
I WOULDN'T HAVE BELIEVED IT EITHER.
BUT I SAW IT.
DID YOU EVER EVEN ASK WHY?
EH...?

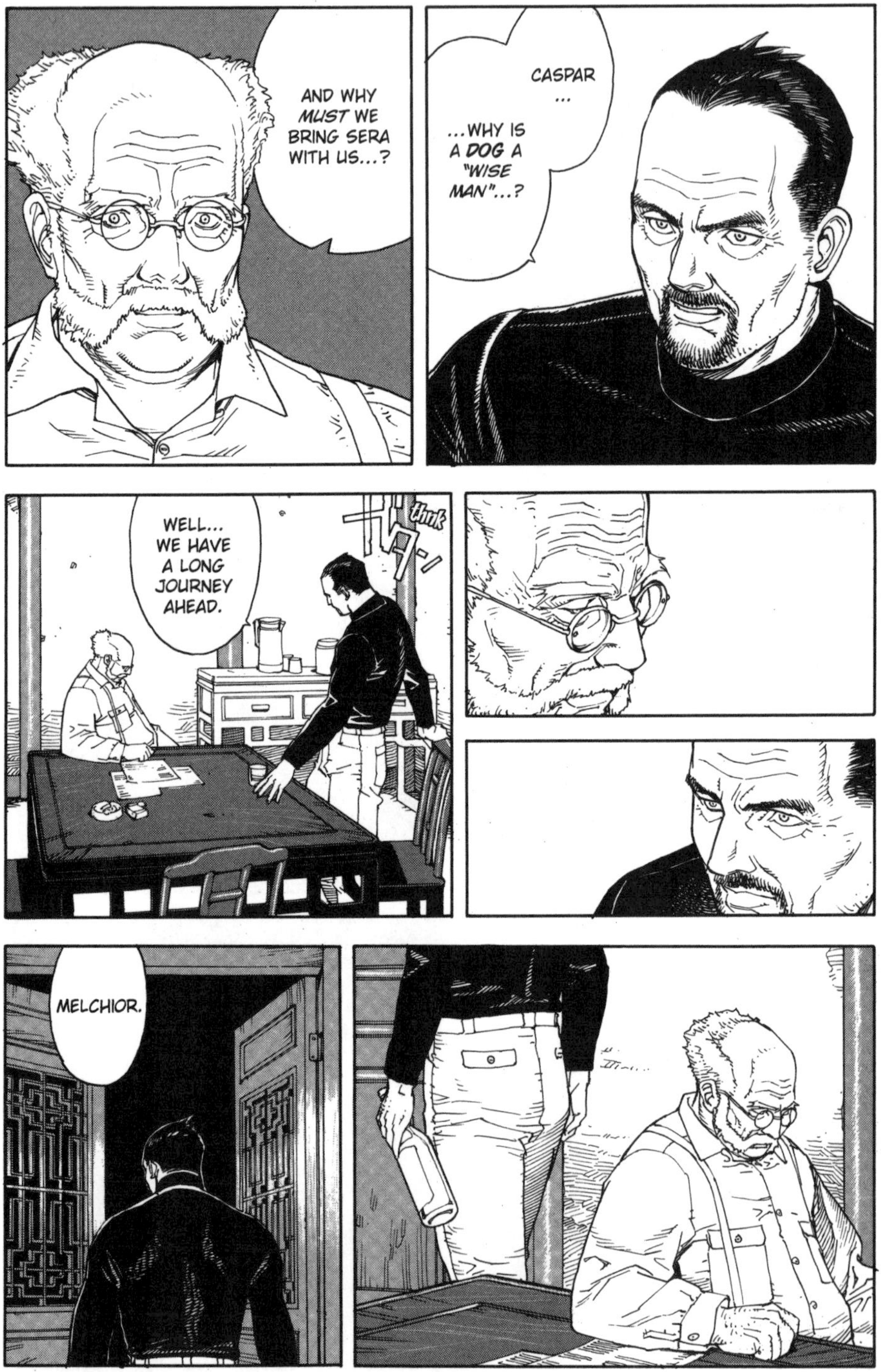
CASPAR ...
...WHY IS A *DOG* A "*WISE MAN*"...?
AND WHY *MUST* WE BRING SERA WITH US...?
WELL... WE HAVE A LONG JOURNEY AHEAD.
thnk
MELCHIOR.

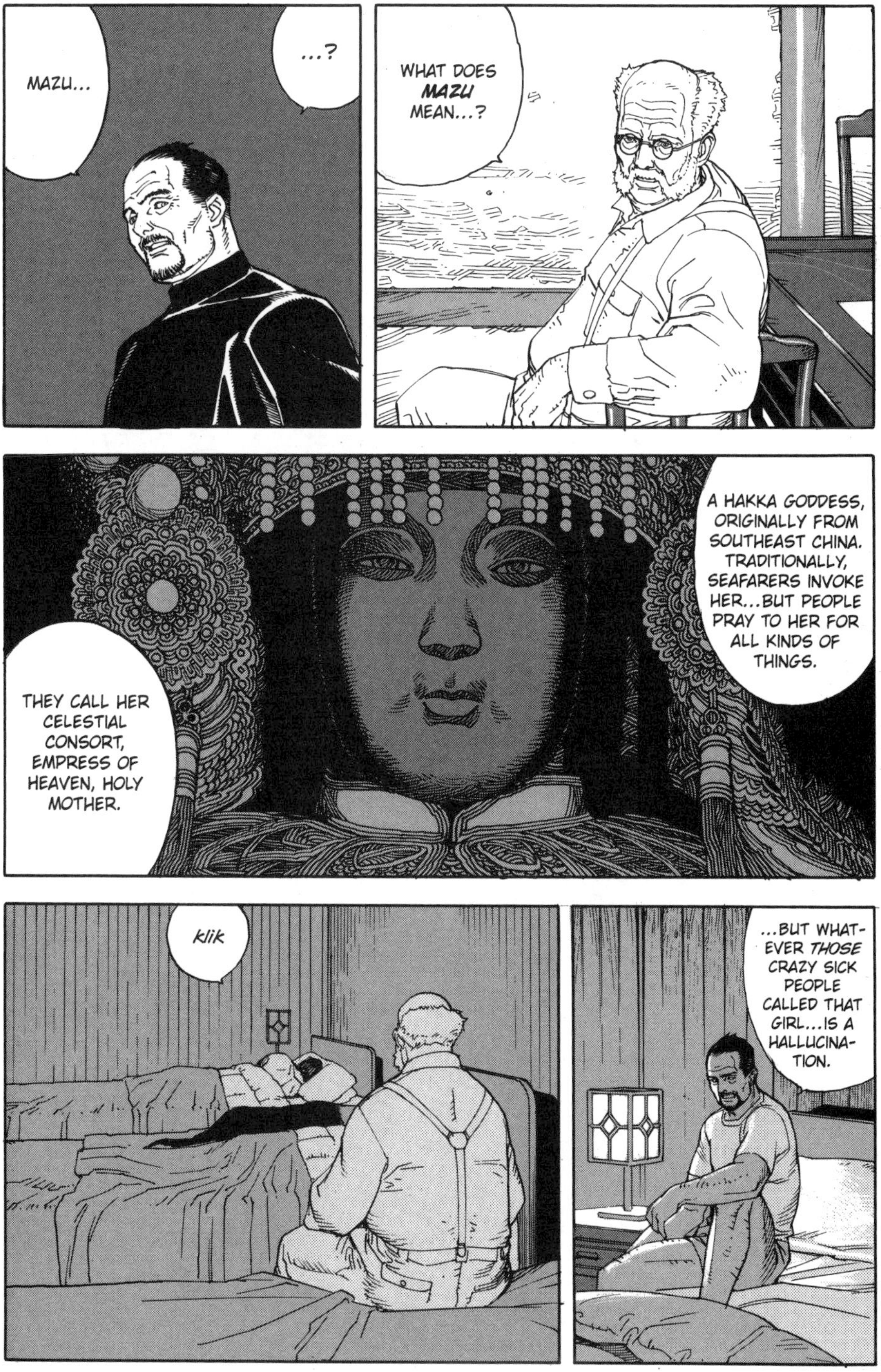
WHAT DOES **MAZU** MEAN...?
...?
MAZU...
A HAKKA GODDESS, ORIGINALLY FROM SOUTHEAST CHINA. TRADITIONALLY, SEAFARERS INVOKE HER...BUT PEOPLE PRAY TO HER FOR ALL KINDS OF THINGS.
THEY CALL HER CELESTIAL CONSORT, EMPRESS OF HEAVEN, HOLY MOTHER.
...BUT WHAT-EVER *THOSE* CRAZY SICK PEOPLE CALLED THAT GIRL...IS A HALLUCINA-TION.
klik

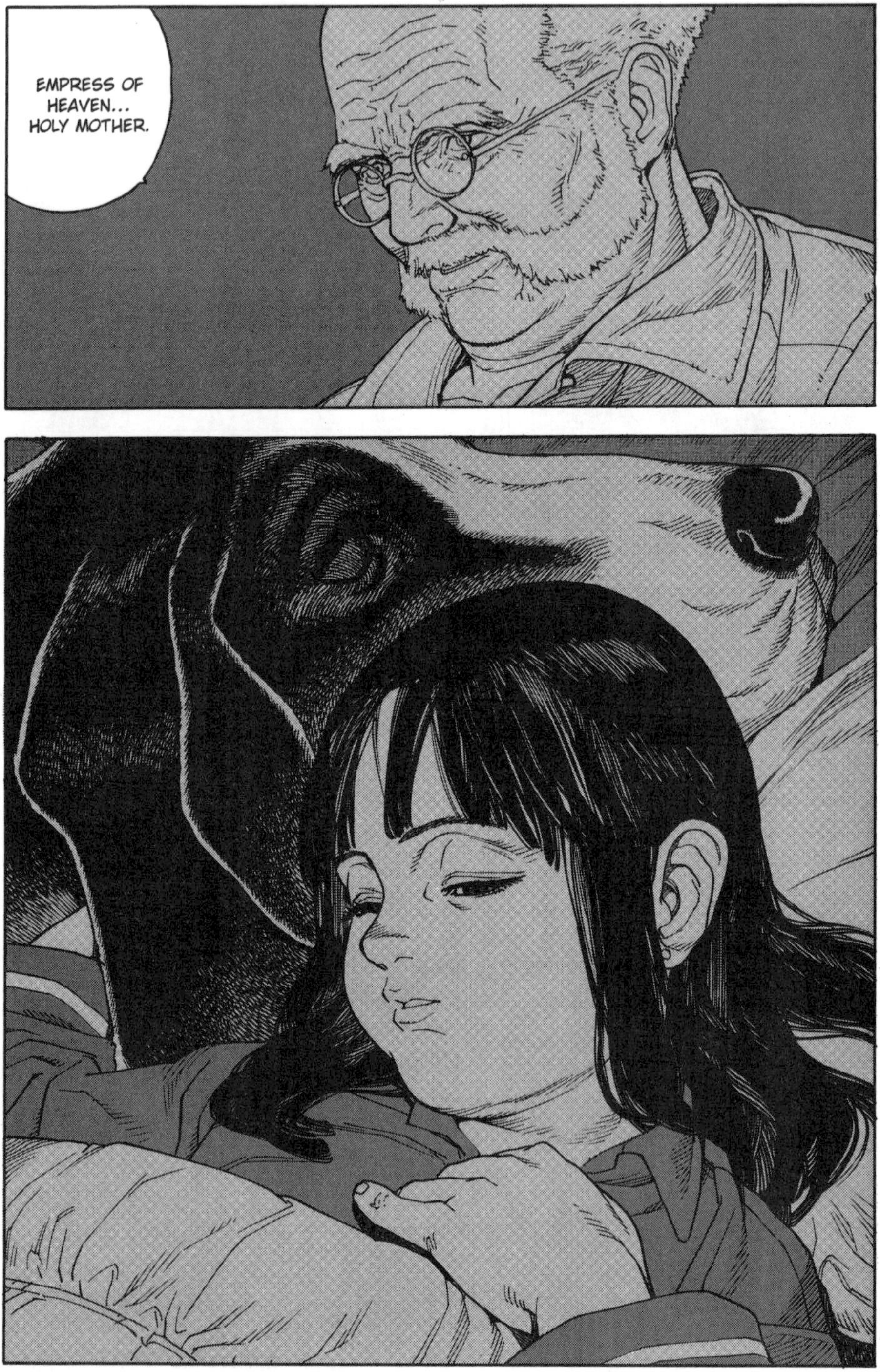
EMPRESS OF HEAVEN... HOLY MOTHER.

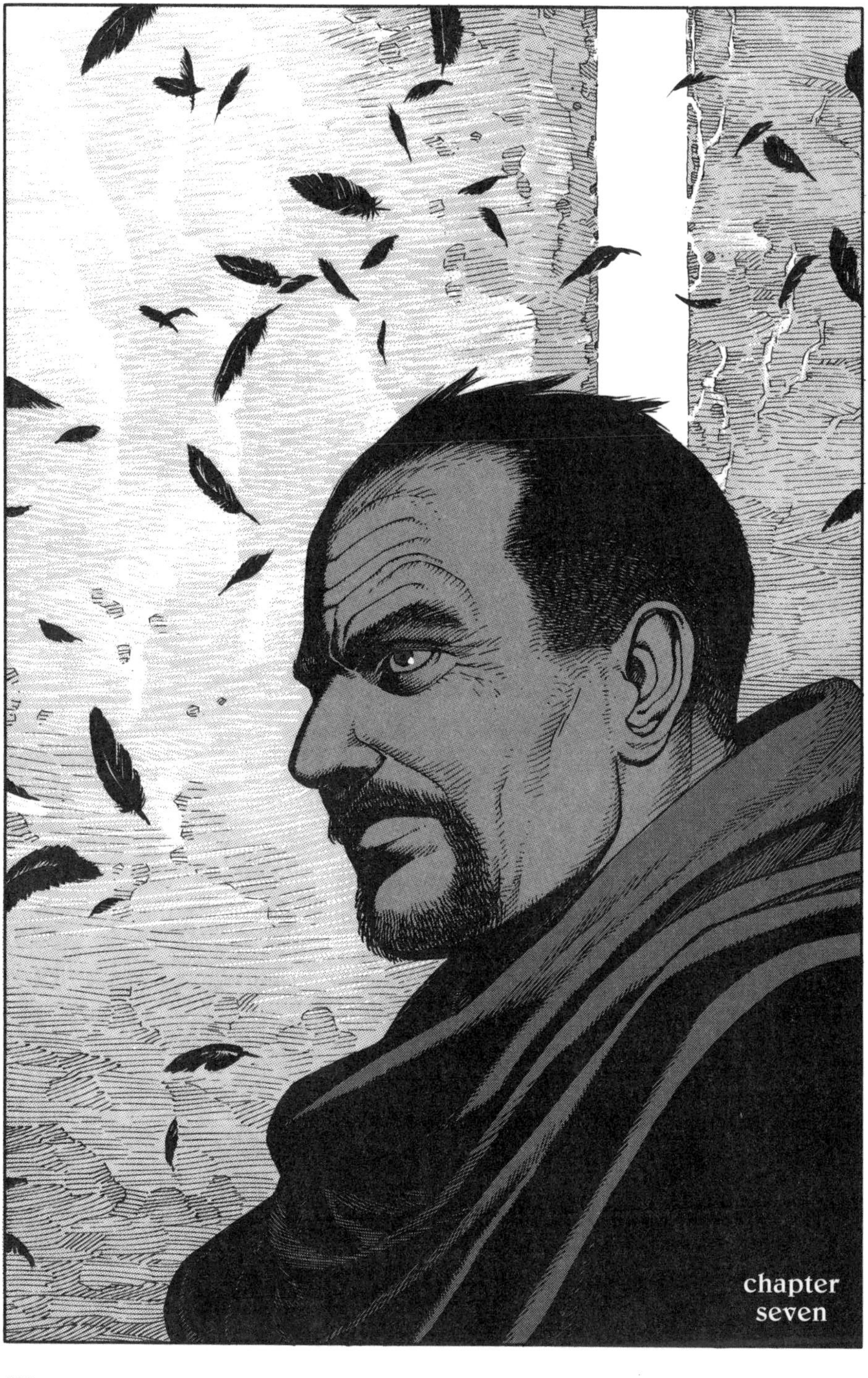
chapter
seven

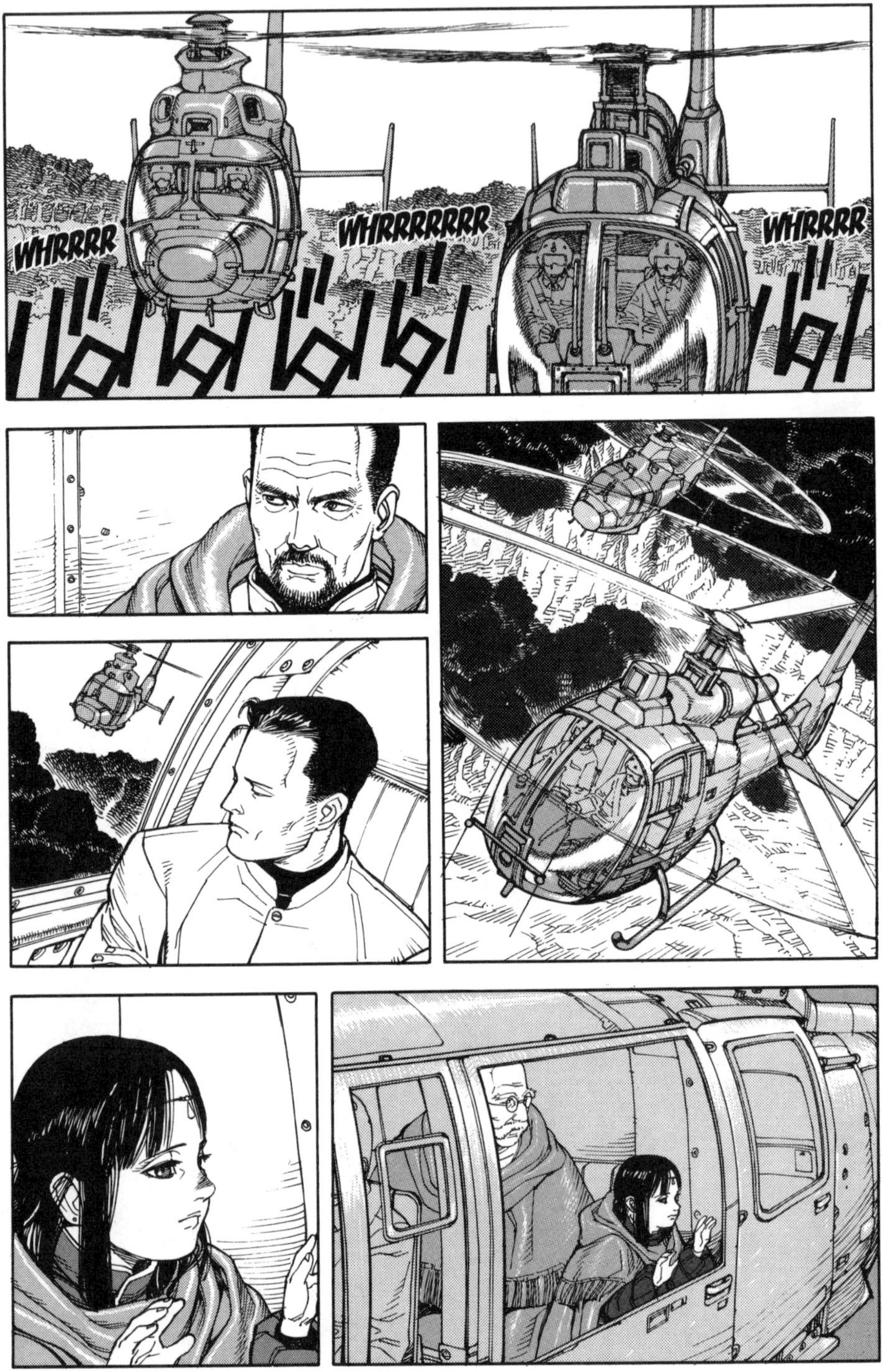
WHRRRR
WHRRRRRRR
WHRRRR

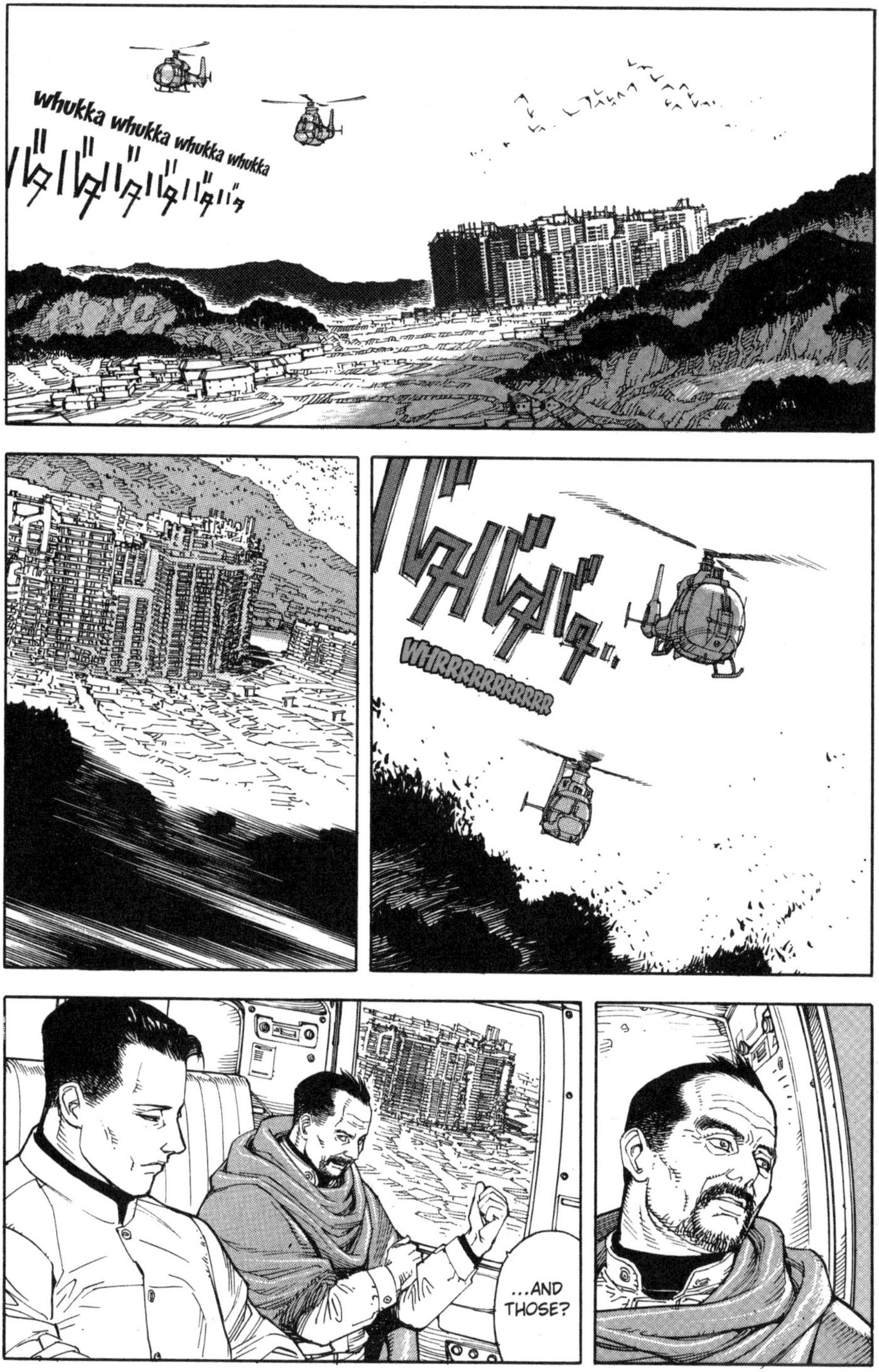
whukka whukka whukka whukka
バタバタバタバタバタ
WHRRRRRRRRRRR
...AND THOSE?

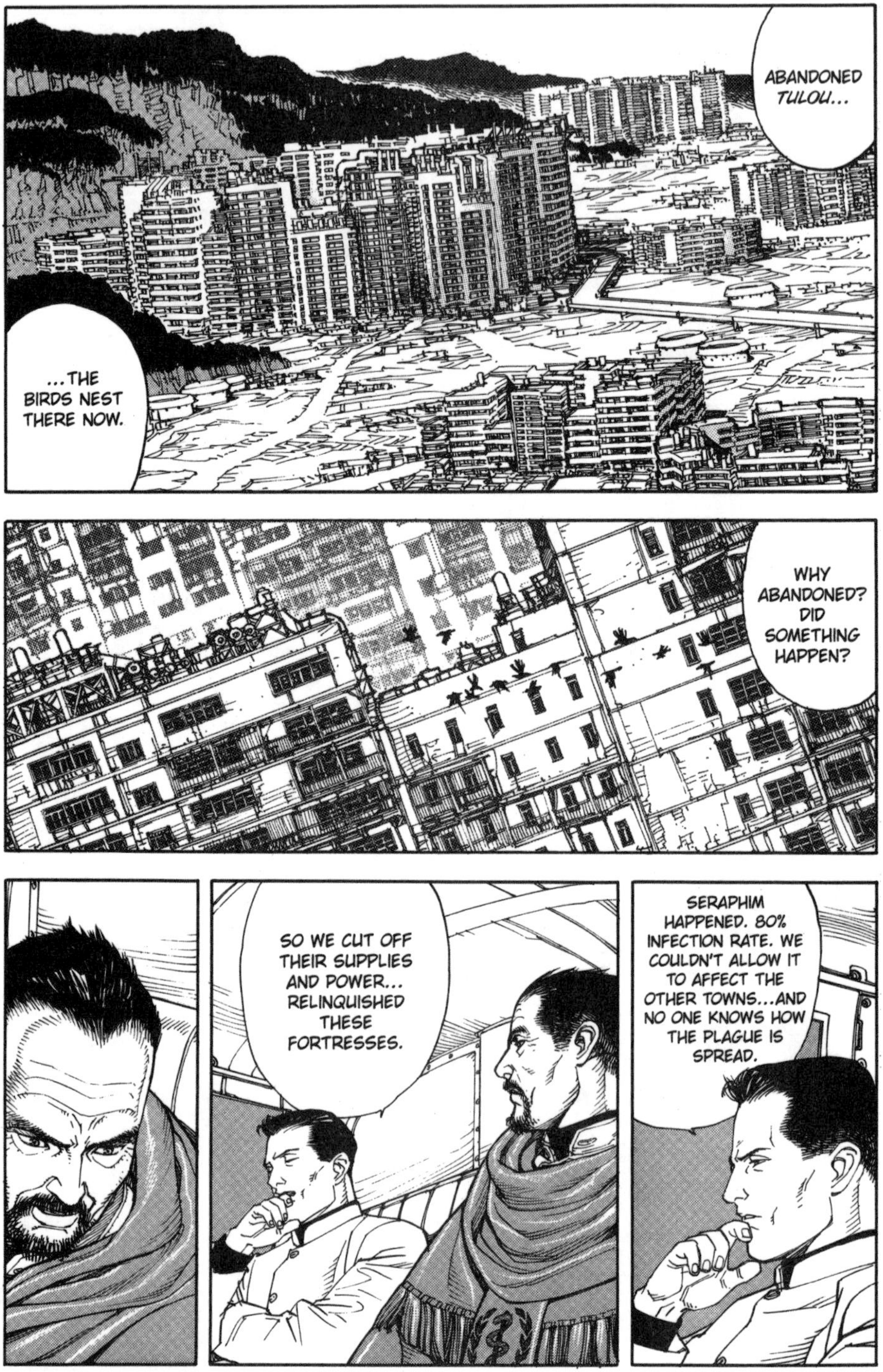
ABANDONED *TULOU*...
...THE BIRDS NEST THERE NOW.
WHY ABANDONED? DID SOMETHING HAPPEN?
SERAPHIM HAPPENED. 80% INFECTION RATE. WE COULDN'T ALLOW IT TO AFFECT THE OTHER TOWNS...AND NO ONE KNOWS HOW THE PLAGUE IS SPREAD.
SO WE CUT OFF THEIR SUPPLIES AND POWER... RELINQUISHED THESE FORTRESSES.

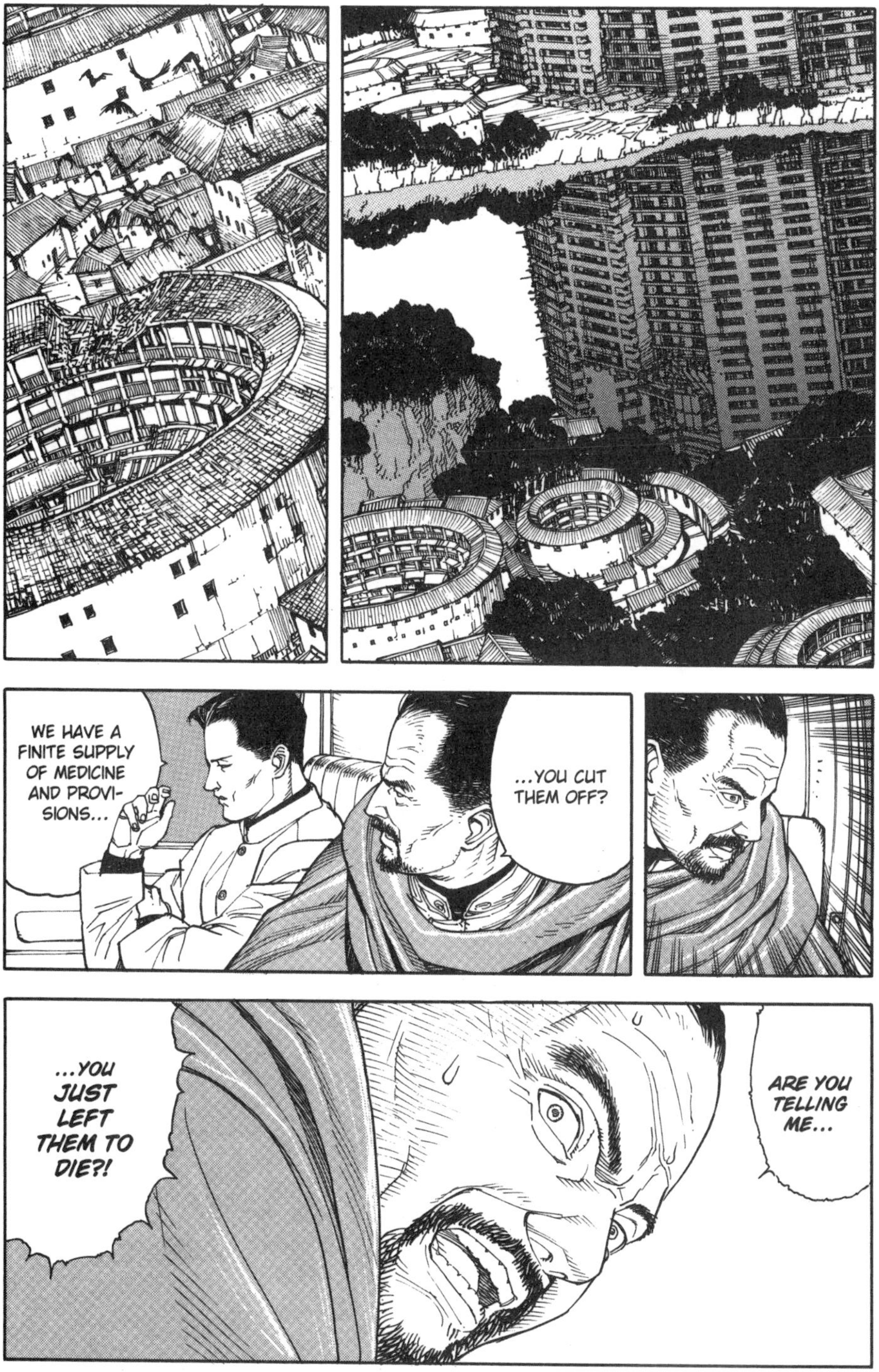
...YOU CUT THEM OFF?
WE HAVE A FINITE SUPPLY OF MEDICINE AND PROVISIONS...
ARE YOU TELLING ME...
...YOU JUST LEFT THEM TO DIE?!

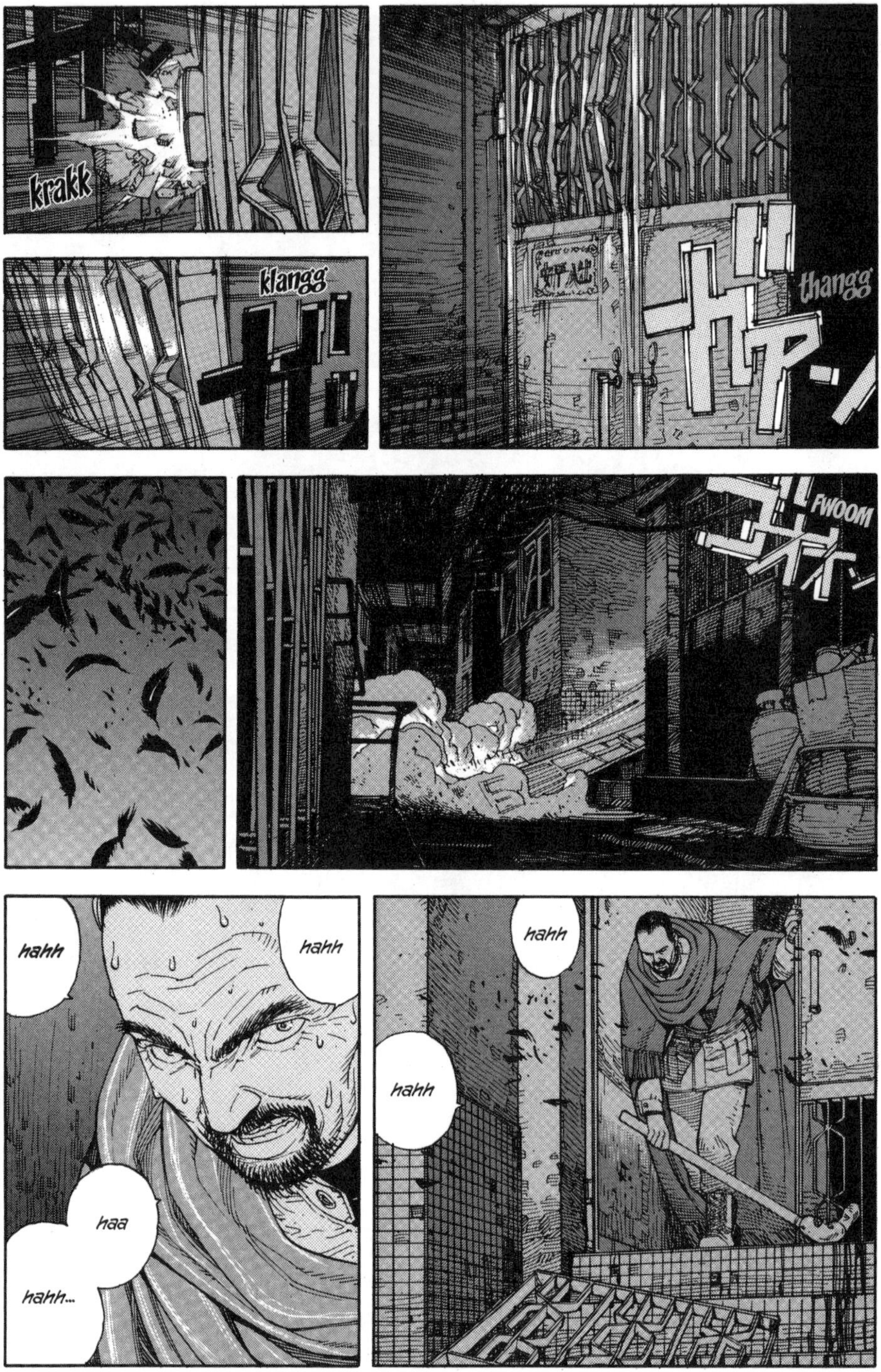
thangg
krakk
klangg
FWOOM
hahh
hahh
hahh
hahh
haa
hahh...

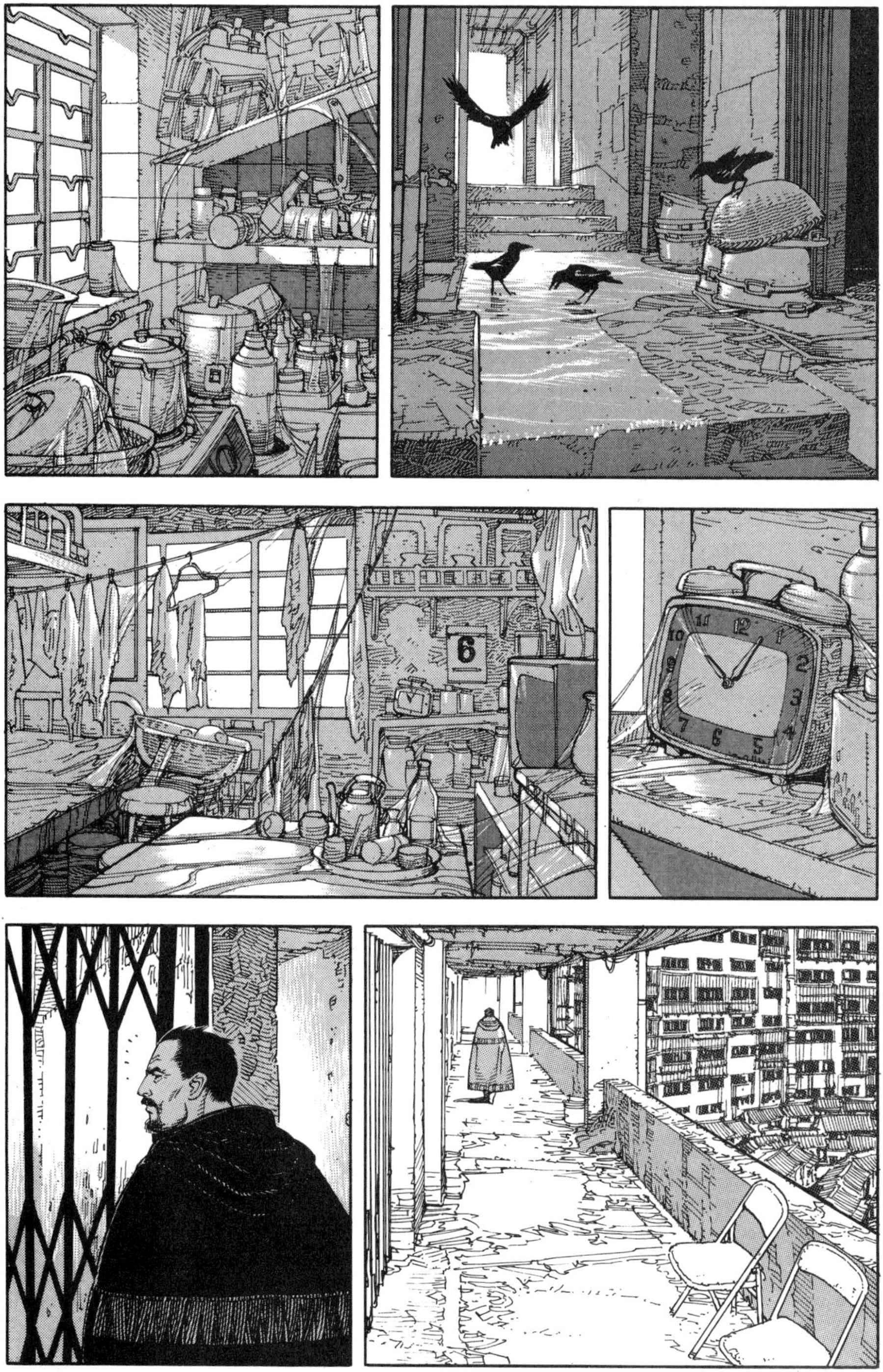

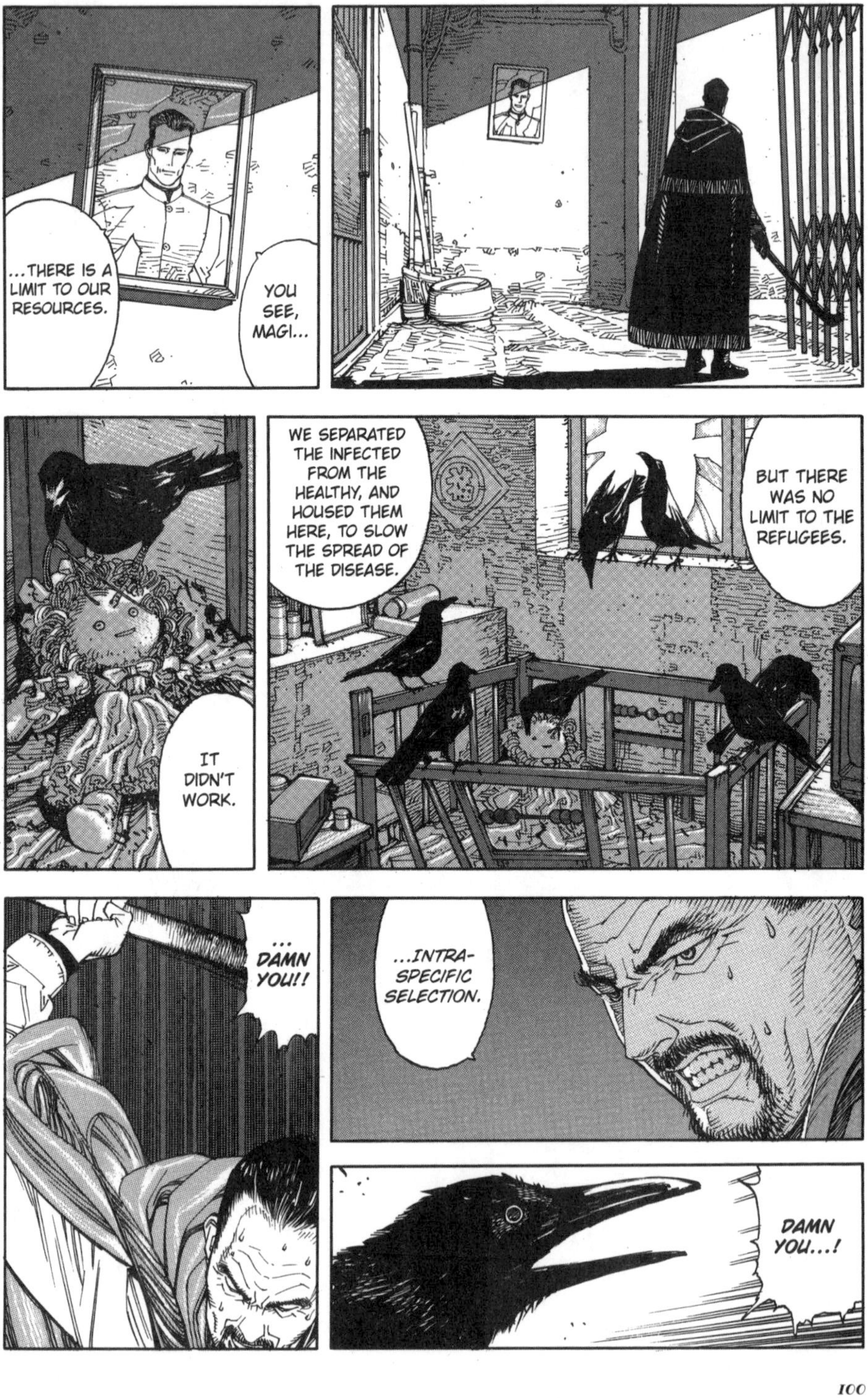
YOU SEE, MAGI...
...THERE IS A LIMIT TO OUR RESOURCES.
BUT THERE WAS NO LIMIT TO THE REFUGEES.
WE SEPARATED THE INFECTED FROM THE HEALTHY, AND HOUSED THEM HERE, TO SLOW THE SPREAD OF THE DISEASE.
IT DIDN'T WORK.
...INTRA-SPECIFIC SELECTION.
DAMN YOU...!
...DAMN YOU!!

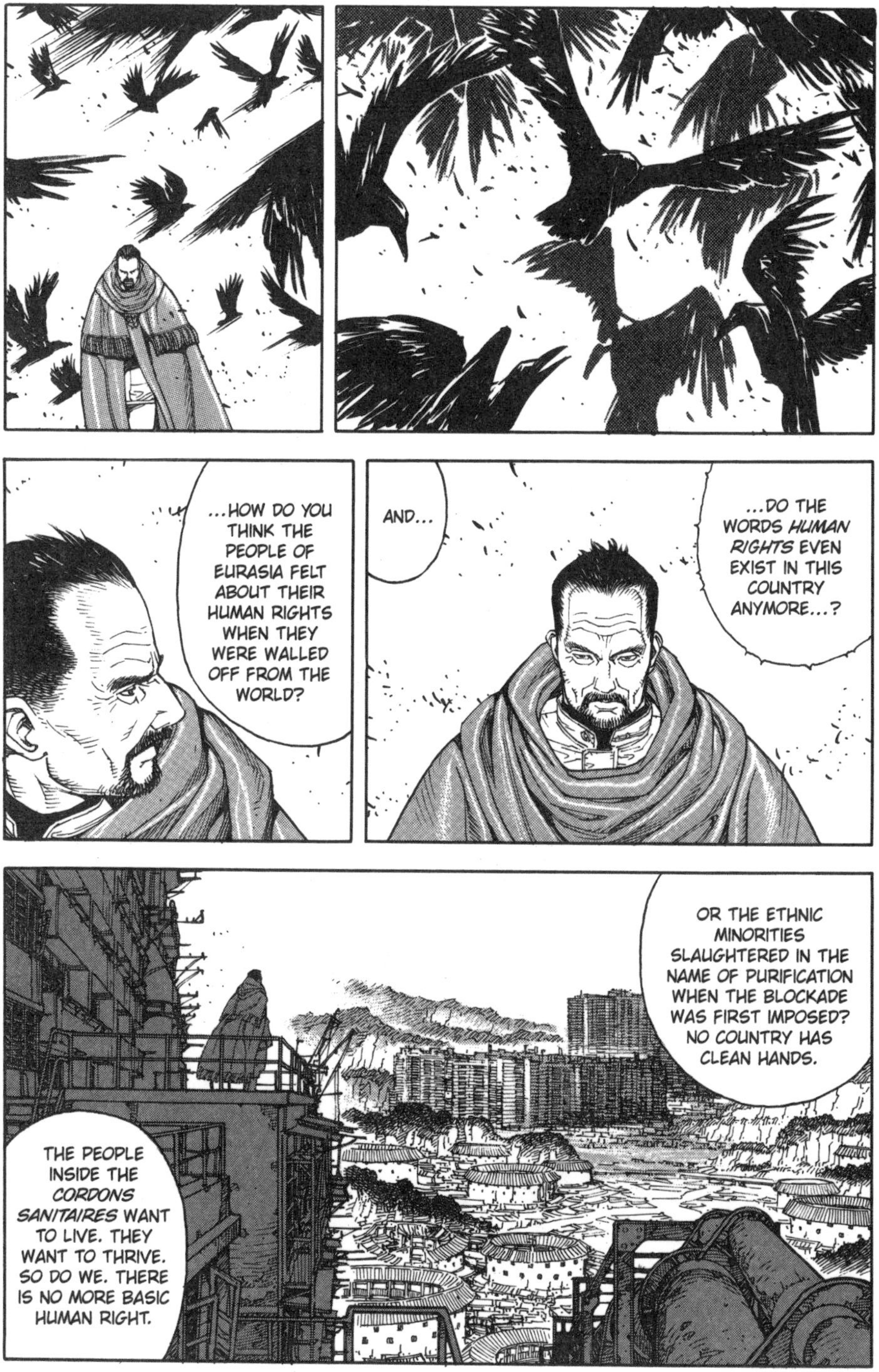
...DO THE WORDS *HUMAN RIGHTS* EVEN EXIST IN THIS COUNTRY ANYMORE...?
AND...
...HOW DO YOU THINK THE PEOPLE OF EURASIA FELT ABOUT THEIR HUMAN RIGHTS WHEN THEY WERE WALLED OFF FROM THE WORLD?
OR THE ETHNIC MINORITIES SLAUGHTERED IN THE NAME OF PURIFICATION WHEN THE BLOCKADE WAS FIRST IMPOSED? NO COUNTRY HAS CLEAN HANDS.
THE PEOPLE INSIDE THE *CORDONS SANITAIRES* WANT TO LIVE. THEY WANT TO THRIVE. SO DO WE. THERE IS NO MORE BASIC HUMAN RIGHT.

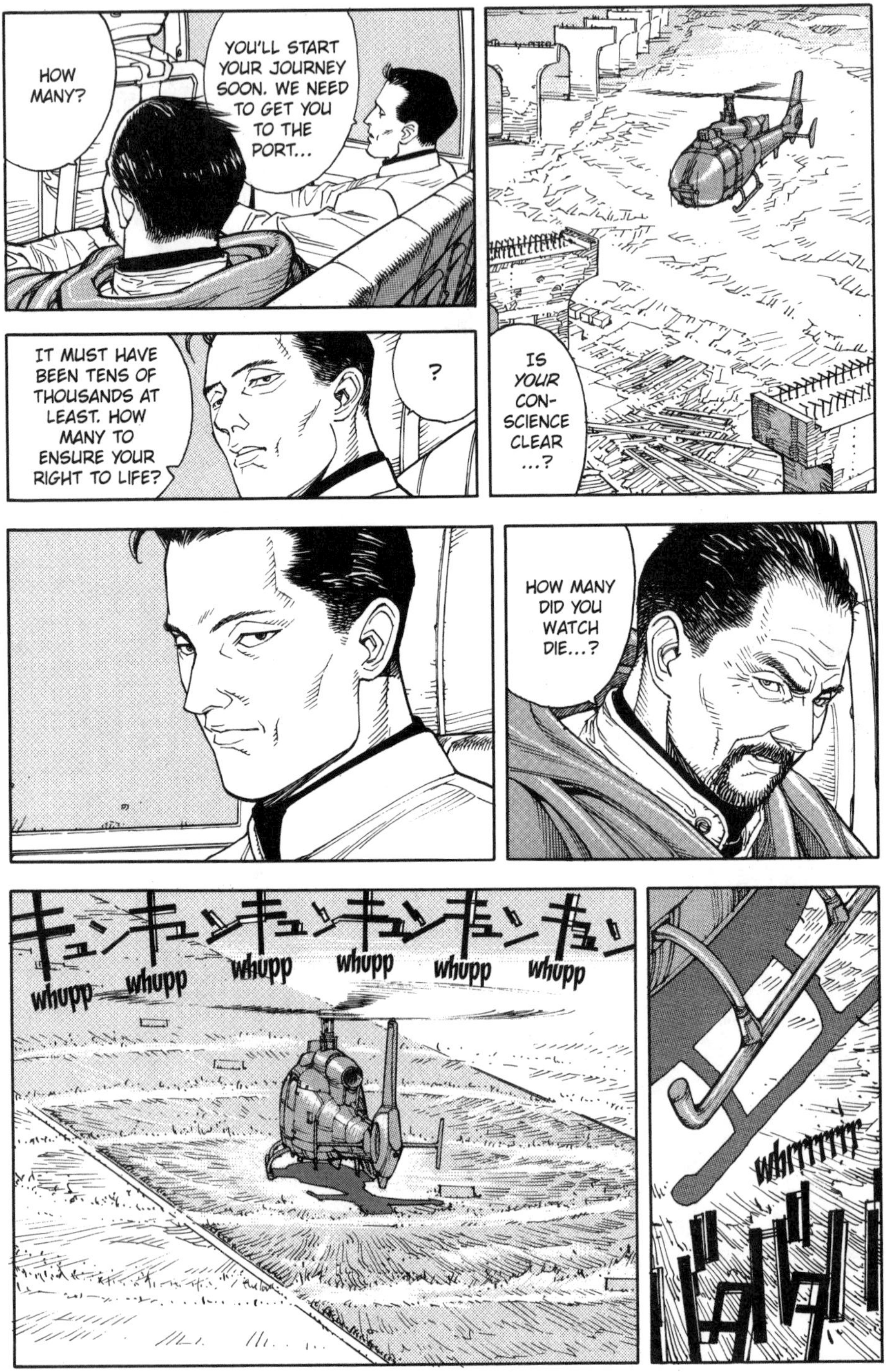
IS YOUR CON- SCIENCE CLEAR ...?
YOU'LL START YOUR JOURNEY SOON. WE NEED TO GET YOU TO THE PORT...
HOW MANY?
?
IT MUST HAVE BEEN TENS OF THOUSANDS AT LEAST. HOW MANY TO ENSURE YOUR RIGHT TO LIFE?
HOW MANY DID YOU WATCH DIE...?
whrrrrrr
whupp whupp whupp whupp whupp whupp

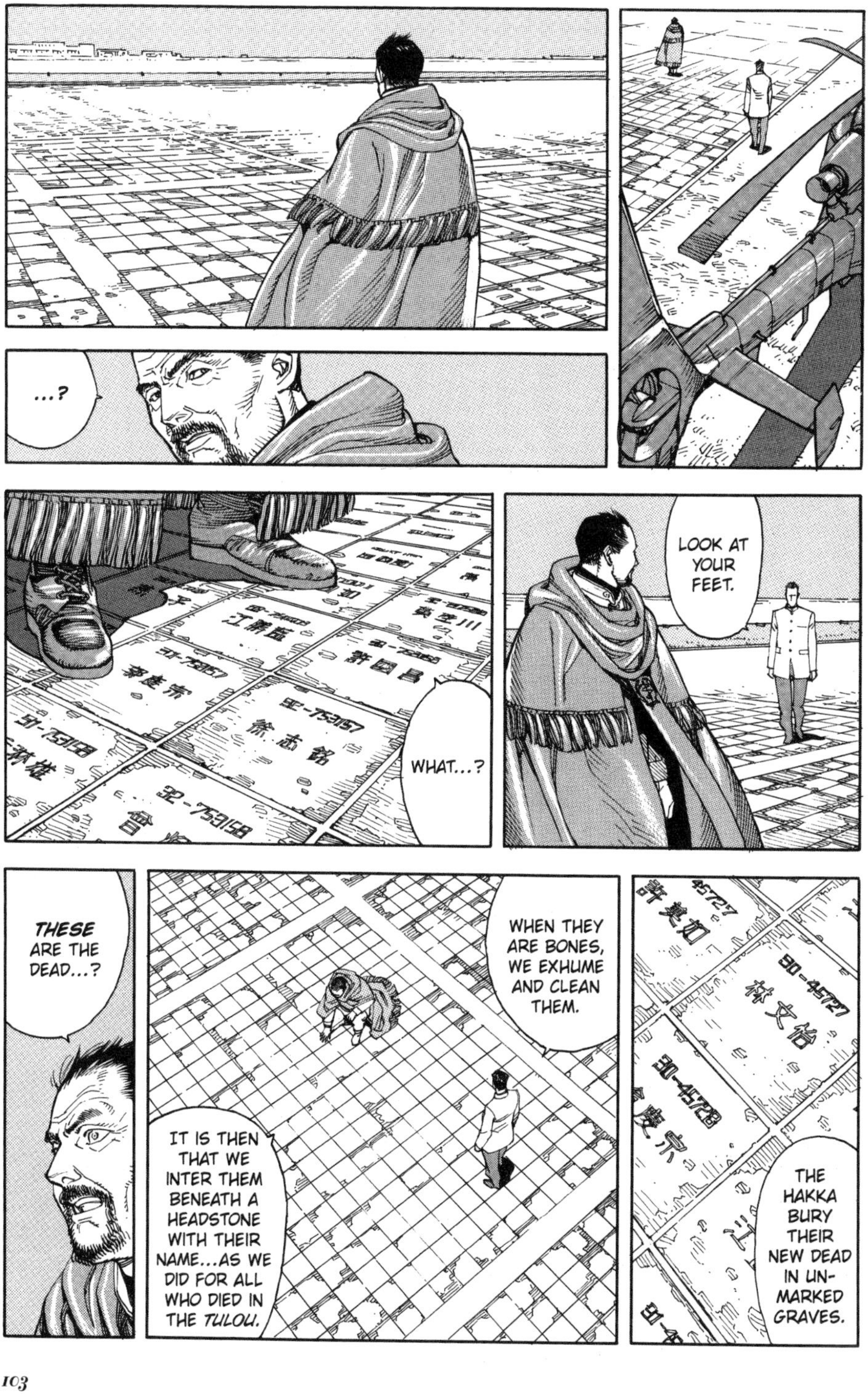
...?
LOOK AT YOUR FEET.
WHAT...?
THE HAKKA BURY THEIR NEW DEAD IN UN-MARKED GRAVES.
WHEN THEY ARE BONES, WE EXHUME AND CLEAN THEM.
IT IS THEN THAT WE INTER THEM BENEATH A HEADSTONE WITH THEIR NAME...AS WE DID FOR ALL WHO DIED IN THE *TULOU*.
THESE ARE THE DEAD...?

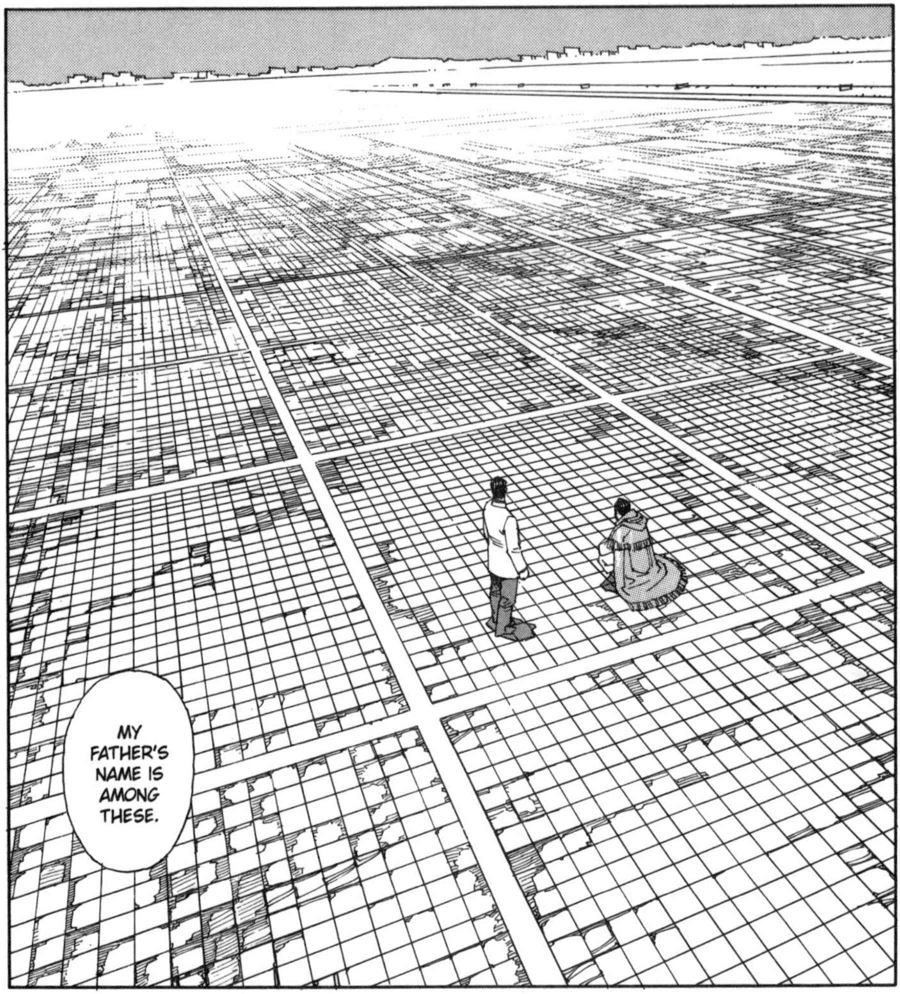
MY FATHER'S NAME IS AMONG THESE.

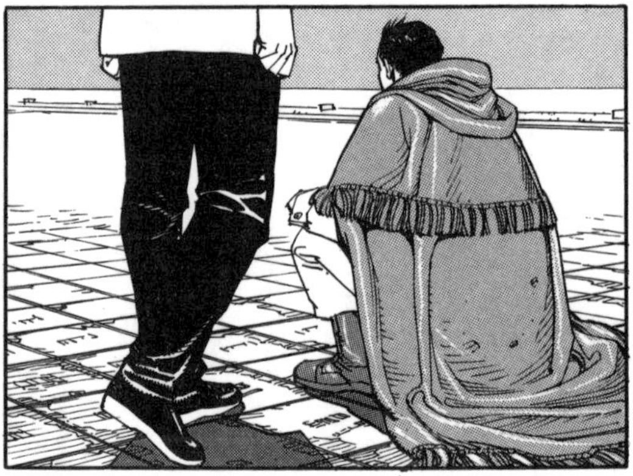

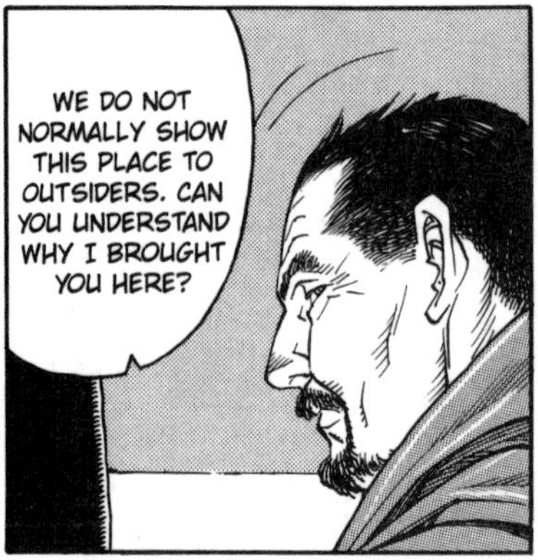
WE DO NOT NORMALLY SHOW THIS PLACE TO OUTSIDERS. CAN YOU UNDERSTAND WHY I BROUGHT YOU HERE?

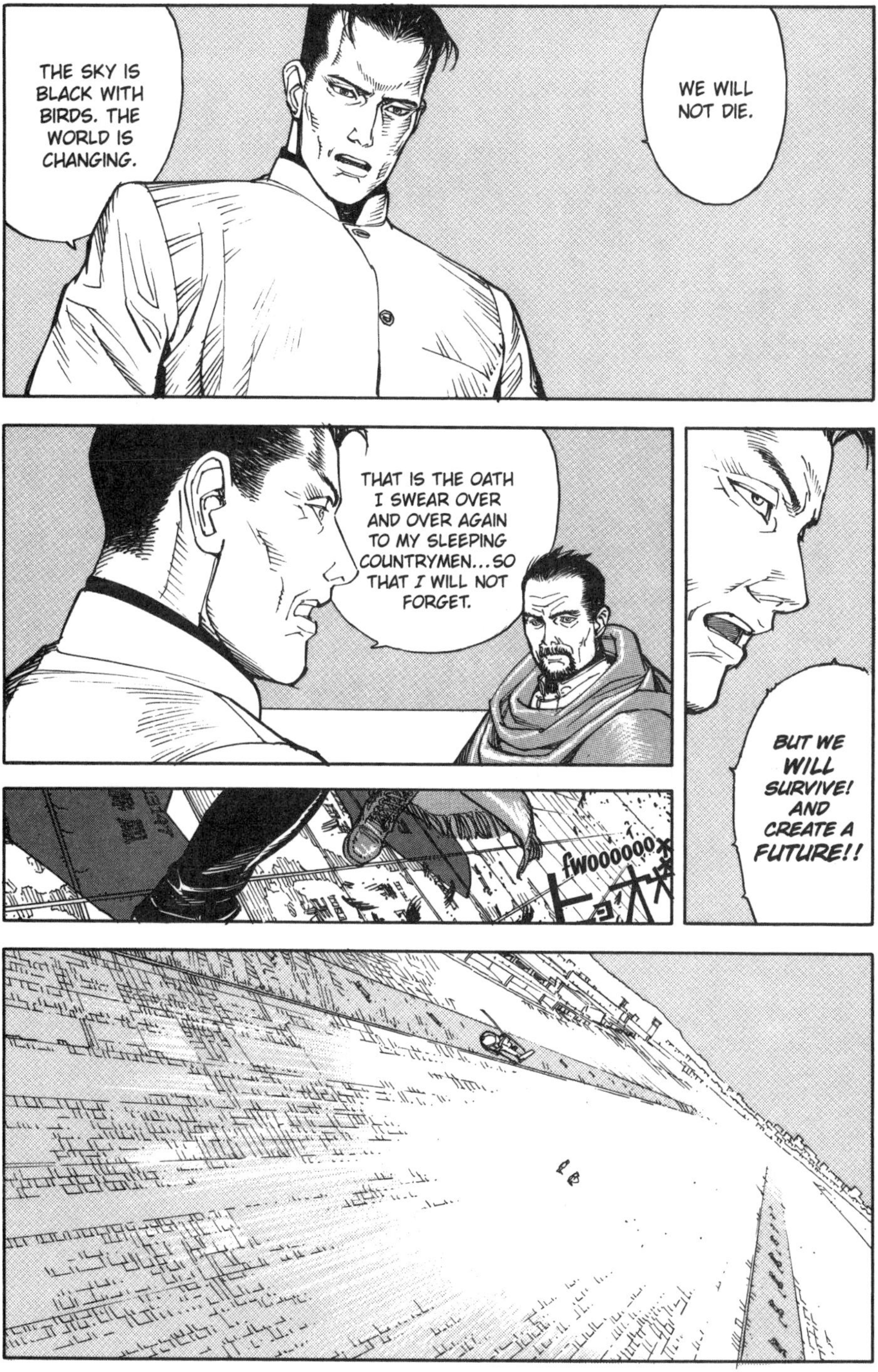
WE WILL NOT DIE.
THE SKY IS BLACK WITH BIRDS. THE WORLD IS CHANGING.
BUT WE WILL SURVIVE! AND CREATE A FUTURE!!
THAT IS THE OATH I SWEAR OVER AND OVER AGAIN TO MY SLEEPING COUNTRYMEN...SO THAT I WILL NOT FORGET.
fwoooooo

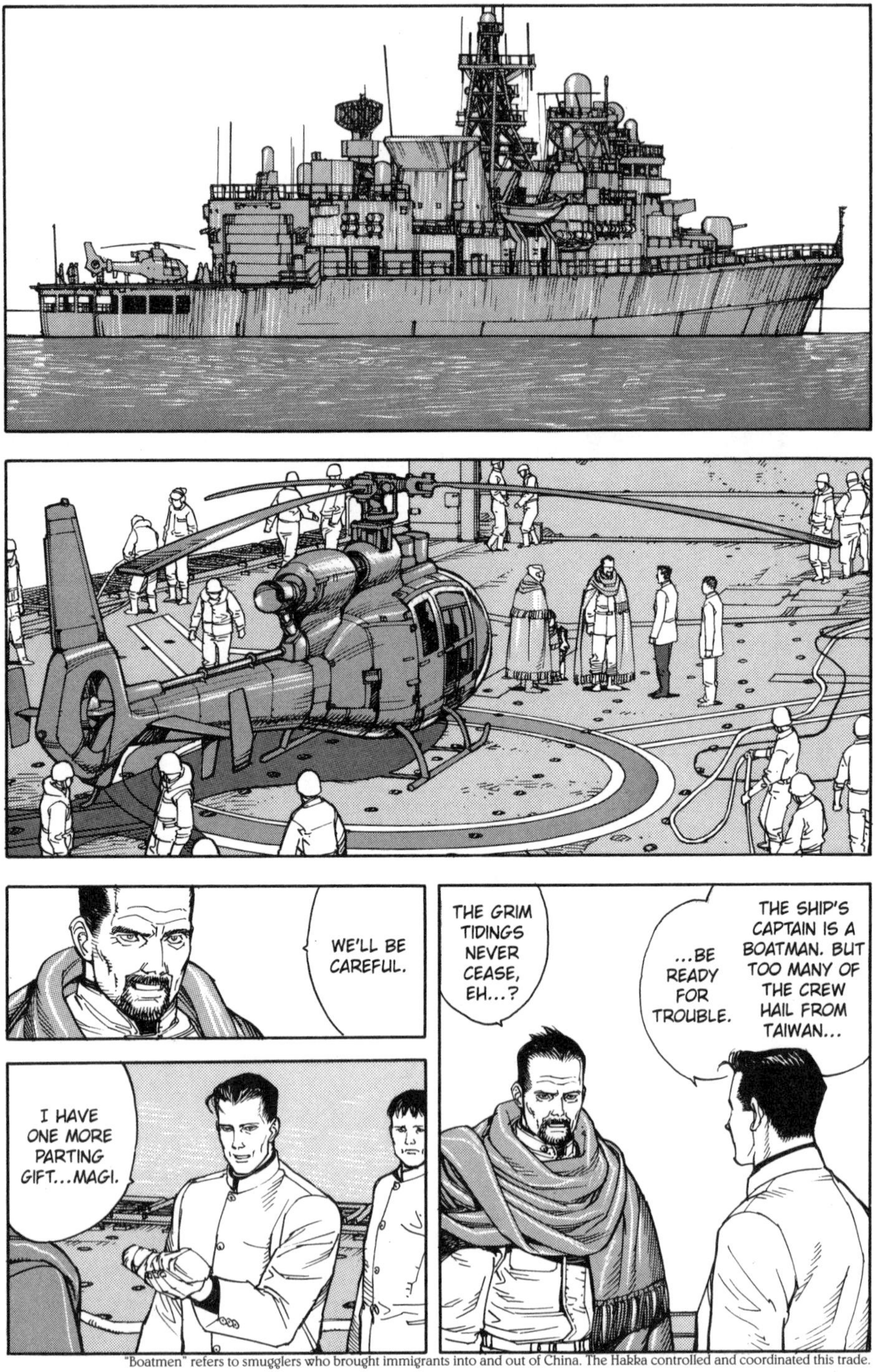
THE SHIP'S CAPTAIN IS A BOATMAN. BUT TOO MANY OF THE CREW HAIL FROM TAIWAN...
...BE READY FOR TROUBLE.
THE GRIM TIDINGS NEVER CEASE, EH...?
WE'LL BE CAREFUL.
I HAVE ONE MORE PARTING GIFT...MAGI.

"Boatmen" refers to smugglers who brought immigrants into and out of China. The Hakka controlled and coordinated this trade.

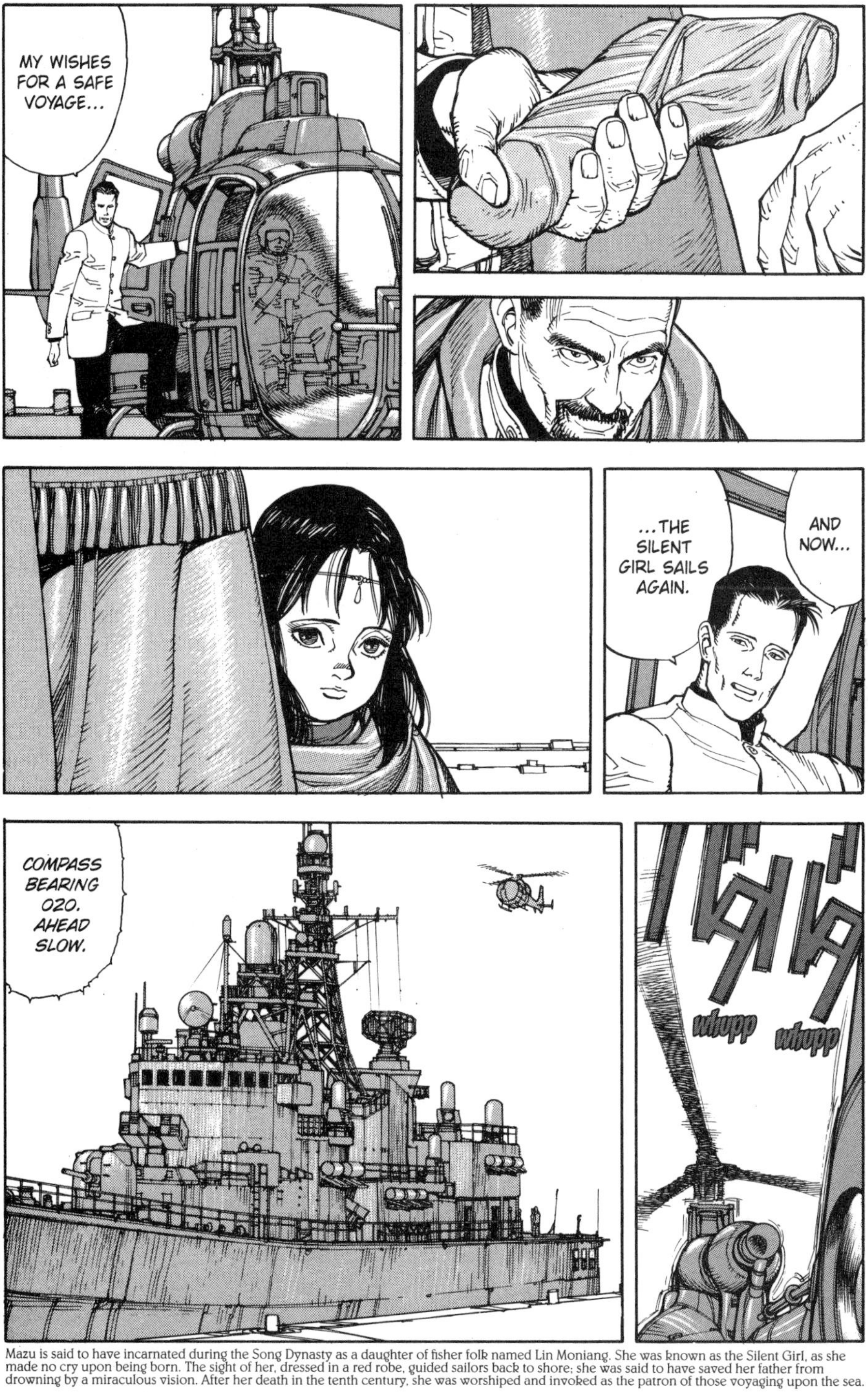
MY WISHES FOR A SAFE VOYAGE...
AND NOW...
...THE SILENT GIRL SAILS AGAIN.
whopp whopp
COMPASS BEARING 020. AHEAD SLOW.

Mazu is said to have incarnated during the Song Dynasty as a daughter of fisher folk named Lin Moniang. She was known as the Silent Girl, as she made no cry upon being born. The sight of her, dressed in a red robe, guided sailors back to shore; she was said to have saved her father from drowning by a miraculous vision. After her death in the tenth century, she was worshiped and invoked as the patron of those voyaging upon the sea.

chugg chugg chugg chugg

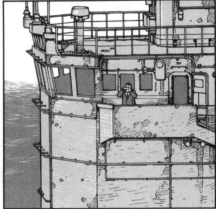

chapter eight

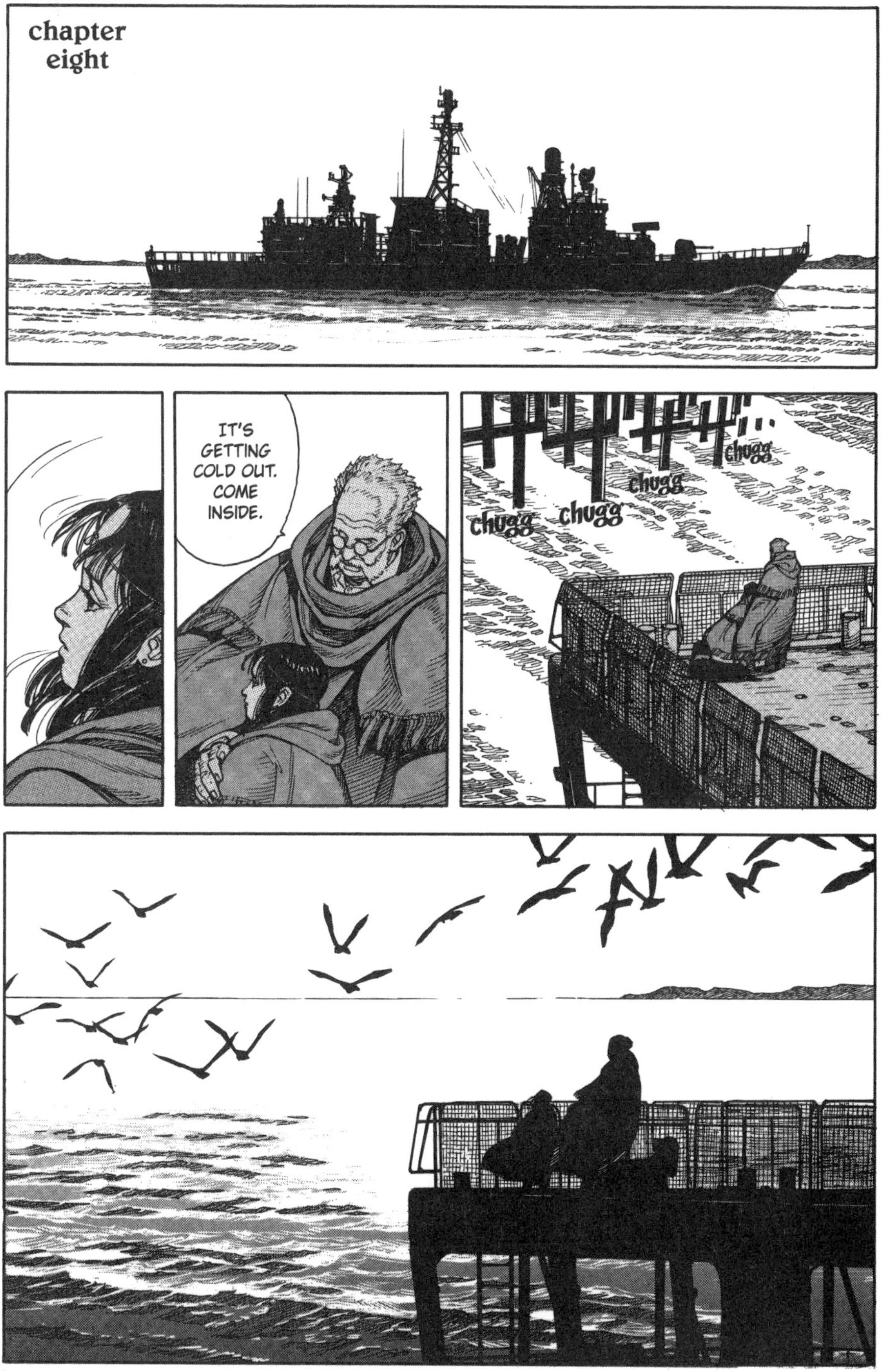
chugg
chugg
chugg
chugg
IT'S GETTING COLD OUT. COME INSIDE.

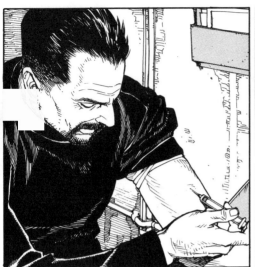

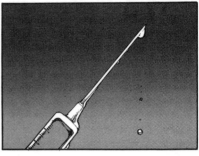

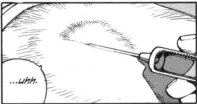

...uhh.
rattle
hahh...
whoooon
chak
...AH, MAGI, SIR. DINNER IS SERVED IN MAGI BALTHAZAR'S QUARTERS...
DINNER CAN WAIT.
WE'VE DROPPED SPEED. WHY?

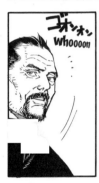

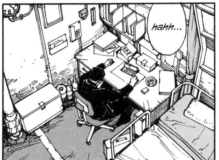

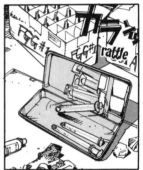

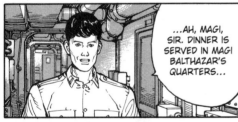

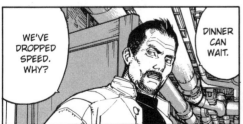

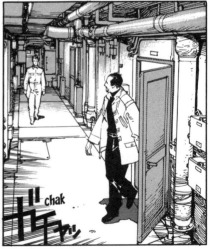

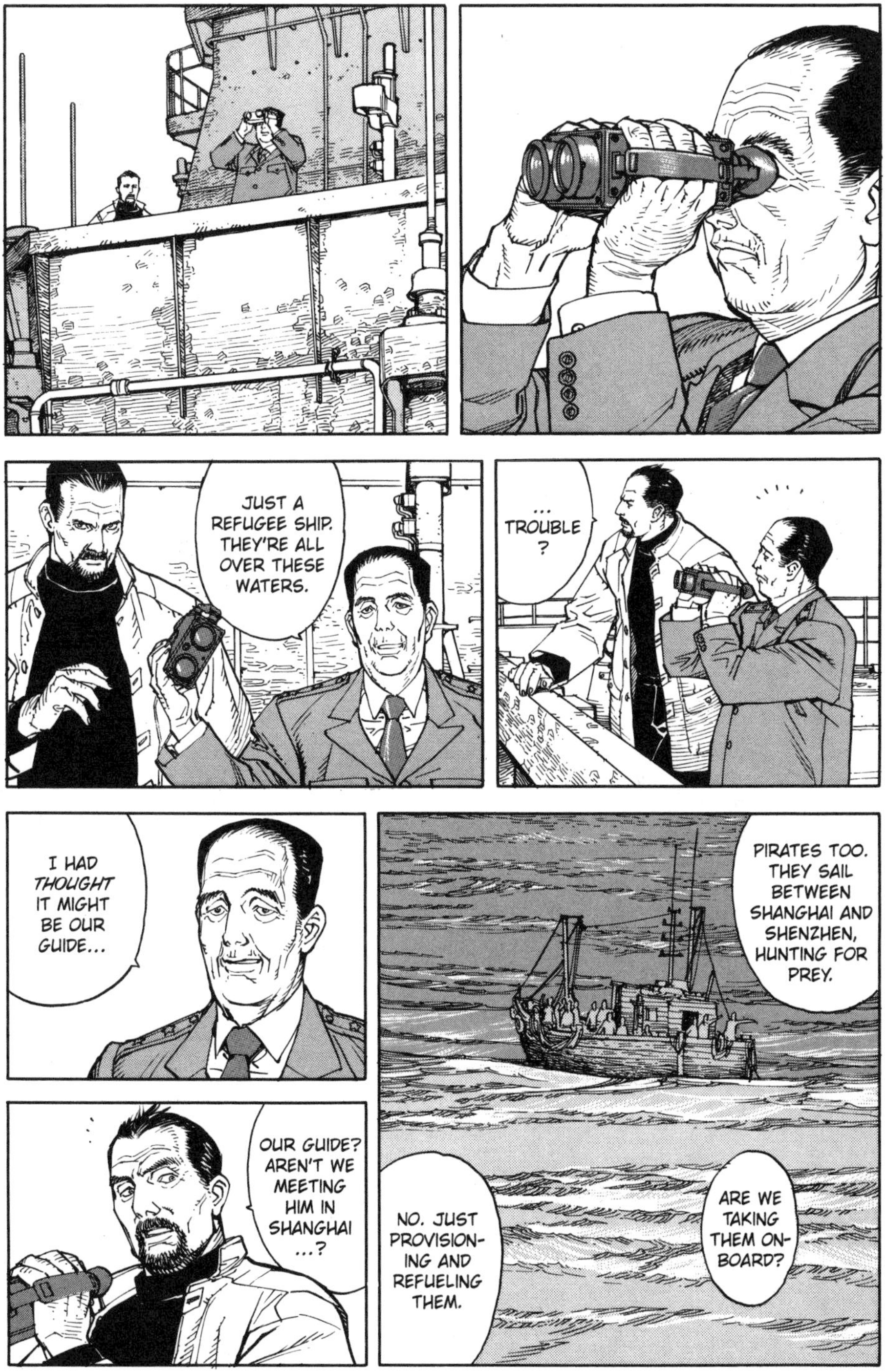

... TROUBLE ?
JUST A REFUGEE SHIP. THEY'RE ALL OVER THESE WATERS.
PIRATES TOO. THEY SAIL BETWEEN SHANGHAI AND SHENZHEN, HUNTING FOR PREY.
ARE WE TAKING THEM ON-BOARD?
NO. JUST PROVISION-ING AND REFUELING THEM.
I HAD *THOUGHT* IT MIGHT BE OUR GUIDE...
OUR GUIDE? AREN'T WE MEETING HIM IN SHANGHAI ...?

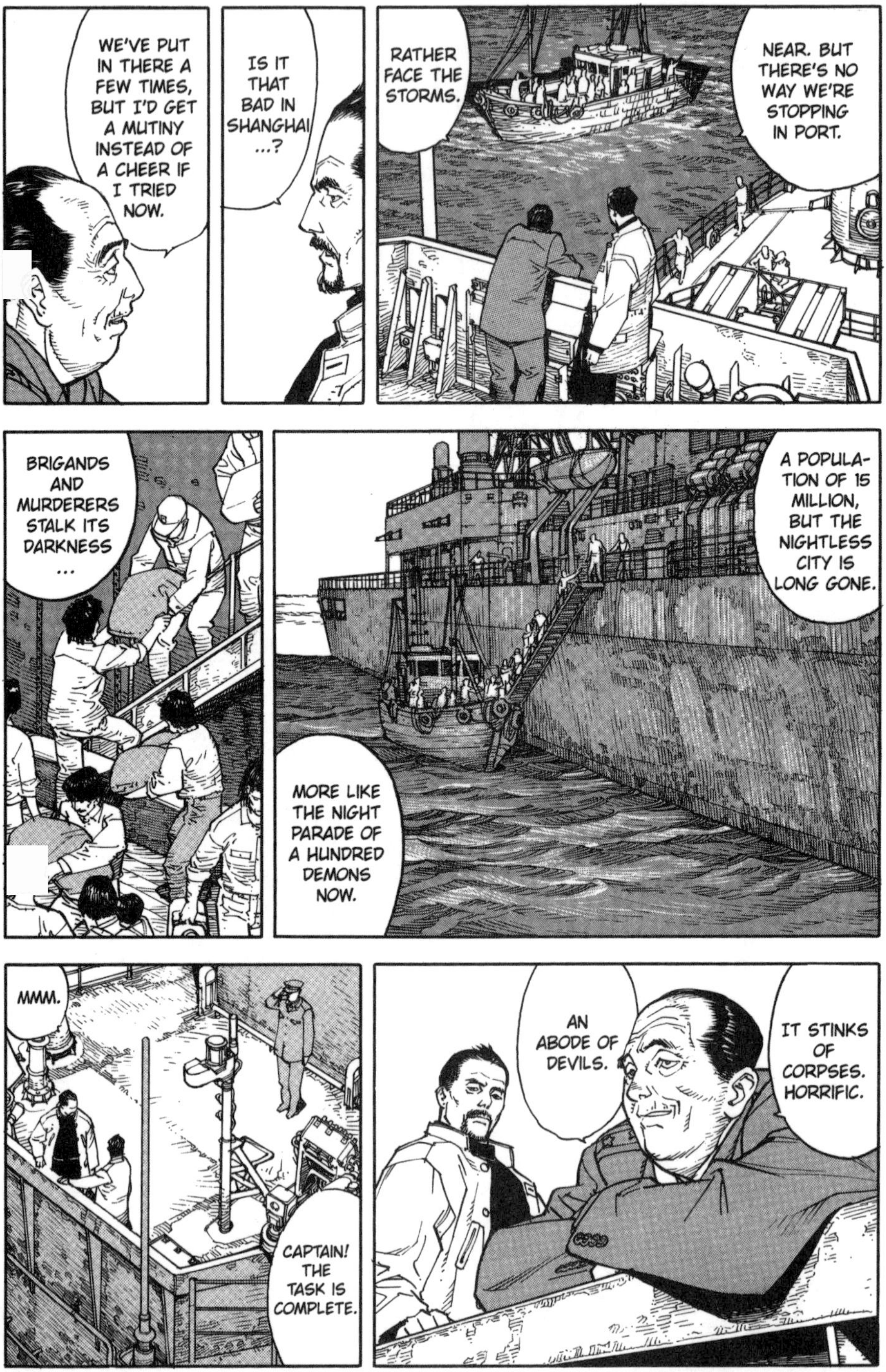
NEAR. BUT THERE'S NO WAY WE'RE STOPPING IN PORT.
RATHER FACE THE STORMS.
IS IT THAT BAD IN SHANGHAI ...?
WE'VE PUT IN THERE A FEW TIMES, BUT I'D GET A MUTINY INSTEAD OF A CHEER IF I TRIED NOW.
A POPULATION OF 15 MILLION, BUT THE NIGHTLESS CITY IS LONG GONE.
MORE LIKE THE NIGHT PARADE OF A HUNDRED DEMONS NOW.
BRIGANDS AND MURDERERS STALK ITS DARKNESS ...
IT STINKS OF CORPSES. HORRIFIC.
AN ABODE OF DEVILS.
CAPTAIN! THE TASK IS COMPLETE.
MMM.

The nightless city (*fuyajoo*) is a euphemism for a red-light district, whereas the night parade of one hundred demons (*hyakki yagyoo*) is a belief in Japanese folklore that a train of supernatural creatures make their way through the streets on certain summer nights, slaying or spiriting away anyone without occult protection.

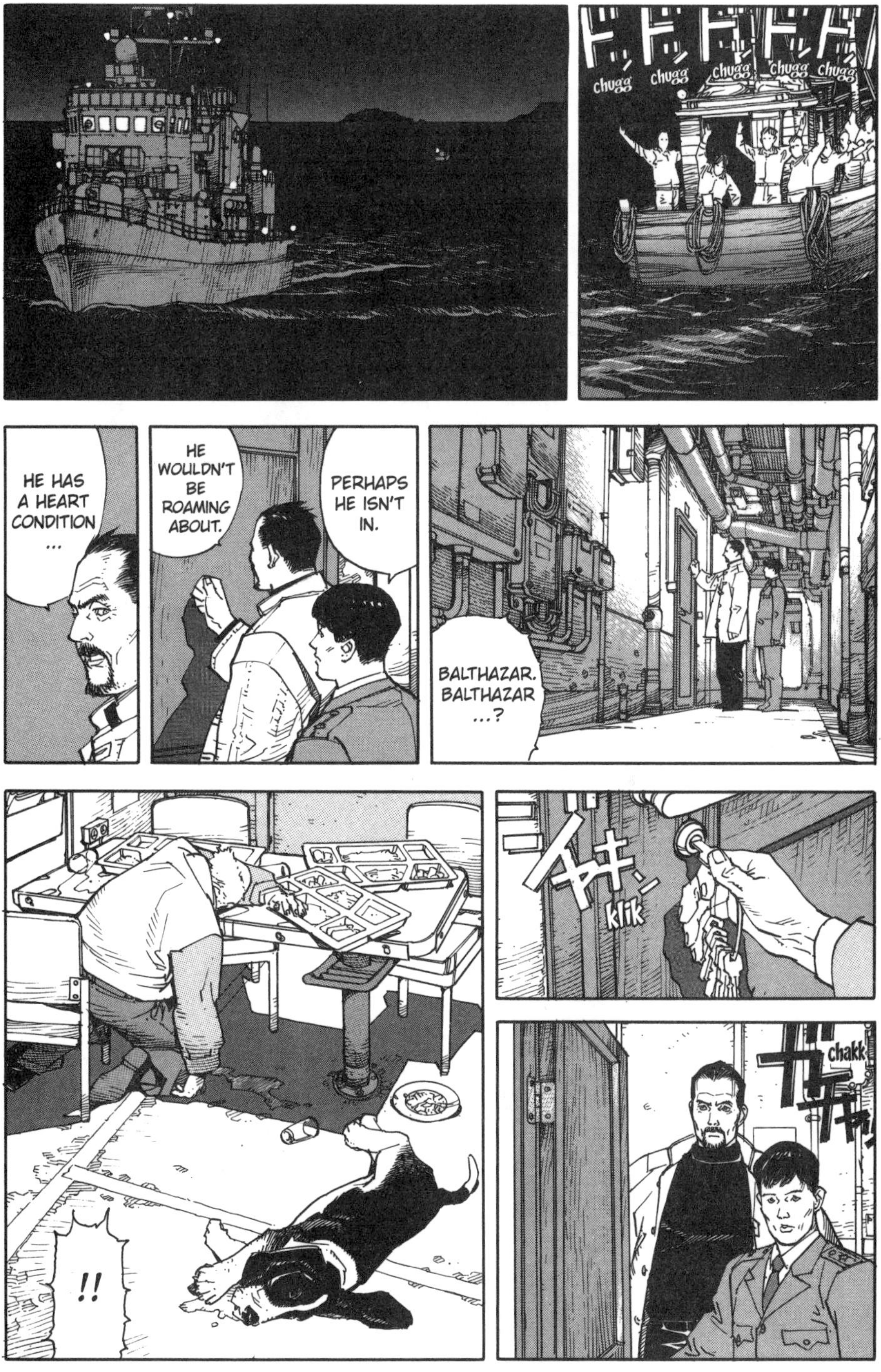
chugg
chugg
chugg
chugg
chugg
BALTHAZAR. BALTHAZAR ...?
PERHAPS HE ISN'T IN.
HE WOULDN'T BE ROAMING ABOUT.
HE HAS A HEART CONDITION ...
klik
chakk
!!

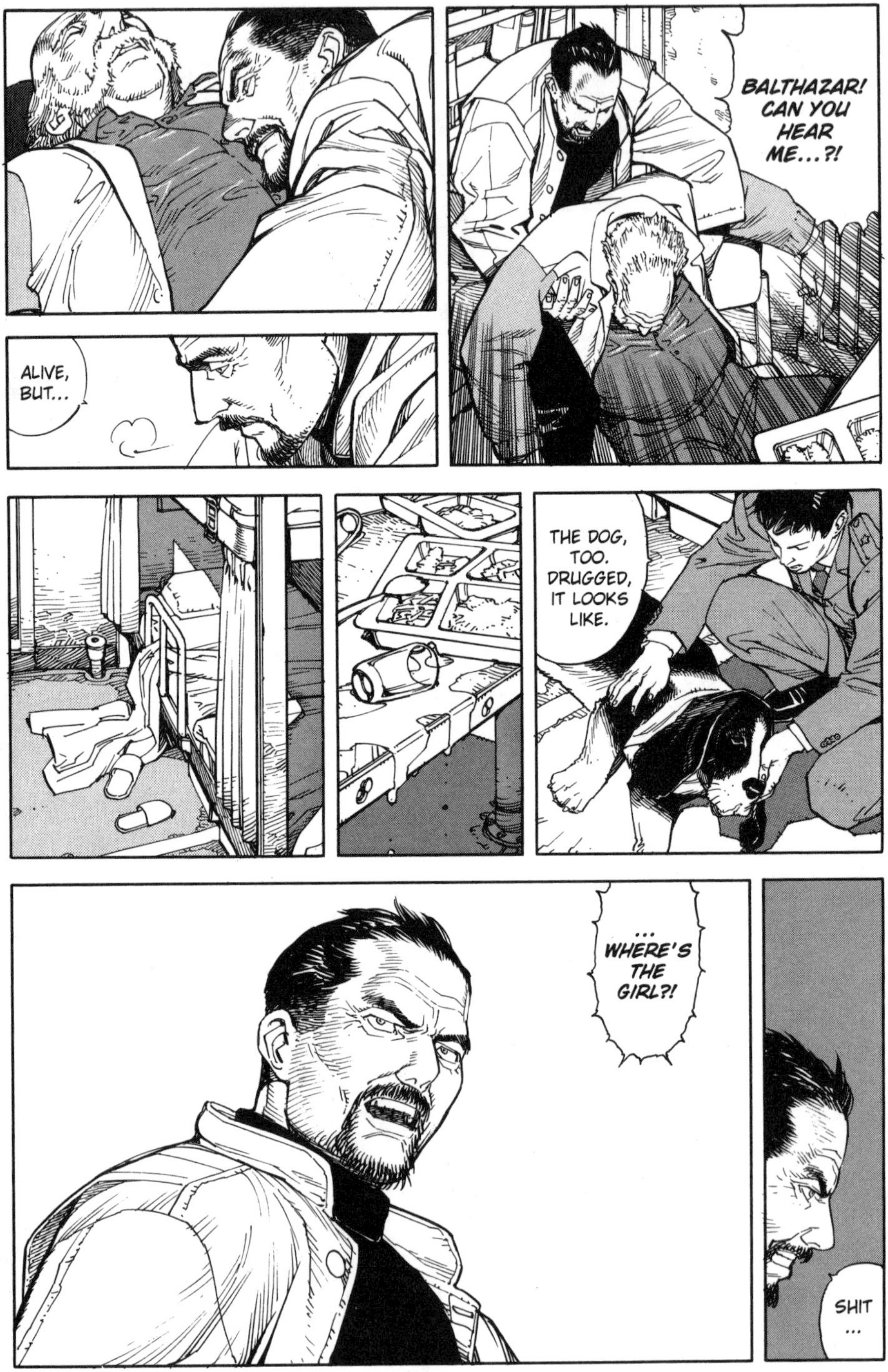
BALTHAZAR! CAN YOU HEAR ME...?!
ALIVE, BUT...
THE DOG, TOO. DRUGGED, IT LOOKS LIKE.
SHIT...
...WHERE'S THE GIRL?!

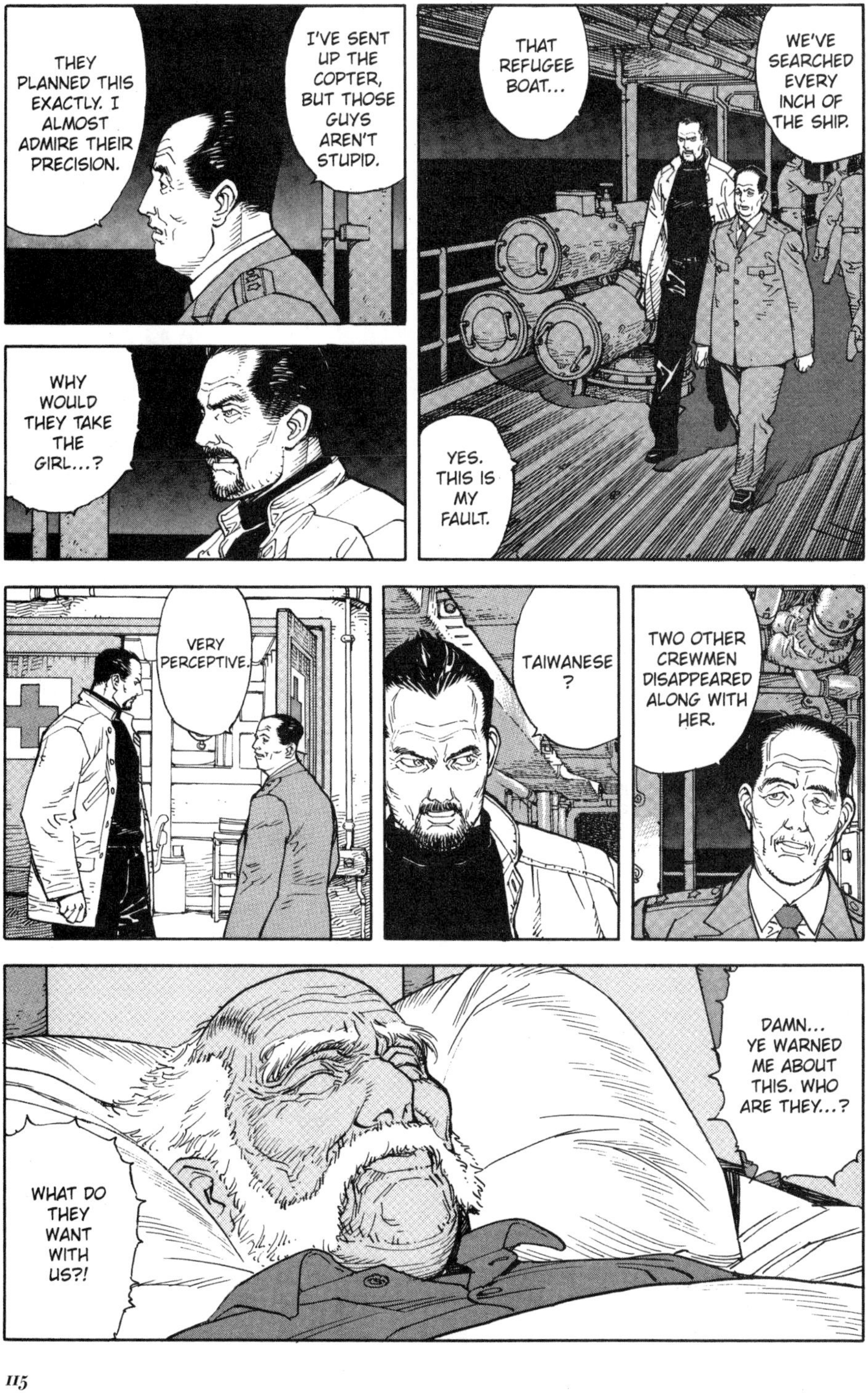
WE'VE SEARCHED EVERY INCH OF THE SHIP.
THAT REFUGEE BOAT...
YES. THIS IS MY FAULT.
I'VE SENT UP THE COPTER, BUT THOSE GUYS AREN'T STUPID.
THEY PLANNED THIS EXACTLY. I ALMOST ADMIRE THEIR PRECISION.
WHY WOULD THEY TAKE THE GIRL...?
TWO OTHER CREWMEN DISAPPEARED ALONG WITH HER.
TAIWANESE ?
VERY PERCEPTIVE.
DAMN... YE WARNED ME ABOUT THIS. WHO ARE THEY...?
WHAT DO THEY WANT WITH US?!

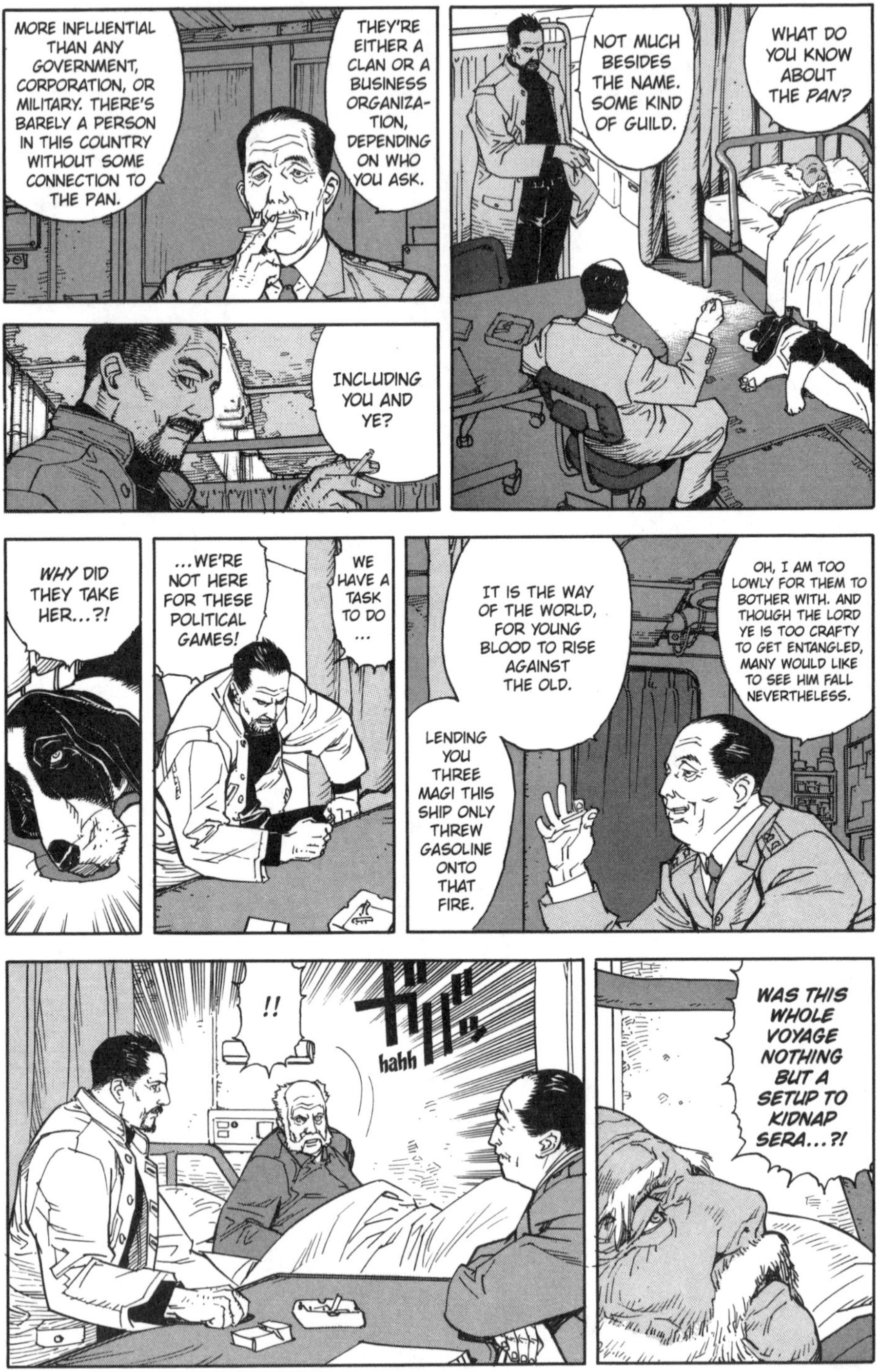
WHAT DO YOU KNOW ABOUT THE *PAN*?
NOT MUCH BESIDES THE NAME. SOME KIND OF GUILD.
THEY'RE EITHER A CLAN OR A BUSINESS ORGANIZA-TION, DEPENDING ON WHO YOU ASK.
MORE INFLUENTIAL THAN ANY GOVERNMENT, CORPORATION, OR MILITARY. THERE'S BARELY A PERSON IN THIS COUNTRY WITHOUT SOME CONNECTION TO THE PAN.
INCLUDING YOU AND YE?
OH, I AM TOO LOWLY FOR THEM TO BOTHER WITH. AND THOUGH THE LORD YE IS TOO CRAFTY TO GET ENTANGLED, MANY WOULD LIKE TO SEE HIM FALL NEVERTHELESS.
IT IS THE WAY OF THE WORLD, FOR YOUNG BLOOD TO RISE AGAINST THE OLD.
LENDING YOU THREE MAGI THIS SHIP ONLY THREW GASOLINE ONTO THAT FIRE.
WE HAVE A TASK TO DO ...
...WE'RE NOT HERE FOR THESE POLITICAL GAMES!
WHY DID THEY TAKE HER...?!
WAS THIS WHOLE VOYAGE NOTHING BUT A SETUP TO KIDNAP SERA...?!
hahh
!!

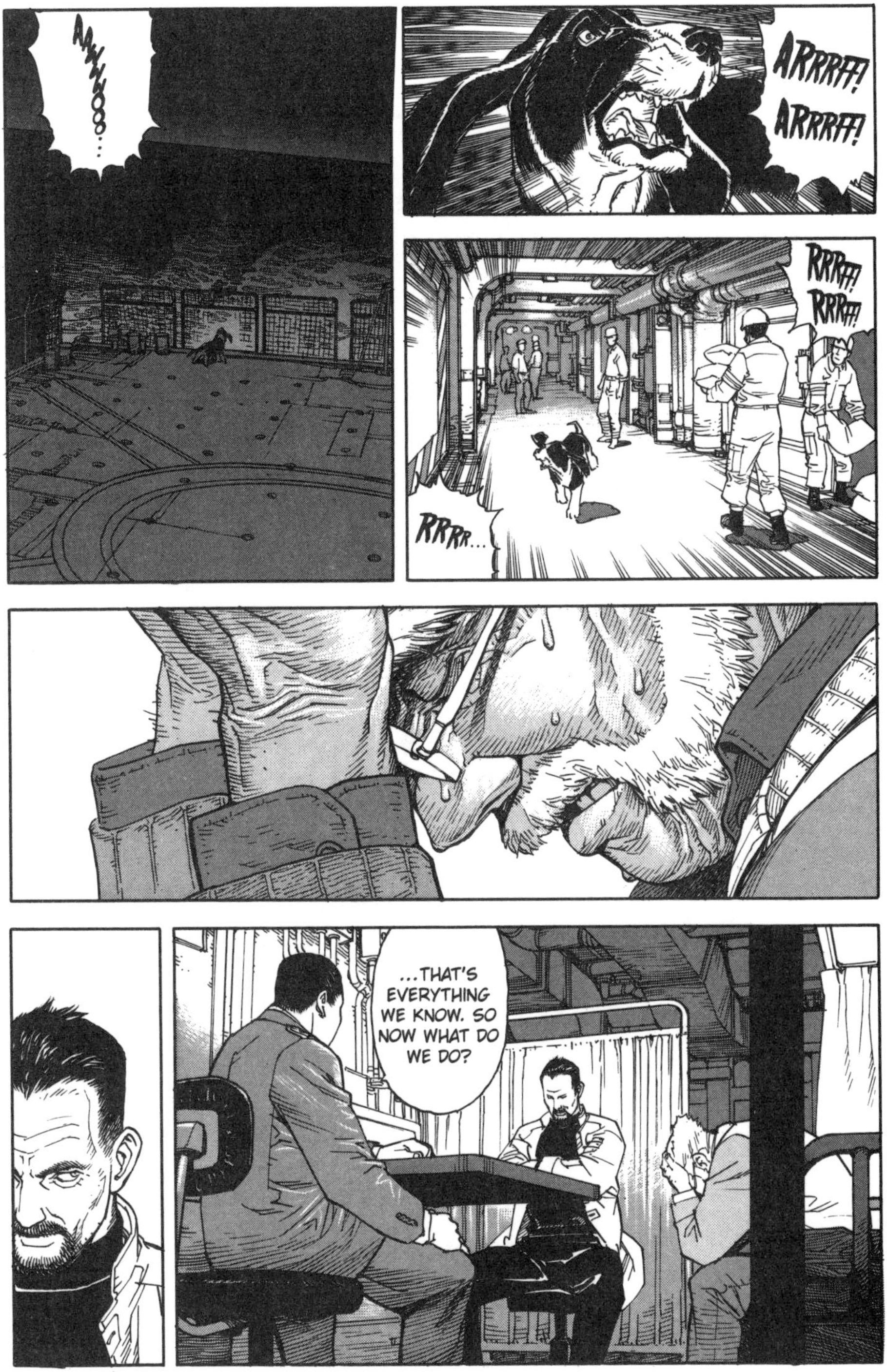
ARRRFF!
ARRRFF!
RRRFF!
RRRFF!
RRRR...
AAWWOOO...
...THAT'S EVERYTHING WE KNOW. SO NOW WHAT DO WE DO?

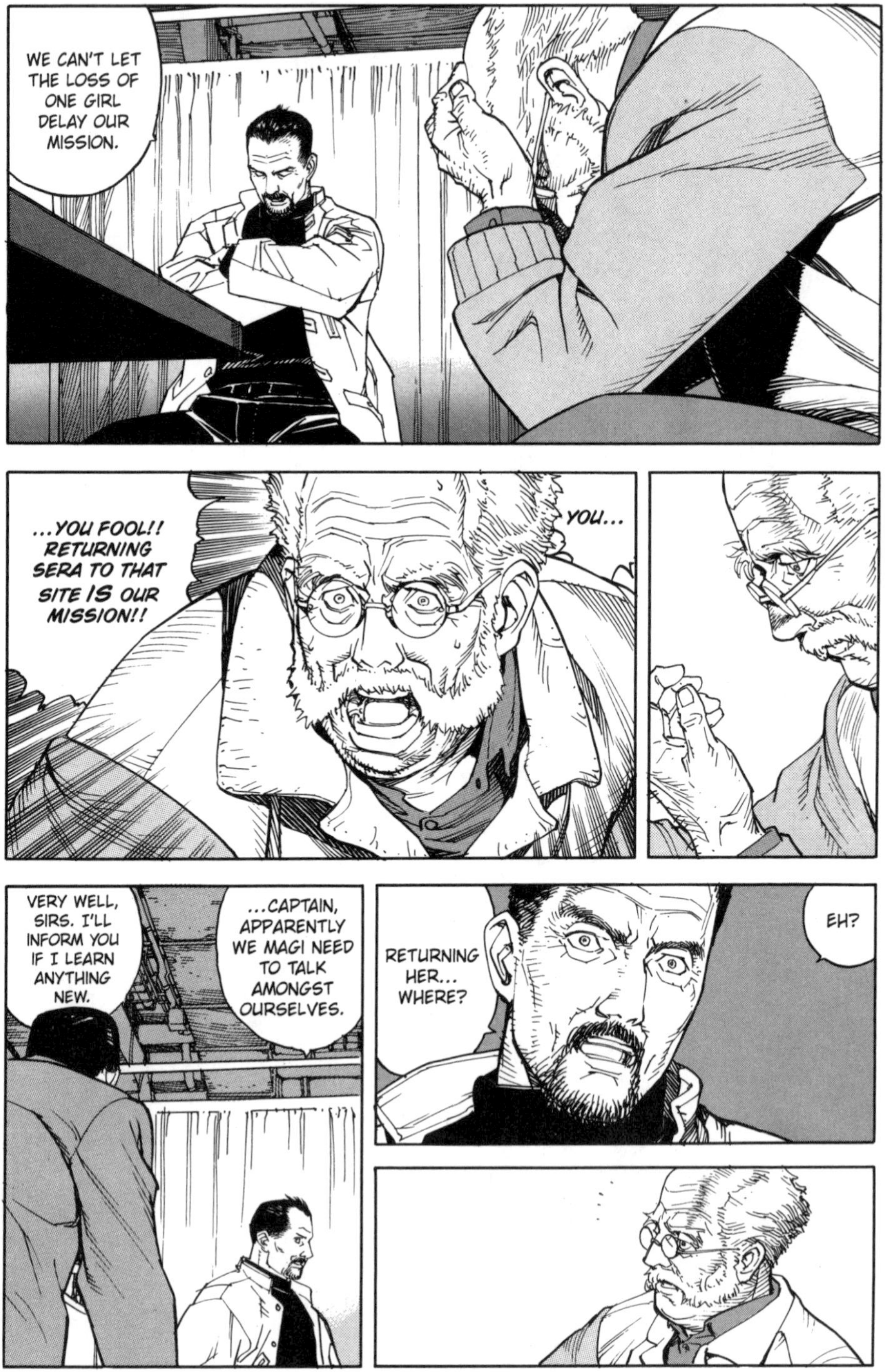
WE CAN'T LET THE LOSS OF ONE GIRL DELAY OUR MISSION.
YOU...
...YOU FOOL!! RETURNING SERA TO THAT SITE IS OUR MISSION!!
EH?
RETURNING HER... WHERE?
...CAPTAIN, APPARENTLY WE MAGI NEED TO TALK AMONGST OURSELVES.
VERY WELL, SIRS. I'LL INFORM YOU IF I LEARN ANYTHING NEW.

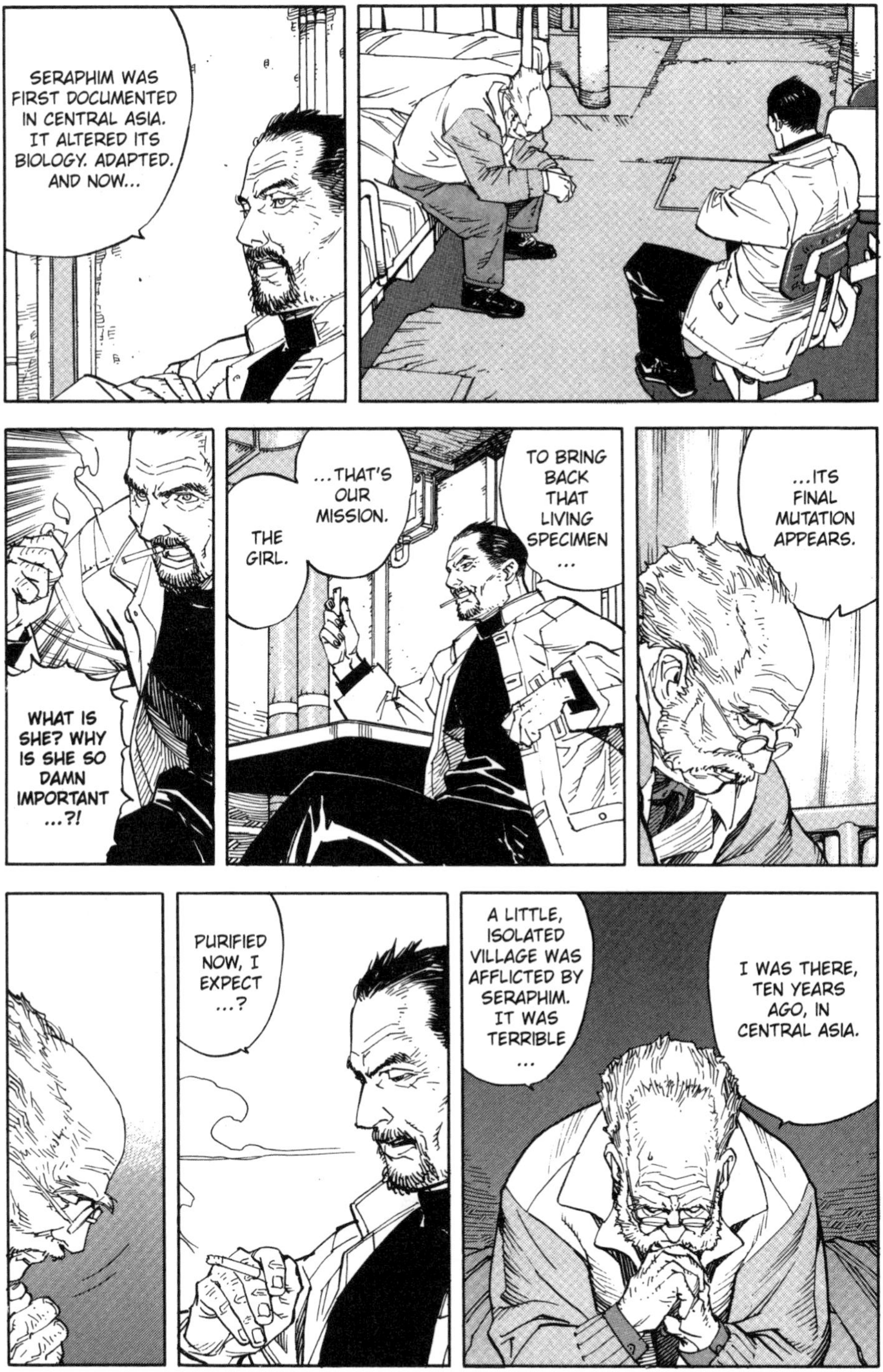
SERAPHIM WAS FIRST DOCUMENTED IN CENTRAL ASIA. IT ALTERED ITS BIOLOGY. ADAPTED. AND NOW...
...ITS FINAL MUTATION APPEARS.
TO BRING BACK THAT LIVING SPECIMEN ...
...THAT'S OUR MISSION.
THE GIRL.
WHAT IS SHE? WHY IS SHE SO DAMN IMPORTANT ...?!
I WAS THERE, TEN YEARS AGO, IN CENTRAL ASIA.
A LITTLE, ISOLATED VILLAGE WAS AFFLICTED BY SERAPHIM. IT WAS TERRIBLE ...
PURIFIED NOW, I EXPECT ...?

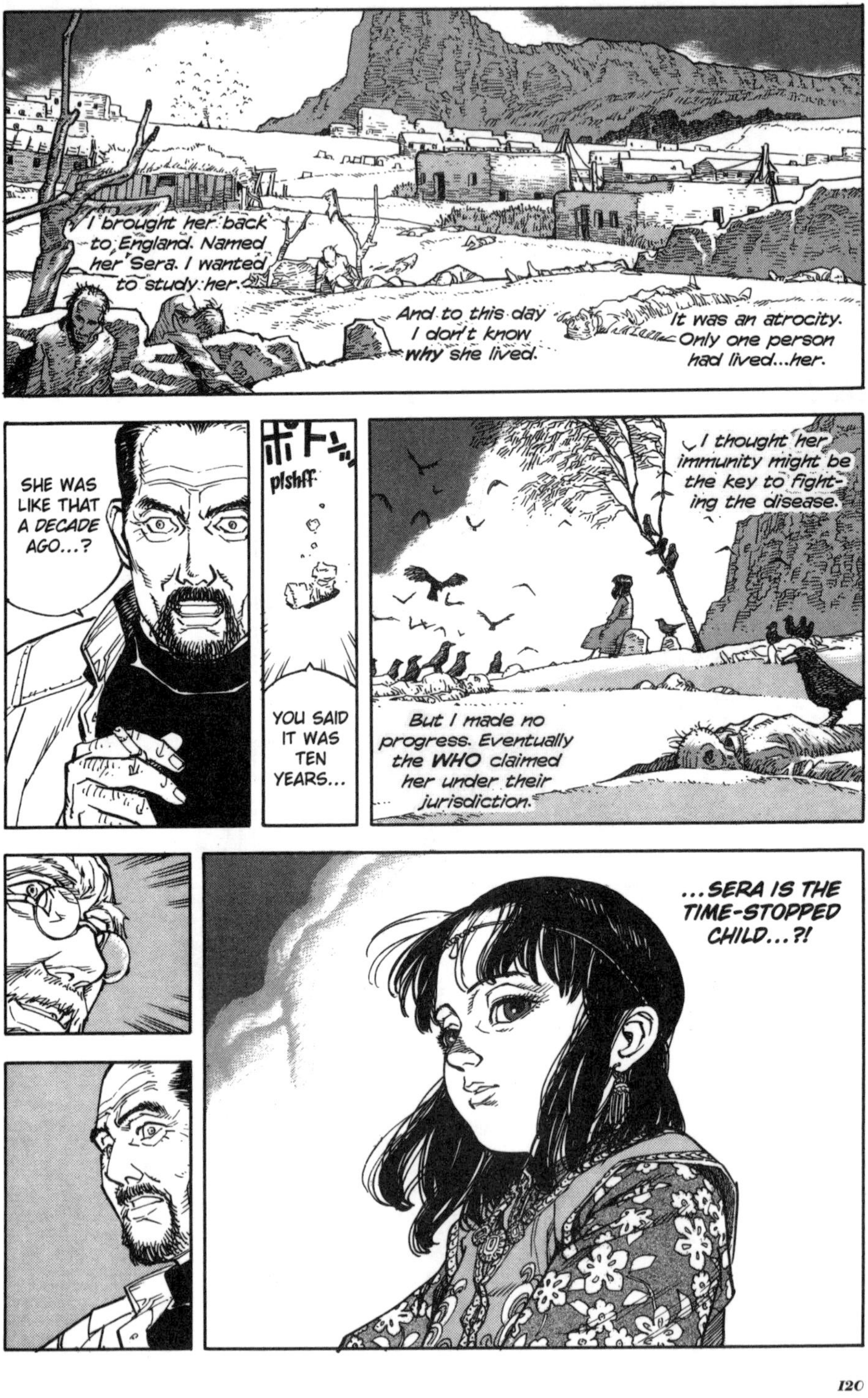
It was an atrocity. Only one person had lived...her.
And to this day I don't know why she lived.
I brought her back to England. Named her Sera. I wanted to study her.
I thought her immunity might be the key to fight-ing the disease.
But I made no progress. Eventually the WHO claimed her under their jurisdiction.
ポトンッ
plshff
YOU SAID IT WAS TEN YEARS...
SHE WAS LIKE THAT A DECADE AGO...?
...SERA IS THE TIME-STOPPED CHILD...?!

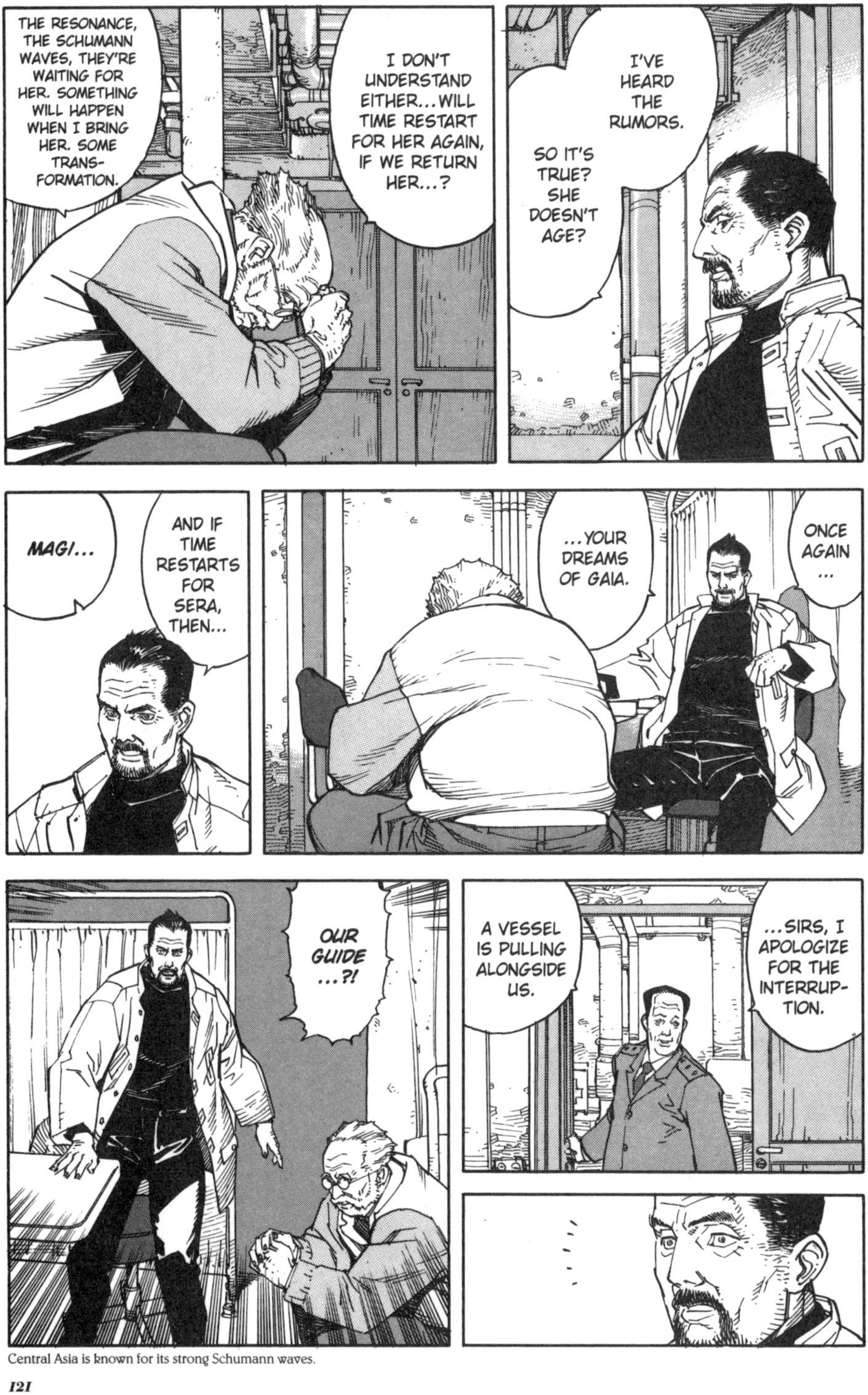
I'VE HEARD THE RUMORS.
SO IT'S TRUE? SHE DOESN'T AGE?
I DON'T UNDERSTAND EITHER...WILL TIME RESTART FOR HER AGAIN, IF WE RETURN HER...?
THE RESONANCE, THE SCHUMANN WAVES, THEY'RE WAITING FOR HER. SOMETHING WILL HAPPEN WHEN I BRING HER. SOME TRANSFORMATION.
ONCE AGAIN ...
...YOUR DREAMS OF GAIA.
AND IF TIME RESTARTS FOR SERA, THEN...
MAGI...
...SIRS, I APOLOGIZE FOR THE INTERRUPTION.
A VESSEL IS PULLING ALONGSIDE US.
OUR GUIDE ...?!

Central Asia is known for its strong Schumann waves.

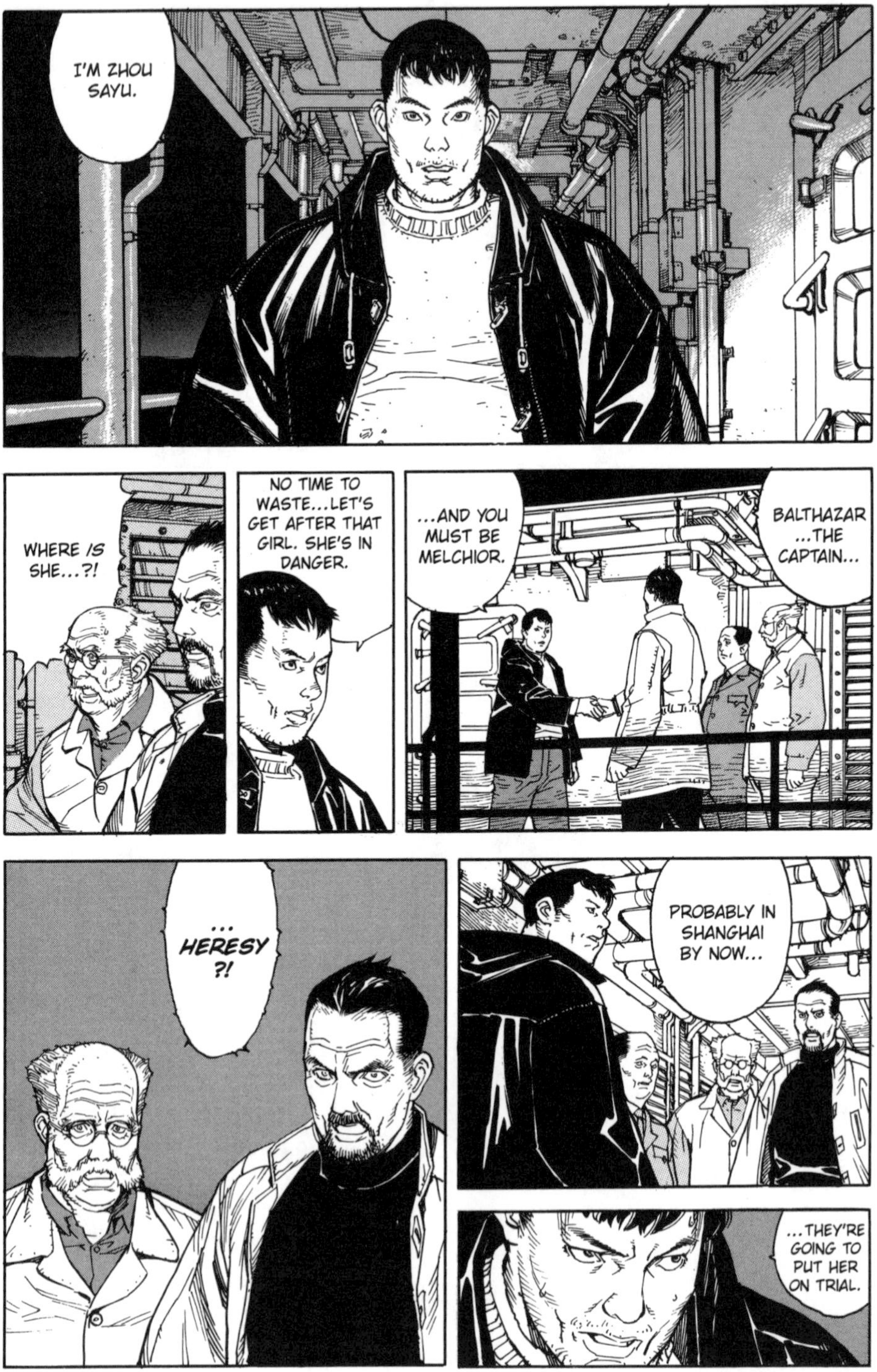
I'M ZHOU SAYU.
BALTHAZAR ...THE CAPTAIN...
...AND YOU MUST BE MELCHIOR.
NO TIME TO WASTE...LET'S GET AFTER THAT GIRL. SHE'S IN DANGER.
WHERE IS SHE...?!
PROBABLY IN SHANGHAI BY NOW...
...THEY'RE GOING TO PUT HER ON TRIAL.
...HERESY?!

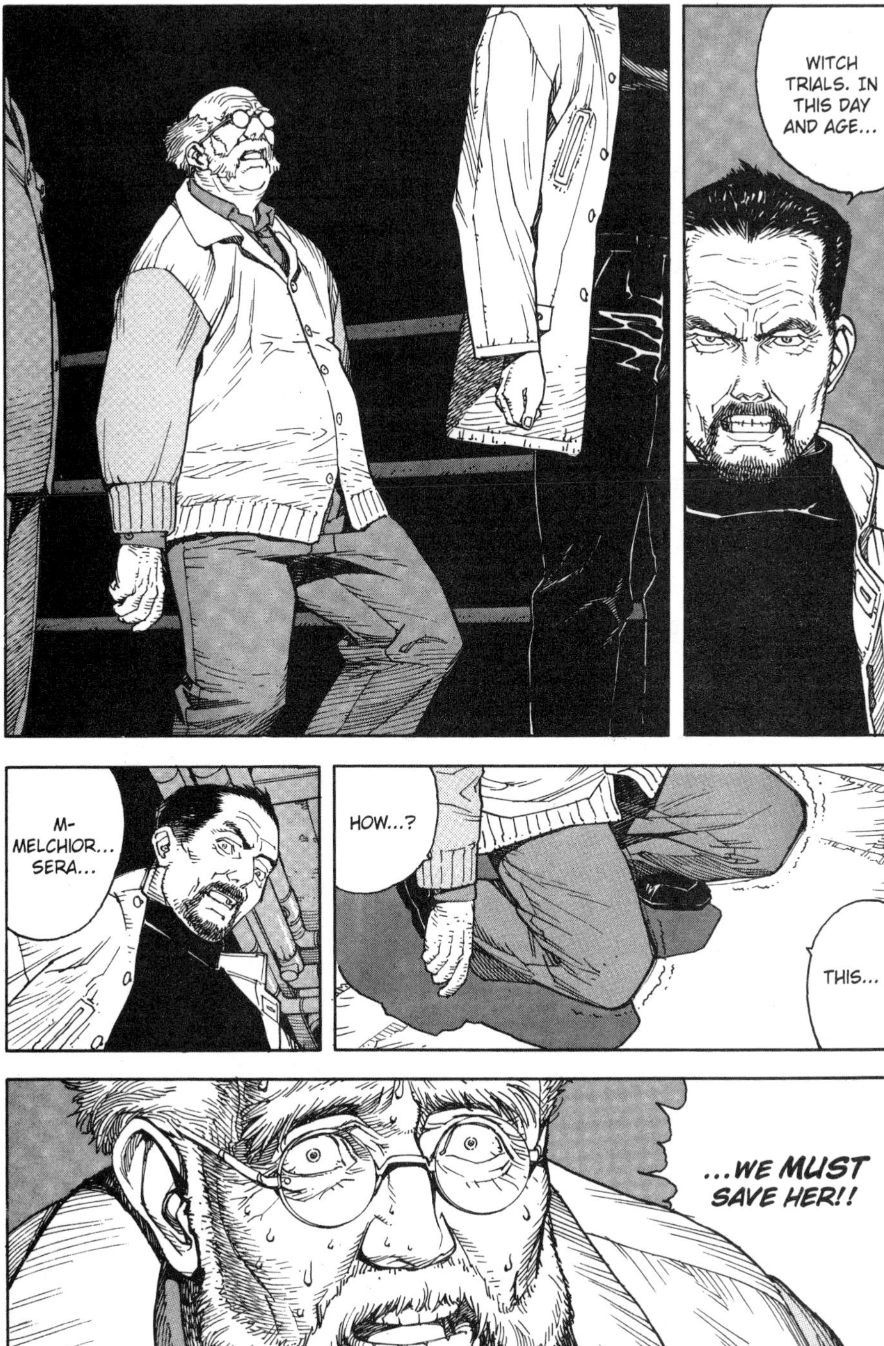
WITCH TRIALS. IN THIS DAY AND AGE...
HOW...?
THIS...
M- MELCHIOR... SERA...
...WE MUST SAVE HER!!

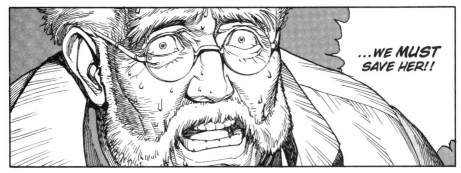

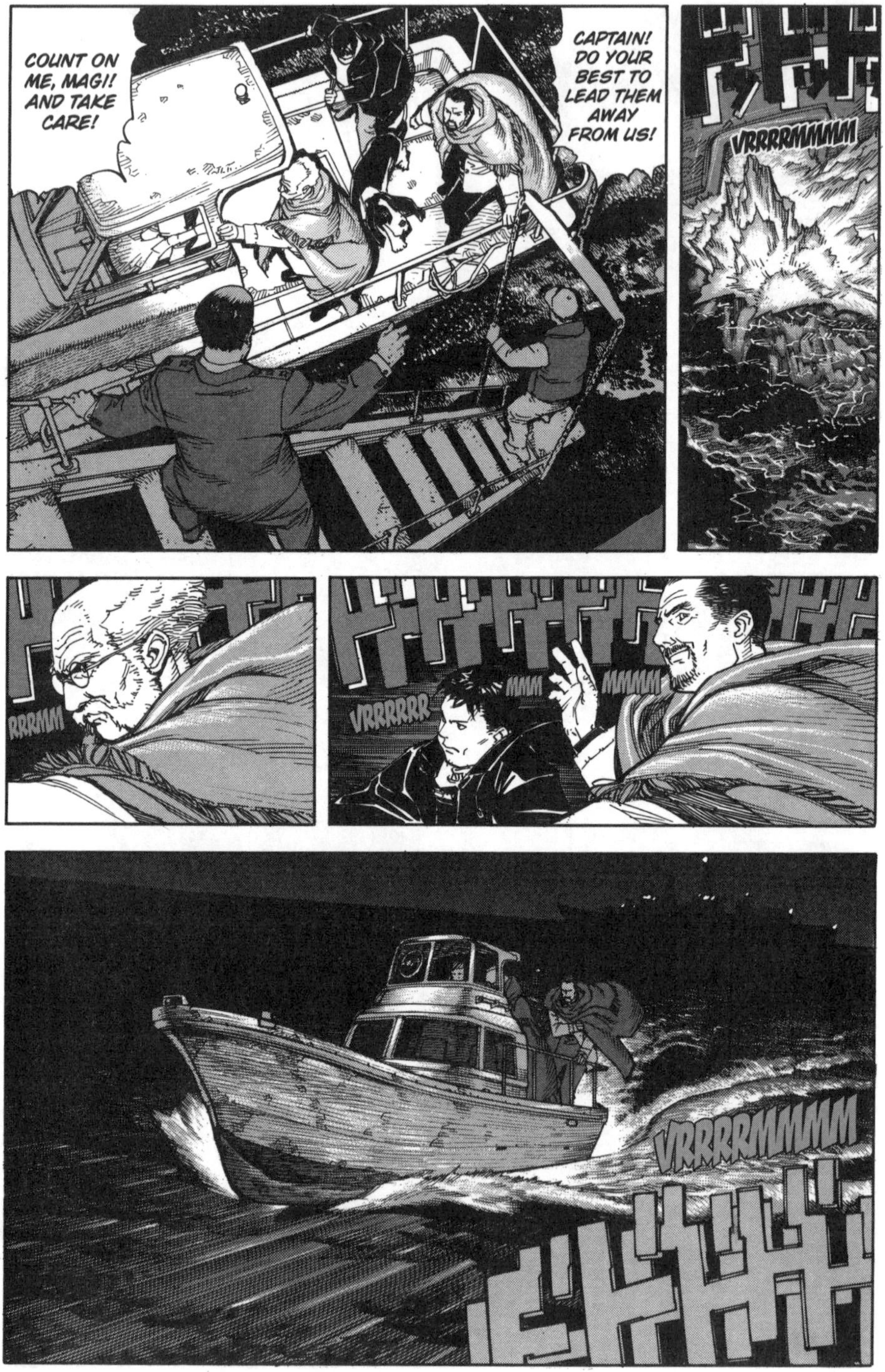
VRRRRMMMMM
CAPTAIN! DO YOUR BEST TO LEAD THEM AWAY FROM US!
COUNT ON ME, MAGI! AND TAKE CARE!
MMMMM
MMM
VRRRRRR
RRRMM
VRRRMMMMM

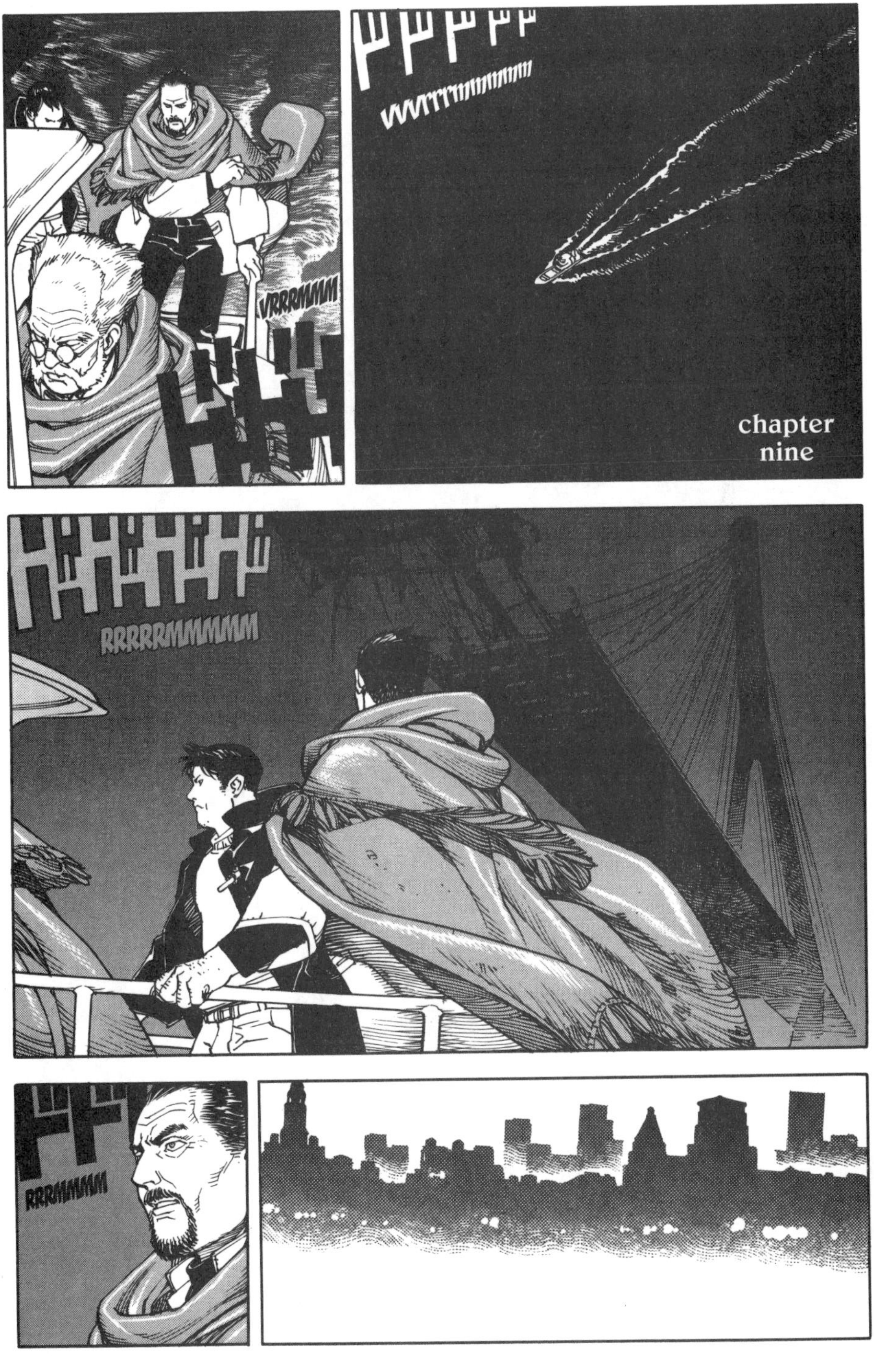
VVVRRRMMMMMMMM
chapter
nine
VRRRMMMM
RRRRRMMMMMMM
RRRMMMMM

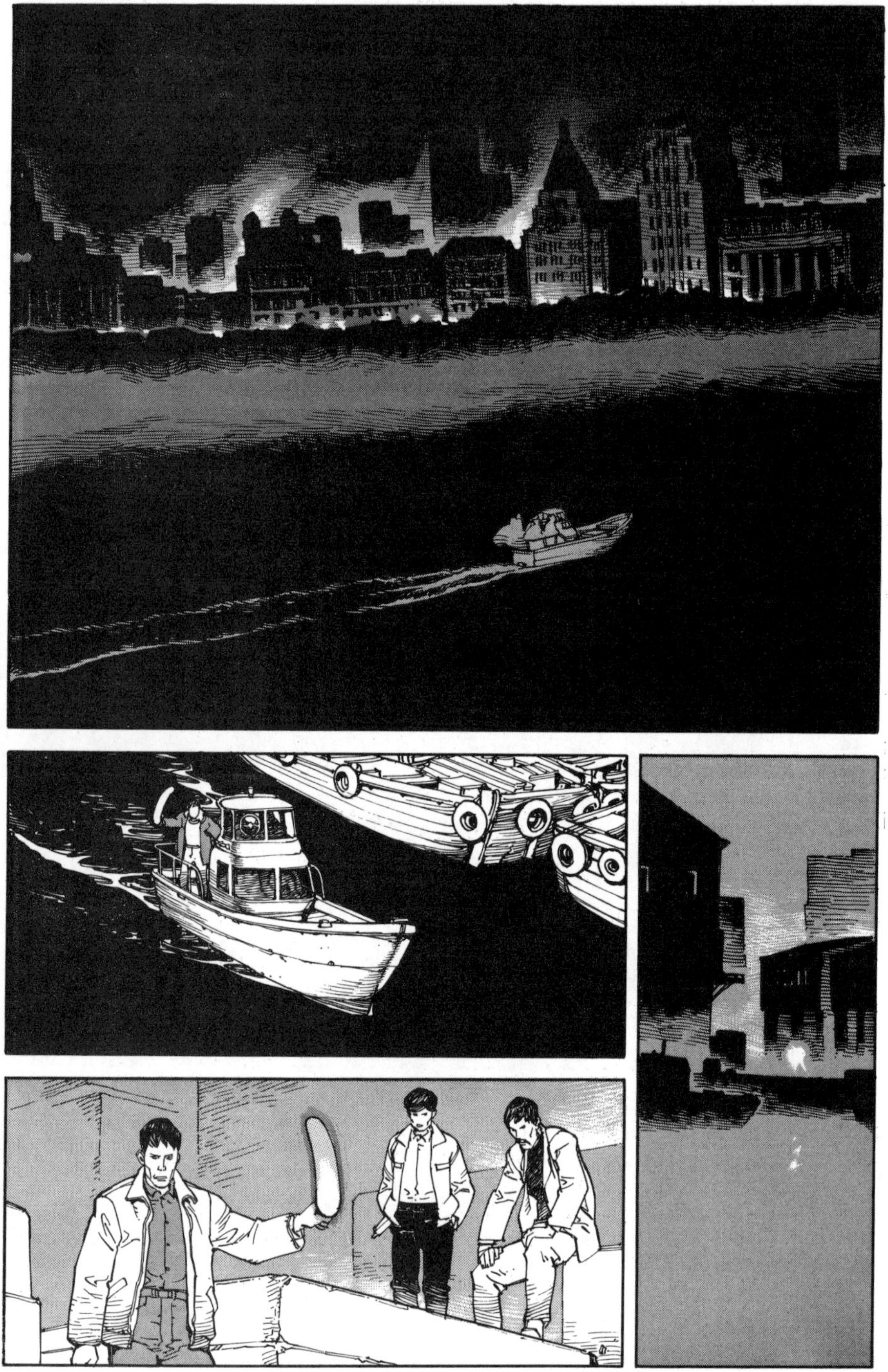

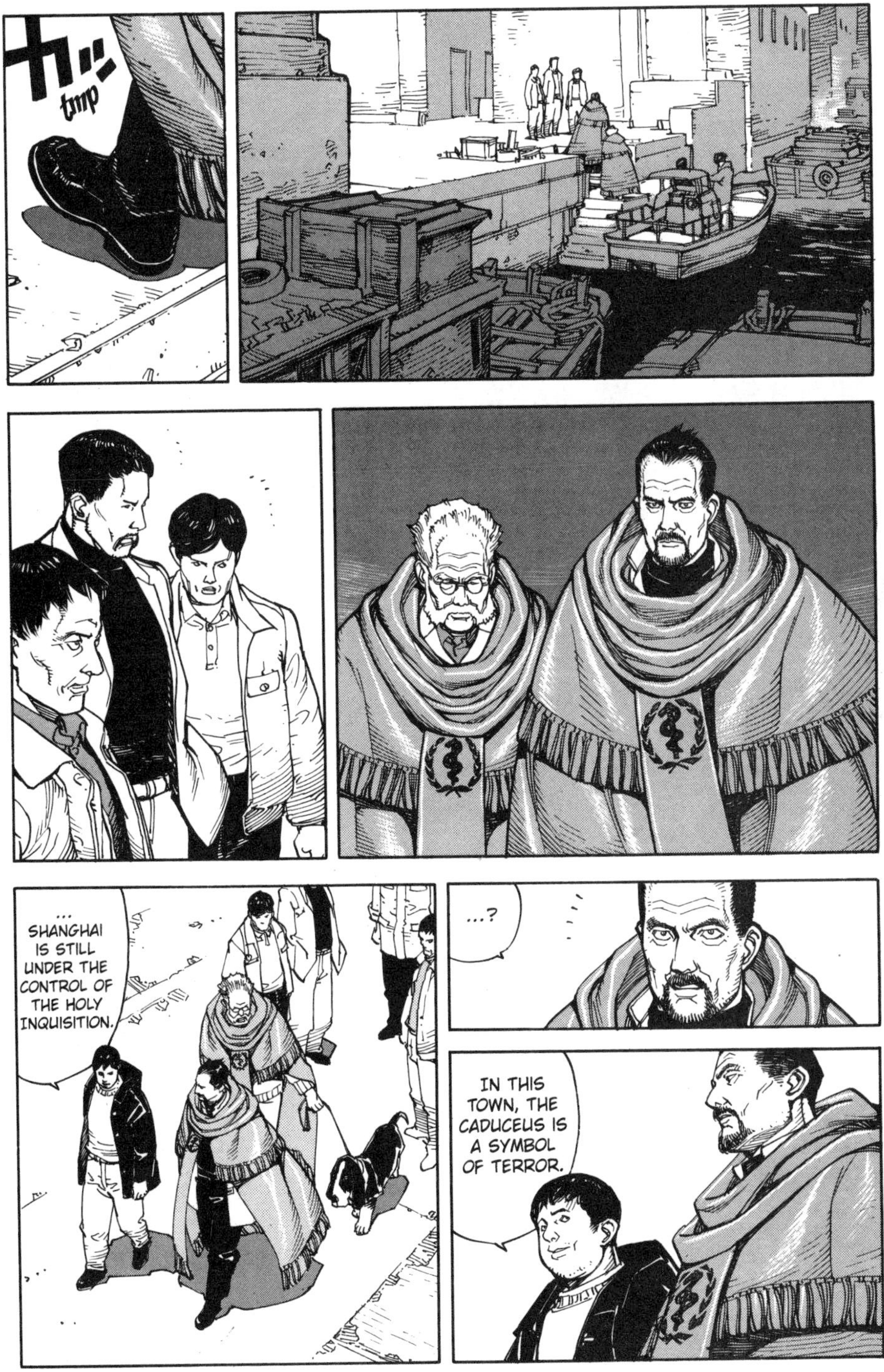
カッ
tmp
...?
IN THIS TOWN, THE CADUCEUS IS A SYMBOL OF TERROR.
... SHANGHAI IS STILL UNDER THE CONTROL OF THE HOLY INQUISITION.

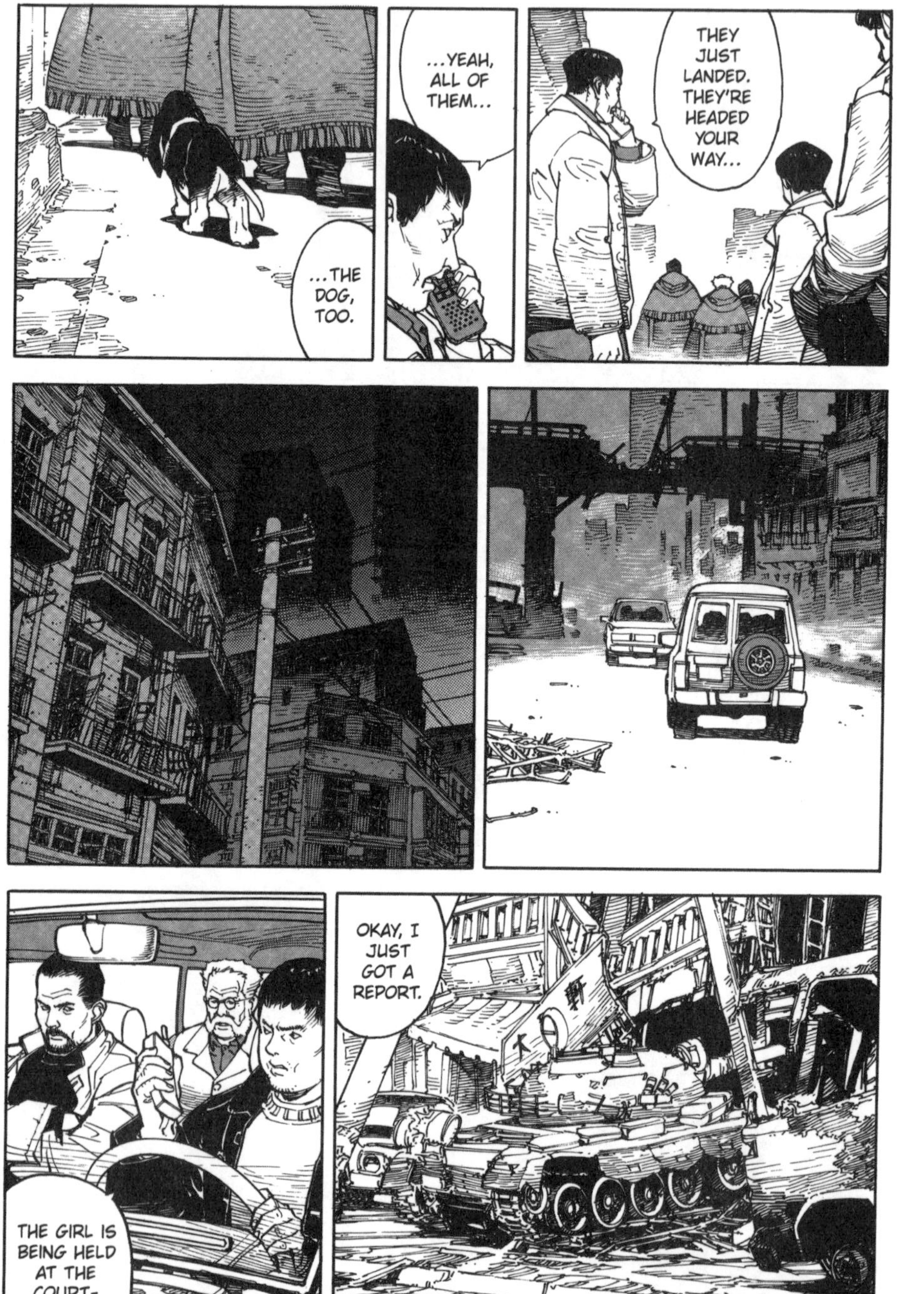
THEY JUST LANDED. THEY'RE HEADED YOUR WAY...
...YEAH, ALL OF THEM...
...THE DOG, TOO.
OKAY, I JUST GOT A REPORT.
THE GIRL IS BEING HELD AT THE COURT-HOUSE.

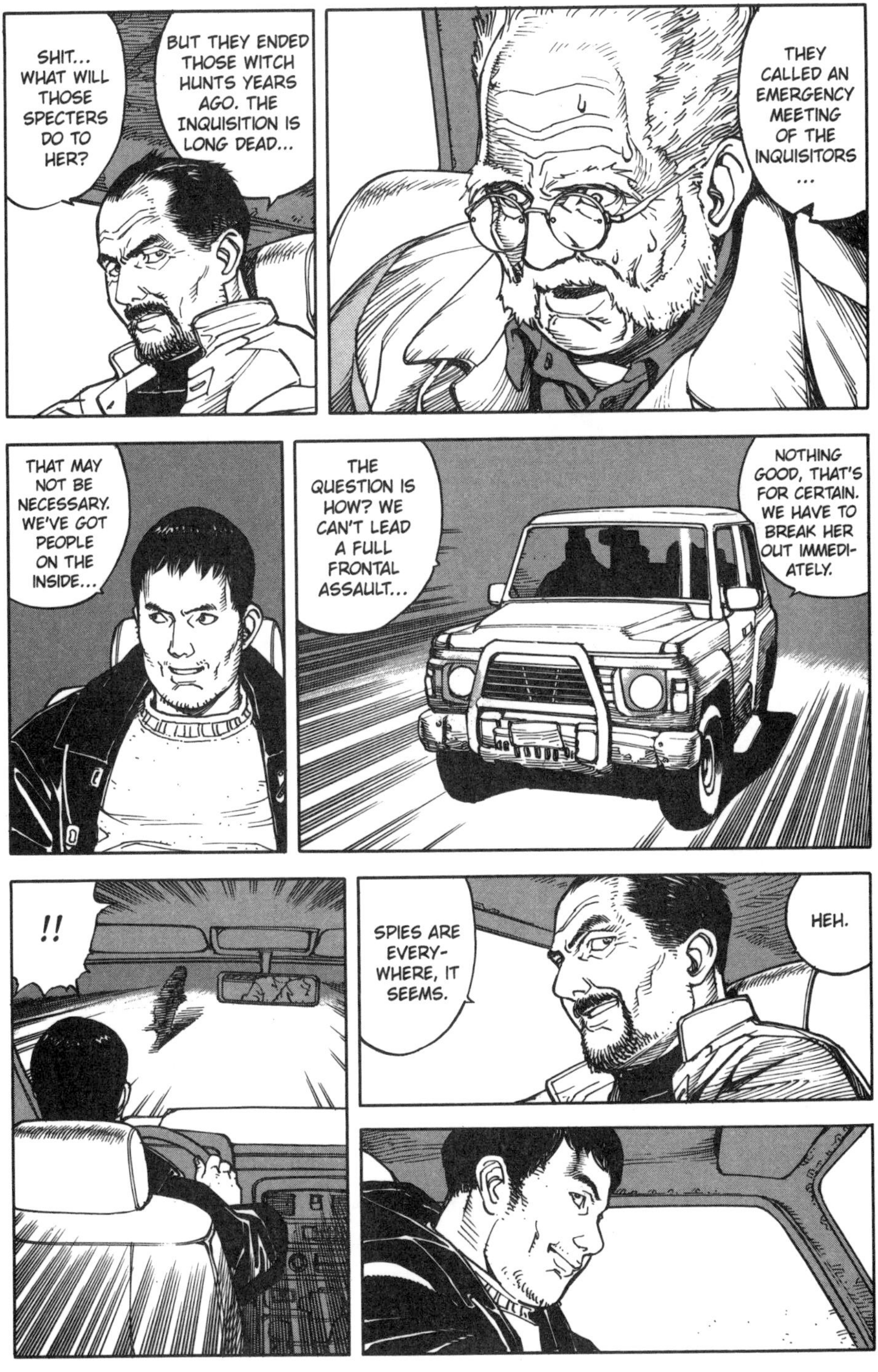
THEY CALLED AN EMERGENCY MEETING OF THE INQUISITORS ...
BUT THEY ENDED THOSE WITCH HUNTS YEARS AGO. THE INQUISITION IS LONG DEAD...
SHIT... WHAT WILL THOSE SPECTERS DO TO HER?
NOTHING GOOD, THAT'S FOR CERTAIN. WE HAVE TO BREAK HER OUT IMMEDI-ATELY.
THE QUESTION IS HOW? WE CAN'T LEAD A FULL FRONTAL ASSAULT...
THAT MAY NOT BE NECESSARY. WE'VE GOT PEOPLE ON THE INSIDE...
HEH.
SPIES ARE EVERY-WHERE, IT SEEMS.
!!

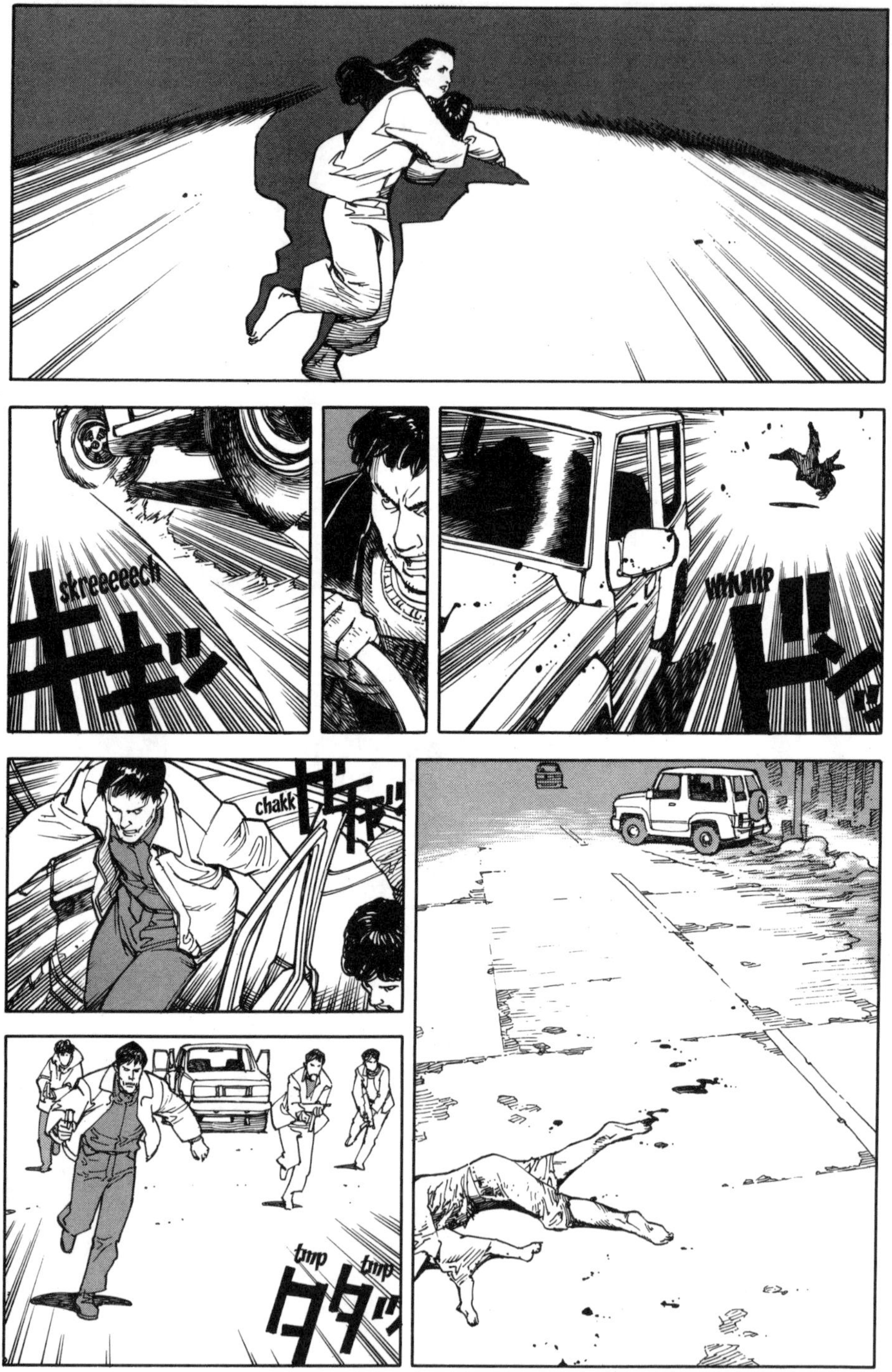
WHUMP
ドッ!!
skreeeeeech
キギッ
chakk
ガチャッ
tmp tmp
タタッ

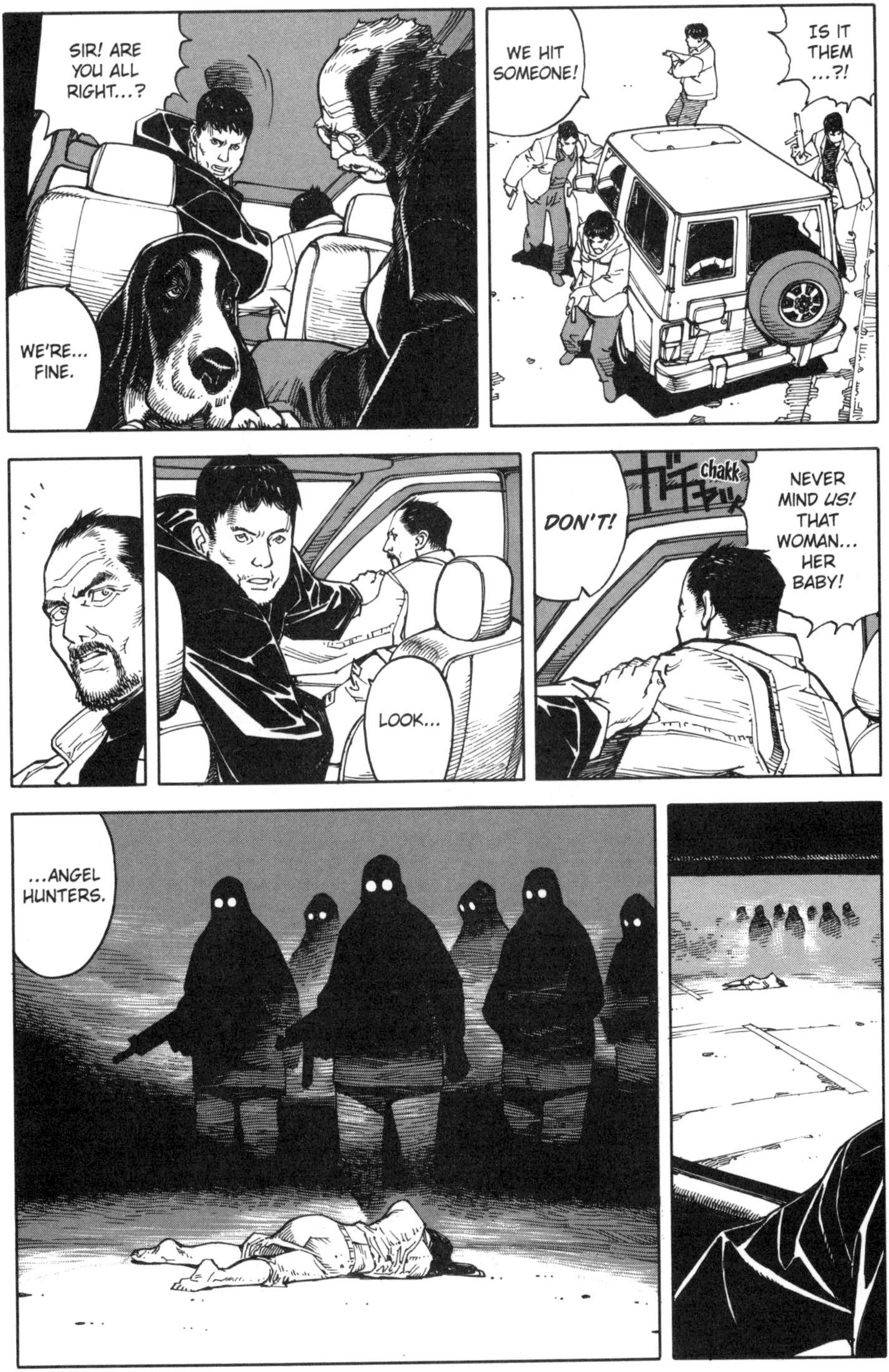
IS IT THEM ...?!
WE HIT SOMEONE!
SIR! ARE YOU ALL RIGHT...?
WE'RE... FINE.
NEVER MIND *US!* THAT WOMAN... HER BABY!
chakk
DON'T!
LOOK...
...ANGEL HUNTERS.

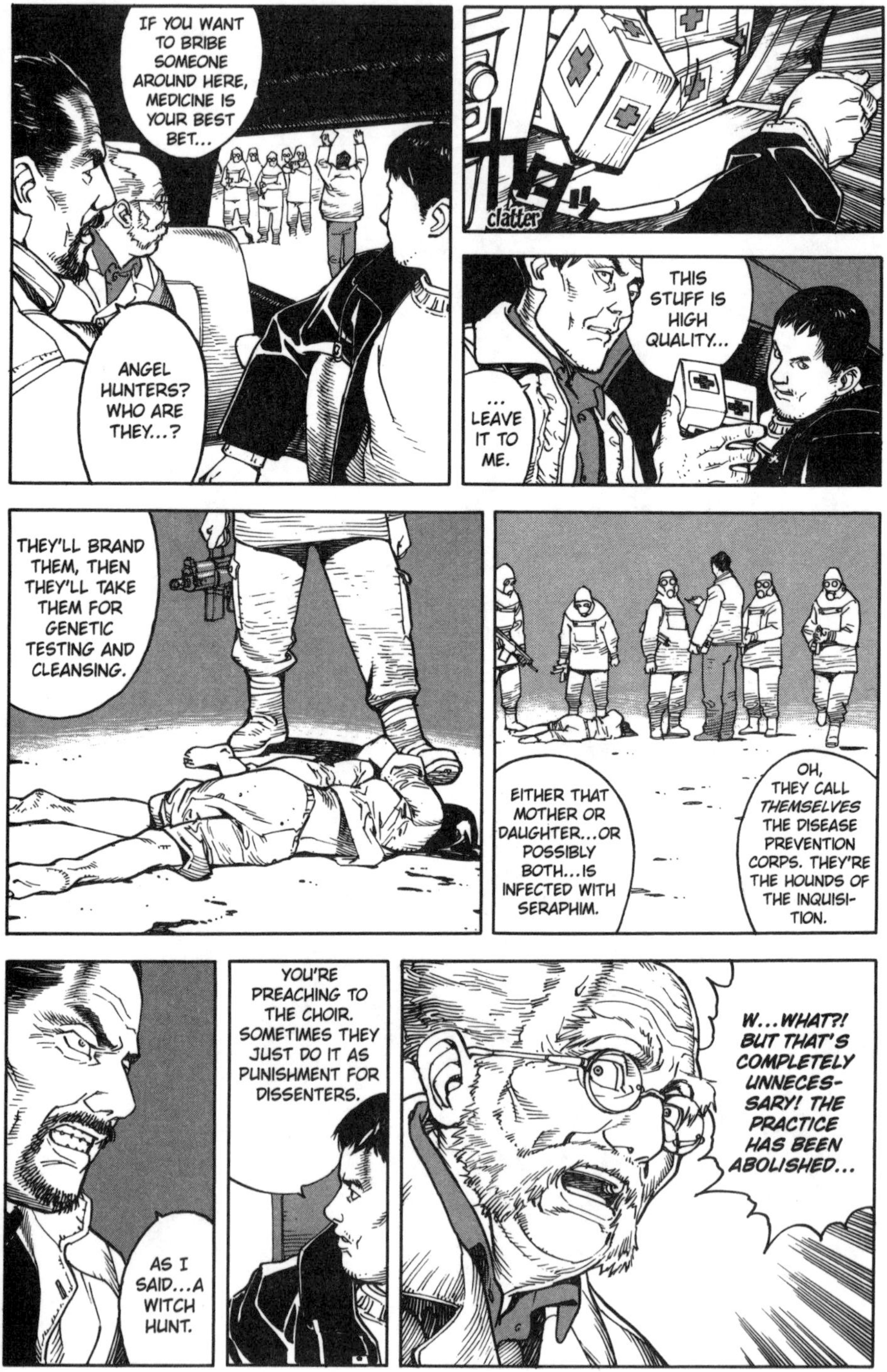
clatter
THIS STUFF IS HIGH QUALITY...
... LEAVE IT TO ME.
IF YOU WANT TO BRIBE SOMEONE AROUND HERE, MEDICINE IS YOUR BEST BET...
ANGEL HUNTERS? WHO ARE THEY...?
OH, THEY CALL *THEMSELVES* THE DISEASE PREVENTION CORPS. THEY'RE THE HOUNDS OF THE INQUISITION.
EITHER THAT MOTHER OR DAUGHTER...OR POSSIBLY BOTH...IS INFECTED WITH SERAPHIM.
THEY'LL BRAND THEM, THEN THEY'LL TAKE THEM FOR GENETIC TESTING AND CLEANSING.
W...WHAT?! BUT THAT'S COMPLETELY UNNECES-SARY! THE PRACTICE HAS BEEN ABOLISHED...
YOU'RE PREACHING TO THE CHOIR. SOMETIMES THEY JUST DO IT AS PUNISHMENT FOR DISSENTERS.
AS I SAID...A WITCH HUNT.

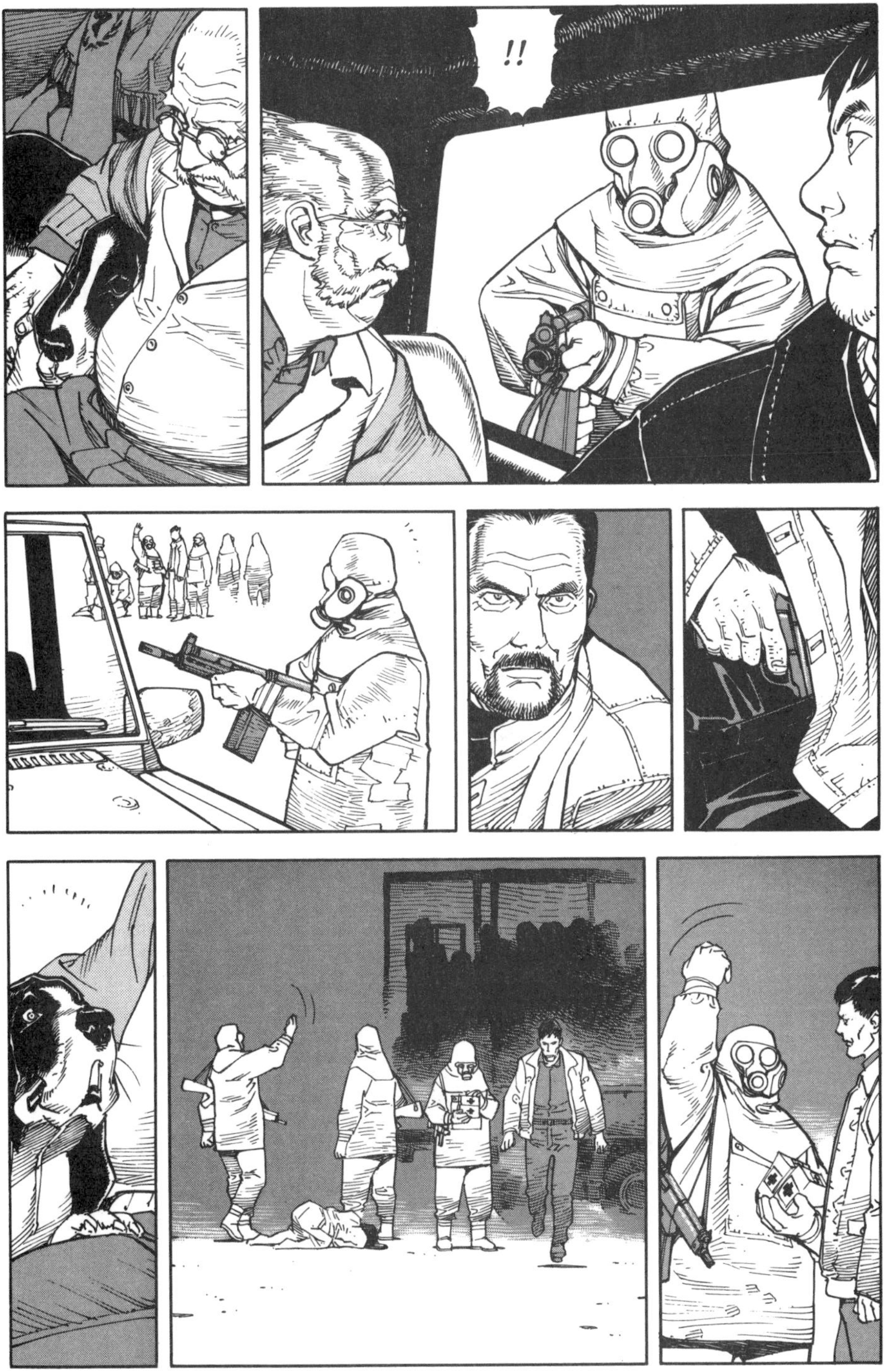
!!

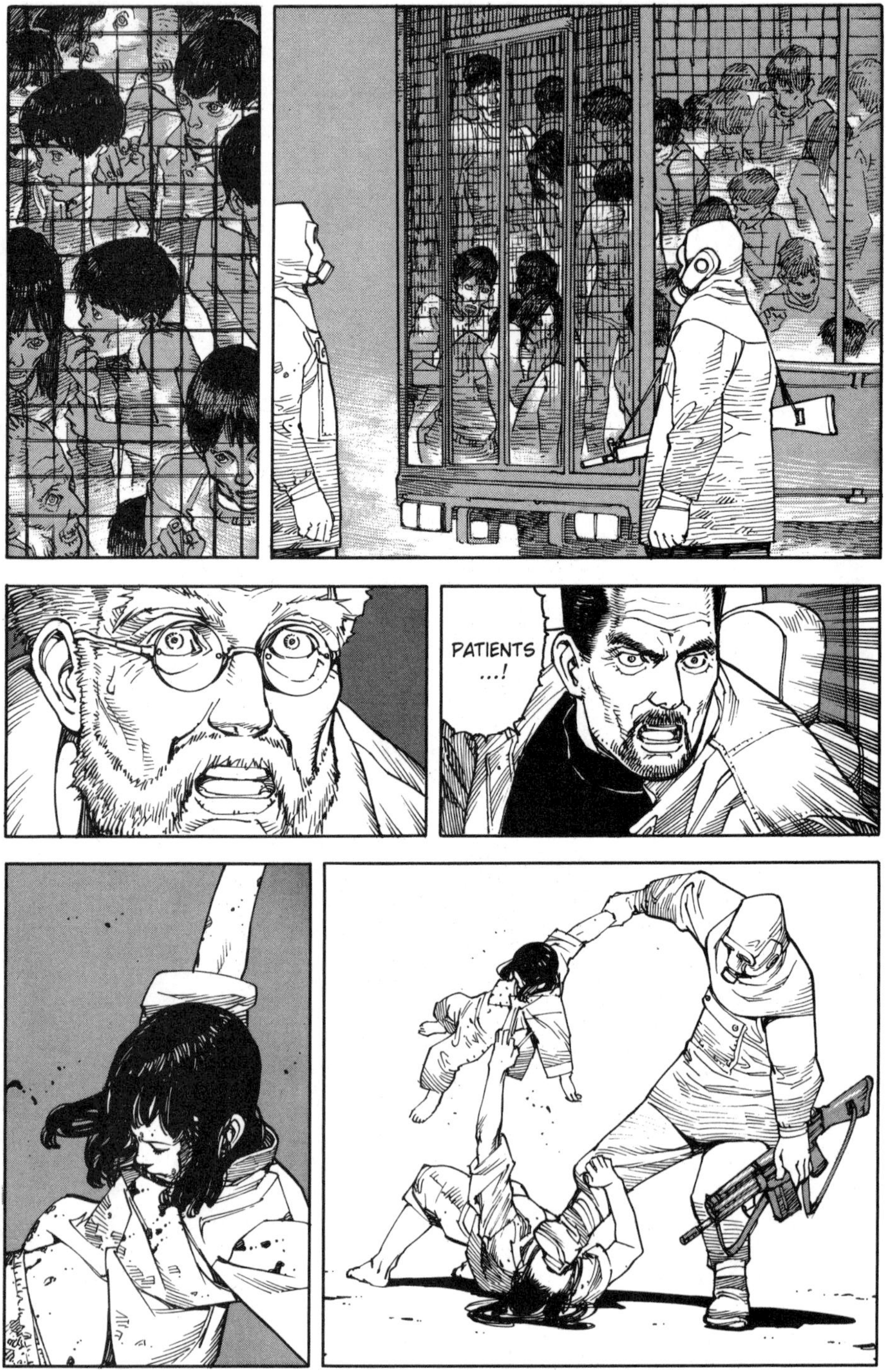
PATIENTS ...!

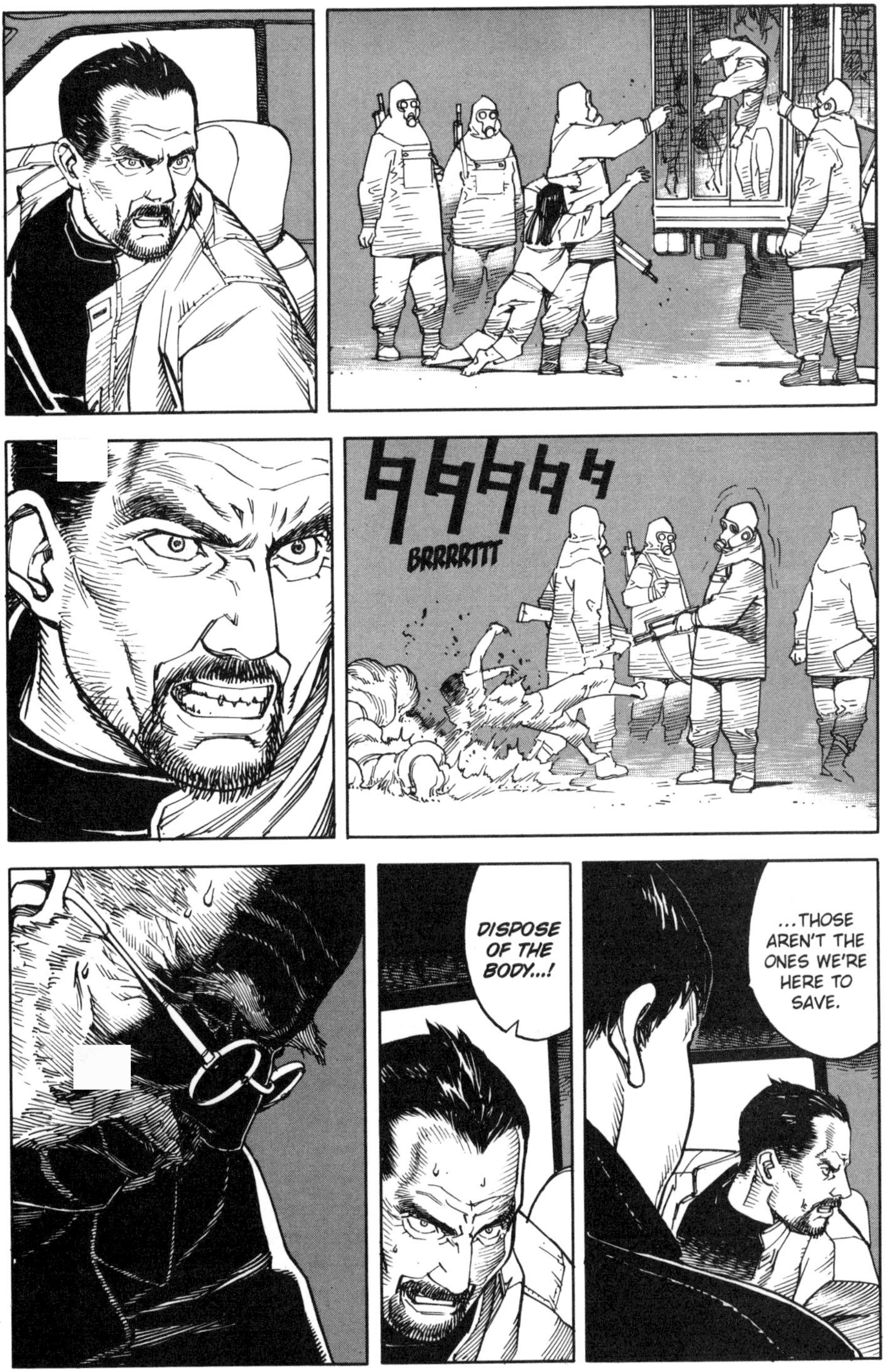
BRRRRTTT
...THOSE AREN'T THE ONES WE'RE HERE TO SAVE.
DISPOSE OF THE BODY...!

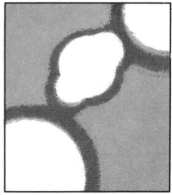

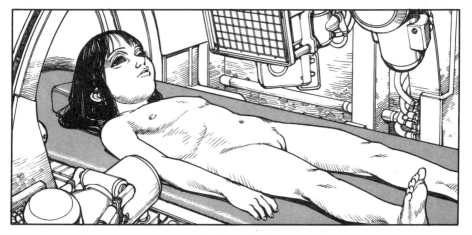

WE'LL HAVE THE FULL ANALYSIS RESULTS TOMORROW... BUT SHE IS THE ONE.

AND SO...?

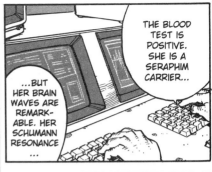
THE BLOOD TEST IS POSITIVE. SHE IS A SERAPHIM CARRIER...

...BUT HER BRAIN WAVES ARE REMARK- ABLE. HER SCHUMANN RESONANCE ...

MIRACULOUS. LOOK HERE.

...

...

WHAT DOES IT MEAN ...?

IT'S NOT POSSI- BLE!

THIS...

...CAN THIS BE?

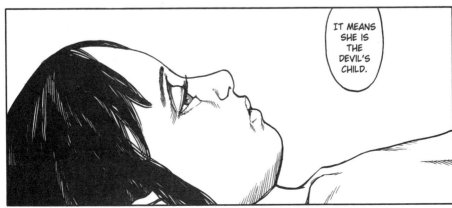
IT MEANS SHE IS THE DEVIL'S CHILD.

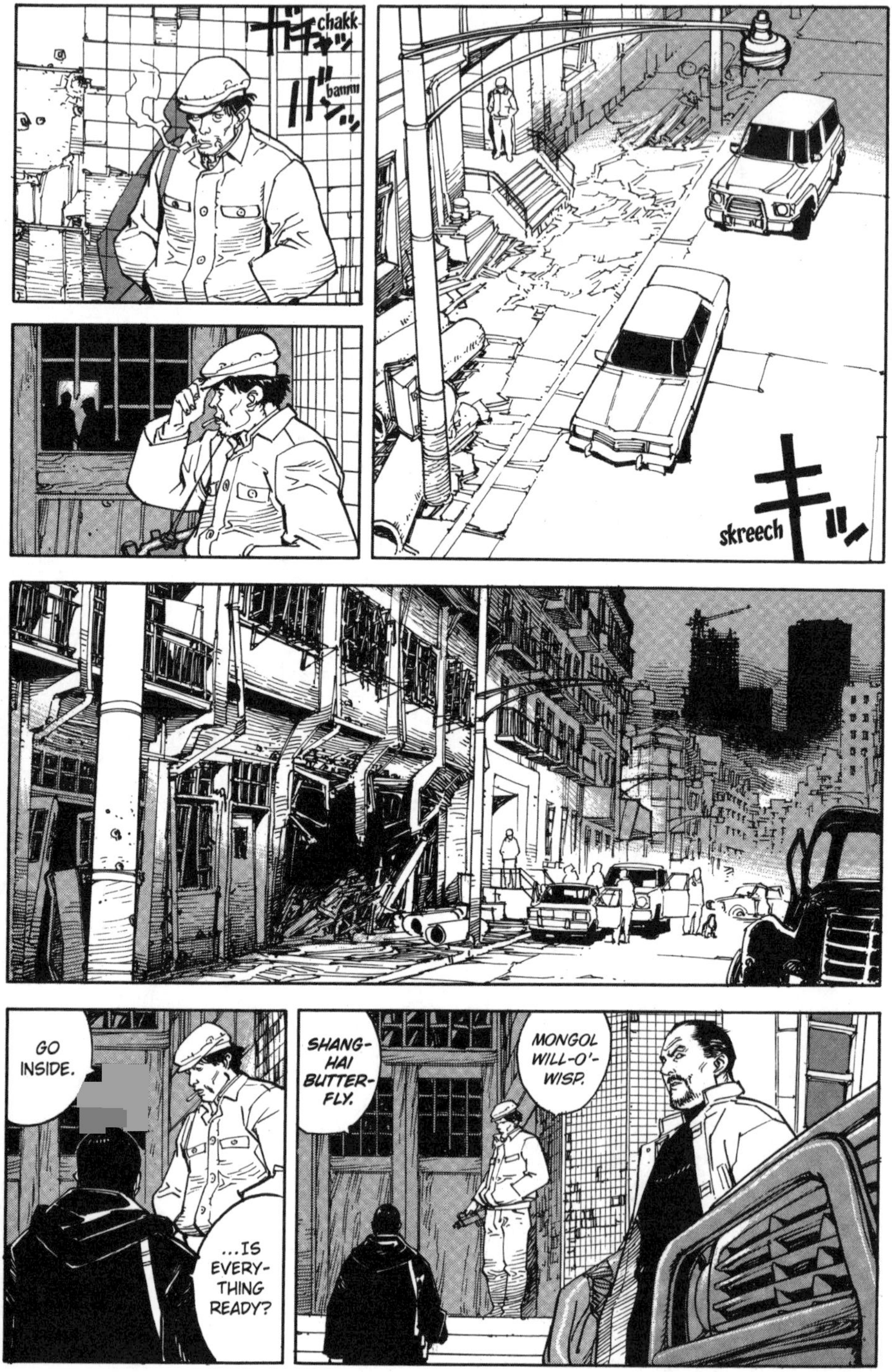

skreech
chakk
bannn
MONGOL WILL-O'-WISP.
SHANG-HAI BUTTER-FLY.
GO INSIDE.
...IS EVERY-THING READY?

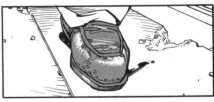

squitch

ズッ

whirl

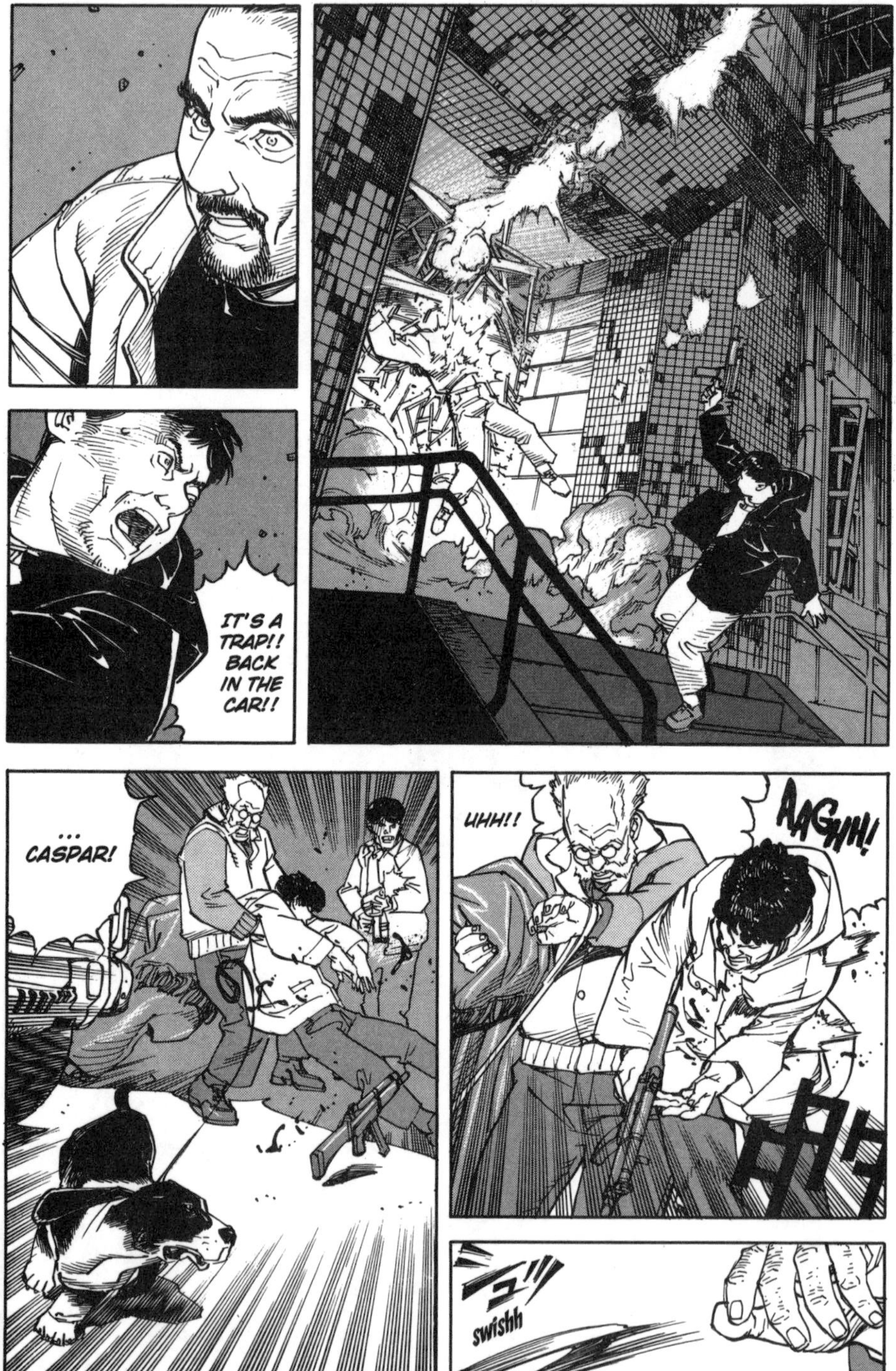

IT'S A TRAP!! BACK IN THE CAR!!
UHH!!
AAGHH!
swishh
... CASPAR!

chapter ten

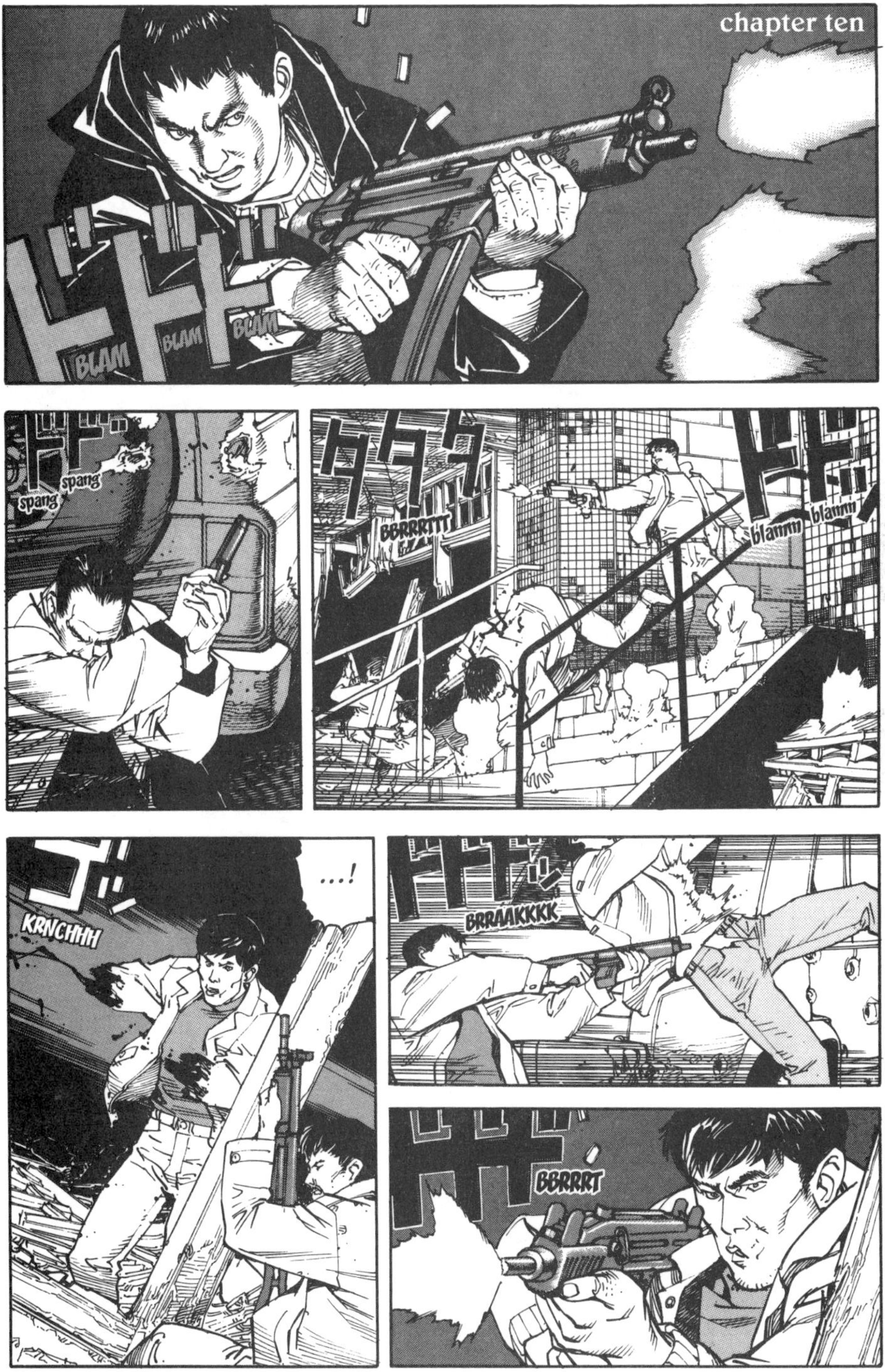
BLAM
BLAM
BLAM
BBRRRTTT
blammm
blammm
spang
spang
BRRAAKKKK
BBRRRT
...!
KRNCHHH

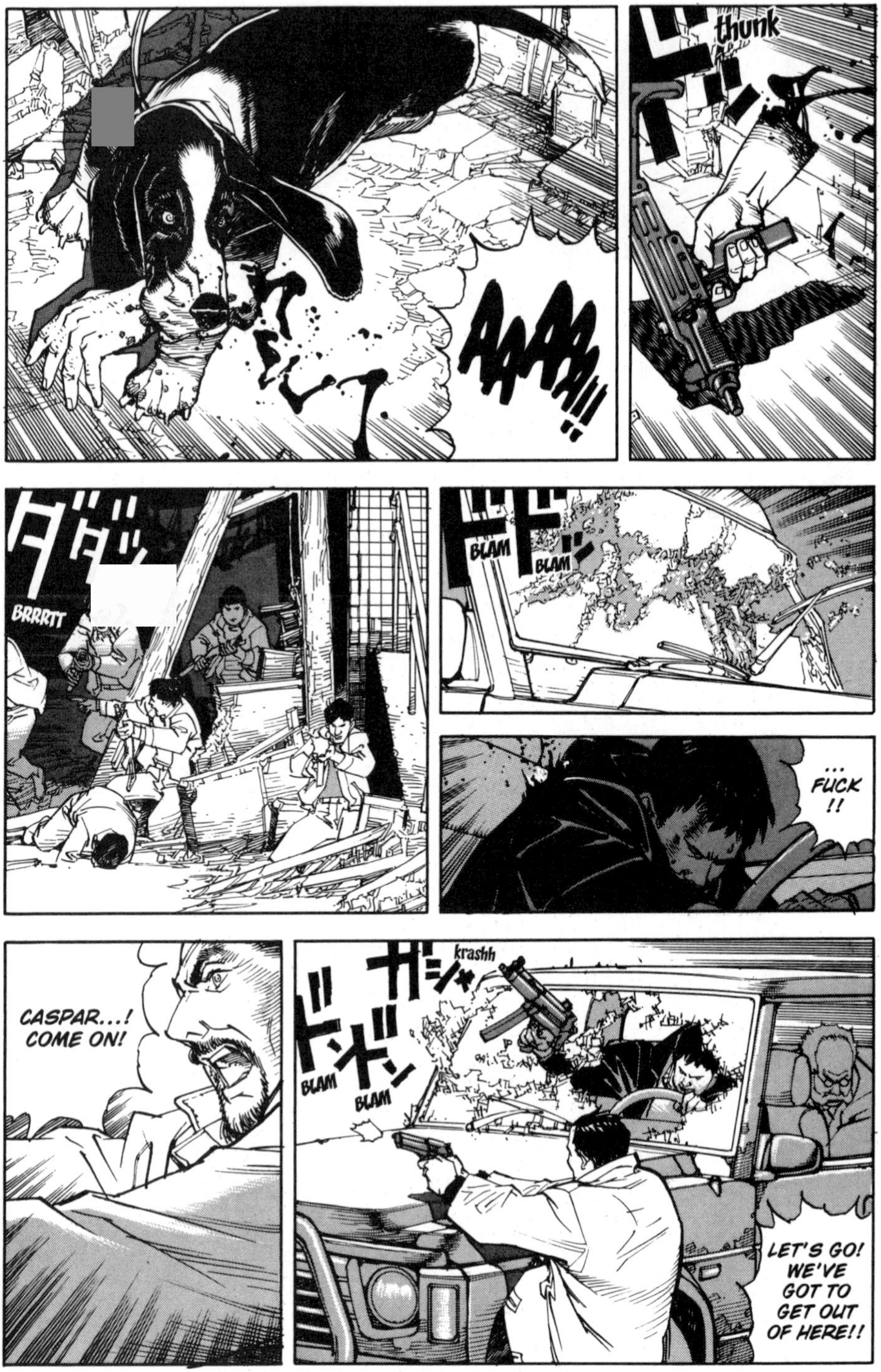
thunk
AAAAA!!!
BLAM
BLAM
... FUCK !!
BRRRTT
krashh
BLAM
BLAM
LET'S GO! WE'VE GOT TO GET OUT OF HERE!!
CASPAR...! COME ON!

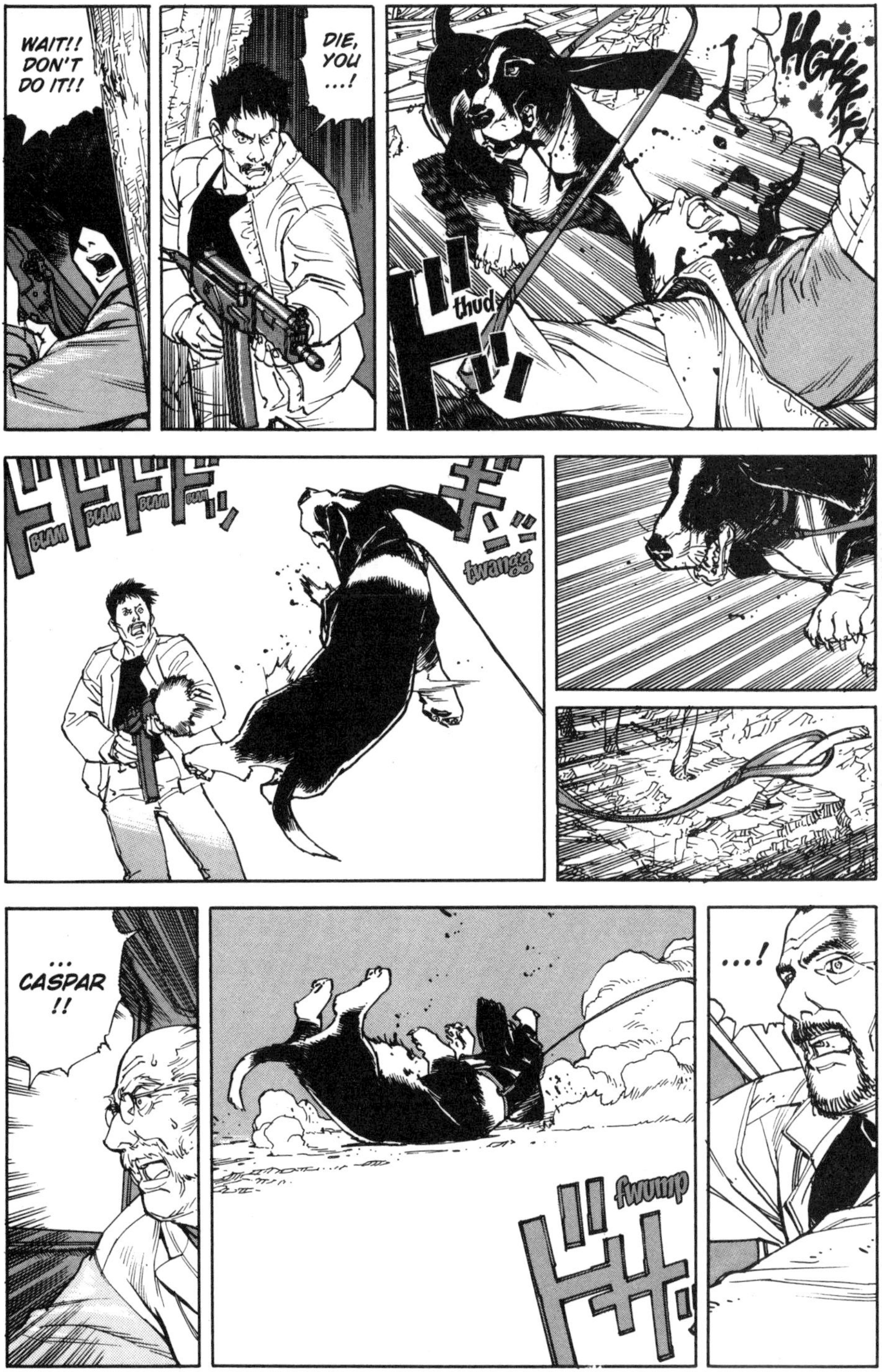
HGHKK
thud
DIE, YOU ...!
WAIT!! DON'T DO IT!!
twangg
BLAM BLAM BLAM BLAM
...!
fwump
... CASPAR !!

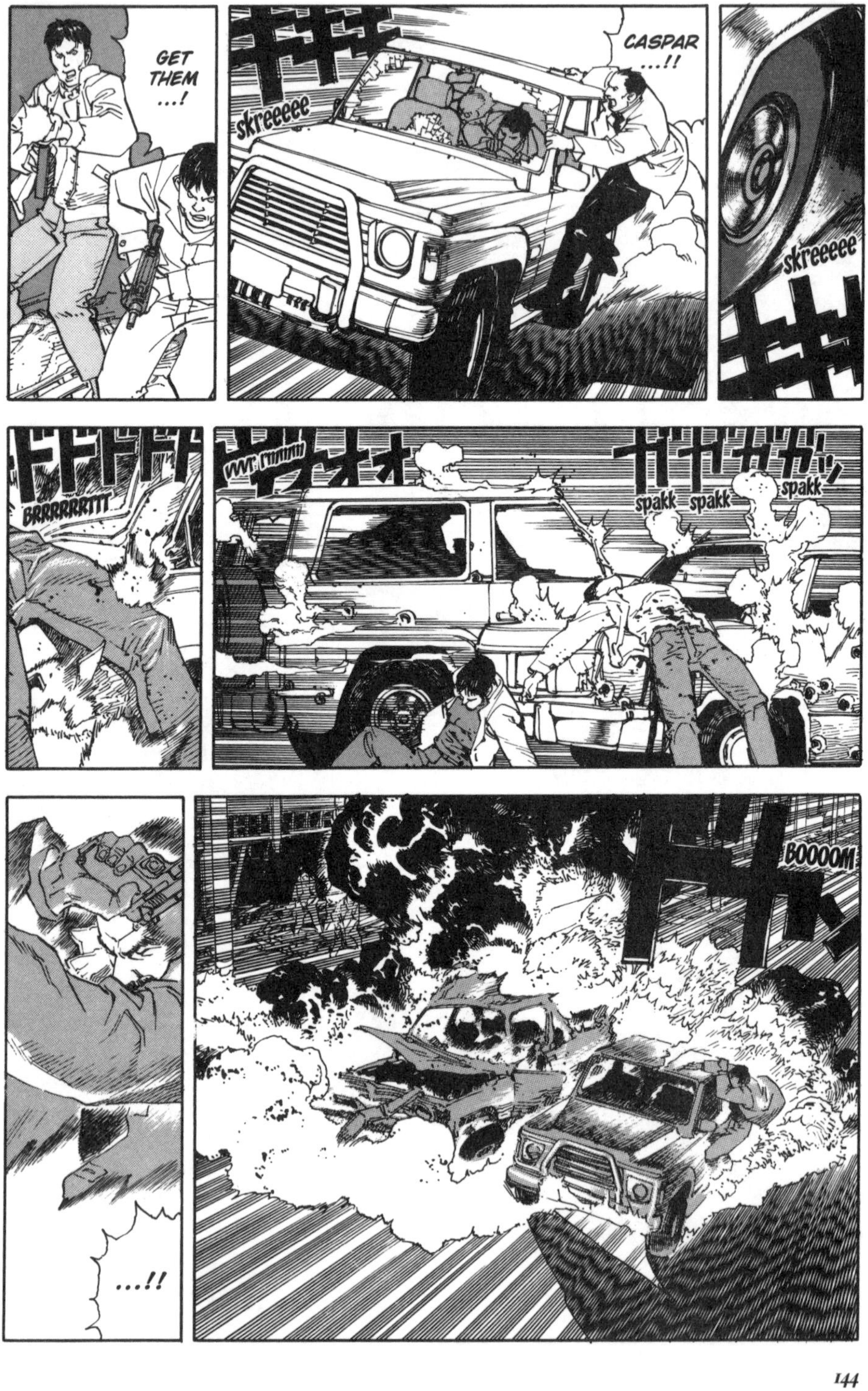
skreeeee
skreeeee
CASPAR ...!!
GET THEM ...!
spakk spakk spakk
BRRRRRRTTT
BOOOOM
...!!

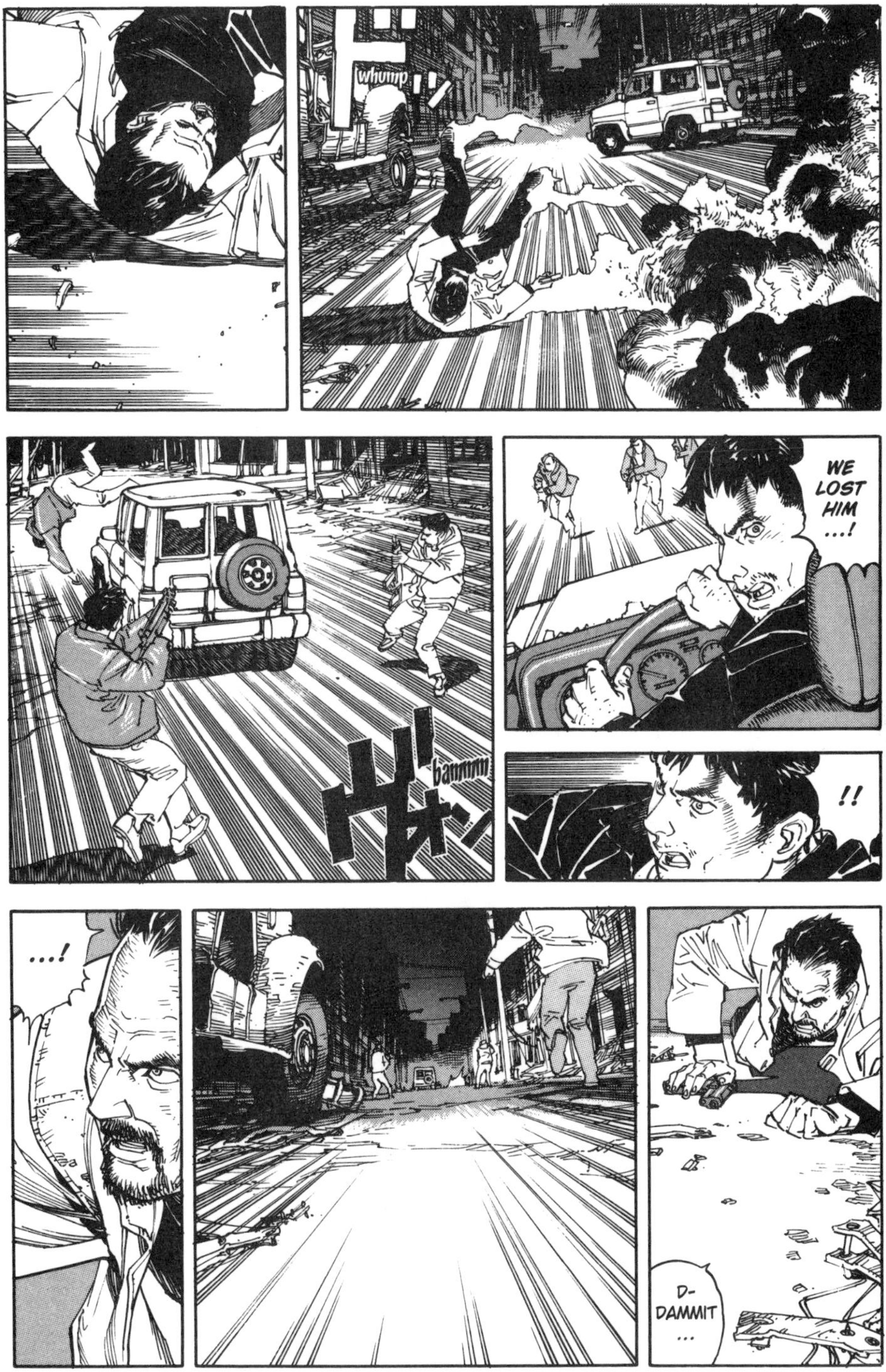
whump
WE LOST HIM ...!
!!
bammm
D-DAMMIT ...
...!

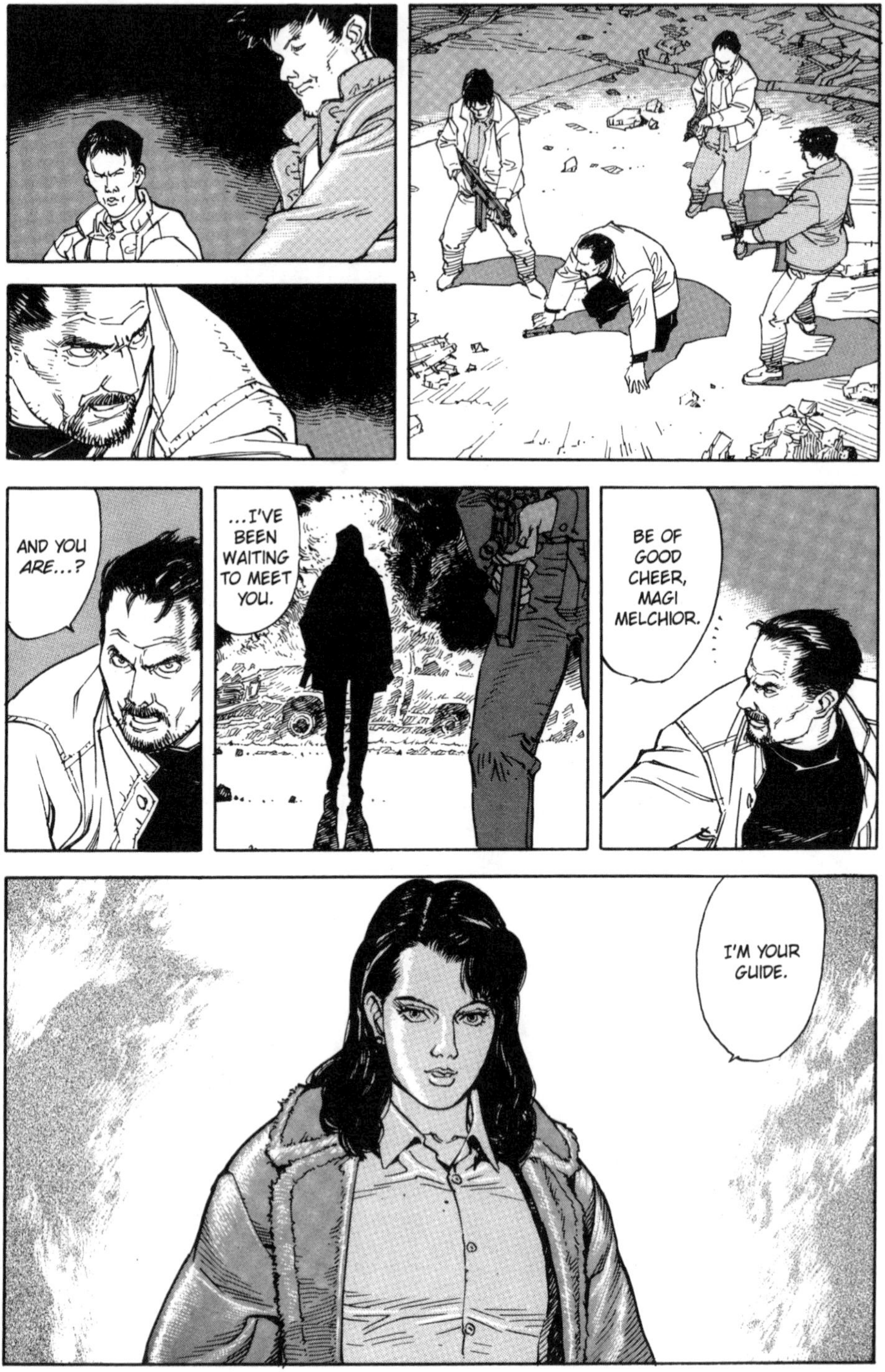
BE OF GOOD CHEER, MAGI MELCHIOR.
...I'VE BEEN WAITING TO MEET YOU.
AND YOU ARE...?
I'M YOUR GUIDE.

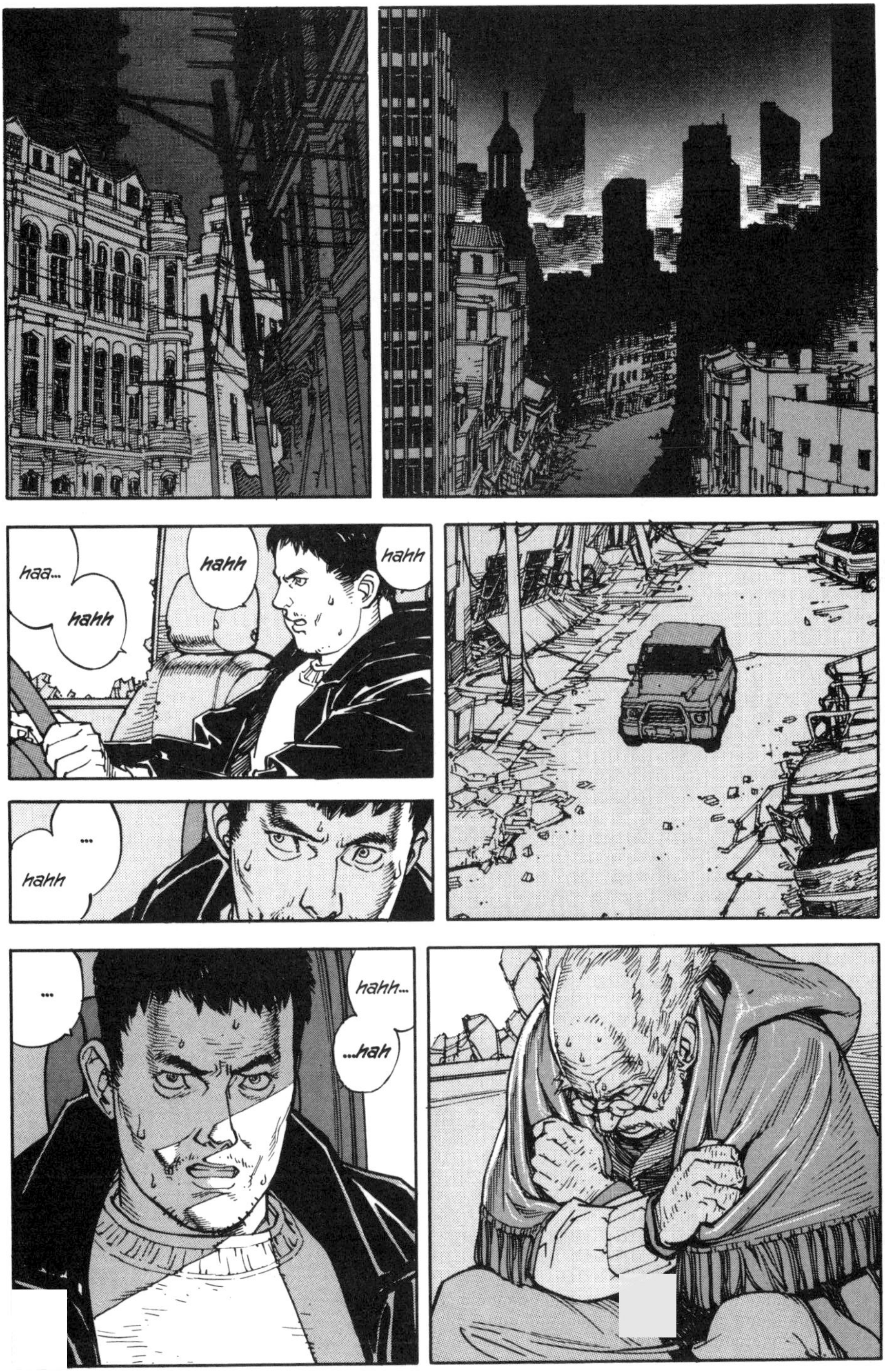
hahh
hahh
haa...
hahh
...
hahh
hahh...
...hah
...

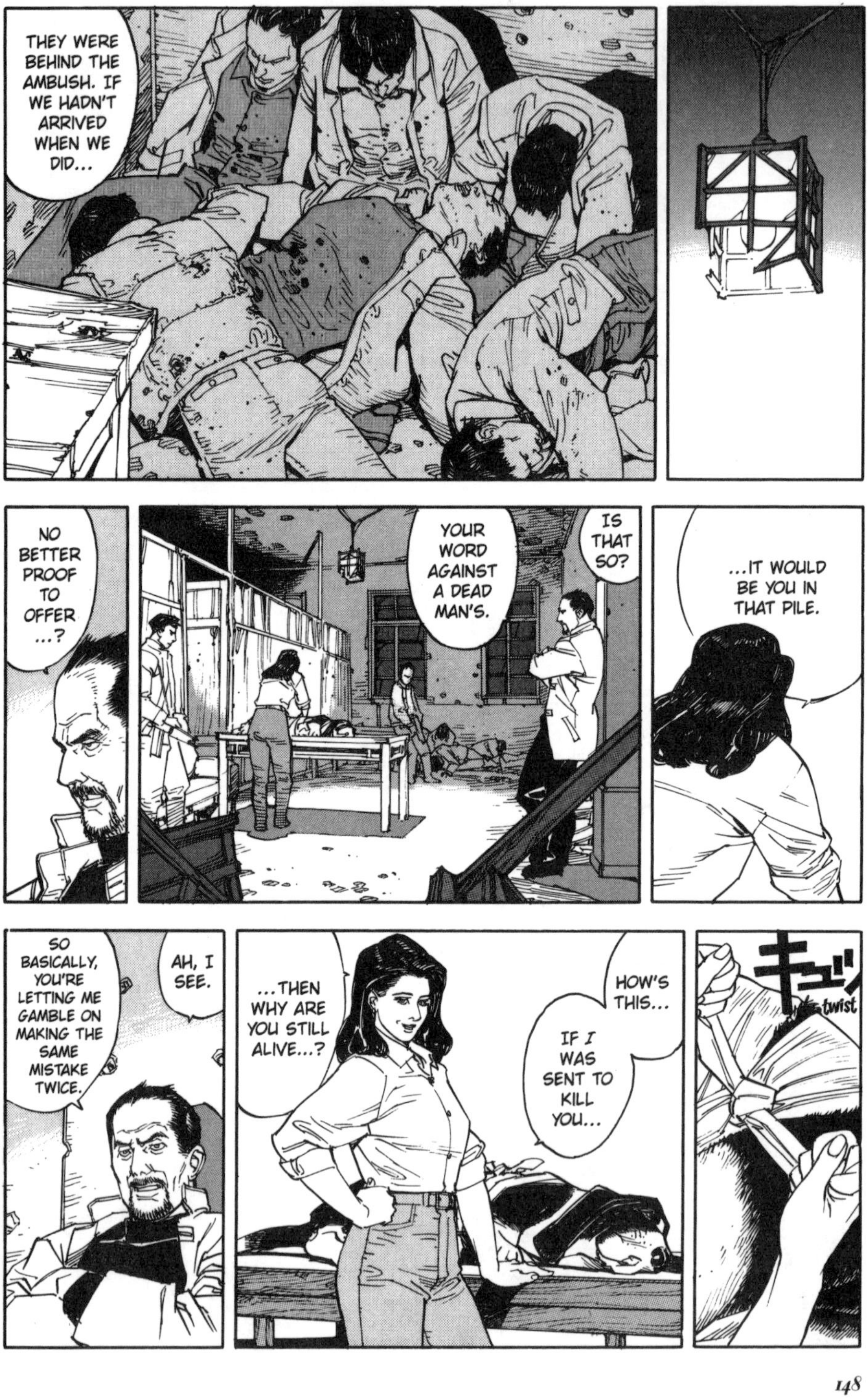

THEY WERE BEHIND THE AMBUSH. IF WE HADN'T ARRIVED WHEN WE DID...
...IT WOULD BE YOU IN THAT PILE.
IS THAT SO?
YOUR WORD AGAINST A DEAD MAN'S.
NO BETTER PROOF TO OFFER...?
twist
HOW'S THIS...
IF *I* WAS SENT TO KILL YOU...
...THEN WHY ARE YOU STILL ALIVE...?
AH, I SEE.
SO BASICALLY, YOU'RE LETTING ME GAMBLE ON MAKING THE SAME MISTAKE TWICE.

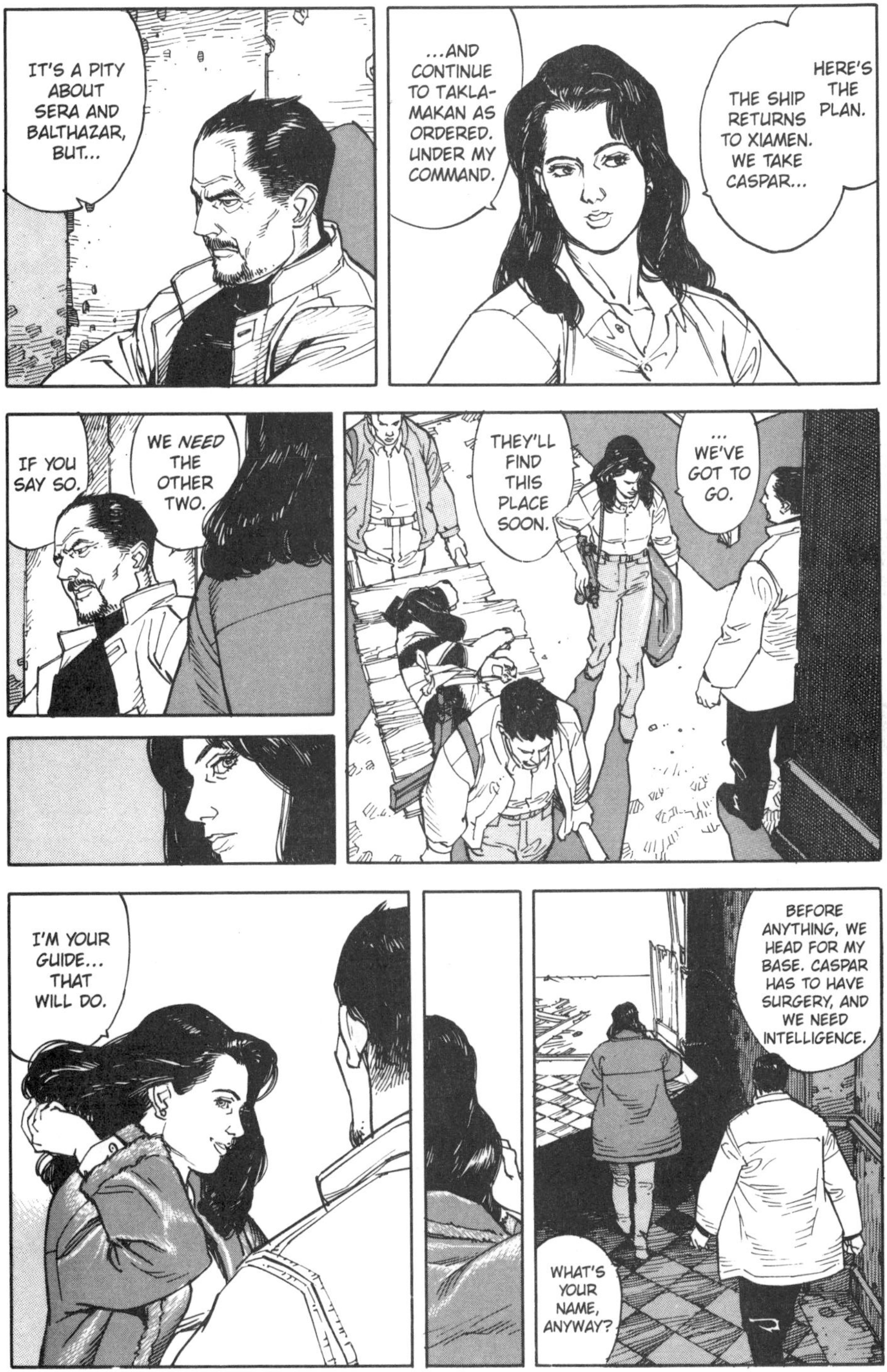
HERE'S THE PLAN.
THE SHIP RETURNS TO XIAMEN. WE TAKE CASPAR...
...AND CONTINUE TO TAKLA-MAKAN AS ORDERED. UNDER MY COMMAND.
IT'S A PITY ABOUT SERA AND BALTHAZAR, BUT...
... WE'VE GOT TO GO.
THEY'LL FIND THIS PLACE SOON.
WE *NEED* THE OTHER TWO.
IF YOU SAY SO.
BEFORE ANYTHING, WE HEAD FOR MY BASE. CASPAR HAS TO HAVE SURGERY, AND WE NEED INTELLIGENCE.
WHAT'S YOUR NAME, ANYWAY?
I'M YOUR GUIDE... THAT WILL DO.

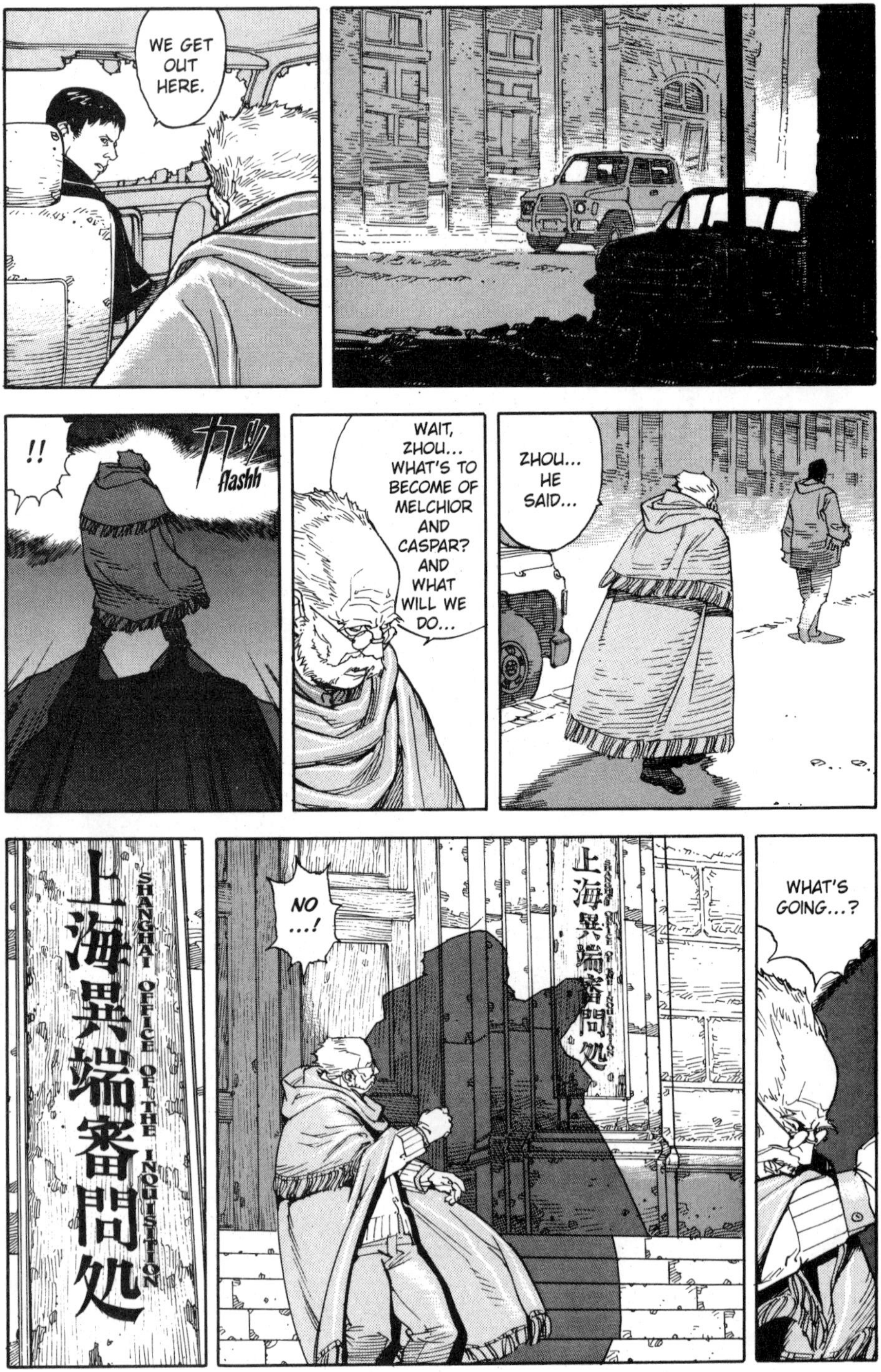
WE GET OUT HERE.
ZHOU... HE SAID...
WAIT, ZHOU... WHAT'S TO BECOME OF MELCHIOR AND CASPAR? AND WHAT WILL WE DO...
flashh
!!
WHAT'S GOING...?
NO ...!
上海異端審問処
SHANGHAI OFFICE OF THE INQUISITION
上海異端審問処
SHANGHAI OFFICE OF THE INQUISITION

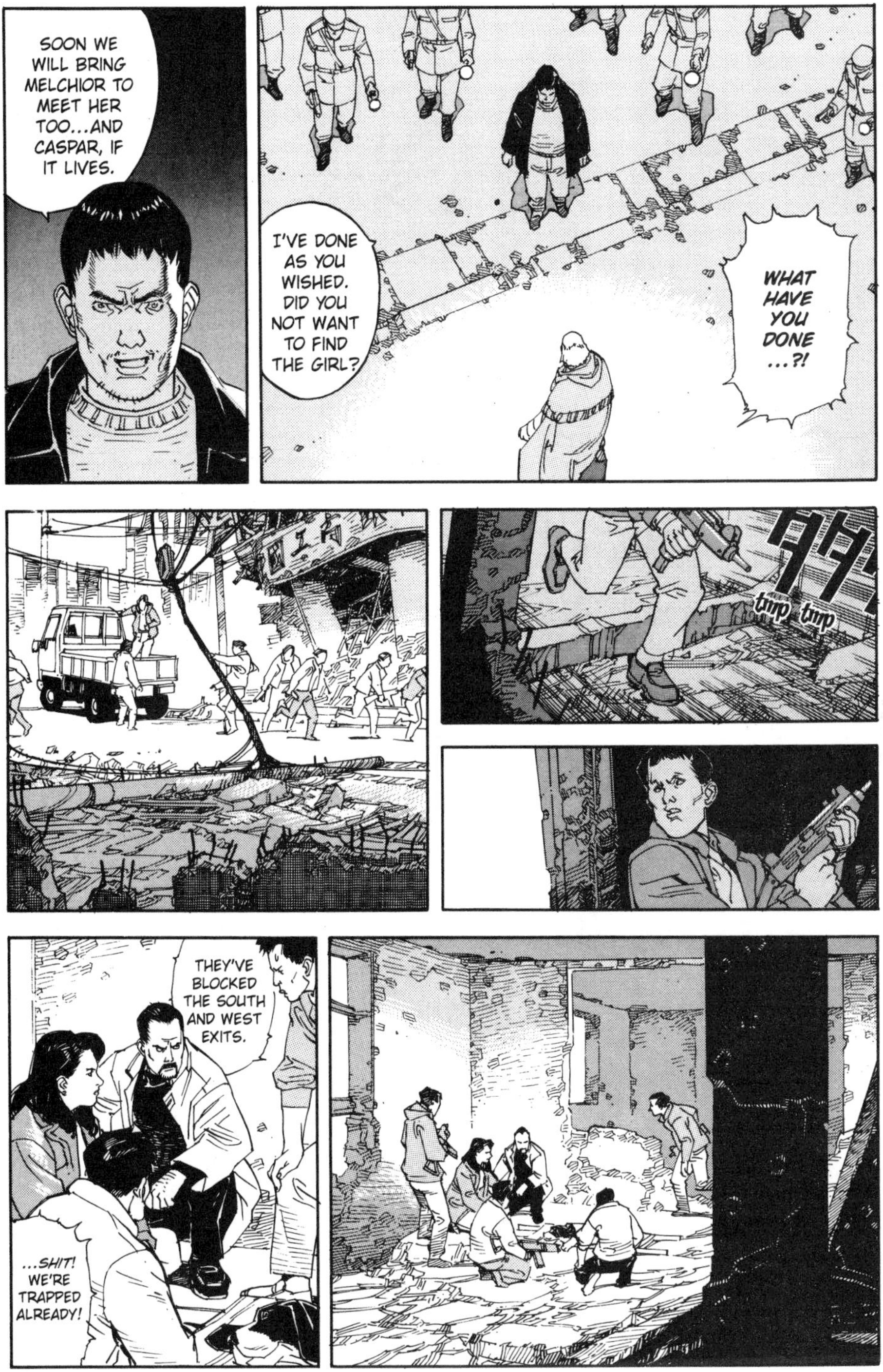
WHAT HAVE YOU DONE ...?!
I'VE DONE AS YOU WISHED. DID YOU NOT WANT TO FIND THE GIRL?
SOON WE WILL BRING MELCHIOR TO MEET HER TOO...AND CASPAR, IF IT LIVES.
tmp tmp
THEY'VE BLOCKED THE SOUTH AND WEST EXITS.
...SHIT! WE'RE TRAPPED ALREADY!

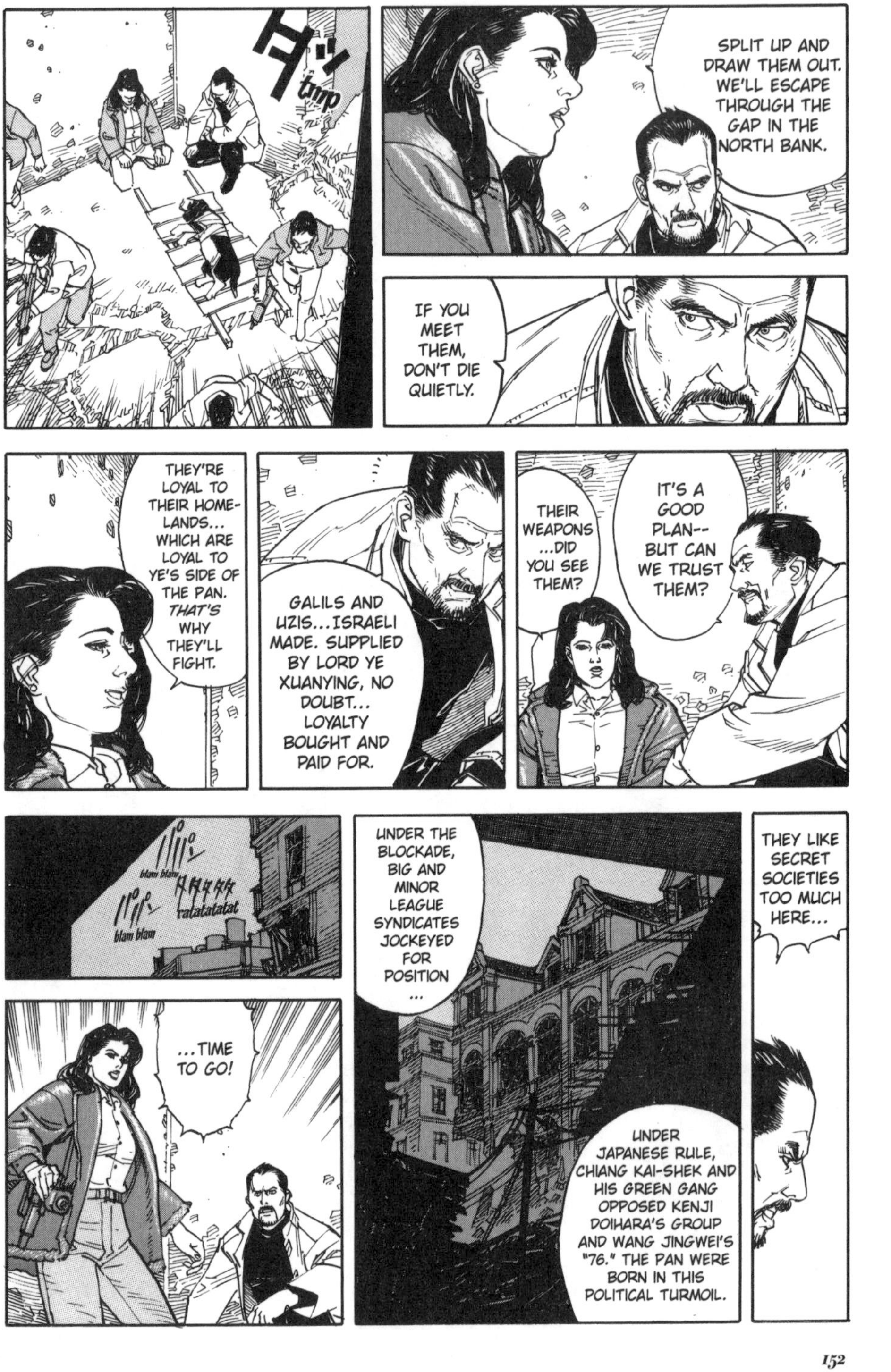
SPLIT UP AND DRAW THEM OUT. WE'LL ESCAPE THROUGH THE GAP IN THE NORTH BANK.
IF YOU MEET THEM, DON'T DIE QUIETLY.
tmp
IT'S A GOOD PLAN-- BUT CAN WE TRUST THEM?
THEIR WEAPONS ...DID YOU SEE THEM?
GALILS AND UZIS...ISRAELI MADE. SUPPLIED BY LORD YE XUANYING, NO DOUBT... LOYALTY BOUGHT AND PAID FOR.
THEY'RE LOYAL TO THEIR HOMELANDS... WHICH ARE LOYAL TO YE'S SIDE OF THE PAN. *THAT'S* WHY THEY'LL FIGHT.
THEY LIKE SECRET SOCIETIES TOO MUCH HERE...
UNDER THE BLOCKADE, BIG AND MINOR LEAGUE SYNDICATES JOCKEYED FOR POSITION ...
UNDER JAPANESE RULE, CHIANG KAI-SHEK AND HIS GREEN GANG OPPOSED KENJI DOIHARA'S GROUP AND WANG JINGWEI'S "76." THE PAN WERE BORN IN THIS POLITICAL TURMOIL.
blam blam
ratatatatat
blam blam
...TIME TO GO!

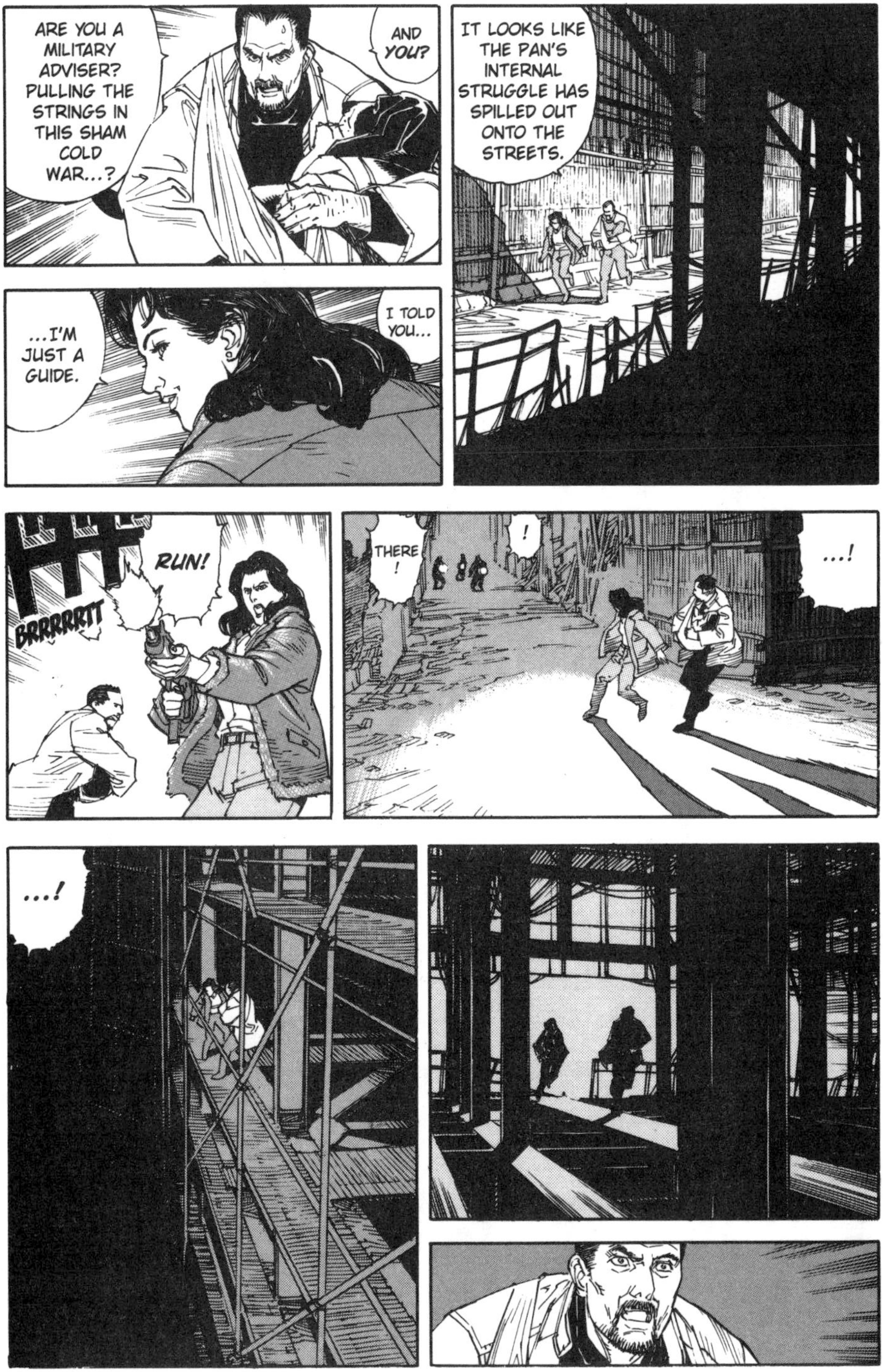
IT LOOKS LIKE THE PAN'S INTERNAL STRUGGLE HAS SPILLED OUT ONTO THE STREETS.
AND *YOU?*
ARE YOU A MILITARY ADVISER? PULLING THE STRINGS IN THIS SHAM COLD WAR...?
I TOLD YOU...
...I'M JUST A GUIDE.
...!
!
THERE !
RUN!
BRRRRRITT
...!

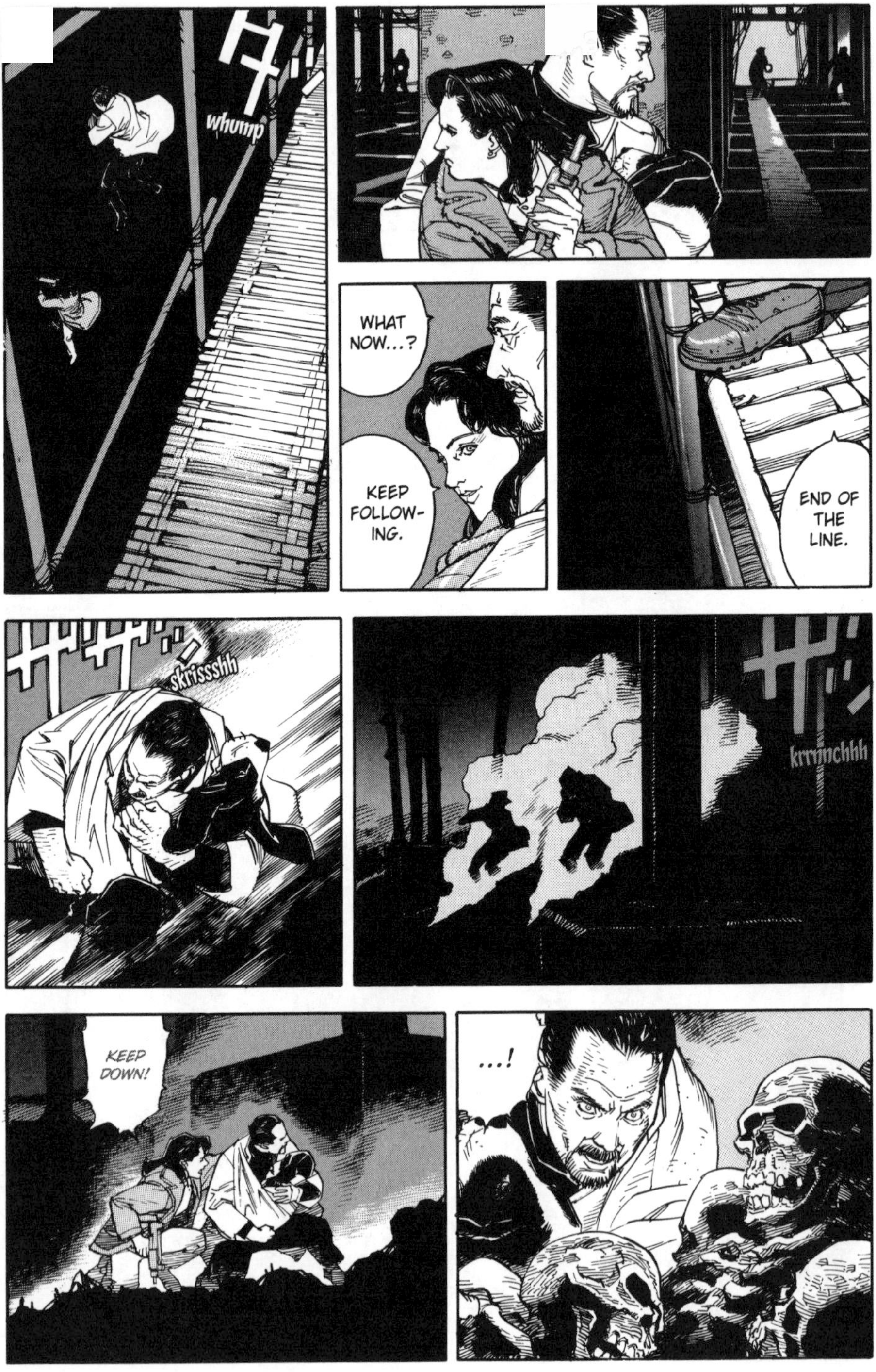
END OF THE LINE.
WHAT NOW...?
KEEP FOLLOWING.
whump
krrrnchhh
skrissshh
...!
KEEP DOWN!

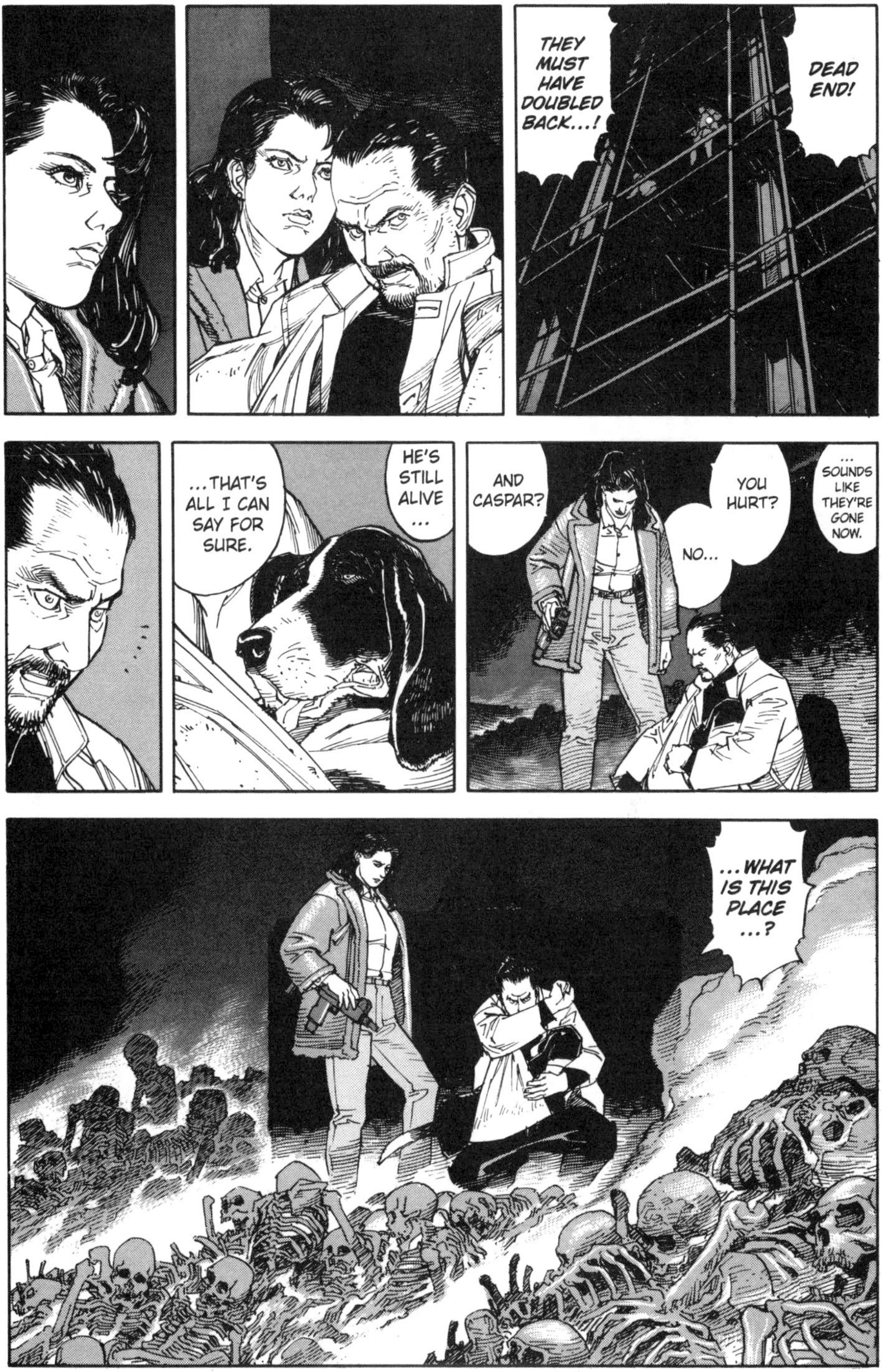
DEAD END!
THEY MUST HAVE DOUBLED BACK...!
...SOUNDS LIKE THEY'RE GONE NOW.
YOU HURT?
NO...
AND CASPAR?
HE'S STILL ALIVE ...
...THAT'S ALL I CAN SAY FOR SURE.
...WHAT IS THIS PLACE ...?

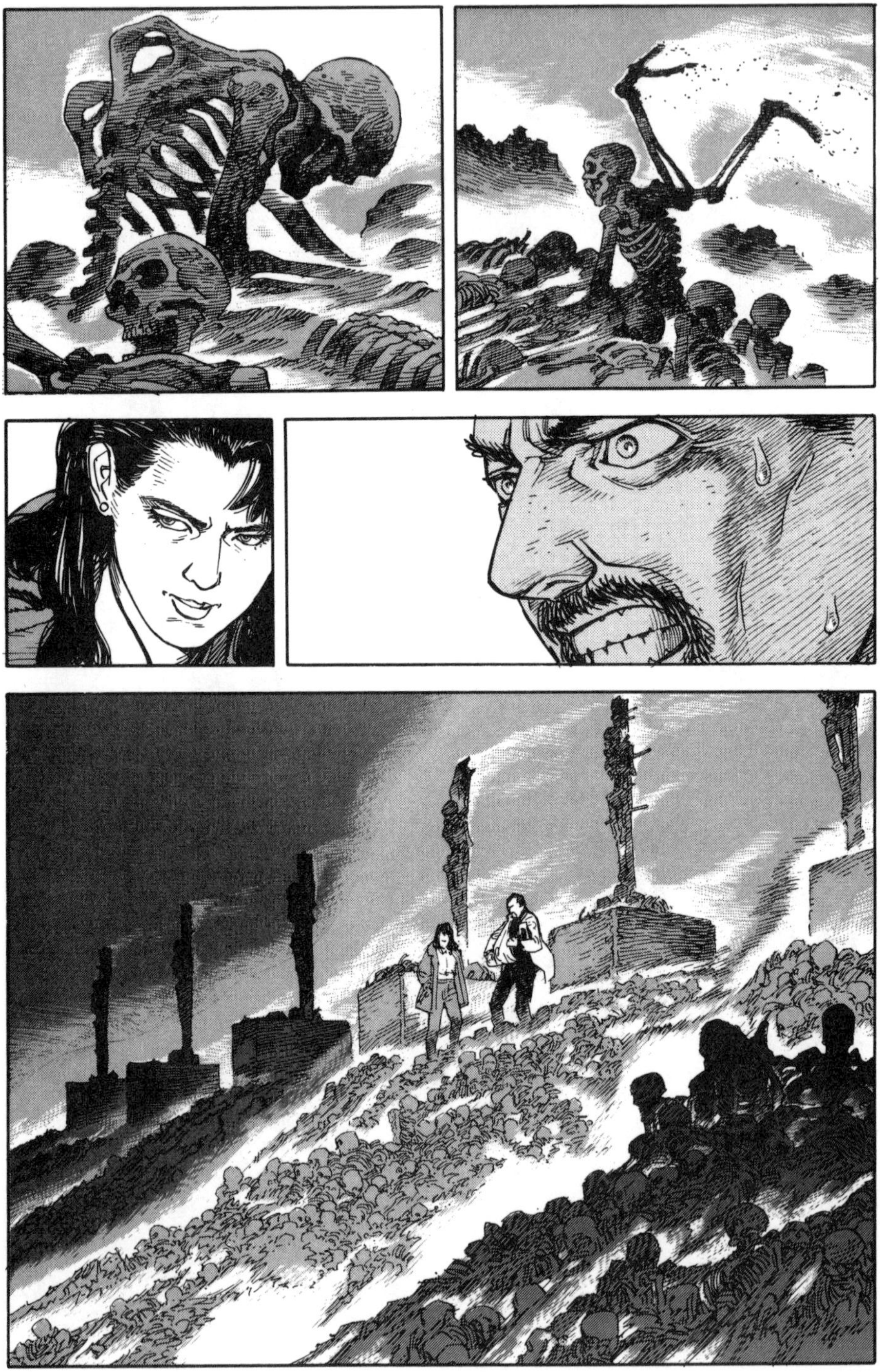

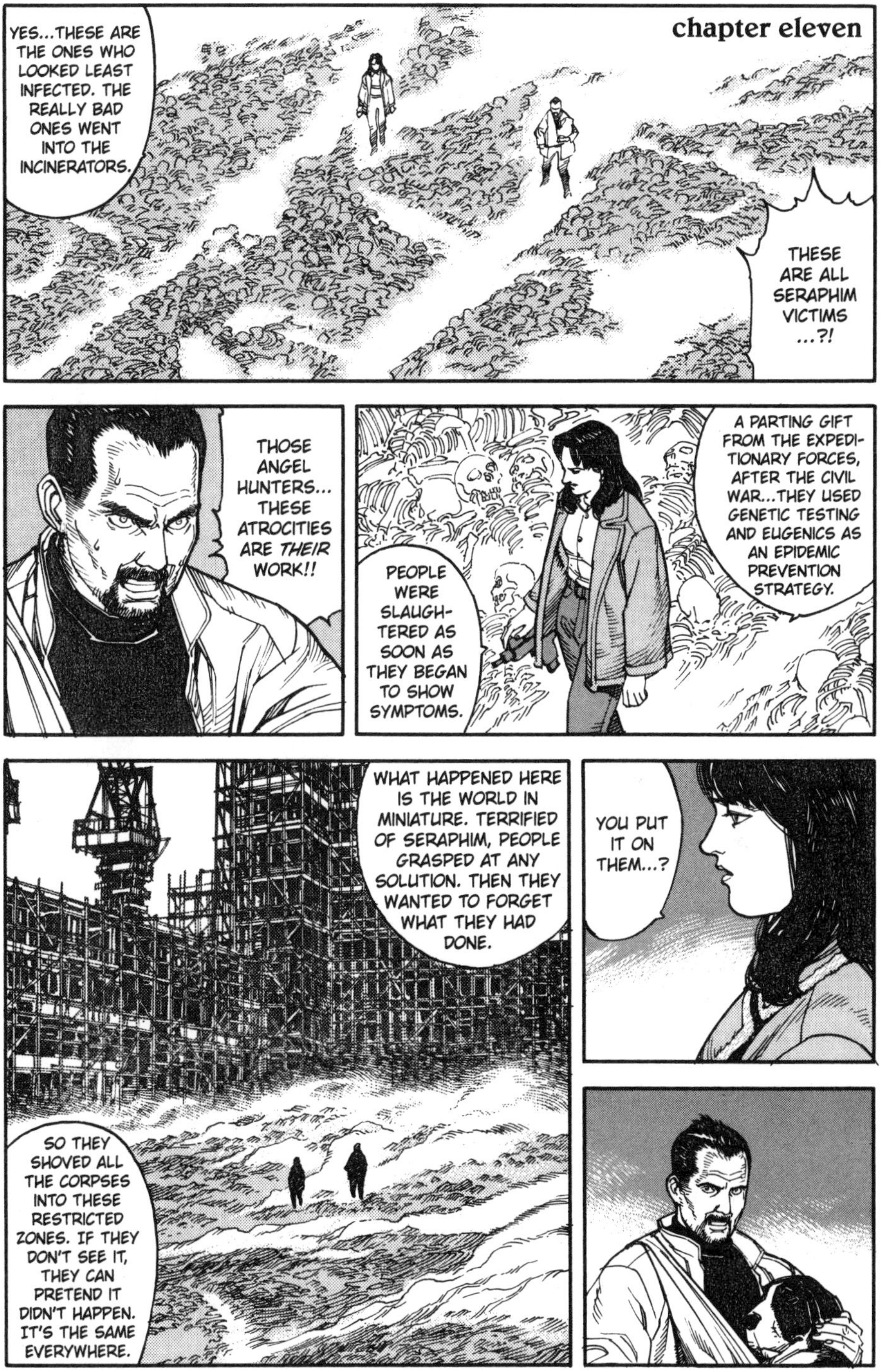
chapter eleven
THESE ARE ALL SERAPHIM VICTIMS ...?!
YES...THESE ARE THE ONES WHO LOOKED LEAST INFECTED. THE REALLY BAD ONES WENT INTO THE INCINERATORS.
A PARTING GIFT FROM THE EXPEDITIONARY FORCES, AFTER THE CIVIL WAR...THEY USED GENETIC TESTING AND EUGENICS AS AN EPIDEMIC PREVENTION STRATEGY.
PEOPLE WERE SLAUGHTERED AS SOON AS THEY BEGAN TO SHOW SYMPTOMS.
THOSE ANGEL HUNTERS... THESE ATROCITIES ARE *THEIR* WORK!!
YOU PUT IT ON THEM...?
WHAT HAPPENED HERE IS THE WORLD IN MINIATURE. TERRIFIED OF SERAPHIM, PEOPLE GRASPED AT ANY SOLUTION. THEN THEY WANTED TO FORGET WHAT THEY HAD DONE.
SO THEY SHOVED ALL THE CORPSES INTO THESE RESTRICTED ZONES. IF THEY DON'T SEE IT, THEY CAN PRETEND IT DIDN'T HAPPEN. IT'S THE SAME EVERYWHERE.

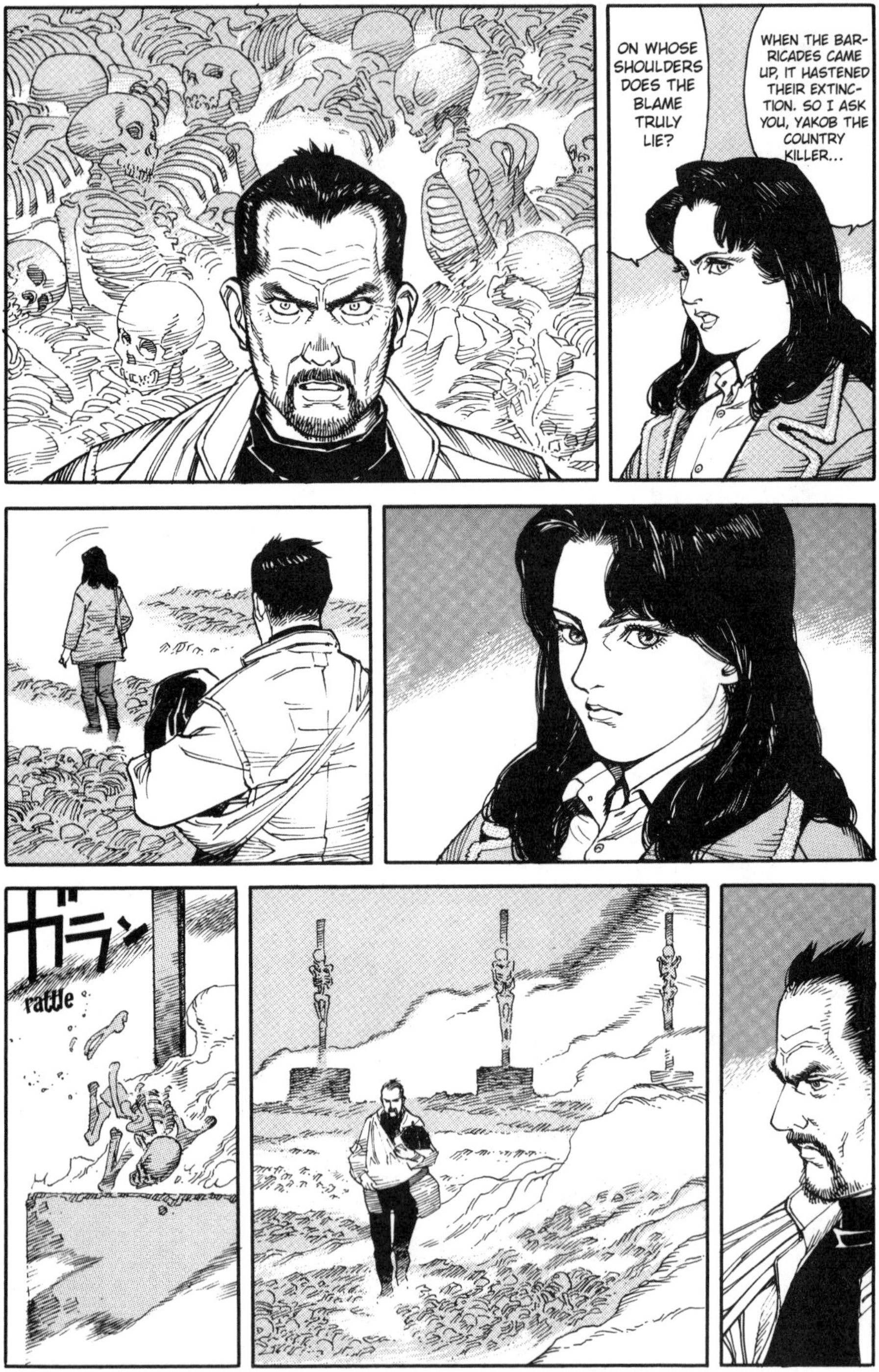
WHEN THE BAR-RICADES CAME UP, IT HASTENED THEIR EXTINC-TION. SO I ASK YOU, YAKOB THE COUNTRY KILLER...
ON WHOSE SHOULDERS DOES THE BLAME TRULY LIE?
ガラン
rattle

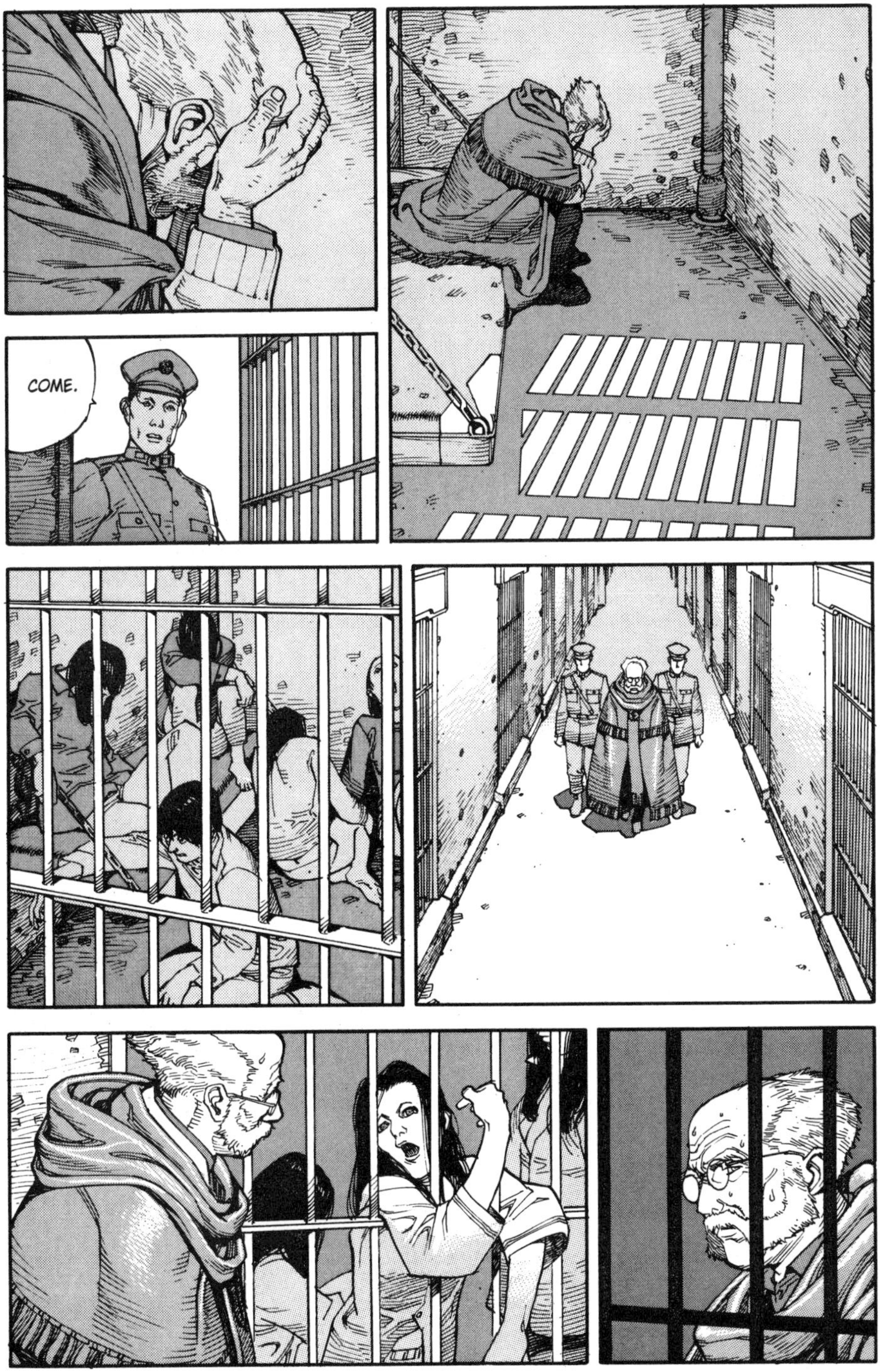
COME.

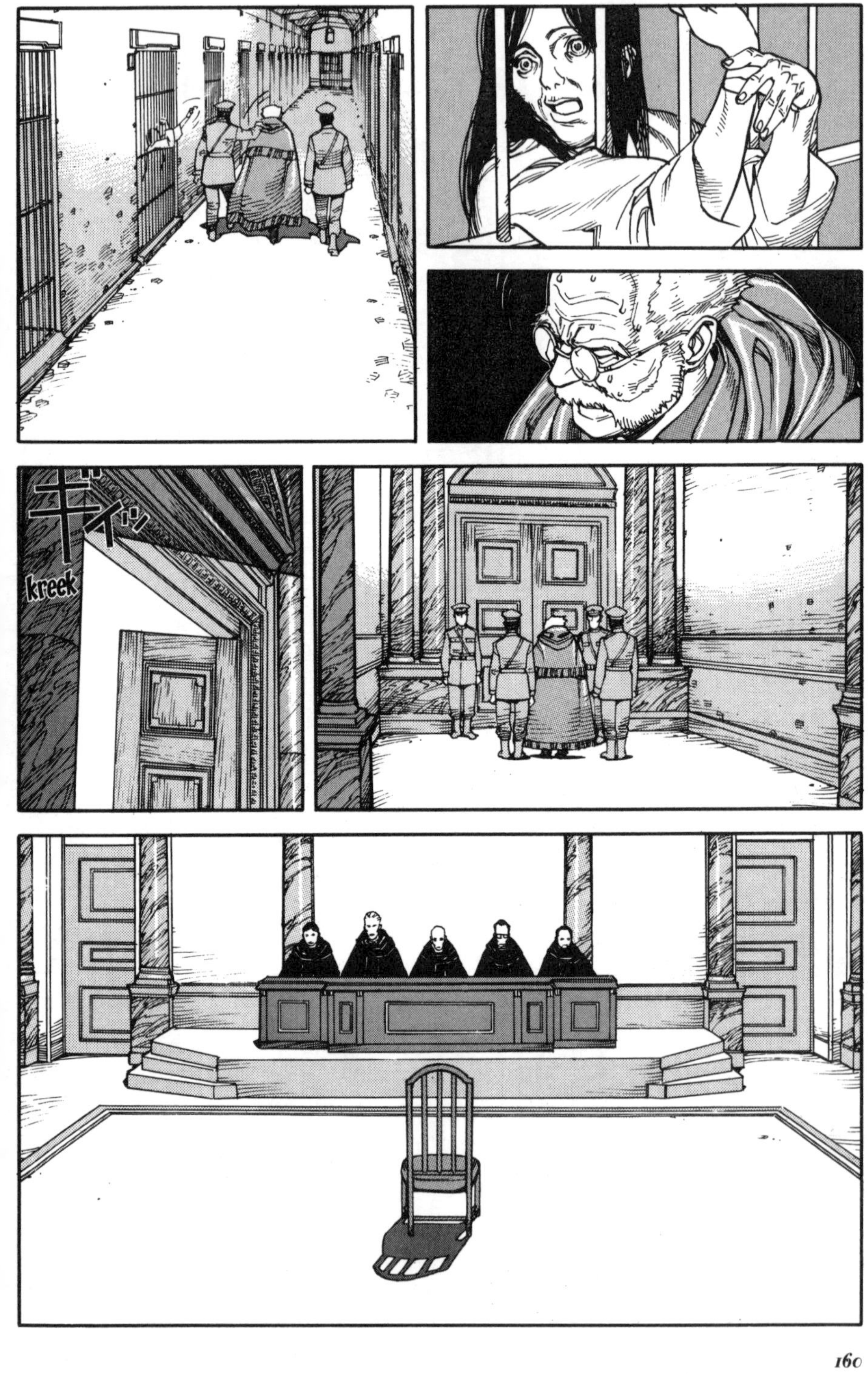
ギイッ
kreek

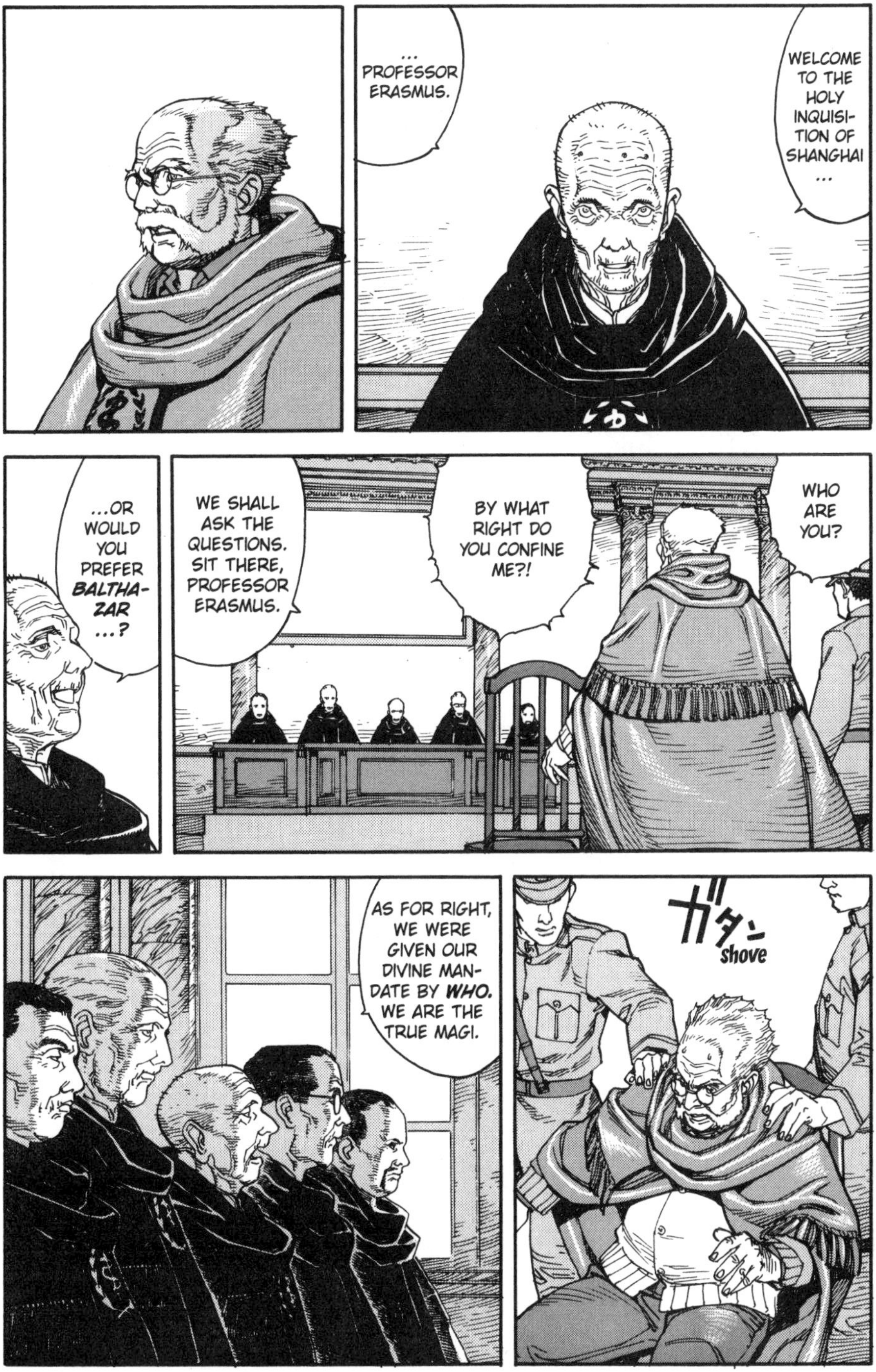
WELCOME TO THE HOLY INQUISITION OF SHANGHAI ...
... PROFESSOR ERASMUS.
WHO ARE YOU?
BY WHAT RIGHT DO YOU CONFINE ME?!
WE SHALL ASK THE QUESTIONS. SIT THERE, PROFESSOR ERASMUS.
...OR WOULD YOU PREFER ***BALTHAZAR*** ...?
ガタン
shove
AS FOR RIGHT, WE WERE GIVEN OUR DIVINE MANDATE BY ***WHO***. WE ARE THE TRUE MAGI.

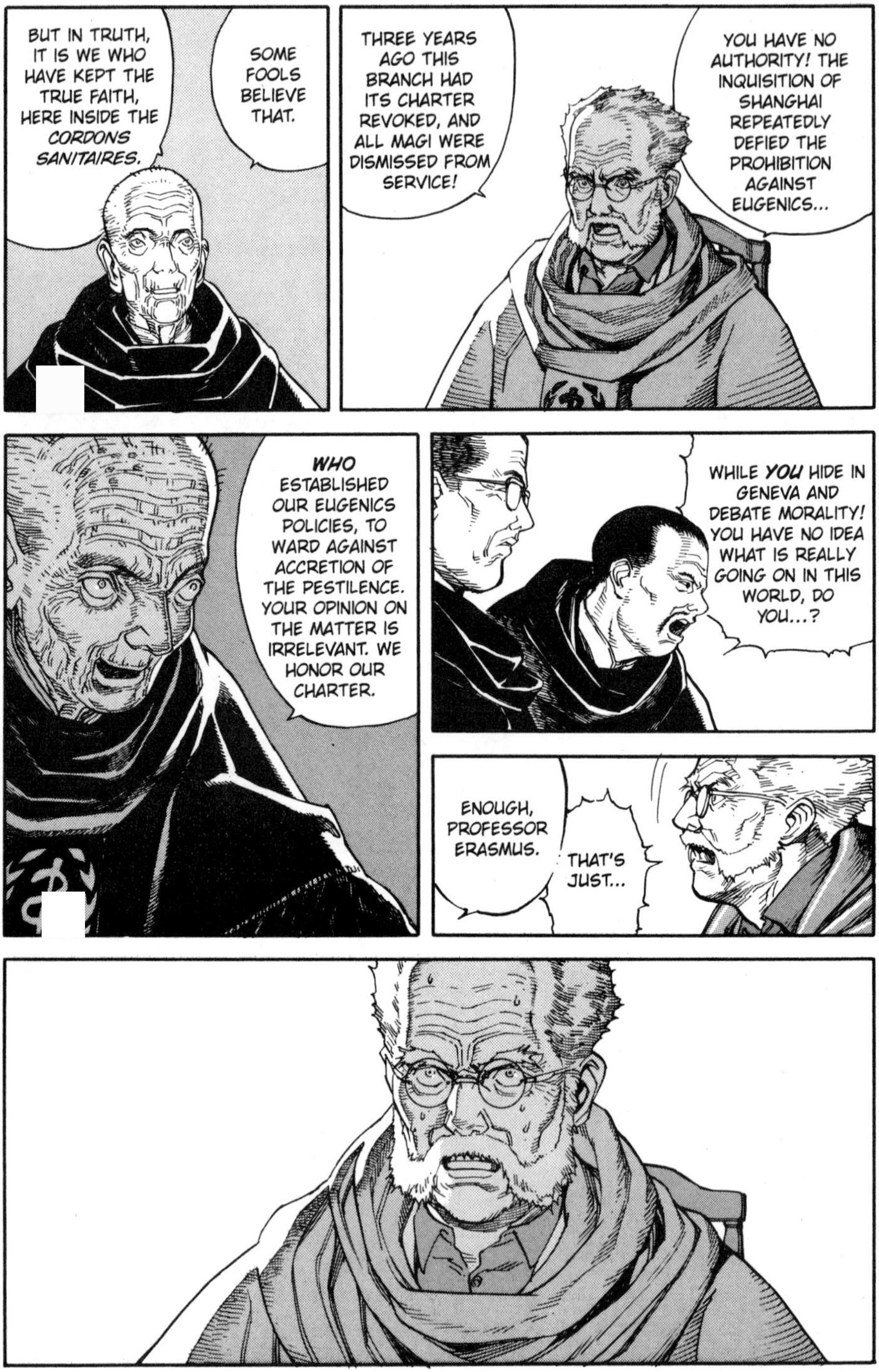
YOU HAVE NO AUTHORITY! THE INQUISITION OF SHANGHAI REPEATEDLY DEFIED THE PROHIBITION AGAINST EUGENICS...
THREE YEARS AGO THIS BRANCH HAD ITS CHARTER REVOKED, AND ALL MAGI WERE DISMISSED FROM SERVICE!
SOME FOOLS BELIEVE THAT.
BUT IN TRUTH, IT IS WE WHO HAVE KEPT THE TRUE FAITH, HERE INSIDE THE *CORDONS SANITAIRES*.
WHILE ***YOU*** HIDE IN GENEVA AND DEBATE MORALITY! YOU HAVE NO IDEA WHAT IS REALLY GOING ON IN THIS WORLD, DO YOU...?
THAT'S JUST...
ENOUGH, PROFESSOR ERASMUS.
WHO ESTABLISHED OUR EUGENICS POLICIES, TO WARD AGAINST ACCRETION OF THE PESTILENCE. YOUR OPINION ON THE MATTER IS IRRELEVANT. WE HONOR OUR CHARTER.

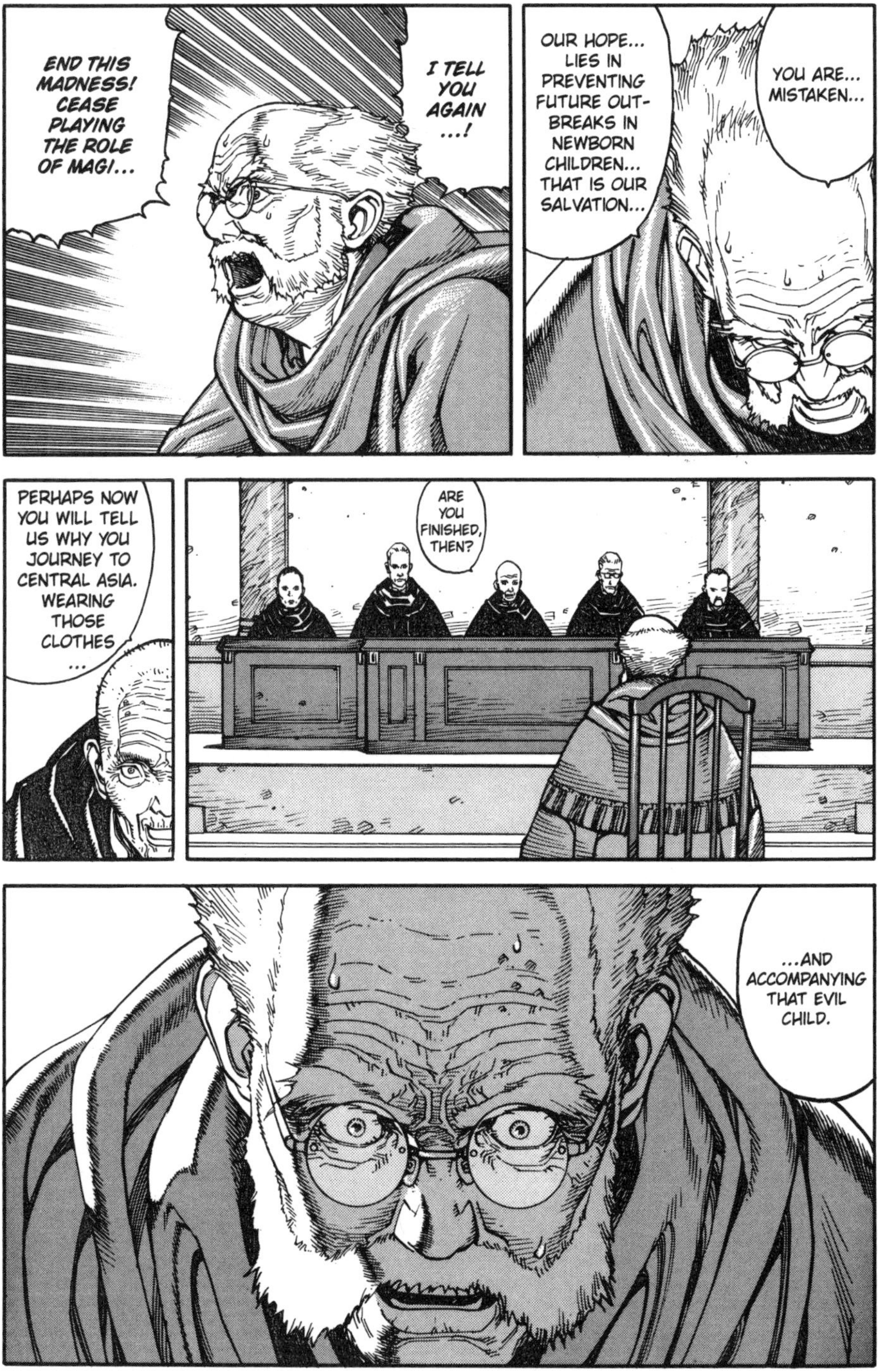
YOU ARE... MISTAKEN...
OUR HOPE... LIES IN PREVENTING FUTURE OUT-BREAKS IN NEWBORN CHILDREN... THAT IS OUR SALVATION...
I TELL YOU AGAIN ...!
END THIS MADNESS! CEASE PLAYING THE ROLE OF MAGI...
ARE YOU FINISHED, THEN?
PERHAPS NOW YOU WILL TELL US WHY YOU JOURNEY TO CENTRAL ASIA. WEARING THOSE CLOTHES ...
...AND ACCOMPANYING THAT EVIL CHILD.

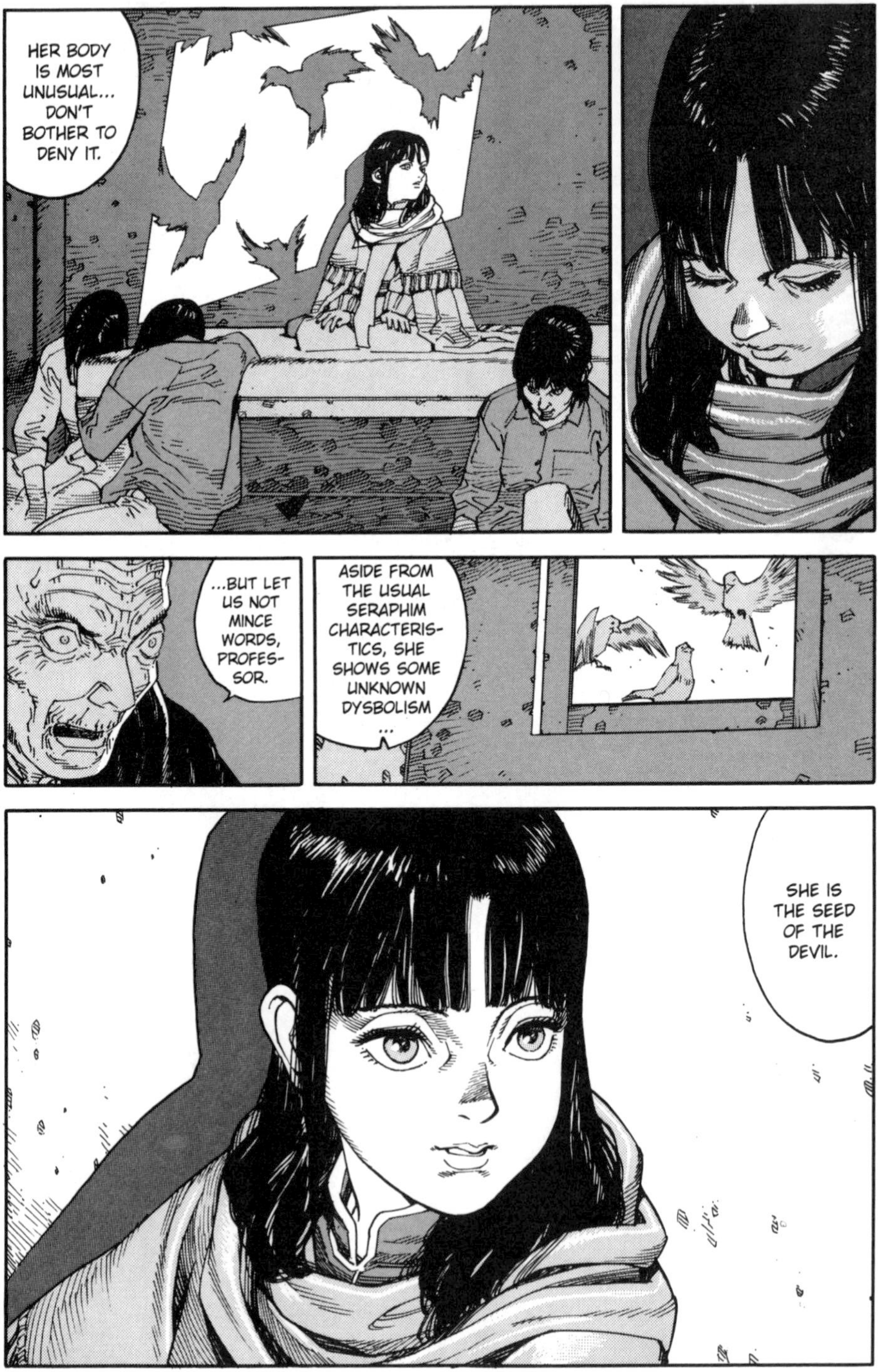
HER BODY IS MOST UNUSUAL... DON'T BOTHER TO DENY IT.
ASIDE FROM THE USUAL SERAPHIM CHARACTERIS-TICS, SHE SHOWS SOME UNKNOWN DYSBOLISM ...
...BUT LET US NOT MINCE WORDS, PROFES-SOR.
SHE IS THE SEED OF THE DEVIL.

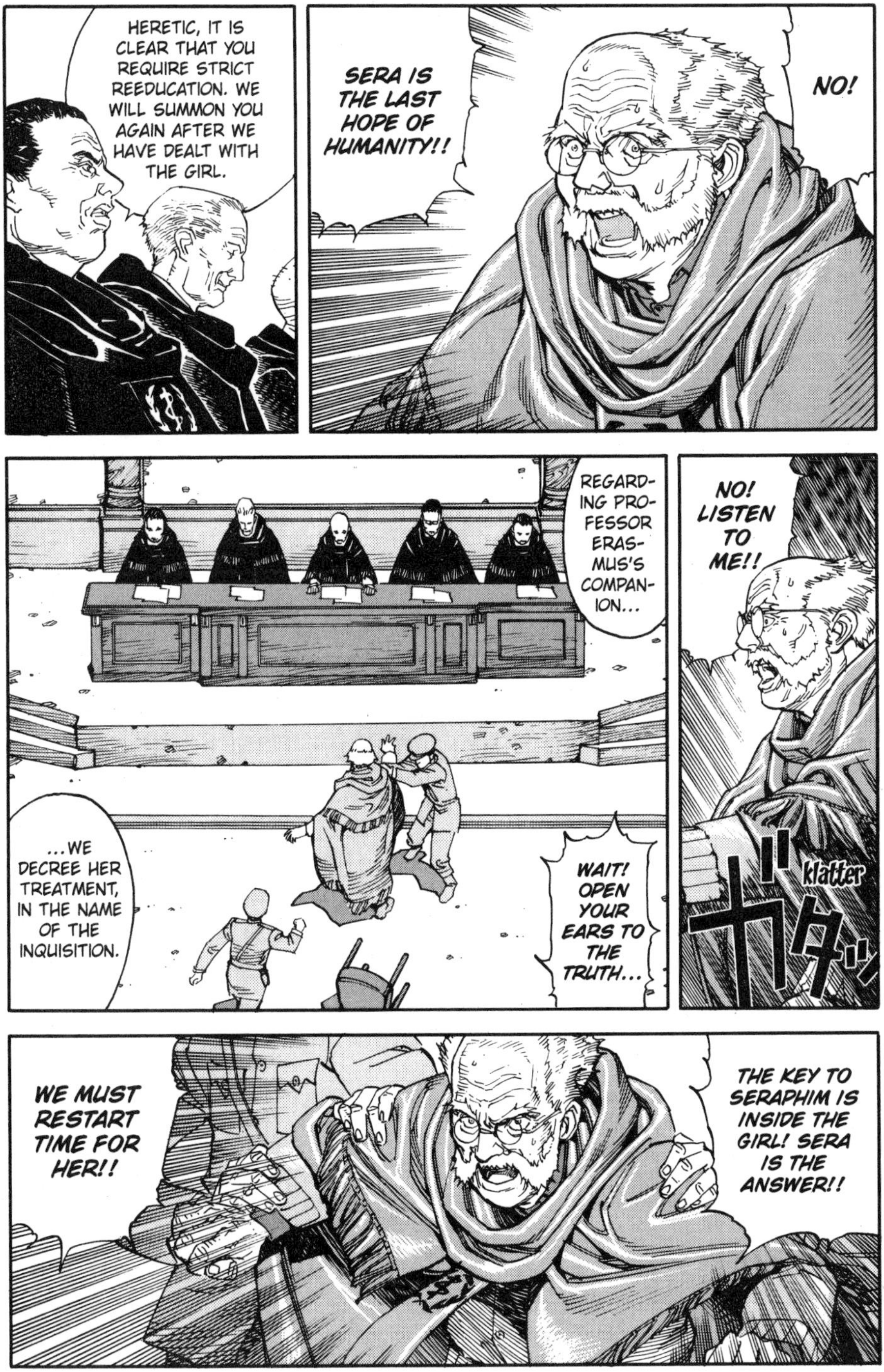
NO!
SERA IS THE LAST HOPE OF HUMANITY!!
HERETIC, IT IS CLEAR THAT YOU REQUIRE STRICT REEDUCATION. WE WILL SUMMON YOU AGAIN AFTER WE HAVE DEALT WITH THE GIRL.
NO! LISTEN TO ME!!
klatter
ガタッ
REGARDING PROFESSOR ERASMUS'S COMPANION...
...WE DECREE HER TREATMENT, IN THE NAME OF THE INQUISITION.
WAIT! OPEN YOUR EARS TO THE TRUTH...
THE KEY TO SERAPHIM IS INSIDE THE GIRL! SERA IS THE ANSWER!!
WE MUST RESTART TIME FOR HER!!

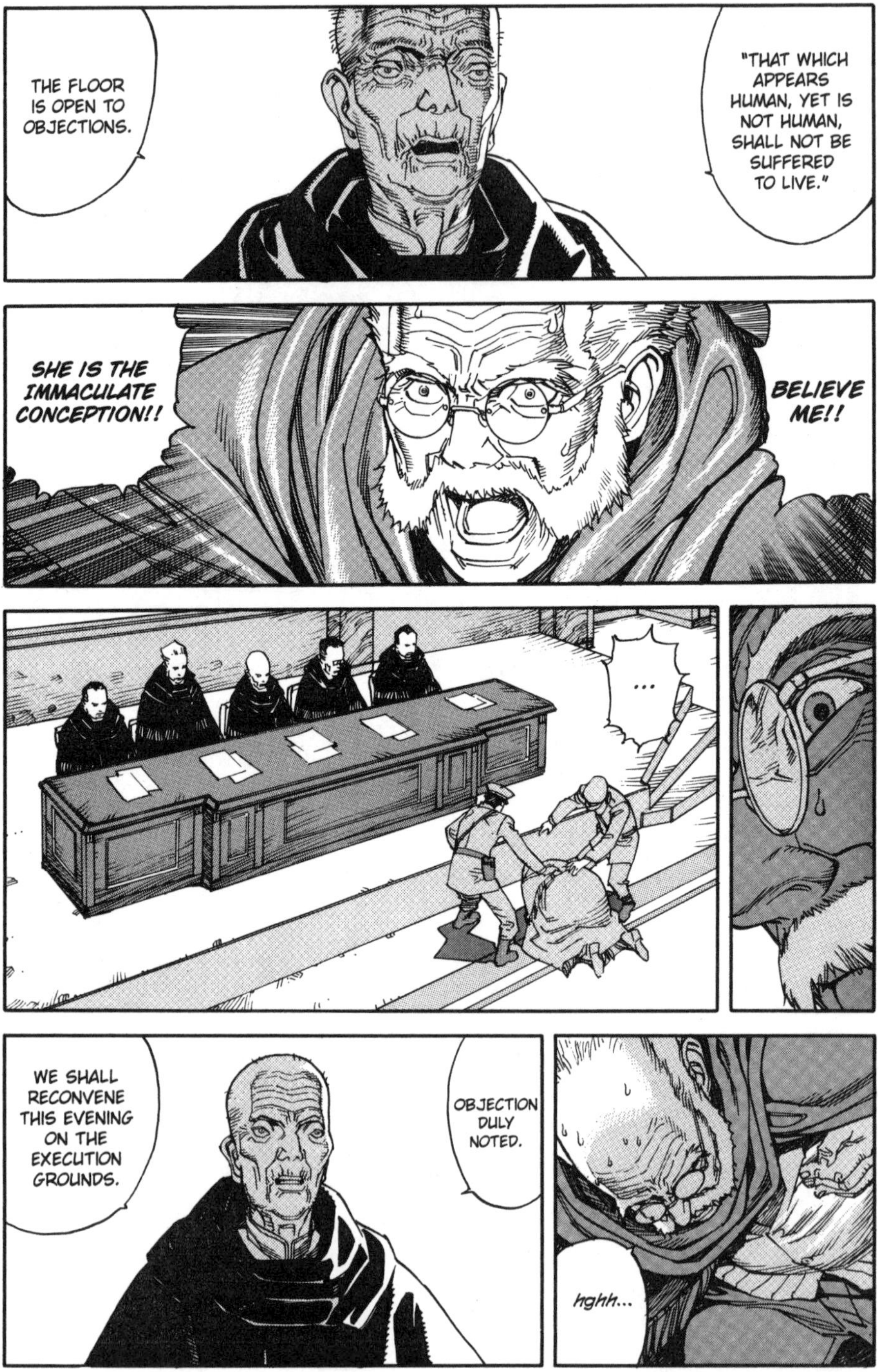
"THAT WHICH APPEARS HUMAN, YET IS NOT HUMAN, SHALL NOT BE SUFFERED TO LIVE."
THE FLOOR IS OPEN TO OBJECTIONS.
BELIEVE ME!!
SHE IS THE IMMACULATE CONCEPTION!!
...
hghh...
OBJECTION DULY NOTED.
WE SHALL RECONVENE THIS EVENING ON THE EXECUTION GROUNDS.

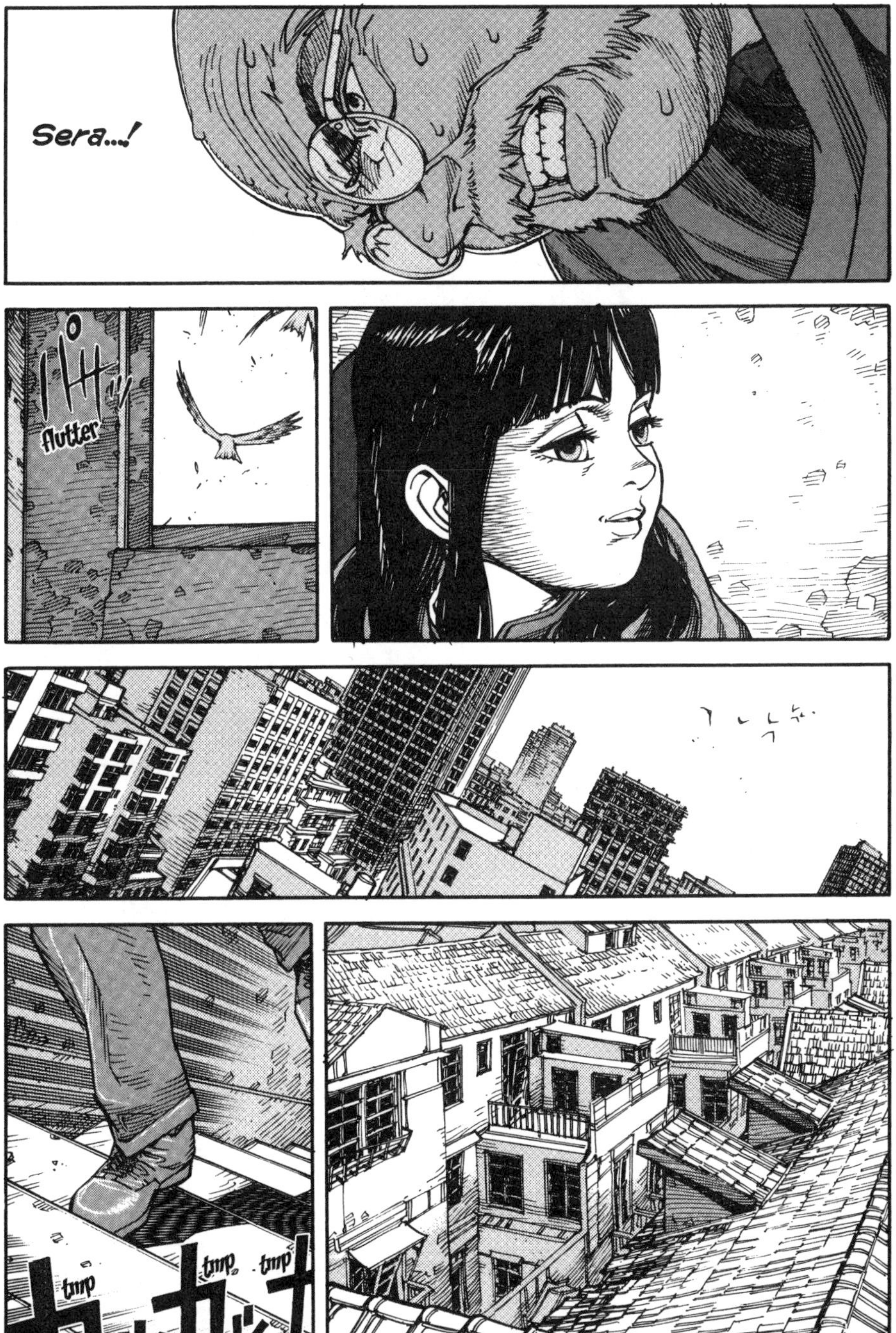
Sera...!
flutter
tmp
tmp
tmp

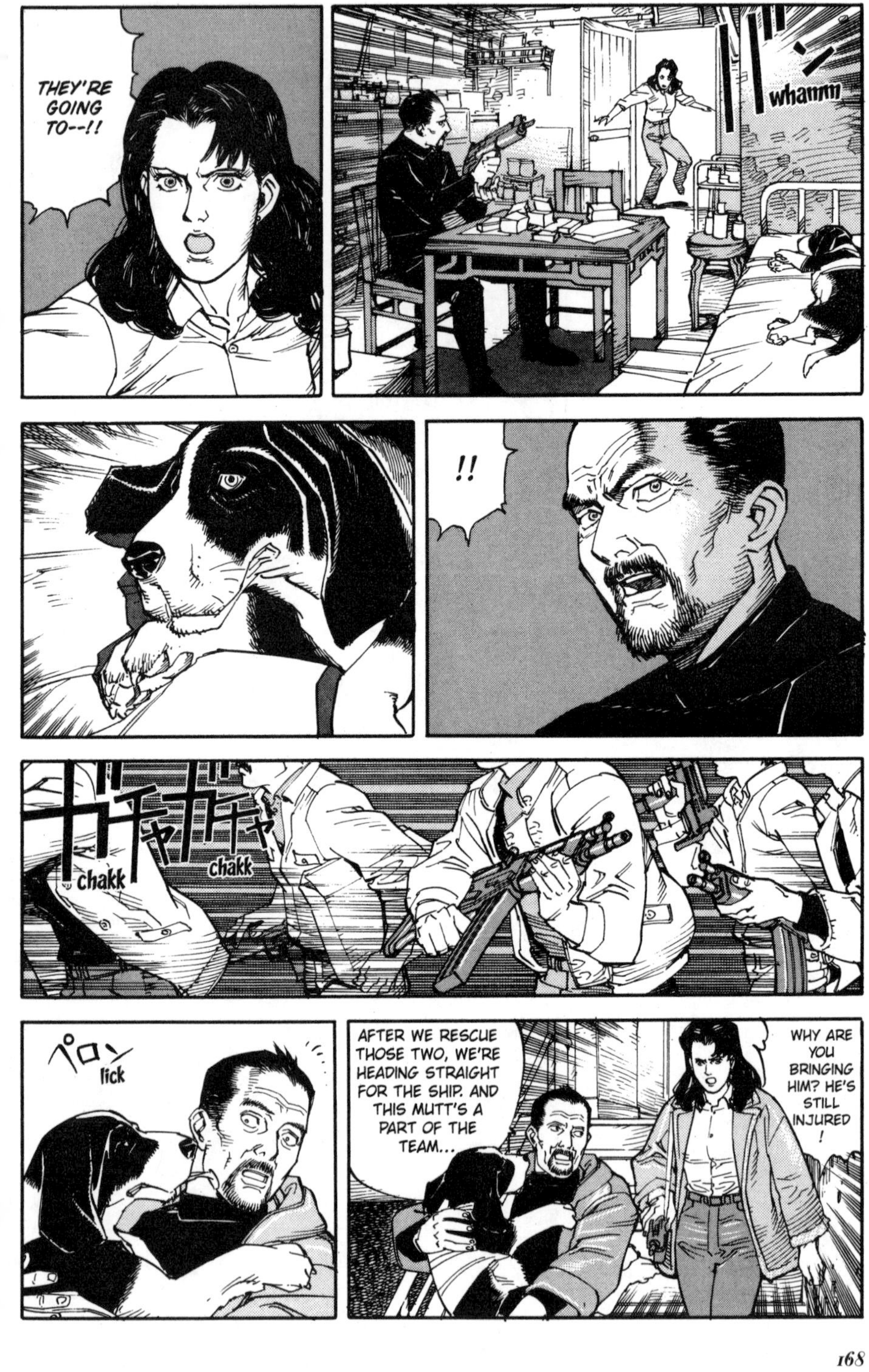
whamm
THEY'RE GOING TO--!!
!!
ガチャガチャ
chakk
chakk
WHY ARE YOU BRINGING HIM? HE'S STILL INJURED!
AFTER WE RESCUE THOSE TWO, WE'RE HEADING STRAIGHT FOR THE SHIP. AND THIS MUTT'S A PART OF THE TEAM...
ペロン
lick

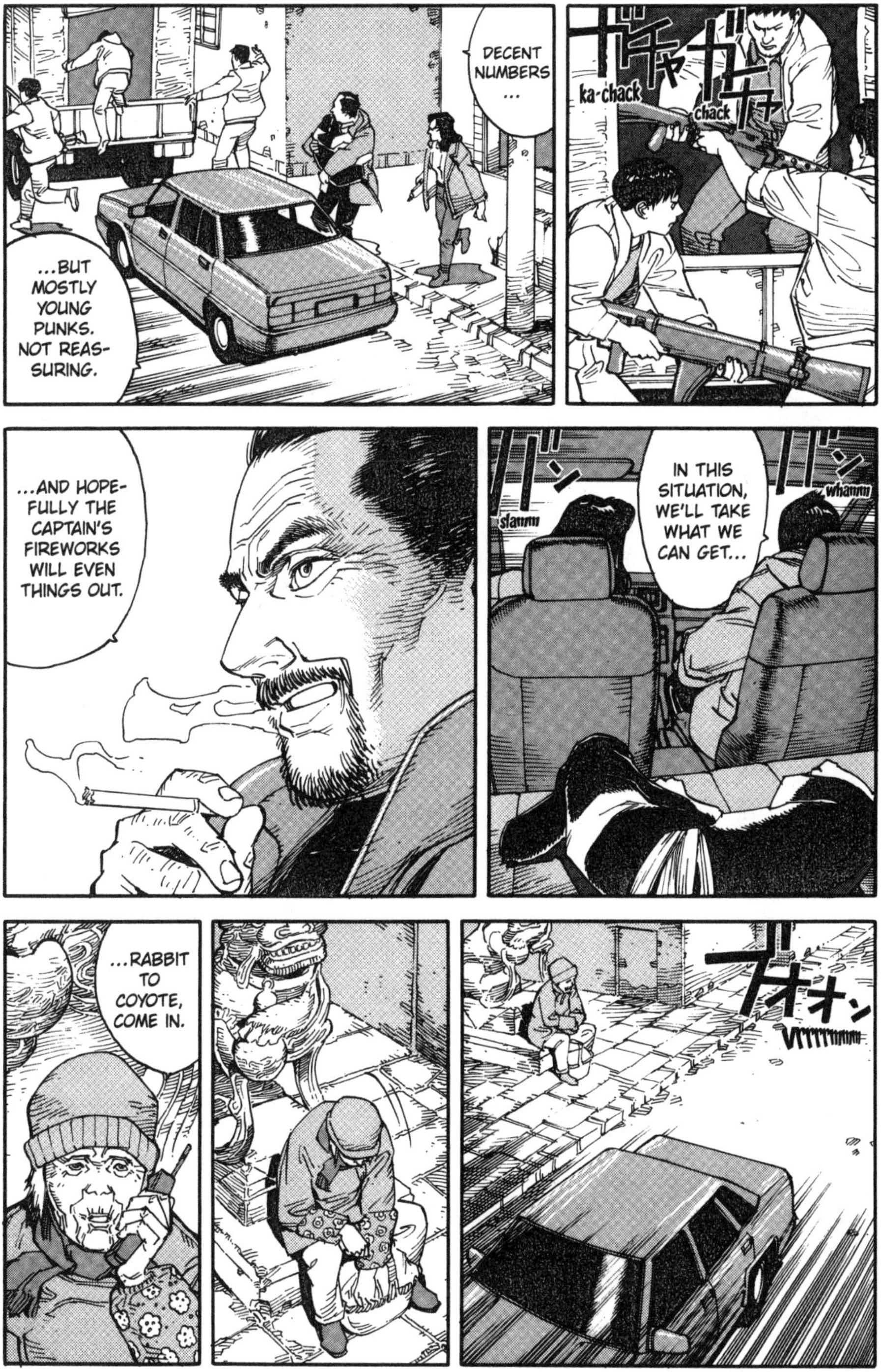
ka-chack
chack
DECENT NUMBERS ...
...BUT MOSTLY YOUNG PUNKS. NOT REAS-SURING.
whammm
slammm
IN THIS SITUATION, WE'LL TAKE WHAT WE CAN GET...
...AND HOPE-FULLY THE CAPTAIN'S FIREWORKS WILL EVEN THINGS OUT.
vrrrrmmm
...RABBIT TO COYOTE, COME IN.

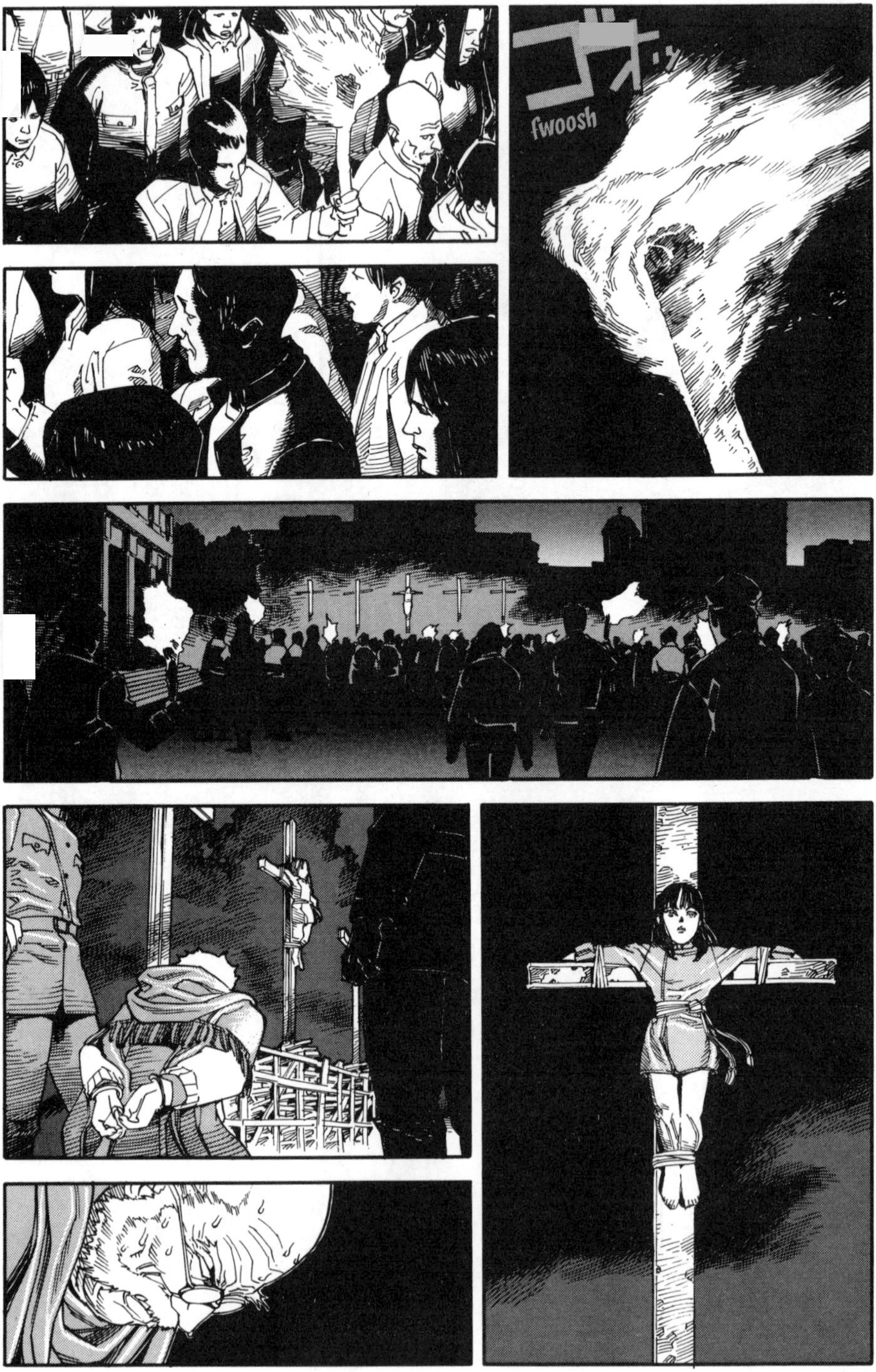
fwoosh

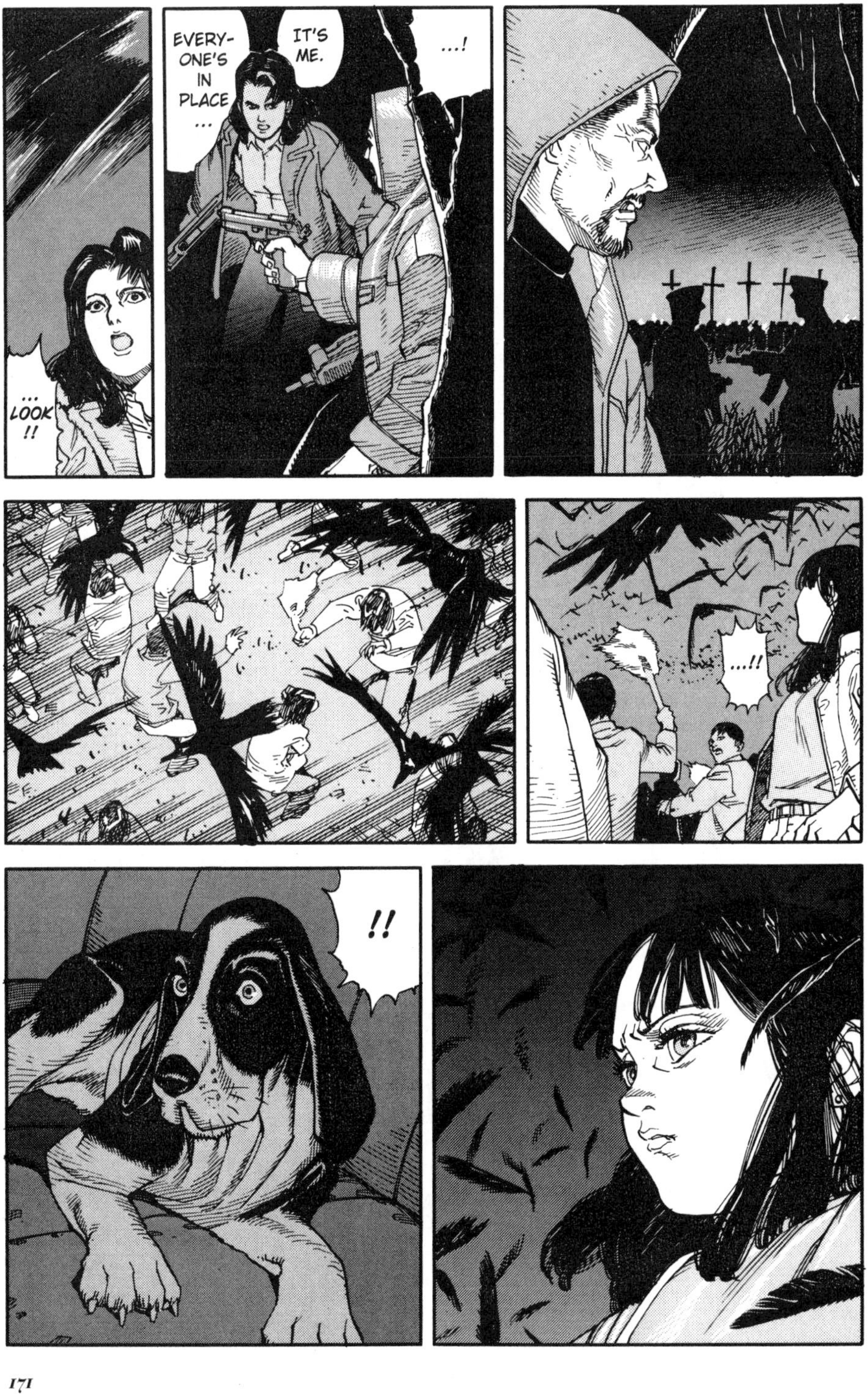
...!
IT'S ME.
EVERY-ONE'S IN PLACE ...
... LOOK !!
...!!
!!

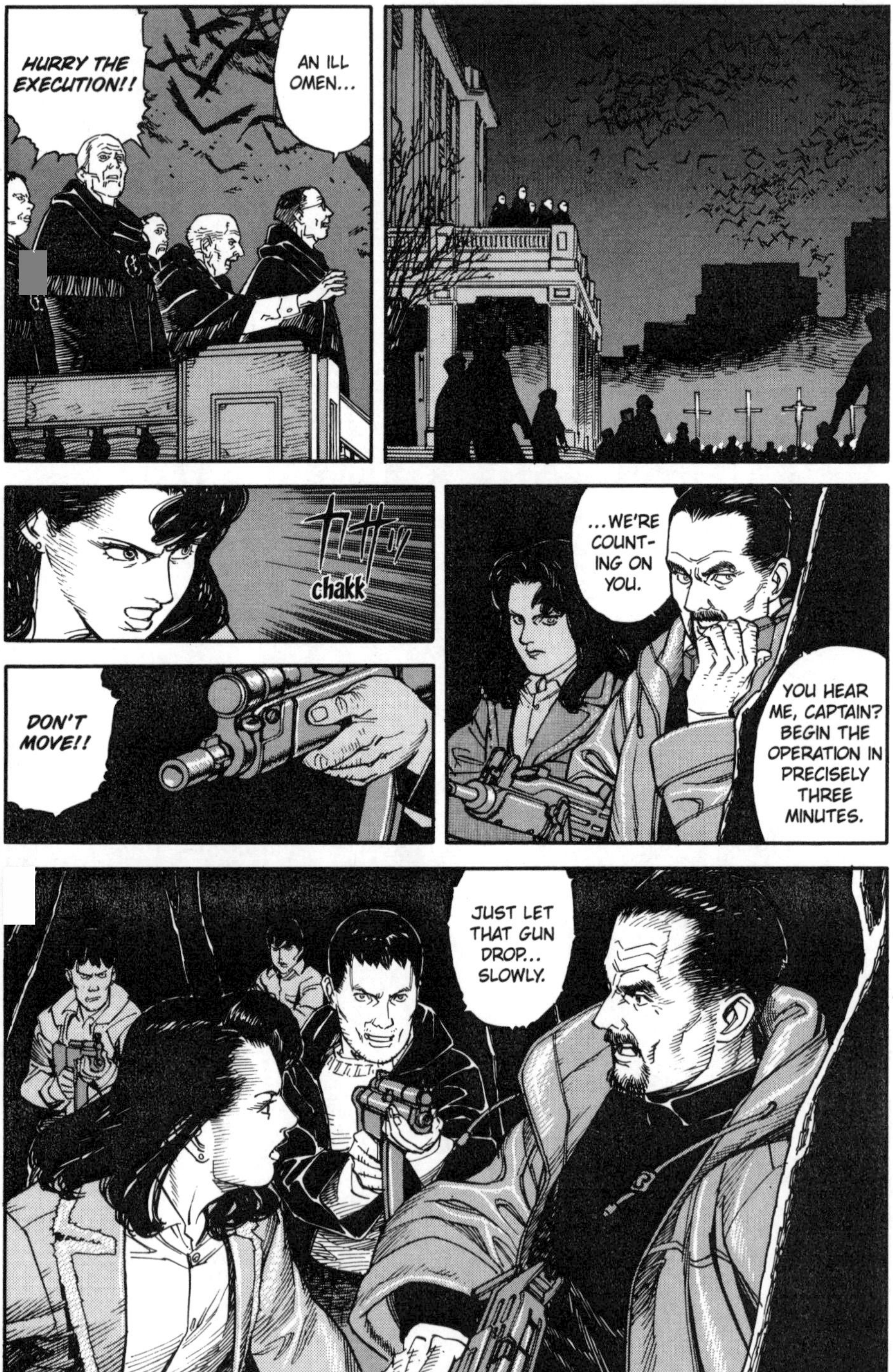
AN ILL OMEN...
HURRY THE EXECUTION!!
...WE'RE COUNTING ON YOU.
YOU HEAR ME, CAPTAIN? BEGIN THE OPERATION IN PRECISELY THREE MINUTES.
chakk
DON'T MOVE!!
JUST LET THAT GUN DROP... SLOWLY.

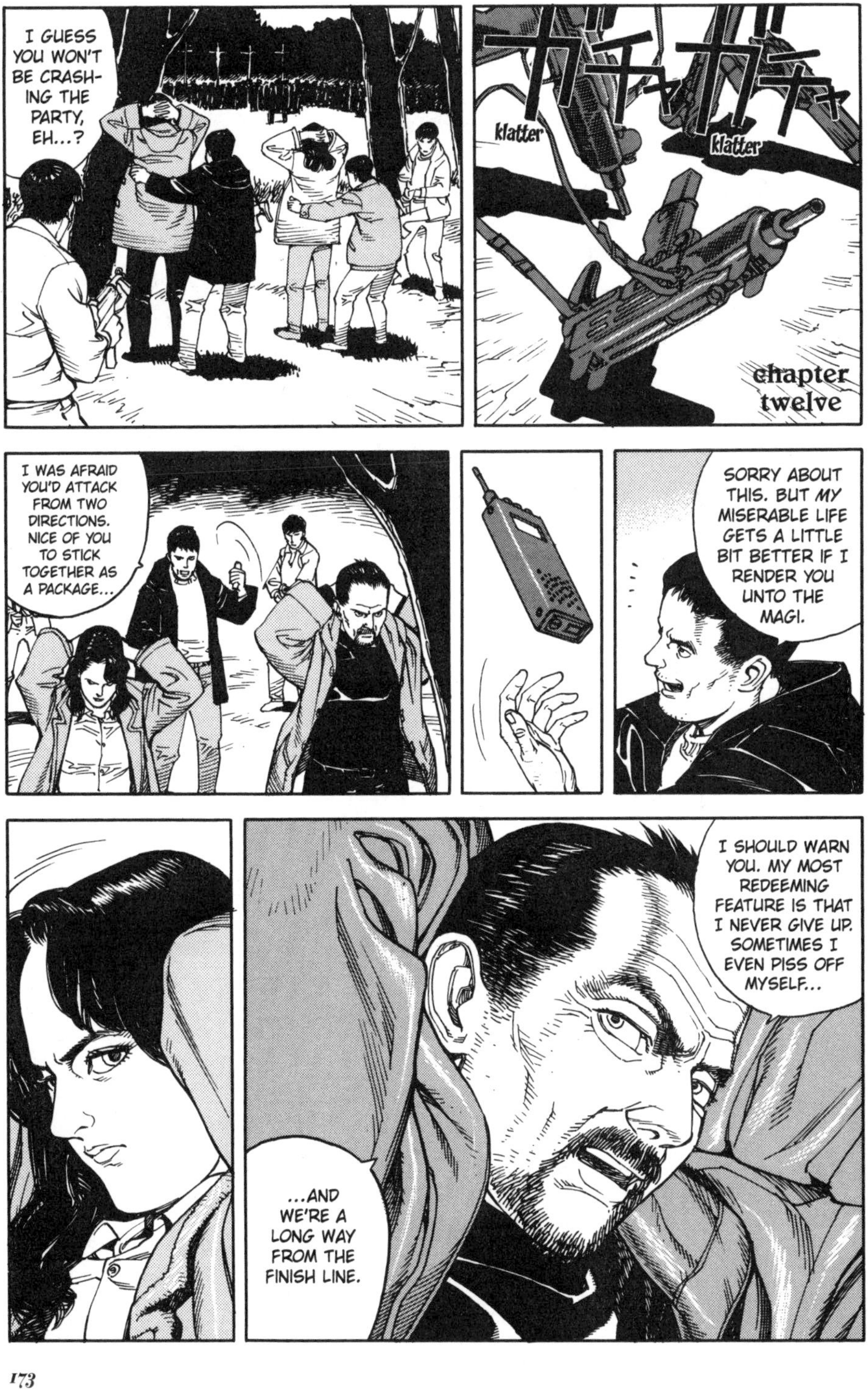
ガチャガチャ
klatter
klatter
chapter twelve
I GUESS YOU WON'T BE CRASHING THE PARTY, EH...?
SORRY ABOUT THIS. BUT MY MISERABLE LIFE GETS A LITTLE BIT BETTER IF I RENDER YOU UNTO THE MAGI.
I WAS AFRAID YOU'D ATTACK FROM TWO DIRECTIONS. NICE OF YOU TO STICK TOGETHER AS A PACKAGE...
I SHOULD WARN YOU. MY MOST REDEEMING FEATURE IS THAT I NEVER GIVE UP. SOMETIMES I EVEN PISS OFF MYSELF...
...AND WE'RE A LONG WAY FROM THE FINISH LINE.

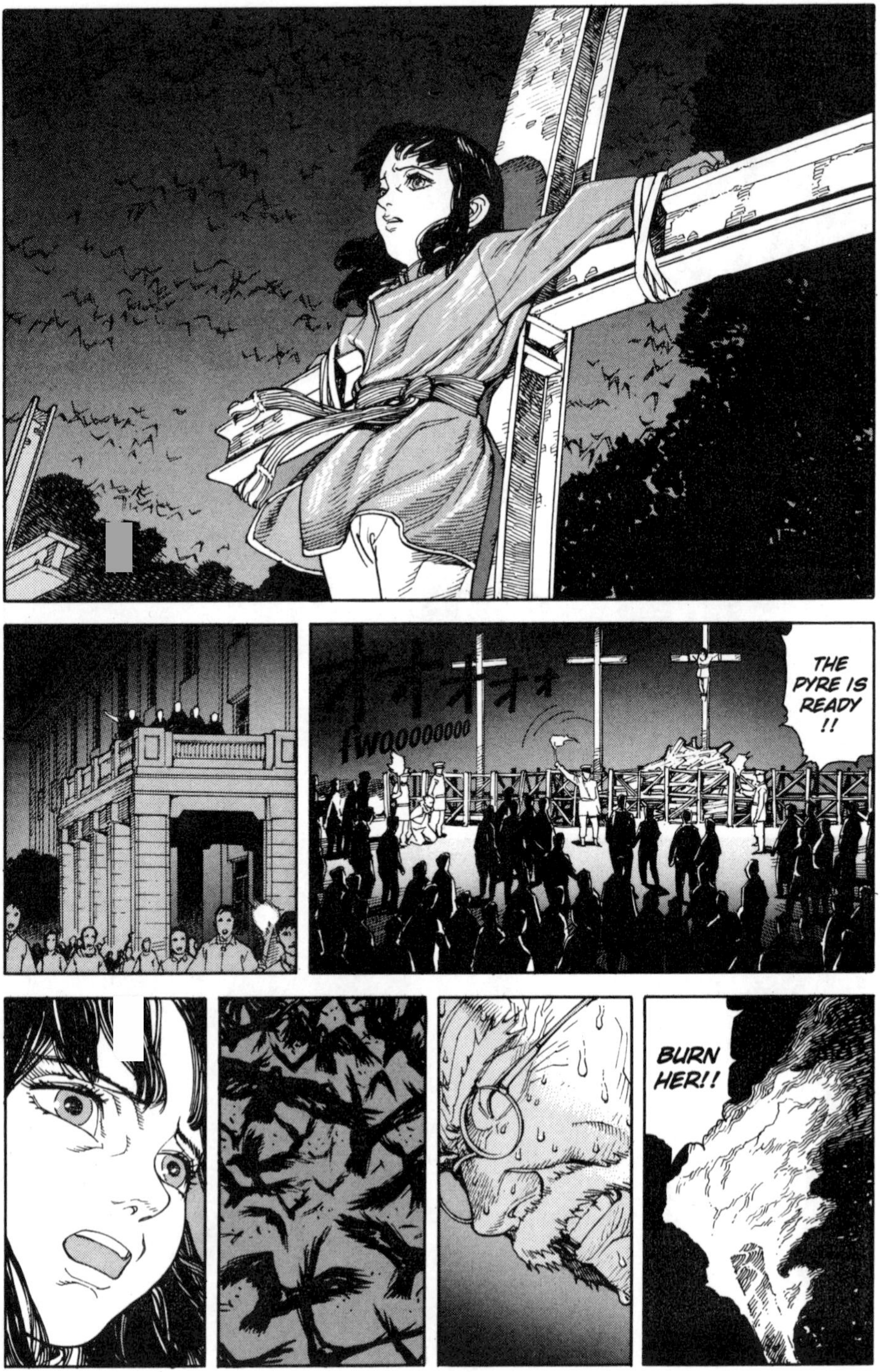
オオオォ
fwaoooooooo
THE PYRE IS READY !!
BURN HER!!

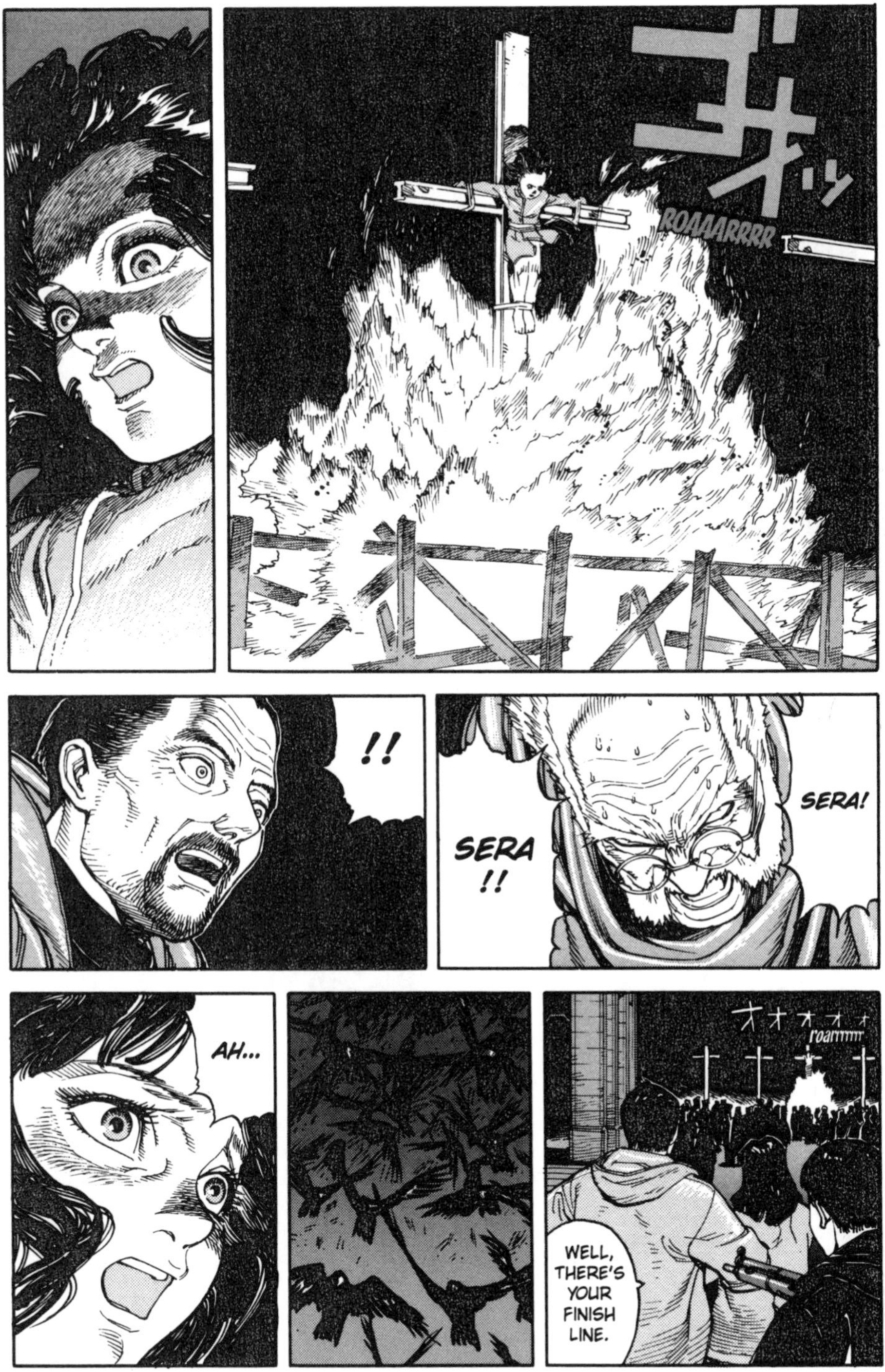
ゴォッ
ROAAARRRR
SERA!
SERA !!
!!
オオオオォ
roarrrrr
WELL, THERE'S YOUR FINISH LINE.
AH...

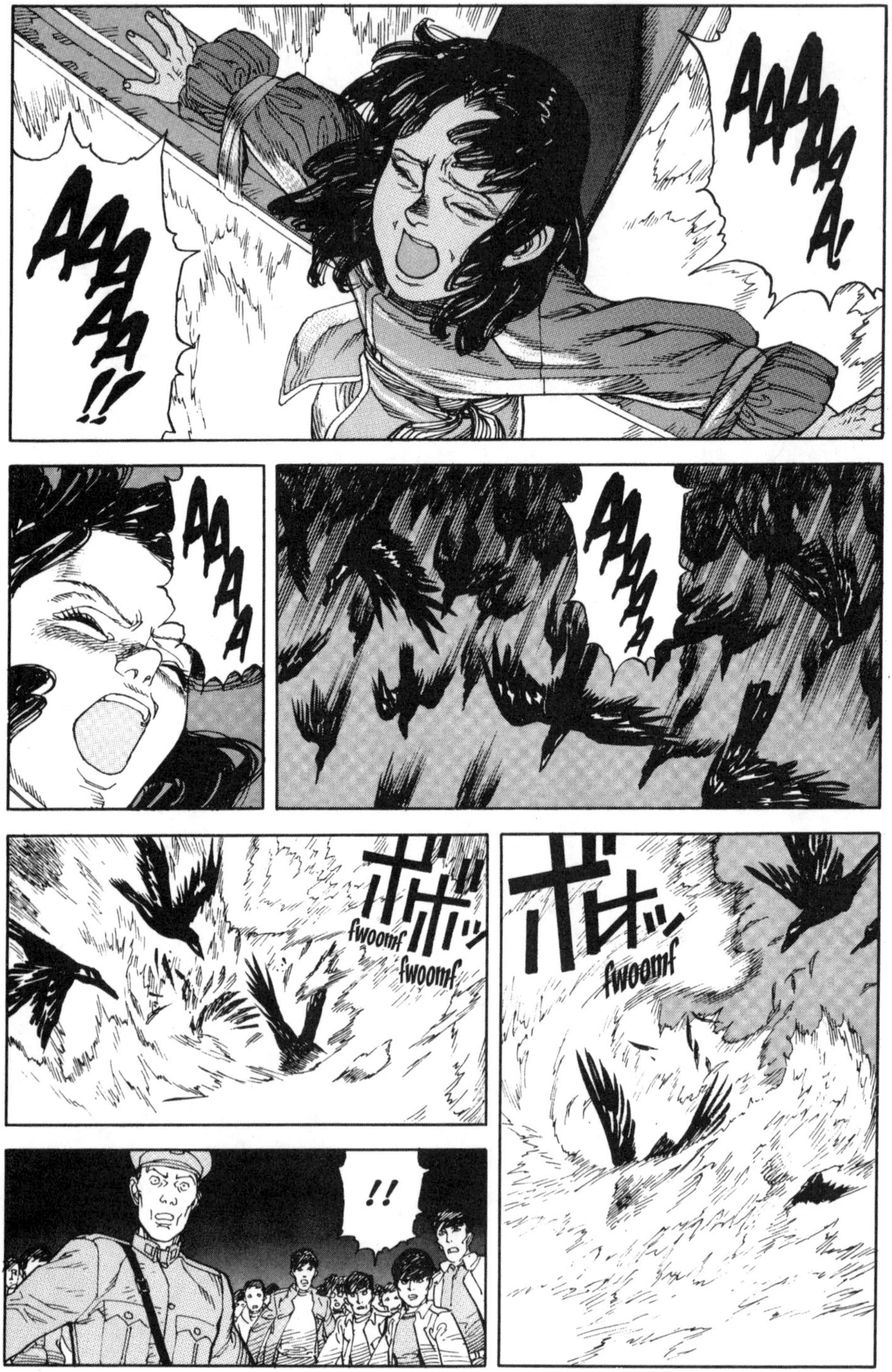
AAAAAAA!
AAAAAAA!!
AAAAAA
AAAAA
ボオッ
fwoomf
ボボッ
fwoomf
fwoomf
!!

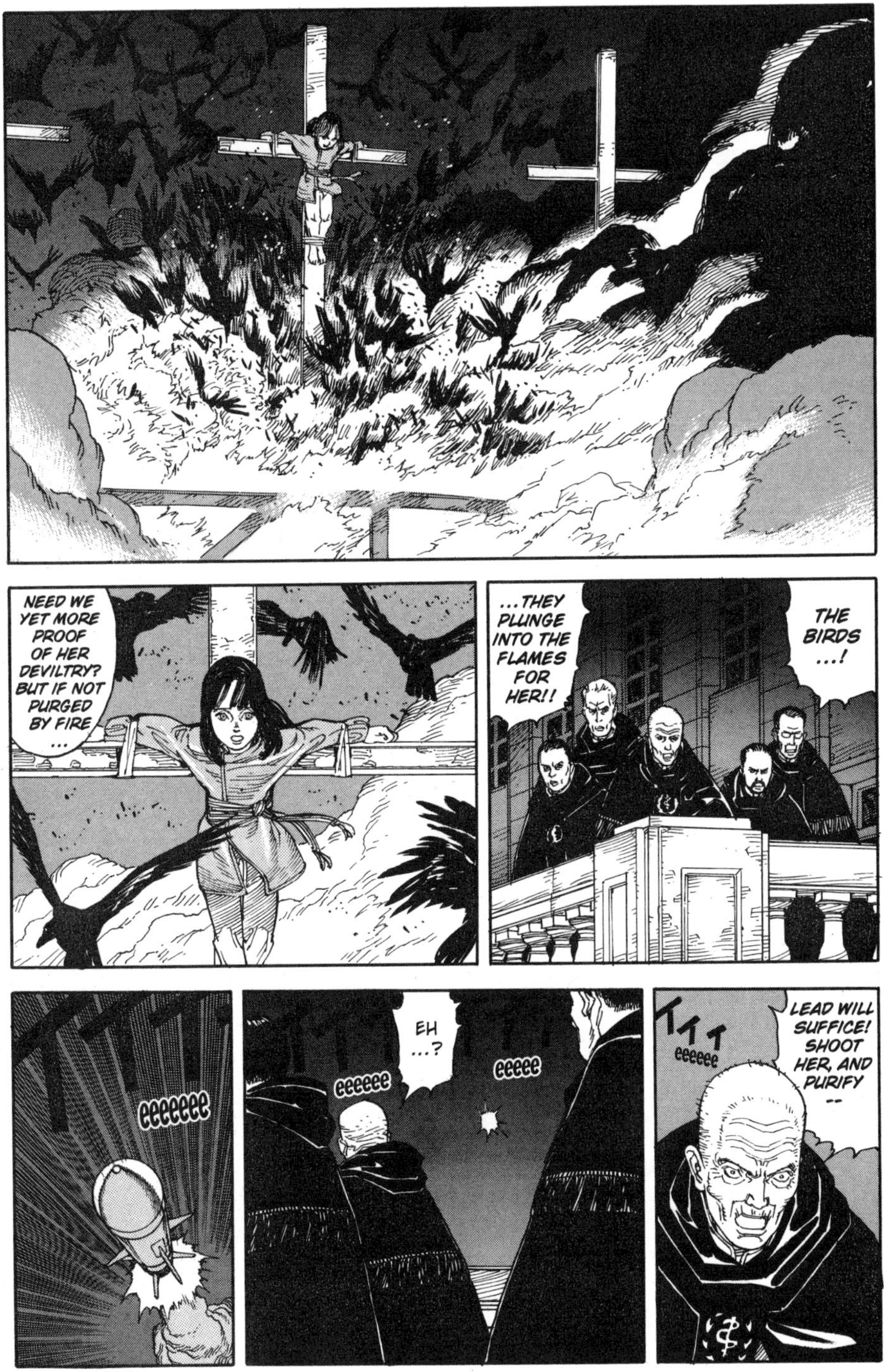
THE BIRDS ...!
...THEY PLUNGE INTO THE FLAMES FOR HER!!
NEED WE YET MORE PROOF OF HER DEVILTRY? BUT IF NOT PURGED BY FIRE ...
LEAD WILL SUFFICE! SHOOT HER, AND PURIFY --
eeeeee
eeeee
EH ...?
eeeeee
eeeeeee

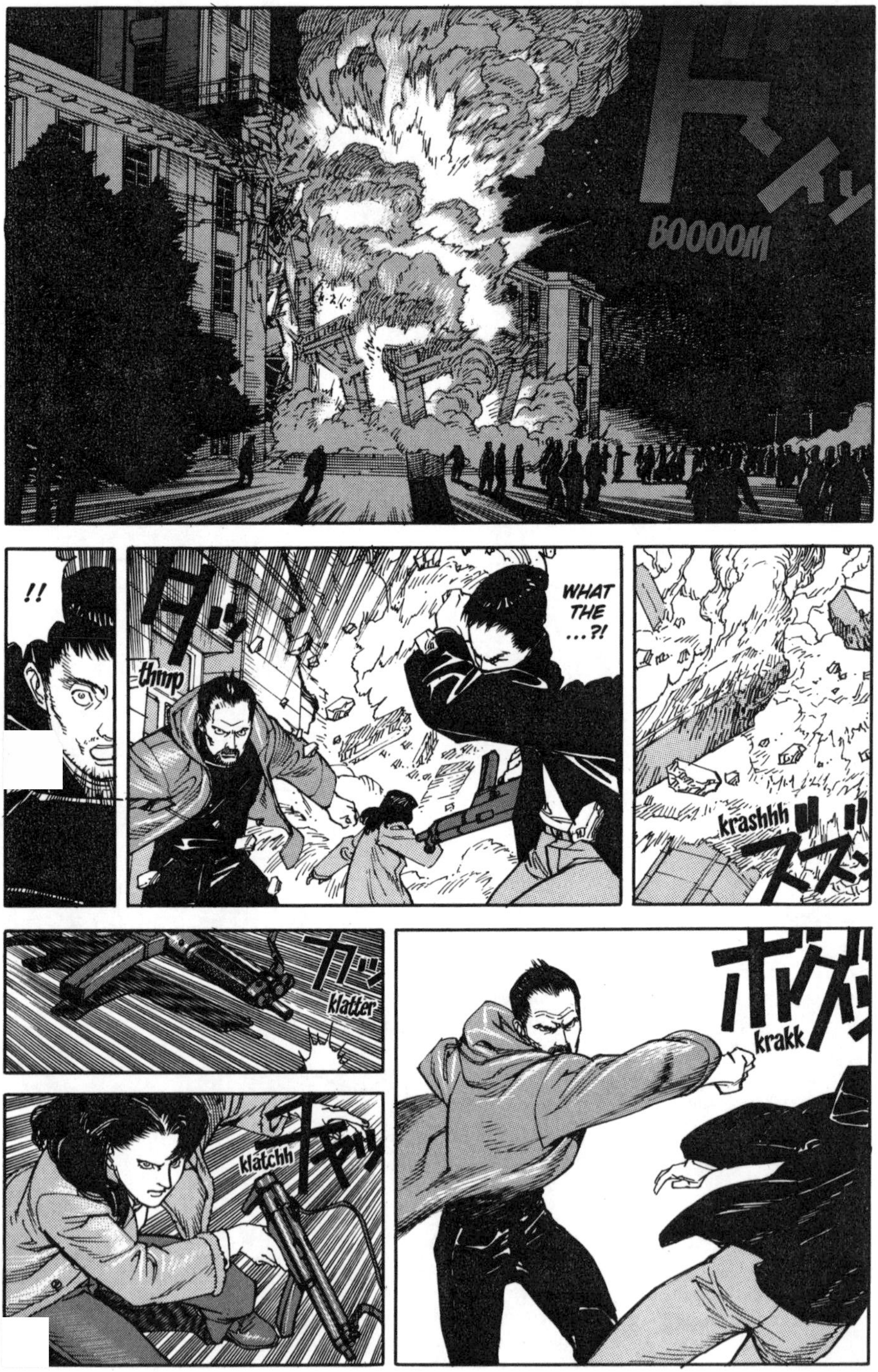
BOOOM
krashhh
WHAT THE ...?!
thimp
!!
krakk
klatter
klatchh

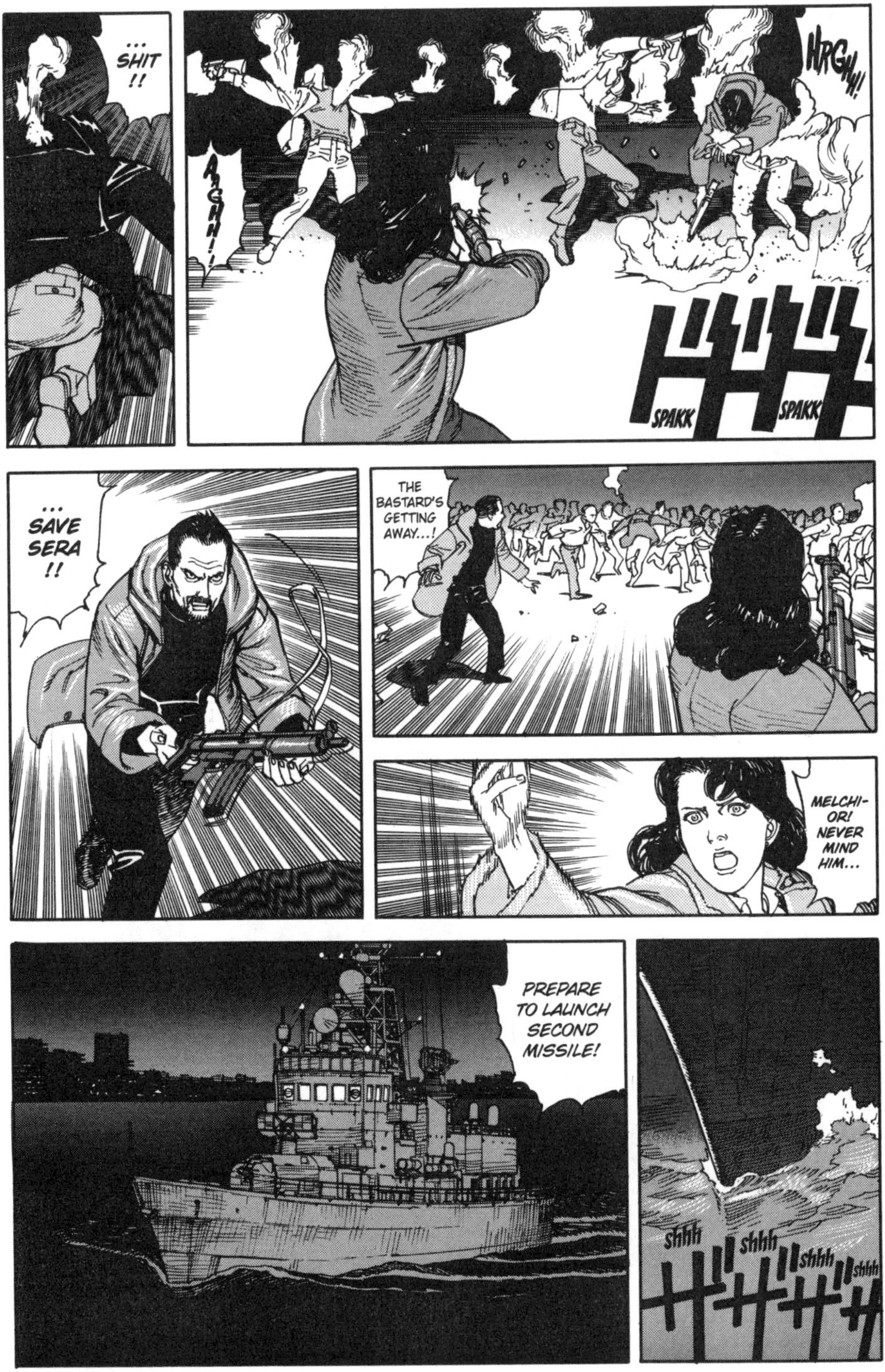
HRGHH!
ANGHH!!
SPAKK
SPAKK
...SHIT!!
THE BASTARD'S GETTING AWAY...!
MELCHIOR! NEVER MIND HIM...
...SAVE SERA!!
shhh
shhh
shhh
shhh
PREPARE TO LAUNCH SECOND MISSILE!

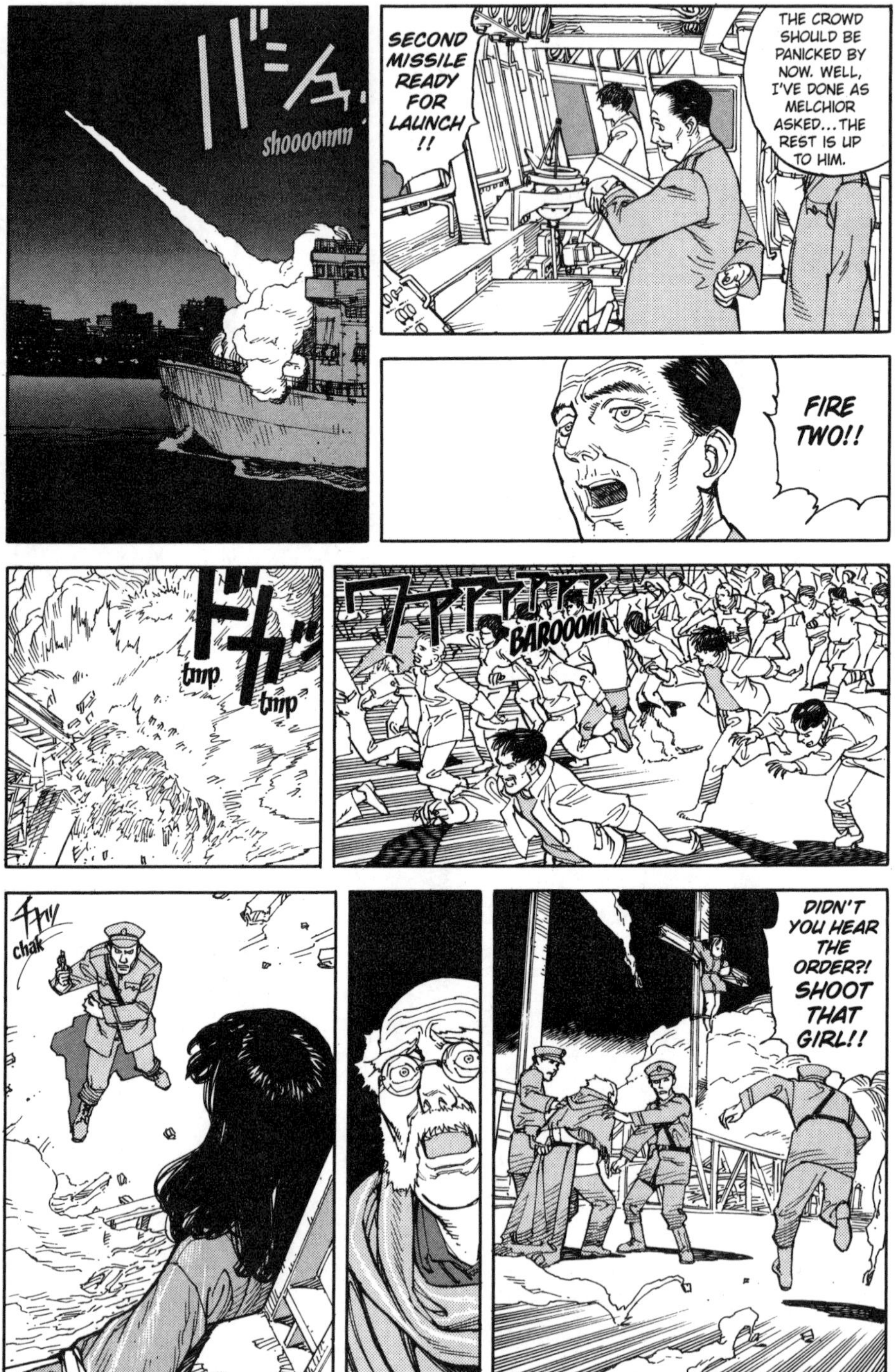
THE CROWD SHOULD BE PANICKED BY NOW. WELL, I'VE DONE AS MELCHIOR ASKED...THE REST IS UP TO HIM.
SECOND MISSILE READY FOR LAUNCH!!
FIRE TWO!!
shoooonnn
BAROOOM
ドカッ
tmp
tmp
DIDN'T YOU HEAR THE ORDER?! SHOOT THAT GIRL!!
chak

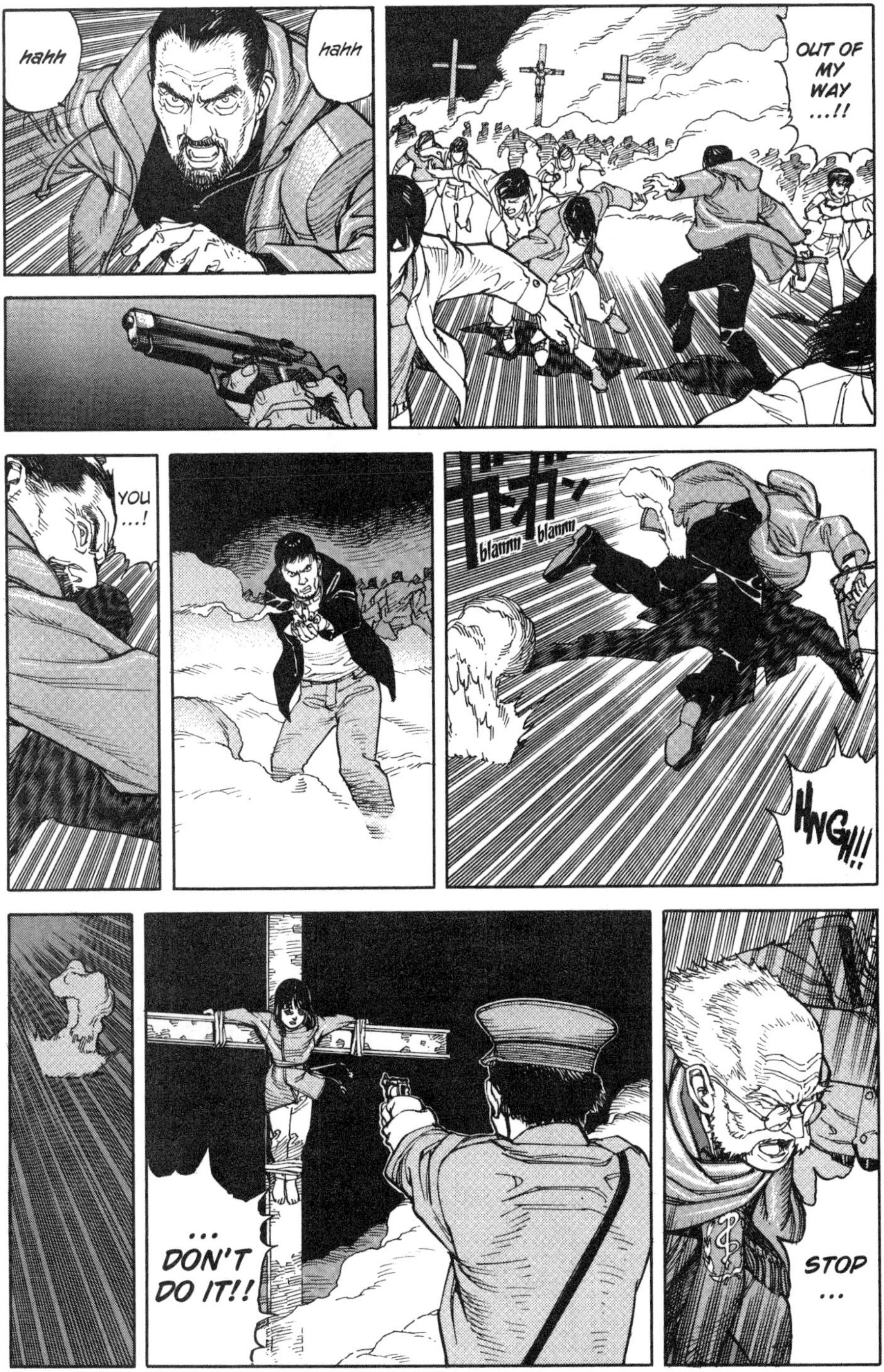
OUT OF MY WAY ...!!
hahh
hahh
blammm blammm
HNGH!!
YOU ...!
STOP ...
... DON'T DO IT!!

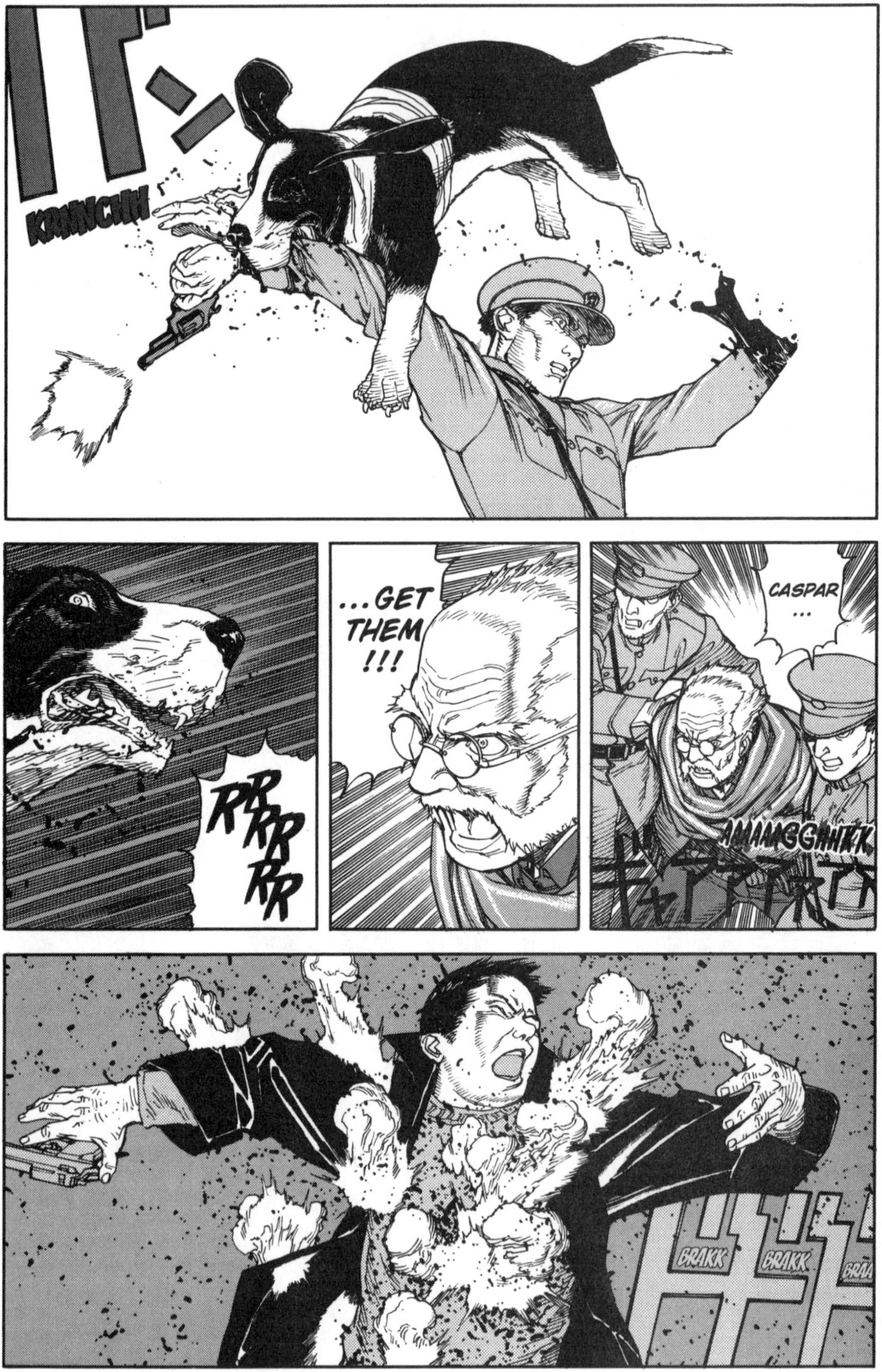
KRNNCHH
CASPAR ...
AAAAAGGHHKK
...GET THEM !!!
RRRRRRR
BRAKK BRAKK BRAA

RRRRRR

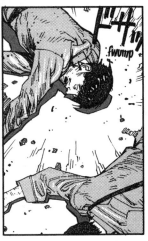

fwump

MELCHIOR
...

ARE YOU
ALL RIGHT,
BALTHAZAR
...?

RRRMMF
!!

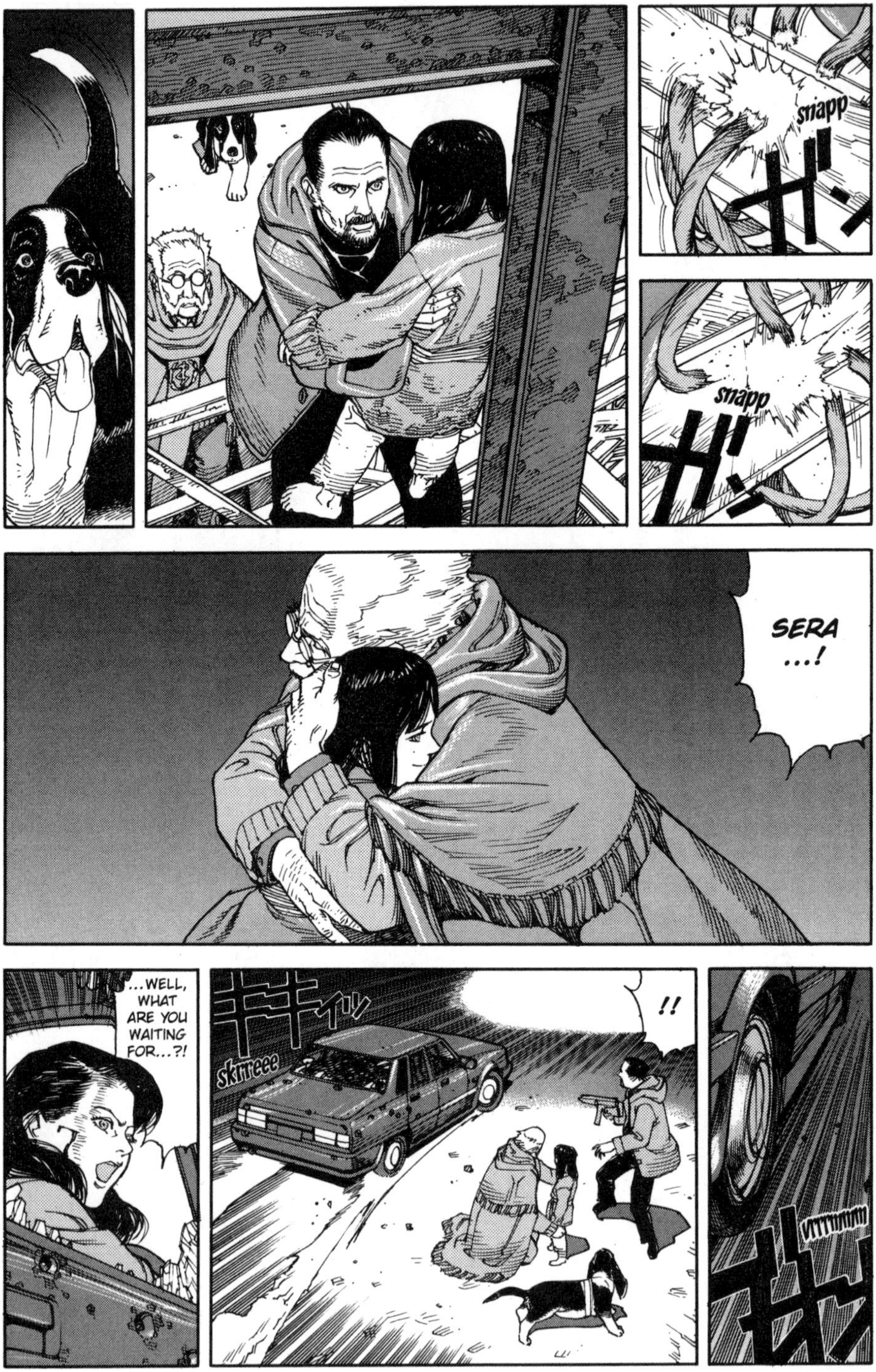
snapp
snapp
SERA ...!
vrrrmmm
skrreee
!!
...WELL, WHAT ARE YOU WAITING FOR...?!

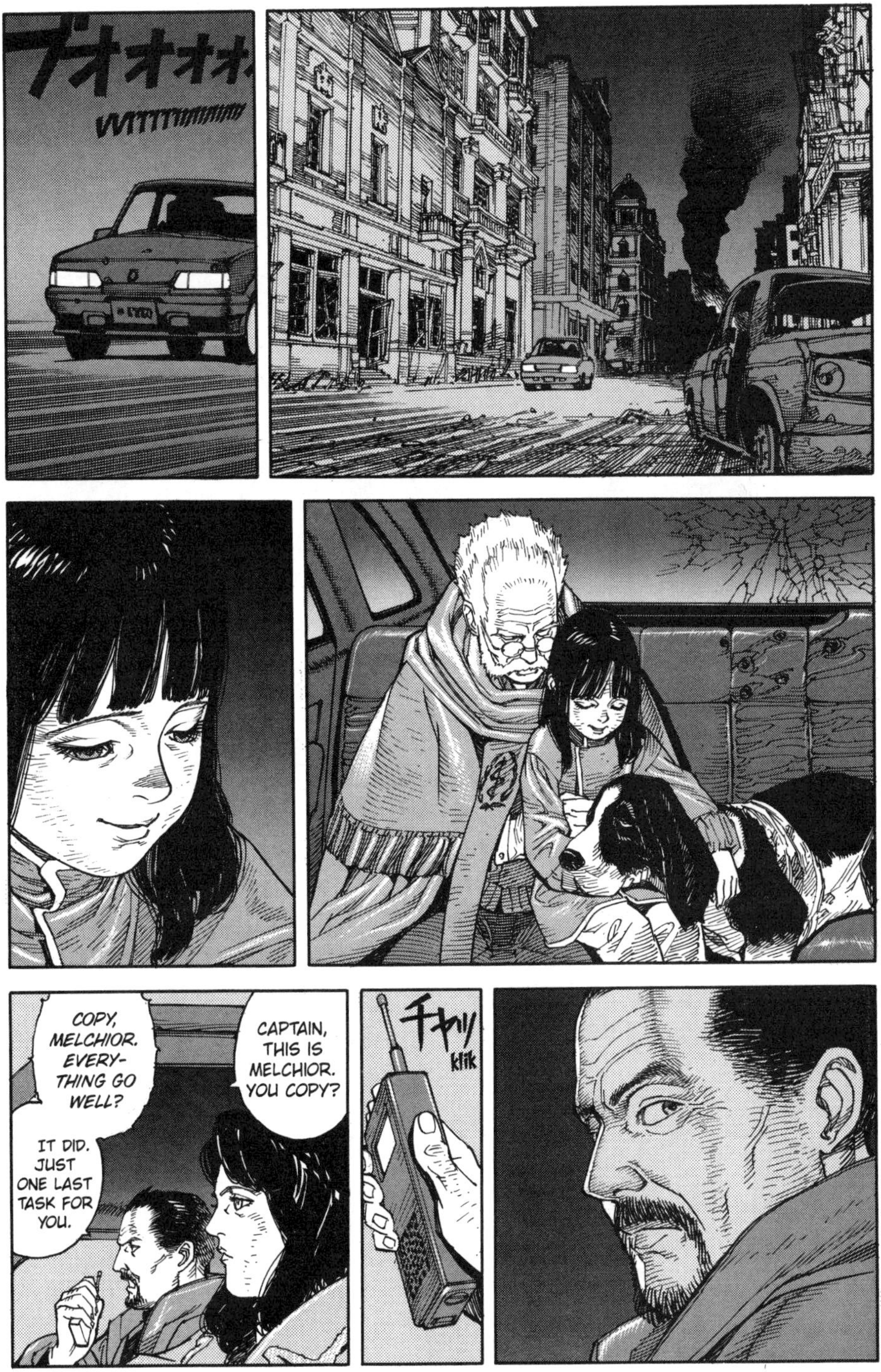
ブオオオオ
VVITTTTTTTT
チャリ
klik
CAPTAIN, THIS IS MELCHIOR. YOU COPY?
COPY, MELCHIOR. EVERY-THING GO WELL?
IT DID. JUST ONE LAST TASK FOR YOU.

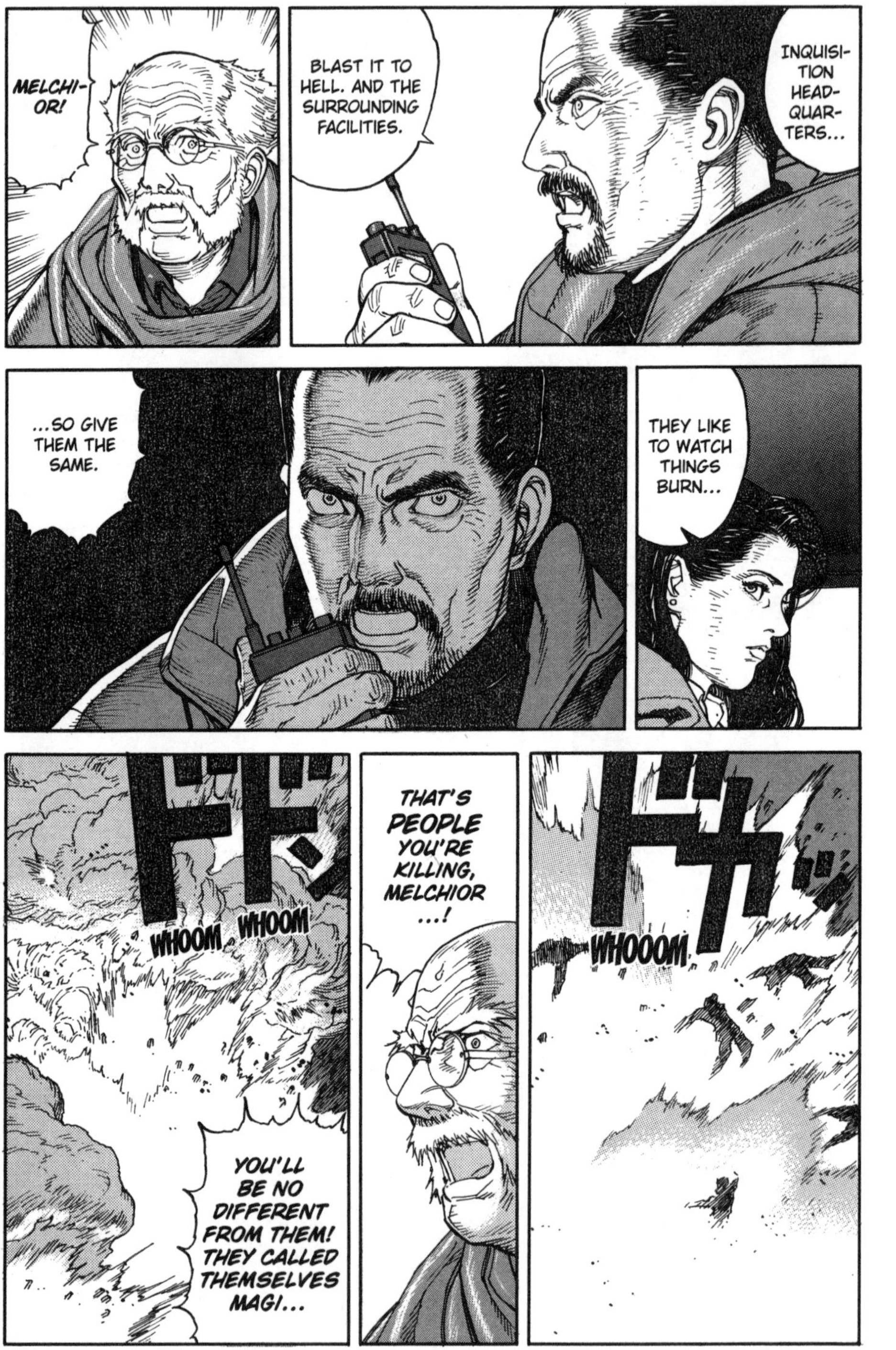
INQUISITION HEADQUARTERS...
BLAST IT TO HELL. AND THE SURROUNDING FACILITIES.
MELCHIOR!
THEY LIKE TO WATCH THINGS BURN...
...SO GIVE THEM THE SAME.
WHOOOM
THAT'S PEOPLE YOU'RE KILLING, MELCHIOR ...!
WHOOM WHOOM
YOU'LL BE NO DIFFERENT FROM THEM! THEY CALLED THEMSELVES MAGI...

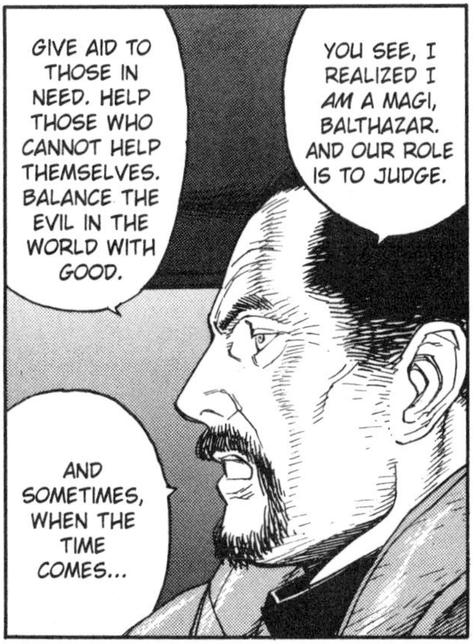
YOU SEE, I REALIZED I AM A MAGI, BALTHAZAR. AND OUR ROLE IS TO JUDGE.
GIVE AID TO THOSE IN NEED. HELP THOSE WHO CANNOT HELP THEMSELVES. BALANCE THE EVIL IN THE WORLD WITH GOOD.
AND SOMETIMES, WHEN THE TIME COMES...
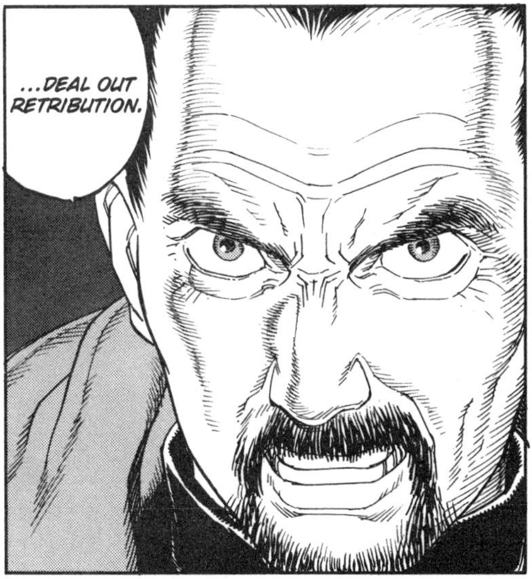
...DEAL OUT RETRIBUTION.
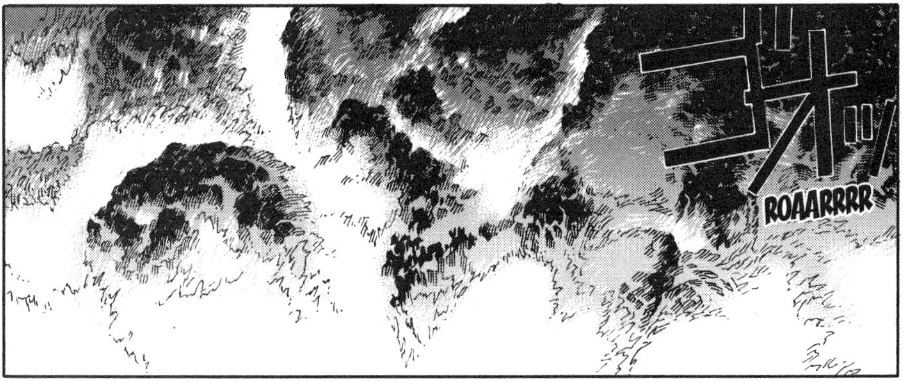
ゴオッ
ROAARRRR
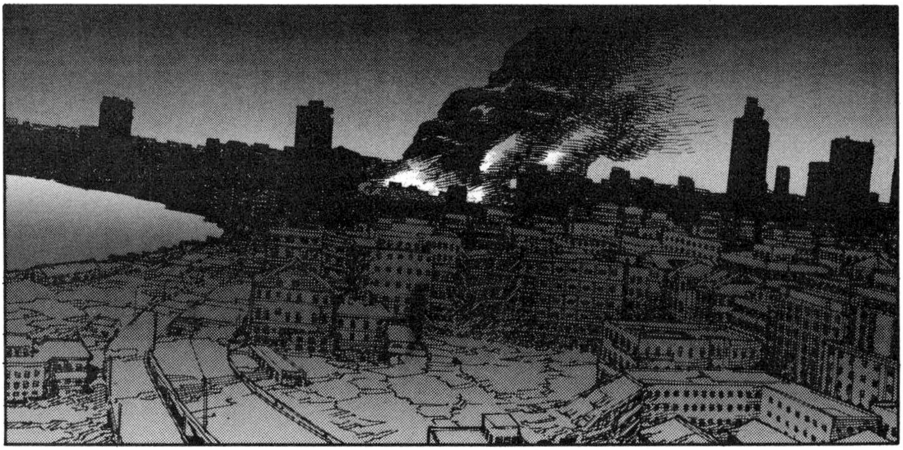

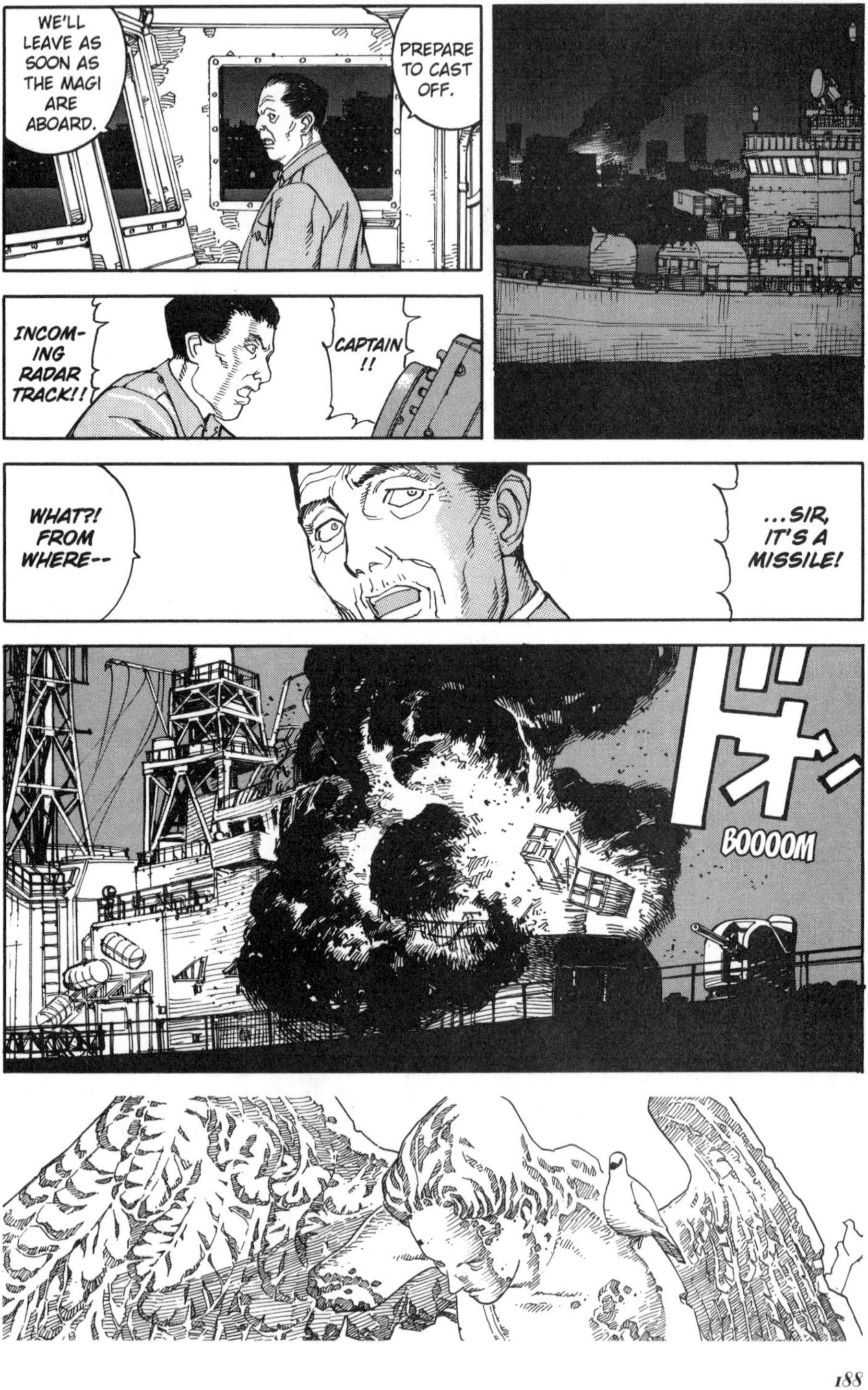
PREPARE TO CAST OFF.
WE'LL LEAVE AS SOON AS THE MAGI ARE ABOARD.
CAPTAIN !!
INCOMING RADAR TRACK!!
...SIR, IT'S A MISSILE!
WHAT?! FROM WHERE--
ドオ
BOOOOM

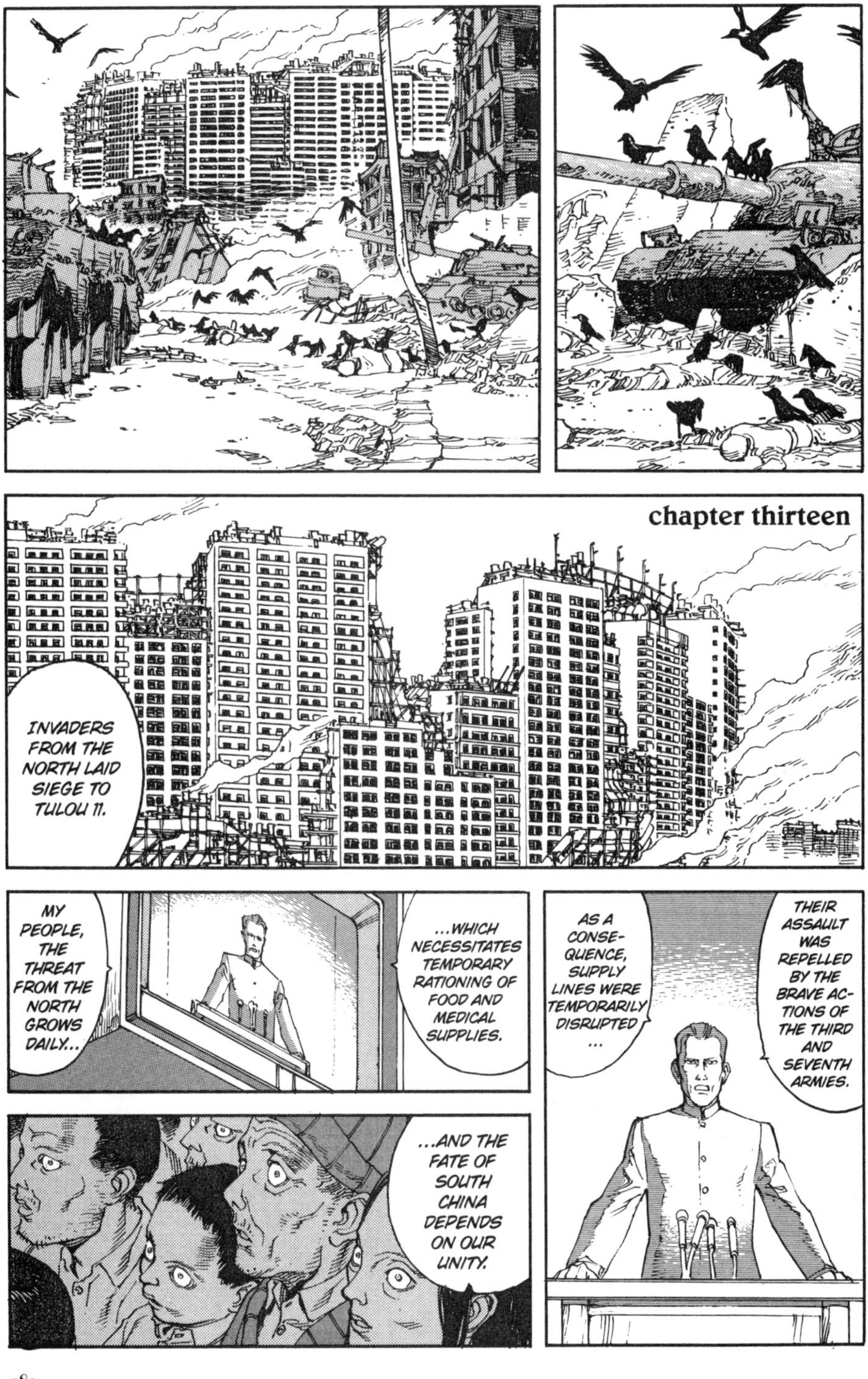
chapter thirteen
INVADERS FROM THE NORTH LAID SIEGE TO TULOU 11.
THEIR ASSAULT WAS REPELLED BY THE BRAVE ACTIONS OF THE THIRD AND SEVENTH ARMIES.
AS A CONSEQUENCE, SUPPLY LINES WERE TEMPORARILY DISRUPTED ...
MY PEOPLE, THE THREAT FROM THE NORTH GROWS DAILY...
...WHICH NECESSITATES TEMPORARY RATIONING OF FOOD AND MEDICAL SUPPLIES.
...AND THE FATE OF SOUTH CHINA DEPENDS ON OUR UNITY.

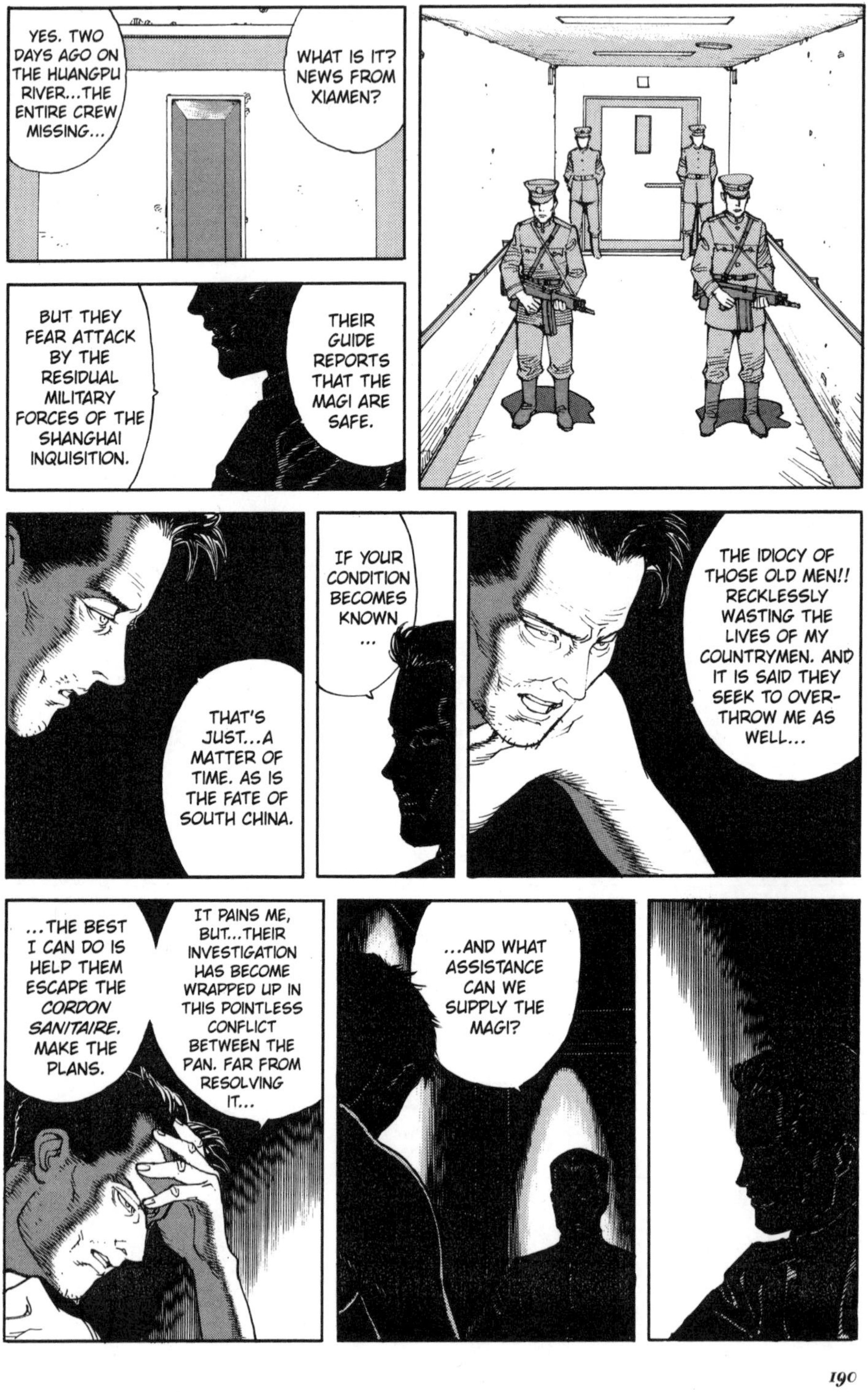
WHAT IS IT? NEWS FROM XIAMEN?
YES. TWO DAYS AGO ON THE HUANGPU RIVER...THE ENTIRE CREW MISSING...
THEIR GUIDE REPORTS THAT THE MAGI ARE SAFE.
BUT THEY FEAR ATTACK BY THE RESIDUAL MILITARY FORCES OF THE SHANGHAI INQUISITION.
THE IDIOCY OF THOSE OLD MEN!! RECKLESSLY WASTING THE LIVES OF MY COUNTRYMEN. AND IT IS SAID THEY SEEK TO OVER-THROW ME AS WELL...
IF YOUR CONDITION BECOMES KNOWN ...
THAT'S JUST...A MATTER OF TIME. AS IS THE FATE OF SOUTH CHINA.
...AND WHAT ASSISTANCE CAN WE SUPPLY THE MAGI?
IT PAINS ME, BUT...THEIR INVESTIGATION HAS BECOME WRAPPED UP IN THIS POINTLESS CONFLICT BETWEEN THE PAN. FAR FROM RESOLVING IT...
...THE BEST I CAN DO IS HELP THEM ESCAPE THE *CORDON SANITAIRE.* MAKE THE PLANS.

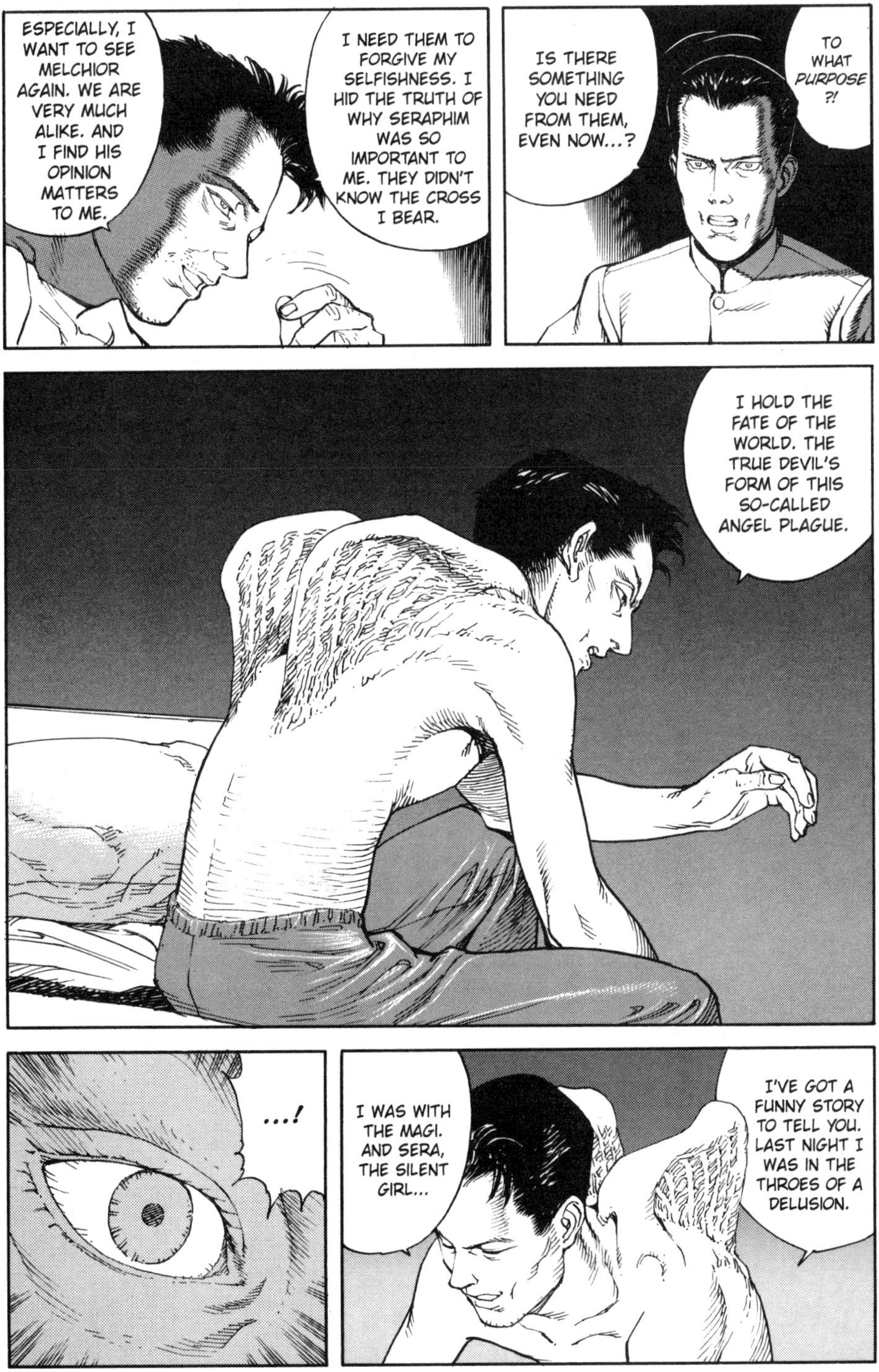
TO WHAT *PURPOSE* ?!
IS THERE SOMETHING YOU NEED FROM THEM, EVEN NOW...?
I NEED THEM TO FORGIVE MY SELFISHNESS. I HID THE TRUTH OF WHY SERAPHIM WAS SO IMPORTANT TO ME. THEY DIDN'T KNOW THE CROSS I BEAR.
ESPECIALLY, I WANT TO SEE MELCHIOR AGAIN. WE ARE VERY MUCH ALIKE. AND I FIND HIS OPINION MATTERS TO ME.
I HOLD THE FATE OF THE WORLD. THE TRUE DEVIL'S FORM OF THIS SO-CALLED ANGEL PLAGUE.
I'VE GOT A FUNNY STORY TO TELL YOU. LAST NIGHT I WAS IN THE THROES OF A DELUSION.
I WAS WITH THE MAGI. AND SERA, THE SILENT GIRL...
...!

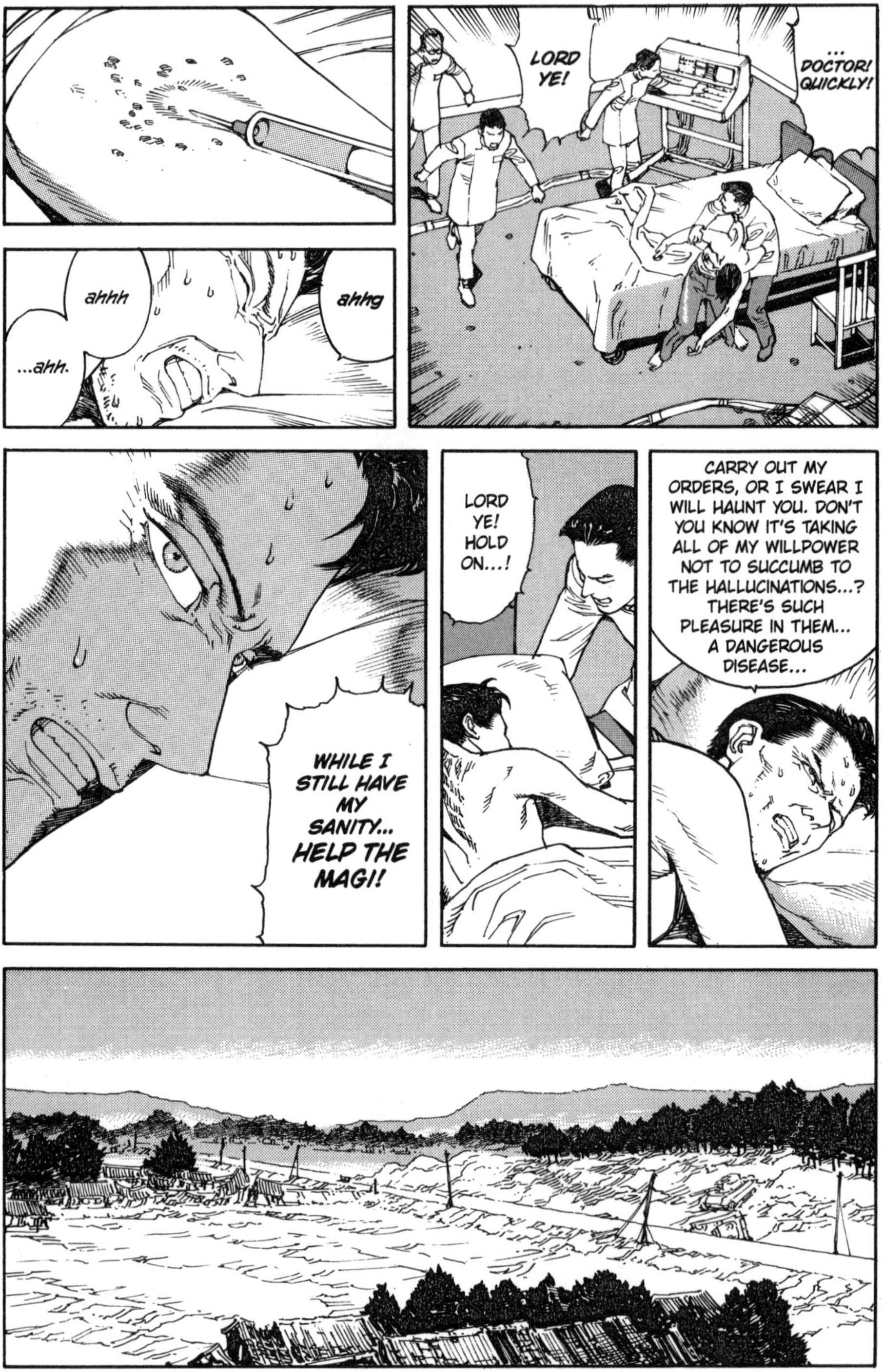
...DOCTOR! QUICKLY!
LORD YE!
ahhg
ahhh
...ahh.
CARRY OUT MY ORDERS, OR I SWEAR I WILL HAUNT YOU. DON'T YOU KNOW IT'S TAKING ALL OF MY WILLPOWER NOT TO SUCCUMB TO THE HALLUCINATIONS...? THERE'S SUCH PLEASURE IN THEM... A DANGEROUS DISEASE...
LORD YE! HOLD ON...!
WHILE I STILL HAVE MY SANITY... HELP THE MAGI!

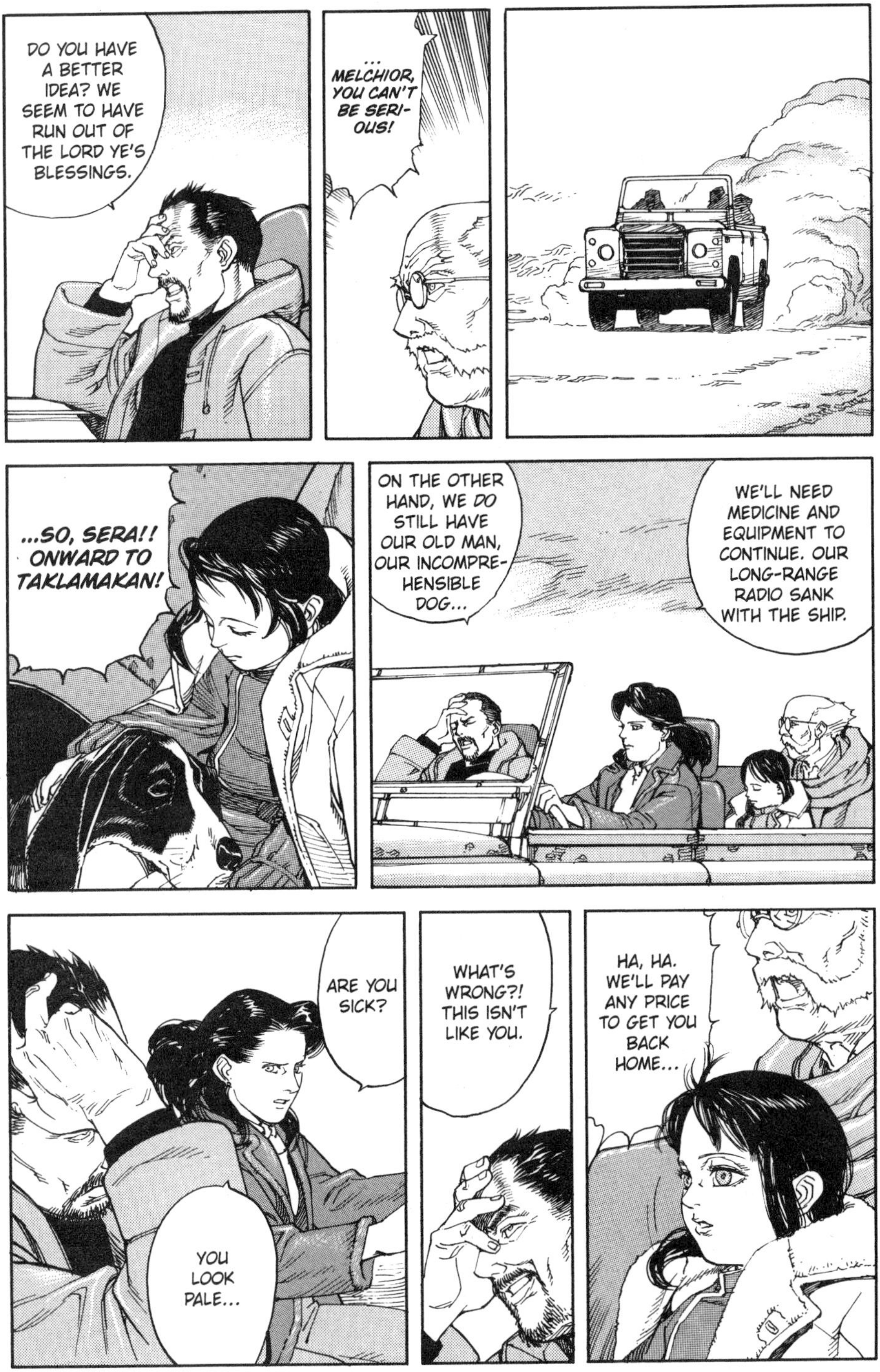
...MELCHIOR, YOU CAN'T BE SERIOUS!
DO YOU HAVE A BETTER IDEA? WE SEEM TO HAVE RUN OUT OF THE LORD YE'S BLESSINGS.
WE'LL NEED MEDICINE AND EQUIPMENT TO CONTINUE. OUR LONG-RANGE RADIO SANK WITH THE SHIP.
ON THE OTHER HAND, WE *DO* STILL HAVE OUR OLD MAN, OUR INCOMPREHENSIBLE DOG...
...SO, SERA!! ONWARD TO TAKLAMAKAN!
HA, HA. WE'LL PAY ANY PRICE TO GET YOU BACK HOME...
WHAT'S WRONG?! THIS ISN'T LIKE YOU.
ARE YOU SICK?
YOU LOOK PALE...

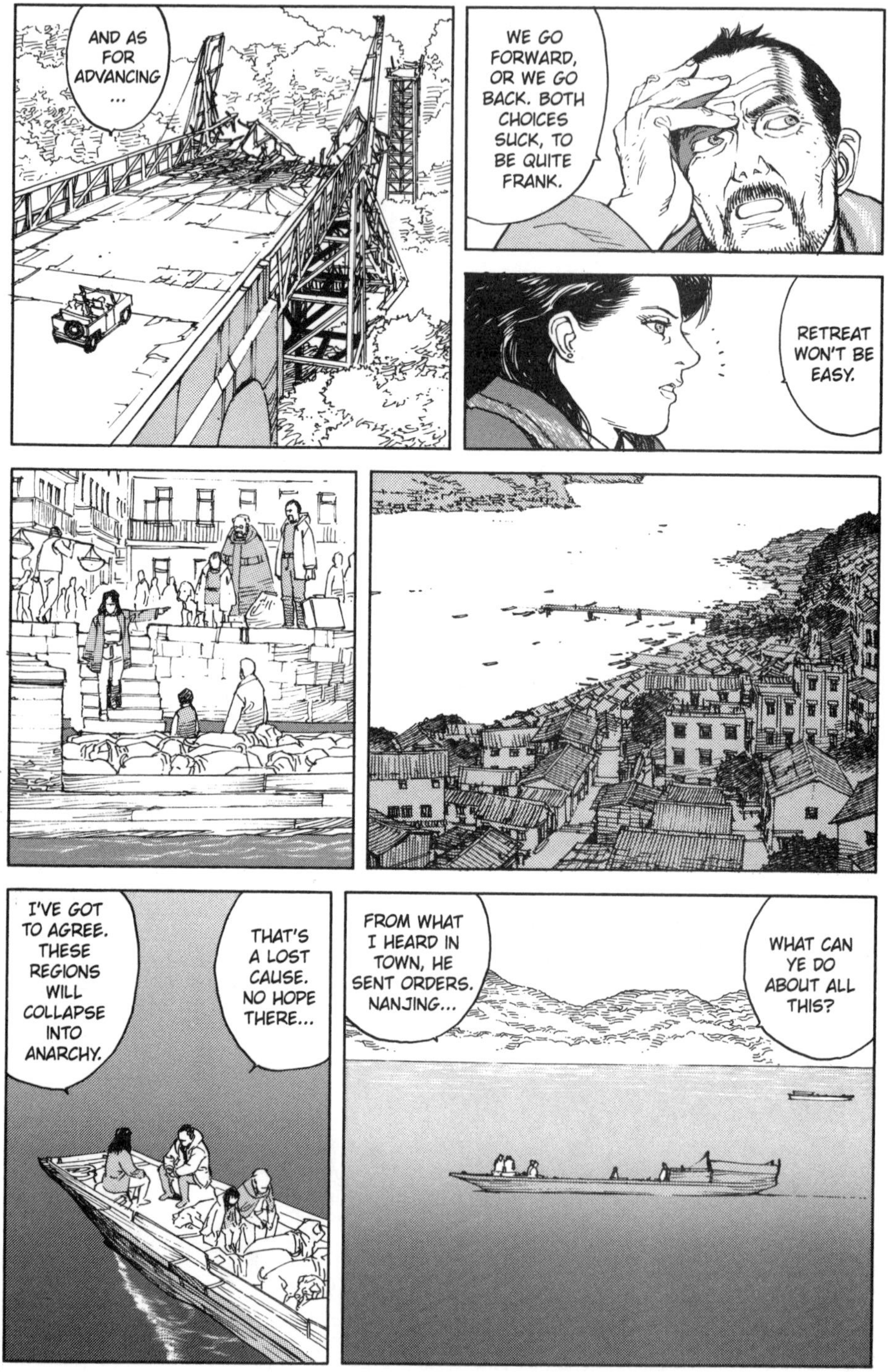
WE GO FORWARD, OR WE GO BACK. BOTH CHOICES SUCK, TO BE QUITE FRANK.
RETREAT WON'T BE EASY.
AND AS FOR ADVANCING ...
WHAT CAN YE DO ABOUT ALL THIS?
FROM WHAT I HEARD IN TOWN, HE SENT ORDERS. NANJING...
THAT'S A LOST CAUSE. NO HOPE THERE...
I'VE GOT TO AGREE. THESE REGIONS WILL COLLAPSE INTO ANARCHY.

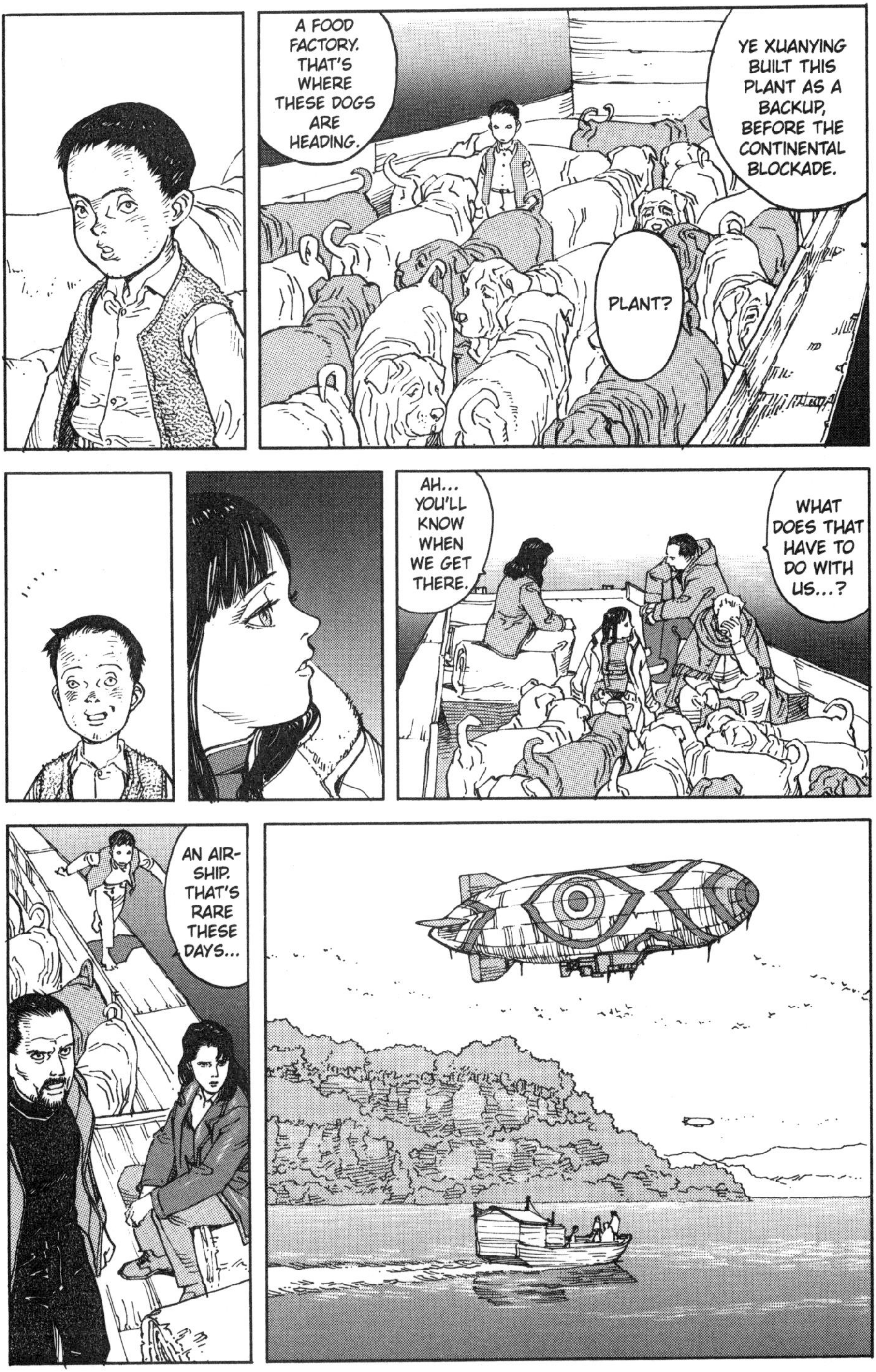
YE XUANYING BUILT THIS PLANT AS A BACKUP, BEFORE THE CONTINENTAL BLOCKADE.
A FOOD FACTORY. THAT'S WHERE THESE DOGS ARE HEADING.
PLANT?
WHAT DOES THAT HAVE TO DO WITH US...?
AH... YOU'LL KNOW WHEN WE GET THERE.
.....
AN AIR-SHIP. THAT'S RARE THESE DAYS...

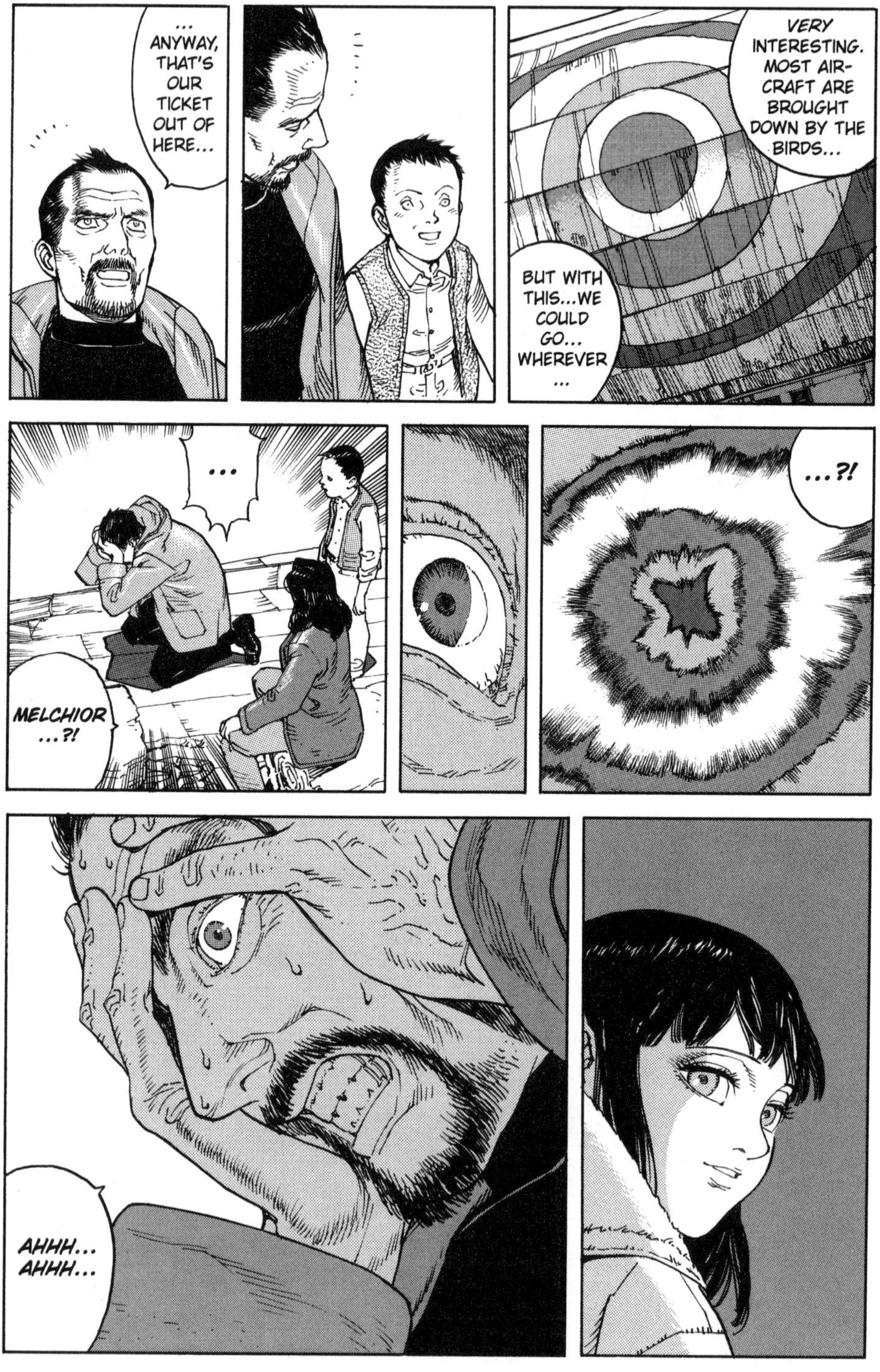

... ANYWAY, THAT'S OUR TICKET OUT OF HERE...
VERY INTERESTING. MOST AIRCRAFT ARE BROUGHT DOWN BY THE BIRDS...
BUT WITH THIS...WE COULD GO... WHEREVER ...
...
MELCHIOR ...?!
...?!
AHHH... AHHH...

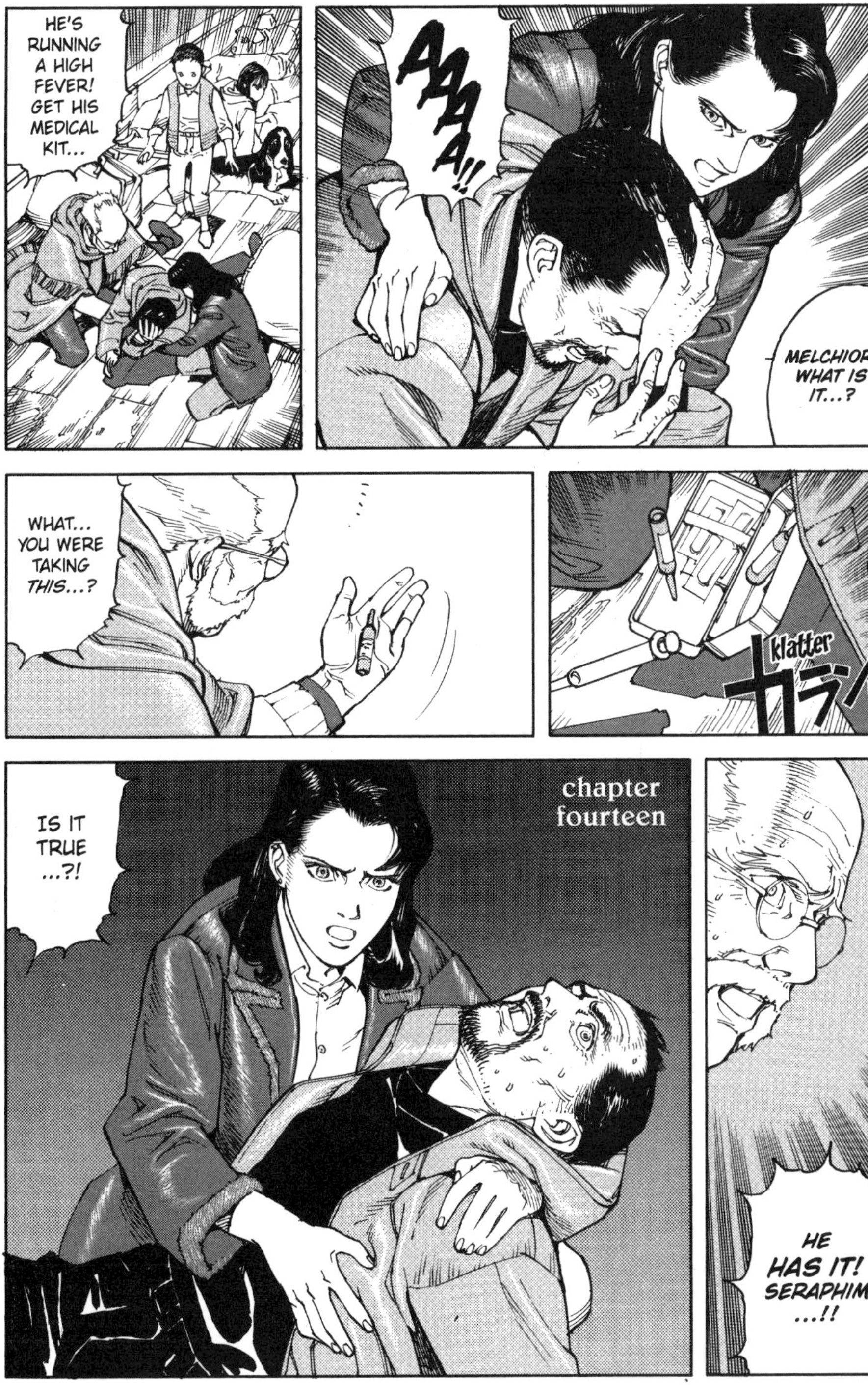
AAAA!!
MELCHIOR, WHAT IS IT...?
HE'S RUNNING A HIGH FEVER! GET HIS MEDICAL KIT...
klatter
カラン
WHAT... YOU WERE TAKING THIS...?
HE HAS IT! SERAPHIM ...!!
chapter fourteen
IS IT TRUE ...?!

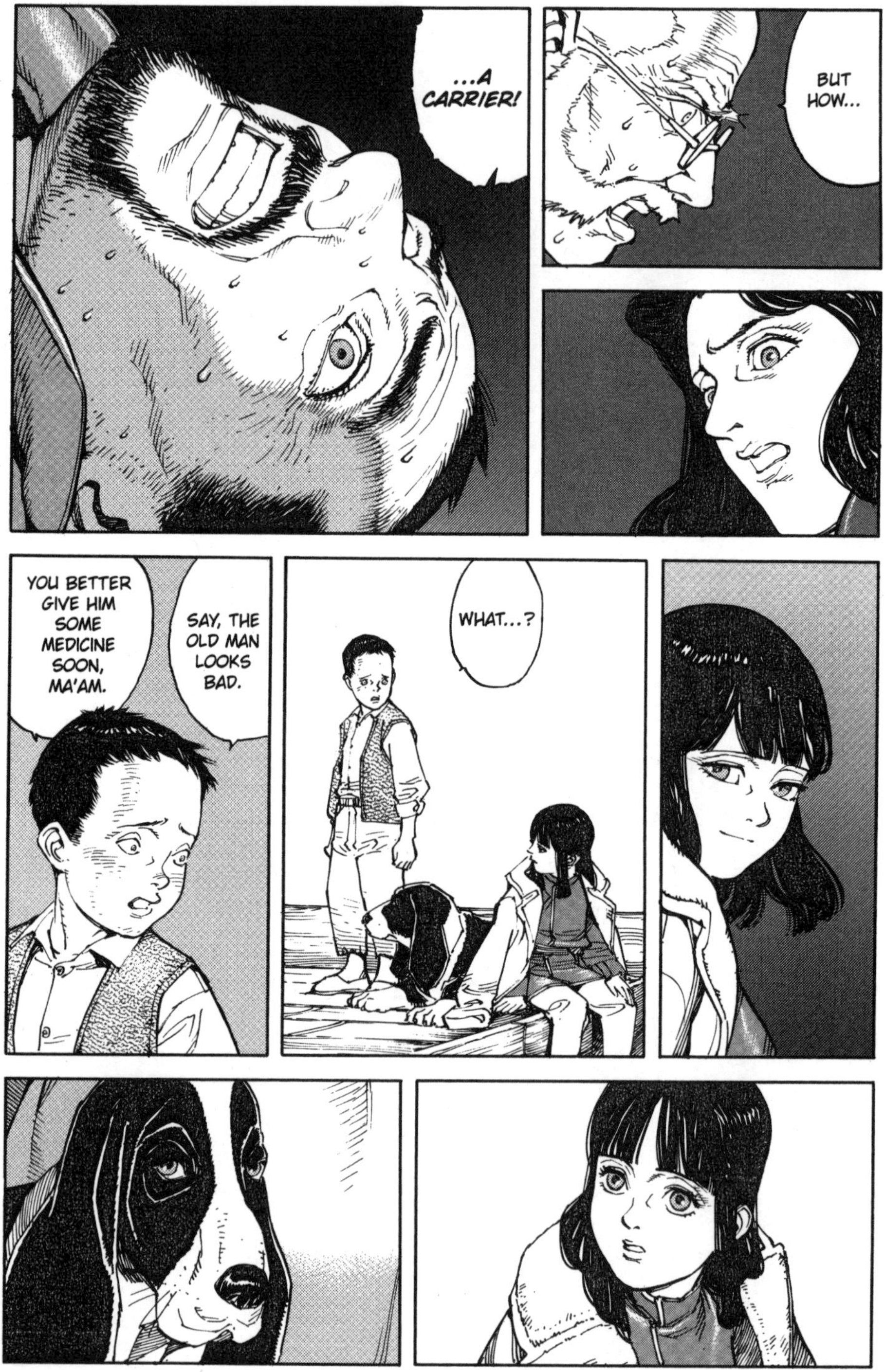
BUT HOW...
...A CARRIER!
WHAT...?
SAY, THE OLD MAN LOOKS BAD.
YOU BETTER GIVE HIM SOME MEDICINE SOON, MA'AM.

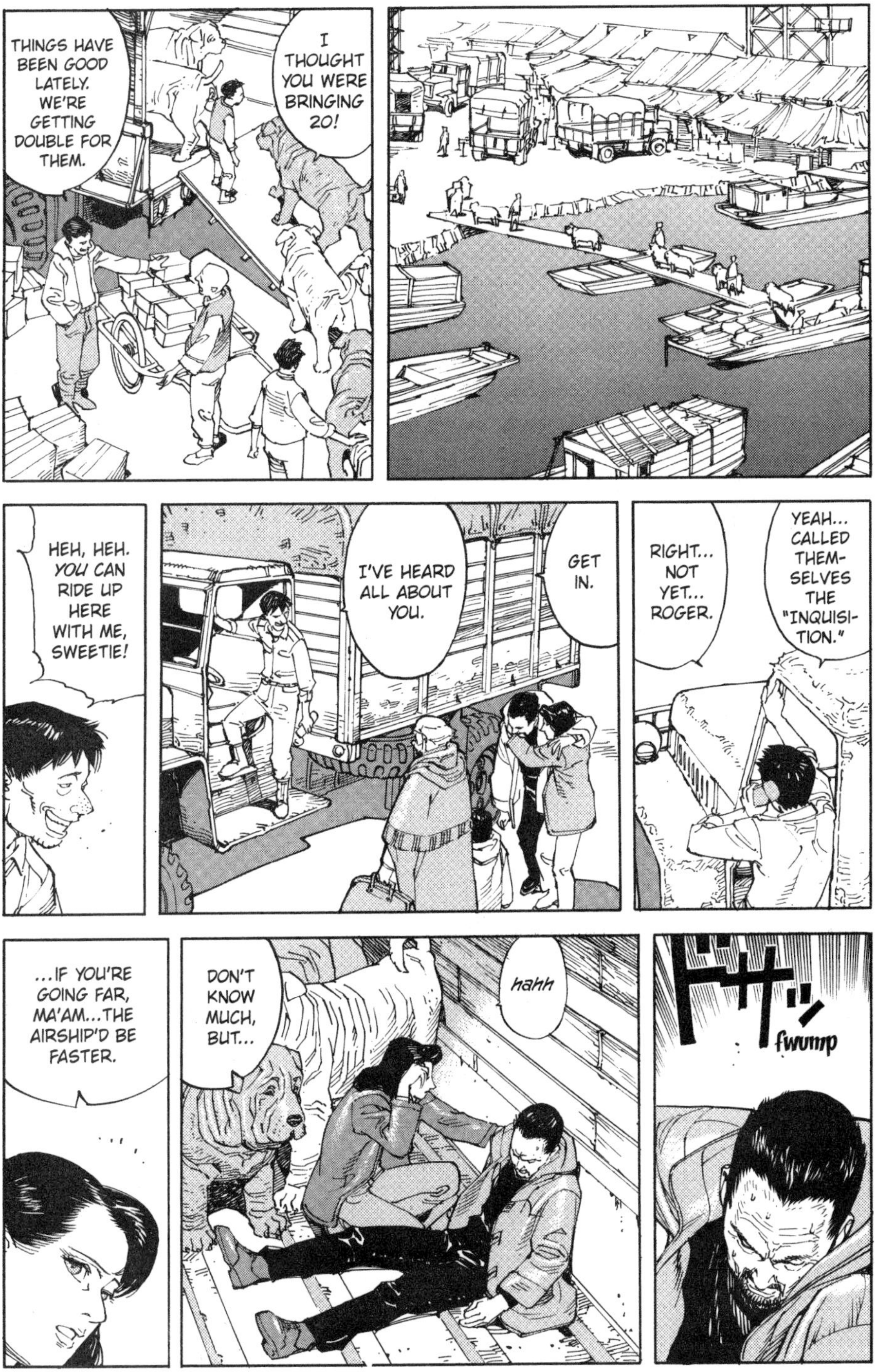
I THOUGHT YOU WERE BRINGING 20!
THINGS HAVE BEEN GOOD LATELY. WE'RE GETTING DOUBLE FOR THEM.
YEAH... CALLED THEMSELVES THE "INQUISITION."
RIGHT... NOT YET... ROGER.
GET IN.
I'VE HEARD ALL ABOUT YOU.
HEH, HEH. *YOU* CAN RIDE UP HERE WITH ME, SWEETIE!
ドサッ
fwump
hahh
DON'T KNOW MUCH, BUT...
...IF YOU'RE GOING FAR, MA'AM...THE AIRSHIP'D BE FASTER.
...,

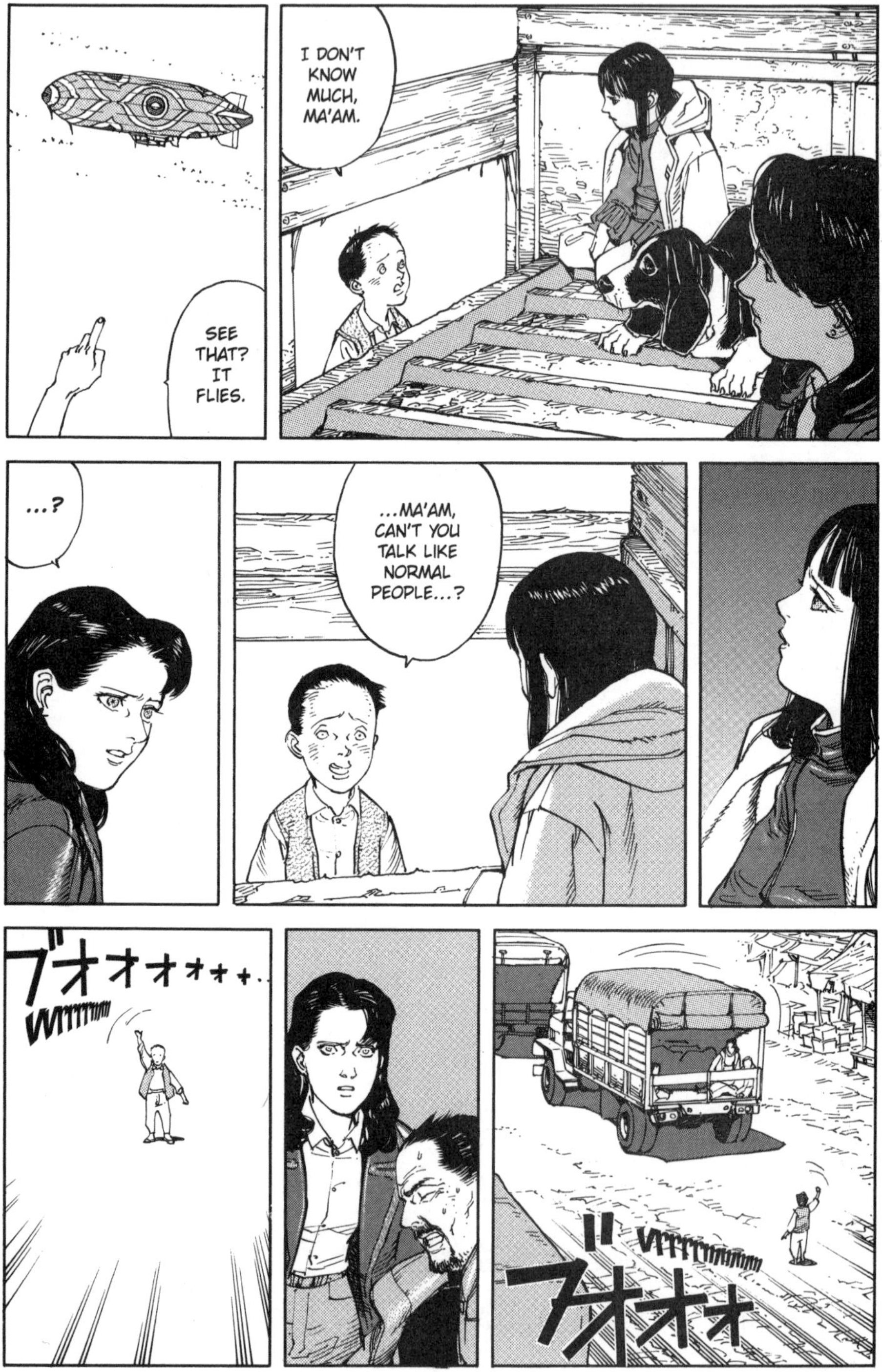
I DON'T KNOW MUCH, MA'AM.
SEE THAT? IT FLIES.
...MA'AM, CAN'T YOU TALK LIKE NORMAL PEOPLE...?
...?
ブオオオ
VRRRRMMMMMMMM
ブオオオォォォ...
VRRRRRRRRR

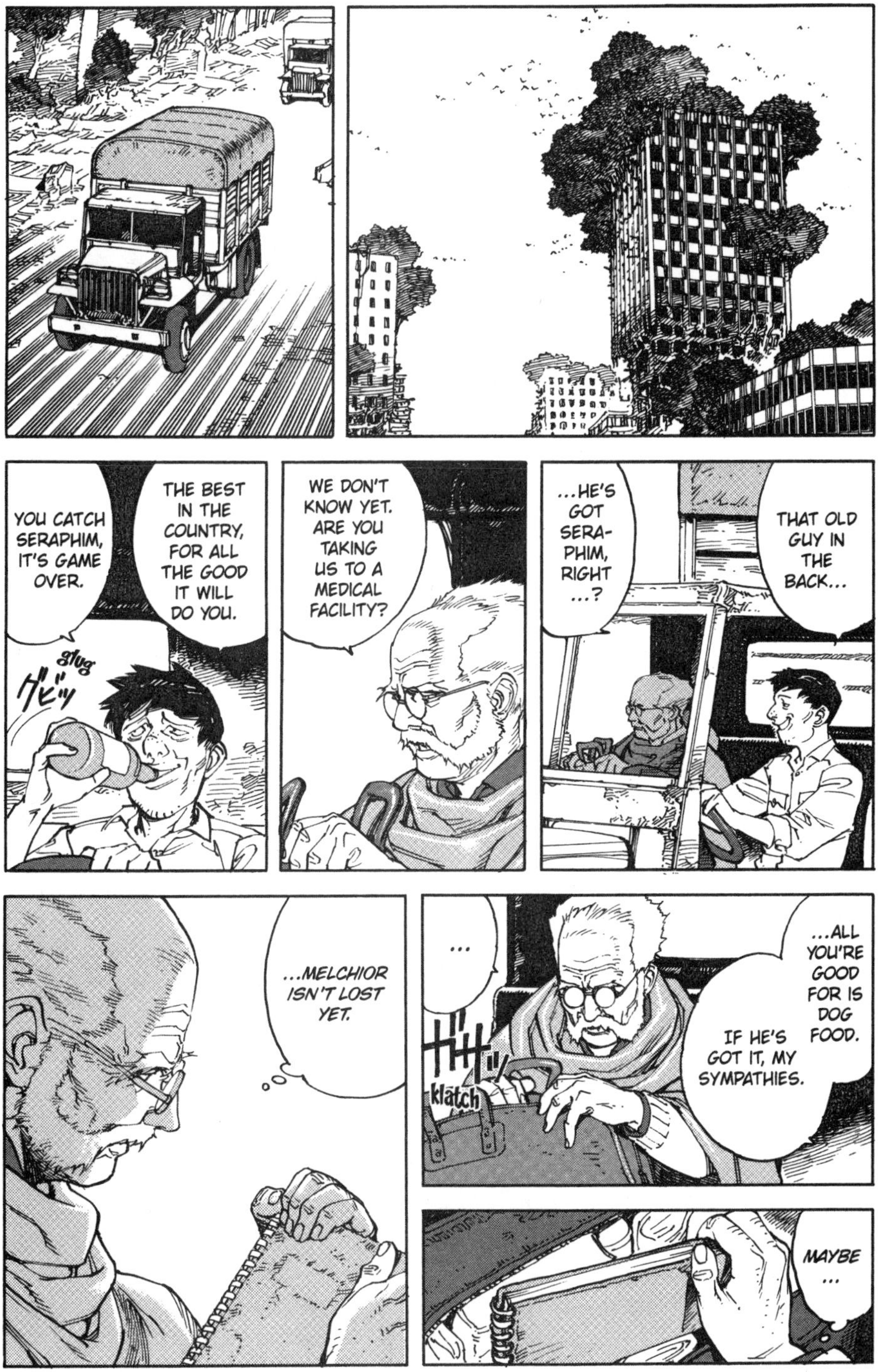
THAT OLD GUY IN THE BACK...
...HE'S GOT SERA-PHIM, RIGHT ...?
WE DON'T KNOW YET. ARE YOU TAKING US TO A MEDICAL FACILITY?
THE BEST IN THE COUNTRY, FOR ALL THE GOOD IT WILL DO YOU.
YOU CATCH SERAPHIM, IT'S GAME OVER.
glug
グビッ
...ALL YOU'RE GOOD FOR IS DOG FOOD.
IF HE'S GOT IT, MY SYMPATHIES.
...
klatch
MAYBE ...
...MELCHIOR ISN'T LOST YET.

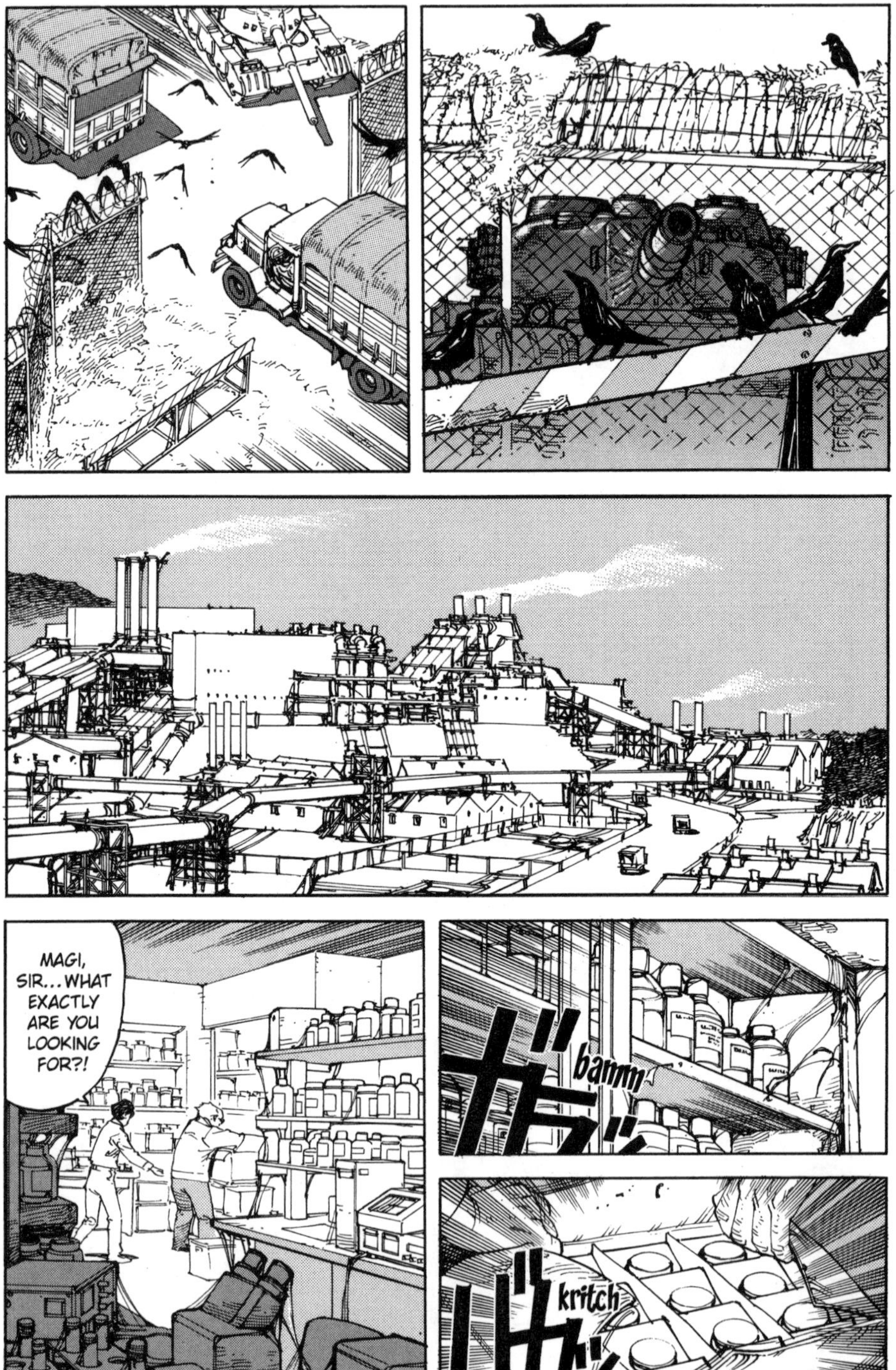
bamm
kritch
MAGI, SIR...WHAT EXACTLY ARE YOU LOOKING FOR?!

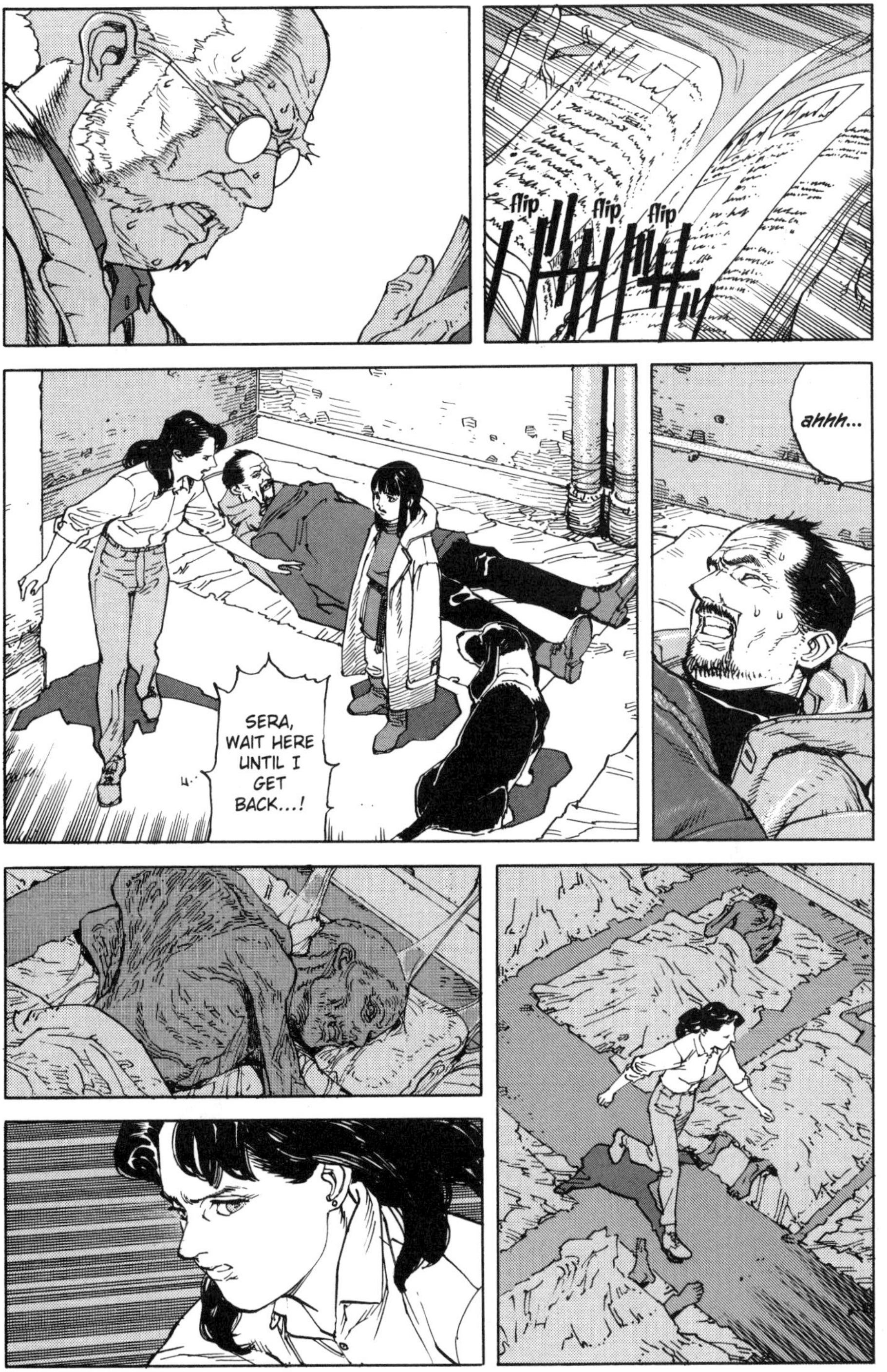
flip flip flip
ahhh...
SERA, WAIT HERE UNTIL I GET BACK...!

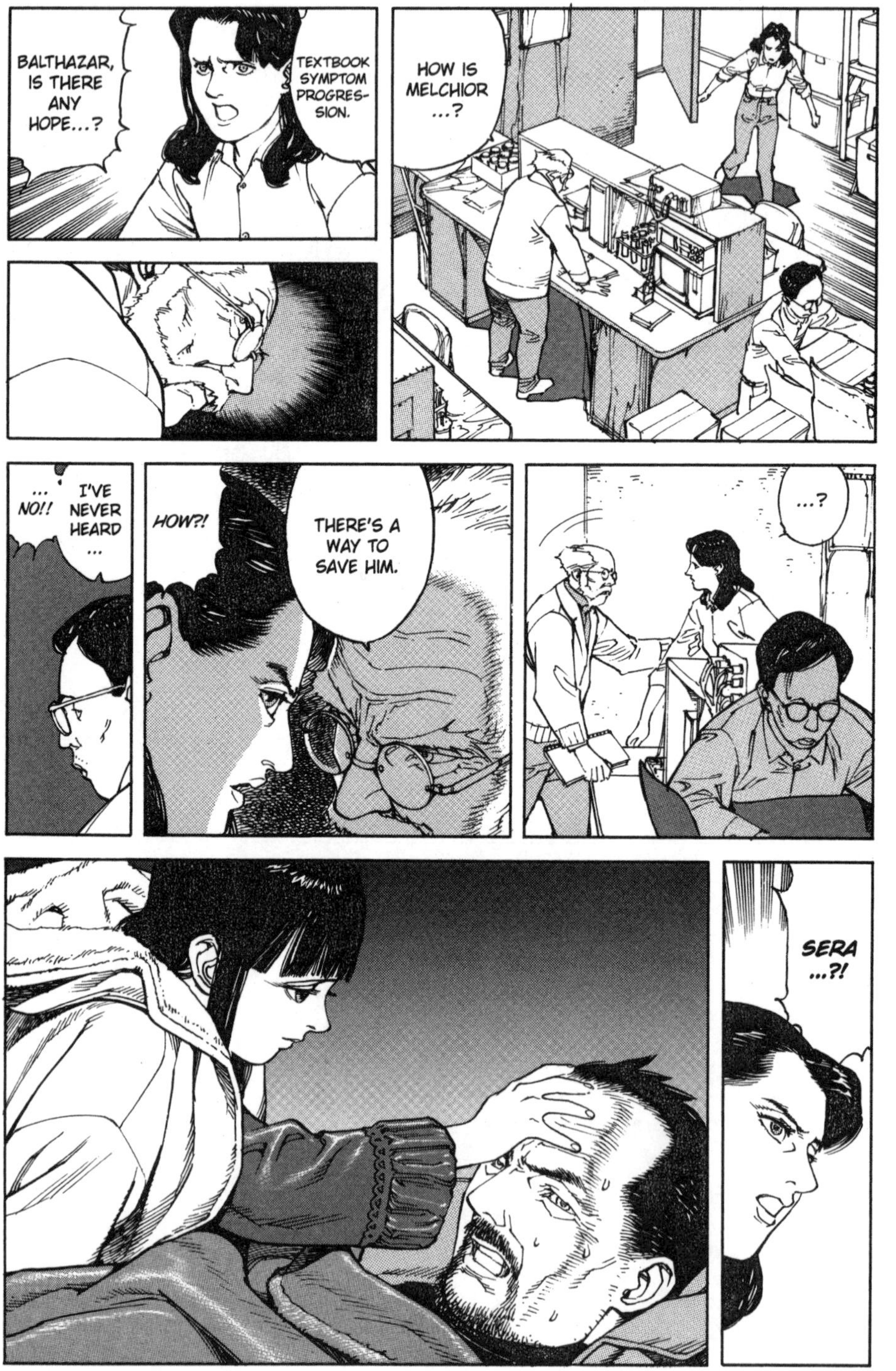
HOW IS MELCHIOR ...?
TEXTBOOK SYMPTOM PROGRES-SION.
BALTHAZAR, IS THERE ANY HOPE...?
...?
THERE'S A WAY TO SAVE HIM.
HOW?!
I'VE NEVER HEARD ...
... NO!!
SERA ...?!

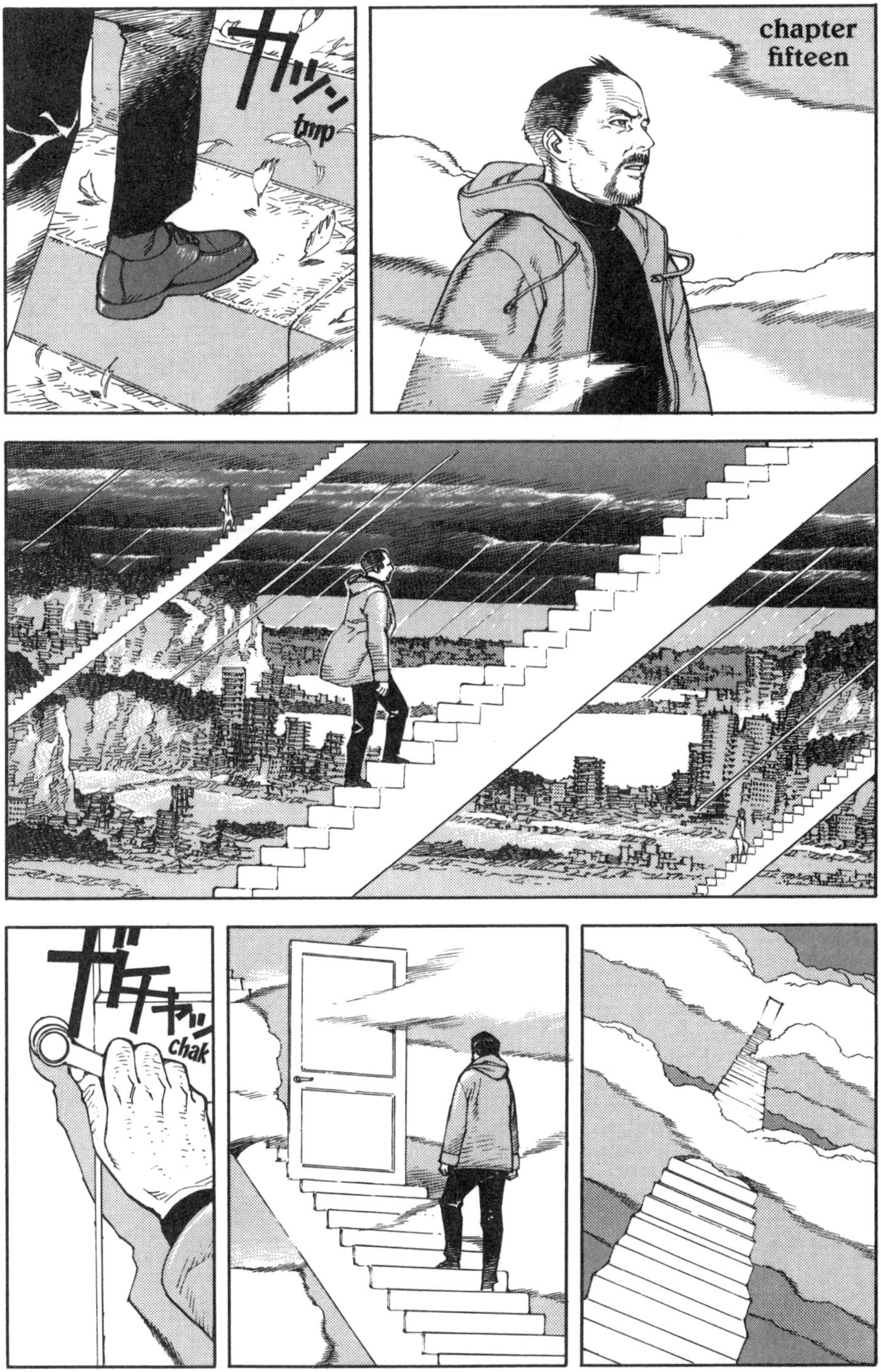
chapter fifteen
tmp
ガチャッ
chak

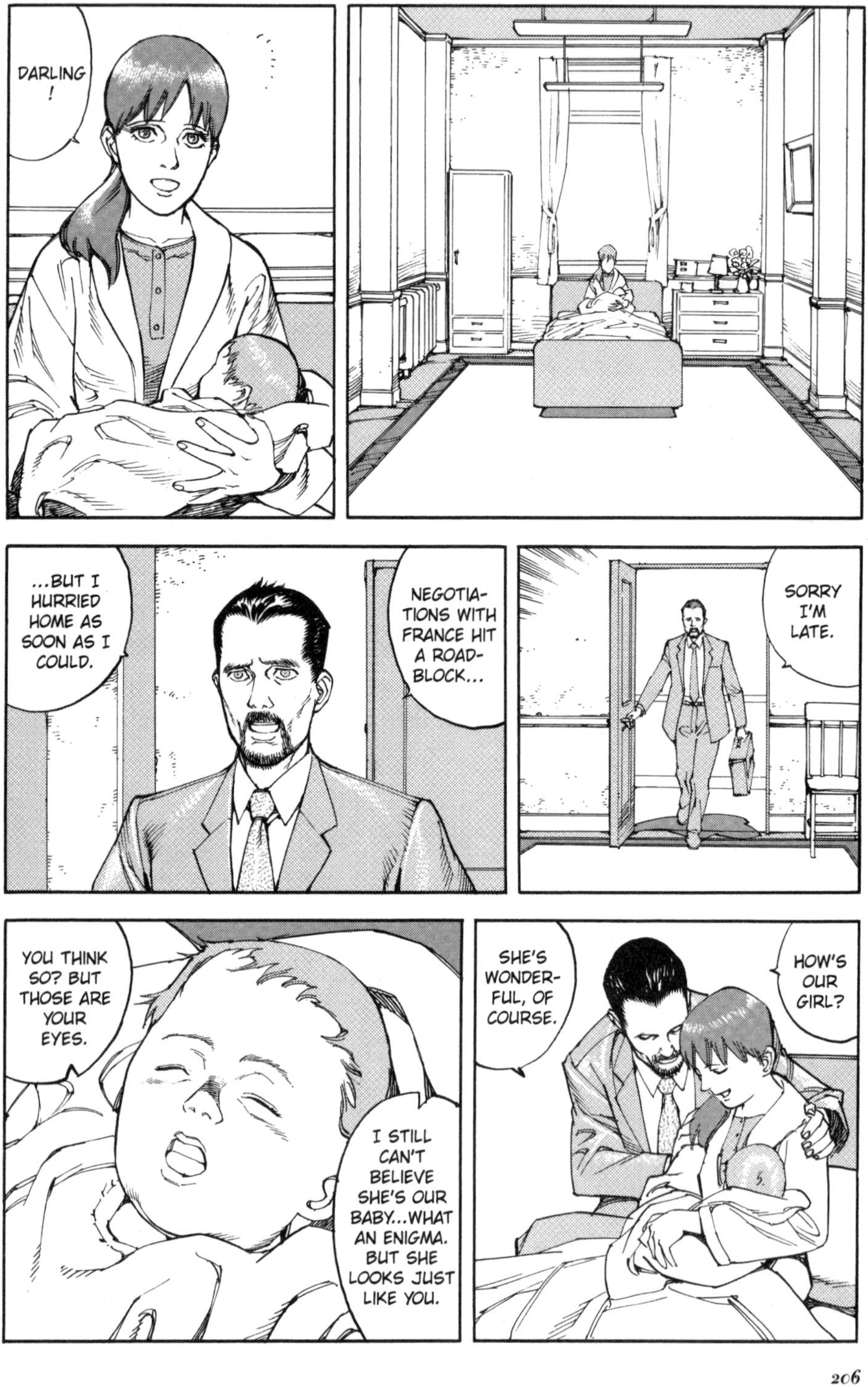
DARLING!
SORRY I'M LATE.
NEGOTIA-TIONS WITH FRANCE HIT A ROAD-BLOCK...
...BUT I HURRIED HOME AS SOON AS I COULD.
HOW'S OUR GIRL?
SHE'S WONDER-FUL, OF COURSE.
I STILL CAN'T BELIEVE SHE'S OUR BABY...WHAT AN ENIGMA. BUT SHE LOOKS JUST LIKE YOU.
YOU THINK SO? BUT THOSE ARE YOUR EYES.

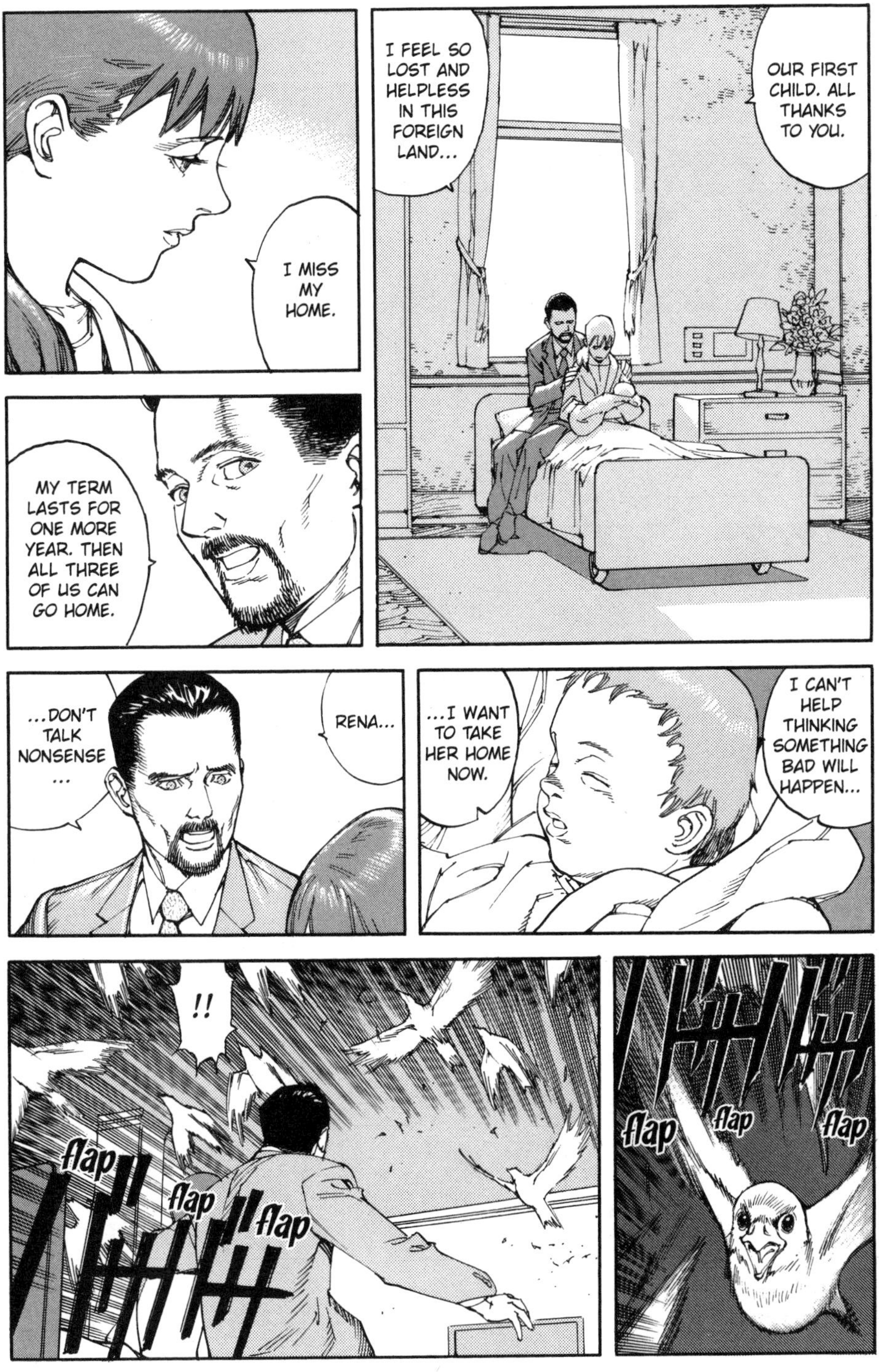
OUR FIRST CHILD. ALL THANKS TO YOU.
I FEEL SO LOST AND HELPLESS IN THIS FOREIGN LAND...
I MISS MY HOME.
MY TERM LASTS FOR ONE MORE YEAR. THEN ALL THREE OF US CAN GO HOME.
I CAN'T HELP THINKING SOMETHING BAD WILL HAPPEN...
...I WANT TO TAKE HER HOME NOW.
RENA...
...DON'T TALK NONSENSE ...
flap
flap
flap
!!
flap
flap
flap

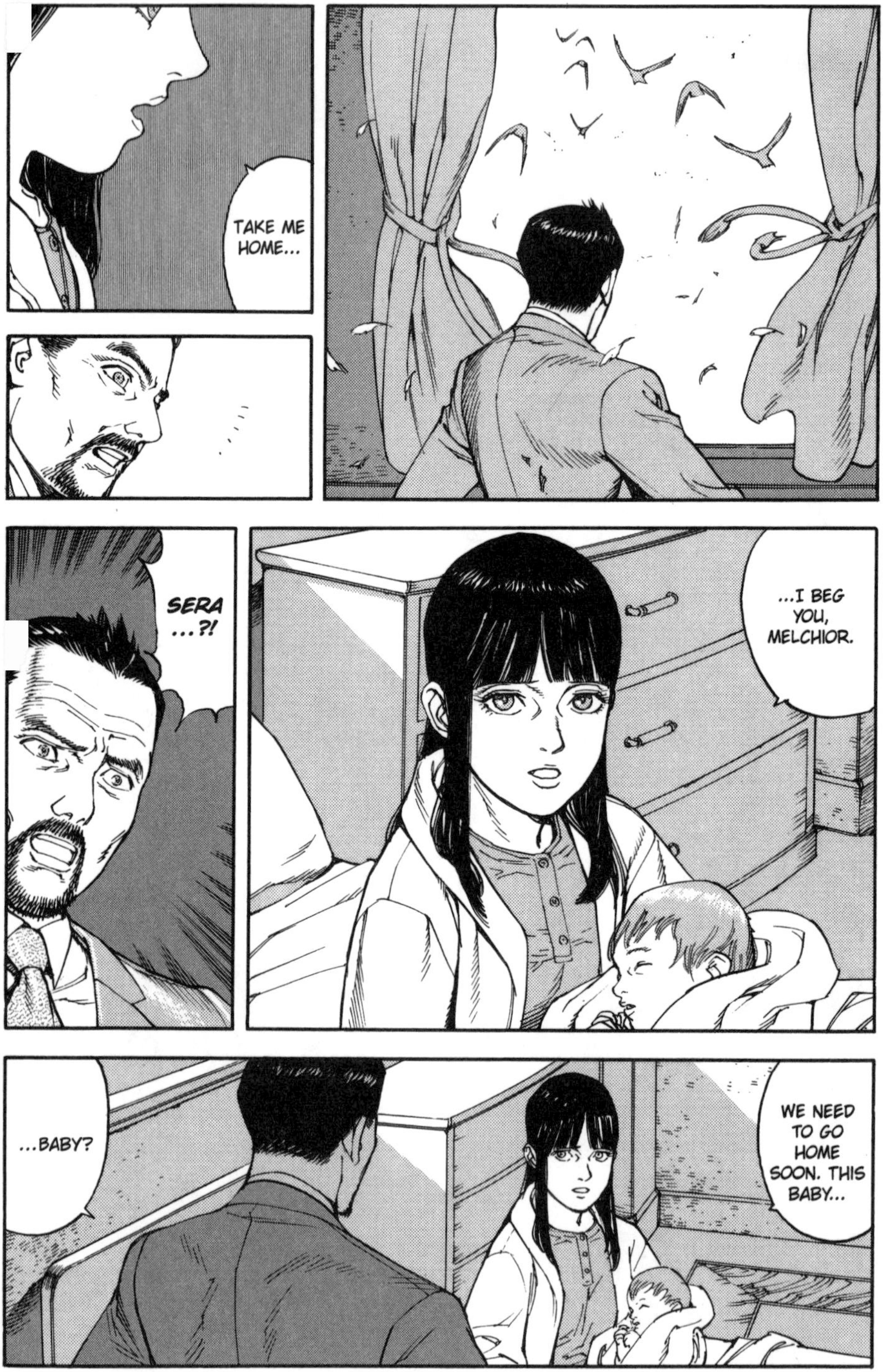
TAKE ME HOME...
...I BEG YOU, MELCHIOR.
SERA ...?!
WE NEED TO GO HOME SOON. THIS BABY...
...BABY?

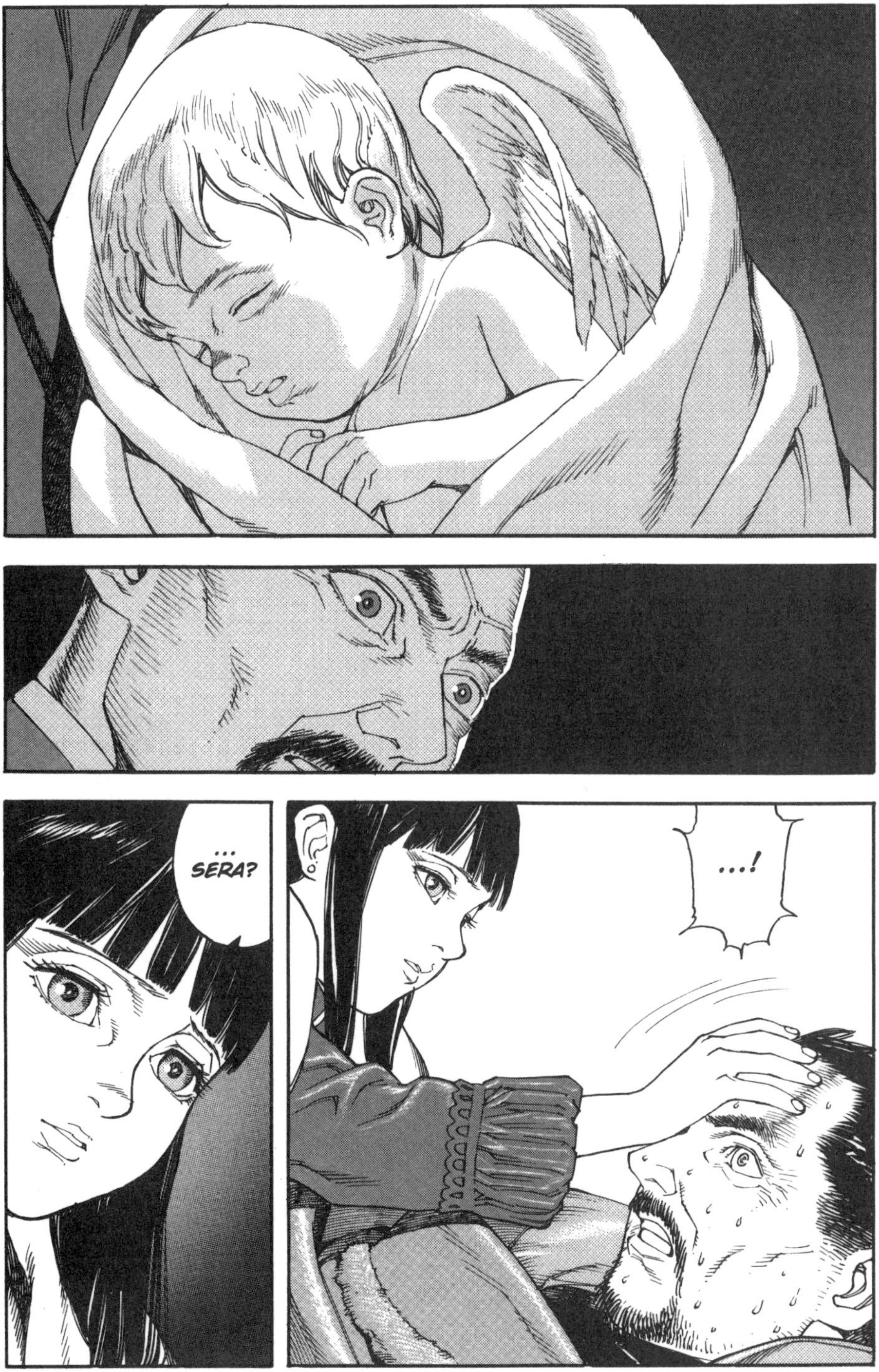
...!
... SERA?

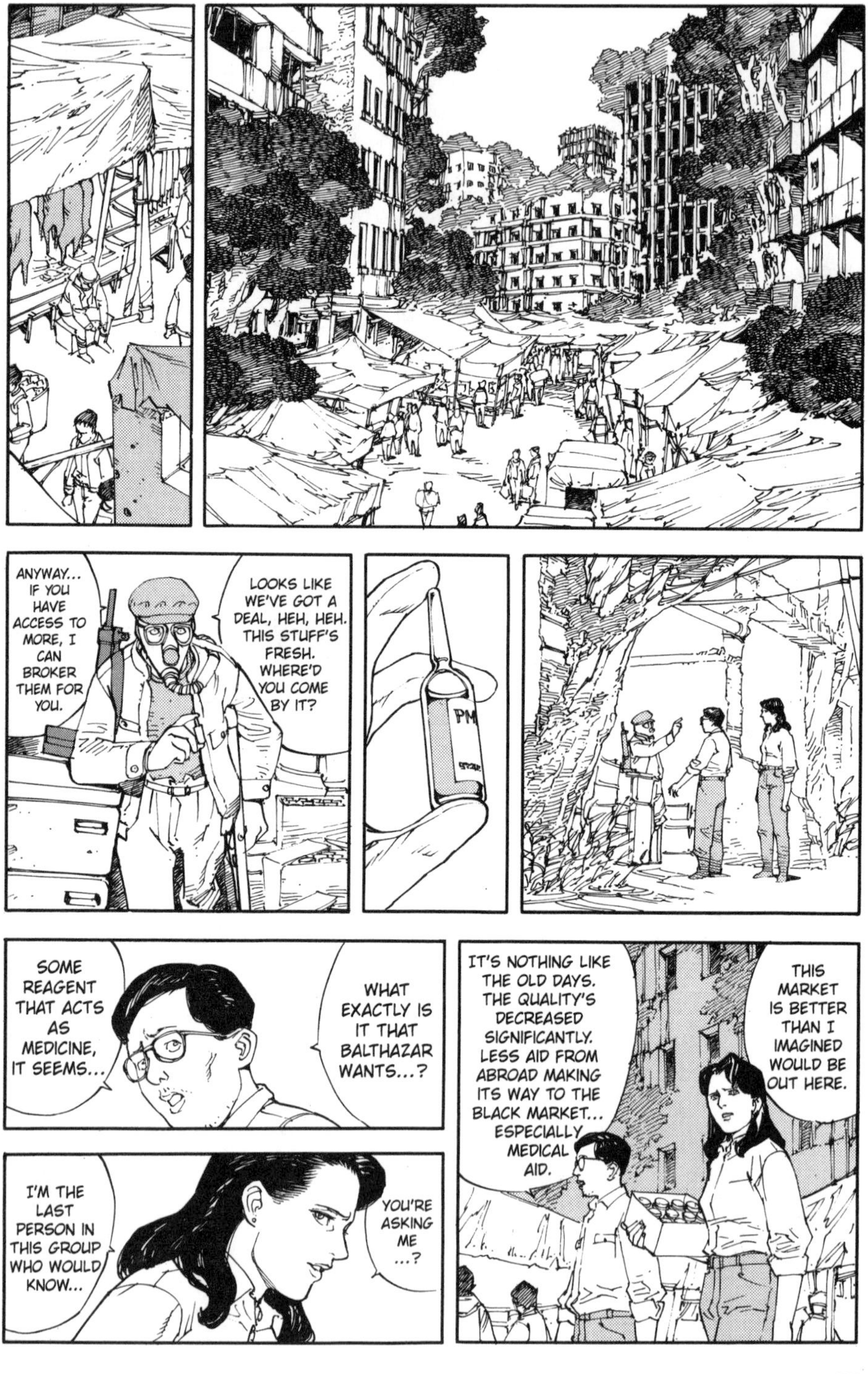
LOOKS LIKE WE'VE GOT A DEAL, HEH, HEH. THIS STUFF'S FRESH. WHERE'D YOU COME BY IT?
ANYWAY... IF YOU HAVE ACCESS TO MORE, I CAN BROKER THEM FOR YOU.
THIS MARKET IS BETTER THAN I IMAGINED WOULD BE OUT HERE.
IT'S NOTHING LIKE THE OLD DAYS. THE QUALITY'S DECREASED SIGNIFICANTLY. LESS AID FROM ABROAD MAKING ITS WAY TO THE BLACK MARKET... ESPECIALLY MEDICAL AID.
WHAT EXACTLY IS IT THAT BALTHAZAR WANTS...?
SOME REAGENT THAT ACTS AS MEDICINE, IT SEEMS...
YOU'RE ASKING ME ...?
I'M THE LAST PERSON IN THIS GROUP WHO WOULD KNOW...

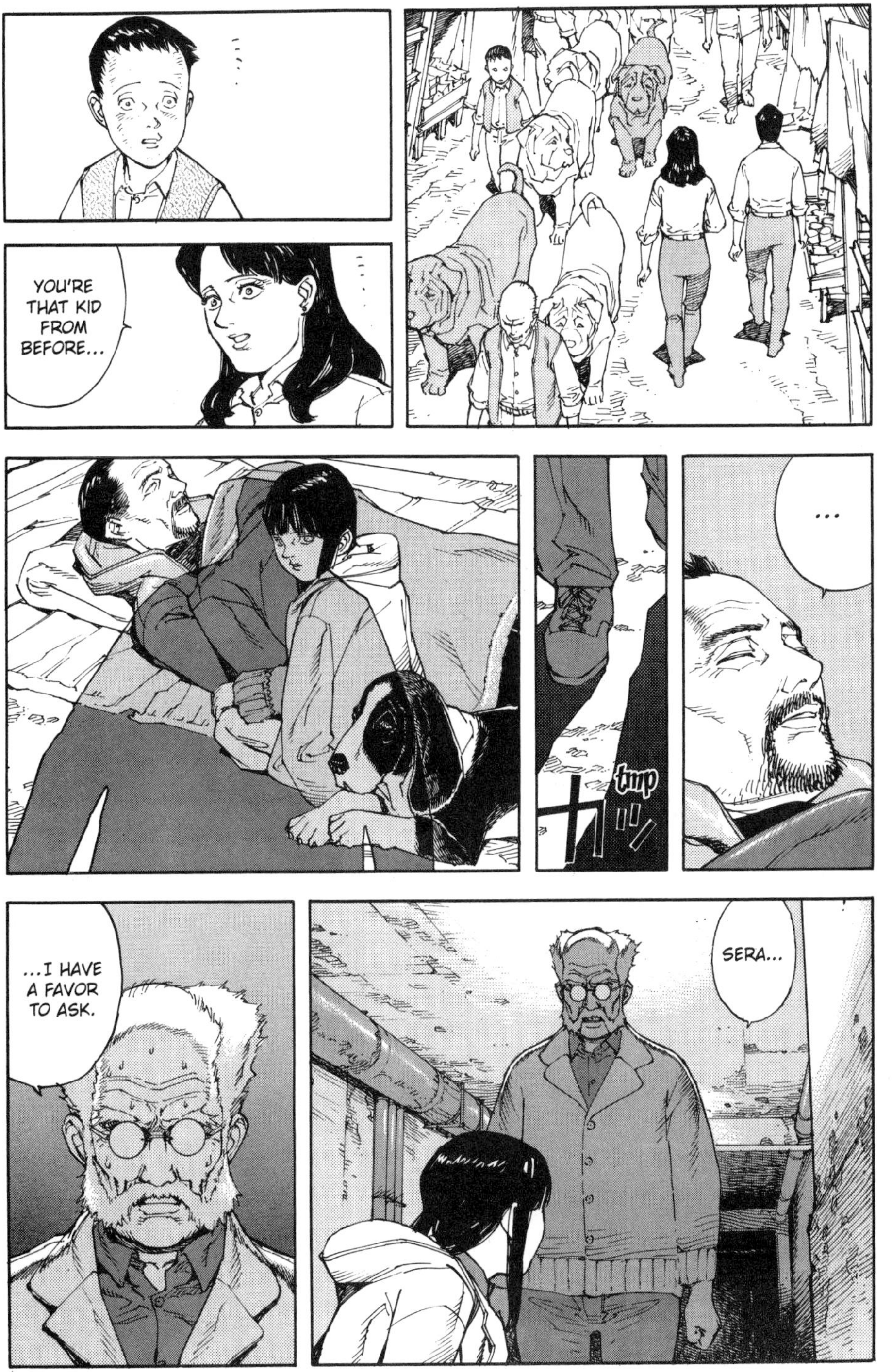
YOU'RE THAT KID FROM BEFORE...
...
tmp
SERA...
...I HAVE A FAVOR TO ASK.

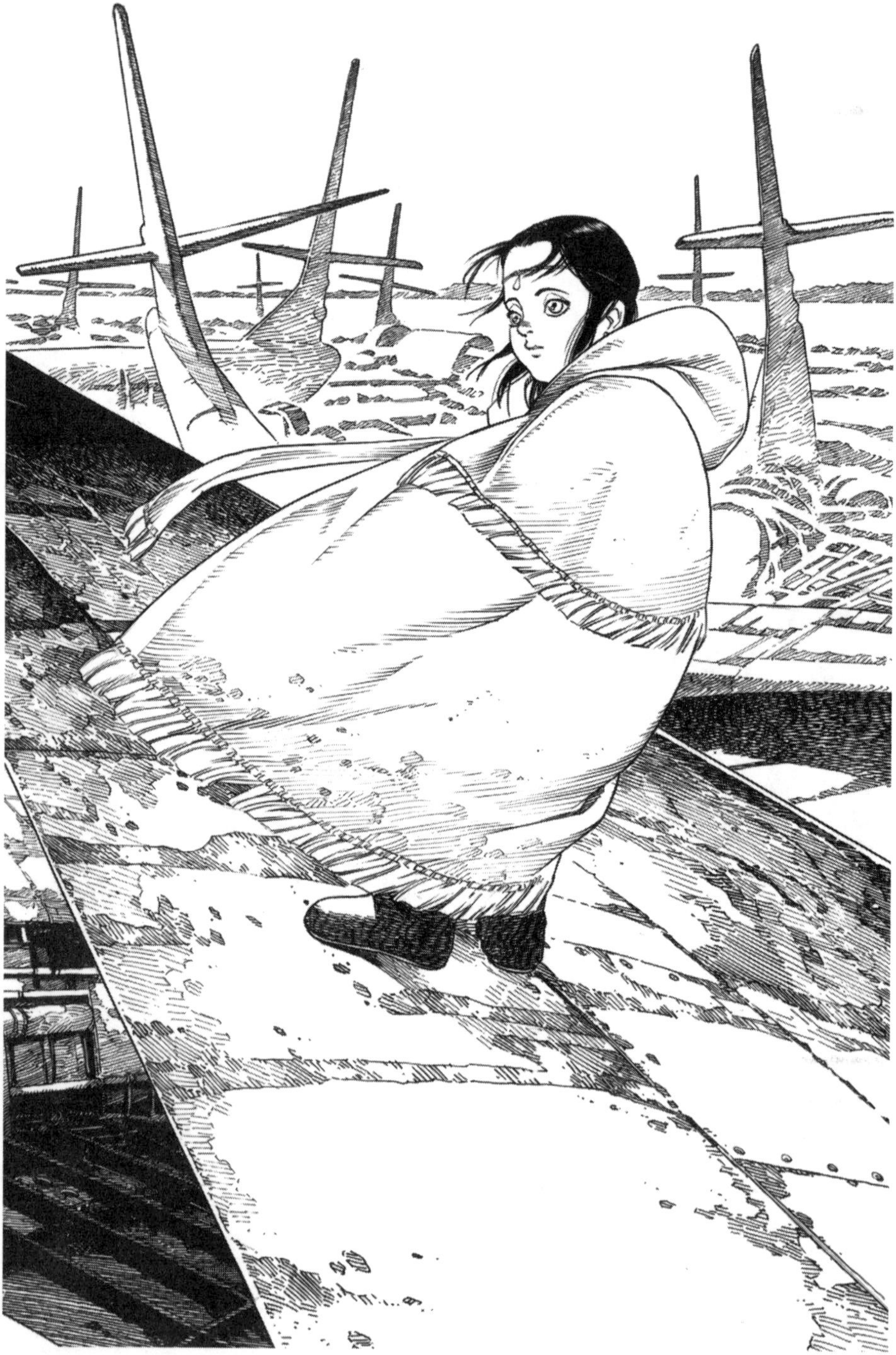

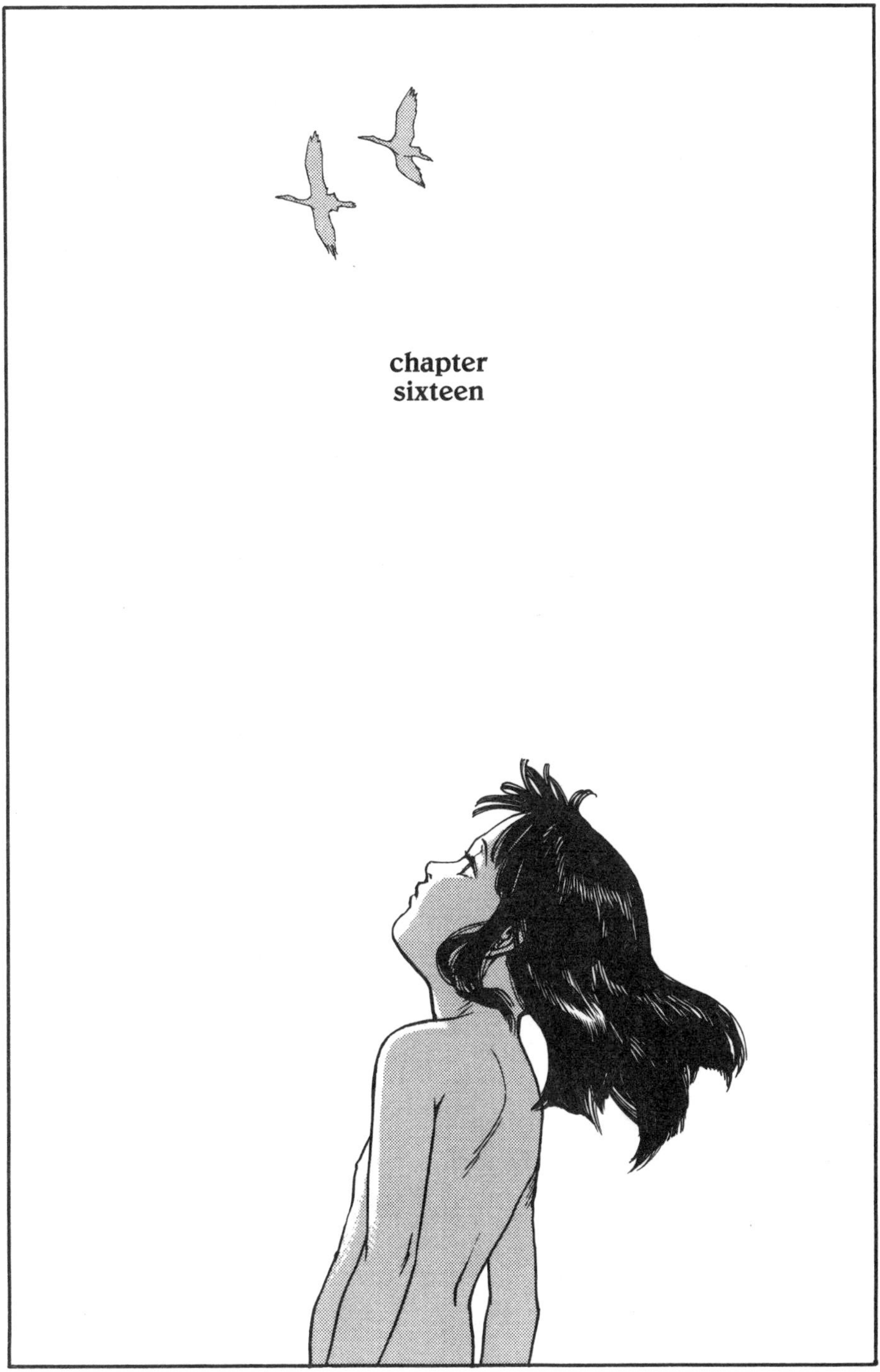

chapter
sixteen

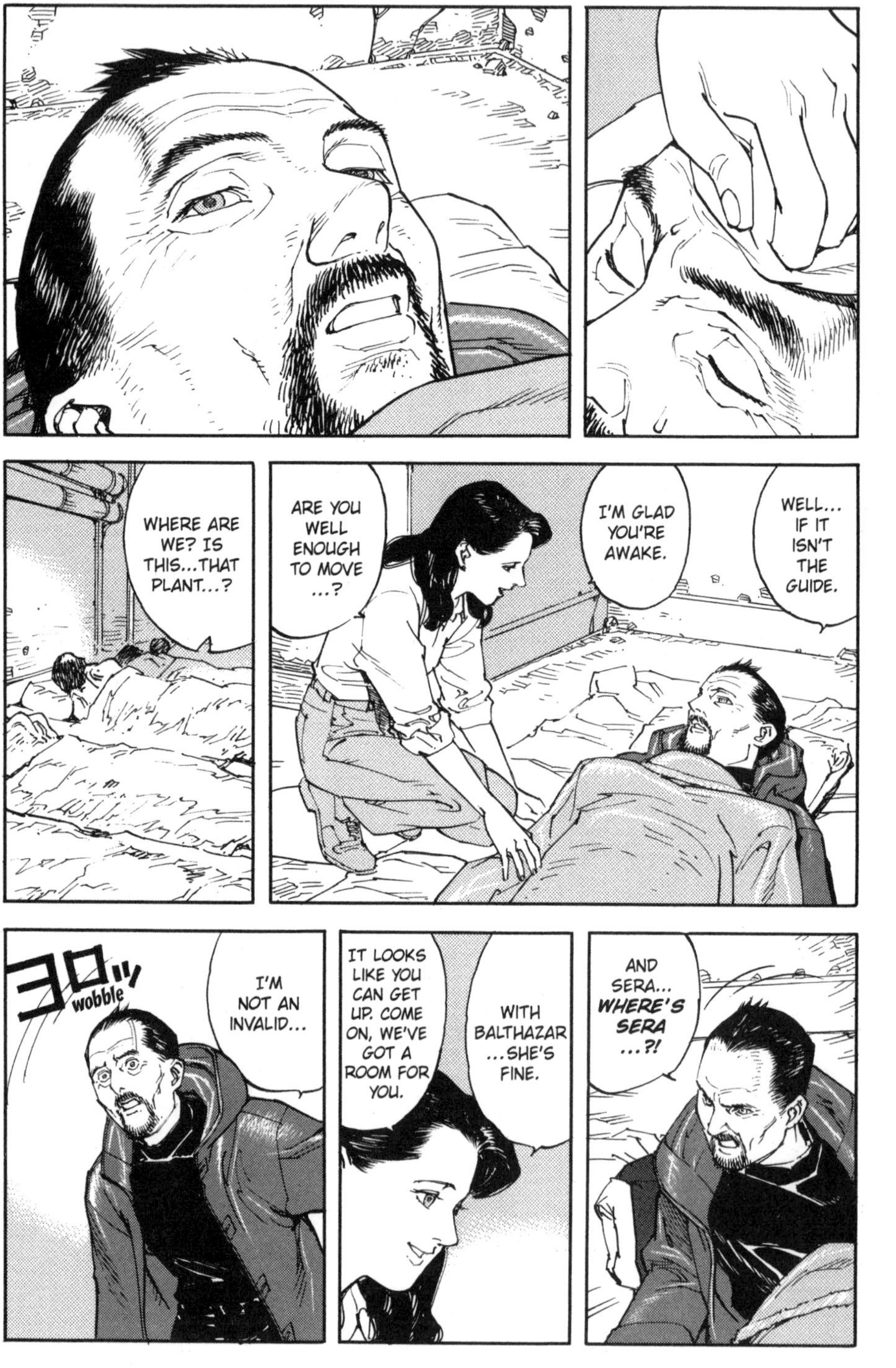
WELL... IF IT ISN'T THE GUIDE.
I'M GLAD YOU'RE AWAKE.
ARE YOU WELL ENOUGH TO MOVE ...?
WHERE ARE WE? IS THIS...THAT PLANT...?
AND SERA... WHERE'S SERA ...?!
WITH BALTHAZAR ...SHE'S FINE.
IT LOOKS LIKE YOU CAN GET UP. COME ON, WE'VE GOT A ROOM FOR YOU.
I'M NOT AN INVALID...
ヨロッ
wobble

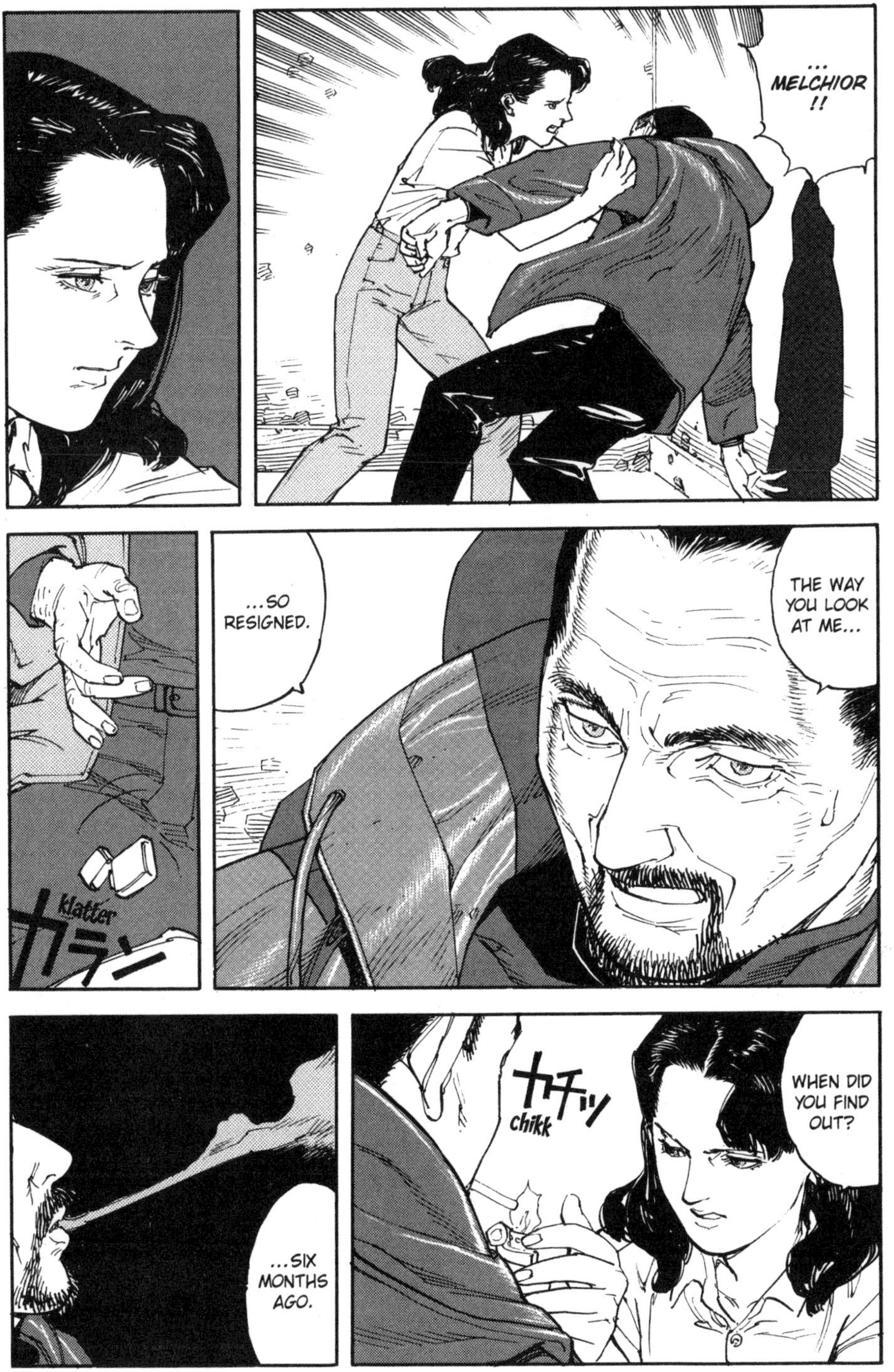
...
MELCHIOR
!!
THE WAY YOU LOOK AT ME...
...SO RESIGNED.
klatter
カラン
カチッ
chikk
WHEN DID YOU FIND OUT?
...SIX MONTHS AGO.

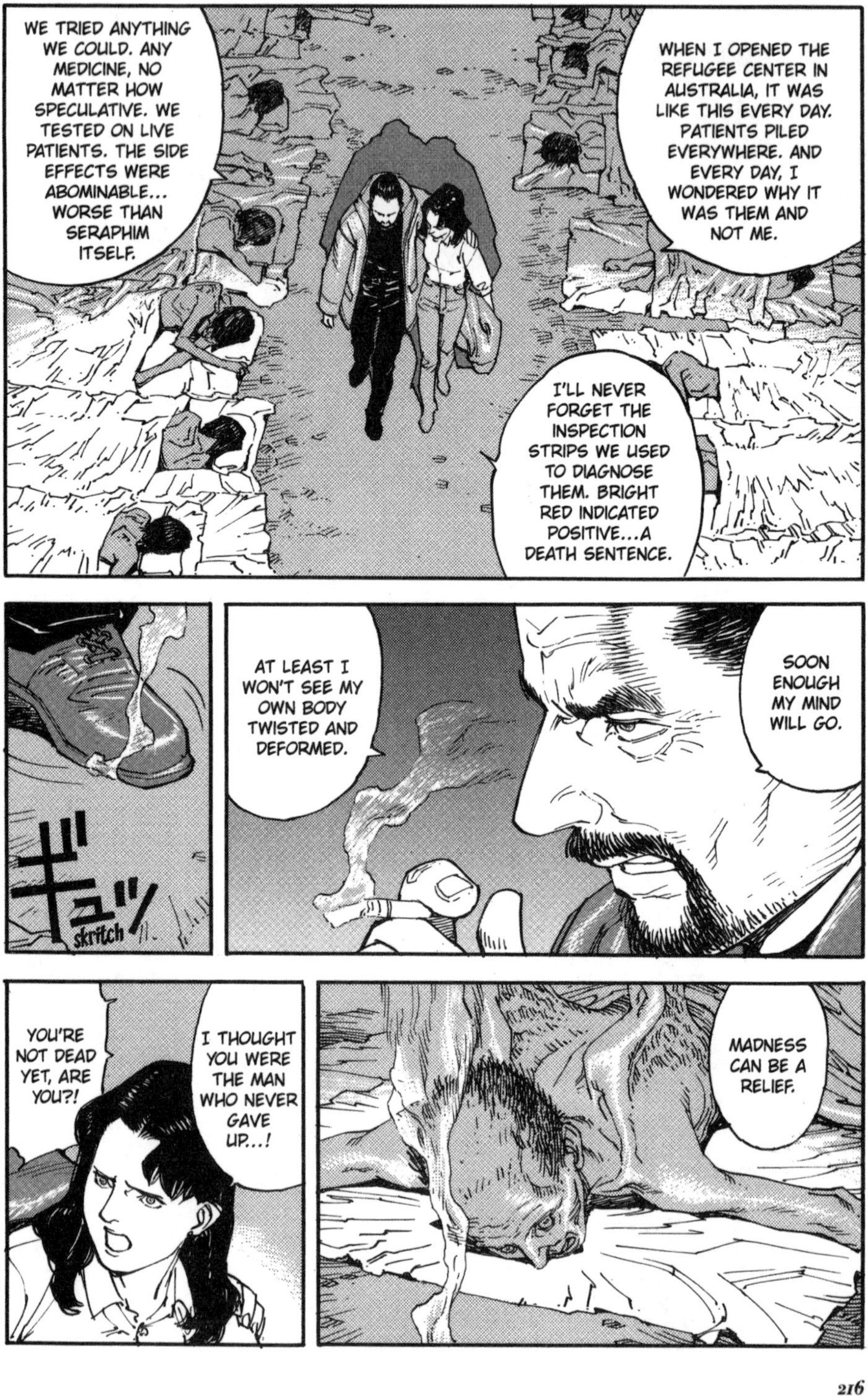
WHEN I OPENED THE REFUGEE CENTER IN AUSTRALIA, IT WAS LIKE THIS EVERY DAY. PATIENTS PILED EVERYWHERE. AND EVERY DAY, I WONDERED WHY IT WAS THEM AND NOT ME.
WE TRIED ANYTHING WE COULD. ANY MEDICINE, NO MATTER HOW SPECULATIVE. WE TESTED ON LIVE PATIENTS. THE SIDE EFFECTS WERE ABOMINABLE... WORSE THAN SERAPHIM ITSELF.
I'LL NEVER FORGET THE INSPECTION STRIPS WE USED TO DIAGNOSE THEM. BRIGHT RED INDICATED POSITIVE...A DEATH SENTENCE.
SOON ENOUGH MY MIND WILL GO.
AT LEAST I WON'T SEE MY OWN BODY TWISTED AND DEFORMED.
ギュッ
skritch
MADNESS CAN BE A RELIEF.
I THOUGHT YOU WERE THE MAN WHO NEVER GAVE UP...!
YOU'RE NOT DEAD YET, ARE YOU?!

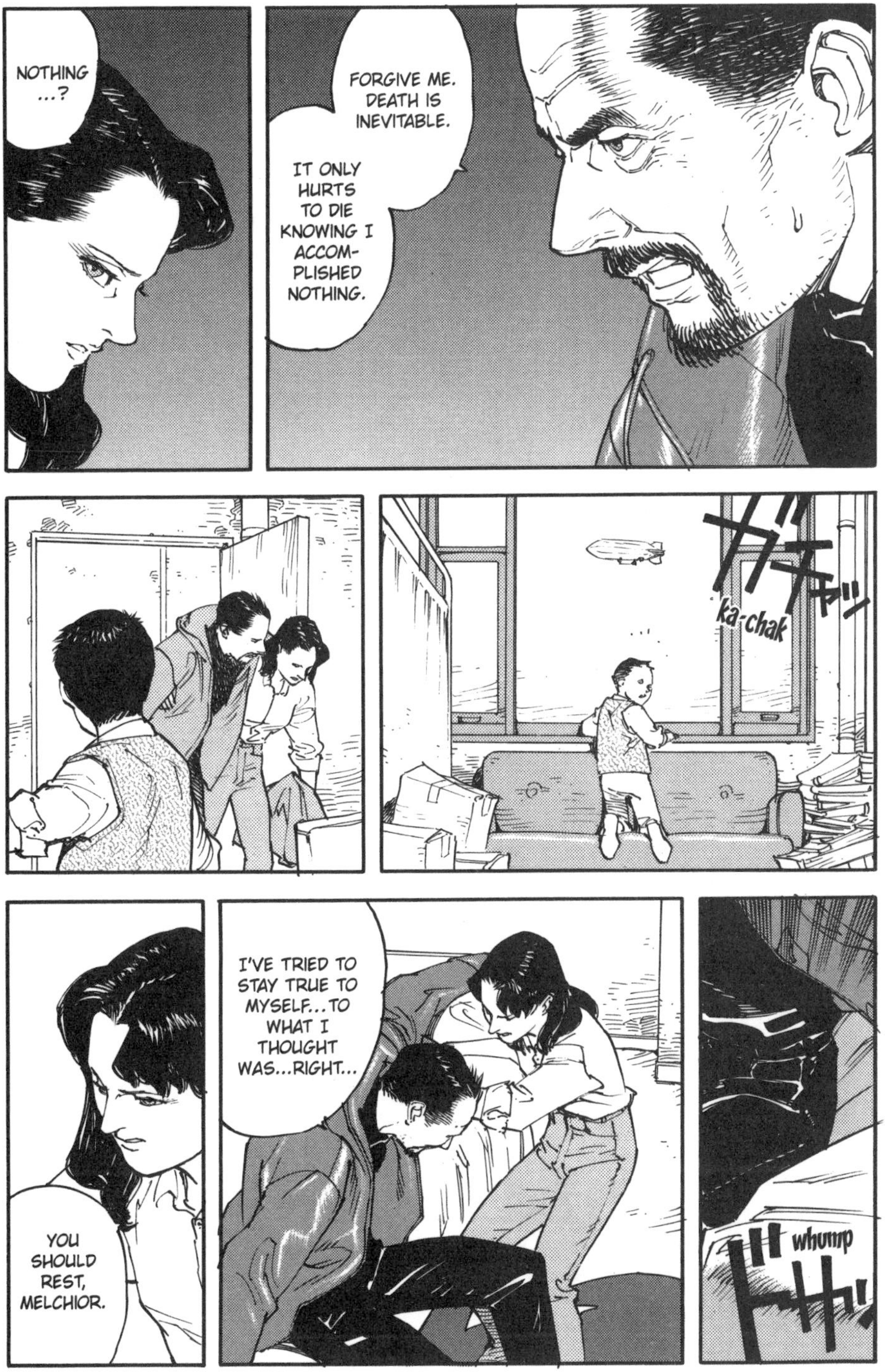
FORGIVE ME. DEATH IS INEVITABLE.
IT ONLY HURTS TO DIE KNOWING I ACCOMPLISHED NOTHING.
NOTHING ...?
ka-chak
whump
I'VE TRIED TO STAY TRUE TO MYSELF...TO WHAT I THOUGHT WAS...RIGHT...
YOU SHOULD REST, MELCHIOR.

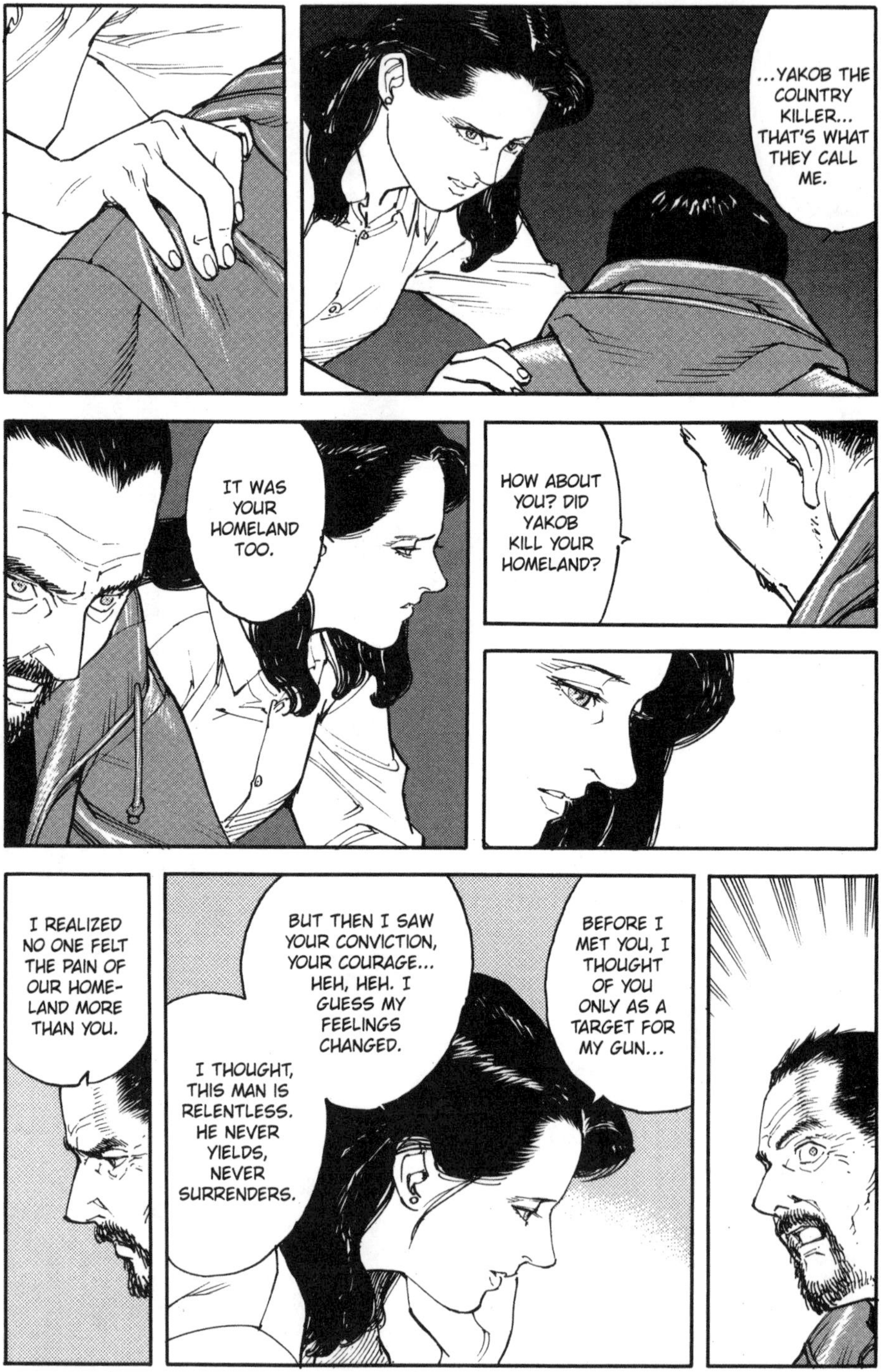
...YAKOB THE COUNTRY KILLER... THAT'S WHAT THEY CALL ME.
HOW ABOUT YOU? DID YAKOB KILL YOUR HOMELAND?
IT WAS YOUR HOMELAND TOO.
BEFORE I MET YOU, I THOUGHT OF YOU ONLY AS A TARGET FOR MY GUN...
BUT THEN I SAW YOUR CONVICTION, YOUR COURAGE... HEH, HEH. I GUESS MY FEELINGS CHANGED.
I THOUGHT, THIS MAN IS RELENTLESS. HE NEVER YIELDS, NEVER SURRENDERS.
I REALIZED NO ONE FELT THE PAIN OF OUR HOME-LAND MORE THAN YOU.

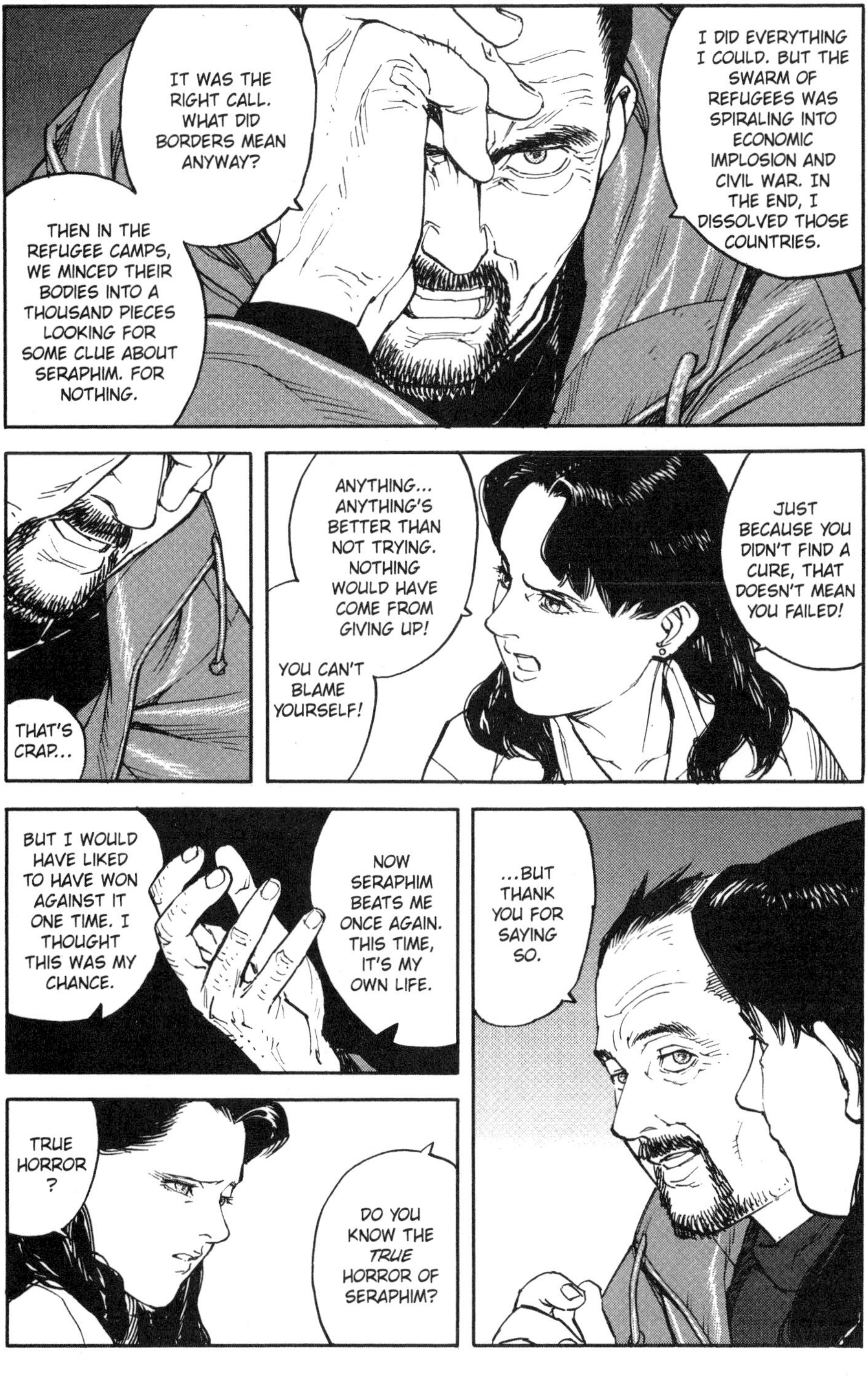
I DID EVERYTHING I COULD. BUT THE SWARM OF REFUGEES WAS SPIRALING INTO ECONOMIC IMPLOSION AND CIVIL WAR. IN THE END, I DISSOLVED THOSE COUNTRIES.
IT WAS THE RIGHT CALL. WHAT DID BORDERS MEAN ANYWAY?
THEN IN THE REFUGEE CAMPS, WE MINCED THEIR BODIES INTO A THOUSAND PIECES LOOKING FOR SOME CLUE ABOUT SERAPHIM. FOR NOTHING.
JUST BECAUSE YOU DIDN'T FIND A CURE, THAT DOESN'T MEAN YOU FAILED!
ANYTHING... ANYTHING'S BETTER THAN NOT TRYING. NOTHING WOULD HAVE COME FROM GIVING UP!
YOU CAN'T BLAME YOURSELF!
THAT'S CRAP...
...BUT THANK YOU FOR SAYING SO.
NOW SERAPHIM BEATS ME ONCE AGAIN. THIS TIME, IT'S MY OWN LIFE.
BUT I WOULD HAVE LIKED TO HAVE WON AGAINST IT ONE TIME. I THOUGHT THIS WAS MY CHANCE.
DO YOU KNOW THE *TRUE* HORROR OF SERAPHIM?
TRUE HORROR ?

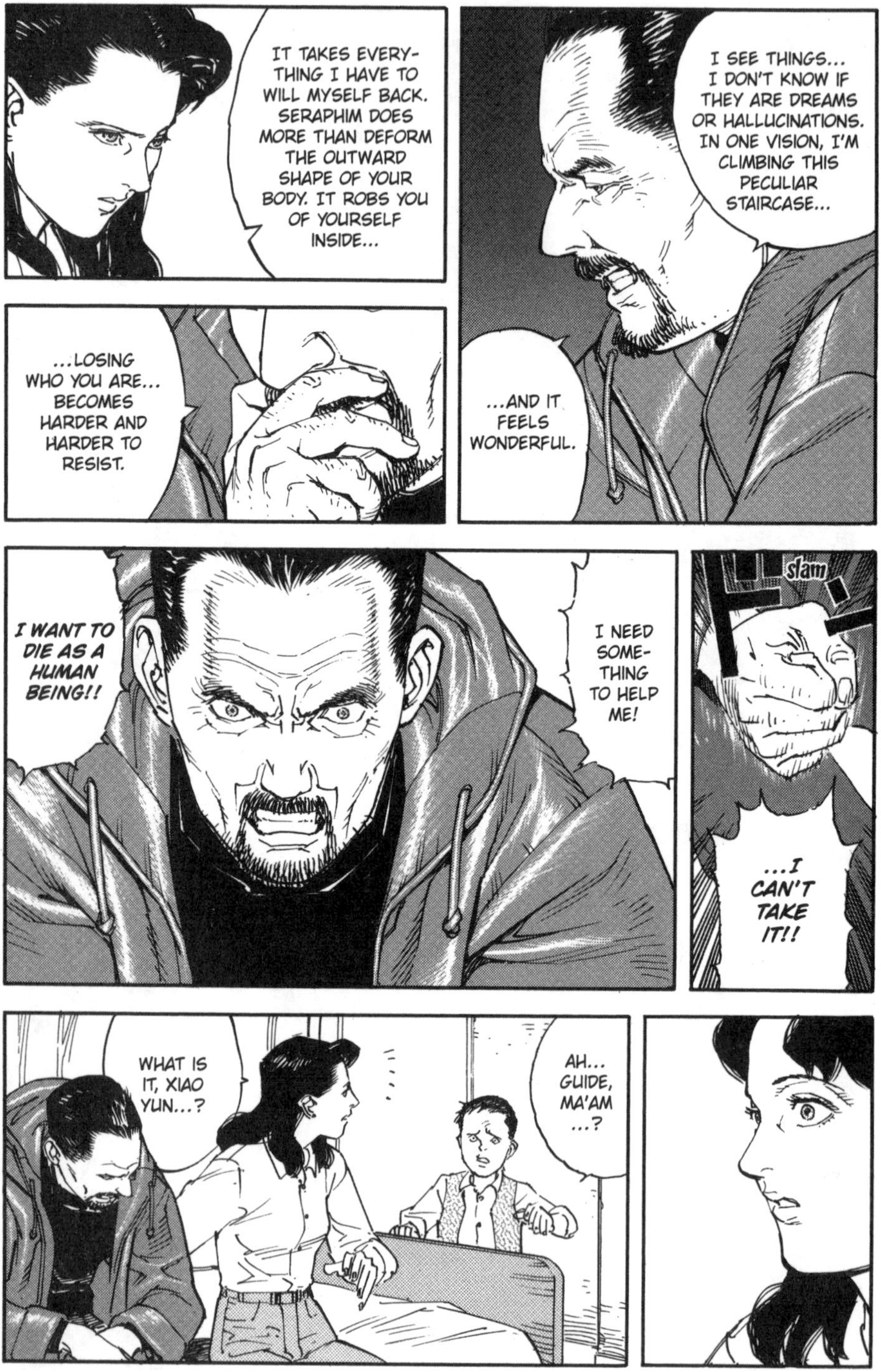
I SEE THINGS... I DON'T KNOW IF THEY ARE DREAMS OR HALLUCINATIONS. IN ONE VISION, I'M CLIMBING THIS PECULIAR STAIRCASE...
...AND IT FEELS WONDERFUL.
IT TAKES EVERY-THING I HAVE TO WILL MYSELF BACK. SERAPHIM DOES MORE THAN DEFORM THE OUTWARD SHAPE OF YOUR BODY. IT ROBS YOU OF YOURSELF INSIDE...
...LOSING WHO YOU ARE... BECOMES HARDER AND HARDER TO RESIST.
slam
...I CAN'T TAKE IT!!
I NEED SOME-THING TO HELP ME!
I WANT TO DIE AS A HUMAN BEING!!
AH... GUIDE, MA'AM ...?
...
WHAT IS IT, XIAO YUN...?

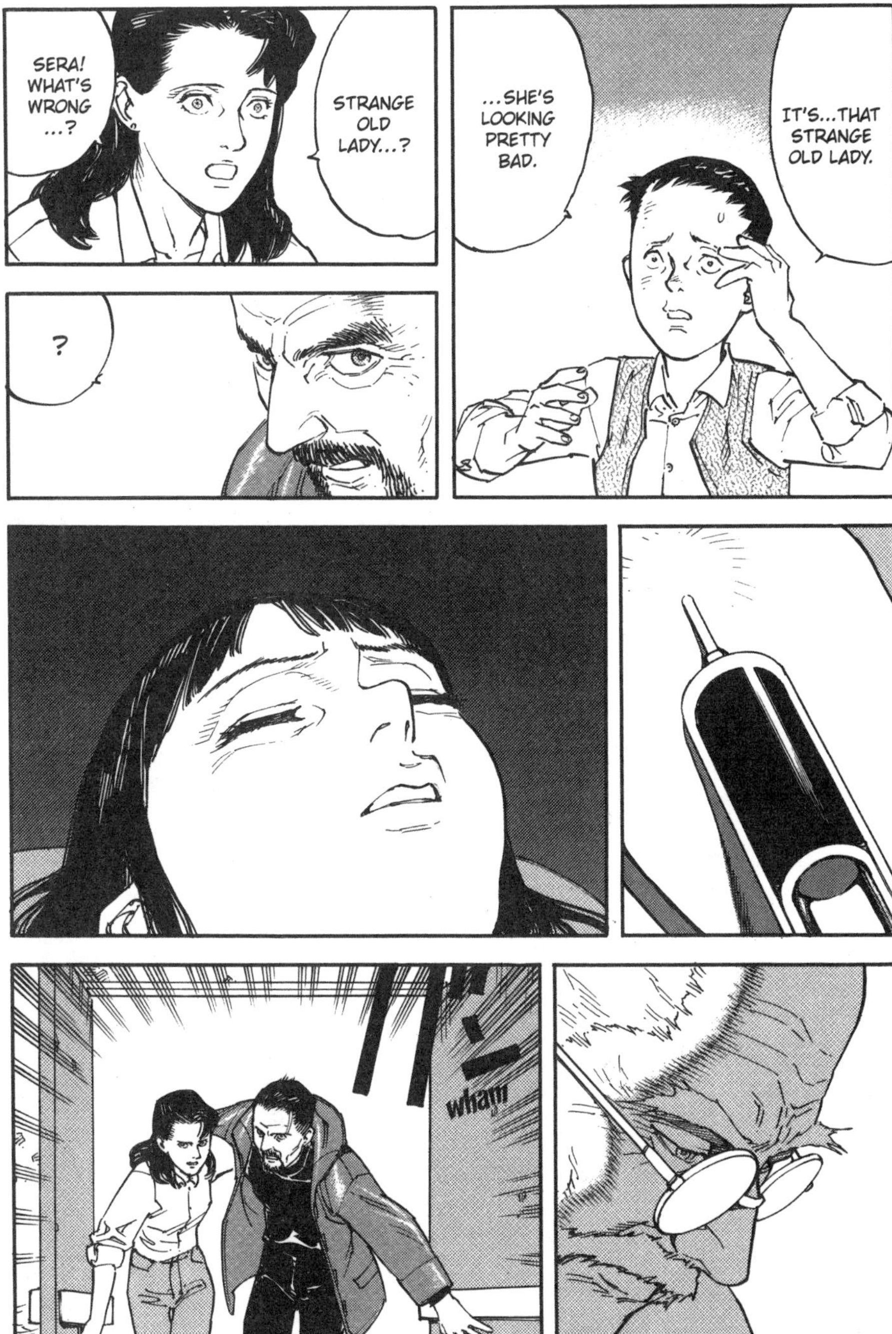
IT'S...THAT STRANGE OLD LADY.
...SHE'S LOOKING PRETTY BAD.
STRANGE OLD LADY...?
SERA! WHAT'S WRONG ...?
?
wham

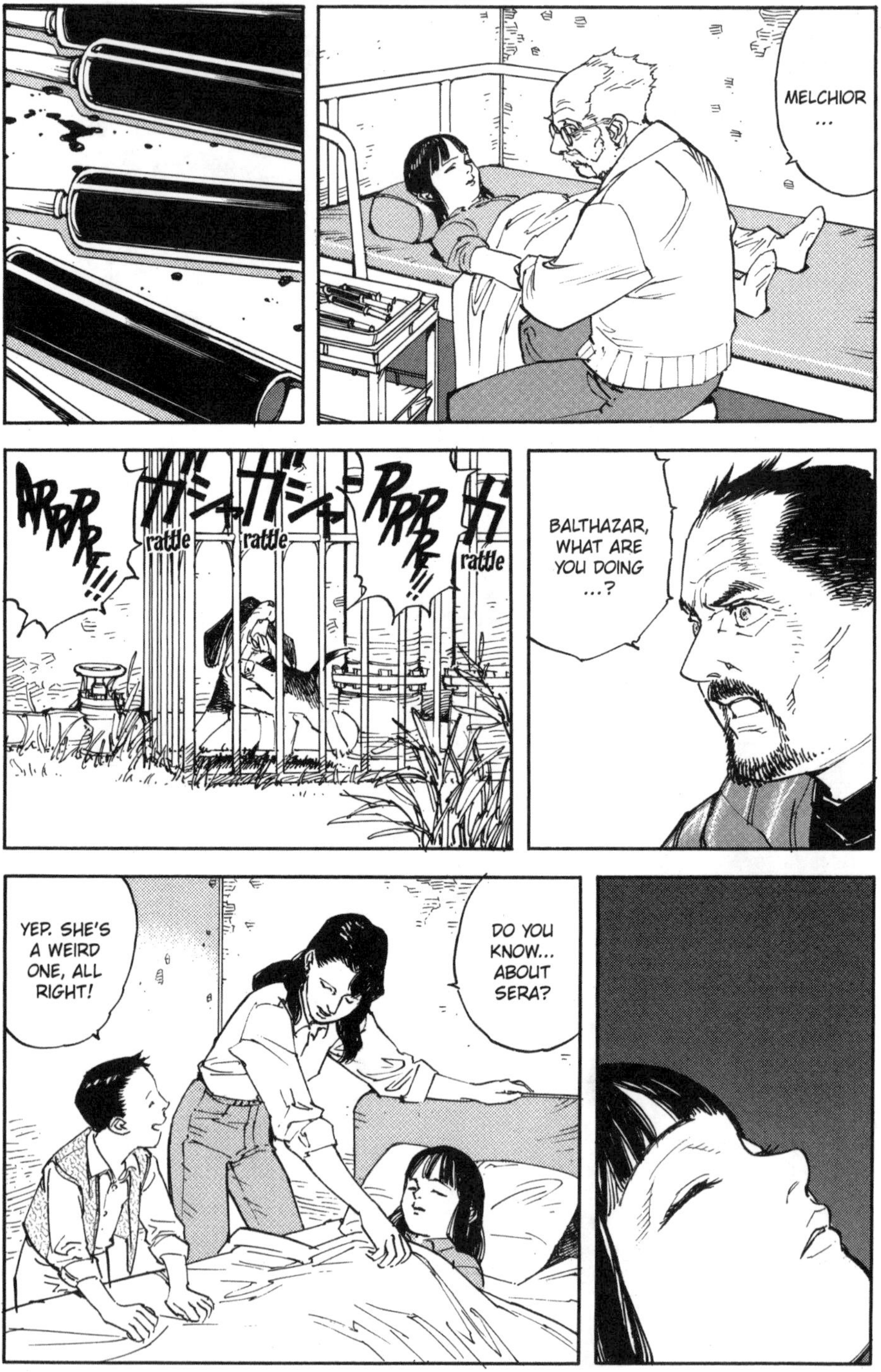
MELCHIOR ...
BALTHAZAR, WHAT ARE YOU DOING ...?
ガ
rattle
RRRRF!!!
ガシャ
rattle
ガシャ
rattle
ARRRRF!!!
DO YOU KNOW... ABOUT SERA?
YEP. SHE'S A WEIRD ONE, ALL RIGHT!

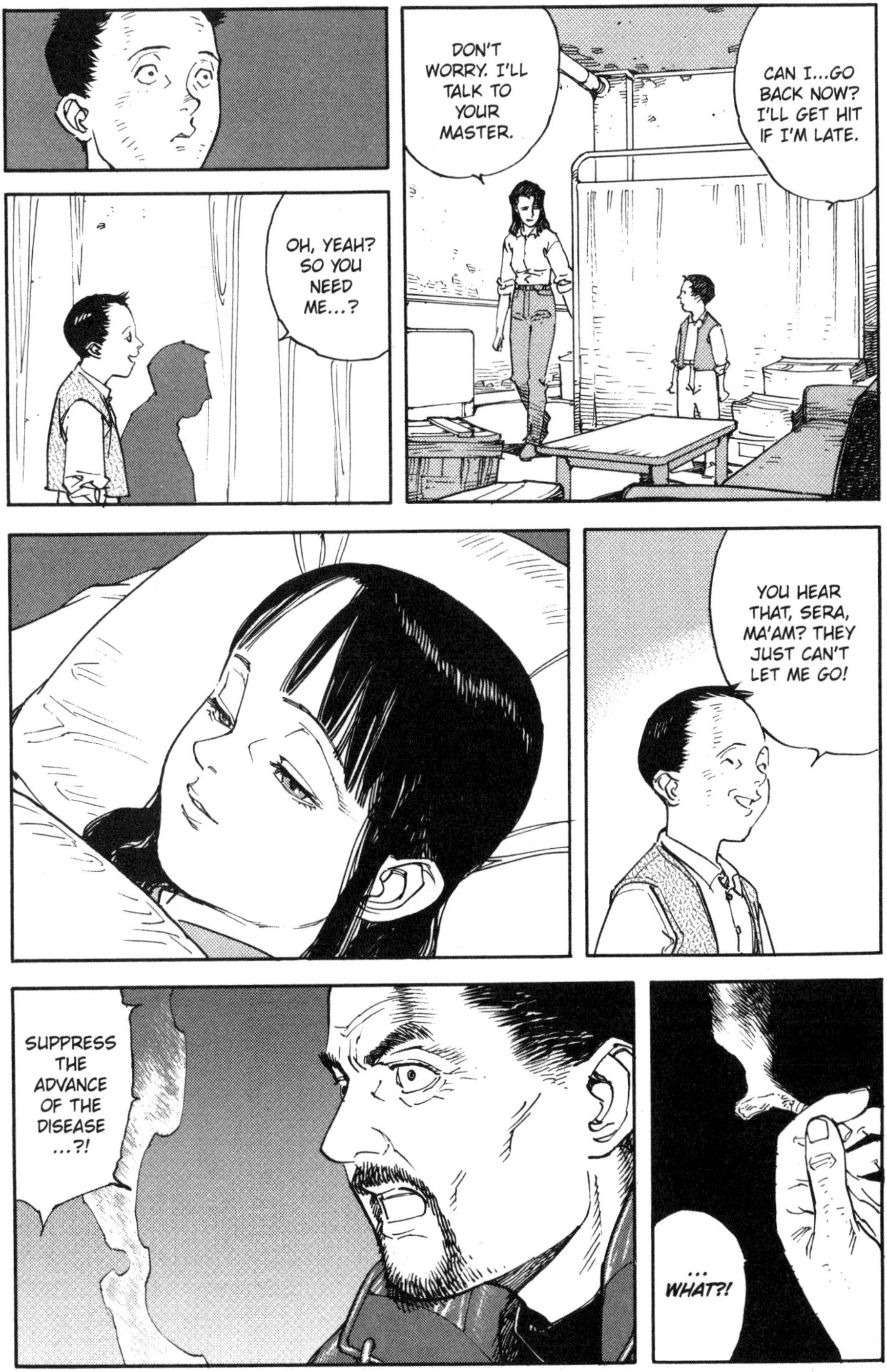
CAN I...GO BACK NOW? I'LL GET HIT IF I'M LATE.
DON'T WORRY. I'LL TALK TO YOUR MASTER.
OH, YEAH? SO YOU NEED ME...?
YOU HEAR THAT, SERA, MA'AM? THEY JUST CAN'T LET ME GO!
...WHAT?!
SUPPRESS THE ADVANCE OF THE DISEASE ...?!

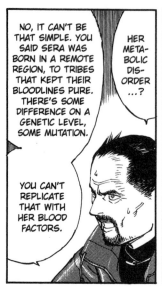

A TREATMENT MADE FROM SERA'S BLOOD. IT INHIBITS SERAPHIM'S PROGRESSION.
YOU KNOW MOST DON'T LAST A YEAR AFTER INFECTION. SERA HAS BEEN ALIVE FOR MORE THAN TEN.
HER METABOLIC DISORDER ...?
NO, IT CAN'T BE THAT SIMPLE. YOU SAID SERA WAS BORN IN A REMOTE REGION, TO TRIBES THAT KEPT THEIR BLOODLINES PURE. THERE'S SOME DIFFERENCE ON A GENETIC LEVEL, SOME MUTATION.
YOU CAN'T REPLICATE THAT WITH HER BLOOD FACTORS.
WHY HAVE YOU KEPT THIS A SECRET?
NOT JUST ME...A FEW OTHERS KNOW. THE POLITICAL POWER OF A CURE WOULD BE IMMEASURABLE.
SO WE HIDE IT.
HIDE IT? IDIOTS!! A DISCOVERY OF THIS MAGNITUDE... YOU HAVE NO RIGHT TO KEEP IT FROM THE PUBLIC!
WHAT ABOUT SERA'S RIGHTS?! SHE ALONE IS THE SOURCE OF THIS SERUM! CAN YOU IMAGINE HOW THEY'D FIGHT OVER HER?!
I WILL NEVER ALLOW...
...NO... THAT *IS* JUST AN EXCUSE.
...I JUST DIDN'T WANT TO LOSE HER.

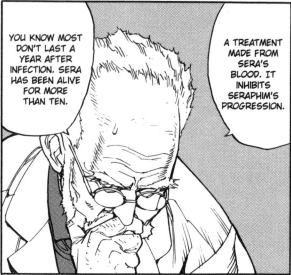

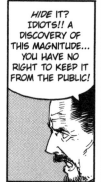

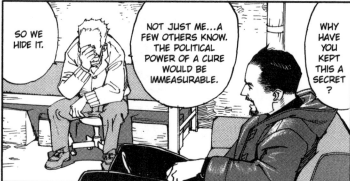

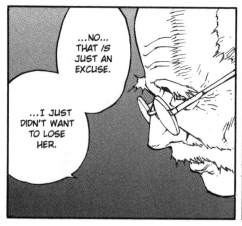

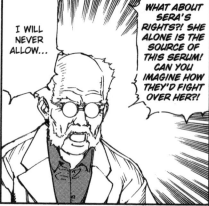

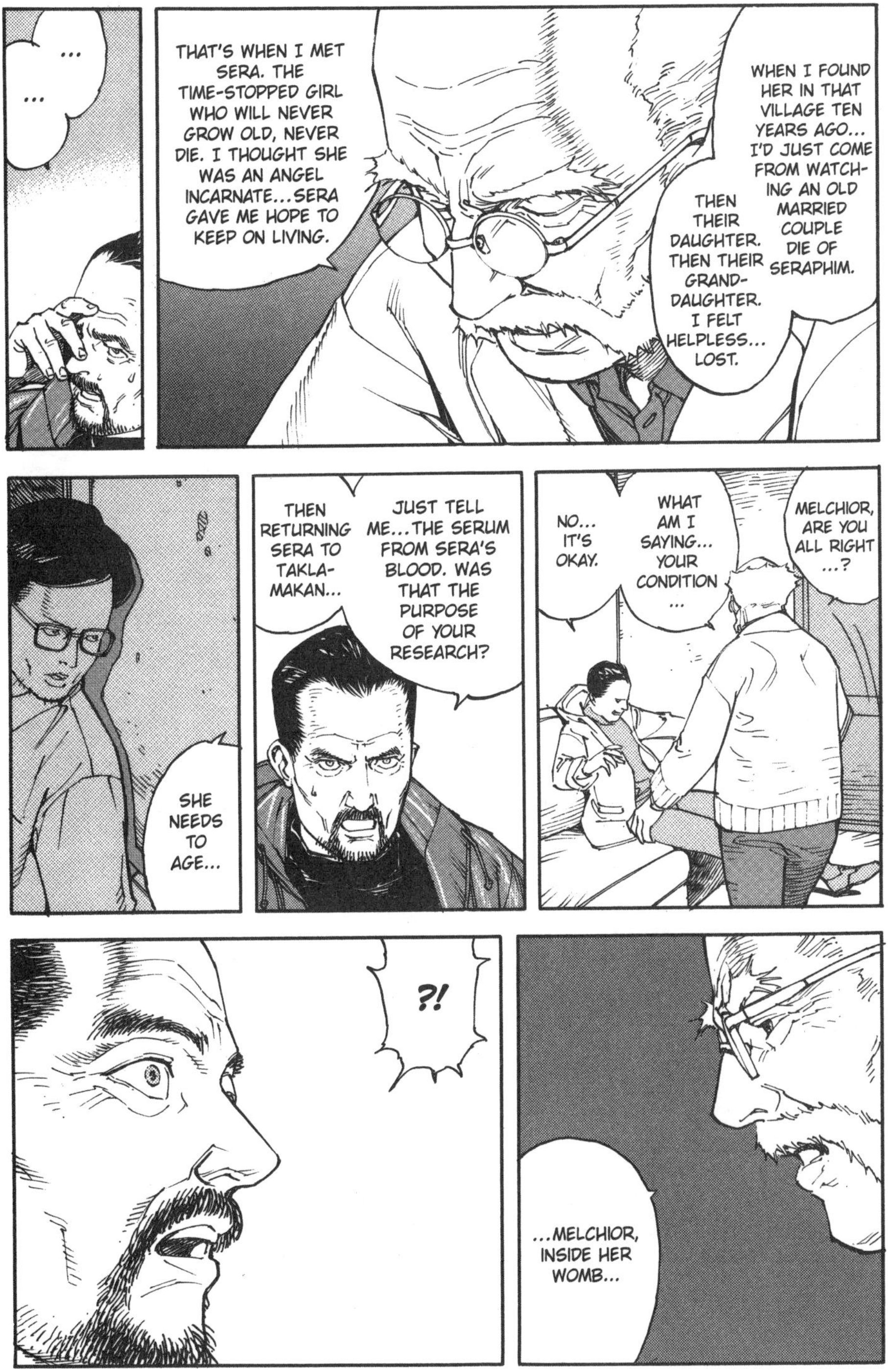
WHEN I FOUND HER IN THAT VILLAGE TEN YEARS AGO... I'D JUST COME FROM WATCHING AN OLD MARRIED COUPLE DIE OF SERAPHIM.
THEN THEIR DAUGHTER. THEN THEIR GRAND-DAUGHTER. I FELT HELPLESS... LOST.
THAT'S WHEN I MET SERA. THE TIME-STOPPED GIRL WHO WILL NEVER GROW OLD, NEVER DIE. I THOUGHT SHE WAS AN ANGEL INCARNATE...SERA GAVE ME HOPE TO KEEP ON LIVING.
... ...
MELCHIOR, ARE YOU ALL RIGHT ...?
WHAT AM I SAYING... YOUR CONDITION ...
NO... IT'S OKAY.
JUST TELL ME...THE SERUM FROM SERA'S BLOOD. WAS THAT THE PURPOSE OF YOUR RESEARCH?
THEN RETURNING SERA TO TAKLA-MAKAN...
SHE NEEDS TO AGE...
...MELCHIOR, INSIDE HER WOMB...
?!

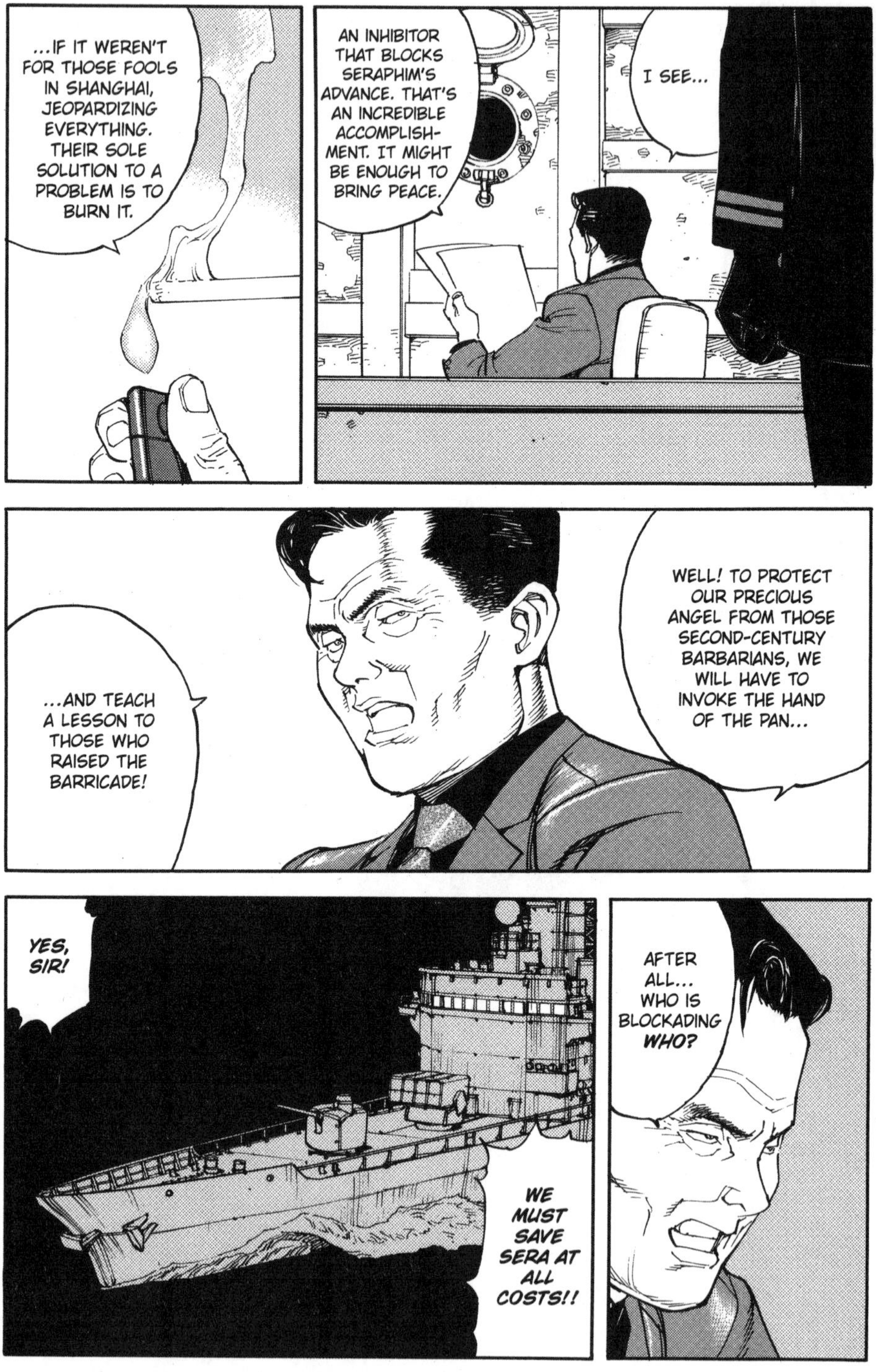
I SEE...
AN INHIBITOR THAT BLOCKS SERAPHIM'S ADVANCE. THAT'S AN INCREDIBLE ACCOMPLISHMENT. IT MIGHT BE ENOUGH TO BRING PEACE.
...IF IT WEREN'T FOR THOSE FOOLS IN SHANGHAI, JEOPARDIZING EVERYTHING. THEIR SOLE SOLUTION TO A PROBLEM IS TO BURN IT.
WELL! TO PROTECT OUR PRECIOUS ANGEL FROM THOSE SECOND-CENTURY BARBARIANS, WE WILL HAVE TO INVOKE THE HAND OF THE PAN...
...AND TEACH A LESSON TO THOSE WHO RAISED THE BARRICADE!
AFTER ALL... WHO IS BLOCKADING *WHO?*
WE MUST SAVE SERA AT ALL COSTS!!
YES, SIR!

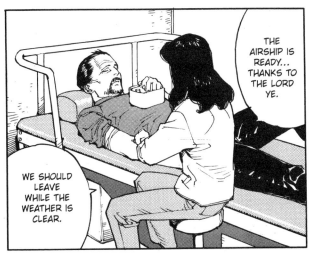

THE AIRSHIP IS READY... THANKS TO THE LORD YE.
WE SHOULD LEAVE WHILE THE WEATHER IS CLEAR.
I'LL LIVE AS LONG AS THIS MEDICINE HOLDS OUT.
SERA GAVE ME THIS BORROWED TIME...
...NOW WE'LL HAVE TO SEE WHAT SHE WANTS TO DO.
MELCHIOR ...?

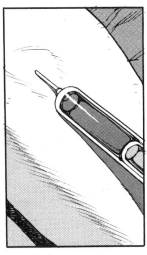

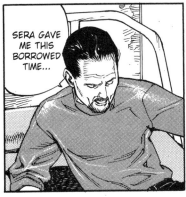

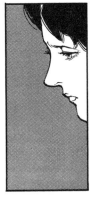

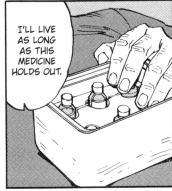

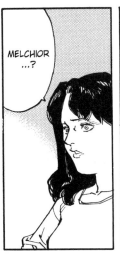

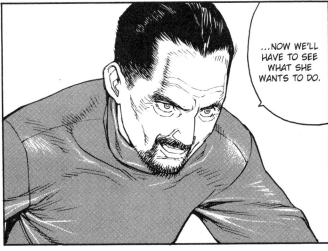

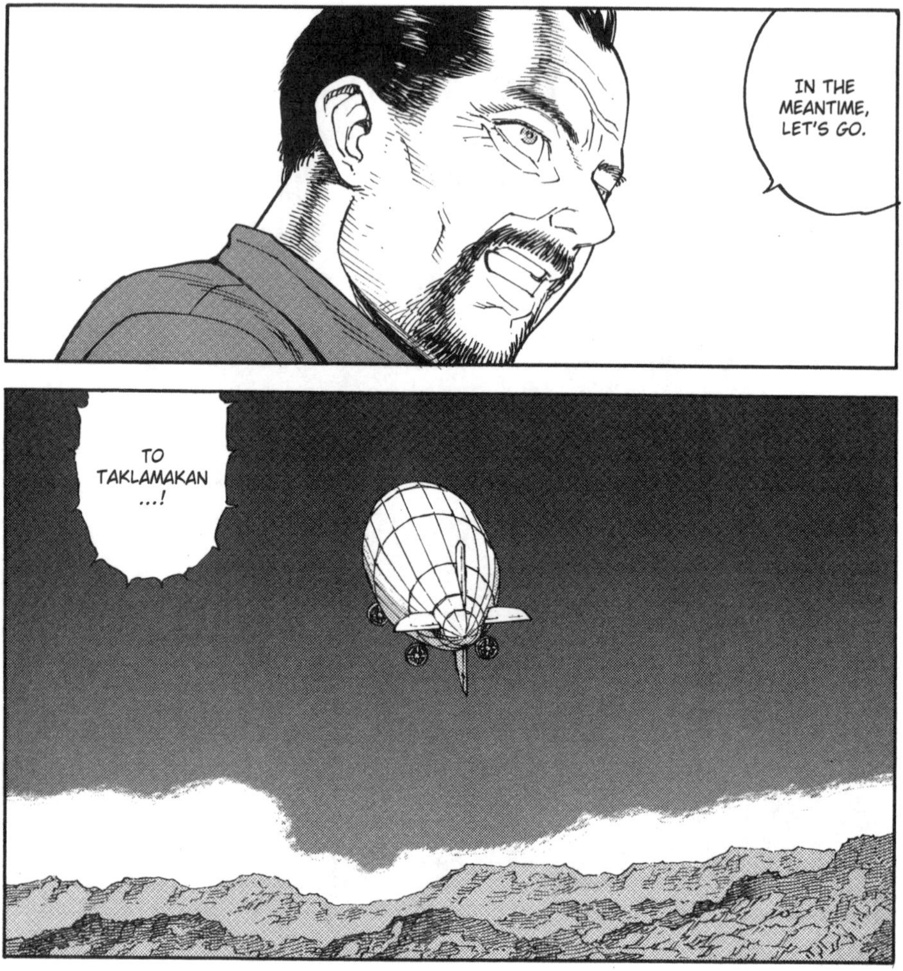
IN THE MEANTIME, LET'S GO.
TO TAKLAMAKAN ...!

Seraphim 266613336 Wings **left off here in November of 1995.**

ABOUT *SERAPHIM 266613336 WINGS*
by Takashi Watanabe

Seraphim 266613336 Wings began serialization in the May 1994 issue of *Animage* magazine, with the final chapter to be published appearing in the November 1995 issue. The story was never finished. This is the first collected edition.

Some changes have been made for the collected edition. During *Seraphim*'s initial run in *Animage*, the credits for the first twelve chapters read, "Satoshi Kon, artist; Mamoru Oshii, writer." For chapters 13–16, the credits read, "Created by Satoshi Kon and Mamoru Oshii." The kanji used for the word *Magi* also changed with chapter 13, but this collected edition has standardized these differences.

The story of *Seraphim* began in March of 1994, when the final chapter of Hayao Miyazaki's long-running manga *Nausicaä of the Valley of the Wind* appeared in *Animage*. *Nausicaä* had been a breakout success, and the editorial department of the magazine was looking for another hit. They commissioned Mamoru Oshii to come up with a series. Oshii created the basic tone and background of the world of *Seraphim*, and wrote the rough outline for the plot. He then brought on Satoshi Kon as the artist, whom he had worked with as a layout supervisor on the film *Patlabor 2*.

The prologue at the beginning of this book was the first published chapter of the serialization. At the time, Oshii said to his editor, "Of all the work I have done in my life, this is my most ambitious." The scale of the story was magnificent. Oshii was enthusiastic, and had his eye on possibly animating the series in the future. Satoshi Kon was more cautious, saying, "Regarding this new serialization with Oshii, I want to take our time, and work slowly and carefully."

Kon got his wish. The two met constantly, working out details of the story with meticulous planning and intention. Working from Oshii's script, Kon questioned Oshii over any uncertainty. He paused working until he received a sufficient answer.

As Kon became more involved in the story, he became more assertive in his opinions, questioning Oshii's story and making suggestions on how to improve it, often saying, "How about if we . . ." Oshii incorporated more and more of Kon's ideas. This resulted in a unique world, charming and detailed, with no obvious distinction between the two men's work.

Eventually, this back-and-forth style took its toll. Discord sprang up over their respective roles, and there was a dispute over the credit for the work. The conflict grew until finally the series was put on hiatus.

Satoshi Kon has passed away. Speculating too deeply about the situation behind *Seraphim* is an exercise in foolishness, one that we wish to avoid. However, looking back, it is easy to imagine the difficulties arising from two men creating a single work, both of whom were proud to wear the title of "director."

Reading *Seraphim* can be an exercise in frustration, especially when you flip to that final page and know that you never get to see how the story ends. But by then the story has gripped you and won't let you go easily. You can't help but imagine the possibilities.

Mamoru Oshii built his world as a logical construction, one which Satoshi Kon then expanded and evolved with his art. *Seraphim* is like a dream—a transient moment, a fragment half-remembered—but one that was real nonetheless.

Takashi Watanabe was the editor in charge of Seraphim *at the time of its original serialization in* Animage *during 1994–95. He is currently head of the visual art department of the media station of Kadokawa Shoten. We express our gratitude for his comments, which originally ran in the Japanese edition of* Seraphim 266613336 Wings, *published in 2011.*

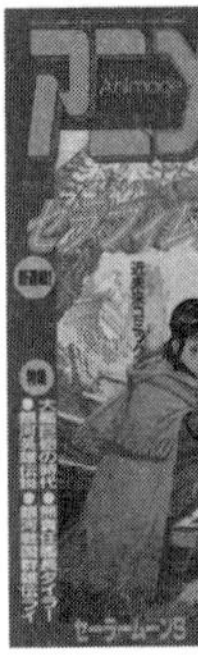
アニメージュ
5

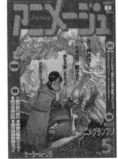

Cover to the May 1994 issue of *Animage* that contained the prologue of *Seraphim 266613336 Wings*.

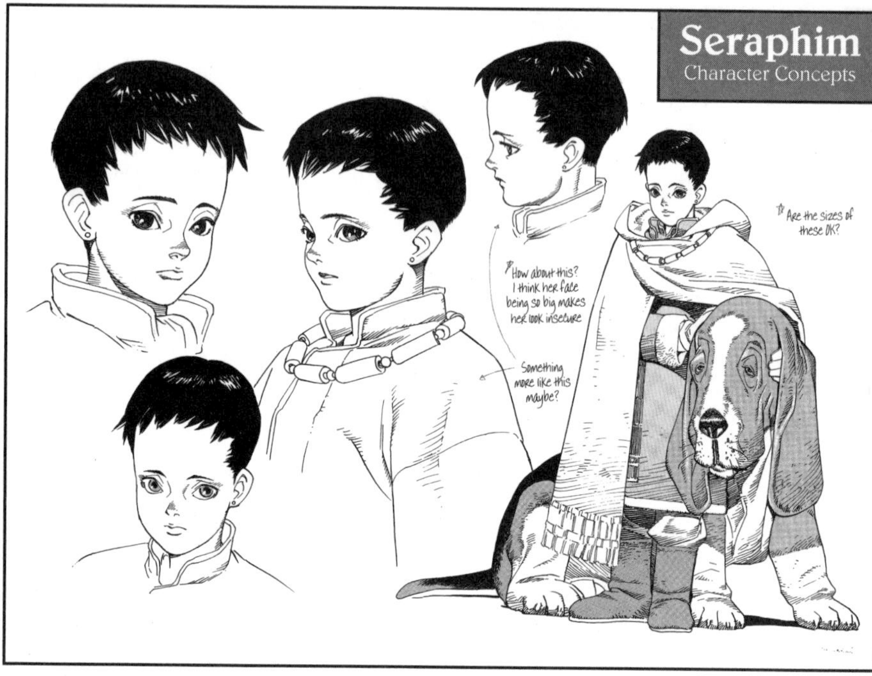
Seraphim
Character Concepts
How about this? I think her face being so big makes her look insecure
Something more like this maybe?
Are the sizes of these OK?

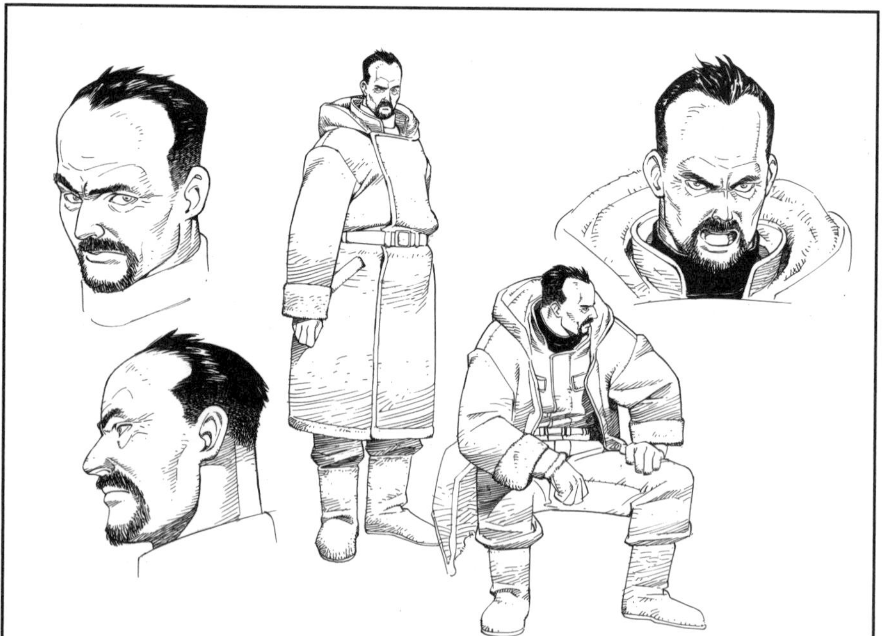

This gallery is from the proposal submitted for *Seraphim*, showing early design concepts for the characters. It was saved together with the original manuscript, and we are grateful for the permission to feature it here, for the first time, in the collected edition of the manga.

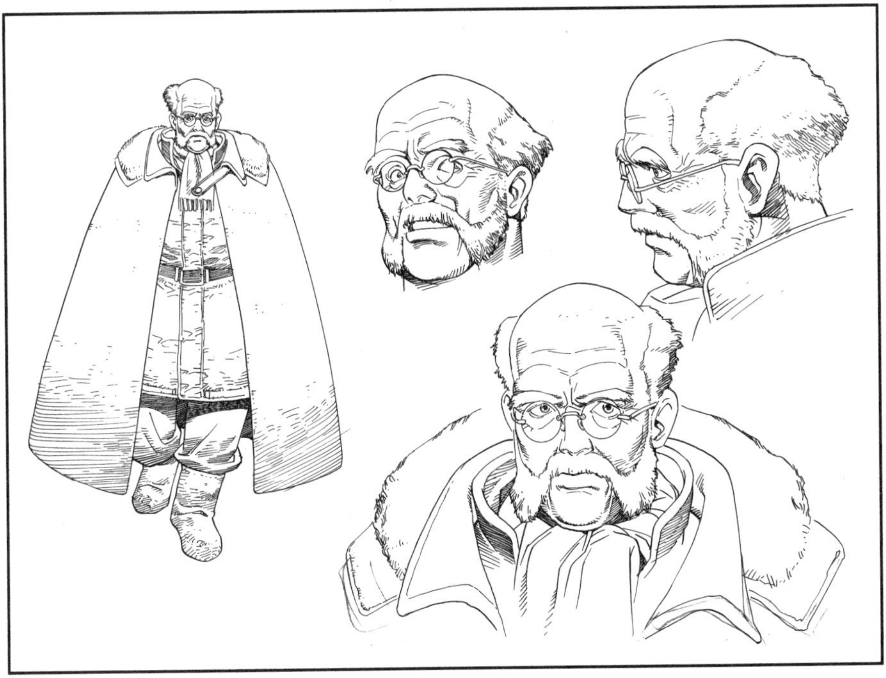

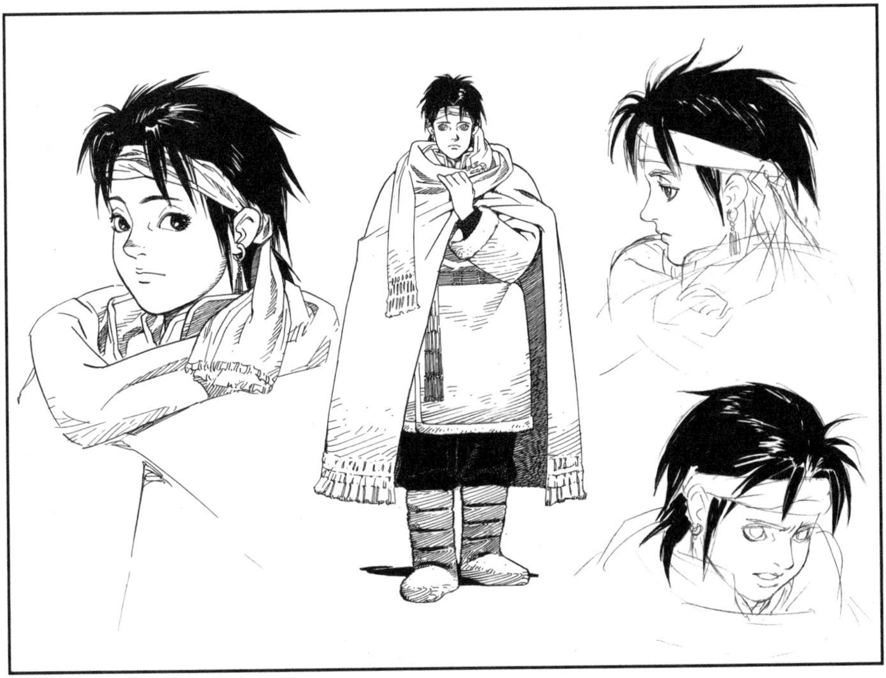

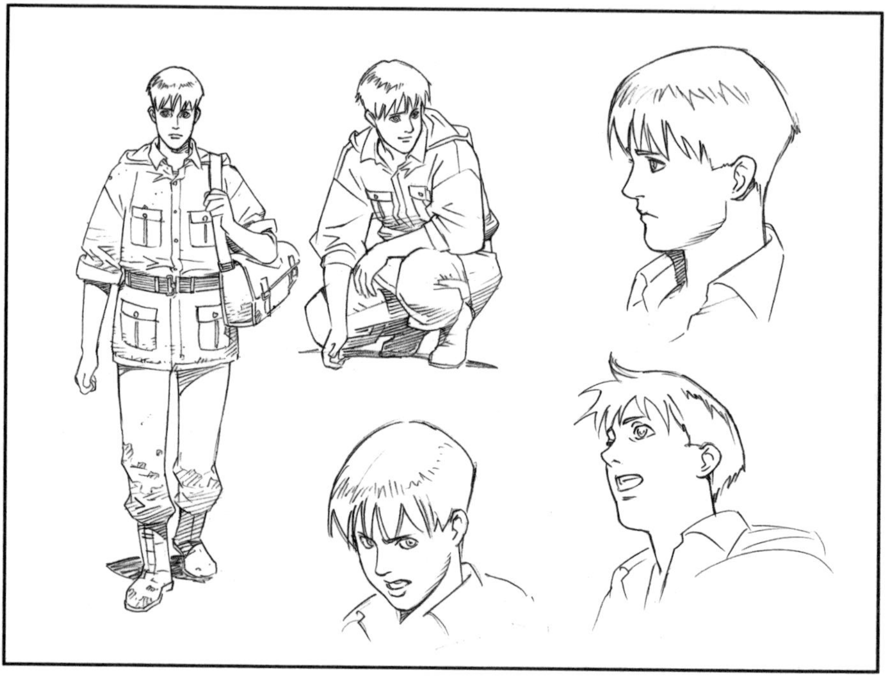

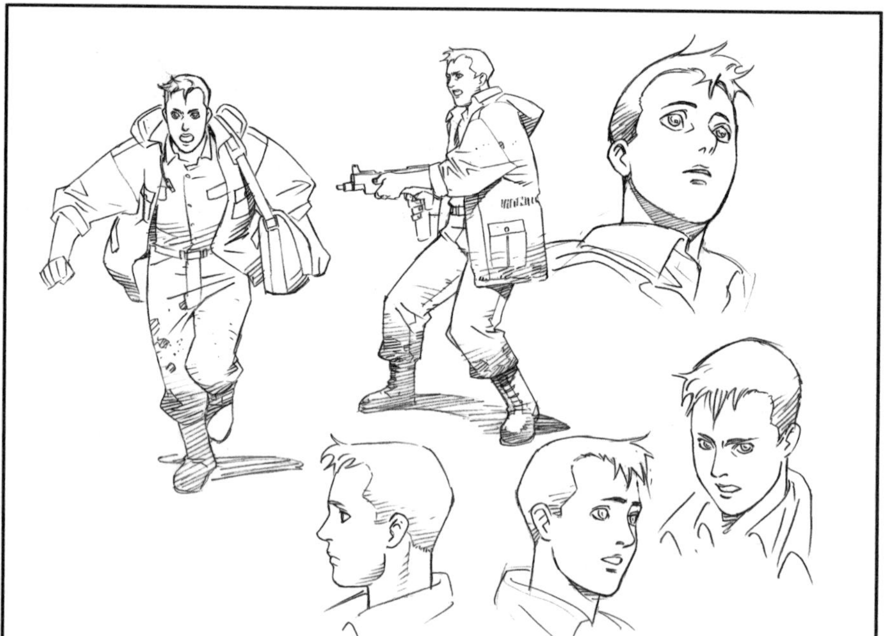

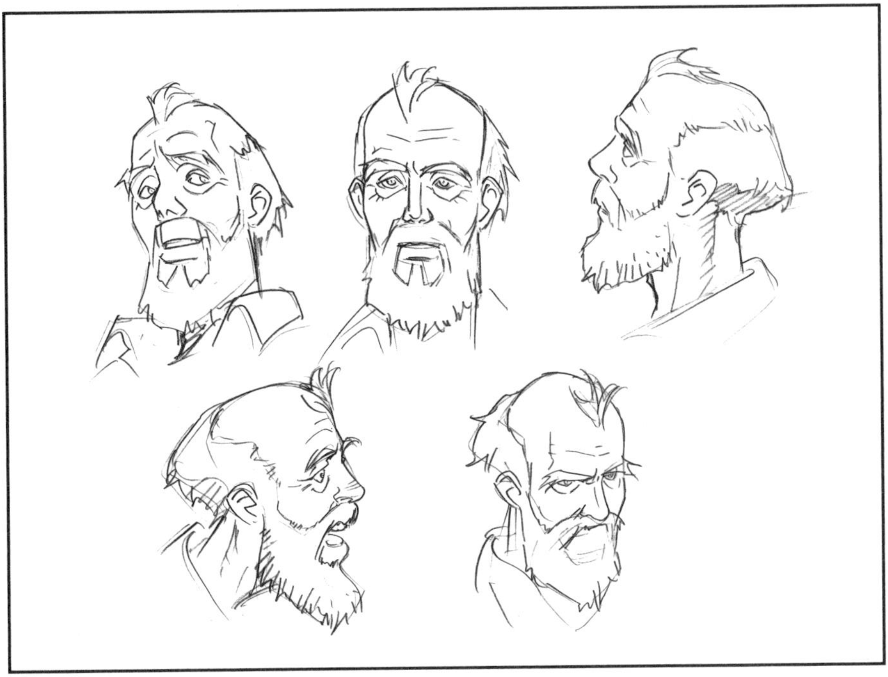

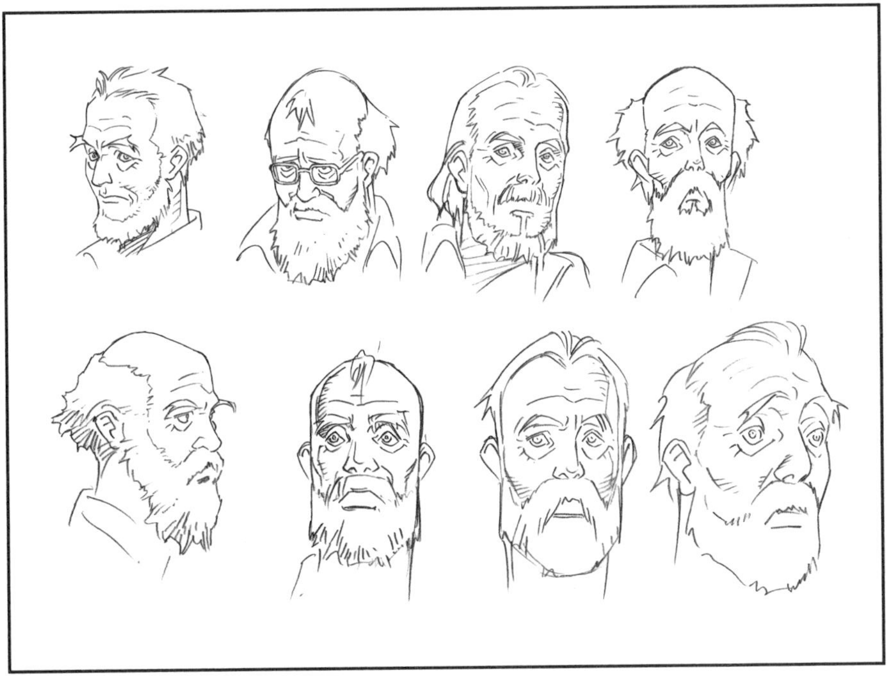

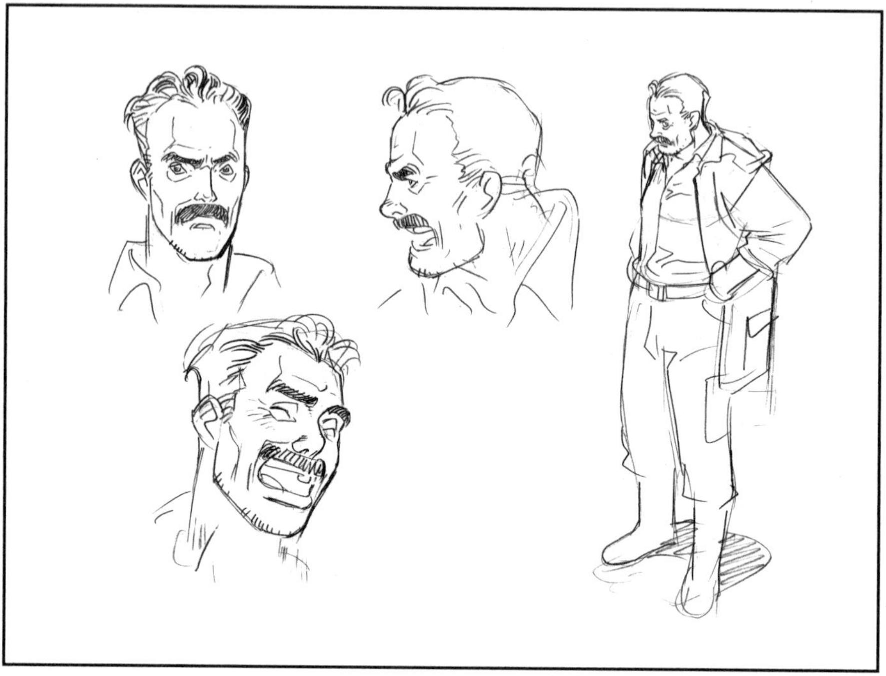

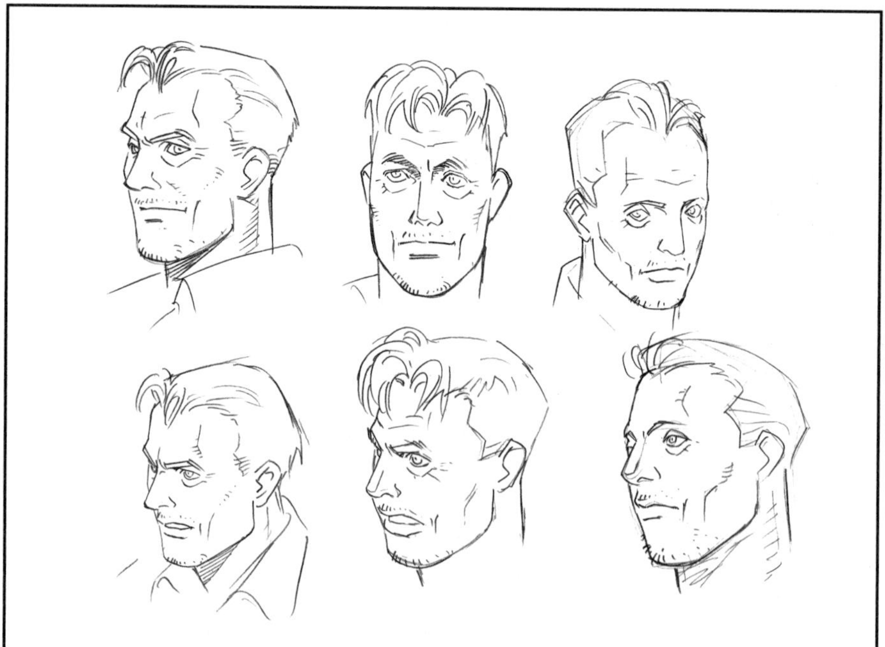

Editor
CARL GUSTAV HORN

Translated by
ZACK DAVISSON

Lettering and Retouch by
IHL

Special Thanks to
MICHAEL GOMBOS

Designer
SANDY TANAKA

President and Publisher
MIKE RICHARDSON

English-language version produced by
Dark Horse Comics

SERAPHIM 266613336 WINGS

Published by
Dark Horse Manga
A division of Dark Horse Comics LLC
10956 SE Main Street
Milwaukie, OR 97222

DarkHorse.com

To find a comics shop in your area, visit comicshoplocator.com

First edition: February 2015
ISBN 978-1-61655-608-2

3 5 7 9 10 8 6 4 2
Printed in the United States of America

AFTERWORD TO THE ENGLISH-LANGUAGE EDITION
by Carl Gustav Horn

Neither Mamoru Oshii nor Satoshi Kon are best known for their work in manga, and furthermore, this manga, just like Kon's *OPUS*, is unfinished. For all those reasons, I thought that, rather than just leaving it here—with that blimp heading off to Taklamakan—some attempts at explanation and context might be in order.

First, a disclaimer, or warning: this essay risks being mistaken for one long, parodic tribute to *Seraphim*'s footnotes and asides. But while the fact that Mamoru Oshii and Satoshi Kon did a manga twenty years ago together entitled *Seraphim 266613336 Wings* has never been a secret, this work *has* remained fairly obscure for most of the past two decades; it wasn't collected as a graphic novel in Japan until 2011. If you had wanted to read this story, even in its original language, you would have had to track down the seventeen separate issues of *Animage* in which it was originally serialized. You are likely only now getting the

chance, then, to encounter *Seraphim*, this "lost" work by Oshii and Kon. We often consider manga and anime separately. But this particular story was made by two manga creators who were also anime creators—and that fact makes for a story of its own, about, among other things, *Animage*, the extraordinary magazine that *Seraphim* came from.

Seraphim was part of a period of creative collaboration between Mamoru Oshii and Satoshi Kon during the first half of the 1990s. It was in the second half of the 1990s that Oshii and Kon—both now going their separate ways—earned their international reputation as filmmakers. When the laser disc version of *Ghost in the Shell* was released in Japan in the summer of 1996, it came with a reproduction of a handwritten fan letter from James Cameron: high praise not only because of Cameron's mainstream success but because at the time he was working with budgets twenty times those available to Oshii. Kon received appreciation through a different yet complementary angle from Darren Aronofsky, who optioned the live-action remake rights to *Perfect Blue* while he himself was still known as a low-budget indie filmmaker; Aronofsky's 1998 movie *Pi*, made for only $60,000, won him the Directing Award at that year's Sundance Film Festival.

The late Satoshi Kon was twelve years younger than Mamoru Oshii, which makes his early death in 2010 all the harder. That is speaking only as an admirer of his anime and manga, which is a very different thing from all those who lost him as a person in their lives: his wife, Kyoko, whom we must thank, as he thanked her; his parents; his comrade in filmmaking, producer Masao Maruyama; his friend since high school and fellow manga artist Seiho Takizawa; and the many, many people he knew both inside and out of the industry. But I don't doubt that those who encountered Satoshi Kon as a person also share, with us strangers around the world, that admiration for his work. Our feelings here, at least, can be joined to theirs.

Kon drew *Seraphim* in the same studio where he did his work for the 1993 film *Patlabor 2* and the 1995 film *Memories*. Although the last chapter of *OPUS* is only drawn sketchily, you can make out the poster for *Memories* on the left side of panel 4 of page 357; on the next page, Kon discusses *Memories* and characterizes *Seraphim* as his "my bastard child. Yeah, that's not finished either" (I briefly considered using that as a pull quote on the back of this manga).

Memories is an anthology of three short anime films ("Magnetic Rose," "Stink Bomb," and "Cannon Fodder"), produced and codirected by *Akira*'s Katsuhiro Otomo. Kon wrote the screenplay and drew the design model sheets (called *settei*, these are the style guides to be used by the animators) for the first (and generally regarded as the best of the three), "Magnetic Rose." In that last chapter of *OPUS*, you see Kon himself discussing how, in the midnineties, he was transitioning into being a full-time anime creator. This is, of course, the field in which he became best known, yet it was something of a second career for him.

By 1984, and while still in college, Kon had broken into the professional manga world, his work appearing in one of Kodansha's weekly manga magazines, *Young*. Thirty years later *Young* is still a major seller—indeed, only the highest-selling manga magazines can maintain the expense of a weekly production schedule; other manga magazines are biweekly or, as is most common, monthly. In 1984 *Young* was a red-hot venue for Kon's talent, as at that time it was serializing Katsuhiro Otomo's *Akira*. Several of those stories from his early pro days, as well as his earlier amateur manga, are reprinted in Vertical's forthcoming anthology *Satoshi Kon's Complete Short Stories—Dream Fossil*, slated for release in the summer of 2015.

Kon, like many artists of his generation, had been motivated and influenced by Otomo, who had already established himself as a critical favorite in the 1970s, some years before *Akira* made him a phenomenal mainstream success. He would later join Otomo as an assistant on *Akira*, and Otomo would bring Kon into his first work in animation. Kon made his anime debut in 1991, doing background design on *Roujin Z*, written by Otomo and directed by Hiroyuki Kitakubo, a friend of Otomo's later to become well known for his 2000 film *Blood: The Last Vampire* (like *Seraphim*, a project strongly associated with Mamoru Oshii). In 1992, a year after *Roujin Z*'s release, Kon began to collaborate with Oshii on anime as well, during the early production of the film sometimes considered Oshii's neglected masterpiece, the political thriller *Patlabor 2* ("neglected" in part because, as its name might imply, *P2* is a sequel in a larger storyline and thus perhaps not as accessible as *Ghost in the Shell*).

Although Japan has one of the biggest economies on earth, its anime productions (as suggested above) almost never receive the budgets needed to permit the smooth movement associated with Western animated films or TV shows. "Smoothness" is much too simplistic a measure by which to judge the animation that gets made in Japan, whose best artists have found ways to convey expressive movements with a stylized economy and individual artistic technique. Still, those same Japanese animators know only too well what they could achieve with more money, and even Hayao Miyazaki's films, which generally had higher budgets than Oshii's or Kon's, were indie productions by the standards of Pixar, Disney, or DreamWorks.

Yet there is an argument to be made that it is the Japanese who, over the decades, have pushed animated filmmaking further as *filmmakers*. Japan can and does make anime suitable for children and the family, be it as different as the *Pokémon* films or the works of Studio Ghibli—but it is difficult to imagine a major American animation studio greenlighting a film definitely *not* suitable for children, such as Kon and Oshii have made. When we consider the development of cinema as a whole, the issue goes far beyond any notions of animated nudity or gore. Imagine how limited live-action filmmaking would have remained, were it required that any major studio film, no matter how sophisticated, still be appropriate for kids.

The script is only one important way that anime can—it *can*; it by no means always *will*—make something interesting and engaging on a lesser budget; others are through emphasis on the film's art design, cinematography, and storyboarding (Matt Groening once challenged critics with the question: "Can you use '*mise en scène*' in a review that anyone will finish reading?"). Such a progressive approach by Oshii to filmmaking in animation was detailed by Ryusuke Hikawa in *Patlabor 2: The Movie Archives*, a book available with the Limited Collector's Edition of the DVD. As Hikawa notes, it was in *Patlabor 2* that Mamoru Oshii made the radical decision to allot twice as much of the film's production time to these nonanimation aspects as he did to the actual animation, a decision that not only made the most of the limited budget, but paid off handsomely in the creative impression made by the movie upon audiences.

Although it has elements of speculative fiction, *Patlabor 2* was a film set in a real version of 1990s Tokyo, and it was Satoshi Kon's sense for urban spaces that brought him into the project. Working from Oshii's storyboards—cartoony in look, but directorial in flow—Kon was one of the six principal artists on the film who created detailed, realistic layouts (these layouts looked not unlike penciled manga panels, but were drawn with the proportions of a film frame) to determine how each individual scene was going to look, and work, before it was actually animated. The sequences in *Patlabor 2* that were classified as street scenes (as opposed to, for example, interior shots) were assigned to Kon, who ended up arranging nearly one hundred of the individual shots in the finished film. As the movie's impact depended on its extraordinary political events—terrorism and martial law—being seen to occur in a recognizable, normal, and workaday Tokyo, Satoshi Kon's contributions to Mamoru Oshii's film were vital.

Seraphim 266613336 Wings: A Manga for an Anime Magazine

Patlabor 2 opened in Japanese theaters in August of 1993; as Takashi Watanabe, its Japanese editor, relates in his previous essay, *Seraphim 266613336 Wings* began its run in *Animage* magazine less than a year later. From Watanabe's remarks, it can be presumed that the interim involved a great deal of back-and-forth between them. Here, there must have been something of a reversal; Oshii at this point was far more experienced in anime than Kon, but it was Kon who had more experience in manga (Oshii had worked in manga before, as will be related later), and Watanabe gives us a sense of a creator who approached *Seraphim* without undue deference to his partner: "Kon questioned Oshii over any uncertainty. He paused working until he received a sufficient answer."

In this essay, I make many remarks about Oshii's contributions to *Seraphim* as if I were certain it was he who made them and not Kon—yet, as Watanabe explained, their work was always collaborative, and in the last four chapters they were no longer credited separately for story and art, but as cocreators. In truth, the official credits of a work don't always tell the whole story; Kon himself suggests this in *OPUS*. However, Watanabe also mentions that "Oshii created the basic tone and background of the world of *Seraphim*, and wrote the rough outline for the plot," and that the first twelve chapters of *Seraphim* did credit the writing to Oshii—it's based on this (plus my sense of the differences in style and interests between the two creators) that I make such assertions.

The target demographic and editorial culture of a magazine naturally have a great influence upon the kind of manga that are chosen to appear in it. Japan is famous for its manga magazines—the thick, phone book–sized periodicals (of which *Shonen Jump* is only the most successful example) that might serialize ten, fifteen, or twenty separate manga stories in every issue. Even in an era of declining circulations, Japan in 2015 still has dozens of different manga magazines that are released on a regular basis. The straight-to-graphic-novel approach is very rare in Japan, and nearly every single manga you will find on sale in a North American bookstore was originally serialized in such a magazine.

Nearly, but not all; it shows the lingering power of manga within Japanese media that even many Japanese periodicals that *aren't* manga magazines will nevertheless still include at least some manga content in addition to their regular columns and feature articles. In other words, within the Japanese publishing industry, manga are not restricted only to their own "neighborhoods." Dark Horse's current series *New Lone Wolf and Cub* is one such example; whereas the original *Lone Wolf and Cub* did in fact run in a manga magazine, Futabasha's *Action* (home also, and at the same time, to some of the early works of Katsuhiro Otomo), its sequel *New Lone Wolf and Cub* ran in Shogakukan's sensationalist current-affairs magazine, *Weekly Post*. This was not unusual; it was *Weekly Post's* rival publication *Modern Weekly* that serialized Dark Horse's *Path of the Assassin* and *Samurai Executioner* (not to mention Shigeru Mizuki's *Onward towards Our Noble Deaths*, available in English from Drawn and Quarterly).

As noted above, Satoshi Kon began his career in what then and now is one of the main stages of the professional manga world, Kodansha's magazine *Young*, the home of *Akira* and *Ghost in the Shell* (and in later years *Chobits* and *xxxHolic*). *OPUS*, which was Kon's manga project following *Seraphim*, appeared in a different manga magazine aiming for a similar demographic as *Young*, *Comic Guy's [sic]*, published by Gakken—a magazine that did indeed cease publication in the midnineties, just as its fictional counterpart in *OPUS*, *Comic Guard*, did. But *Seraphim* was serialized in *Animage*, and, as its name might suggest, it is not a manga magazine, but an anime magazine, devoted mainly to covering the anime industry.

Manga and anime often do have a close relationship, as the account of Kon's career itself demonstrates, and *Seraphim*, a collaboration between two manga creators brought together by their work on anime, exemplifies. There is significant overlap between the two fan bases in Japan; they are often cross-marketed. Yet it is in Japan, the native market for both media, where their differences are most keenly felt. The industries have separate economics. Anime generally relies on sales of physical goods to make its profits (such as DVDs and merchandise), just as manga relies upon graphic-novel sales—but anime makes itself known to its customers through digital means, airing on TV or streaming online. Many manga are now available digitally, but with its dozens of print magazines, it remains an intensely physical industry at its core; just to produce *Shonen Jump* alone means printing over a billion (with a b) pages of manga every week. The media also differ greatly in their pricing models; graphic novels are generally cheap in Japan, whereas anime DVDs are generally expensive. As Katsuya Terada remarks in Dark Horse's recent *Dragon Girl and Monkey King*, a further difference between anime and manga is that the latter can be created with far less personnel and money.

Those are some economic reasons for separating anime from manga—but there are artistic reasons as well that (as they must within any industry) form their own links back to the economic ones. *Animage*, the original home of *Seraphim*, was founded in 1978, which means it predates some of the most prominent manga magazines, including *Young*. But *Animage*, it might be said, was a magazine founded not only to promote the anime that were on TV and in the movie theaters (anime wasn't released on home video until the 1980s) but the basic idea that the word *anime* should be used to assert a special artistic—and marketing—identity distinct from the word *manga*. This idea was by no means obvious or universal at the time. A scene in GAINAX's semi-biographical *Otaku no Video* recalls waiting in line for the debut of Miyazaki's *Nausicaä* in 1984, and how the way young fans insisted it be called *anime* instead of *manga* sounded affected to regular people. Even Miyazaki himself, as late as one 1987 interview, spoke of his own films as *manga eiga*, "manga movies," despite the fact only one of them had been a direct adaptation of a manga story. The term in part reflected his generation's usage; Miyazaki had begun at Toei in the 1960s, a studio that customarily branded its own semiannual releases as the *manga matsuri*, "manga festival," again despite often featuring content not adapted from manga.

The seeming confusion might be more easily understood if we translate *manga*—at least, in this context—as the English word *cartoon*, with connotations similar to those *cartoon* has in English. That is, it could mean either still drawings or animation—their content entertaining and funny perhaps, but seen as basically for children, not to be taken too seriously. Animators themselves didn't necessarily have a problem with that term, taking pride in their craft and what it was capable of (when it was permitted to reach its potential, and when it had the budget—a problem that doesn't change whether you call it *manga eiga* or *anime*, *cartoons*, or *animation*). Nor did the first national anime fan club in the United States, the C/FO, founded in 1977, which stood for "Cartoon/Fantasy Organization"—not a hint of weaboo in the name. The rebellion against terms like *manga* and *cartoon* to describe what we now call *anime* was in part a shift in generation, as a younger rose against the previous; in part a shift in branding; in part a justified sense that it was indeed time to assert a separate identity from manga.

Animage declared that identity boldly, even snootily—its first issue launched with the iconic *Space Battleship Yamato* approaching readers on the cover, a hit anime not based upon a manga. The magazine's 580-yen cost might not at first seem like prestige pricing, but in 1978 it was considerably more than what a manga graphic novel cost, and over three times the price of an issue of *Shonen Jump*. *Animage's* founding editor in chief, Hideo Ogata, understood the promotional use such a magazine could have to the industry. Yet from the beginning *Animage* also carried articles about what was not hot, stylish, or even on sale, with photo features on Japanese animated works made years in the past—in some cases, before its readers were even born. The idea, of course, was to suggest to fans that the medium they were presently excited about had a history to be proud of for its own sake, and to remind people that the hot anime of the moment were the latest stage in a long creative heritage in which techniques had been slowly refined, and one generation of animators had trained the next.

The manga stories that ran in *Animage* (one or two per issue, sometimes with additional short gag-manga features) were, as might be expected, often done by creators who worked in anime. Miyazaki's *Nausicaä* is the most famous of all, but the magazine's very first manga, *Kogane no senshi* (Golden warrior), was by Yuki Hijiri, best known in manga for his *Locke the Superman* (running to this day in *Young King Ours* magazine, the home of *Drifters*, *Hellsing*, and *Trigun*), but who had been the character designer for two of the pivotal robot anime of the late seventies, *Voltes V* and *Daimos*. *Chito*, which ran intermittently in *Animage* during the late 1980s, was cocreated by Yukio Kaizawa, later director of *Zatch Bell* and *Digimon Tamers*. *Yadamon* in the early 1990s was by SUEZEN, pen name of longtime

GAINAX key animator and animation director Fumio Iida, today working with Hideaki Anno on the *Evangelion* movies. And in 1984–85, a decade before *Seraphim*, Mamoru Oshii had written a manga in *Animage* entitled *Todo no Tsumari* (When all's said and done), drawn by another animation director still active today, Yuji Moriyama, most famous for his *Project A-Ko.*

Animage has never been the only anime magazine in Japan. Readers might remember from the 2000s *Newtype USA*, an impressive English-language edition of the Japanese anime magazine *Newtype*, first published by Kadokawa in 1985. *Newtype*, with its bold use of double-page graphic layouts (themselves reminiscent of the widely influential *Life* magazine), shook things up and provided *Animage* with strong competition. *Animedia* magazine from 1981, published by Gakken, is another longtime survivor in Japan; its 1999 spinoff, the monthly *Megami* (Goddess) emphasized cute-girl characters (*Newtype* had placed increased emphasis on mecha design within anime) and is likely better known to English-language fans than its parent magazine. Other anime magazines have come and gone, and some offered their own distinctive viewpoints. But *Animage* is the longest-running anime magazine, and, as such, provides a baseline for historical comparison as the industry and medium have changed.

Animage, whenever copies of it could be obtained, had its own special meaning to fans outside Japan. In the 1980s, years before one could casually search images from any anime online (let alone watch them online), the magazine, with its design illustrations and layouts full of TV show and movie stills, gave foreign fans a sense of what was going on in anime, even if they had no easy way to actually view the anime itself. But *Animage* represented more than that; like a missionary with a picture Bible, you could simply show it to anyone you were trying to convince that exciting things were going on in Japan. Handsome and square bound, its issues sometimes nearly half an inch thick, it was a portable scene. Nor was *Animage* indifferent to its foreign influence; although the magazine's articles were (naturally) written in Japanese, it would occasionally report on international fans and even print their letters to the magazine.

This wasn't incidental; as is so often the case in life, it came down to having a key person care and make an effort, and with *Animage*, that person was Hideo Ogata. Cheerful and extroverted, he was a confident ambassador for his nation's pop culture at a time when the Japanese government (and even most of Japan's entertainment industry) had no idea that they were living in "Cool Japan." When I was sixteen, making my first trip there in 1987, he gave me an hour of his time in the *Animage* office to look at our fanzines and talk about the prospects for anime in America—this, when there as yet was no anime home video licensing industry in the United States. A few months later, he came to America, where I served as his chauffeur in a borrowed old Mercedes, which amused him no end—not least because sixteen is too young to drive a car in Japan—and he warned from the back seat that if I was trying to be a Benz-driving Lupin III, he intended to be the Fujiko of this caper. He had brought along an English dub of Hayao Miyazaki's third film, *Castle in the Sky*, the first made under a new production unit called Studio Ghibli. Hideo Ogata had helped to plan the film out. I was driving him to a local anime club meeting to show it—we're talking maybe twenty people. It was as if Jann Wenner had parachuted behind the Iron Curtain to meet some kids trading rock cassette tapes.

Mr. Ogata died in 2007; in his eulogy (which you can read in full in *Turning Point*, published in English by Viz), Hayao Miyazaki said of him, "He loved being called a Don Quixote, and charged into windmills and castle gates over and over. And he wound up fostering several people in his line of work, who learned by cleaning up the chaos he created. By following the holes Ogata-san created on his many impetuous charges and the footsteps he left behind, we actually were able to discover many unanticipated new openings and routes . . . Hideo Ogata-san. Our editor of legend . . ." He is mine as well.

Animage, Mamoru Oshii, and Satoshi Kon

Studio Ghibli had begun as a subsidiary of Tokuma Shoten, the publisher of *Animage*; eventual Ghibli studio president Toshio Suzuki was Ogata's successor as editor in chief of *Animage*. Hideo Ogata would, like Suzuki, be a planner and producer on various Ghibli films, a role that concluded for Ogata with Isao Takahata's 1994 film *Pom Poko*. But one of the other people he fostered (and for whom he created chaos) was Mamoru Oshii. Unlike Ghibli's Miyazaki or Takahata, who had established careers well before the first issue of *Animage* hit the stands, Oshii's anime career began in the same era that the magazine did, in 1977 at Tatsunoko Productions.

Ogata helped to plan out the production of Mamoru Oshii's first movie based on the director's own original concept—1985's *The Angel's Egg*, which was itself produced by Tokuma Shoten. A collaboration with Yoshitaka Amano (later to become world-renowned for *Final Fantasy*) who designed the look of the film's characters and world, *The Angel's Egg* is oddly atypical as an Oshii work in that, far from being full of exchanges of dialogue, the movie has almost no dialogue at all (and is entirely devoid of basset hounds). Yet it is perhaps the most experimental and private of his anime films, and thus in a sense the most "Oshii."

Certainly it contains a number of motifs we will see again in this manga, including the phylogenetic tree Oshii would most famously use as the backdrop to the Major's duel with the tank at the end of *Ghost in the Shell*—in *Seraphim*, Dr. Erasmus, a.k.a.

Balthazar, mentions that he resided in England, and the museum seen in chapter 1, with its seated statue of Darwin, is a similar but not exact evocation of the Natural History Museum in London. The nameless, quiet, cloaked girl (and quasi-mother) of *The Angel's Egg*, with her heavy upward gaze, is reminiscent of Sera, and the hunt of the fishermen in that movie puts me in mind of the bird chasers of *Seraphim*'s chapter 4. Yet without a doubt it is *The Angel Egg*'s depiction of an angel as a grotesque, ossified visage of death that *Seraphim* most strongly echoes.

This whole line of discussion fits some of the common images we might have of Mamoru Oshii's films, and of the director himself: cryptic, foreboding, the directionless pilgrim drifting past familiar yet ever unresolved symbols. But this isn't the Mamoru Oshii *Animage* readers knew early in his career; between October of 1981 and March of 1984, he was the director of one of the most fan-beloved shows of the decade, *Urusei Yatsura*, based on the Rumiko Takahashi manga of the same name. The *Animage* readers' poll for the best single TV anime episode of 1982 was won by Oshii's "Kimi sarishi nochi" (After you've gone), episode 44 of *Urusei Yatsura*—incidentally, the episode that, when I saw it at thirteen, taught me the as-yet-unnamed concept of *moe* (I saw it in that most *moe* of cities, Oakland). In the pages of *Animage* he was presented to the readers with a familiar tone, not as any kind of sensei but as "Oshii-kun" or even "Mamoru-chan"—during 1985–86 *Animage* ran a series of four-panel gag strips about the making of *The Angel's Egg* entitled *Ganbare! Mamoru-chan* (Go for it, Mamoru-chan!). His droopy features (which he just as often lit up with a smile) were depicted in caricatures as cute rather than just gloomy; he was kind of *moe* himself.

Although Mamoru Oshii has never achieved the same level of prominence as Hayao Miyazaki (no other anime director has), he shares with Miyazaki the fact that in the 1980s both directors were much closer to the tastes of the hardcore anime fans whose readership *Animage* sought (and attempted to cultivate and sometimes curate). The process of Oshii and Miyazaki gradually gaining recognition outside that community, and moving into the realm of the avant-garde or (in Miyazaki's case) general audiences, was also a process of gradual drift away from their earlier fan base, as the directors changed the kind of anime they wanted to make. Perhaps this is because "*otaku* never learn anything," as Miyazaki said in *The Kingdom of Dreams and Madness*—but then, it was Miyazaki who had the biggest *otaku* of all, Hideaki Anno, voice the protagonist of his final and most personal film.

Here is a fact that will illustrate it: In November 1995, thirteen years after he had won that *Animage* poll, Mamoru Oshii's most famous film, *Ghost in the Shell*, was released in Japan. Yet *Ghost in the Shell* never made the front of *Animage*—it was the first Oshii feature anime not to be a cover story for the magazine. Both of his *Urusei Yatsura* films had made the cover, as had *The Angel's Egg* and *Patlabor 1* and *2*. Outside Japan, *Ghost in the Shell* was the most talked-about anime movie since 1988's *Akira* (which did make the cover of *Animage* twice in its time). But that month the cover story instead was on Hideaki Anno's *Neon Genesis Evangelion*, which had just made its debut on Japanese television. It was the first of five cover stories *Evangelion* would receive in less than a year. In that same November 1995 issue, *Seraphim* ceased its serialization with chapter 16.

I don't think it was because of any final falling-out with *Animage*; Oshii would do a retrospective interview for them just a few years later in 1998, to celebrate the magazine's twentieth anniversary; that year *Animage* also did a special feature on Oshii's *G.R.M.—The Record of Garm War*, a long-gestating project of his that finally saw release in 2014 as *Garm Wars: The Last Druid*, a Canadian-Japanese coproduction starring Lance Henriksen. If I had to guess why *Ghost in the Shell* didn't make the cover of *Animage*, my blunt inclination as an *otaku* is to think that it was because *Ghost in the Shell* had no cute boy or girl characters to feature. There had already been some disconnect as Oshii's approach to anime had evolved; the *Animage* cover for Oshii's *Patlabor 2* in 1993 had featured the character Noa Izumi—in earlier incarnations of the series, its perky heroine—rather than the older cast members who were now the actual lead characters of the film.

The unusually adult and rather affectless look of *Ghost in the Shell*'s cyborg protagonist, Major Kusanagi, was a deliberate change from the lively, cute, and sexy manga character originally created by Shirow Masamune. One way to understand the point is to imagine if Oshii's 1984 film *Urusei Yatsura 2: Beautiful Dreamer* had changed the appearance of Rumiko Takahashi's Lum-chan in the same way that *Ghost in the Shell* had changed the appearance of Shirow's Kusanagi. This change was in harmony with the movie's theme of humanity in departure from itself, and fit its visual aesthetic of a convincing next-generation world—and I believe the change greatly contributed to giving *Ghost in the Shell* credibility with wider international audiences. But by the same token, the character designs made it less

appealing (or, perhaps, recognizable) as an "anime" to hardcore Japanese fans. To suggest the landscape of anime culture against which *Ghost in the Shell* made its debut in Japan, 1995's other *Animage* cover stories besides the *Evangelion* one (which was of Rei Ayanami, naturally), were devoted to *Macross 7* (three times), *Magic Knight Rayearth* (twice), *I Can Hear the Sea* (twice), and *Sailor Moon S*, *Wedding Peach*, *Azakukin Cha Cha* and *Gundam Wing* (once each). All of these anime starred cute young characters.

In the 1990s, neither Kon nor Oshii's work fit easily with that aesthetic. So you will perceive a certain irony that *Seraphim 266613336 Wings*, destined to be an obscure, unfinished manga, made the cover of *Animage* (as shown in Takashi Watanabe's reminiscence), while *Ghost in the Shell*—a famous anime film with several spinoffs and sequels, currently in development as a live-action film by DreamWorks—did not. But giving *Seraphim* the cover showed how seriously the magazine took the launch of the manga in May of 1994. And perhaps it showed also how *Animage*, which as a monthly magazine had to respond to tastes and didn't necessarily dislike what was popular (for what was popular was usually at least fun or engaging, and sometimes it was also exciting and dynamic), had nevertheless not abandoned its editorial ideals—its search to also push and challenge its readers as fans, not just indulge them as fans.

If Miyazaki was from the generation of anime creators that established themselves before *Animage*, and Oshii was from the generation that established themselves along with *Animage*, Satoshi Kon was from the generation that had grown up reading *Animage*. The magazine began publication when he was in junior high school—he once spoke of his excitement over *Mobile Suit Gundam* and all the "otakuesque conversations" he used to have about it as "the errors in my youth, although they're not really errors"—evoking (as a true *otaku* might) the famous quote from *Gundam's* Char Aznable, "One does not care to acknowledge the mistakes of one's youth." And Kon, who broke out of the original *otaku* generation (he was only three years younger than Hideaki Anno) would come to embody one of the lost battles of *Animage's* editorial ideals, for unlike Miyazaki or Oshii, Kon never experienced a time when his work met the taste of the readers of the magazine that he too read when he was a teen.

We can again find the comparison within *Animage* itself; that same readers' poll for best TV anime episode that Oshii had won with *Urusei Yatsura* in 1982 had Satoshi Kon's *Paranoia Agent* nowhere to be seen when it aired in 2004; the show didn't even make *Animage* readers' top twenty for the year. It can be objected that the comparison is unfair, as *Paranoia Agent* aired on the premium service WOWOW (but then, so did *Cowboy Bebop*, which was very popular with *Animage* readers—even if *Bebop* still came second in the 2000 poll to the ultimate in cute and charming anime, *Cardcaptor Sakura*), and Oshii, with *Urusei Yatsura*, had been adapting a popular manga rather than trying out an original concept (but then, *Cowboy Bebop* had been an original concept).

Of course, this isn't the point—the point is that while Satoshi Kon was one of anime's most progressive directors, his approach to anime simply wasn't all that popular with anime fans in Japan. It wasn't the case that *Animage* didn't cover *Paranoia Agent*;

they did, as they covered his entire directorial career. The magazine had made a powerful endorsement of Kon just by symbolically giving him—with *Seraphim*—the manga space that Miyazaki had previously occupied. But none of Kon's works ever broke the top twenty in the annual *Animage* poll—not *Perfect Blue*, not *Millennium Actress*, not *Tokyo Godfathers*, not *Paprika*.

Kon's movies didn't make much money at the Japanese box office, either—but Miyazaki's *Spirited Away* was Japan's *highest-earning film of all time*, and even it only made number seven in that year's *Animage* readers' poll. That was how far the ways had parted. In the 1980s, *Animage* readers were Miyazaki's most ardent fans; they knew who he was back when the average Japanese person had never heard of him (or of Studio Ghibli, for that matter). By 2001 the magazine's readers simply liked things like *Fruits Basket*, *s-CRY-ed*, and *Sister Princess* better than *Spirited Away*, and were not ashamed to tick their ballots accordingly. The Oscar-winning Miyazaki, the Oshii and Kon praised by foreign critics and directors—the hardcore Japanese fans weren't necessarily against all that, or against their films. But neither was this what they really wanted most out of anime—or, perhaps, what *Animage's* editors wished that they wanted most.

I wonder what *Animage's* readers made of *Seraphim*. Takashi Watanabe remarks that the manga was conceived with the hope of being another hit like *Nausicaä*. If you were to pitch *Seraphim*, it could indeed sound a lot like *Nausicaä*—an extraordinary young woman, seen as a prophesied savior by some, journeys into a postapocalyptic world still riven by sectarian conflict, accompanied by older men as her protectors . . .

But that's only to illustrate how different the two manga actually are. *Nausicaä*, like *Dune* or *The Lord of the Rings* (two works to which it has been compared), certainly expresses ideas that are relevant to the politics and society of the real world. Yet, despite its dreadnought birds and angel plague, *Seraphim* takes place in the real world in a way that *Nausicaä* does not. Its intrigues are not those of the imaginary Torumekian Empire and the Doroks, but of China and its Hakka minority, just across the water from Japan; places and people that exist not a thousand years in an imagined future, but right now, today.

The contrast lies as much in the art as in the story. *Nausicaä*'s unruled panel borders, its sepia ink, the soft line of its character drawings, the rounded and organic look even of its machines, give a suggestion of handcraft and folklore befitting Miyazaki's aesthetics. Kon's art in *Seraphim* took inspiration from Katsuhiro Otomo's oddly radical character realism (one is tempted to call it "that small-eyed manga look"), embrace of the present and future, and clean draftsmanship that often looks as if it came off an architect's, rather than a cartoonist's, table.

These are observations, not criticisms. *Nausicaä* is an *exercise* in imagination; it reflects an imaginary world built up by Miyazaki, a world that (as with the SF or fantasy novels to which it is compared) readers are fascinated to experience. By contrast, *Seraphim* suggests the discovery of the complexities of the real world, although this is itself complicated by the way the readers (like the Magi) may feel as if they are on a surprise field trip to a historical minefield, and, as will be examined, by *Seraphim*'s particular view of history. *Seraphim* is, of course, like

Nausicaä, a work of fiction—but if Miyazaki shaped his narrative by molding a fantasy, Oshii defined his by choosing to cut a certain shape out of a larger reality.

The World of *Seraphim*

Seraphim was running in *Animage* magazine at the same time I was beginning my career at Viz Media's former *Animerica* magazine, as a contributor and assistant under editors Trish Ledoux and Julie Davis. As you might expect, *Animage*, together with *Newtype*, was an inspiration and a resource for *Animerica*, which although much smaller in page count adopted a similar format of anime coverage combined with a manga section (in fact one of the manga *Animerica* serialized was *Urusei Yatsura*). This might seem odd, but at the time, we wondered whether the then-new *Neon Genesis Evangelion* wasn't taking some of its inspiration from *Seraphim*. I say "odd" because nobody could mistake one work for the other, but we were thinking of such elements as a real-life humanitarian organization falling under the influence of a cult-like cabal and now having the military assets of Japan and the United States under their command, angels as a sinister, apocalyptic motif, the Magi, the conversation between two antagonists in a vast, standardized cemetery. Some readers might have also noted *Seraphim*'s mention of "Schumann resonances," which would be a plot point in another later noteworthy anime TV series of the 1990s, *Serial Experiments Lain*.

Seraphim features no plugsuited teens in giant robots (actually, they're—sorry, wrong back of manga) and its hero is a bearded, middle-aged dude, whereas in *Evangelion* that guy would have been the

villain. And while taking some inspiration might be one thing, I don't really think that *Evangelion* is ripping off *Seraphim*, although that would have made awesome clickbait, if only it weren't printed on this here paper (Cure Seraphim with this one old weird tip). People at *Evangelion*'s Studio GAINAX read the manga when it was coming out, of course; everyone in the industry read *Animage*. But more simply than that, they knew Oshii and Kon; one of *Evangelion* character designer Yoshiyuki Sadamoto's early professional jobs had been as a key animator on *The Angel's Egg*, and Oshii had helped the studio that same year, lending equipment support to their 16mm live-action *The Counterattack of Yamata no Orochi*. GAINAX had worked with Kon fairly recently; he did the *settei* design model sheets (the same role he would play on "Magnetic Rose") on their early 1990s anime feature-film proposal *Aoki Uru*. It was originally to have been directed by Hideaki Anno; the project's collapse led to the development of *Evangelion* instead (as it has now been revived as *Uru in Blue* and is slated for a 2018 release, GAINAX can take pride in having beaten even Oshii's *Garm Wars* for unmadeness).

Perhaps the most significant difference between *Seraphim* and *Evangelion* is one that's so obvious it might escape comment: whereas *Evangelion* was set in and largely concerned Japan, *Seraphim* has little or nothing to do with the home country of its creators. It would be only natural for those reading the manga in *Animage* to have wondered what happened to Japan in the future the manga depicts; and it offers a curt answer early on, in chapter 2. Oftentimes, a manga set in a foreign country (or, in the case of fantasy or SF, in an imaginary land) might have a Japanese main character to serve as a point of identification for the reader. But there are no characters identified as Japanese in *Seraphim*, and whatever the political charge may be in a Japanese creator depicting a China that is warring and divided, it must be of a different kind from that usually associated with Japanese nationalism (compare *Seraphim* to another 1990s manga, *The First President of Japan*), for if there is no "China" anymore in *Seraphim*, there is also evidently no Japan, and Oshii notes specifically that its Self-Defense Force (a nationalist icon, as many countries' militaries are) could not save it when the crisis came.

A contemporary reader might naturally see *Seraphim*'s depiction of a pandemic in  China associated with birds as a monstrous symbol for avian influenza, a.k.a. "bird flu," the highly lethal H5N1 virus strain that the real-life WHO has indeed worked strenuously to combat. But, as with *Patlabor 2* preceding 9/11, what might look like over-the-top metaphors when they come after events may seem more like an artist's prophetic visions when they come before. According to the WHO's history of H5N1, the virus known as "bird flu" was first known to infect human beings in 1997, almost two years after *Seraphim* ceased running. It also seems appropriate to note that the August 12, 2014, issue of the *New York Times* remarked how the Ebola outbreak in West Africa has revived the practice of the *cordon sanitaire*—that is, sealing off disease-hit regions by military force—maintaining that this was the first time the tactic had been used in almost a century.

Most of the footnotes you'll see on the manga pages were also in the original Japanese version of *Seraphim*. I considered the idea of moving the information to a notes section in the back, but thought it would be better to keep them where they were, to better preserve a sense of how the readers in *Animage* experienced the story. The notes on pages 47 and 112 were not in the original Japanese version, but I felt they might be useful to add here; conversely, the original version had notes in the prologue and in chapter 1 explaining that the seraphim are the highest order of angels (a perspective that reflects Christian but not necessarily Jewish tradition), and that the Magi are another name for the Three Wise Men who searched for Jesus, but I felt these might not be necessary for English-language readers.

In addition, there was originally a footnote in chapter 6 explaining that the caduceus is the symbol of the WHO. This would appear to have been a mistake; the symbol of the WHO (as seen on the robes of the Magi) is the rod of Asclepius, the Greek god of medicine, with a single snake entwined about it. But as a slip of the pen—if it in fact was—this would have ironically fit the argument Melchior was having with Lord Ye, as the caduceus was the double-snaked staff of Hermes; in 1932 Stuart L. Tyson, writing of the frequent confusion between the two symbols, noted that Hermes was the "god of the high-road and the market-place . . . the patron of commerce and the fat purse."

In real life, the World Health Organization (WHO) is a United Nations agency. The WHO as depicted in *Seraphim* isn't completely dissimilar to the real organization: it does concern itself with global public-health issues, in particular pandemics such as avian flu or Ebola, it is headquartered in Geneva, and its logo is similar to the one shown in the manga, which has the olive branches and the rod of Asclepius (the real logo also has the stylized map of the world found on the United Nations flag). *Seraphim*'s WHO is (to put it mildly) very different in tone, however; whereas the actual organization has the expected controversies that come when bureaucracy and politics interact with life-and-death matters, the WHO in this manga's future seems to have adopted the style

and mannerisms of a religious order of centuries past, one able to conduct inquisitions and command military assets.

This bizarre repainting of the WHO, changed from the bureaucrats, doctors, and researchers of reality to the robed inquisitors of *Seraphim*, can in part be seen as a trapping of a postapocalyptic story; I was reminded of the "scientific heresy" trial in the original *Planet of the Apes* (the Shanghai Inquisition are presented as extremists, but the Magi that recruit Balthazar and Melchior don't exude a bedside manner either). Our modern world has never yet had to face pandemics on the scale of those seen in the ancient and medieval worlds—events where entire continents lost a third or fourth of their population. It's not implausible that such a massive social disruption might be seen as discrediting the modern values of science and humanism, especially if these very values were seen as having been helpless against the plague itself. Even before Melchior is recruited as a Magi, he's shown in chapter 2 as angry at the talk of Gaian mysticism among the ostensibly scientific researchers in the refugee camp; he struggles to hold on to a rational perspective on Seraphim, telling Lord Ye, "It's just a disease."

But this change for the manga also serves another kind of dramatic shading particularly associated with Oshii—the use of religious, and especially Christian, motifs. In the real world, after all, pandemics may twist or bloat or disfigure their victims, but they don't cause them to sprout an angel's wings. The strange religious tone to Oshii's fictional WHO, therefore, seems no stranger than the fictional disease they profess to contain; not only the fact but the nature of *Seraphim*'s pandemic would seem to have shaped the survivors' culture of the manga's postapocalyptic world (a darkly Gaian perspective, perhaps).

There may be a third part to it, however. The WHO, as mentioned, is in real life a United Nations agency. Oshii's film *Patlabor 2* had begun with a disaster met by a Japanese UN peacekeeping force in an unnamed Southeast Asian country. The setting and premise were directly inspired by the real-life UN peacekeeping operation in Cambodia during 1992–93, which was overseen by Japanese diplomat Yasushi Akashi, and which represented the first participation of the Japanese Self-Defense Force in an overseas deployment, although a noncombatant role.

Besides the WHO, another UN agency that figures in *Seraphim* is the United Nations High Commission for Refugees (UNHCR); Melchior, also known as "Yakob, the country killer," is shown to have worked for the UNHCR. The *Seraphim* manga was serialized during 1994–95; in real life, during this same period, both the WHO and the UNHCR were—again, for the first time—headed up by Japanese individuals— Hiroshi Nakajima and Sadako Ogata,

respectively. Naturally, this caused increased discussion of both organizations in the Japanese media, and it is possible that Oshii was influenced here, as with *Patlabor 2*, to bring them as topical elements into the plot of *Seraphim*.

The depiction of UN agencies and missions in these early nineties works of Oshii seems to show them as ambivalent at best and dangerous and sinister at worst. Taken literally, they might remind one of the UN as it has also often been depicted in American conspiracy culture (I remember once driving to Dallas to attend an anime convention, and seeing a billboard above the I-45 asking, "COULD TEXAS BE OCCUPIED BY UNITED NATIONS TROOPS?"). Certainly an author doesn't have to personally believe in conspiracy theories in order to employ them in their work (of course, the same could be said of the beliefs publicly professed by political and religious leaders), but conspiracy and a conspiratorial view of history is a perhaps underexamined theme in Oshii's work— even more than *Seraphim*, it suffuses his 2000 novel *Blood: The Last Vampire—Night of the Beasts*, also available in English from Dark Horse.

You might have also noticed that as we get into the second half of the story, the footnotes disappear (as they did in the Japanese original). This may perhaps be because by this point in the narrative, the background and motifs of the story have been established. But it occurred to me that another possibility is that it simply reflects a difference between Kon and Oshii's approach to scripting, as Kon gradually took a larger role in writing *Seraphim*. Still another uncertainty here lies over all these speculations, considering the unknown extent to which editor Takashi Watanabe (rather than

Oshii or Kon) determined which elements in the script should receive a footnote and composed the content of those footnotes.

As I write all this, I feel I'm obsessing over details of details—and, of course, risking that exercise in foolishness the original editor warned of. Yet it is also true that Oshii and Kon's works are studied around the world. Therefore I want to acknowledge both my speculation, and my lack of complete certainty, about what precisely can be ascribed to whom in discussing the notes and narrative of *Seraphim*—what I wonder about, not just what I think or presume I know.

Many Chinas, Many Futures

Japanese has the most complicated writing system of any of the world's major languages, using not only kanji (ideograms originally imported from Chinese, in which they are called *hanzi*), but also kana (a phonetic syllabary the Japanese developed by abstracting kanji), as well as the Roman alphabet (imported from the West, naturally). Although this is, of course, an English version of *Seraphim*, you can see examples of all three kinds of writing here and there as graphic elements within the manga, such as the English in Sera's dossier in chapter 4 (it was English in the original manga as well) or the *hanzi* on the tombstones that Lord Ye shows Melchior. The many sound FX in the manga are all written in kana, as manga FX typically are. But these multiple modes of script are used in writing Japanese dialogue as well; and can have aspects difficult to convey when this dialogue is lettered in English; after all, we use only one script in writing our language, the Roman alphabet. Japanese can feature not only wordplay as can English, but a

"script play" for which there is no exact English equivalent. *Seraphim* uses this approach in its earliest pages to literally set the scene of the manga and the unstable context in which the story takes place.

In *Seraphim*'s prologue, there is a line that appears in English: "And as for Red China . . ." In the original Japanese dialogue, the line was "*Chuugokujin nan ka ni . . .*" *Chuugokujin* was written in Japanese using kanji, as 中国人—it means "(the) Chinese (people.)" But in the original dialogue, that same word was also given a small subtitle that used kana, as レッドチャイナ—which is a phonetic way of spelling out the English phrase "Red China," the term often used during the Cold War to refer to the nation formally known as the People's Republic of China. In other words, the original dialogue was written in a way that simultaneously "said" two different things in two different languages. Either might be correct to use, and, as the character is evidently an American, the English phrase was used. Yet using *either* doesn't quite capture the Japanese technique Oshii is employing here, for he used both. Even if the English dialogue were to try to use both, as in "And as for the Chinese . . . Red China . . . ," it still wouldn't convey it, for it was not one reading after the other, but two readings at once, as if it was permitted to view it from different sides.

When I was eighteen years old, my cultural heroes were Japanese, but my political heroes were Chinese. For a few weeks in the spring of 1989, the entire world looked toward the city of Beijing as a symbol of courage and ideals—something that, sadly, seems very hard to believe today. That year had begun for me when I saw an import tape of Katsuhiro Otomo's film *Akira*, not yet then released in English. Its scenes of a great Asian city in rebellion and under martial law seemed to reflect the coming moment with a prescient urgency that anime rarely possesses. The massacre of the pro-democracy movement and its supporters in Beijing on the evening of June 3, 1989—an event that, twenty-five years later, can still not be freely discussed where it occurred—was what motivated me to study China in school. Or rather, the different Chinas, for there are many, just as there are many Japans, and many Americas. I wanted to begin with the China that those people had died for, and the China that had killed them.

Seraphim 266613336 Wings takes place almost entirely in China, and its fictional plot touches upon actual persons, groups, and events in modern Chinese history. The fragmented land reflected in the map in chapter 6 may seem fanciful in 2015, with China on track to soon become the largest economy in the world, but there are Chinese old enough to remember a map that indeed had different lines. The nation we usually refer to as simply as China today—that is, the People's Republic of China—is young as a political entity; it was founded in 1949, just two years before Mamoru Oshii was born. Yet China is one of the world's oldest continuous human civilizations, and the idea that it has needed to catch up with the West is itself relatively recent. Even as Europe began to modernize in the seventeenth and eighteenth centuries, Enlightenment thinkers such as Leibniz and Voltaire argued that China's enduring system of imperial government administered by a scholar class had much to teach Europe, itself divided and torn by conflict.

By the early twentieth century, however, that once-respected ancient system in China had collapsed—a consequence both of the long-building pressure of internal demographics, and of the politically volatile influence of outside philosophy, technology, trade, subversion, and military invasions. Much of the first half of the twentieth century in China was dominated by a convoluted and violent struggle to establish a new Chinese state that could restore stability while achieving modernization. The issue was further inflamed by the fact the ruling imperial dynasty, the Qing, was Manchu, a people from China's northeast periphery, adding an ethnic nationalist tone to the struggle, blaming "foreign" rule for China's weakness (although the powerful China of the seventeenth and eighteenth centuries had also been ruled over by the Qing). In addition to all this, outside powers exerted considerable effort to affect the struggle for China's future, and a particular role was played by China's near neighbors, the Soviet Union and Japan.

Both nations had themselves only recently modernized. Each had its own strong ideological pitch to make to China—the Soviets as the vanguard of historical progress and revolutionary anti-imperialism, the Japanese as the first modern Asian nation, and the one that had successfully resisted foreign takeovers. Both nations, of course, also sought to shape events in China to maximize their own power and influence, and these ideologies (though not completely insincere—human nature is more complicated than that, even for imperialists) were tools to that end. During this half-century period, Japan colonized, invaded, and occupied various parts of China—sometimes actually developing the economy and infrastructure, very oftentimes oppressing the Chinese in a style that ranged from everyday bayonetings and shootings to theatrical levels of cruelty and villainy, with Japanese generals running private drug rings and bioweapons programs. Millions of Chinese died as a consequence of Japanese foreign policy and militarism.

The Qing had ultimately been overthrown by the Nationalist movement under Sun Yat-Sen, whose political party of the same name, known as the Kuomintang, or KMT, established a short-lived republic that held multiparty elections in 1913 (this election, held over a century ago, was perhaps the closest mainland China has ever come to democracy). However, in a struggle that makes Oshii's *Kerberos Saga* look clear and simple, the military forces that had provided the muscle for the revolution were reluctant to cede or share power, their officers becoming independent warlords that ruled much of China until the late 1920s. In 1921 the Chinese Communist Party (CCP) was founded, but originally had little strength compared to the KMT, which, under its new ruler, General Chiang Kai-Shek, became authoritarian, along Leninist principles of centralized leadership. Originally in a united front with the KMT, the Communists were purged in the late 1920s as the warlords were suppressed, and the bare remnants of their forces eventually had to retreat deep into China's interior in the famous "Long March" of 1934–35.

As the Japanese (who, like the Soviets, had at different times armed, trained, and financed multiple factions) began their most serious assault on China in the 1930s, the KMT bore the brunt of the resistance; Allied propaganda at the time sometimes depicted Chiang as a fellow anti-Axis leader, alongside Roosevelt, Churchill, and Stalin (this, by the way, is why the five

permanent members of the UN Security Council are China, the US, the UK, and Russia, as well as France—the UN was originally based around the Allied Powers of World War II). In the aftermath, however, Chiang lost the struggle to unite China to the CCP during four years of renewed civil war, during which the Communists found much public support, owing to the corruption and brutality of the KMT. The Kuomintang government retreated in 1949 to the island of Taiwan, setting up a regime in exile; even today, under democracy, they remain Taiwan's largest political party. The KMT continued to be regarded as the legal government of China by the UN until the early 1970s, even though by then, for practical purposes, most nations dealt with the Communists that ruled the Chinese mainland—in those days known as "Red China" to distinguish it from the KMT government on Taiwan.

The Communists had been led to victory by a remarkable political and military strategist named Mao Zedong—a man who eventually proved to be as ruthless, callous, and heedless of the lives of the Chinese as the Japanese had been. Mao, having solidified his position after the Long March, became chairman of the Communist Party (in his lifetime he was commonly known as "Chairman Mao") that established the People's Republic of China in 1949. Americans have the leader of *our* revolution, George Washington, only on the one-dollar bill; in China, Mao is on the one, the five, the ten, the twenty, the fifty, and the one hundred *renminbi*. As *Seraphim* suggests in its remarks on the Great Leap Forward, Mao's rule of China, which lasted until his death in 1976, was in fact often lacking in either stability or modernization—Mao professed to believe, and perhaps actually did, that it was necessary to sacrifice the first to achieve his notion of the second. Millions more Chinese died as a consequence of Mao's rule.

Mamoru Oshii's high-school activist days in late-sixties Japan (which are evoked in *Blood: The Last Vampire—Night of the Beasts*) coincided with Mao's infamous Cultural Revolution in China, in which he encouraged millions of young people to attack objects and people connected (or claimed to be) with traditional culture, authority, bureaucracy, capitalism—anything that might stand in the way of creating a truly revolutionary society. It was conducted with an apocalyptic fervor, sometimes literally—in 1967, radical students even mobbed the test site of China's first H-bomb, running toward the mushroom cloud afterward shouting, "Long live Chairman Mao!" Mao indeed allowed himself to be presented as a messiah; his quasi-divine image—and personal insulation from the poverty and suffering inflicted by his policies—was something like that of the Kim dynasty of North Korea. But unlike the Kims, Mao Zedong ruled the largest nation on Earth, and he was a figure taken very seriously around the world, both as a threat and as an inspiration. Even the Beatles, in their 1968 song "Revolution," felt the need to advise their young fans that they shouldn't "go carrying around pictures of Chairman Mao." Japan had its own Maoist-influenced militant group, the United Red Army, which is the subject of *Red*, a current manga by *Dance till Tomorrow*'s Naoki Yamamoto; Oshii discusses his own experiences from that era with Yamamoto in *Red* Volume 2.

The original Japanese footnote in chapter 4 that explained who people such as Hong Xiuquan, Sun Yat-Sen, and Zhu De had been did not explain Deng Xiaoping and Zhao Ziyang—perhaps because in the early 1990s Deng and Zhao, both now deceased, would have been contemporary names to the manga's readers. For anyone familiar with modern Chinese history, there would have been a tremendous jolt in the dialogue Melchior so casually rattles off: "Ye Jianying was marshal of the People's Liberation Army . . . It was he who forged the Southern Republic of China with Deng and Zhao Ziyang. Followed by his son, Ye Xuanping . . . Xuanying's the fourth of his line. During the active measures, his father dreamed of establishing a permanent home for the Hakka people."

Ye Xuanying—the character in the manga known as "Lord Ye"—is, as far as I know, a fictitious person, but the others, including his putative elders Ye Jianying and Ye Xuanping, were real people, important political figures in twentieth-century China, some of whom at times were fierce rivals to each other. *Seraphim*, as a work of fiction, suggests that they were all part of a cabal centered on their shared Hakka ethnicity. As a very (very) rough American equivalent, imagine a manga that claimed that Robert McNamara, John F. Kennedy, Ronald Reagan, Tip O'Neill, and Richard Daley had all conspired to break off a portion of the United States to become a homeland for Irish Americans.

Melchior, of course, speaks of all this in a cynical, even contemptuous fashion, but the end of the chapter presents Lord Ye's more benign view of *Seraphim*'s Hakka conspiracy, toward a nobler purpose than a simple ethnic state: "The country was maturing into a true democracy . . . a process the Hakka were shepherding. Our great work . . . until that chance was snatched away." In other words, in *Seraphim* Oshii presents a view of modern

Chinese history based on a conspiracy theory where an ethnic minority lies behind many of its upheavals and revolutions, but working toward an admirable end; with our last glimpse of Lord Ye in chapter 13, the somewhat-ambiguous character is revealed as a true ally of the Magi.

The Map Is Not the Territory

Seraphim's views on the role of the Hakka in Chinese history were possibly influenced by Mary S. Erbaugh's paper "The Secret History of the Hakkas: The Chinese Revolution as a Hakka Enterprise," which appeared in the December 1992 issue of *The China Quarterly*, less than two years before the debut of *Seraphim*. The paper, which is available on Portland State University's website, is recommended to anyone interested in further examining the uses of history within this manga, although under the heading "Some Caveats," Erbaugh herself notes, "Taboo topics tempt researchers toward conspiracy theories and reductionism. Consideration of Hakka ties helps to clarify the view of modern China, but they are never explanatory in isolation. The high tide of Hakka leadership appears to rest on revolutionary status as much as ethnicity. The Hakka are only one of hundreds of subgroups which won the revolution, and ethnic bonds compete with dozens of other demands, even for Hakka politicians."

Oshii proffers all these names with a certain vagueness in time and space that perhaps befits Oshii the science-fiction fan—a person who (as he mentions in his afterword to Ryu Mitsuse's *10 Billion Days and 100 Billion Nights*, published in English through Viz's Haikasoru imprint) managed to convince himself as a young student radical that interviewing his favorite SF author was all in the cause of the revolution. For example, the remark in *Seraphim* that Lord Ye is fourth of his line might be understood as saying he is the grandson of the real-life Ye Xuanping, born in 1924 and former mayor of Guangzhou, China's third-largest city. The "active measures" Melchior refers to is a term used to describe subversion efforts conducted by Soviet intelligence throughout the history of the USSR (that is, between 1917 and 1991). The phrase is associated with the controversial Mitrokhin Archive, as detailed in Christopher Andrew's *Sword and the Shield*; like Erbaugh's paper, published in 1992 and another possible influence on *Seraphim*.

Seraphim made its debut in 1994; if the manga is meant to be future history, it takes place in at least 2004, going by Balthazar's remark that he found Sera ten years before. There is also the possibility, however, that

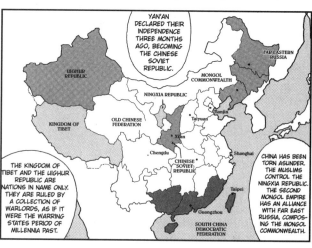

YAN'AN DECLARED THEIR INDEPENDENCE THREE MONTHS AGO, BECOMING THE CHINESE SOVIET REPUBLIC.
UIGHUR REPUBLIC
MONGOL COMMONWEALTH
FAR EASTERN RUSSIA
NINGXIA REPUBLIC
KINGDOM OF TIBET
OLD CHINESE FEDERATION
Tianjin
Taiyuan
Xi'an
Chengdu
CHINESE SOVIET REPUBLIC
Shanghai
Taipei
Guangzhou
SOUTH CHINA DEMOCRATIC FEDERATION
CHINA HAS BEEN TORN ASUNDER. THE MUSLIMS CONTROL THE NINGXIA REPUBLIC. THE SECOND MONGOL EMPIRE HAS AN ALLIANCE WITH FAR EAST RUSSIA, COMPOSING THE MONGOL COMMONWEALTH.
THE KINGDOM OF TIBET AND THE UIGHUR REPUBLIC ARE NATIONS IN NAME ONLY. THEY ARE RULED BY A COLLECTION OF WARLORDS, AS IF IT WERE THE WARRING STATES PERIOD OF MILLENNIA PAST.

Seraphim depicts some sort of alternate history, and shows a China that was already changed by events in the past, not just the future. Oshii has worked in this subgenre, most notably through his long-running multimedia *Kerberos Saga*, which includes his scripts for Hiroyuki Okiura's anime film *Jin-Roh* and for the manga *Hellhounds: Panzer Cops*, published in 1994 by Dark Horse. More recently, and perhaps relevant to the approach of *Seraphim*, his novel *Rolling Thunder: Pax Japonica* tartly inverts the geopolitical issues of Oshii's youth by imagining Japan as a hegemon fighting its own Vietnam War in 1966 (the year of *Blood: The Last Vampire*, Oshii fans will note). Whereas in many Japanese stories of this type, Japan becomes more powerful due to having somehow won World War II, in Oshii's more sophisticated approach, it was an unanticipated result of a change that had happened long before—in this world, the Confederacy won the Battle of Antietam, leading to a US that remained divided and weakened in this alternate twentieth century, and also permitting Oshii to draw ironic parallels between the North-South conflicts of America and those of Vietnam.

In the real 1994 in which *Seraphim* debuted, Ye Jianying had been dead for eight years; his son Ye Xuanping was then a vice chair of the Chinese People's Political Consultative Conference, a sort of "upper house" within the strictly limited parliamentary aspect of Chinese politics. Deng Xiaoping and Zhao Ziyang were also both alive in 1994, but in quite different circumstances. Both men had held high office at the time of the 1989 pro-democracy movement; it was Deng, as chair of China's Central Military Commission, who had ordered the army to suppress it, whereas Zhao, then general secretary of the Chinese Communist Party, had publicly supported the demonstrators. Five years later, Deng was formally retired from politics but in fact remained the most influential leader in China, whereas Zhao had been purged and remained under house arrest. The idea that these different men would work together to found a separatist nation in southern China based on their shared Hakka ethnicity is problematic (as the students politely say) from several angles, and even as a conceit of conspiratorial or alternate history, it might be seen as an outrageous slur on their reputations by many Chinese. Others might just think the idea bizarre. But in an ethnically and culturally diverse nation of 1.3 billion people, it's unlikely that everyone indeed sees the idea of China in the same way. Other than officially.

Governments are rarely enthusiastic about separatism, even through peaceful and democratic means, as seen in the United Kingdom's recent campaign to keep Scotland within their union. But in looking at that map in chapter 6 of *Seraphim*, I can't help but reflect on how in real life China takes even the *symbolic* image of national unity to levels seen in no other country. To illustrate the point, consider that China, as a nation, is larger in area, and stretches farther from east to west, than the lower forty-eight states of the US. Now go look at any map that shows global time zones, and compare the two nations. You'll see that China has only *one* time zone; it would be as if Los Angeles, Denver, and Houston all had to set their clocks to match the ones in Washington, DC. Or—so as to not make this a US vs. China thing—compare it to the different time zones inside other big nations in the Eastern Hemisphere, whether democratic (Australia) or not so much (Russia). China is a nation that has launched space stations, yet even the curvature of the Earth cannot be permitted to take precedence over national unity on the map. If it is noon in Beijing, it must likewise be noon in Lhasa and Kashi.

Alternate maps of the United States, showing it with different internal or external boundaries, are not uncommon: whether made for satirical purposes (as in the "Jesusland" maps that followed the 2004 US election), in the social sciences (as in Colin Woodward's 2012 bestseller *American Nations: A History of the Eleven Rival Regional Cultures of North America*), or to imagine a future or alternate history (such as the maps of a divided America in Frank Miller and Dave Gibbons's *Give Me Liberty*, or Harry Turtledove's *How Few Remain*). But the map of the divided China Lord Ye shows Melchior in chapter 6 would not be acceptable in China, even in a work of science fiction. I noticed another startling thing about the map: several major Chinese cities are placed on it, but not Beijing; it should be just to the northwest of Tianjin. The omission was in the original manga as well; no blunter symbolism could be made

that this is no longer the People's Republic of China.

I fear that I'm missing a very obvious point while I discuss this, and by *obvious*, I mean it's right there in the title. Not the 266613336 *Wings* part (the number is an esoteric cipher decoded by the word that follows it: 266,613,336 divided by 2—a pair of wings—gives 133,306,668, the total number of angels that sided with Lucifer and were cast out of heaven, in the figure traditionally attributed to the medieval reckoning of Peter of Spain). I meant the *Seraphim* part, which in the manga is the name given to a plague, after its effects.

Seraphim is a story that makes debatable use of actual Chinese history, people, and cultures. But then, it takes place not in the China we know, but in a China (and a world) ravaged by a pandemic implied to have killed off a large percentage of the Earth's population. Great plagues of the past such as the Black Death have caused profound political and economic disruptions; in fact, a bubonic plague outbreak played its own role in destabilizing

late Imperial China in the mid-nineteenth century. In other words, add the social upheavals of a devastating pandemic to the equation, and the idea of leaders long devoted to the People's Republic of China instead supporting a split along regional lines seems a bit less outrageous. Oshii might well have noted in writing *Seraphim* that (even without a war or plague) this is just what had happened recently to another great multiethnic Communist power, the Soviet Union. In 1991, less than three years before *Seraphim*'s debut, the USSR—a political entity that had, after all, existed longer than the People's Republic of China—split up into fifteen different nations, some of which were led by people who had previously held top offices within the Soviet system; for example, the new nation of Georgia's head of state was Eduard Shevardnadze, the former Soviet foreign minister.

That is still perhaps more of a literary conceit than a comparison; the PRC was not the USSR (indeed, the political split between China and the Soviet Union was a major theme in the latter half of the Cold War) and Eduard Shevardnadze, a Georgian, was nowhere near as invested in the idea of the Soviet Union as Deng Xiaoping, a Hakka, was in the idea of the People's Republic of China. Shevardnadze was born into a USSR that already existed, but Deng was forty-five years old when the PRC was founded, the culmination of a cause he had been working toward as a revolutionary since he was a teenager. Deng, born in 1904 and dying in 1997, had a life that spanned the turbulence of twentieth-century Chinese power politics, of which he was its great survivor and eventual victor. Purged twice by Mao (during the Cultural Revolution, Deng, who had been a cabinet minister and vice premier, was

reassigned to factory work, building tractors), Deng was the tortoise to Mao's wild hare, and when Mao died in 1976, it was he who pushed for an end to radical politics and who set in motion the emphasis on economic development for which China has become known ever since.

In 1994, however, when *Seraphim* made its debut, China was not yet the colossus it is today. Just twenty years ago, China's economy was still smaller than Canada's. It was Japan in 1994 that still had the second-largest economy in the world—a position they had held since the 1960s, and continued to hold until they lost it in 2010, to China. In the last years of his life, Deng Xiaoping, trying to rebuild his political support after the suppression of the democracy movement, made a famous speaking tour to Shenzhen, Guangzhou, and Zhuhai—all cities in the area of the "South China Democratic Federation" that Lord Ye leads in *Seraphim*. It was on this tour that he was credited with his famous slogans, "To get rich is glorious" and "Some areas [meaning, South China] must get rich before others."

This was provocative in a country whose leadership had come up under the communist egalitarianism preached by Chairman Mao, but it gave powerful encouragement to the local culture of entrepreneurship and export, and may have inspired *Seraphim* in its conception of South China as an independent, mercantile nation—at the end of chapter 2, the manga even refers to it as the "Special Economic Zone," a PRC term for areas allowed more free-market activity, first applied to south coastal China in the 1980s. As a sort of historical consolation prize, the map in chapter 6 also contains a "Chinese Soviet Republic" centered in Yan'an. The

Chinese Soviet Republic was the name of a provisional revolutionary government run by Mao in the 1930s, and Yan'an is where Mao famously rebuilt the party after the Long March. Perhaps, Oshii is saying, as history turns, the Maoists too may get their chance again.

And Came into the Land
of the People of the East

Something will have occurred to Oshii fans long before now. *Seraphim*, as discussed before, was being made at the same time as was the movie *Ghost in the Shell*. The two are like a polarized image, each turned to a different angle, for each gives a different vision of a Chinese future. Just as the movie made the deliberate decision to change the look and style of Major Kusanagi from the original manga, the movie changed the setting of the story from the manga's fictional "Newport City" in Japan to a fictional city inspired by Hong Kong—a place with grit and grime, but also a wired, thriving metropolis, not the fortress *tulou*, full of afflicted victims and under siege, that we see in *Seraphim*.

It's important not to elide the two places, which is why I speak of a "Chinese" future and not just that of "China." The real-life Special Economic Zone of south China directly borders Hong Kong; although it too is not on the map in chapter 6, Hong Kong would be just to the south of Guangzhou. We saw what that border means in the recent democracy protests in Hong Kong. Two years after *Seraphim* ceased its run and *Ghost in the Shell* premiered, the People's Republic of China reacquired administration of Hong Kong under the policy of "one country, two systems," under which Hong Kong would be permitted to retain its democratic and legal protections until 2047. It is, therefore (together with nearby Macau) presently the only part of the People's Republic of China with such political freedoms, and the recent Hong Kong protests would have been quickly and firmly suppressed had they happened anywhere else within its administration—it was, in fact, the most prominent protest movement in China since the massacre in Beijing in 1989.

Not everyone in Hong Kong agreed with the protestors, by any means. But what they were fighting for was the freedom to be Chinese and yet disagree; for Chinese people to have the right to decide for themselves as individuals what it can mean to be Chinese, not to have the definition and the rules enforced upon them. The tension between the individual and nationalism exists in many places, for a "strong nation" seems to often require not only defense from external threats, but from the perhaps greater internal enemy of differing opinions as to what exactly the nation should be. It's certainly an issue in our country as well. Perhaps something we often despair of, our disunity and disorder in America, is part of the price we must pay; perhaps freedom can't have it both ways. The alternatives include an imposed unity, and the imposed appearance of unity. The difference between the China of Hong Kong and the China of Guangzhou is the freedom to draw a line.

China today is reclaiming the place it has had throughout much of recorded history— that of one of the world's richest and most powerful nations. In the alternate-future China of *Seraphim*, Shanghai was a darkened "abode of devils" ruled by witch-burning inquisitors. In the real future China, Oshii became the supervising director for

"Shanghai Skygate: The Door of the Sky," a short film made to promote the Shanghai World Financial Center in 2011—at the time, the second-tallest building in the world. Its curved, prism-like face and trapezoidal aperture at the top are indeed a romantic cyberpunk vision. Built with Japanese funds, the aperture at the top was originally to have been in the shape of a circle. It was objected that this would have looked too much like a rising sun.

I couldn't help but notice that whereas Melchior's remark to Lord Ye in chapter 4 that Caspar is "not your supper" was marked in the original Japanese (and here) with a footnote saying, "The Hakka Chinese are often stereotyped as dog eaters," no such footnote accompanied his line a few pages earlier, "Think of them as the 'Jews of China,' if that helps. Purveyors of political discord and uprisings."

In Japan, manga lettering and captions (such as those you can see on the first few pages of *OPUS*) are often done by the editorial staff of the manga magazine in which the story appears, rather than by a freelance specialist, as is the norm in English-language editions of manga (and in comic books). It's therefore again uncertain whether the footnotes that appeared in the original Japanese edition of *Seraphim* were at the behest of the creators or the editor. Although many Chinese are hostile or indifferent to the idea, dog eating is, in fact, not uncommon in parts of China, in both Hakka and non-Hakka areas (the practice can be found in Korea, Vietnam, and the Philippines as well)—despite the footnote, *Seraphim* later portrays matter-of-factly dogs being raised for food, which is the usual way dog meat is obtained in China, rather than by catching dogs on the street.

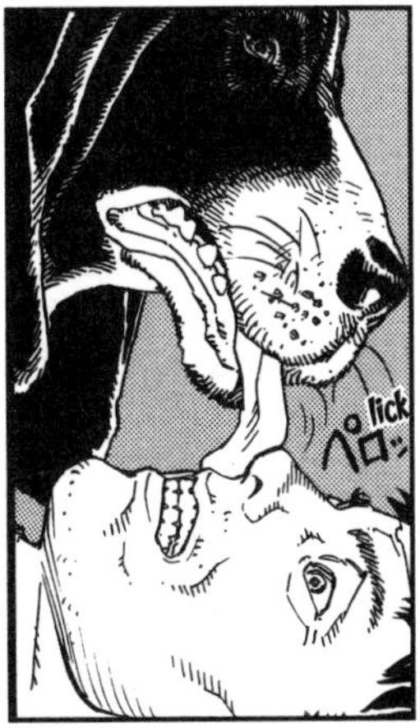
ペロッ
lick

Melchior's comment on "the Jews" can perhaps be compared to Oshii's placement of the Rothschild family into the backstory of his 2000 novel *Blood: The Last Vampire—Night of the Beasts*, which quotes extensively from Sanshiro Yokoyama's *Rosuchairdoka: Yudaya kokusai zaibatsu no koubou* (The Rothschilds: The rise and fall of a Jewish international financial combine), published in 1995 by Kodansha—the inference is that the "Red Shield" organization of the *Blood* franchise takes its inspiration from the English meaning of *Rothschild*. "Inference" is perhaps unduly coy; the *Blood+* anime series has an organization called Cinq Flèches—"five arrows," which is also the logo of the real-life N M Rothschild & Sons investment-banking firm; in the anime, the five members of Cinq Flèches share the names of the five sons (Amschel, Salomon, Nathan, Carl, and James) of the founder of the Rothschild dynasty, Mayer Rothschild.

In *Blood*, Oshii has a character use the story of the Rothschilds to denounce anti-Semitism, and in *Seraphim*, if a character suggests that "the Hakka" and "the Jews" have both played the role of subversive elements in history, it seems worth noting that the manga develops a positive image of Lord Ye, who likewise comes to admire Melchior, saying, "We are very much alike." Melchior is in many respects the protagonist of *Seraphim*, yet his own homeland is

never clearly stated. But his real name is Yakob, and after his dream of the ascending staircase in chapter 15, there seems less doubt that he is named for the Old Testament patriarch who—after a struggle with a strange being that will not give its name, alternately described as a man, an angel, or God—was renamed Israel.

In Paul Johnson's *A History of the Jews*, this struggle is described as "perhaps the most mysterious and obscure passage in the entire Bible . . . The term 'Israel' may mean he who fights Gods, he who fights for God, he whom God fights, or whom God rules, the upright one of God, or God is upright. There is no agreement. Nor has anyone yet provided a satisfactory account of what the incident means." There is something in those words that reminds me of the works of Mamoru Oshii himself. And if it is mysterious and obscure, then there might be reason in dismissing it. But Oshii knows that it is these things above all that people do not dismiss.

With an Alien People Clutching Their Gods

Takashi Watanabe quotes Oshii saying at the time of *Seraphim's* beginning, "Of all the work I have done in my life, this is my most ambitious"—a strong statement, considering everything he already accomplished up to that point. After Satoshi Kon passed away, Oshii demonstrated his continuing interest in *Seraphim* by writing a text prologue to the manga, *Sankenja reihai-hen*. *Hen* is a suffix in titles that might be translated "(the) book (of)" or "volume."

Sankenja reihai is derived from the usual way "The Adoration of the Magi" is translated into Japanese, 東方三博士の礼拝—*Toohoo sanhakase no reihai*. *Toohoo* (said "tohh-hohh") means "east," with the connotation of direction. *Reihai* means "adoration." *San* is three, whereas *hakase* is a not uncommon title used to refer to someone (such as a professor) that connotes knowledge and wisdom; the not especially wise young scientist Hakase Shinonome from *Nichijou* takes her name from the term. For the title of the prologue, Oshii uses not *sanhakase* for "Three Wise Men," but the more old-fashioned-sounding 三賢者—*sankenja*, *kenja* meaning "sage" or "wise man."

You'll remember Watanabe's remark that in the *Seraphim* manga, "the kanji used for the word *magi* also changed with chapter 13, but this collected edition has standardized these differences." Interestingly, the kanji used in the collected edition were neither *sanhakase* nor *sankenja*, but 審問官—*shimmonkan*, "inquisitor." Unlike the first two terms, *shimmokan* wouldn't ordinarily be associated in Japanese with the biblical Magi, but in *Seraphim*, of course, the term fits the job description. The reader may notice the first two kanji in the name on the sign of Shanghai Inquisition in chapter 10. The association of *shimmokan* with the Magi is made by the same subtitle technique discussed earlier with "*Chuugokujin*/Red China"—in the original Japanese collected version of *Seraphim*, the kana マギ—"Magi" written phonetically—are added alongside *shimmokan* whenever the term is used.

Sankenja reihai-hen, the *Seraphim* prologue, appeared in the March 2011 issue of the manga magazine *Comic Ryu* (like *Animage*, also published by Tokuma). The prologue featured an illustration by Katsuya Terada, whom in 2000 Oshii had personally requested to design the characters of *Blood: The Last Vampire* (the illustration can be seen on page 120 of Dark Horse's *Dragon Girl and Monkey King: The Art of Katsuya Terada*). At the time of the prologue's release, it was announced that a full *Seraphim* novel would be forthcoming from Oshii in 2012; however, it has not appeared to date.

Despite the creative conflicts to which Watanabe alludes, and Kon's referring to *Seraphim* as his "bastard child," Kon might very well have had some lingering affection for the traditions behind *Seraphim*; it certainly seems worth remarking that his 2003 film *Tokyo Godfathers* takes inspiration from John Ford's 1948 movie *3 Godfathers*, and of course both took inspiration from the story of the Magi. Loose inspiration, of course—the Bible says little

about their career as action heroes—but in this, works like *Seraphim* and *Tokyo Godfathers* only join the great body of folklore that, like a long-traveling fair, surrounds the citadels of canon. There were plenty of legends about the Magi in the Middle Ages, too, not least because of the legend-like vagueness with which they are described in the Book of Matthew. Oshii, who liked to drop a little Greek in Balthazar's plea to Caspar in chapter 5, would be aware that the exact nationality of the Magi is never mentioned in the Bible—Matthew 2:1 says only that they came from ἀπὸ ἀνατολῶν—*apo anatolon*, translated as "from the east," but which literally means "from the rising sun." A Japanese, adding their own telling to the tradition, could take delight in that.

We're fortunate that we have at least two book-length treatments in English on the creators of *Seraphim*, both of which were resources for this afterword—Brian Ruh's *Stray Dog of Anime: The Films of Mamoru Oshii*, just recently issued in a 2014 second edition from Palgrave Macmillan, and Andrew Osmond's 2009 *Satoshi Kon: The Illusionist*, from Stone Bridge Press. Both works emphasize Oshii and Kon's anime rather than their manga works, in part because of the relative obscurity of the latter—but not improperly either, as it was their anime that built their international reputations. Mamoru Oshii, at least, is still with us, and still making anime as well as live-action movies. Yet even the hero of an Oshii film once said, "The world cannot live at the level of its great men."

To offer one more scriptural quote, as that director might: "Man shall not live by bread alone, but by every word that proceedeth out of the mouth of God." Anime is a thing of the imagination, and those motivated to watch it and write about it are often inspired by their notion of a creative spirit, and the wonders it has worked. But it is anime's bread, rather than every word that proceedeth out of the mouth of a director (or marketer, or manga editor) that concerns Jonathan Clements in another book to recommend, his bracing and well-researched 2013 *Anime: A History*, published by the British Film Institute.

Clements considers anime as something a century old; not to dust off isolated obscurities, but to display the continuities and evolution in tradecraft and industry practices—no less so than in the history of Hollywood—that link figures like Kon and Oshii (who were themselves followed into the industry by younger generations) to those who came before them. But unlike *Animage*'s history of anime, in Clements' macro view, Kon and Oshii are indeed only figures—names mentioned in passing (a side remark of Clements's on Kon speaks to the bread in its own way), rather than mighty pillars one must pass between to enter the temple of anime. I would perhaps like that to be true, as the editors of *Animage* would have. Perhaps it should be true. But it is not true. Plenty of people watch far more anime than I, yet have never yet seen a work by Kon or Oshii. They're the ones going to church every week, as opposed to people who just call themselves spiritual.

Clements doesn't take his view out of a lack of respect or admiration for those directors, but because the anime industry existed before them, and went on in their absence, and would not have vanished or even hardly diminished its output (or revenues) had Kon or Oshii never existed. It is the same in Hollywood or any of the world's major film traditions: respected directors die, but media conglomerates, studios, and craft unions are collective bodies that live on, passing along their networks, capital, and knowledge. If Satoshi Kon and Mamoru Oshii *are* artists you admire, whose work you wish *were* more representative of anime, you can understand them further precisely by reading not only Ruh and Osmond, but Clements as well, for he is talking not about their careers, but the systems within which their careers have existed and developed. Clements also proffers a refreshing—and perhaps British—skepticism toward every dramatic claim of the struggling, suffering artist, suggesting the industry does not lack for skiving, idle buggers. Kon's own *OPUS* more than hints at this, of course.

Anime is more than a genre. But perhaps it is still less than a medium, and remains something like a demographic. Many who love it take a fierce pride—with the anger, with the heat of fierceness—in how well, in the end, Kon used his time. Not everyone can be like Kon, but it may also be that not everyone chooses to be like Kon. *Animage* has never quite given up. Oddly enough, *Ghost in the Shell 2: Innocence* (called in Japan simply *Innocence*) *did* make the cover of *Animage* in 2004—but then, it would have been somewhat awkward not to, as the film was coproduced by Toshio

Suzuki, and at tremendous expense by anime standards, with a reported budget of US$20 million. And Isao Takahata's *The Tale of the Princess Kaguya* (starring a cute young girl!) made the cover of the January 2014 issue. That first issue of *Animage* in 1978 carried a feature on Takahata's *Horus, the Prince of the Sun*. Even then, the movie was ten years in the past. Some have lived and worked; some have labored and died young.

We live in an age where a person's last public words may be a tweet. Satoshi Kon's, a few hours before his death, were 「古くさいというより、古びた価値観にいまだに憬れているのかもしれないが。」("It's not so much that I have an old way of thinking, but rather, that I still yearn to see the values prized by yesteryear.") The soul leaves the mouth in the form of a bird.

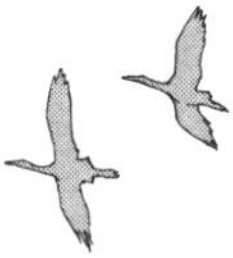

—*CGH*

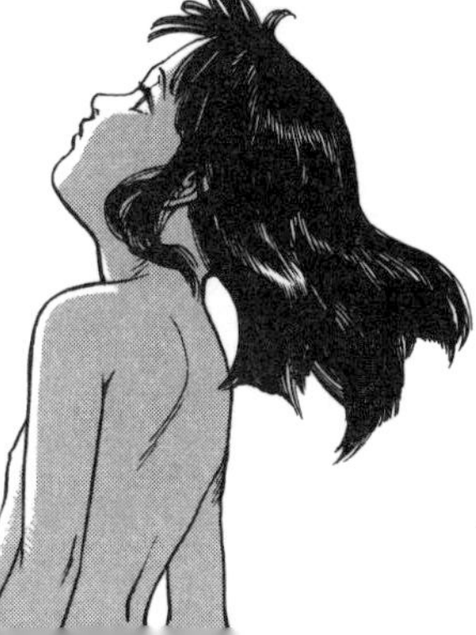

ALSO AVAILABLE FROM DARK HORSE

SATOSHI KON'S
OPUS

OPUS is Kon's metafictional tale of Chikara Nagai—a creator under pressure to finish his latest graphic novel, *Resonance*—who finds that the harshest critic of the shock ending he's got planned is the character who'll have to die in it! Nagai's strengths and weaknesses as a creator are tested beyond their limits as his present and his past, and the worlds of the manga and of reality, become the levels of a maze he may never escape . . . let alone get a chance to resolve the story!

NOW ON SALE! $19.99 US/$21.99 CAN   ISBN 978-1-61655-606-8

STOP!

THIS IS THE BACK OF THE BOOK!

This manga collection is translated into English, but arranged in right-to-left reading format to maintain the artwork's visual orientation as originally drawn and published in Japan. If you've never read comics this way before, take a look at the diagram below to give yourself an idea of how to go about it.

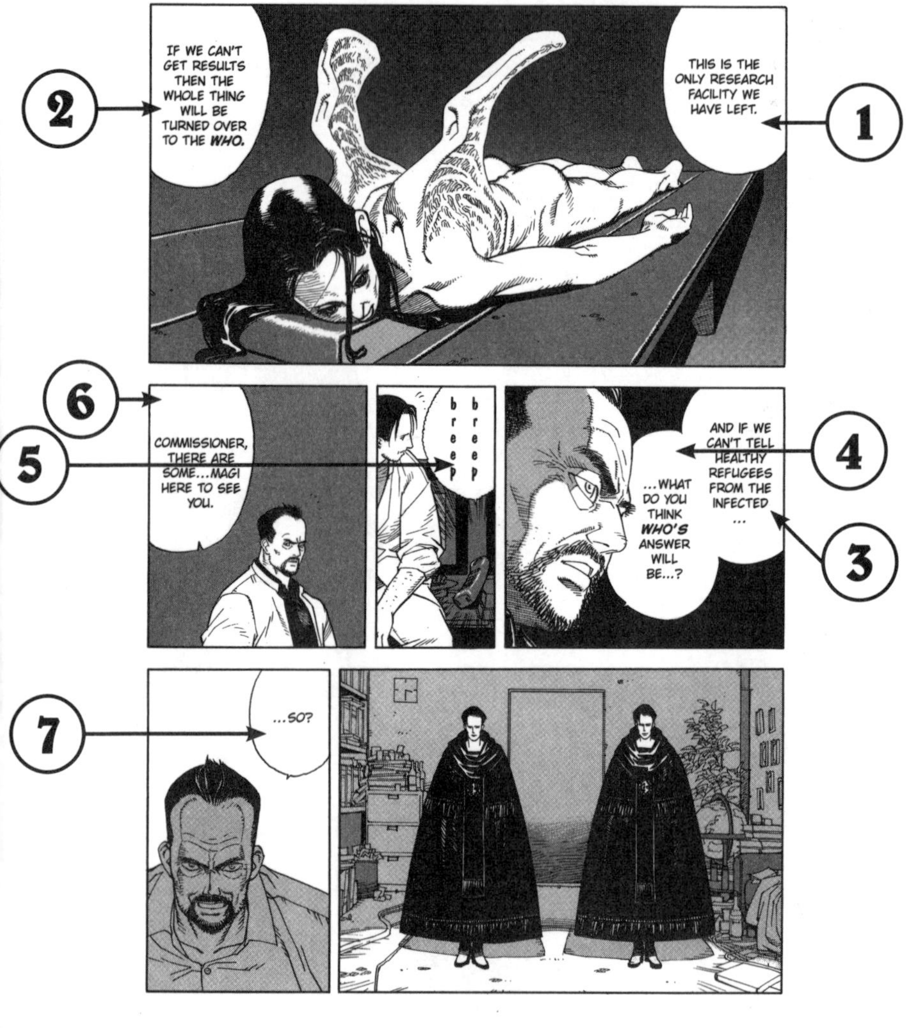
1
THIS IS THE ONLY RESEARCH FACILITY WE HAVE LEFT.
2
IF WE CAN'T GET RESULTS THEN THE WHOLE THING WILL BE TURNED OVER TO THE *WHO.*
3
AND IF WE CAN'T TELL HEALTHY REFUGEES FROM THE INFECTED...
4
...WHAT DO YOU THINK *WHO'S* ANSWER WILL BE...?
5
breep breep
6
COMMISSIONER, THERE ARE SOME...MAGI HERE TO SEE YOU.
7
...SO?